Mathematical Modelling of Contemporary Electricity Markets

Mathematical Modelling of Contemporary Electricity Markets

Edited by

Athanasios Dagoumas

ACADEMIC PRESS

An imprint of Elsevier

Academic Press is an imprint of Elsevier
125 London Wall, London EC2Y 5AS, United Kingdom
525 B Street, Suite 1650, San Diego, CA 92101, United States
50 Hampshire Street, 5th Floor, Cambridge, MA 02139, United States
The Boulevard, Langford Lane, Kidlington, Oxford OX5 1GB, United Kingdom

Notices
Knowledge and best practice in this field are constantly changing. As new research and experience broaden our
understanding, changes in research methods, professional practices, or medical treatment may become
necessary.

Practitioners and researchers must always rely on their own experience and knowledge in evaluating and using
any information, methods, compounds, or experiments described herein. In using such information or methods
they should be mindful of their own safety and the safety of others, including parties for whom they have a
professional responsibility.

To the fullest extent of the law, neither the Publisher nor the authors, contributors, or editors, assume any
liability for any injury and/or damage to persons or property as a matter of products liability, negligence or
otherwise, or from any use or operation of any methods, products, instructions, or ideas contained in the material
herein.

Library of Congress Cataloging-in-Publication Data
A catalog record for this book is available from the Library of Congress

British Library Cataloguing-in-Publication Data
A catalogue record for this book is available from the British Library

ISBN: 978-0-12-821838-9

For information on all Academic Press publications
visit our website at https://www.elsevier.com/books-and-journals

Publisher: Brian Romer
Acquisitions Editor: Graham Nisbet
Editorial Project Manager: Sam W. Young
Production Project Manager: Nirmala Arumugam
Cover Designer: Greg Harris

Typeset by SPi Global, India

Contents

Part I
Modelling market fundamentals of electricity markets

1. Forecasting energy demand with econometrics

Theodosios Perifanis

2. An econometric approach for Germany's short-term energy demand forecasting

Symeoni Soursou (Eleni)

3. A novel adaptive day-ahead load forecast method, incorporating non-metered distributed generation: A comparison of selected European countries

B. Sinkovics, I. Taczi, I. Vokony, and B. Hartmann

4. Forecasting week-ahead hourly electricity prices in Belgium with statistical and machine learning methods

Evangelos Spiliotis, Haris Doukas, Vassilios Assimakopoulos, and Fotios Petropoulos

Contributors

Numbers in parentheses indicate the pages on which the authors' contributions begin.

Nicholas Apergis (289), University of Derby, Derby, United Kingdom

Ángel Arcos-Vargas (209), School of Engineering, Department of Industrial Engineering and Management Science, University of Seville, Seville, Spain

Vassilios Assimakopoulos (59), School of Electrical and Computer Engineering, National Technical University of Athens, Athens, Greece

Anastasios Bakirtzis (127), Department of Electrical and Computer Engineering, Aristotle University of Thessaloniki (AUTH), Thessaloniki, Greece

Pablo Benalcazar (237), Mineral and Energy Economy Research Institute of the Polish Academy of Sciences, Department of Policy and Strategic Research, Division of Energy Economics, Kraków, Poland

Pandelis Biskas (127), Department of Electrical and Computer Engineering, Aristotle University of Thessaloniki (AUTH), Thessaloniki, Greece

David Canca (209), School of Engineering, Department of Industrial Engineering and Management Science, University of Seville, Seville, Spain

Stamatios Chondrogiannis (127), European Commission, Joint Research Centre (JRC), Ispra, Italy

Athanasios S. Dagoumas (349), Energy and Environmental Policy Laboratory, School of Economics, Business and International Studies, University of Piraeus, Piraeus, Greece

Haris Doukas (59), School of Electrical and Computer Engineering, National Technical University of Athens, Athens, Greece

B. Hartmann (39), Budapest University of Technology and Economics, Budapest, Hungary

Sam Hartnett (279), Energy Web, Zug, Switzerland

Jacek Kamiński (237), Mineral and Energy Economy Research Institute of the Polish Academy of Sciences, Department of Policy and Strategic Research, Division of Energy Economics, Kraków, Poland

Nikolaos E. Koltsaklis (111, 317), Energy and Environmental Policy Laboratory, School of Economics, Business and International Studies, University of Piraeus, Piraeus, Greece

Evangelos Kotsakis (225), European Commission—Joint Research Centre, Ispra, VA, Italy

Agis Koumentakos (191), Energy & Environmental Policy Laboratory, School of Economics, Business and International Studies, University of Piraeus, Piraeus, Greece

Stavros Lazarou (225), Department of Electrical and Electronic Engineering Educators, School of Pedagogical and Technological Education (ASPETE), Heraklion Attikis, Athens, Greece

Antonios Marinopoulos (127), European Commission, Joint Research Centre (JRC), Petten, The Netherlands

Ilias Marneris (127), Department of Electrical and Computer Engineering, Aristotle University of Thessaloniki (AUTH), Thessaloniki, Greece

Jesse Morris (279), Energy Web, Zug, Switzerland

Andreas Ntomaris (127), Department of Electrical and Computer Engineering, Aristotle University of Thessaloniki (AUTH), Thessaloniki, Greece

Fernando Núñez (209), School of Engineering, Department of Industrial Engineering and Management Science, University of Seville, Seville, Spain

Ioannis Panapakidis (157, 333), Department of Electrical and Computer Engineering, University of Thessaly, Volos, Greece

Anthony Papavasiliou (173), UCLouvain, Louvain la Neuve, Belgium

John A. Paravantis (295), Department of International and European Studies, University of Piraeus, Piraeus, Greece

Theodosios Perifanis (3), Energy and Environmental Policy Laboratory, Department of International and European Studies, School of Economics, Business and International Studies, University of Piraeus, Piraeus, Greece

Fotios Petropoulos (59), School of Management, University of Bath, Bath, United Kingdom

Michael L. Polemis (289), Department of Economics, University of Piraeus, Greece and Hellenic Competition Commission, Athens, Greece

Marta Poncela-Blanco (127), European Commission, Joint Research Centre (JRC), Ispra, Italy

B. Sinkovics (39), Budapest University of Technology and Economics, Budapest, Hungary

Symeoni Soursou (Eleni) (17), Energy and Environmental Policy Laboratory, Department of International and European Studies, School of Economics, Business and International Studies, University of Piraeus, Piraeus, Greece

Evangelos Spiliotis (59), School of Electrical and Computer Engineering, National Technical University of Athens, Athens, Greece

I. Taczi (39), Budapest University of Technology and Economics, Budapest, Hungary

Konstantinos Tasiopoulos (95), Energy and Environmental Policy Laboratory, University of Piraeus, Piraeus, Greece

Eleftherios C. Venizelos (259), Energy & Environmental Policy Laboratory, School of Economics, Business and International Studies, University of Piraeus, Piraeus, Greece

Ioannis Vlachos (279), Energy Web, Zug, Switzerland

I. Vokony (39), Budapest University of Technology and Economics, Budapest, Hungary

Shutang You (75), Department of Electrical Engineering and Computer Science, The University of Tennessee, Knoxville, TN, United States

Yao Zhang (75), Shaanxi Province Key Laboratory of Smart Grid, Xi'an Jiaotong University, Xi'an, China

Preface

The book aims at examining a challenging task, namely mathematical modelling of contemporary electricity markets. Liberalization of electricity markets, technological and policy developments create needs for advanced and robust mathematical models toward quantifying and tackling those developments. This book aims to provide different mathematical formulations, developed for capturing new challenges and approaches in contemporary electricity markets, including both new as well as traditional methodologies. The book includes different approaches (i.e., optimization, econometrics, neural networks, blockchain, cooptimization, energy system models, simulation) applied in modelling different problems/challenges of electricity markets.

I would like to thank all the contributors for providing chapters of high quality and responding in time and professionally to all my requests. The engagement of several experts, who have strong and long-lasting experience in real problems of electricity markets, enables the development of a book that I hope will be useful to energy experts for their daily operations. The engagement of several staff, from the Energy and Environmental Policy Laboratory of the University of Piraeus that I am directing, enables the provision of a more coherent and structured book, which is the main problem in case of books consisting of chapters from different contributors.

The period, when the book was edited, as well as the majority of the chapters were written, was also challenging, as the whole world faced the COVID-19 outbreak. This period challenged not only the energy sector and the whole economy, but also personal beliefs, as uncertainty is evident and extremely difficult to be predicted. This period enabled me to spend more hours with my family, my wife Maria and my children Stergios and Panagiota, as well as understanding the commitments of my parents, my father Stergios and my recently gone mother Agoritsa, on the mental and moral cultivation of myself and my siblings. I am devoting this book to my family and my parents.

Finally, few days ago I was elected from a special committee of the Hellenic Parliament as President of the Hellenic Regulatory Authority of Energy, where my new duties include responsibilities on regulation and market monitoring of electricity and natural gas markets in Greece. The last chapter, written in spring 2020 under my scientific identity, tackles market concentration issues for those markets. I plan, if there is time available, to implement this scientific dissemination strategy for other market design issues, as well as for introducing modern theories in regulation, such as nudging techniques.

We hope that the readers will find the book useful.

Athanasios Dagoumas

Introduction

Athanasios Dagoumas

Energy and Environmental Policy Laboratory, Department of International and European Studies, School of Economics, Business and International Studies, University of Piraeus, Piraeus, Greece

Any scientific book usually aims to respond to the following main questions:

- What is the need of the book? What is the aim and scope of the book?
- What problems does the book solve?
- What are the features of the book?
- What is its contribution in the literature? Are there competitive recent books? How this book distinguishes itself from the competition?
- What is the structure of the book and how it was selected? Does its nature (book of chapters) affect its coherence and quality?

1 Which is the need for the book? What are its aims and scope?

The need for this book derives from the dynamic evolution of contemporary electricity markets, due to liberalization processes, technological and policy developments. Electricity markets are facing rapid reforms and liberalization processes all over the world which create new forms of markets, i.e., day-ahead, intraday, balancing. Moreover, technological challenges lead to the penetration of new technologies both in the supply and the demand side, affecting electricity market needs. Distributed energy sources, stochastic renewables, dynamic demand, electric storage, electric vehicles, artificial intelligence, and internet of things create new challenges for the contemporary power markets. Moreover, policy challenges, such as energy security, security of supply, market concentration, decarbonization due to raising of environmental awareness, shocks in the markets, and issues related to energy planning, are important issues for electricity markets. But, as in case of any commodity market, the examination of its market fundamentals, as well as its interlinkage with other markets, is always an important task.

The quantification of those developments with advanced and robust modelling techniques is very important. This book aims to provide different mathematical models developed for capturing new challenges and approaches in competitive electricity markets. The book includes different approaches (i.e., optimization, econometrics, neural networks, blockchain, cooptimization, energy system models, simulation) in modelling electricity markets. The book captures the developments mainly in the European electricity markets, as the vast majority of its contributors provide applications mainly for European markets. However, the book does not focus on a specific market, i.e., European, as the contributions are invaluable for anyone interested in mathematical modelling for electricity market.

2 What problems does the book solve?

The book provides solutions to the following issues:

- Technology and policy developments are rapid in the electricity sector, so mathematical models for capturing those developments are expanding to capture them
- The specific problems faced by readers are forecasting market fundamentals of power markets (demand, supply, prices), forecasting renewables, integration of dynamic demand, optimization of energy and ancillary services, dispatching

power units in different market types, market concentration, integration of electric vehicle and storage in electricity markets, evolution of new market types, bidding under uncertainty in electricity markets, interlinkage with other commodities markets. Those problems are tackled by the relevant mathematical models and applications.

- The book is expected to familiarize readers with electricity markets' models, to identify the importance for developing robust quantitative tools, and to help readers on developing/using relevant models that are important for their daily responsibilities and modelling developments.

3 What are the features and benefits of the book?

The main features and benefits of the book are as follows:

- Provide different modelling techniques for electricity markets modelling
- Assess new challenges in contemporary electricity markets
- Assess different types of electricity markets
- Familiarize energy experts with quantitative skills needed in competitive electricity markets
- Familiarize energy investors with markets' risk by stressing the multidimensionality of electricity markets

4 Who is the target audience

The book captures mainly the needs of energy experts; however, it could also be useful as a textbook, especially in post-graduate studies and for doctoral students. Therefore the target audience is:

- Energy experts working with electricity companies, system operators, energy exchanges, and regulators
- Master/PhD students expanding their quantitative skills for competitive electricity markets
- Analysts in the power sector and in academia
- Electricity market analysts, electricity traders, heads of energy management and energy trading division, electricity retailers, risk analysts in banking and in electric utilities, energy investors

The book aims to improve the understanding of the abovementioned personnel in power markets operations, to improve their modelling capabilities for electricity markets as well as the understanding of the modelling outputs, to improve their strategy in participation in electricity markets, and to improve their understanding in decision making in energy investments.

5 What is the contribution of the book in the literature?

The literature is extensive concerning mathematical modelling on power markets. Each chapter incorporates several scientific papers, including review papers that organize recent developments. However, the literature in relevant books is limited. There exist several books that tackle modelling and other challenges for contemporary electricity markets, from which the author chooses the most relevant to his knowledge, in order to justify the usefulness, contribution, and complementarity of this book. Kariniotakis (2017) focuses on renewable energy forecasting, providing extended applications and methodologies which however focus only on renewables. Therefore the proposed book captures a wider audience in the power sector. Sioshansi (2008) examines market design, implementation, and performance issues of competitive electricity markets. This book captures more recent challenges of contemporary electricity markets, while it also focuses more on mathematical models rather than on design of competitive electricity markets. Therefore it is more useful to energy experts in daily operations. Conejo et al. (2010) focus on decision making under uncertainty in electricity markets, providing robust methodological approaches to crucial challenges related to tackling uncertainty in electricity markets. This book captures new technology and policy developments, as well as modelling techniques and applications. Sioshansi (2013) provides new paradigms, new challenges, and new approaches concerning the evolution of global electricity markets, focusing more on the design of electricity markets. This book focuses on modelling new challenges and provision of new techniques. Biggar and Reza (2014) examine economic issues of electricity markets, standing as a useful textbook on market fundamentals of power markets. This book focuses on mathematical models for electricity markets, therefore the audience is different as it targets more on energy experts. Lin and Magnago (2017) examine theories and applications in electricity markets, standing as a textbook providing the basic concepts of electric power systems, microeconomics, and optimization techniques. This book focuses on mathematical models for electricity markets, therefore the audience is different as it targets more on energy experts. The review undertaken reveals that the book contributes to the literature by examining mathematical modelling on electricity markets, focusing on new challenges and approaches. Finally, the book, although being a book of chapters, has engaged several staff from the Energy and Environmental Policy Laboratory of the University of Piraeus, with personal engagement of the editor, in order to enhance coherence of the book and create a structure that resembles a textbook. Therefore its audience concerns mainly energy experts, but could be useful as a textbook, especially in postgraduate studies and doctoral students.

6   What is the structure of the book? Does its nature (book of chapters) affect its coherence and quality?

The structure was based on extensive literature review made and discussed in previous section. Firstly, a review has been undertaken on existing books toward identifying the need for issuing this book and its structure. Moreover, the extensive experience of the Energy and Environmental Policy laboratory staff of the University of Piraeus on energy modelling and provision of models/software to energy companies enhanced the capability to enhance the coherence of the book, providing chapter contributions on different modelling techniques and for technological/policy challenges not covered by other contributors. Therefore the structure was done with a double purpose:

- to assist energy experts on their specific problems and to familiarize them on using and developing models for their needs
- but also, as a textbook, especially in postgraduate studies, doctoral students, and analysts to help them understand the capability of each modelling technique.

The book is split into *four different parts* examining how:

- market fundamentals (Part 1),
- forms of electricity markets (Part 2),
- technology challenges (Part 3), and
- policy challenges (Part 4)

of electricity markets are modeled, respectively.

Part 1 concerns *modelling market fundamentals* of electricity markets. It consists of six chapters. The term market fundamentals might not be accurate, as readers would expect chapters on demand and supply forecasting. Demand forecasting is examined in Chapters 1, 2, and 3, with different methodologies, while supply forecasting is examined in different aspects: how supply (from network assets) affects network demand in Chapter 3, as well as forecasting uncertainty from supply (in case of wind assets) in Chapter 4. This part also includes Chapter 5 on forecasting electricity prices, as well as on linking electricity with other commodity prices in Chapter 6. Therefore market factors could be more appropriate as a term, but we chose to use market fundamentals.

Chapter 1, authored by Theodosios Perifanis, focuses on energy demand forecasting with econometrics. Demand forecasting is of crucial importance in the liberalized electricity markets, both for long- and short-term needs. Short-term forecasting is dependable on many variables, i.e., weather, hour, season, working or public holiday day, which however do not incorporate important economic indicators, such as income/economic activity, as those figures are not measured in the short term. Those indicators are used for long-term forecasting. This is the focus of this chapter, applying econometrics to investigate the relationship between economic (price and GDP) and weather conditions (number of heating and cooling degrees) in three European markets: Denmark, France, and Spain. Demand's reactions are investigated both in the long and short term, providing evidence on different elasticities on the examined countries, although facing similar market regulatory environment.

Chapter 2, authored by Simoni Soursou, provides an econometric approach for Germany's short-term energy demand forecasting using traditional modelling techniques. This study seeks to assess different time series forecasting techniques for energy demand. Using an extensive sample of hourly observations for actual electricity load, under the Box-Jenkins framework different ARMA and ARMAX models for Germany's energy demand are developed. Furthermore, a regression analysis is realized to compare our estimates.

Chapter 3, authored by B. Sinkovics, I. Taczi, I. Vokony, and B. Hartmann, provides a novel adaptive day-ahead load forecasting method, incorporating nonmetered distributed generation. The method provides a comparison of selected European countries. This chapter reveals, similar to Chapter 1, the need for tailored solutions for each application, due to the considerably varying conditions of each country. Long short-term memory networks are a subtype of recurrent neural networks using a unique node architecture called cells. This is one of the most widely used state-of-the-art models for predictions, where temporal dependencies are important. The chapter makes a hypothesis that the proliferation of nonmetered residential photovoltaic plants significantly affects the accuracy of load forecasts. The introduced long short-term memory load predictor was applied to transmission system operator frequency control areas with various load scales and renewable penetration. The developed model has outperformed national forecasts and has identified potential effects of nonmetered distributed generation. This comparison reinforced the hypothesis of the authors that residential photovoltaic entities play an important role in the characteristics of the daily load curves, and the performance of load forecasts can be improved by taking such data into consideration, when developing forecasting algorithms.

Chapter 4, authored by Yao Zhanga and Shutang You, examines probabilistic forecasting toward modelling uncertainties in electricity markets, by proving a wind power example. This work first develops an enhanced k-nearest neighbor (KNN) algorithm to find similar weather condition days in historical dataset. Then a novel kernel density estimator (KDE) is developed and applied to derive the probability density of wind power generation from k-nearest neighbors. Logarithmic transformation is utilized to reduce the skewness of wind power density, and the boundary kernel method is used to eliminate the density leak at the bounds of wind power density. In addition, an outlier detection tool is employed to remove the data of wind power output being zero in a successive 48-h period due to wind turbine maintenance. An advantage of this approach is that it could provide both point forecasts and probabilistic forecasts for wind power generation. Evaluation results, on the public dataset from the 2014 Global Energy Forecasting Competition, demonstrate the high accuracy and reliability of the methodology.

Chapter 5, authored by Evangelos Spiliotis, Haris Doukas, Vassilios Assimakopoulos, and Fotios Petropoulos, focuses on forecasting of week-ahead hourly electricity prices in Belgium with statistical and Machine Learning (ML) methods. Electricity price forecasting is influenced by numerous variables, such as weather conditions, electricity consumption, and seasonal factors. This chapter provides an overview of both statistical and ML approaches. It compares the forecasting performance of two popular ML methods, namely neural networks and random forest, to that of traditional, statistical ones by considering the electricity market in Belgium. The results indicate that ML methods provide better forecasts, both in terms of accuracy and bias. External variables improve the performance of both statistical and ML approaches; however, the improvements in the latter group are relatively more substantial.

Chapter 6, authored by Konstantinos Tasiopoulos, focuses on modelling interlinked commodities' prices, examining the linkage of electricity prices with natural gas prices. Several econometric methodologies are applied to examine both the price transmission mechanism and the volatility spillovers between the Title Transfer Facility (TTF) natural gas price and the wholesale electricity day-ahead prices regarding the case of Netherlands. Evidence of an asymmetric cointegrating relationship found with natural gas prices causing electricity prices both in the long and in the short run. The asymmetric relationship suggested that TTF price decreases cause faster adjustments to ELC prices than increases, whereas electricity price adjustments do not seem to influence TTF prices. Furthermore, the chapter studies the partial covolatility spillovers with the implementation of a diagonal BEKK model. Results signified that covolatility spillovers do exist between two variables with the spillovers effects moving toward different directions.

Part 2 concerns *modelling different forms of electricity markets*. It consists of five chapters. It considers different forms of electricity markets, namely day-ahead, examined in Chapters 7 and 8; intraday, examined in Chapter 8; and balancing markets, examined in Chapters 8 and 9. Moreover, it examines markets from the perspective of market participants. Chapter 10 examines portfolio optimization from the retailers' perspective, while Chapter 11 examines electricity portfolio optimization for a market perspective with vertical integration.

Chapter 7, authored by Nikolaos E. Koltsaklis, describes an optimization model for the economic dispatch problem in power exchanges. The chapter considers recent developments in the process of European power markets' integration toward adopting a common clearing algorithm among European power exchanges under the title EUPHEMIA (acronym for Pan-European Hybrid Electricity Market Integration Algorithm), which provides several options and products to the market participants. This chapter proposes an optimization-based methodological framework for the optimal economic dispatch problem in power exchanges, further enhancing block order options of the EUPHEMIA algorithm. More specifically, through the development of a mixed integer linear programming (MILP) model and utilizing an iterative process, it quantifies the impacts of the proposed new options to the optimal power mix, the resulting market clearing prices, and on the welfares achieved by the market participants. The model incorporates all the current market products of the EUPHEMIA algorithm, as well as introduces new market products such as the flexibility provision of the main aspects of block orders (minimum acceptance ratio, price offer, and block time limits). The applicability of the proposed approach has been assessed in the Hellenic power system and its interconnections in Southeast Europe, providing a robust and systematic methodological formation, being able to address the new market operating challenges of low carbon flexible power systems.

Chapter 8, authored by Stamatios Chondrogiannis, Marta Poncela-Blanco, Antonios Marinopoulos, Ilias Marneris, Andreas Ntomaris, Pandelis Biskas, and Anastasios Bakirtzis, focuses on power system flexibility, providing a methodological analytical framework based on unit commitment and economic dispatch modelling. This chapter contributes in posing new challenges to modern power systems in terms of adequacy and operational security due to the penetration of stochastic renewables, presenting a step-wise methodological framework for assessing power system flexibility. It combines preliminary model independent analyses with simulations based on a Unit Commitment and Economic Dispatch (UCED) model, representing the sequence of Day-Ahead, Intraday, and Balancing Markets, along with System's operational constraints such as Reserve requirements. Monte Carlo simulations are employed for capturing the effects of renewables and load variability, different hydro conditions, and contingencies in generating assets. A discussion on some key modelling challenges, such as of storage, Demand Response (DR), level of aggregation of generating units, maintenance requirements, and temperature dependency of demand is also provided. The main focus of the work is on the development of an appropriate set of indicators in order to infer meaningful information on power system flexibility needs, challenges, available resources, and potential solutions. Indicators are developed to gain insights on potential undesired effects in the behavior of power markets, such as the probability of negative prices or high price volatility, while the probability of RES curtailment resulting from inadequate flexibility in the power system is also assessed.

Chapter 9, authored by Anthony Papavasiliou, examines modelling cross-border interactions of EU balancing markets, providing a focus on scarcity pricing. The goal of scarcity pricing is to reflect more accurately the incremental value of reserve capacity in real-time operations, and thereby to create a more favorable environment for investment in resources that can offer reserve services to the system. Scarcity pricing has recently been expanded in various US markets and is being increasingly considered as a viable option forward for EU market design. The consideration of scarcity pricing by certain EU member states raises the question of how a unilateral implementation of the mechanism might affect neighboring markets. The chapter presents a simple stochastic equilibrium model for understanding the effects of a unilateral implementation of scarcity pricing on a two-zone illustrative example. It focuses on the implications of scarcity pricing on balancing market equilibrium and the backpropagation of scarcity adders in day-ahead markets. The chapter provides insights derived from the model and their institutional relevance.

Chapter 10, authored by Ioannis Panapakidis, focuses on the retailers' profit maximization with the assistance of price and load forecasting processes. The scope of the developed methodology is to maximize retailers' profits through the solution of a profit maximization problem. The system marginal prices are assumed a stochastic variable. Instead of treating the system price as a stochastic variable where a set of scenarios are formulated, a computational intelligence based forecasting system can be implemented in order to decrease the optimization problem complexity. Also, another source of stochasticity is the consumers' load patterns. In this case, a short-term load forecasting system can aid on the strategic decision of the retailer such as the amount of the electricity procurement and tariff structure. Two crucial variables, i.e., price and load, are not simulated via stochastic programming; instead of this, accurate forecasting algorithms are implemented to provide better predictions.

Chapter 11, authored by Agis Koumentakos, focuses on electricity portfolio optimization through the development of a Mixed Integer Linear Programming (MILP) model. The chapter proposes an optimization-based methodological framework for the optimal economic portfolio management of a provider. The latter has the ability to produce electricity from its natural gas power plant, buying from the day-ahead spot market or curtailing part of the demand through Demand Response (DR) programs. More specifically through the development of a mixed integer linear programming (MILP) model, it quantifies the proposed new alterations of the Spot Market products as well as considering the consumer behavior in Demand Response programs. The model incorporates the ability of the provider to meet the demand via three different options as mentioned before. As far as the Spot Market products are concerned, it integrates the abilities of base load contract (BLC), three kinds of peak load contracts (12, 4, 2-h PLCs), and standard hourly products. The last option of Demand Response refers to load curtailment, with an upper constraint on the curtailed power reflecting the consumer's behavior in terms of participation, response, and persistence. The comparison among the three different models leads to a significant cost minimization of 9% in the provider's total cost.

Part 3 concerns *modelling technology challenges in electricity markets*. It consists of five chapters. It examines the participation of different technologies in electricity markets, such as storage assets in Chapter 12, dynamic demand assets with Blockchain technology in Chapter 13, cross-sectoral technologies such as Combined Heat and Power (CHP) assets in Chapter 14, as well as interconnection assets in Chapter 15. Finally, it assesses innovative technologies, such as energy web application in Chapter 16 that enables peer-to-peer trading among customers (increasingly, prosumers) and distributed energy resources, as well as suggesting grid architecture design that that could challenge the traditional role of system operators.

Chapter 12, authored by Ángel Arcos-Vargas, David Canca, and Fernando Núñez, examines business opportunities in the day-ahead markets by storage integration, providing an application to the German case. In order to develop a potential business model based on energy arbitrage, a Linear Mixed-Integrated Programming model is developed to obtain optimal strategies for buying and selling electricity by energy storage systems considering a full year of hourly electricity prices. For each configuration (battery size/inverter size), the model provides an optimal business strategy. Given the size of each yearly model and since we are interested in obtaining the best strategy for each battery-converter combination until the actual capacity of the battery is small enough to get profitable results, a sequential year-by-year solution framework has been implemented. By applying this resolution scheme, the optimization procedure provides the optimal operation strategy for each configuration. This strategy is then used to compute some financial indicators in order to select the optimal configuration. The optimization procedure is applied to the German wholesale electricity market in 2019, obtaining the optimal operation policy, as well as guidance to the research centers on the impact that the different improvements to the storage systems would have.

Chapter 13, authored by Stavros Lazarou and Evangelos Kotsakis, focuses on the integration of dynamic demand in electricity markets, examining how Blockchain 3.0 as an enabler of microgrid energy exchange, demand response, and storage. This chapter provides the relevant bibliography and analyzes Blockchain 3.0 technology, giving emphasis to storage and demand management microgrid applications. Blockchain 3.0 provides operational advantages such as reduced transaction costs due to the absence of a trusted authority and the lack of single point of failure but it requires relatively increased computational resources and enhanced measures to safeguard privacy. Existing blockchain implementations include Bitcoin, Ethereum, Hyperledger, Corda, Tendermint, Chain Core, Quorum. Each one of these demonstrates different characteristics and they have better fit to different energy market applications. Blockchain energy markets could be organized on Implementation, System Local, and Entities level.

Chapter 14, authored by Pablo Benalcazar and Jacek Kamiński, focuses on optimizing Combined Heat and Power (CHP) operational planning for participating in day-ahead power markets: The case of a coal-fired CHP system with thermal energy storage is examined. This chapter presents a Mixed Integer Linear Programming (MILP) approach for solving the operation planning problem (commonly referred in the literature as the "day plan") of a coal-fired CHP system. The system comprises a CHP plant (equipped with an extraction-condensing steam turbine driven by two pulverized coal-fired boilers), two auxiliary boilers, and a tank thermal energy storage. The objective of the mathematical model is the minimization of the operating costs of the CHP system considering the heat demand of a district heating network and the potential revenues from the sales of electricity in the local power market. An illustrative example based on a typical cogeneration system operating in Central and Eastern Europe is used to demonstrate the applicability of the proposed approach. Two scenarios are investigated to highlight the advantages of the model in dealing with the cooptimization of heat and power.

Chapter 15, authored by Eleftherios C. Venizelos, provides a statistical analysis of power flows based on system marginal price differentials between two power systems. In this chapter, a statistical analysis on ex-post historical power data is introduced. The application of the methodology is performed on ex-post historical data of imports from Italy to Greece, considering a period of over 4 years. The main contribution of this study is the definition of the probability density function of power flows (PDFs), based on the system marginal price differentials (SMPds) between two power systems. In order to define the PDFs of power flows, the initial data are classified according to the interconnection capacity and the direction characterization of power flows (economical or noneconomical). Then, for every classification, a further partitioning of the spectrum of SMPds is performed and for every resulted subrange of the spectrum, a representative flow state (i.e., range of power flow percentages) is defined. So, for a given value of SMPd, this model has a result, a forecast of the power flows, since the SMPd value belongs to a unique subrange of the initial spectrum, which in turn corresponds to a defined flow state. The present methodology can assist on the trading activity, in terms of power flow forecasting and trading pattern recognition, valuable to market players. Also, it can contribute to the optimization of the role of the system operator, in terms of cross-border power flows and the capacity schedule of the power system.

Chapter 16, authored by Sam Hartnett, Jesse Morris, and Ioannis Vlachos, focuses on describing a Decentralized Flexibility Marketplace fostering Transmission System Operator (TSO)-Distribution System Operator (DSO) cooperation. The physical, financial, and political systems used to deliver electricity—collectively, our grid architecture—must evolve to reflect the novel characteristics of a grid where phenomena traditionally bound within the bulk power system—generation, balancing, markets—occur among customers at the distribution level at scale. This fast-moving energy transition has resulted in some peculiar side effects, namely, transmission system operators (TSOs) that are starting to look and act like distribution system operators (DSOs), and vice versa. The role of system operators, as well as their cooperation, is becoming important. It is a growing "turf war" of sorts in which TSOs want to reach down into distribution grid assets and customer relationships (conversely, DERs want to reach up into wholesale markets), and where retail market DSOs want to shepherd some of the functions and processes normally reserved for wholesale markets and transmission grids. The chapter evolutionary comments that the debate -about the appropriate scope for reenvisioned TSOs and DSOs- focuses on the wrong question. This chapter aims at challenging the traditional role of system operators, as we should focus on grid architecture design decisions that put customers (increasingly, prosumers) and their DERs at the center.

Part 4 concerns *modelling policy challenges in electricity markets*. It consists of five chapters. It examines different policy challenges, such as electricity supply shocks in Chapter 17; energy planning issues on different power systems, examined in Chapters 18 and 19; energy security tackled from a geopolitical dimension in Chapter 20; as well as market concentration issues, examined through an ex-ante market monitoring and regulation mechanism in Chapter 21.

Chapter 17, authored by Nicholas Apergis and Michael L. Polemis, focuses on forecasting electricity supply shocks, by providing a Bayesian panel VAR analysis. The goal of this chapter is to investigate the relationship and the possible spillovers between electricity supply shocks and US macroeconomic performance, given that there is considerable evidence that this relationship has been unstable over time. The analysis uses monthly seasonally adjusted regional data from the US states, over a 15-year period, and combines a novel identification strategy for electricity supply shocks based on inequality constraints, with the estimation of a time-varying Bayesian panel VAR model (TVBPVAR). The main novelty of this chapter is that it combines the employment of a TVBPVAR model with accounting for the decomposition of electricity supply per fuel mixture and linking its possible interactions with the US macroeconomic conditions across US states. The empirical findings are in alignment with the existing literature, suggesting that GDP per capita increases after a positive electricity supply shock irrelevant to the source of energy that generates it. This finding confirms the important role of electricity for economic growth across US states.

Chapter 18, authored by Nikolaos E. Koltsaklis, provides an assessment of the Western Balkans power systems, focusing on the case study of Serbia. This chapter presents a generic mixed integer linear programming model that has been used for the solution of the unit commitment problem, implementing a cooptimization of the energy and reserves market. The applicability of the developed framework has been assessed for the determination of the optimal annual operating scheduling of the Serbian power system, taking also into consideration its interconnections with all the neighboring power systems. A successive solution of all the dates of a whole year has been executed, where the outputs of a specific date comprise the inputs of the next date. The outputs of the model show the dominance of the installed lignite-fired units, the importance of the hydroelectric units in terms of both security of supply and balancing services provider, as well as the influence of other more liquid power exchanges on the Western Balkans power systems. The wholesale marginal price of the Serbian power system is proved to be highly correlated with the corresponding Hungarian one. The proposed optimization approach can provide useful insights on market participants, regulatory authorities, system operators, and policymakers regarding the formation of cost-competitive and decarbonized energy roadmaps, by highlighting the critical phases and the challenges of each design stage.

Chapter 19, authored by Ioannis Panapakidis, provides an evaluation of capacity expansion scenarios for the Hellenic electric sector. During the last years, fossil fuels covered the largest share of the produced electricity of the Greek electric sector. In the near term, many units' decommissioning is expected, a fact that provides the landscape for more investments in gas-fired plants and renewable energy resources. The present study analyzes the current state of the Hellenic energy system, focusing on the historical evolution of electricity consumption and electricity generation. Different scenarios of future power system expansion are examined. The scenarios are compared to the baseline scenario of the 10-year transmission system development plan issued by Independent Power Transmission Operator (IPTO) SA. The objective is to examine the impact of various power generation technologies on the capacity expansion costs and the emission of environmental pollutants and to provide a detailed study for interested parties concerning the expected benefits and limitations of increased penetration of various sources on the power system.

Chapter 20, authored by John A. Paravantis, focuses on the formulation and estimation of an energy security index, providing a geopolitical review of quantitative approaches. This chapter reviews the research literature that has aimed to formulate and estimate energy security quantitatively. Energy security is defined as an entity containing dimensions and components represented by metrics. Adopting a geopolitical perspective that is lacking, selected quantitative approaches used for the computation of energy security indexes are reviewed. Many simple (disaggregate) indicators, composite (aggregate) indicators, and complex indexes of energy security are mentioned. Complementary qualitative techniques such as interviews are discussed. Reviewed works were found to analyze energy security metrics using numerical (scoring/ranking, weighting, organizing into a matrix); statistical (z-score approaches, correlation analysis, consumer surveys); multivariate statistical (multiple regression, Principal Component Analysis, Factor Analysis, Cluster Analysis on static of time series data); econometric (time series approaches); multicriteria decision making (Analytic Hierarchy Process, Fuzzy Analytical Hierarchical Process, Preference Ranking Organization Method for Enrichment Evaluations); (accident) risk assessment; complexity (time series analysis coupled with path dependency and lock-in concepts, Agent-Based Models); risk assessment (covering energy, social, institutional and political factors); game theoretic; and qualitative (e.g., interviews, expert panels) methods and techniques. Public perceptions were occasionally taken into consideration. Regarding the scope of the reviewed research, several works examine case studies of a single or a few countries; others analyze more countries, usually located in a region (such as Europe or Asia); some studies concentrate on regions or provinces. The chapter is concluded with a roundup of main points.

Chapter 21, authored by Athanasios S. Dagoumas, describes an ex-ante market monitoring and regulation mechanism for market concentration in electricity and natural gas markets. Market concentration is a sensitive and contradicting issue in power and natural gas markets. Market concentration is usually tackled under Competition Authorities, through ex-post and ad-hoc evaluation of each case. This creates an uncertainty on whether a market participant is considered to have dominant position in a market, as well as on what and when is allowed for a participant to do concerning its bidding and tariffs formation strategies. The Directorate General for Competition in Europe considers that "if a company has a market share of less than 40%, it is unlikely to be dominant"; however, there is not specific threshold which identifies a dominant position. On the other hand, National Regulatory Authorities for Energy are responsible for the regulation and market monitoring of power and natural gas markets; however, they do not tackle market concentration issues with a coherent and permanent methodology. This chapter describes an ex-ante Market Monitoring and Regulation Mechanism for Market Concentration in Power and Natural Gas Markets. The mechanism concerns the available capacity in both supply and demand sides. In the supply side, it estimates the available capacity of all market participants, considering the capacity per resource type (i.e., lignite, natural gas, large hydro, renewables), market participation type (i.e., FiT, FiP, commissioning), interconnection (entry) point type, and existence of bilateral contracts. It imposes a common threshold, i.e., 40% or 50%, for both aggregate and disaggregate markets, namely capacity of each resource/entry point type. In the demand side, it considers load, storage, and pumping as well as export interconnections. However, regulation can exclude resource/entry point types with low capacity under a third threshold linked to the value of the second threshold. The mechanism also considers the relative size of market participants in the supply and demand side, implementing a fourth threshold linked to the value of the third threshold. The mechanism is a coherent and permanent mechanism. The mechanism provides indicative results concerning the Hellenic power market. It can assist Energy Regulators to design clear rules on tackling market concentration ex-ante, to be implemented by the Transmission System Operators.

We hope that the readers will find the book useful.

References

Biggar, D.R., Reza, H.M., 2014. The Economics of Electricity Markets. Wiley-IEEE Press. Available from: https://www.wiley.com/en-us/The+Economics+of+Electricity+Markets-p-9781118775752.

Conejo, A.J., Miguel, C., Morales, J.M., 2010. Decision Making Under Uncertainty in Electricity Markets. Springer. Available from: https://www.springer.com/gp/book/9781441974204.

Kariniotakis, G., 2017. Renewable Energy Forecasting: From Models to Applications. Elsevier. Available from: https://www.elsevier.com/books/renewable-energy-forecasting/kariniotakis/978-0-08-100504-0.

Lin, J., Magnago, F.H., 2017. Electricity Markets: Theories and Applications. Wiley-IEEE Press. Available from: https://www.wiley.com/en-us/Electricity+Markets%3A+Theories+and+Applications-p-9781119179351.

Sioshansi, F., 2008. Competitive Electricity Markets: Design, Implementation, Performance. Elsevier. Available from: https://www.elsevier.com/books/competitive-electricity-markets/sioshansi/978-0-08-047172-3.

Sioshansi, F., 2013. Evolution of Global Electricity Markets: New Paradigms, New Challenges, New Approaches. Elsevier. Available from: https://www.elsevier.com/books/evolution-of-global-electricity-markets/sioshansi/978-0-12-397891-2.

Part I

Modelling market fundamentals of electricity markets

Chapter 1

Forecasting energy demand with econometrics

Theodosios Perifanis

Energy and Environmental Policy Laboratory, Department of International and European Studies, School of Economics, Business and International Studies, University of Piraeus, Piraeus, Greece

Acronyms

ANFIS	adaptive network-based fuzzy inference system
ANN	artificial neural networks
AR	autoregressive
ARIMA	autoregressive integrated moving average
ARMA	autoregressive moving average
ARTV	autoregressive based time varying
BEMD	bivariate empirical mode decomposition
BP	back propagation
EEU	European Energy Union
EFUNN	evolving fuzzy neural network
EMD	empirical mode decomposition
FFNN	feedforward neural network
FID	final investment decision
GARCH	generalized autoregressive conditional heteroskedasticity
GDP	gross domestic product
GP	Gaussian processes
IRF	impulse response functions
LEAP	Long-Range Energy Alternative Planning system
MAPE	mean absolute percentage error
MARS	multivariate adaptive regression spline
MLR	multiple linear regression
NNM	neural network models
NPV	net present value
PI	prediction intervals
SARIMA	seasonal autoregressive integrated moving average
SVR	support vector regression

1 Introduction

Electricity is now conceived as an energy commodity. To be perceived as that a lot have changed. Many countries have taken the initiative for energy unbundling. This opened the market for several stakeholders. Further, market coupling brought the possibility of regional trading. An excellent example of this is European Energy Union which aims at a fully integrated and efficient market. As thus European countries share a regulatory framework. Trading in country or regional markets requires high quality information. Decision making based on not so accurate information, let alone misinformation, will turn into severe losses for power companies, traders, and market stakeholders. Moreover, final investment decisions (FIDs) are taken on the grounds of future fundamentals (demand and supply). Sharp forecasting is a challenge for all market stakeholders.

Mathematical Modelling of Contemporary Electricity Markets. https://doi.org/10.1016/B978-0-12-821838-9.00001-3

What is crucial for price discovery is demand forecasting both in long- and short-term horizon, since supply capacity is constant at least in the short-term. This is difficult in electricity markets as apart from the horizon (day, month, and year etc.), or the hour itself (day or night), or the season (winter, summer, etc.), there are weather, economic, or other conditions. Forecasting horizons should be discriminated accordingly. Additionally, electricity demand is subject to high volatility. Suppliers must have a transparent view of the demand side. Econometrics come to supply an objective forecasting toolbox for this challenge. However, econometrics is not the single toolbox for demand forecasting. Many use it as a component of their forecasting methodology. Econometrics use past data to forecast future values. This is a disadvantage since many challenges like distributed energy sources, energy transition or environmental regulations lay ahead. Therefore, it is difficult to forecast electricity demand since it is in a phase of transition. We try to present the most representative literature review on demand forecasting. For most of the cases, econometrics are one of the applied methods in combination with others in the forecasting procedure. Further, these methodologies vary depending on available data, sequence and the market. Long-term forecasting is mostly based on economic, demographic and weather factors. Instead, short-term forecasting is focused on more specific data like the aggregated demand per household, the number of households, hourly trends, and types of day i.e. public holiday or working day. We start the literature review with short-term forecasting to end with long-term forecasting.

An et al. (2013) use MFES methodology which integrates multi-output FFNN (feedforward neural network) with empirical mode decomposition (EMD) based signal filtering and seasonal adjustment. This removes the seasonal components and interference of noise signals from demand series. Last, demand series are modeled by FFNN approach. Vu et al. (2017) suggest an autoregressive based time varying (ARTV) model for forecasting short-term electricity demand. Their model allows coefficients to be updated at pre-set time intervals. This, in turn, updates coefficients to enhance the relationship between electricity demand and historical data. Further, data collection and usage are improved by an adjustment procedure including a similar-day-replacement technique and a data shifting algorithm. Their results are better than those of AR, ARMA, PARMA and neural network models (NNM). Son and Kim (2017) improve data selection with the support vector regression (SVR) and fuzzy-rough feature with particle swarm optimization algorithms. This methodology identified 10 variables out of 19 as most appropriate for electricity demand forecasting. In turn the SVR algorithm was applied for the forecasting model using electricity demand data and 10 variables. The SVR model performed better in forecasting the rise and fluctuation of residential electricity demand with less variables. Again, the model was compared against standard models like ARIMA, multiple linear regression (MLR) and artificial neural network ANN models. Morita et al. (2017) suggest an "upscaling model" which projects a small number of representative households' electricity demand to the aggregated electricity demand of several hundred households. In addition, they use a simple 1 h forecasting model to modify a day-ahead forecasted demand. This method is favorable during summer and winter. Lebotsa et al. (2018) use a complex forecasting model with the application of partially linear additive quantile regression models for forecasting short-term electricity demand during peak hours. After that, a bounded variable mixed integer linear programming technique is applied to discover the optimal number of power generation units to switch on or off. Their results for the South African market are that gas fired generation units are too costly, while coal fired units are favorable. Laouafi et al. (2017) propose that since load demand is too complex and influenced by a variety of factors, then there is not a single forecasting method which could satisfactorily perform through all periods. As a result, they apply an adaptive exponential smoothing method in combination with forecasts of other five individual models. To improve the forecasting accuracy of the combination of the primary models, they apply a data filter and the trimmed mean. Last, their methodology does not require ample resources. Elamin and Fukushige (2018) propose a seasonal autoregressive integrated moving average (SARIMAX) model with exogenous variables as main effects and interaction variables (cross effects) to predict hourly load demand data. The model with the interactions had better predictive ability than that without interactions. Exogenous variables and their interactions should be included. Al-Musaylh et al. (2019) apply an artificial neural network model with climatic variables for 6-h and daily electricity demand forecasting. Their model was better than other standard models like multivariate adaptive regression spline (MARS), multiple linear regression (MLR), and autoregressive integrated moving average (ARIMA) model. When they integrated their model with MARS and MLR models, then they had even better results by the hybrid ANN. Al-Musaylh et al. (2018) propose that the MARS and SVR models are better in forecasting electricity demand in the short-run. Xiong et al. (2014) propose an interval forecasting method i.e. they do not predict a single value but rather a range. They also propose a hybrid method integrating bivariate empirical mode decomposition (BEMD) and support vector regression (SVR) with the extension of empirical mode decomposition (EMD). However, their research is restricted to one-step-ahead forecasting. Adeoye and Spataru (2019) take into consideration nine categories of household appliances occupancy patterns of household members, weather conditions, type of day and day-light hours to model electricity demand. They separate electricity demand in residential and rural components. Their hybrid model derived by bottom-up and top-down methodologies only had deviations due to the sudden power generation shutdowns. Yang et al. (2016) take the forecasts by back propagation (BP) neural networks, adaptive network-based fuzzy inference system (ANFIS) and difference seasonal autoregressive integrated moving average (diff-SARIMA) models, then the forecasts are multiplied by optimal weights and later summed up for the final forecast. BP and ANFIS can account for nonlinear effects, while diff-ARIMA can account for linearity and seasonality. Van der Meer et al. (2018) utilize Gaussian processes (GPs) for probabilistic forecasting. They tested various combinations of covariance functions. Their results suggest that the dynamic GPs bring out better results with sharper prediction intervals (PIs) than the static GP. Last, they examined the forecasting ability between direct and indirect strategies to suggest that the former produce sharper PIs. Chang et al. (2011) use an evolving fuzzy neural network framework (EFUNN) with weighted factors to forecast monthly demand. Their results are better than those of MAPE for the Taiwanese market. Wang et al. (2012) apply a PSO optimal Fourier methodology, seasonal ARIMA (S-ARIMA), and combinations between the aforementioned models. The combination of the models has more accurate forecasts. De Felice et al. (2015) use both linear and non-linear (based on support vector machine) regression methodologies to propose the relationship between summer average temperature patterns over Europe and Italian electricity demand. Further, their analysis is supplemented by a probabilistic approach. Li et al. (2020) also use a hybrid method. They start with Fourier decomposition to derive fluctuation characteristics. Then the conditions of linearity and stationarity sequences are satisfied to mute seasonal patterns. Further, the sine cosine optimization algorithm is used to choose the penalty and kernel parameters of support vector machine.

Zhu et al. (2011) propose a hybrid model including a moving average procedure, a combined method and an adaptive particle swarm optimization algorithm or else (MA-C-WH) model. This is developed for time series with trend and seasonality. Further, the introduced model can adjust trend and seasonality, while the APSO algorithm searches for its weighted coefficients. Their model performs well in trend forecasting as well as in seasonal forecasting. Yukseltan et al. (2017) used past data to develop a linear regression model in terms of the harmonics of the daily, weekly and seasonal variations and a modulation by seasonal harmonics was developed. Their contribution is that no weather information is needed since they incorporate the modulation of diurnal variations by seasonal harmonics. Pessanha and Leon (2015) use decomposition methodology to forecast energy consumption. The components are the average consumption per consumer unit, electrification rate and the number of households. The suggested model combines macroeconomic scenarios, demographic projection, and assumptions for ownership and efficiency of electric appliances. Oh et al. (2016) use both top-down and bottom-up approaches. Further, they put their proposals like an innovative absorbent-based dehumidifier and an indirect evaporative cooling under two scenarios. The business as usual and the high conservative scenario. This is how they forecasted future energy demand. Mirjat et al. (2018) apply a Long-Range Energy Alternatives Planning System (LEAP) to forecast Pakistan's 2015–50 demand. Then they propose their suggestions under different supply scenarios. After that they evaluate different outcomes with NPV methodology. He et al. (2017) use classical econometric methods in combination with system dynamics. Econometrics were used for factor screening and quantitative relationships, while the systems dynamics method for demand forecasting. It is a hybrid methodology as well, whose performance is enhanced due to integration. Their results show that power consumption shifts from energy-intensive industries to tertiary industry and residents. Angelopoulos et al. (2019) suggest an ordinal regression method for power demand forecasting and they find that economic development, and energy efficiency have the greatest influence. Weather conditions are also a driver. Günay (2016) use both multiple and artificial neural networks (ANN) to forecast electricity demand. His methodology considers population, gross domestic product (GDP) per capita, inflation and average summer temperature. On the contrary, winter temperatures and unemployment were insignificant. The hybrid methodology continues with forecasting the value of statistically significant drivers by ANN models, and these are simulated in a multilayer perception ANN model forecasting demand. The forecasted demand in 2028 is double that of 2013. Pérez-García and Moral-Carcedo (2016) find that economic growth, average consumption per household, non-residential intensity and demographic components can well forecast electricity demand in Spain. Shao et al. (2015) use again a hybrid model which is a combination of the semi-parametric model with fluctuation feature decomposition technology. Their model is tested in two different Chinese regions and has satisfactory results against standard forecasting methodologies (SVM, ARIMA, and BP). Its results are probability forecasts of the total power consumption. Last, Khalifa et al. (2019) use scenario analysis for the Qatari electricity consumption. They use GDP and population growth as the main drivers. In addition, they include electricity efficiency as the muter of long-run elasticity of consumption. They conclude that efficiency is crucial for future electricity consumption.

Through the literature review, we can suggest that no applied method as a stand-alone forecasting method is considered as optimal. Most of the researchers use hybrid methodologies which include the merits of different methodologies while their disadvantages are smoothed. Econometrics play a crucial role in variable selection, future values, and relationship investigation. However, they use past data to make their projections, while they are susceptible to aggregation. Further, most of the researchers consider economic development, demographics and weather conditions as the main factors which can forecast electricity demand. We develop an econometric model by using economic variables and weather conditions to account for long- and short-run elasticities. We develop our methodology in the following parts.

2 Methodology

Our effort is to calculate both long- and short-run elasticities. To proceed, we transform our data into natural logarithms. Since our data are natural logarithms then their first differences are the respective returns. Initially, we test our data for stationarity. The first test we use is that of Elliot, Rothenberg and Stock (ERS) (1996) which is a modification of the Augmented Dickey-Fuller (ADF) test (Said and Dickey, 1984), and sometimes is referred as ADF (GRS) test. Further, we confirm our first results with the Zivot and Andrews (1992) test. To conduct the tests, we compare their values with the respective 5% critical values. Non-stationary series can create spurious models whose results are not credible. If all our time series are I(1) meaning that they are not stationary at levels, but they are stationary at their first differences, then we can construct VAR models to check for cointegration. We conduct the Johansen (1992) procedure which involves the estimation of VARs and then the estimation of the error correction mechanism. Our residuals for both the VARs and VECM are tested for serial correlation, heteroscedasticity, and normality.

Given a VAR(p) of I(1) variables (ignoring intercept and deterministic trends)

$$X_t = \Phi_1 X_{t-1} + \ldots + \Phi_p X_{t-p} + e_t \tag{1.1}$$

Then there is an error correction representation of the form ($X_t = X_{t-1} + \Delta X_t$) and then we can have:

$$\Delta X_t = \Pi X_{t-1} + \sum_{i=1}^{p-1} \Phi_i^* \Delta X_{t-i} + e_t \tag{1.2}$$

When Π and Φ^* are the functions of the $\Phi's$. More in detail

$$\Phi_j^* = -\sum_{i=j+1}^{p} \Phi_i, \ j = 1, \ldots, p-1 \tag{1.3}$$

$$\Pi = -\left(I - \Phi_1 - \ldots - \Phi_p\right) = -\Phi(1) \tag{1.4}$$

The characteristic polynomial is

$$I - \Phi_1 z - \ldots - \Phi_p z^p = \Phi(z) \tag{1.5}$$

We apply the Johansen (1992) procedure which examines whether a long-run co-movement of the variables exists. Initially, we calculate the optimum lag order for our VARs. Akaike (1973) criterion suggests two lags for France and Spain, while for the Danish market suggests one. We then test for cointegration with the Johansen test i.e. whether a long-run relationship exists between the data in these three different markets. We compare the Max-Eigen Statistics with their respective 5% and 1% critical values. If our cointegration tests suggest that there is a long-run relationship among the variables for each market, then we can proceed. Then, we present the respective cointegration equations with their normalized cointegration coefficients. The numbers in parentheses are the respective standard errors, which from we can tell whether a coefficient is statistically significant or not (divide the coefficient with its standard error). Since our results confirm that a cointegrating equation exists, then we can proceed with the short-run dynamics. The cointegrating equation is the mechanism which corrects short-run deviations from the long-run equilibrium. We then construct three VECMs (vector error correction models). Our short-run dynamics are the first differences (the coefficients are the respective short-run elasticities), while the cointegrating equation is the error correction term.

Additionally, to our long- and short-run elasticities, we derive the impulse response functions (IRFs) from our respective VARs. The IRFs track the response of one variable to shocks in the error terms in a VAR. More simply, it tracks the influence of a one-time shock to one of the innovations on current and future values of the endogenous variables (Greene, 2003). For the analysis to be correct, the innovations should be contemporaneously uncorrelated. Our VARs lag order is determined under the Akaike criterion. This assumes that there is no lag omission which would lead into bias, nor there is higher lag structure which can give irrelevant lags in the equation whose estimations are inefficient (Clarke and Mirza, 2006). Since our VARs are well specified, we can derive our impulse response functions. This is a supplementary analysis which will complete our results.

3 Methodology application

3.1 Data

Our aim is to study different electricity markets and detect the differences between them. To do so, we study three European markets. We study the Danish, French, and Spanish market. Our intension is to research one Scandinavian, one Central, and one Southern market. These markets are now parts of a greater electricity grid, but they are not completely coupled. Further, they experience different weather and economic conditions.

Our research period spans from 1985 to 2017. This period includes a financial crisis (2008) and a period of economic stress for peripheral European economies (2010–17), while the central and northern countries did not experience the same financial crisis. Further, we study countries within the European Union which means that their convergence can provide a ceteris paribus intensifying their market structures. Our data are annual since some of our data are not monitored differently. The last implies that aggregation is present since a whole year provides enough time for crisis' or special conditions' effects to be smoothed.

We use the Gross Domestic Product at 2015 levels (OVGD) or average of national growth rates weighted with current value in Euros. This variable is the factor representing economic growth. Additionally, we include electrical energy prices in Euros for a kilowatt-hour. Our prices are for households i.e. DC and consumption between 2500 and 5000 KWh. We also included the number of heating and cooling degree days to account for weather conditions. These are the independent variables which are studied against the dependent of total electricity net consumption in billion kilowatt-hours. The GDP data for each country are supplied by AMECO database. Prices and number of heating and cooling degree days are supplied by Eurostat, while total demand (consumption) is supplied by EIA. We transformed our data into natural logarithms to obtain the respective elasticities.

Finally, we denote consumption as CON, price as PRICE, GDP as GDP, number of heating and cooling degree days as HEAT and COOL respectively.

3.2 Long-run

As already mentioned we test our data for stationarity. As already mentioned our results by the stationarity tests verify that the data are I(1). All our data are I(1) meaning that they are stationary at first differences (Table 1.1). The result let us proceed with the Johansen (1992) procedure and the construction of VARs. Our variables follow a long-run co-movement i.e. they are cointegrated in each electricity market. We present the results of Max-Eigen Statistic with the corresponding 1% and 5% critical values in Table 1.2.

Our markets are cointegrated and thus our cointegrating equation for each market is:

$$\text{DENCON} = -\underset{(0.2772)}{1.1209}\text{DENPRICE} + \underset{(0.5767)}{2.1748}\text{DENGDP} + \underset{(0.2831)}{0.5465}\text{DENHEAT} + \underset{(0.0078)}{0.0026}\text{DENCOOL} - \underset{(5.3123)}{18.6776}\text{C} \quad (1.6)$$

$$\text{FRACON} = -\underset{(0.0859)}{0.3858}\text{FRAPRICE} + \underset{(0.1086)}{0.6856}\text{FRAGDP} - \underset{(0.2527)}{1.6527}\text{FRAHEAT} - \underset{(0.0301)}{0.0550}\text{FRACOOL} \quad (1.7)$$

$$\text{SPACON} = -\underset{(0.0240)}{0.3305}\text{SPAPRICE} + \underset{(0.0823)}{0.5497}\text{SPAGDP} + \underset{(0.0755)}{0.3755}\text{SPAHEAT} - \underset{(0.0246)}{0.0634}\text{SPACOOL} + \underset{(0.0027)}{0.0272}\text{TREND} \quad (1.8)$$

For the Danish market, the price is statistically significant and elastic. The price elasticity is over one implying that a 1% price increase would decrease consumption (demand) by 1.12%. Consumers are quite sensitive to price changes. This might imply high substitution, as consumers can turn to other energy sources at low costs. Further, consumption is even more sensitive to GDP changes as 1% increase of GDP would increase consumption by 2.17%. As it is expected both relationships have the correct sign (negative for price and positive for GDP). So far Danish consumers are sensitive to the first two variables. Additionally, the number of heating degree days are statistically significant adding to the consumption. Their influence is very low (0.54) and as a result inelastic. Finally, the influence of the number of cooling days is statistically insignificant. The difference of statistical significance between heating and cooling days implies the prevailing weather conditions in the Scandinavian country. Last, the intercept (constant) is also significant.

As for the French market, the price elasticity is inelastic (−0.38). French consumers are less sensitive to price changes. Profoundly, electricity has low substitution, and price increases have low influence on consumption. In addition, France covers the majority of its electricity needs from nuclear generation. This dependence on nuclear energy might have removed incentives for any diversification of energy sources. This would increase substitution and competition among power sources. Additionally, French consumption increases inelastically to GDP increases (0.68). If GDP increases

TABLE 1.1 Unit root tests.

	Elliot, Rothenberg and Stock (ERS)			Zivot and Andrews (1992) test			
	Test value	Critical values		Test value	Critical values		Order of integration
		5%	10%		5%	10%	
Denmark							
DENCON	−1.1165	−1.9500	−1.6200	−3.8586	−4.8000	−4.5800	I(1)
DENPRICE	0.0728	−1.9500	−1.6200	−2.6086	−4.8000	−4.5800	I(1)
DENGDP	0.7483	−1.9500	−1.6200	−4.3516	−4.8000	−4.5800	I(1)
DENHEAT	−1.7960	−1.9500	−1.6200	−4.0300	−4.8000	−4.5800	I(1)
DENCOOL	−1.3151	−1.9500	−1.6200	−4.1511	−4.8000	−4.5800	I(1)
France							
FRACON	−0.1173	−1.9500	−1.6200	−2.4694	−4.8000	−4.5800	I(1)
FRAPRICE	0.3972	−1.9500	−1.6200	−2.9263	−4.8000	−4.5800	I(1)
FRAGDP	0.0798	−1.9500	−1.6200	−2.7983	−4.8000	−4.5800	I(1)
FRAHEAT	−1.5167	−1.9500	−1.6200	−4.0889	−4.8000	−4.5800	I(1)
FRACOOL	−1.3322	−1.9500	−1.6200	−3.3437	−4.8000	−4.5800	I(1)
Spain							
SPACON	−0.4309	−1.9500	−1.6200	−2.4735	−4.8000	−4.5800	I(1)
SPAPRICE	−0.3500	−1.9500	−1.6200	−1.5223	−4.8000	−4.5800	I(1)
SPAGDP	−0.2884	−1.9500	−1.6200	−3.3776	−4.8000	−4.5800	I(1)
SPAHEAT	−1.8448	−1.9500	−1.6200	−4.6228	−4.8000	−4.5800	I(1)
SPACOOL	−1.5474	−1.9500	−1.6200	−4.7577	−4.8000	−4.5800	I(1)
First differences							
Denmark							
D(DENCON)	−2.1489	−1.9500	−1.6200	−6.2031	−4.8000	−4.5800	I(0)
D(DENPRICE)	−3.9233	−1.9500	−1.6200	−6.6284	−4.8000	−4.5800	I(0)
D(DENGDP)	−2.4843	−1.9500	−1.6200	−5.6048	−4.8000	−4.5800	I(0)
D(DENHEAT)	−5.2039	−1.9500	−1.6200	−6.6090	−4.8000	−4.5800	I(0)
D(DENCOOL)	−2.4643	−1.9500	−1.6200	−5.1379	−4.8000	−4.5800	I(0)
France							
D(FRACON)	−2.8898	−1.9500	−1.6200	−7.3731	−4.8000	−4.5800	I(0)
D(FRAPRICE)	−2.3143	−1.9500	−1.6200	−5.8227	−4.8000	−4.5800	I(0)
D(FRAGDP)	−3.3742	−1.9500	−1.6200	−5.7651	−4.8000	−4.5800	I(0)
D(FRAHEAT)	−4.6200	−1.9500	−1.6200	−6.2670	−4.8000	−4.5800	I(0)
D(FRACOOL)	−3.5449	−1.9500	−1.6200	−5.0780	−4.8000	−4.5800	I(0)
Spain							
D(SPACON)	−2.0215	−1.9500	−1.6200	−5.1043	−4.8000	−4.5800	I(0)
D(SPAPRICE)	−2.5479	−1.9500	−1.6200	−5.2362	−4.8000	−4.5800	I(0)
D(SPAGDP)	−2.6932	−1.9500	−1.6200	−5.0149	−4.8000	−4.5800	I(0)
D(SPAHEAT)	−3.4143	−1.9500	−1.6200	−7.0326	−4.8000	−4.5800	I(0)
D(SPACOOL)	−3.1206	−1.9500	−1.6200	−5.2646	−4.8000	−4.5800	I(0)

Both tests were conducted with a constant. The number of lags is decided by the Schwarz (1978) criterion.

TABLE 1.2 Cointegration test (Johansen).

Johansen's maximum likelihood method test for cointegration relationship

Null hypothesis, H_0	Alternative hypothesis, H_1	Max eigen statistic	Critical value	
			1%	5%
Danish electricity market				
Danish electricity consumption: VAR = 1, variables DENCON, DENPRICE, DENGDP, DENHEAT, DENCOOL Trend assumption: No deterministic trend, restricted constant				
Maximum eigen statistic				
$r = 0$	$r = 1$	45.0754[a]	40.2952	34.8058
$r \leq 1$	$r = 2$	27.9778	33.7329	28.5880
French electricity market				
French electricity consumption: VAR = 2, variables FRACON, FRAPRICE, FRAGDP, FRAHEAT, FRACOOL Trend assumption: Linear deterministic trend				
Maximum eigen statistic				
$r = 0$	$r = 1$	40.3139[a]	39.3701	33.8768
$r \leq 1$	$r = 2$	21.0035	32.7152	27.5843
Spanish electricity market				
Spanish electricity consumption: VAR = 2, variables SPACON, SPAPRICE, SPAGDP, SPAHEAT, SPACOOL Trend assumption: Linear deterministic trend (restricted)				
Maximum eigen statistic				
$r = 0$	$r = 1$	42.9384[a]	39.3701	38.3310
$r \leq 1$	$r = 2$	28.0078	32.7152	32.1183

[a]Denotes significance at $\alpha = 0.01$.
[b]Denotes significance at $\alpha = 0.05$.
r denotes the number of cointegrating equations.

1%, then consumption will increase 0.68%. This might also imply the saturation of consumers with ample energy from the nuclear generation. An increase in total output will not have great influence over consumption. Further, the number of heating degree days have a negative sign and they are elastic. On the contrary, the coefficient of the number of cooling degree days has again negative sign but it is insignificant. Our long-term analysis highlights differences in the first two markets. While in the Danish market we have elastic relationships for total consumption with price and GDP, in France we have inelastic.

Our last market is that of Spain. Spanish market's elasticity is again inelastic (-0.33). In addition, consumption has an elasticity of 0.54% to GDP changes. Our results are very close to that of France since both first coefficients are statistically significant and with the expected signs. The Spanish consumption is influenced by both heating and cooling degree days, as they are both statistically significant. As for the heating degree days' coefficient is positive while for the cooling is negative. Trend is also significant.

Our so far long-term analysis presents evidence that price and GDP are the main drivers for consumption in the long-term. Price has, as expected, a negative relationship while GDP has a positive. Economic development requires more electricity since capital intensive operations demand quantities. Last, the number of heating and cooling degree days are statistically significant depending on the weather conditions.

3.3 Short run

Our long-term models presented evidence of the trends in electricity consumption in the long-run since our so far analysis presents the long-run equilibrium. A correction mechanism brings short-run deviations back into the long-run equilibrium. Our results are presented in Tables 1.3–1.5, where we present our VECM results. Each coefficient of the variables represents the short-run elasticity. The ECT term denotes the error correction term, which is the respective speed of adjustment toward the long-run equilibrium. It must be definitely negative and statistically significant.

For the Danish market the short-run price coefficient or elasticity is negative and inelastic (-0.12). This is a change since the long-run elasticity is (-1.12). This is following the LeChatelier principle (Milgrom and Roberts, 1996) since in the long-run consumers can respond greater than in the short-run. The same is for the GDP elasticity since it is positive and lower than one. Again, we have a compliance to the same principle. In the short-run, the elasticity of the number of heating degree days is ten times less. This means that the variable influences electricity consumption much less in the short-run. As for the coefficient of cooling degree days is again statistically insignificant. What is most important is that the elasticities which are significant in the long-run are also significant in the short-run. They are lower since responses in the short-run are less abrupt. Last, the ECT term is -0.27 meaning that temporary deviations will be corrected 27% during the first year i.e. if we are off the consumption curve, then consumption will adjust toward its long-run level by 27% during the first year.

As for the French market, electricity price is statistically insignificant meaning that consumers do not change their demand due to price changes, at least in the short-term. Important to notice is that price is significant in the long-run. Additionally, the short-run elasticity of GDP is significant, positive and inelastic. However, the short-run elasticity is almost identical than the long-run (0.70 against 0.68). This implies that electricity consumption follows the same pattern irrespectively of the time horizon. Consumption does not change abruptly to GDP changes. This might be explained by the reason that GDP is posted annually while it is too difficult to perceive changes in shorter iterations. Further, the number of heating degrees are significant, positive and inelastic. We have a change of sign between the two time-horizons (long/short term).

TABLE 1.3 Danish electricity market; results of Vector Error-Correction Model (VECM).

Variables	D(DENCON)	Stand. error	Prob.
D(DENPRICE)	-0.1252^a	0.0428	0.0070
D(DENGDP)	0.6639^a	0.0802	0.0000
D(DENHEAT)	0.0541^a	0.0175	0.0046
D(DENCOOL)	-0.0001	0.0003	0.6835
$(ECT)_{t-1}$	-0.2731^a	0.0263	0.0000
Diagnostics		Prob. F	Prob. X^2
R^2	0.8734		
Adjusted R^2	0.8547		
Durbin Watson	1.3105		
J. Bera	1.0320		
Prob. J. Bera	(0.5968)		
LM test		0.1873	0.1344
Harvey test		0.9772	0.9578

[a]Denotes significance at $\alpha = 0.01$.
[b]Denotes significance at $\alpha = 0.05$.
The Durbin Watson stat is higher than R^2 and Adj R^2 suggesting that our model is not spurious. The parenthesis beneath J. Bera is the respective probability. Serial correlation is tested with 2 lags (Breusch-Godfrey LM test, null hypothesis of no correlation). Harvey test accounts for heteroscedasticity (null hypothesis of homoscedasticity).

TABLE 1.4 French electricity market; results of Vector Error-Correction Model (VECM).

Variables	D(FRACON)	Stand. error	Prob.
Constant	0.0036	0.0036	0.3360
D(FRAPRICE)	0.0443	0.0615	0.4776
D(FRAGDP)	0.7044[a]	0.1514	0.0001
D(FRAHEAT)	0.2594[a]	0.0202	0.0000
D(FRACOOL)	0.0020	0.0024	0.4057
$(ECT)_{t-1}$	−0.0654[a]	0.0115	0.0000
Diagnostics		Prob. F	Prob. X^2
R^2	0.8733		
Adjusted R^2	0.8489		
Durbin Watson	2.4291		
J. Bera	1.4100		
Prob. J. Bera	(0.4940)		
LM test		0.4708	0.3778
Harvey test		0.0607	0.0842

[a]Denotes significance at $\alpha = 0.01$.
[b]Denotes significance at $\alpha = 0.05$.
The Durbin Watson stat is higher than R^2 and Adj R^2 suggesting that our model is not spurious. The parenthesis beneath J. Bera is the respective probability. Serial correlation is tested with 2 lags (Breusch-Godfrey LM test, null hypothesis of no correlation). Harvey test accounts for heteroscedasticity (null hypothesis of homoscedasticity).

TABLE 1.5 Spanish electricity market; results of Vector Error-Correction Model (VECM).

Variables	D(SPACON)	Stand. error	Prob.
Constant	0.0093	0.0060	0.1337
D(SPAPRICE)	−0.1297[b]	0.0471	0.0106
D(SPAGDP)	0.7700[a]	0.1761	0.0002
D(SPAHEAT)	−0.0295	0.0378	0.4425
D(SPACOOL)	0.0006	0.0099	0.9458
$(ECT)_{t-1}$	−0.2780[a]	0.0766	0.0012
Diagnostics		Prob. F	Prob. X^2
R^2	0.6767		
Adjusted R^2	0.6145		
Durbin Watson	2.0986		
J. Bera	0.6126		
Prob. J. Bera	(0.7361)		
LM test		0.7757	0.7152
Harvey test		0.1841	0.1845

[a]Denotes significance at $\alpha = 0.01$.
[b]Denotes significance at $\alpha = 0.05$.
The Durbin Watson stat is higher than R^2 and Adj R^2 suggesting that our model is not spurious. The parenthesis beneath J. Bera is the respective probability. Serial correlation is tested with 2 lags (Breusch-Godfrey LM test, null hypothesis of no correlation). Harvey test accounts for heteroscedasticity (null hypothesis of homoscedasticity).

The ECT term is again negative and significant verifying the robustness of our model. The speed of adjustment is (-0.06) implying that only a 6% correction will occur in the first year. Adjustments are quite slow for the French market.

As for the Spanish market, the price elasticity is negative and lower than that of the long-run. Both remain inelastic implying low substitution. The LeChatelier principle is verified. The extremely low elasticity (-0.12) highlights that there might be low diversity in energy sources, while electricity demand covers inelastic needs. The short-run elasticity of GDP is positive, inelastic and higher than the respective long-run. This might be explained by the short-term needs of electrification during periods of economic development. Spanish development requires, short-term, more quantities i.e. it is more energy intensive in this time horizon. The speed of adjustment is higher than that of France and almost identical to that of Denmark.

3.4   Impulse response functions (IRFs)

We derive our IRFs from the unrestricted VARs for each market. The diagrams trace the response of each VAR variable to its innovation and to the innovations of the other variables. We use a 10-year horizon. We confirm the negative relationship between consumption and price starting from the first row of the diagrams in Fig. 1.1 for Danish consumption. One standard deviation shock of GDP causes positive reaction to consumption, while the bounds of confidence become wide after the fourth year. Again, IRFs confirm the positive relationship between GDP and consumption. The responses to the number of heating and cooling degrees are negligible confirming the low coefficient of heating and the statistical insignificance of cooling. Further, the bounds of confidence for heating and cooling become wide after the second year meaning that the response of consumption becomes insignificant.

As for the second market (France), Fig. 1.2 shows that our IRFs confirm the negative relationship between consumption and price. The greatest response is after 2 years and since then the impact fades out. Additionally, the confidence bounds

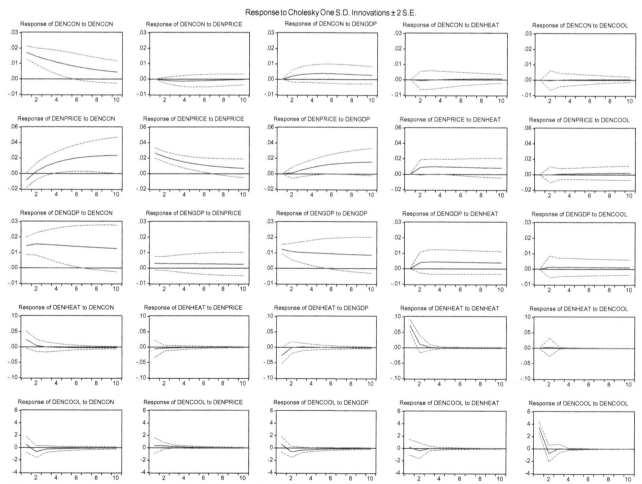

FIG. 1.1   Impulse response functions for the Danish electricity market. *(Source: Author's calculations.)*

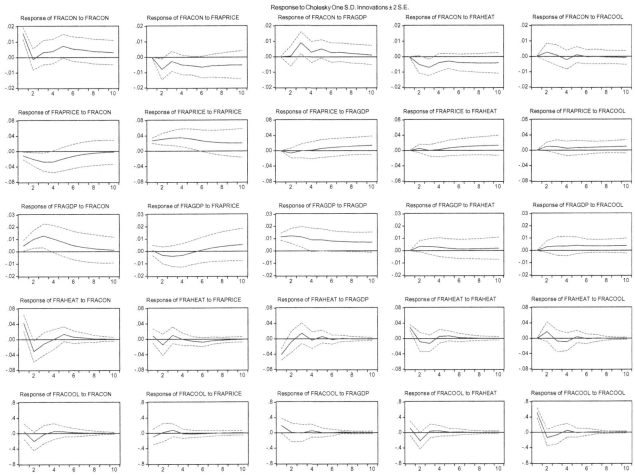

FIG. 1.2 Impulse response functions for the French electricity market. *(Source: Author's calculations.)*

become wide since the second year making the response insignificant. Consumption has again a positive response to GDP, and its greater response is during the third year. The diagram does confirm the negative relationship between heating and consumption. Last, the response to cooling is negligible.

The diagrams of the first row in Fig. 1.3 for the Spanish market again confirm our elasticities. Consumption has a negative relationship with price, while the confidence bounds become very wide from the beginning. GDP holds a positive relationship with consumption, but the response is very close to zero verifying our low elasticities. As for the heating and cooling diagrams, the response of consumption is almost negligible confirming our low elasticities. However, the IRFs do not confirm the positive sign of the number of heating degrees. The confidence bounds start widening from the beginning making significance less possible.

4   Conclusions

Electricity demand forecasting is important but also poses a lot of challenges. It is of utter importance since electricity markets are lately liberalized. Further, many countries proceed to market coupling, while they share a common regulatory framework. A great example of how state-run markets are transformed into free markets and then to regionals is that of the European Energy Union. Since price discovery is more an issue of fundamentals, then stakeholders should have a timely and accurate picture of those fundamentals. Supply side remains largely constant in the short-run since investment in capacity cannot change from day to day. What is volatile is the demand. Demand is subject to greater volatility since hour (day or night), or season (winter or summer), or other characteristics have their own influence. Further, electricity markets are ones of the latest liberalized and as a result in transition. New regulatory frameworks, environmental restrictions, energy transition, electric storage and distributed energy sources create a very dynamic environment stakeholders must cope with.

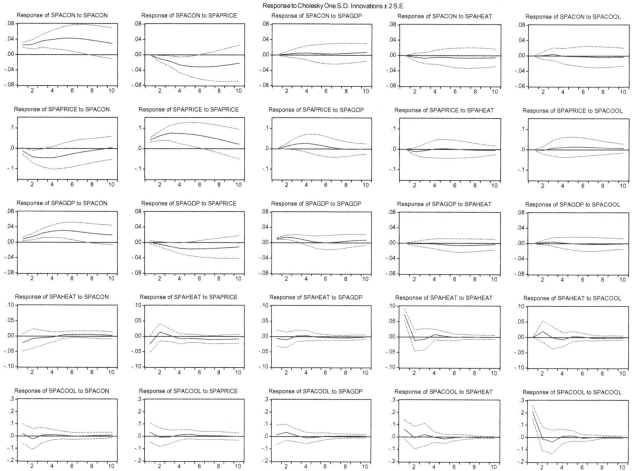

FIG. 1.3 Impulse response functions for the Spanish electricity market. *(Source: Author's calculations.)*

In this difficult task (demand forecasting), econometrics can play a significant role. Econometrics, for example, use data that they are not used in neural networks. Economic fundamentals like GDP, employment or industrial production are not posted daily, let alone hourly. These can reveal trends in energy consumption. Additionally, FIDs (final investment decisions) appraisals require long- and short-term forecasting, something which econometrics can supply. The VECM modelling we developed covers both horizons (long- and short-term). As a result, econometrics can cover large areas of forecasting. Econometrics can also derive elasticities i.e. responses to certain changes. In addition, econometrics can adjust to certain markets or regions. For example, our results presented great differences in price sensitivity among the markets. In the long-run, Danish consumers overreact to price changes (−1.12), while French and Spanish consumers hold a much milder stance (−0.38 and −0.33 respectively). The ability of econometrics to adjust to the data creates a lot of opportunities for application of prudent policies depending on the market characteristics. Societies do not respond in the same way to price changes, or environmental taxes or regulations. Seasonal temperatures also create different consuming profiles. Electricity pricing is among the issues which econometrics can be useful for. The aforementioned methods are important for policymaking and business decisions. Many other methodological approaches work without taking into consideration market characteristics. Moreover, econometrics can be applied for variables' selection. Econometrics already have a firm base for variable selection and trimming. Removing seasonal trends is one of them. Last, econometrics, as a well-established science, can well cover many needs like volatility modelling (GARCH modelling) and forecasting.

Last, econometrics should be applied in combination with other methodologies from other fields. A disadvantage of econometrics is that they use past data to forecast future values. In addition, econometrics are subject to much aggregation. To avoid those issues, scientists should preferably apply hybrid methodologies to combine the merits of each component. Forecasting needs to be as more precise as possible since market failures can have great impact on corporations and market participants.

References

Adeoye, O., Spataru, C., 2019. Modelling and forecasting hourly electricity demand in West African countries. Appl. Energy 242, 311–333. https://doi.org/10.1016/j.apenergy.2019.03.057.

Akaike, H., 1973. Information theory and an extension of the maximum likelihood principle. In: Second International Symposium on Information Technology, pp. 267–281.

Al-Musaylh, M.S., Deo, R.C., Adamowski, J.F., Li, Y., 2018. Short-term electricity demand forecasting with MARS, SVR and ARIMA models using aggregated demand data in Queensland, Australia. Adv. Eng. Inform. 35, 1–16. https://doi.org/10.1016/j.aei.2017.11.002.

AL-Musaylh, M.S., Deo, R.C., Adamowski, J.F., Li, Y., 2019. Short-term electricity demand forecasting using machine learning methods enriched with ground-based climate and ECMWF Reanalysis atmospheric predictors in southeast Queensland, Australia. Renew. Sust. Energy Rev. 113, 109293. https://doi.org/10.1016/j.rser.2019.109293.

An, N., Zhao, W., Wang, J., Shang, D., Zhao, E., 2013. Using multi-output feedforward neural network with empirical mode decomposition based signal filtering for electricity demand forecasting. Energy 49, 279–288.

Angelopoulos, D., Siskos, Y., Psarras, J., 2019. Disaggregating time series on multiple criteria for robust forecasting: the case of long-term electricity demand in Greece. Eur. J. Oper. Res. 275, 252–265. https://doi.org/10.1016/j.ejor.2018.11.003.

Chang, P.C., Fan, C.Y., Lin, J.J., 2011. Monthly electricity demand forecasting based on a weighted evolving fuzzy neural network approach. Int. J. Electr. Power Energy Syst. 33, 17–27. https://doi.org/10.1016/j.ijepes.2010.08.008.

Clarke, J.A., Mirza, S., 2006. A comparison of some common methods for detecting Granger noncausality. J. Stat. Comput. Simul. 76, 207–231. https://doi.org/10.1080/10629360500107741.

De Felice, M., Alessandri, A., Catalano, F., 2015. Seasonal climate forecasts for medium-term electricity demand forecasting. Appl. Energy 137, 435–444.

Elamin, N., Fukushige, M., 2018. Modeling and forecasting hourly electricity demand by SARIMAX with interactions. Energy 165, 257–268. https://doi.org/10.1016/j.energy.2018.09.157.

Elliott, B.Y.G., Rothenberg, T.J., Stock, J.H., 1996. Efficient tests for an autoregressive unit root. Econometrica 64, 813–836.

Greene, W.H., 2003. Econometric Analysis, fifth ed. Prentice Hall.

Günay, M.E., 2016. Forecasting annual gross electricity demand by artificial neural networks using predicted values of socio-economic indicators and climatic conditions: case of Turkey. Energy Policy 90, 92–101. https://doi.org/10.1016/j.enpol.2015.12.019.

He, Y., Jiao, J., Chen, Q., Ge, S., Chang, Y., Xu, Y., 2017. Urban long term electricity demand forecast method based on system dynamics of the new economic normal: the case of Tianjin. Energy 133, 9–22. https://doi.org/10.1016/j.energy.2017.05.107.

Johansen, S., 1992. Cointegration in partial systems and the efficiency of single-equation analysis. J. Econ. 52, 389–402. https://doi.org/10.1016/0304-4076(92)90019-N.

Khalifa, A., Caporin, M., Di Fonzo, T., 2019. Scenario-based forecast for the electricity demand in Qatar and the role of energy efficiency improvements. Energy Policy 127, 155–164. https://doi.org/10.1016/j.enpol.2018.11.047.

Laouafi, A., Mordjaoui, M., Haddad, S., Boukelia, T.E., Ganouche, A., 2017. Online electricity demand forecasting based on an effective forecast combination methodology. Electr. Power Syst. Res. 148, 35–47. https://doi.org/10.1016/j.epsr.2017.03.016.

Lebotsa, M.E., Sigauke, C., Bere, A., Fildes, R., Boylan, J.E., 2018. Short term electricity demand forecasting using partially linear additive quantile regression with an application to the unit commitment problem. Appl. Energy 222, 104–118. https://doi.org/10.1016/j.apenergy.2018.03.155.

Li, R., Jiang, P., Yang, H., Li, C., 2020. A novel hybrid forecasting scheme for electricity demand time series. Sustain. Cities Soc. 55, 102036. https://doi.org/10.1016/j.scs.2020.102036.

Milgrom, P., Roberts, J., 1996. The LeChatelier principle. Am. Econ. Rev. 86, 173–179. https://doi.org/10.2307/2118261.

Mirjat, N.H., Uqaili, M.A., Harijan, K., Walasai, G.D., Mondal, M.A.H., Sahin, H., 2018. Long-term electricity demand forecast and supply side scenarios for Pakistan (2015–2050): a LEAP model application for policy analysis. Energy 165, 512–526. https://doi.org/10.1016/j.energy.2018.10.012.

Morita, K., Shiromaru, H., Manabe, Y., Kato, T., Funabashi, T., Suzuoki, Y., 2017. A study on estimation of aggregated electricity demand for one-hour-ahead forecast. Appl. Therm. Eng. 114, 1443–1448. https://doi.org/10.1016/j.applthermaleng.2016.09.162.

Oh, S.J., Ng, K.C., Thu, K., Chun, W., Chua, K.J.E., 2016. Forecasting long-term electricity demand for cooling of Singapore's buildings incorporating an innovative air-conditioning technology. Energy Build. 127, 183–193. https://doi.org/10.1016/j.enbuild.2016.05.073.

Pérez-García, J., Moral-Carcedo, J., 2016. Analysis and long term forecasting of electricity demand trough a decomposition model: a case study for Spain. Energy 97, 127–143. https://doi.org/10.1016/j.energy.2015.11.055.

Pessanha, J.F.M., Leon, N., 2015. Forecasting long-term electricity demand in the residential sector. Procedia Comput. Sci. 55, 529–538. https://doi.org/10.1016/j.procs.2015.07.032.

Said, S.E., Dickey, D.A., 1984. Testing for unit roots in autoregressive-moving average models of unknown order. Biometrika 71 (3), 599–607. https://doi.org/10.2139/ssrn.2882101.

Schwarz, G., 1978. Estimating the dimension of a model. Ann. Stat. 6, 461–464.

Shao, Z., Gao, F., Yang, S.L., Yu, B.G., 2015. A new semiparametric and EEMD based framework for mid-term electricity demand forecasting in China: hidden characteristic extraction and probability density prediction. Renew. Sust. Energy Rev. 52, 876–889. https://doi.org/10.1016/j.rser.2015.07.159.

Son, H., Kim, C., 2017. Short-term forecasting of electricity demand for the residential sector using weather and social variables. Resour. Conserv. Recycl. 123, 200–207. https://doi.org/10.1016/j.resconrec.2016.01.016.

Van der Meer, D.W., Shepero, M., Svensson, A., Widén, J., Munkhammar, J., 2018. Probabilistic forecasting of electricity consumption, photovoltaic power generation and net demand of an individual building using Gaussian processes. Appl. Energy 213, 195–207.

Vu, D.H., Muttaqi, K.M., Agalgaonkar, A.P., Bouzerdoum, A., 2017. Short-term electricity demand forecasting using autoregressive based time varying model incorporating representative data adjustment. Appl. Energy 205, 790–801. https://doi.org/10.1016/j.apenergy.2017.08.135.

Wang, Y., Wang, J., Zhao, G., Dong, Y., 2012. Application of residual modification approach in seasonal ARIMA for electricity demand forecasting: a case study of China. Energy Policy 48, 284–294.

Xiong, T., Bao, Y., Hu, Z., 2014. Interval forecasting of electricity demand: a novel bivariate EMD-based support vector regression modeling framework. Int. J. Electr. Power Energy Syst. 63, 353–362.

Yang, Y., Chen, Y., Wang, Y., Li, C., Li, L., 2016. Modelling a combined method based on ANFIS and neural network improved by DE algorithm: a case study for short-term electricity demand forecasting. Appl. Soft Comput. J. 49, 663–675. https://doi.org/10.1016/j.asoc.2016.07.053.

Yukseltan, E., Yucekaya, A., Bilge, A.H., 2017. Forecasting electricity demand for Turkey: modeling periodic variations and demand segregation. Appl. Energy 193, 287–296. https://doi.org/10.1016/j.apenergy.2017.02.054.

Zhu, S., Wang, J., Zhao, W., Wang, J., 2011. A seasonal hybrid procedure for electricity demand forecasting in China. Appl. Energy 88, 3807–3815. https://doi.org/10.1016/j.apenergy.2011.05.005.

Zivot, E., Andrews, D.W.K., 1992. Evidence on the Great Crash the oil price shock and the unit root hypothesis. J. Bus. Econ. Stat. 10, 251–270.

Chapter 2

An econometric approach for Germany's short-term energy demand forecasting

Symeoni Soursou (Eleni)

Energy and Environmental Policy Laboratory, Department of International and European Studies, School of Economics, Business and International Studies, University of Piraeus, Piraeus, Greece

1 Introduction

The magnitude of energy demand during the last decades has been fully recognized, especially, under the spectrum of liberalized economies. The development of deregulated energy markets and the urgency to meet the real energy needs have mirrored the necessity of an effective demand response. Through the context of power markets' efficiency energy scheduling, management and forecasting are yielding market-based instruments (Cugliari and Poggi, 2018).

For this reason, energy demand forecasting is at the core of energy economic research. A plethora of different approaches tries systematically to analyze and provide a safety net for future predictions willing to meet actual load. Various factors are explaining the significance of accurate electricity forecasts both at a macroeconomic and microeconomic scale. On the macroeconomic side, energy forecasts can be a useful compass for environmental and energy policies, whereas on a microeconomic perspective they help in the well-functioning of different industry's segments (utilities, traders, suppliers) (Luo et al., 2018).

Furthermore, the global surge in energy consumption, concerns about the energy dependence, greening the economies and the penetration of RES favor the development and the adoption of more accurate forecasting models (Javier Campillo, 2012).

As Nalcaci mentions load forecasting is a crucial process regarding the planning and the operation of electric power systems directly connected national security and the daily operation of society as well as to the development of the economy (Nalcaci et al., 2018). Thus, the precision of electric load forecasting is of great significance to power system management and energy generating capacity scheduling, "as these accurate forecasts lead to substantial savings in operating and maintenance costs, and correct decisions for future development" (Mahmoud and Hammad, 2020). Moreover, it depicts the first step to improve future generation, transmission and distribution facilities.

Nevertheless, the precision of electricity load forecasting is not often in the position to fulfill our desired expectations as it is affected by social activities, country policies, economic growth and climate change (Zhanga et al., 2017). To deal with these issues more complex systems, such as the artificial neural networks, are adapted to energy demand quest (Al-Shareef et al., 2008).

Another, challenging issue during the forecasting process is to treat holidays. Zien dedicates a detailed study examining the effects of bank holidays on the German electricity market, providing an extensive variety of methods and models (Ziel, 2018). The study uses two core models a univariate and a multivariate as well, following in both cases "a Fourier approximation of the annual seasonal component" (Ziel, 2018). Both the models are enriched with different dummy variables. The results indicate that the overall forecasting is improved significantly if dummies for holidays are embedded, reaching to 80% accuracy.

Finding a suitable forecasting model for an exact electricity network is claimed to be much difficult as none of the forecasting models and methods can be generalized for demand patterns (Zhanga et al., 2017). According to Lin et al., there are two sorts of electric load forecasting models; the multi-factor/cross-sectional forecasting method which concentrates on the search of the causal relations between forecasting values and various influencing factors. The second is the faster and far easier time series forecasting method which is depended on historical series and is also classified into machine learning models, statistical models and hybrid models (Lin et al., 2017).

Mathematical Modelling of Contemporary Electricity Markets. https://doi.org/10.1016/B978-0-12-821838-9.00002-5

Furthermore, it is critical to mention that the load forecast literature suggests the categorization of energy forecasting on a time horizon basis. So, many researchers have sorted load forecasting into four distinct groups:

- *Long-term load forecasting (LTLF)* that ranges from 1 year to 20 years emphasizing the construction of new generations and strategic planning, development of power supply and delivery system.
- *Medium-term load forecasting (MTLF)* that varies from 1 week to a year representing maintenance planning, scheduling fuel buys, trade in energy and assessment of revenue.
- *Short-term load forecasting (STLF)* that ranges from 1 h to a week and it is very significant for daily utility operations, generation plan and electricity transmission.
- **Very short-term load forecasting** *(VSTLF)* that varies from a few minutes to an hour and is mainly used for real-time control.

Historical data concerning the energy consumption is widely used to project the future consumption in terms of short-term load forecasting. Besides, short-term forecasting uses weather data or seasonal dummies as independent variables. Many researchers employ regression analysis with the aim of OLS, where the actual load is treated as a dependent variable, while weather-climate information and calendar variables enrich the model as explanatory.

One of the most popular models in this category is the Tao's Vanilla, the landmark approach during the Global Energy Forecasting Competition 2012 (GEFCom2012). The model incorporates temperature, linear trend and calendar variables as well. Building on this model Jian Luo, Tao Hong and Meng Yue present in their recent study a dynamic regression model willing to augment predictions accuracy for the very short-term load forecasts. Adding the lagged load values and using methods for anomaly detection they finally employ a threshold model ((Luo, 2018).

Except for the multiple regression, stochastic time series and weighted regression can be found in the literature. Nonetheless, recent studies focus on machine learning methods, mainly the artificial neural networks (ANN), fuzzy regression and support-vector machine. Currently, the support-vector machine—which simulates ANN—is preferred for short-run predictions as it offers a higher level of accuracy. The development of artificial neural networks is due to their superior forecast accuracy and their ability to analyze complex and non-linear relationships. For instance, Charytoniuk and Chen suggest a set of ANNs to predict the load dynamics (Charytoniuk and Chen, 2000). Taylor accounting to minute-to-minute electricity values in United Kingdom fits an autoregressive integrated moving average model (ARIMA) and two exponential smoothing techniques (Taylor, 2008). Jebarah, assessing the Malaysia's and following Taylor's steps applies four different forecasting methods time series regression, double and triple exponential smoothing, ARIMA and finally constructs an ANN, obtaining a mean absolute percentage error of −0.16 from the univariate ANN (Jebaraj, 2017).

Mandal et al. using neural networks for the very short-term forecasts have achieved a mean absolute percentage error (MAPE) of 0.8% for a 1 h ahead forecasts and 2.43% for 6 h ahead forecasts as well (Mandal et al., 2006). Furthermore, Al-Shareef with the aim of a neural network has achieved a 1.12% level of accuracy for 1 h-ahead forecasting (Al-Shareef et al., 2008). Currently, the support-vector machine—a method that simulates ANN—has been proven as the best alternative to ANN providing that it offers better results in short-run predictions.

Other forecasting models also refer to Wu and Shahidehpour (2010) who displayed a hybrid ARMAX-GARCH (generalized autoregressive conditional heteroskedastic) adaptive wavelet neural network model, and tested it using PJM market information. Moreover, Welch and Bishop (Welch and Bishop, 2004) suggest the Kalman filter (KF) as a set of math equations in the state space that can give an effective computational (repetive) means to assess the state of an observed process.

The grey system (GM) introduced by Deng Julong in 1982 and refers to systems that lack information, like operation mechanism, structure message and behavior document (Julong, 1989). In grey system theory, the development of a dynamic model with a group of differential equations is called grey differential model (GM) and relies on the generating series rather than on the raw one (Julong, 1984). Additionally, Weron describes similar-day and exponential smoothing (ES) as important forecasting methods. The first model is based on examining historical information for days with features similar to the predicted day and taking those historical values as predictions of future prices (Weber, 2006). Exponential smoothing is a pragmatic approach to prediction, through which the prediction is constructed by an exponentially weighed average of past observations (Weron, 2014).

As far as the long-term forecasting serves as a significant policy instrument to meet the increasing demand, potential shortages and capacity issues. Long-term forecast incorporates technology, implemented policies and consumer behavior indicators. The majority of the long-term attempts arise from econometrics. The electricity demand is explained through the economic theory while many criteria affecting the electricity output are taken into account. Widen et al. proposed a Markov chain model for household electricity consumption in Sweden (Widén and Wäckelgård, 2010). Alternatively, some researchers apply the conditional demand analysis for final household consumption (Javier Campillo, 2012).

So, examining different forecasting techniques and providing some recommendations is of paramount importance. This study following the step of previous attempts wishes to examine the electricity forecast methods concerning short-term predictions, suggesting a comparative analysis for Germany's load. We choose Germany as our reference country for certain reasons.

Germany is among the most robust industrialized economies and consequently a heavy energy consumer. Also, Germany is a significant player in the European Power Market and has become a net-exporter for neighboring countries (IEA, 2020). However, it is critical to mention that country's total electricity consumption is relatively steady over the last decade at around 530 TWh (IEA, 2020). Furthermore, Germany is in the process of radically changing its energy sector obeying to European guidelines and its national climate policies. While during the last decades Germany achieved a successful transition to a more diversified energy system and finally variable energy production, such as solar and wind generation are broadly influenced by meteorological conditions. Table 2.1 provides a synopsis of previous studies.

This study aims to assess different econometric forecasting methods and investigate the factors that ameliorate the results of the forecasts. The state-of-the-art of time-series analysis is used. The starting point of our empirical attempt is the application of a univariate Autoregressive model-AR (p). Thus, a univariate AR (p), MA (q), ARMA (p, q) and ARIMA (p, q, d) model for German load will be constructed. We will proceed to the appropriate Autoregressive Moving Average-ARMA (p, q) model following the Box-Jenkins steps (Box, 1976). While seeking to improve our estimates exogenous variables expressing the meteorological conditions and the electricity prices are nested. Hence, ARMAX models are developed for the sake of higher forecasting accuracy. Afterwards, a regression analysis takes place as a suitable alternative to ARMAX models. Also, we proceed to the exponential smoothing technique.

This chapter is organized as follows: the next section describes Germany's electricity market; the status and the future advancements that potentially would influence the electricity demand. The third section highlights the methods and formulas that will be applied and provides an extensive description of the data used as well. Then, we proceed to forecasts

TABLE 2.1 Previous studies.

Author	Title	Methods	Year
Ziel, F.	Modelling public holidays in load forecasting: a German case study	Univariate, multivariate model with dummy variables	2018
Charytoniuk, W. & Chen, M.	Very short-term load forecasting using artificial neural network	ANN	2000
Taylor, J.W.	An evaluation of methods for very short-term load forecasting using minute-by-minute British data	ARIMA, exponential smoothing	2008
Luo, J., Hong, T. & Yue, M	Real-time anomaly detection for very short-term load forecasting	Dynamic regression model-threshold	2018
Jebaraj, S.	Electricity demand forecasting for Malaysia using artificial neural network	Time series regression, double moving average model, double and triple exponential smoothing model, ARIMA, ANN	2017
Coşkun Hamzaçebi	Primary sources planning based on demand forecasting: the case of Turkey	Grey Systems Theory GM(91,1) & Grey Seasonal Forecasting Method	2016
Abdoulaye Camara, Wang Feixing & Liu Xiuqin	Energy consumption forecasting using seasonal ARIMA with artificial neural networks models	SARIMA Model & ANN	2016
Nor Hamizah Miswan, Rahaini Mohd Said, Nor Hafizah Hussin, Khairum Hamzah, and Emy Zairah Ahmad	Comparative performance of ARIMA and DES models in forecasting electricity load demand in Malaysia	ARIMA and Double Exponential Smoothing	2016
Jamal Fattah, Latifa Ezzine, Zineb Aman, Haj El Moussami, and Abdeslam Lachhab	Forecasting of demand using ARIMA model	ARIMA	2018

analysis, presenting the results, the advantages, and disadvantages of each empirical method. The last section provides important remarks and recommendations for further work.

2   German energy landscape

Germany in response to the provisions of the First European Energy Package for electricity markets in 1996 proceeds to major structural changes in the power sector. Moving toward a "a market-based system," the German government adopts the National Energy Act in 1998 which brings an end to the previous status of vertically integrated monopolies, while it foresees price setting and a certain degree of unbundling in supply and transmission (IEA, 2020). Complete unbundling is applied through the implementation of the Second Energy Package that also poses the third-party access as a prerequisite for the liberalized European markets. Germany incorporates into national law the aforementioned measures under the National Energy Act of 2005 which provides a significant degree of freedom on supplier's choice both to industrial and end-user consumers.

Considering the advancements in European Energy Market and the implementation of the Target Model, the stake for Germany is to achieve its energy and climate targets for 2050. In the spirit of European energy and environmental policies, Germany has launched an extensive national plan for transition from Electricity Market 2.0 to Energy Market 2.0. The BMWi roadmap includes 12 drivers for the fulfillment of 2030 and 2050 targets among them the advancements in power generation and transmission, an ambitious increase in the share of renewables −65% until 2030 according to the 2018 governmental planning as well as coupling in transport, heating and industry (IEA, 2020).

Renewable energy sources, such as wind, solar and bioenergy, are making rapid progress replacing a large part of German's conventional power, while this trend will continue to grow in the future years. In 2017, wind generation has become the second source of electricity production exceeding natural gas and nuclear energy (IEA, 2020). As IEA mentions in the country's 2020 report, renewables also provide a safety net for potential energy outages and urge Germany to sustain a stable level of self-sufficiency at approximately 40% of electricity supply. The total installed capacity of clean energy sources has risen to 32% between 2010 and 2017. The biggest deployment concerns solar and wind generation which account to 42.3GW and 56GW of installed capacity respectively.

In addition, both the fast renewables' penetration and the developments in interconnected European grid permit Germany to become a net electricity exporter for neighboring countries like Netherlands, Poland and Austria.

Germany is firmly on track to entail the gradual elimination of coal by 2038 and the electricity generation that derives from nuclear by the end of 2022. Refocusing its efforts on achieving stronger emissions reductions mainly in heating and transport, the German government has recently adopted the Climate Protection Programme 2030 as a significant move in the right direction. The plan is cognizant of the distributional effects of climate policies and intends to ensure a level playing field across stakeholders and sectors. Regulatory and policy reforms assist Germany to accomplish a sustainable, cost-efficient and equitable passage to meet its aspiring energy transition objectives (Zhanga et al., 2017).

These targets are anticipated to lead a decrease in greenhouse gas emissions (GHG) by 80–95% by 2050 and at the same time guarantee the growth and competitiveness of the German economy. The major drivers of the Energiewende are environmental sustainability and climate protection, as well as high-tech development, reduction in energy imports and economic growth (Velte, 2018).

Germany has also diversified a liberal market, a well-connected supply infrastructure, oil supply sources and high oil emergency reserves that all contribute to maintain the country's solid security of oil supply. Furthermore, it has ensured a rather high level of natural gas supply security, in spite of its reliance on imports. However, the phasing out of both coal and nuclear generation will raise Germany's demand for natural gas in electricity generation. Consequently, the security of natural gas supply has been a top priority for the government (IEA, 2020).

3   Data and methodology

The scope of this study is twofold; first of all, to delineate the most widely used econometric approaches on power forecasting by emphasizing on their mathematical expression. And second to highlight their precision. At the core of our analysis is the short-term forecasting, while Germany's electricity demand serves as the reference point to execute 1 h-ahead forecasts. The sample used provides hourly observations for the German load, capturing a time horizon near to 5 years. For the construction of the baseline model, the obtained sample contains hourly data from the Open Power System Data (Data) platform that has been used to cover the period from December 31, 2014 to March 31, 2019. At the core of our analysis is the short-term forecasting and specifically, 1 h-ahead forecasts.

We build an autoregressive (AR) and moving average (MA) models that will lead us to the application of an ARMA model which are appropriate for stationary stochastic processes. For that purpose, all the necessary unit root tests take place together with the graphical representation of the univariate model. Afterwards, we enrich the ARMA model with independent variables; we incorporate temperature and electricity price to improve the forecast estimates. This leads to the adoption of different ARMAX models. In addition, a regression analysis takes place to compare our results. Finally, we proceed to ETS-Exponential Smoothing which permits the investigation of non-linear relationships.

3.1   Variables description

Table 2.2 provide the description of the variables used in our analysis. We use the variables' mathematical expression, i.e. all variables are transformed in logarithms. Lnload contains information for Germany's electricity Load in MW. The explanatory variable lnprice illustrates the German electricity prices in euro for the period under examination. The data are obtained from the Open Power System Data platform which provides power data for 37 European countries acquired from Entso-e Transparency Platform and Entsoe's Power Statistics. Concerning the meteorological data, it is obtained from the Renwables.ninja databank which provides hourly geographically aggregated weather data across the globe from 1980 to 2019 and valuable information for renewables generation[a] from Nasa's hourly weather data.[b] The variable for temperature (lntemperature) is expressed in Celsius degrees. Regarding to solar and wind power generation they are obtained from the same platform (data R. P.)[c] and are expressed in MW. Moreover, we use two additional variables in order to assess renewables output. So, lnairdens describes the air density which is an important factor for wind farms generation and is measured in kg/mm3, whereas lnirrad represents irradiance measured in W/m^2.

3.2   Methods and formulas

The initial pivot for time series predictions is the application of Box-Jenkins methodology (Box G. a., 1976) for autoregressive (AR), moving average (MA), autoregressive moving average (ARMA) and autoregressive integrated moving average models (ARIMA). Univariate time series models or the so called "atheroretical models" are a fruitful instrument in forecasting process, given that the future values of the dependent variable Y_t can be explained from its past values and its stochastic error terms.

Aljandal (2017) states that the Box-Jenkins approach to time series modelling comprises extracting predictable movements from the observed information via a series of iterations. The univariate Box-Jenkins methodology is purely a predicting tool that follows a four-phase procedure: model identification, estimation, diagnostics and forecasting (Aljandal, 2017).

Analytically, a specific type of Box-Jenkins model is identified by using different statistics computed from an analysis of the historical information (Box, 2008). Time series stationarity is also a prerequisite. The variance and the mean must be

TABLE 2.2 Variables description.

Variable name	Variable description	Source
lnload	Actual load in MW	Open Power System Data-Entso-e Transparency
lnprice	Electricity price ahead in euro	Open Power System Data
lntemperature	Temperature °C	Renewables.ninja (T2M in MERRA-2)
lnsolar	PV hourly capacity in MW	Renewables.ninja
lnwind	Wind (onshore & offshore) hourly capacity in MW	Renewables.ninja, (ninja_wind_country_DE_current-merra-2_corrected—Version: 1.3)
lnirrad	W/m^2	Renewables.ninja (SWGDN and SWTDN in MERRA-2)
lnairdens	kg/mm3	Renewables.ninja (RHOA in MERRA-2)

a. https://www.renewables.ninja/#/country.

b. https://science.nasa.gov/earth-science/earth-science-data/data-information-policy.

c. https://doi.org/10.1016/j.energy.2019.08.068.

constant over time supposing that the values of Y_t are stationary. The stationarity can be defined through the appropriate unit roots tests and also through the autocorrelation function (ACF) and partial autocorrelation function (PACF) which indicates the autocorrelation of lagged values. This leads to the optimal model's "identification." Since identified the "best model" is assessed so that the fitted values come as close as possible to capture the pattern displayed by the existing data. The final model is used to predict the time series and to develop confidence internals, which calculate the uncertainty connected with the prediction (Aljandal, 2017).

To determine the baseline model, i.e. the appropriate AR (p) model, the graphical representation of time series, all the necessary unit roots and the ACF and partial PACF will be presented. If the German load is a non-stationary process or random walk, then it is necessary to differencing and decomposing it. Also, the graphical representations of autocorrelation and partial autocorrelation will lead to the right AR (p) and MA (q) respectively.

3.2.1 AR (p) and MA (q)

Based on Box-Jenkins (Box G. a., 1976), Harvey (Harvey, 1989) an AR of order p, AR (p) adopted to our case will be written as follows:

$$Inload_t = \delta + a_1 \, Inload_{t-1} + a_2 \, Inload_{t-2} + \ldots + a_p \, Inload_{t-p} + \epsilon_t - 1 < a < 1 \tag{2.1}$$

Where, $Inload_t$ is the dependent variable for load, δ illustrates a constant, a_1, a_2, a_p are unknown parameters, ϵ_t is the stochastic term and p the time lag. The median of an AR (p) is given by the following equation:

$$\mu = E(Inload_t) = \frac{\delta}{1 - a_1 - .. - a_2 a_p} \tag{2.2}$$

While autocorrelation and partial autocorrelation functions aim to determine the appropriate order of p, alternatively, using Yule-Walker equations we can obtain the autocorrelation coefficient, ρ and the partial autocorrelation coefficients.

MA (q)

A moving average model of order q is expressed as:

$$Y_t = \mu + \epsilon_t + \beta_1 \epsilon_{t-1} + \beta_2 \epsilon_{t-2} + \ldots + \beta_q \epsilon_{t-q} \tag{2.3}$$

Where ϵ_t is defined as $(0, \sigma^2_\epsilon)$. The β_1, β_2, β_q are simply coefficients and μ is a constant given that

$$E(Y_t) = \mu \tag{2.4}$$

3.2.2 ARMA and ARMAX

ARMA modelling is also an econometric technique dedicated to univariate models, whilst it is the combination of an autoregressive (AR) and moving average (MA) model respectively. Thus, two conditions have to be met for an ARMA model: *stationarity and invertibility* (Box G. a., 1976). The term invertibility describes the ability of an AR (1) or MA (1) model to be transformed to a MA (∞) and AR (∞) respectively (Vamvoukas, 2008).

The mathematical expression of an ARMA models is expressed as follows:

$$Y_t = \delta + \alpha_1 Y_{t-1} + \alpha_2 Y_{t-2} + \cdots + \alpha_p Y_{t-p} + \epsilon_1 + \beta_1 \epsilon_{t-1} + \beta_2 \epsilon_{t-2} + \cdots + \beta_q \epsilon_{t-q} \tag{2.5}$$

If the time series Y_t is stationary, then the median is defined:

$$E(Y_t) = \mu = \frac{\delta}{1 - a_1 - a_1 - .. - a_p} \tag{2.6}$$

Assuming a general ARMA model of order (p, q) and the case of $s \leq q$ the initial value of the autocorrelation coefficient ρ_s depends on the initial values of α_p and β_p (Vamvoukas, 2008) . While if $s > q$ is in effect, then the ARMA's ρ_s and γ_s are identical to these of AR (p):

$$Y_t = \alpha_1 Y_{t-1} + \alpha_2 Y_{t-2} + \cdots + \alpha_p Y_{t-v} \text{ for } s > q \tag{2.7}$$

And

$$\rho_s = \alpha_1 \rho_{s-1} + a_2 \rho_{s-2} + \ldots + \alpha_p \rho_{s-p} \text{ for } s > q \tag{2.8}$$

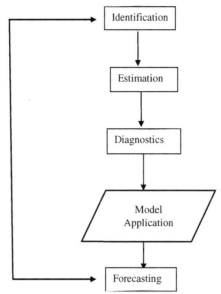

FIG. 2.1 Box-Jenkins methodology: 4 Step Evolution of ARMA/ARIMA Models.

Finally, under the ARMAX framework, independent variables may be included in the ARMA process (Md Hasanuzzaman, 2019). This special multivariate ARMA or ARIMA models allow the existence of independent variables in two distinct ways; first the independent variables take part during the specification process (Hamilton, 1994), otherwise they *reduce to the Box-Jenkins ARIMA models in the dependent variable* (Stata). Fig. 2.1 provide the Box-Jenkins methodology: 4 Step Evolution of ARMA/ARIMA Models.

3.3 Forecasting

3.3.1 AR

As it is mentioned above in the AR context the energy demand is explained *as the linear combination of the past actual values and a random noise* (Islam and Hasanuzzaman, 2020a,b). Considering the simplest AR process, i.e. AR (1) the forecast equation is expressed mathematically as follows:

$$lnload_{T+1} = \delta + a_1\, lnload_T + \epsilon_{T+1} \tag{2.9}$$

Where $\widehat{lnload}_{T+1}$ depicts the prediction with the lowest root mean squared error (Vamvoukas, 2008). Thus,

$$\widehat{lnload}_{T+1} = E_T = [lnload_{T+1}] \tag{2.10}$$

combining the Eqs. (2.9) and (2.10) it is obtained the next function:

$$lnload_{T+1} = E_T\,[\delta + lnload_{T+1} + \epsilon_{T+1}] \tag{2.11}$$

and $E_T[\epsilon_{T+1}] = 0$ if the residuals do not suffer from autocorrelation. Then,

$$lnload_{T+1} = \delta + lnload_{T+1} \tag{2.12}$$

Afterwards, we can calculate the forecast error $\widehat{\epsilon_{T+1}}$ from:

$$\widehat{\epsilon_{T+1}} = lnload_{T+1} - \widehat{lnload}_{T+1} \text{ which leads to } \widehat{\epsilon_{T+1}} = \epsilon_{T+1} \tag{2.13}$$

Finally, the forecast variance is equal to

$$\text{Var}\left(\widehat{\epsilon_{T+1}}\right) = Var(\epsilon_{T+1}) = \sigma_\epsilon^2 \tag{2.14}$$

Whilst the prediction in the $lnload_{T+h}$ period is equal to

$$\widehat{lnload}_{T+1} = \delta + a_1 \, \mathrm{E_T}[lnload_{T+h-1}] = \delta + \alpha_1 lnload_{T+h-1} \tag{2.15}$$

And

$$\mathrm{Var}\widehat{(\epsilon_{T+1})} = \sigma_\in^2 \left(1 + \alpha_1^2 + \alpha_1^4 + \cdots + \alpha_1^{2(h-1)}\right) \tag{2.16}$$

3.3.2 Forecast with MA

Assuming that the variable for energy demand lnload follows a MA (1) process which is expressed as:

$$lnload_t = \mu + \in_t + \beta_1 + \epsilon_{t+1} \tag{2.17}$$

Then taking into account the past values of lnload and seeking to obtain the future values of lnload during the period $T+h$ the subsequent equation is formed:

$$lnload_{T+h} = \mu + \in_{T+h} + \beta_1 + \epsilon_{T+h-1} \tag{2.18}$$

Note, that if the $T=2$ the equals ϵ_{T+1} consequently for the period $T+h$, $\in_T$ will be equal to: ϵ_{T+h-1}.

The prediction for $T+h$ with the smallest value of root mean squared error is determined as:

$$lnload_{T+h} = \mu \tag{2.19}$$

Whereas the variance of forecast error is

$$\mathrm{Var}\left(\widehat{\in_{T+1}}\right) = \sigma_\in^2 \left(1 + \beta_1^2\right) \tag{2.20}$$

However, MA models fit better for one period ahead predictions as it is admitted that for an $h > 1$ the obtained prediction coincides to μ (Vamvoukas, 2008).

3.3.3 Forecast with ARMA (p,q) model

For reasons of simplicity, the energy demand model is presented as an ARMA (1,1) which is expressed mathematically:

$$lnload_t = \delta + a_1 \, lnload_{t-1} + \in_t + \beta_1 \in_{t-1} \tag{2.21}$$

Then, the forecast equation for an ARMA (p,q) for h periods is defined:

$$\widehat{lnload}_{T+h} = \delta + a_1 \, \widehat{ln \, load}_{T+h-1} + \ldots + a_{h-1} \, \widehat{ln \, load}_{T+1} + a_h \, \widehat{ln \, load}_T + \ldots + a_p \, \widehat{ln \, load}_{T-p+h} + \in_t + \beta_h \in_T + \ldots$$
$$+ \beta_q \in_{T-q+h} \tag{2.22}$$

To calculate the forecast error, consider the simplest ARMA of first order (1,1):

$$Lnload_t = \delta + a_1 lnload_{t-1} + \in_1 + \beta_1 \in_{t-1} \tag{2.23}$$

Setting $t=T$ the prediction for $lnload_{T+1}$ can be obtained:

$$\widehat{lnload}_{T+1} = \delta + \alpha_1 lnload_T + \in_{T+1} + \beta_1 \in_T \tag{2.24}$$

Then using the following formula the optimal prediction for $lnload_{T+1}$ is determined; otherwise, the prediction with the smallest mean average squared error (Vamvoukas, 2008):

$$lnload_{T+1} = E_T\{lnload_{T+1}\} = E_T\{\delta + \alpha_1 lnload_T + \in_{T+1} + \beta_1 \in_T\} = \delta + \alpha_1 lnload_T + \beta_1 \in_T \tag{2.25}$$

That yields to the estimation of forecast error as follows:

$$\widehat{E_{T+1}} = lnload_{T+1} - \widehat{lnload}_{T+1} = \in_{T+1} \tag{2.26}$$

While the variance is defined as:

$$\mathrm{Var}\left(\widehat{\in}_{T+1}\right) = (\in_{T+1}) = \sigma_\in^2 \tag{2.27}$$

3.4 Forecasting accuracy

Measuring the accuracy of predictions is a primary goal in forecasting process. There are numerous statistical instruments on examining the results' precision (Ismit Mado, 2018). Wallstrom and Segerstedt suggest that the following formula for forecasting error is (Wallstrom and Segerstedt, 2010):

$$\in_t = E_t - F_t \tag{2.28}$$

Where $\in_t$ represents the forecast error in period t, E_t denotes the actual energy demand after the forecast at period t and F_t denotes the forecast energy demand at the period t. Hence, as Md Hasanuzzaman supports the forecasting error is defined as the deviation of the forecasted value at period t from the real value observed at period t (Md Hasanuzzaman, 2019).

Superior forecasting accuracy arises from a lower forecast error. However, in the case of energy demand forecasting many times is hard to obtain forecast errors with small magnitude. For that purpose statistical metrics such as the mean square error (MSE), the mean absolute error (MAE), the root mean absolute error (RMSE), the mean average percentage error (MAPE), the symmetrical mean average percentage error and the Theil inequality coefficient are widely used.

Our analysis includes the magnitude of RMSE, MAE, MAPE, symmetrical MAPE and Theil inequality coefficient. Table 2.3 provides the mathematical formulas for the metrics that measure forecasting accuracy.

Based on Box-Jenkins methodology we employ different energy demand models for Germany. The next section provides the estimation results as well as assesses the forecasts precision.

4 Results

Our preliminary work concerns the long-run behavior of Germany's energy demand. Fig. 2.2 illustrates the evolution of German energy demand in the course of time. The graph suggests that lnload at level is a stationary white noised stochastic process. Alternatively, we provide the results from a variety of unit roots tests based on SIC selection criterion for the appropriate number of lags. The results of Dickey-Fuller, Philips Perron and KPSS tests also verified that the variable lnload does not suffer from any unit root, as shown in Table 2.4. Hence, lnload is integrated of I(0). Therefore, we apply the ARMA approach instead of ARIMA (p, q, d) which are dedicated to integrated of order one time series, I (1).

The overriding concern to choose the appropriate order of p and q is to examine the ACF and PACF graphs (see Appendix) for lnload. Applying the necessary steps of Box-Jenkins methodology (Box G. a., 1976)—i.e. identification, estimation, diagnostics- an AR of order p (1), an AR (2) and finally an AR (3) are constructed for the energy demand. Likewise, the estimates of ACF lead to the adoption of four distinct MA models due to strong autocorrelation. However, as it mentioned above a moving average model offers satisfying forecast results notably if it is expressed in order 1. So, our forecast attempt is restricted to a MA (1). While all the necessary diagnostics checks are in the Appendix. Figs. 2.3 and 2.4 provide the autocorrelation and partial autocorrelation on lnload time-series respectively.

Proceeding to ARMA approach, we create different models to capture the potential combinations of AR (p) and MA (q). Afterwards, using the Akaike's minimization criterion we select the most efficient ARMA model that is enriched with the chosen independent variables under the ARMAX framework.

TABLE 2.3 Indicators for measuring forecasting accuracy.

Forecast evaluation statistics	Formulas
RMSE	$\sqrt{\sum_{t=T+1}^{T+h} (Y_t - Y_t)^2 / h}$
MAE	$\sum_{t=T+1}^{T+h} \lvert Y_t - Y_t \rvert^2 / h$
MAPE	$100 \sum_{t=T+1}^{T+h} \left[\frac{Y_t - Y_t}{Y_t} / h \right]$
Theil inequality coefficient	$\dfrac{\sqrt{\sum_{t=T+1}^{T+h} (Y_t - Y_t)^2 / h}}{\sqrt{\sum_{t=T+1}^{T+h} Y_t^2 / h} + \sqrt{\sum_{t=T+1}^{T+h} Y_t^2 / h}}$

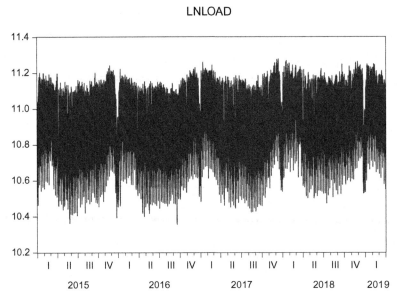

FIG. 2.2   lnload at levels.

TABLE 2.4 Unit root tests.

Variables	Augmented Dickey-Fuller		Phillips-Perron		KPSS		Order of integration
	τ_t	τ_μ	τ_t	τ_μ	$\widehat{\eta}$	$\widehat{\eta}_\mu$	
Levels	−23.42790	−24.47642	−28.95111	−26.27197	4.5432890	231,202	
lnload	(0.0000)	(0.0000)	0.0000	0.0000	(11385.17)[a,b,c]	(5729.914)[a]	I (0)

Note: Dickey-Fuller tests are conducted according to optimal lag selection criteria AIC, SBIC, HIC. The optimal lag length is based on SIC information criterion. Number in parenthesis in Phillips-Perron test indicates the Newey-West lags. MacKinnon approximate p-value are in parentheses.
[a]Denotes significance at 1% level.
[b]Denotes significance at 5% level.
[c]Denotes significance at 10% level.

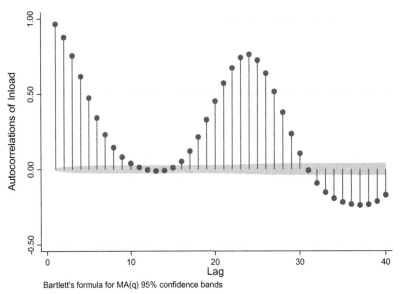

Bartlett's formula for MA(q) 95% confidence bands

FIG. 2.3   Autocorrelation on lnload time-series.

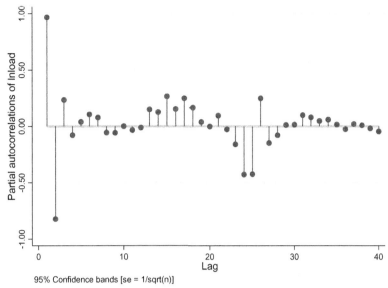

FIG. 2.4 Partial autocorrelation on lnload time-series.

From 25 different estimations of ARMA (p, q), shown in Fig. 2.5, we conclude that the ARMA (4, 3) is the optimal model based on Akaike's criterion (AIC value: −9.28174220131). Then the reference model ARMA (4, 3) is converted to different ARMAX models to ameliorate our estimates; among them two separate models dedicated to weather conditions and prices. Alternatively, we use simple linear regression as in many previous studies, for instance Tao's Vanilla model, to compare forecasting estimates. Finally, we proceed to exponential smoothing which is preferred for energy demand forecasts.

The sample used for the forecast refers to December 31, 2014 to March 31, 2019, while our training sample covers the period during January 1, 2015 and December 31, 2019 including 37,224 hourly observations. The following table presents the estimates of the mean absolute percentage error (MAPE), the mean absolute error (MAE) and the root mean squared error for the forecasts of lnload.

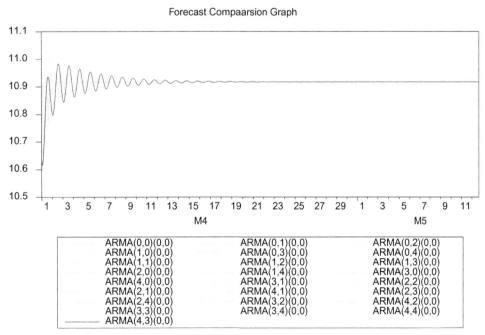

FIG. 2.5 Defining the optimal ARIMA model.

4.1 Measuring forecasting accuracy

This sub-section presents the forecast results obtained from the two AR(p) models, i.e. AR (1), AR(2), the MA(1), the superior ARMA(4,3) and four ARMAX attempts. Table 2.5 contains the stronger forecasting metrics, i.e. MAPE, MAE, RMSE, Symmetric MAPE and Theil's U.

The table above sustains the high level of accuracy with respect to time series predictions (Box, 2008) even in a univariate context. Univariate methods can actually achieve a high level of performance as in Jiang et al. (Jiang et al., 2018), where the ARIMA Model for energy demand has a 0.017 MAPE and 6.18 RMSE respectively. Also, Taylor, De Menezes and Mc Sharry in their study "A Comparison of Univariate Methods for Forecasting Electricity Demand Up to A Day Ahead" prove especially, the magnitude of ARMA models in forecasting (James and Taylor, 2006).

Our estimates show a low forecasting error in relation to previous studies where a sufficient MAPE is close to 6% or 7% as in Hamizah (2016) and Jebaraj et al. (S.). In our case the estimations for MAPE, MAE, RMSE and Theil U are identical for most of the developed models. The similarity in measuring statistics can be explained under the prism of stationarity. Germany's idiosyncratic energy demand that follows a stable path (IEA, 2020) over the last decade is mirrored to the MAPE close to 1%, given that the lnload is a stationary stochastic process without trends and drifts.

The obtained percentages of forecasting error in our case are the same in the AR (1), AR (2) and MA (1) achieving a MAPE at around 1.46. Likewise, for MAE and Theil inequality coefficient. While the RMSE for AR (2) is the same as in ARMAX Model 1. Regarding the ARMA (4, 3) Model we observe that the MAPE is not improved further in comparison to the univariate methods and all the other metrics remain the same. Our estimates are in accordance with Ismail Shah's et al. results who obtained low values of MAPE, MAE and RMSE through the application of an AR and ARMA techniques in their recent study for short-term energy demand (Shah et al., 2019). For instance, the obtained MAPE from their ARMA is 2.51 and 2.50 for the AR respectively. Furthermore, Franco, Blanch et al. evaluating predictions for the day-ahead electricity price in Spanish Power Market also find evidence of higher accuracy in the simplest AR (1) process.

After, fitting the ARMA (4, 3) Model we develop different ARMAX Models adding exogenous variables for meteorological conditions and information about electricity price given that these indicators influence greatly the energy demand. The first ARMAX Model containing the variable for electricity prices, lnprice, improves the percentage of MAPE, while

TABLE 2.5 Error estimation.

Model	MAPE	MAE	RMSE	Symmetric MAPE	Theil inequality coefficient
AR (1)	1.46	0.16	0.19	1.46	0.008
AR (2)	1.46	0.16	0.18	1.46	0.008
MA (1)	1.46	0.16	0.19	1.46	0.008
ARMA (4,3)	1.46	0.16	0.19	1.46	0.008
ARMAX Model 1: (4,3) independent variables lnprice	1.44	0.16	0.18	1.44	0.008
ARMAX Model 2: (4,3) independent variables: lntemperature	1.49	0.16	0.19	1.49	0.008
ARMAX Model 3: (4.3) independent variables: lntemperature, lnirrad, lnairdens	1.32	0.14	0.17	1.32	0.007
ARMAX Model 4: (4.3) independent variables: lntemperature, lnirrad, lnairdens, lnsolar, lnwind	1.14	0.12	0.16	1.14	0.007
ARMAX Model 5: (4.3) independent variables: lntemperature, lnirrad, lnairdens, lnsolar, lnwind, lnprice	1.15	0.12	0.15	1.13	0.007
OLS Model 1: lnload, lnprice	1.28	0.14	0.16	1.28	0.007
OLS Model 2: lnload, lntemperature	1.49	0.16	0.19	1.48	0.008
OLS Model 3: lnload, lntemperature, lnprice, lnwind, lnsolar, lnirrad, lnairdens	0.86	0.09	0.12	0.86	0.005
Simple Exponential Smoothing	26.5	25.5	75.40	30.9	0.9

the other statistics remain uninfluenced. As far as, the ARMAX Model 2, which has as an independent variable the temperature (lntemperature) does not seem to ameliorate the forecast errors. To the contrary, MAPE is worsening (1.49).

On the other hand, when it is enriched with lnirrad and lnairdens respectively, the obtained MAPE ameliorates to 1.32, while the MAE is 0.14 and RMSE reaches to 0.17. The ARMAX Model 4, which nests also the variables for renewables generation yields to better results, achieving a MAPE of 1.14, MAE of 0.12 and a RMSE at around 0.16. While the Theil inequality coefficient remains at 0.007 as in previous model, ARMAX Model 3. Finally, ARMAX Model 5 does not improve the measuring statics.

To conclude, energy demand forecasting accuracy improves further under the ARMAX framework. When meteorological and price information are included to the ARMA model the forecast accuracy increases which is in accordance with several previous studies (Islam and Hasanuzzaman, 2020a). Finally, ARMAX Model 4, which contains additional exogenous variables for PV and wind output over-performs. Fig. 2.6 provides the Actual Vs Forecasting Values for the ARMAX Model 3, while Fig. 2.7 provides the Forecasted Energy Demand for the ARMAX Model 4.

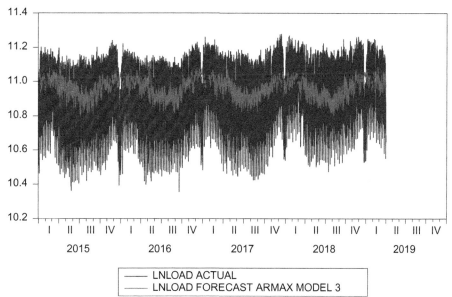

FIG. 2.6 Actual vs forecasting values with ARMAX Model 3.

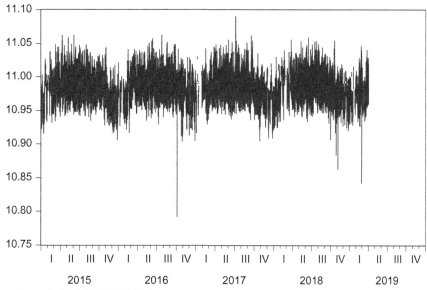

FIG. 2.7 Forecast energy demand with ARMAX Model 4.

This model achieves the optimal MAPE. MAE and RMSE among the other estimated models which is close to ANN forecasts precision. A. Al-Shareef for example develops a neural network with a 1.12% level of accuracy for 1 h-ahead forecasting (Al-Shareef et al., 2008). Likewise, Mandal investigating the neural networks' application for very short-term energy demand predictions obtains a 0.8% MAPE for a 1 h ahead to Consequently, ARMA and especially ARMAX models over-performs in short-term forecasting.

4.2 Comparing linear regression, simple exponential smoothing and ARMAX models

One of the most common econometric methods is the linear regression. Regression analysis is also used as an alternative to time series forecasting. Table 2.7 also includes information on forecasting accuracy of three linear regression models. First we construct a model with the lnprice as independent variable, while the second model uses the lntemperature. Finally, we construct a multivariate regression model including as explanatory variables all the variables used in ARMAX Model 5.

The level of accuracy is still high in the OLS framework. OLS Model 1 gives better results in comparison to ARMAX Model 1. Thus, lnprice ameliorates further energy demand forecasting with OLS estimation. Concerning the models with temperature as independent variable, the observed percentage of MAPE, MAE, RMSE and Theil inequality coefficient are identical. By contrast to the ARMAX framework the model embedded with lnprice performs better in relation to other with lntemperature.

The model which over performs among the three regressions and ARMAX models is the OLS 3—reaching to the lowest MAPE of 0, 86—that incorporates all the additional variables.

Finally, we apply ETS-Exponential Smoothing on lnload. The Error-Trend-Seasonal Exponential Smoothing incorporates the typical exponential smoothing methods and also allows for dynamic non-linear relationships. The optimal model based on the AIC criterion—among 30 performed models—allows for Additive Error, Additive Dampened Trend and non-seasonal effects. Table 2.6 describes the model that fits better, while Table 2.7 provides a comparison among the actual and forecast values of energy demand. Fig. 2.8 provides the Actual & Forecast Lnload values with ETS-Exponential Smoothing.

5 Conclusions

At the core of this analysis is the short-term energy demand forecasting. To evaluate the efficiency of different econometric methods, the Box-Jenkins methodology is fully developed to Germany's hourly energy demand from January 31, 2014 to March 31, 2019.

The starting point is the examination of time series behavior over the course of time and the construction of the simplest univariate models. Considering that the energy demand mix is influenced from various factors like weather conditions, renewables' variable generation and the rate of electricity prices it is critical to examine their impact on forecasting accuracy. Hence, our reference model contains initially data for the actual load. Then, variables for electricity prices and weather data are embedded leading finally to the adoption of a multivariate model like in Tao's Vanilla attempt.

According to unit root tests, Autocorrelation and Partial Autocorrelation Function Graphs the German energy demand appears stationary which guide us to different AR, MA, ARMA and ARMAX models in order to obtain the optimal forecast results.

Our results find evidence on high time-series forecast performance—even on the simplest univariate framework—which are in accordance with numerous previous studies (Jiang et al., 2018; James and Taylor, 2006). Indeed, the univariate models for energy demand achieve a high level of accuracy in Germany's context; for instance, AR (1) and AR (2) obtain a MAPE of 1.46. This is in accordance with the findings of Feng et al. and Box, Jenkins, and Reinsel who also suggest the great magnitude of time series predictions (Jiang et al., 2018; Box, 2008).

However, the metrics of MAPE, MAE, RMSE and Theil inequality coefficient for AR, MA and ARMA models are quasi identical. Whilst the estimates are improved further if the temperature, the price and the renewables generation enter

TABLE 2.6 Results of the optimum model.

Model	Compact LL	Likelihood	AIC[a]	BIC	HQ	AMSE
A,AD,N[a]	−64961.7	78110.0	129,933	129,976	129,947	1.E+100

[a]The optimal AIC criterion among the examined models. This model minimizes the AIC, BIC, and likelihood criteria. See Appendix LL Comparison Table concerning Exponential Smoothing.

TABLE 2.7 Forecasting via ETS-Exponential smoothing.

	Actual value	EX.Smoothing (A.AD. N*)
3/31/2019 14:00	10.743	10.727
3/31/2019 15:00	10.764	10.736
3/31/2019 16:00	10.796	10.780
3/31/2019 17:00	10.835	10.822
3/31/2019 18:00	10.881	10.865
3/31/2019 19:00	10.849	10.917
3/31/2019 20:00	10.837	10.825
3/31/2019 21:00	10.772	10.828
3/31/2019 22:00	10.702	10.720
3/31/2019 23:00	10.651	10.646
4/01/2019 00:00	NA	10.600
4/01/2019 01:00	NA	10.549
4/01/2019 02:00	NA	10.498
4/01/2019 03:00	NA	10.448
4/01/2019 04:00	NA	10.397
4/01/2019 05:00	NA	10.346
4/01/2019 06:00	NA	10.295
4/01/2019 07:00	NA	10.244

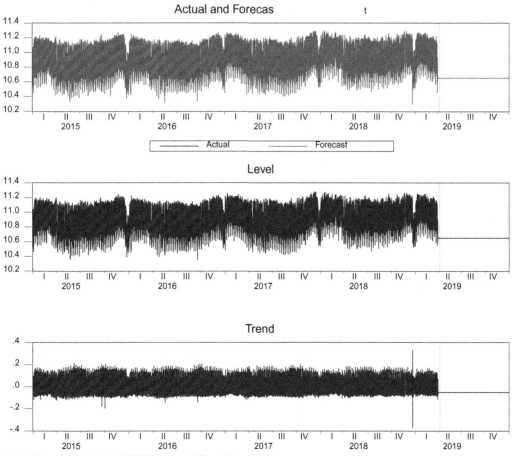

FIG. 2.8 Actual & Forecast Lnload with ETS-Exponential Smoothing.

into the model. Similarly, the OLS estimates increase the level of forecasting accuracy if the explanatory variables are nested.

Furthermore, the ARMAX Model 4 which includes all the independent variables over performs in comparison to other ARMAX Models. Moreover, our OLS estimates ameliorate further the forecasting performance in comparison to ARMAX models. While the OLS Model 3 which incorporates all the potential factors affecting the energy demand output over performs in comparison with the same model in the ARMAX framework.

Finally, the developed energy demand models achieve high rates of precision due to the nature of the German energy demand. The steady increase in renewables energy production in conjunction with the implementation of energy and climate policies has led the country's energy demand in relatively stable energy consumption (IEA, 2020). Furthermore, our findings prove that the country is in the right path regarding its energy diversification and energy security goals.

Our baseline models provide a breeding ground for further research. Non-linear relationships except the ETS-Exponential Smoothing that is presented in this study would be examined through a state-space model or via a multilayer ANN. Also, a neural network using genetic algorithms would give superior results. Similarly, Support Vector Machine or the Lasso Regression would be applied to compare different techniques in energy demand forecasting quest.

Appendix

Autocrrelation & Partial Autocorrelation

Autocorrelation	Partial Correlation		AC	PAC	Q-Stat	Prob
|*******	|*******	1	0.966	0.966	34721.	0.000
|******|	******| |	2	0.877	-0.820	63384.	0.000
|***** |	|** |	3	0.755	0.228	84629.	0.000
|**** |	*| |	4	0.617	-0.075	98781.	0.000
|*** |	| |	5	0.475	0.037	107166	0.000
|** |	|* |	6	0.342	0.106	111528	0.000
|** |	|* |	7	0.230	0.078	113506	0.000
|* |	| |	8	0.144	-0.053	114278	0.000
|* |	| |	9	0.081	-0.059	114525	0.000
| |	| |	10	0.039	0.001	114582	0.000
| |	| |	11	0.012	-0.033	114588	0.000
| |	| |	12	-0.004	-0.012	114588	0.000
| |	|* |	13	-0.012	0.147	114593	0.000
| |	|* |	14	-0.009	0.126	114596	0.000
| |	|** |	15	0.010	0.262	114600	0.000
| |	|* |	16	0.052	0.154	114700	0.000
|* |	|** |	17	0.119	0.245	115229	0.000
|** |	|* |	18	0.214	0.167	116929	0.000
|** |	| |	19	0.329	0.038	120953	0.000
|*** |	| |	20	0.452	0.000	128572	0.000
|**** |	|* |	21	0.571	0.091	140736	0.000
|***** |	| |	22	0.673	-0.024	157601	0.000
|***** |	*| |	23	0.742	-0.157	178125	0.000

Continued

Autocorrelation	Partial Correlation		AC	PAC	Q-Stat	Prob
|******|	***| |	24	0.763	-0.427	199818	0.000
|***** |	***| |	25	0.725	-0.420	219389	0.000
|***** |	|** |	26	0.637	0.234	234510	0.000
|**** |	*| |	27	0.516	-0.135	244447	0.000
|*** |	*| |	28	0.378	-0.084	249776	0.000
|** |	| |	29	0.236	0.011	251855	0.000
|* |	| |	30	0.104	0.015	252258	0.000
| |	|* |	31	-0.007	0.096	252260	0.000
*| |	|* |	32	-0.093	0.080	252580	0.000
*| |	| |	33	-0.154	0.046	253460	0.000
*| |	| |	34	-0.194	0.058	254862	0.000
**| |	| |	35	-0.219	0.016	256645	0.000
**| |	| |	36	-0.233	-0.027	258667	0.000

ETS Smoothing

LNLOAD

Model: A,AD,N - Additive Error, Additive
-Dampened Trend, No Season (Auto E=*, T=
, S=)

Model selection: Akaike Information Criterion

Alpha:	1.000000
Beta:	1.000000
Phi:	0.789873
Initial level:	10.68562
Initial trend:	-0.051278
Compact Log-likelihood	-64961.69
Log-likelihood	78109.97
Akaike Information Criterion	129933.4
Schwarz Criterion	129976.0
Hannan-Quinn Criterion	129946.9
Sum of Squared Residuals	32.79312
Root Mean Squared Error	0.029681

Forecast Comparison Graph

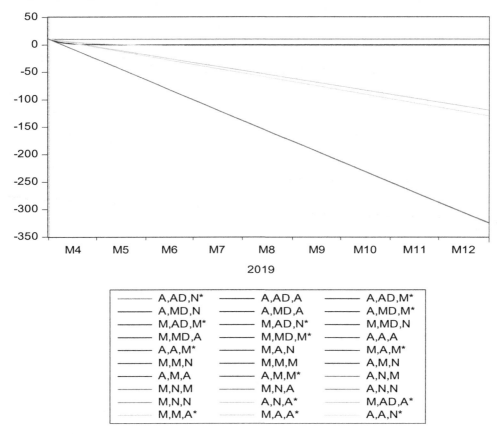

Forecast Comparison Table

	Actuals	A,AD,N*	A,AD,A	A,AD,M*	A,MD,N	A,MD,A
3/31/2019 14:00	10.743	10.727	10.727	10.727	10.727	10.727
3/31/2019 15:00	10.764	10.736	10.735	10.735	10.736	10.735
3/31/2019 16:00	10.796	10.780	10.780	10.780	10.780	10.780
3/31/2019 17:00	10.835	10.822	10.822	10.822	10.822	10.822
3/31/2019 18:00	10.881	10.865	10.865	10.865	10.865	10.865
3/31/2019 19:00	10.849	10.917	10.917	10.917	10.917	10.917
3/31/2019 20:00	10.837	10.825	10.825	10.825	10.825	10.825
3/31/2019 21:00	10.772	10.828	10.827	10.827	10.828	10.827
3/31/2019 22:00	10.702	10.720	10.721	10.721	10.721	10.721
3/31/2019 23:00	10.651	10.646	10.646	10.646	10.647	10.646
4/01/2019 00:00	NA	10.600	10.600	10.600	10.611	10.611
4/01/2019 01:00	NA	10.549	10.549	10.549	10.571	10.571
4/01/2019 02:00	NA	10.498	10.498	10.498	10.540	10.540
4/01/2019 03:00	NA	10.448	10.448	10.448	10.515	10.516
4/01/2019 04:00	NA	10.397	10.397	10.397	10.496	10.497
4/01/2019 05:00	NA	10.346	10.346	10.346	10.481	10.482
4/01/2019 06:00	NA	10.295	10.295	10.295	10.469	10.470
4/01/2019 07:00	NA	10.244	10.244	10.244	10.460	10.461

*14 models failed to converge

AIC Comparison Graph

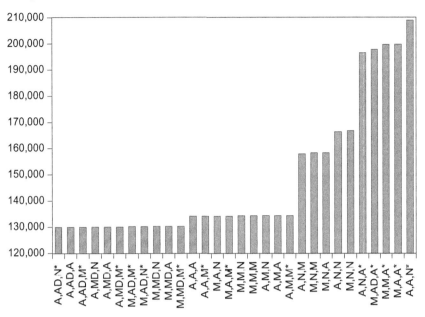

LL Comparison Table

Model	Compact LL	Likelihood	AIC*	BIC	HQ	AMSE
A,AD,N*	-64961.7	78110.0	129933.	129976.	129947.	1.E+100
A,AD,A	-64960.4	78111.3	129935.	129994.	129954.	1.E+100
A,AD,M*	-64963.3	78108.4	129941.	130000.	129959.	1.E+100
A,MD,N	-64989.7	78081.9	129989.	130032.	130003.	0.00600
A,MD,A	-64988.2	78083.4	129990.	130050.	130009.	0.00600
A,MD,M*	-64989.6	78082.1	129993.	130053.	130012.	0.00600
M,AD,M*	-65063.0	78008.6	130140.	130200.	130159.	1.E+100
M,AD,N*	-65077.9	77993.7	130166.	130208.	130179.	1.E+100
M,MD,N	-65102.2	77969.5	130214.	130257.	130228.	0.00602
M,MD,A	-65100.8	77970.9	130216.	130275.	130235.	0.00602
M,MD,M*	-65104.2	77967.5	130222.	130282.	130241.	0.00602
A,A,A	-67026.1	76045.5	134064.	134115.	134081.	0.00768
A,A,M*	-67026.2	76045.5	134064.	134115.	134081.	0.00768
M,A,N	-67036.0	76035.7	134080.	134114.	134091.	0.00768
M,A,M*	-67038.0	76033.7	134088.	134139.	134104.	0.00768
M,M,N	-67133.2	75938.5	134274.	134308.	134285.	0.00778
M,M,M	-67131.8	75939.9	134276.	134327.	134292.	0.00778
A,M,N	-67136.7	75934.9	134281.	134316.	134292.	0.00778
A,M,A	-67135.1	75936.6	134282.	134333.	134298.	0.00778
A,M,M*	-67135.9	75935.8	134284.	134335.	134300.	0.00778
A,N,M	-78954.9	64116.8	157918.	157952.	157929.	0.00778
M,N,M	-79151.4	63920.3	158311.	158345.	158322.	0.00777

Continued

Model	Compact LL	Likelihood	AIC*	BIC	HQ	AMSE
M,N,A	-79160.5	63911.2	158329.	158363.	158340.	0.00777
A,N,N	-83162.5	59909.2	166329.	166346.	166334.	0.00915
M,N,N	-83373.7	59697.9	166751.	166769.	166757.	0.00915
A,N,A*	-98274.8	44796.9	196558.	196592.	196568.	0.01261
M,AD,A*	-98931.2	44140.4	197876.	197936.	197895.	1.E+100
M,M,A*	-99877.9	43193.8	199768.	199819.	199784.	0.01606
M,A,A*	-99904.0	43167.7	199820.	199871.	199836.	0.01608
A,A,N*	-104499.	38572.5	209006.	209040.	209017.	0.01944

References

Aljandal, A., 2017. The Box-Jenkins methodology. In: Multivariate Methods and Forecasting with IBM® SPSS® Statistics. Statistics and Econometrics for Finance. Statistics and econometrics for finance, Springer. In press .doi.org/10.1007/978-3-319-56481-4.

Al-Shareef, A., Mohamed, E., Al-Judaibi, E., 2008. One hour ahead load forecasting using artificial neural network for the western area of Saudi Arabia. World Acad. Sci. Eng. Technol. 37, 219–224.

Box, G.E., 1976. Time Series Analysis, Forecasting and Control. Holden-Day, San Francisco.

Box, G.E., 2008. Time Series Analysis: Forecasting and Control, fourth ed. Wiley, Hoboken, NJ.

Charytoniuk, W., Chen, M., 2000. Very short-term load forecasting using artificial neural networks. IEEE Trans. Power Syst. 15 (1), 263–268.

Cugliari, J., Poggi, J., 2018. Electricity demand forecasting. In: Wiley StatsRef: Statistics Reference Online. John Wiley & Sons, Hoboken, NJ.

Hamilton, J.D., 1994. Time Series Analysis. Princeton University Press, Princeton.

Hamizah, M.R., 2016. Comparative performance of ARIMA and DES models in forecasting electricity load demand in Malaysia. International Journal of Electrical & Computer Sciences IJECS-IJENS 16 (01), 6–9. http://ijens.org/Vol_16_I_01/163601-4949-IJECS-IJENS.pdf.

Harvey, A.C., 1989. Forecasting, Structural Time Series Models and the Kalman Filter. Cambridge University Press, Cambridge.

IEA, 2020. Germany 2020 Enerhy Policy Review.

Islam, M., Hasanuzzaman, M., 2020a. Energy demand forecasting. In: Energy for Sustainable Development: Demand, Supply, Conversion and Management.

Islam, M.M., Hasanuzzaman, M., 2020b. Chapter 1 - Introduction to energy and sustainable development. In: Hasanuzzaman, MD., Nasrudin, Abd Rahim (Eds.), Energy for Sustainable Development,. Academic Press, pp. 1–18. In press http://www.sciencedirect.com/science/article/pii/B9780128146453000018.

Ismit Mado, A.S., December 2018. Applying of double seasonal ARIMA model for electrical power demand forecasting at PT. PLN Gresik Indonesia. Int. J. Electr. Comput. Eng. 8 (6), 4892–4901.

James, W., Taylor, L.M., 2006. A comparison of univariate methods for forecasting electricity demand up to a day ahead. Int. J. Forecast. 22, 1–16.

Javier Campillo, F.V., July 2012. Energy demand model design for forecasting electricity consumption and simulating demand response scenarios in Sweden. In: International Conference on Applied Energy.

Jebaraj, S., 2017. Electricity demand forecasting for Malaysia using artificial neural network. Int. J. Latest Eng. Manage. Res. 02 (04), 65–68.

Jiang, F., Yang, X., Li, S., 2018. Comparison of forecasting India's energy demand using an MGM, ARIMA Model, MGM-ARIMA model, and BP neural network model. Sustainability. 10 (7), 1–17.

Julong, D., 1984. The differential dynamic model (GM) and its implement in long period forecasting of grain. Exploration of Nature 3, 47–50.

Julong, D., 1989. Introduction to grey system theory. J. Grey System 1, 1–24.

Lin, Y., Luo, H., Wang, D., Guo, H., Zhu, K., 2017. An ensemble model based on machine learning methods and data preprocessing for short-term electric load forecasting. Energies 10, 1186.

Luo, J., Hong, T., Yue, M., 2018. Real-time anomaly detection for very short-term load forecasting. J. Mod. Power Syst. Clean Energy 6, 235–243. https://doi.org/10.1007/s40565-017-0351-7.

Mahmoud, A., Hammad, B.J., February 2020. Methods and models for electric load forecasting: a comprehensive review. Logist. Sustain. Transport 11 (1), 51–76.

Mandal, P., Senjyu, T., Urasaki, N., Funabashi, T., July 2006. A neural-network based several-hour-ahead electric load forecasting using similar days approach. Int. J. Electr. Power Energy Syst. 28 (6), 367–372.

Md Hasanuzzaman, N.A., 2019. Energy for Sustainable Development: Demand, Supply, Conversion and Management, first ed. Academic Press.

Nalcaci, G., Özmen, A., Weber, G.W., 2018. Long-term load forecasting: models based on MARS, ANN and LR methods. Central Eur. J. Oper. Res. 27 (2019), 1033–1049. Springer-Verlag GmbH Germany.

Shah, I., Iftikhar, H., Ali, S., Wang, D., 2019. Short-term electricity demand forecasting using components estimation technique. Energies 12 (3), 2532. https://doi.org/10.3390/en12132532.

Taylor, J.W., 2008. An evaluation of methods for very short-term load forecasting using minute-by-minute British data. Int. J. Forecast. 24 (4), 645–658.

Vamvoukas, G., 2008. Modern Econometrics: Analysis and Application. AUEB (Athens University of Economics and Business), Athens.

Velte, H.K., 2018. Mission-Oriented R&I Policies: In-Depth Case Studies. RTD Publications.

Wallstrom, P., Segerstedt, A., 2010. Evaluation of forecasting error measurements and techniques for intermittent demand. International Journal of Production Economics 128 (2), 625–636. https://doi.org/10.1016/j.ijpe.2010.07.013.

Weber, R., 2006. Uncertainty in the Electric Power Industry. Spinger.

Welch, G., Bishop, G., 2004. An Introduction to the Kalman Filter, TR 95-041. University of North Carolina, Chapel Hill, pp. 1–16. http://www.silviosimani.it/kalman_intro.pdf.

Weron, R., 2014. Electricity price forecasting: a review of the state-of-the-art with a look into the future. Int. J. Forecast. 30, 1030–1081.

Widén, J., Wäckelgård, E., June 2010. A high-resolution stohastic model of domestic activity patterns and electricity demand. Appl. Energy 87 (6), 1880–1892.

Wu, L., Shahidehpour, M., 2010. A hybrid model for day-ahead price forecasting. IEEE Trans. Power Syst. 25 (3), 1519–1530.

Zhanga, X., Wang, J., Zhang, K., 2017. Short-term electric load forecasting based on singular spectrum analysis and support vector machine optimized by Cuckoo search algorithm. Electr. Power Syst. Res. 146 (2017), 270–285.

Ziel, F., 2018. Modeling public holidays in load forecasting: a German case study. J. Mod. Power Syst. Clean Energy 6 (2), 191–207.

Further reading

Data, O.P (n.d.). Time-Series. https://open-power-system-data.org/.

data, R.P (n.d.). Renewables.ninja PV (Hourly Data 1980–2019)—ninja_pv_country_DE_merra-2_corrected—Version: 1.3—License: https://creativecommons.org/licenses/by-nc/4.0/.

data, S.E.-S.-d.-W.-h (n.d.) https://science.nasa.gov/earth-science/earth-science-data/data-information-policy. https://renewables.ninja and https://doi.org/10.1175/JCLI-D-16-0758.1.

Feinberg, E.A., Genethliou, D., 2005. Load Forecasting. In: Chow, J.H., Wu, F.F., Momoh, J. (Eds.), Applied Mathematics for Restructured Electric Power Systems. Power Electronics and Power Systems. Springer, Boston, MA. https://doi.org/10.1007/0-387-23471-3_12.

Granger, C.W., 1980. An introduction to long-memory time series models and fractional differencing. J. Time Ser. Anal. 1, 15–29.

Jan, L., 2018. Real-time anomaly detection for very short-term load forecasting. J. Mod. Power Syst. Clean Energy 6 (2), 235–243.

Stata. (n.d.). https://www.stata.com/manuals13/tsarima.pdf. Stata Corporation.

Wind, R. (n.d.). Renewable.ninja Wind (hourly data, split by on/offshore, 1980–2019)—ninja_wind_country_DE_current-merra-2_corrected—Version: 1.3—License: https://creativeco.

Chapter 3

A novel adaptive day-ahead load forecast method, incorporating non-metered distributed generation: A comparison of selected European countries

B. Sinkovics, I. Taczi, I. Vokony, and B. Hartmann
Budapest University of Technology and Economics, Budapest, Hungary

1   Introduction

Short term load forecasts are generally used to predict the electric load of a region or a country for a 1–3-day horizon. Load forecast of single consumers is a very complex task due to the large number of affecting variables, but those random elements partially cancel each other when cumulated for load areas. Therefore, the electricity need of a city, a region or a country is more predictable. The time horizon of the forecast is also important, since most of the input variables (e.g. weather data) are usually available with adequate temporal resolution, 1–3 days in advance, so hourly or quarter-hourly predictions can be prepared. The importance of short-term load forecasting has been highlighted lately because of the liberalization of electricity markets. The introduction of intraday electricity trading has put more emphasis on forecasts for few hour horizons (very short-term load forecasting), which dominantly use the same toolset.

The mathematical problem of short-term load forecasting is not trivial; predictions must consider daily and weekly periodicities, effects of weather, public holidays and other variables (e.g. wholesale electricity prices). Since the consumer portfolio of each country is also specific to certain extent, no exclusive methods are used, but tailored solutions are necessary for each application.

As it is typical in the case of complex technical problems, decomposition of the task may lead to simpler problems and significantly decreased computational needs. Decomposition of short-term load forecasts can be carried out in various ways.

- Forecasts can be prepared using historical data, which usually shows certain trends (e.g. increase of annual electricity consumption). Such trends should be removed from the dataset and their effects must be assessed and considered separately.
- Grouping of available data may lead to more accurate predictions. In this way, the forecasting algorithm can operate using a smaller sample set, avoiding most irrelevant data points. This step does not only decrease computation time, but probably increases the accuracy of the forecasts. A typical application of this is the grouping of the days of the week and public holidays. With the use of clustering algorithms, it can also support handling weather dependence of load curves.
- Certain weather parameters (such as temperature, humidity, wind speed) have a prioritized role; it could be advantageous to handle them separately from other factors influencing power system demand.
- In general, daily load curve patterns can be relatively easily determined. The inaccuracy of daily load forecasts is due to errors in predicting extremes (peak and off-peak periods) of the curve. Thus, decomposition of the prediction of the pattern and the load values is often seen.
- Instead of forecasting the load for all (quarter-)hours of a day, parallel forecasting of individual hours can be also done. As the load of consecutive hours does show high correlation, such decomposition does not necessarily increase the efficiency of the forecast, but it allows the application of those models, which only have single outputs (e.g. time series models).

Furthermore other, even fundamentally different approaches are feasible, and a combined use of the methods is also possible.

Mathematical Modelling of Contemporary Electricity Markets. https://doi.org/10.1016/B978-0-12-821838-9.00003-7

The present chapter focuses on the state-of-the art techniques used for day-ahead load forecasting. It proposes a neural network-based method, which is benchmarked to national forecasts of selected European transmission system operators (TSOs). The novelty of the approach is that it considers the effects of non-metered distributed generation, which is expected to corrupt the efficiency of day-ahead load forecasts. The study is structured as follows. Section 2 presents a comparative review of load forecasting methods, while an introduction to neural networks is given in Section 3. In Section 4, the long short-term memory (LSTM) network developed by the authors is presented and validated. Section 5 discusses the performance of the proposed method in the light of non-metered generation capacities, using historical data of four European countries. Conclusions are summarized in Section 6.

2 Comparative review of load forecasting methodologies

The operation and control of power systems rely on load and generation forecasts at several levels. From online stability assessment to decade-long investment planning, the growing share of distributed generation, especially the non-metered units, increase the complexity of the calculations. This section is a summary of the forecast methods, concentrating on the characteristic changes in the generation mix. The review highlights machine learning methods such as complex neural networks as a promising possible solution.

Table 3.1 summarizes the most important aspects discussed in the literature, such as the subject and time horizon of the forecast, comparison of proposed solutions, information about the applied artificial neural network (ANN) (topology, training) and evaluation of the results. The proposed method of this research is a short-term load forecast (STLF), which includes the non-metered residential power plants. Thus, in practice, it is a load forecast which includes the non-metered

TABLE 3.1 Overview of load forecasting methods.

References	Load forecast	Generation forecast (incl. irrad.)	Time horizon	Model comparison	Neural network information	Training	Performance metrics
Nicolao et al. (2014)	X		24 h	Regression model on similarity	Only applies statistics	–	MAPE
Khuntia et al. (2016)	X		1–24 h	No comparison included	Feedforward ANN	Levenberg-Marquardt	MAPE, coefficient of variation (CV)
Dehalwar et al. (2017)	X		24 h	ANN vs. bagged regression trees	Feedforward ANN	Levenberg-Marquardt	MAPE, mean average error (MAE), daily peak MAPE
Singh et al. (2017)	X		24 h	No comparison included	Feedforward ANN	Levenberg-Marquardt	MAE, MAPE
Webberley and Gao (2013)	X		1 week	Different training methods	Feedforward ANN	Levenberg-Marquardt, Bayesian regularization	MAPE
Xie et al. (2015)	X		24 h	Multiple linear regression vs. ARIMA vs. ANN vs. random forest	Feedforward ANN	Algorithm dependent	MAPE
Ray et al. (2016)	X		24 h	ANN vs. genetic algorithm	Feedforward ANN	Back propagation	MAPE
Ray et al. (2016)	X		24 h	ANN vs. genetic algorithm	Feedforward ANN	Genetic algorithm	MAPE

TABLE 3.1 Overview of load forecasting methods—cont'd

References	Load forecast	Generation forecast (incl. irrad.)	Time horizon	Model comparison	Neural network information	Training	Performance metrics
Rodrigues et al. (2014)	X		24–72 h		Feedforward multilayer perceptron	Levenberg-Marquardt	MAPE +standard deviation error (SDE)+serial correlation
Bashir and El-Hawary (2009)	X		24 h (several cases, even 2 weeks included)	No comparison included	Feedforward multilayer perceptron	Particle swarm	MAPE, absolute percentage error (APE)
Lu et al. (2019)	X		24 h	ARIMA, random forest and LSTM	Hybrid convolutional neural network with LSTM	Forget gate included	MAPE, RMSE, forecast accuracy (FA)
Cui et al. (2019)			24 h	RNN, LSTM and proposed modified LSTM	LSTM	Forget gate included	Relative error (RE), MAPE
Imani (2019)	X		1 h	LSTM vs. LSTM +SVR	LSTM	Support vector regression (SVR)	MAPE, MAE, MSE
Jiang et al. (2018)	X		1 week	LSTM vs. SVR	LSTM	Forget gate included	RMSE, training loss
Liu et al. (2017)	X		24 h	Elman NN vs. LSTM	LSTM	Back propagation	MAPE
Ma et al. (2019)	X		1 week	LSTM vs. iForest—BP vs. iForest—LSTM	iForest—LSTM	Isolation forest	MAPE, RE
Narayan and Hipely (2017)	X		24 h	Feedforward ANN vs. ARIMA vs. LSTM	LSTM	Forward pass +back propagation	RMSE, normalized RMSE
Sun et al. (2005)	X		24 h	Elman vs. feedforward	Elman ANN	Back propagation	MSE
He et al. (2017)	X		24 h/ 1 week	ANN, SVR, extreme learning machine (ELM) vs. DBN	Deep belief network (DBN)	Restricted Boltzmann machine (RBM)	MAPE, RMSE
Ulbricht et al. (2013)		X	2, 12, 24 h	Multivariate regression vs. MARS	Only applies statistics and stochastics	–	RMSE+MAPE
Alzahrani et al. (2014)		X	Not explicitly described	Linear regression vs. ANN	Nonlinear autoregressive wit external input (NARX)	Back propagation	Mean square error (MSE)
Wang et al. (2012)		X	24 h	Historical data series vs. statistical feature parameters	Statistical feature parameters included	Levenberg-Marquardt	MAPE. RMSE, MABE

Continued

TABLE 3.1 Overview of load forecasting methods—cont'd

References	Load forecast	Generation forecast (incl. irrad.)	Time horizon	Model comparison	Neural network information	Training	Performance metrics
Mishra and Palanisamy (2019)		X	1–4 h	RNN vs. LSTM vs. machine learning	LSTM	–	MSE, RMSE
Mukhoty et al. (2019)		X	24 h	LSTM vs. feedforward ANN vs. Gradient Boosted Regression Trees	LSTM	–	MAE, RMSE, training loss
Liao et al. (2019)		X	1–12 h	DAC vs. feedforward ANN	Dense average network	Backpropagation	MAPE, MAE
Lang et al. (2019)		X	24 h	CNN vs. statistical method	1D CNN	–	MSE
Massaoudi et al. (2019)		X	1 year	Extra trees vs. K Nearest Neighbors vs. LSTM vs. NARX-LSTM	NARX-LSTM	–	MAE, RMSE, MAPE

units. Therefore, the review of these methods also contributes to the analysis and categorization of the proposed solution. Besides the comparison in the summary table, other review-oriented research (Kostylev and Pavlovski, 2011; Ulbricht et al., 2013) is also included here to provide a holistic picture in the field of load forecast.

Historically, power systems were designed with a principle that generation should be continuously controlled to follow the load, and the latter had to be predicted to calculate the adequacy of control. Therefore, load forecast methods have a long history, but the evolution of the applied methods shows similarity. Statistical methods (regression) were considered conventional, the stochastic approach improved accuracy and model-based and machine-learning solutions emerged as more accurate solutions (Bashir and El-Hawary, 2009).

Generation forecasting methods for photovoltaic systems is a growing research area, as the share of distributed generation becomes significant at the system level, However, estimation accuracy still needs to be improved for reliable operation (Kostylev and Pavlovski, 2011). As the above table describes, the main directions of forecasting are linear regression, satellite data-based methods, and ANN (with meteorological inputs).

Considering input data generation, the main options are the physical model approach (weather dynamics, more complex from the computation point of view, often referred to as numerical weather prediction—NWP), the statistical solutions and cloud imagery (Ulbricht et al., 2013). Data sources could be weather-related measurement stations, satellite data or total sky imagers (Mayer et al., 2008; Kostylev and Pavlovski, 2011). Statistical approaches include naïve (persistence) and similarity-based (diurnal persistence) predictions, different types of regression (linear, logarithmic, etc.), stochastic solutions like Autoregressive (Integrated) Moving Average (ARMA/ARIMA) and Multivariate Adaptive Regression Splines (MARS), or machine learning methods like ANN, fuzzy logic (Reikard and Hansen, 2019; Ulbricht et al., 2013).

In the model-based solution, weather changes are calculated using a mathematical description. Spatiality and locational dependence is a limitation for those solutions due to less information on cloud movements and weather variability (Kostylev and Pavlovski, 2011). These methods usually provide forecasts by the hour. Examples include the European Center for Medium-Range Weather-Forecasts (ECMWF), the Global Forecast System (GFS, the North American Mesoscale Model (NAM) and the Global Environmental Multiscale Model. Satellite-based forecasting focuses on cloudiness as the crucial factor in the process with the application of motion vector calculation (Kostylev and Pavlovski, 2011).

There are several ways to handle the correlation between electrical load/generation and weather parameters (temperature, solar irradiation, humidity, wind speed, etc.) and to process the input data (eliminating redundancy, creating stochastic variables as model elements, use further important historical data as input time series). Appropriate settings could lead to better forecast accuracy. However, literature for input generation is exceedingly diverse for a simple categorization. Possible solutions include wavelet transformation (Bashir and El-Hawary, 2009), empirical mode decomposition (Cui et al., 2019) or isolation forest cleaning (Ma et al., 2019) of the input data. These result in better input data structures and the identification of key influential factors.

Machine learning methods are commonly used in time series forecasts as an alternative to statistical or stochastic variable approaches. The main advantage of ANN as a solution is its flexibility, generality and ability to handle the nonlinear behavior of the observed variable (Nicolao et al., 2014). Hybrid approaches include the combination of different methods to create a unique model. The feedforward neural network architecture is the most commonly used one, with one hidden layer, as it is provenly effective for any continuous function (Rodrigues et al., 2014), while the recurrent neural network (RNN), usually LSTM, is another commonly used development alternative.

Learning algorithms usually include backpropagation (gradient descent or conjugate gradient with partial derivative) or the Levenberg-Marquardt algorithm, where the latter is effective in reducing complexity and computational effort (Rodrigues et al., 2014). However, there are more advanced solutions, such as particle swarm optimization (PSO), which shows promising results like faster training and less sensitivity to initialization.

In the methodology comparison, two important aspects must be pointed out from Table 3.1: ANN clearly outperforms any statistical or stochastic method by accuracy, which points into the possible development direction. In addition, in the field of ANN, there is room for further improvement: feedforward neural networks with back propagation or Levenberg-Marquardt training have many practical implementations. However, for exact time horizons and system parameters, more complex alternatives such as recurrent structures or PSO-based trainings show better results in the comparisons. Therefore, if the timescale of the application is defined appropriately, an adequate level of accuracy is achievable with advanced ANN structures.

Regarding timescales, there is no clear professional consensus on the classification. Different time horizons and granularity result in diverse methods at each level to suit the specific goals. The underlying principle for the classification is the business process of the system operator or the market participant. The following groups can be defined regarding generation (Kostylev and Pavlovski, 2011; Reikard and Hansen, 2019):

- Short-term (now cast)
  - ○ Intra-hour—15 min to 2 h, ~ minute granularity
    - ▪ Ramping constraints, power quality events (voltage/frequency variations)
  - ○ Hour-ahead—1–6 h, ~ hourly time-steps
    - ▪ Load following, dispatching, intraday markets, balancing markets
- Day-ahead—24–72 h, hourly granularity
  - ○ Unit commitment, energy and reserve market constraints
- Long-term
  - ○ Medium-term—1 week to 2 months, daily time-steps
    - ▪ Asset utilization, operation planning
  - ○ Longer-term—~ years, with daily or monthly data
    - ▪ Generation adequacy, transmission infrastructure planning, investment calculations

The now-cast and daily levels together are generally referred to as short-term load forecast, as opposed to long-term load forecast (LTLF). (Other systems may set up a separate category for medium-term forecasts (Khuntia et al., 2016), similarly to the medium-term in the case of generation.)

In the Chinese technical definitions, the shorter time horizons are divided into ultra-short-term (4–6 h) and short-term (24–72 h) groups (Wang et al., 2012). Meanwhile, the International Energy Agency distinguished real-time, short term and long term data with different spatiality (Mayer et al., 2008). The time-steps are usually 15 min (or 1 h), which suits the settlement periods of electricity markets. The most common time horizon in the previously proposed methods is 24 h, which fits to many operational needs in power systems. Regarding photovoltaic forecasts, shorter time horizons appear more often, than in the case of loads.

Performance evaluation is an utmost part of load and generation forecasting. Table 3.1 shows that the most used metrics are MAPE (mean absolute percentage error), RMSE (root-mean-square error), MAE (mean absolute error) and MBE (mean bias error). The values describe different aspects of forecast quality. Normalization—especially the basis of the process—could lead to misleading conclusions, e.g. one method calculates with rated power, the other with actual power output or with the maximum measured value. Therefore, comparisons between the algorithms mostly appear in review articles in a comprehensive way (Kostylev and Pavlovski, 2011; Ulbricht et al., 2013; Srivastava et al., 2016; Reikard and Hansen, 2019).

Following the discussed partitioning of forecasting methods, this paper focuses on the day-ahead algorithms. The next subsection discusses state-of-the-art load forecast methodologies applied by Transmission System Operators (TSOs).

2.1 Load forecasting methods applied by TSOs

While each country has a different methodology to prepare its load forecast, they usually rely on similar input data and computation methods. Forecasts have to consider the daily and weekly periodicity of power system demand (as load is usually lower on weekends and in the night), the effect of special days (e.g. public holidays), the changes in weather and possibly other factors (e.g. wholesale electricity prices). The exact forecast methodology of system operators is rarely published, but below a brief overview of the practice of selected countries is presented.

Regulations of MAVIR Hungarian TSO prescribe that the error of day-ahead load curve forecast must stay below 5%. To achieve this, forecasting is prepared according to a two-step process. At first, characteristic values of the day are defined, then the shape of the load curve is finalized. Both steps use naïve methods, e.g. historical data of similar days or the experience of operators. The software-aided process is repeated in a successive-approximation iteration, which largely builds on the competence of the personnel. Weather data of multiple suppliers is used, including national (Hungarian Meteorological Service) and private entities. From these weather forecasts the factors of temperature, wind chill, luminance and cloud cover are considered in the load forecast. When determining the shape of the load curve, the operators also consider non-quantifiable factors, e.g. television broadcasted sport events, changes in the law or the simultaneity of good weather and a long weekend (Sinkovics and Hartmann, 2018).

The Australian AEMO produces forecasts with various probability of exceedance for all timeframes, of which the 50% case is used in pre-dispatch. Load forecasts are generated automatically every half-hour without manual intervention. Key inputs for the forecast are historical and real-time actual metered loads, historical and forecast temperature and humidity, non-scheduled forecast of variable renewable energy sources, type of day data and restrictions (Australian Energy Market Operator, 2017).

The load forecast of New Zealand TSO Transpower uses aggregate load and weather data to forecast half-hourly regional load values for 10 areas. Real-time load data is received directly from SCADA, while historical data is provided by the MV90 metering system, which has higher quality than the telemetered SCADA data (less susceptible to problems). Forecast and actual weather data (temperature, wind speed) comes from the national meteorological service (Transpower New Zealand, 2016).

The French TSO's (RTE) load forecasts correspond to power consumers in mainland France, including consumers of public transport networks. Meteorological data comes from the national provider. RTE creates regional forecasts, which are later weighted (most importantly because of the dominance of the Paris region). Statistical forecasting models are used, which rely on temperature and cloud data of multiple weather stations and the historical load of the power system. The forecaster builds the final forecast from the data models and references from the past and the data that is not modeled (e.g. height of the clouds, precipitation) (Réseau de transport d'électricité, 2014).

In Austria, load forecasts are calculated for various horizons, based on a model with the input data historical actual load and the type of the day. Day-ahead load forecasts also use temperature forecast of the following day (Austrian Power Grid, 2020).

In some cases, load forecast methodologies are not known, but certain information has been published in relation to how the generation of variable renewable energy producers is taken into consideration. TenneT uses a weighted combination of several solutions, altogether called "Meta-Forecast." Weights of different forecasts are based on the quality of historical data, the weather-dependency of the model, the number of predictors and the personal experience of operators. Input data is provided by public and private entities (satellite imaging, numerical weather prediction). TenneT also cooperates with the solar inverter manufacturer SMA to utilize real-time production data of photovoltaic units (Gesino, 2013).

The Italian Terna applies their own forecast model (Sibilla—Statistical Integrated Bayesian Information system for Large to Local area Analysis) to create quarter-hourly data, based dominantly on historical data of similar days. Inputs of this model include weather parameters received from the ECMWF model. Sibilla uses neural networks for post-processing and definition of regional values (Nicolao et al., 2014).

In conclusion, TSOs use various approaches for predicting consumer's electricity load. Traditional methods are dominantly naïve and rely largely on the experience of operational personnel. Recent development in machine learning and the increasing computational capacity of industrial systems have however opened the way for the application of more complex tools and the incorporation of weather forecasts.

3   Neural networks—Mathematical background

Due to the robust and versatile application opportunities of ANNs, the introduced STLF model is also based on the principles of this technique. For this reason, general attributes of neural networks are described in this section following an evolutionary approach. Firstly, the basic principles of ANNs (e.g. architecture, operation, backpropagation algorithm) are introduced. Then more specialized algorithms are described focusing on time series forecast. The mathematical explanations were edited for the sake of the cause giving a general comparative overview of vanilla neural models, RNNs and LSTM structures.

A major advantage of ANNs is that they provide flexible and general-purpose models accounting for the nonlinearity of electricity load series, as well as the nonlinear mapping between weather and load variables. In addition, ANNs may be used to learn the dependencies directly from the historical data without explicitly selecting an appropriate model.

The basic units of the ANN are called neurons (or nodes) owing to the bio-inspired origin of this model. These neurons are aggregated into layers, namely input, hidden and output layers. In general, the input data flows through the network sequentially using each weight as a connection. The most conventional fully connected feedforward neural network topology comprises connections between all neighboring layer's nodes (see Fig. 3.1).

Fig. 3.1 shows a general ANN architecture with two inputs, one hidden layer with three neurons and a single output, where variables denote the following:

- X_i—input value/vector.
- $w_{start\ node,\ end\ node}^{layer\ no.}$—network weights.
- b_i—bias term.
- Y—output vector.
- $s_{node\ no.}^{layer\ no.}$—weighted sum of neuron inputs.
- $a_{node\ no.}^{layer\ no.}$—calculated node output using activation function.

Before the training, the input dataset is divided into three parts, namely training, validation and test sets. The training set provides the learning environment for the neural network. In this phase, the algorithm has room to learn nonlinear dependencies in relation to the input-output data. The validation set helps to measure the optimality of the model tuned in the previous step. There are no additional weight updates, it provides information about the optimal number of hidden units or determines a stopping point to avoid overfitting. Then test set examples are used to assess the performance of the trained neural network.

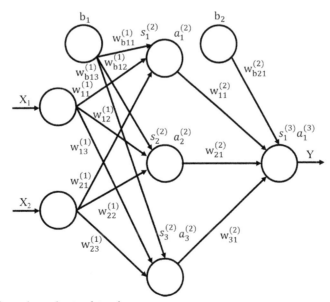

FIG. 3.1   A fully connected feedforward neural network topology.

When data splitting is done first, it is supposed that the network weights are randomly initialized, and the first batch of input data is read into the input layer's memory. In the hidden layer two steps are carried out: summarizing of the weighted inputs, and the calculation of the activated node value. The sum of the first hidden node can be calculated as follows:

$$s_1^{(2)} = b_1 w_{b11}^{(1)} + X_1 w_{11}^{(1)} + X_2 w_{21}^{(1)} \tag{3.1}$$

A node sum in a neural network without the bias term is nothing more than a multiplication of the input with a matrix. The bias value adds another dimension to the input space, improves learning convergence speed, and helps to avoid node values stuck in zero. It is generally a simple generic algebraic term, which enables the system to represent more complex situations.

Node activation depends on the used activation function. In this example sigmoid activation is supposed:

$$a_1^{(2)} = f\left(s_1^{(2)}\right) = \frac{1}{1 + e^{-s_1^{(2)}}} \tag{3.2}$$

Then the same process is carried out to obtain the further hidden node and the output layer results. The prediction performance is showed by a loss or error value. It is free to use custom loss/cost functions, entropy or well-known functions like mean square error.

Then the second phase implements an inverse data flow, which helps to adjust the weights to reduce the error between the output of the network and the target value. This algorithm uses the loss value, and from the backward update the weights of the network using weight derivatives. The most elemental gradient descent algorithm uses simply first-order derivatives of the cost function to adjust weights iteratively:

$$w_i^{k+1} = w_i^k - \alpha \frac{\partial J}{\partial w_i^k} \tag{3.3}$$

where

- J—cost function (e.g. mean squared error).
- α—learning rate.
- k denotes the time steps.

Since gradient descent has some disadvantageous features like difficult learning rate tuning or reliability concerns applying to non-convex problems (stuck in local optima), a more advanced optimization algorithm is used, namely the Levenberg-Marquardt algorithm. While gradient descent is a steepest descent algorithm, the Levenberg-Marquardt algorithm is a variation of Newton's method. This optimization technique combines the benefits of the steepest descent (backpropagation) method and the Gauss-Newton algorithm. Gradient descent has a slow convergence to the (local) optima, because the constant step size does not fit every function gradient. The Gauss-Newton algorithm can estimate proper step sizes for the directions, but the convergent result needs a reasonable quadratic approximation of error function. The advantage of the Gauss-Newton approach over the standard Newton's method is that it does not require calculation of second-order derivatives. The Levenberg-Marquardt algorithm trains an ANN multiple times faster than the usual backpropagation algorithms.

For this reason, the Levenberg-Marquardt method uses a steepest descent algorithm until quadratic approximation is available, then it changes to the Gauss-Newton algorithm. It is traceable in the equation of the method:

$$w_{k+1} = w_k - \left(J_k^T J_k + \mu I\right)^{-1} J_k e_k \tag{3.4}$$

where

- I—the identity matrix.
- μ—a positive number, which express the switching between two algorithms.
- w—the weight vectors (with k iterations).
- J—Jacobian matrix, which gives the second-order error of total error function.

When μ is nearly zero, the equation approaches the Gauss-Newton method; otherwise, it behaves like a steepest descent algorithm.

3.1   RNNs—Transition toward LSTM

In the previous section general attributes of the neural network design were introduced. This is a powerful tool for both regression and classification problems, but extensive research interest resulted better state-of-the-art solutions for partial

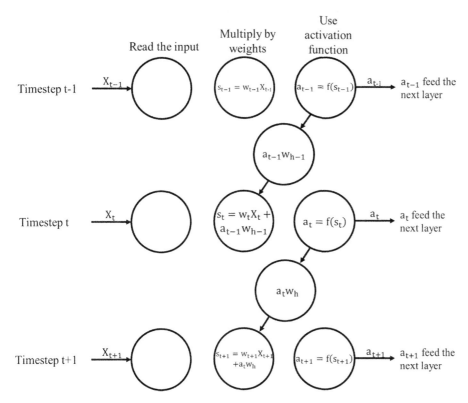

FIG. 3.2 Transition steps of a single recurrent neuron in time.

problems. In the context of a STLF, the sequence patterns of past data are a highly relevant attribute of the dataset. For this reason, a variation of feedforward neural networks called RNNs is used widely with great performance.

RNNs differ from conventional network structures which have an impact on the data feature extraction and exceeds the boundaries of the straightforward information flow. In a sequential fully connected neural network topology, the state of the hidden layers is based only on the input data. Feedforward networks do not remember historical input data at the test time unlike recurrent networks. The latter have a hidden layer recurrence resulting in a more complex mapping method, where the output is no longer a simple function of the input. In general, this can be described as a system memory, because the features of previous information can remain.

The unwrapped recurrence can be defined as an influencer layer, which contains a weighted sum of previous steps' metadata. The recurrence allows to forget irrelevant input features and remember important ones. As usual, this model is also implemented using matrices. Normally, these define the relationship between the current layer and the next one and propagates the input data to the following hidden layer. The recurrence is represented by a new matrix which propagates from the hidden layer to the hidden layer at the next step.

This process is depicted in Fig. 3.2, where the transition steps of a single neuron are detailed. In every timestep the previously introduced mathematical calculations are carried out (input multiplication by corresponding weights, apply activation function). The variables have the same notion as the introduced ones in the previous section. An additional matrix provides the transition between the timesteps which multiply neuron output by recurrent weights. This algorithm operates as a memory cell, and backpropagation though time refresh weights to map only relevant information to the next timestep.

Despite this methodology, the network structure has limitations mapping long-term relationships. Additional problems are vanishing and exploding gradients during the learning process. When the cost function has been calculated in the end of an epoch, it is propagated back through the network and updates the weights. The problem relates to updating the recurring weight, which provides the unrolled temporal loop of hidden layers. If a tanh or sigmoid activation function is used, the first order derivative may be a very small number, which eliminates the influence of past information. The ReLu activation function characteristics handle the vanishing problem but may result in neuron outputs over 1. These values steepen the gradient and may cause too large updates to neural networks during training.

3.2 Long short-term memory

The LSTM networks are a subtype of recurrent ones using a unique node architecture called cells. This is one of the most widely used state-of-the-art model for prediction both for the mid- and the long term. In research fields where time dependencies are important, attributes of the dataset (e.g. neural machine translation, natural language processing, text to image synthesis, etc.) LSTM networks are widely used. This model was created by Hochreiter and Schmidhuber (1997), but due to low interest in AI technologies, the flourishing of the application only started in the 2010s.

As it was discussed, due to the accumulation of error during training, it is easy to cause gradient explosion or gradient disappearance in recurrent networks. In response to this problem, the LSTM network, as an improvement of the traditional RNN, introduces the structure of cells containing memory blocks. These have gates not only for inputs and outputs, but they also contain a forget gate, which is to be discussed later. In the previous neural structures, data flowed through the nodes. Depending on the direction of data flow between the gates, different actions are defined in the LSTMs: read, write and reset. This memory structure provides a better dependency mapping in a long-time span. Therefore, as opposed to the introduced network operation, there is no weight initialization and backpropagation. The LSTM training consists of gate actuation and the parametrization of data buffering.

The operational logic implemented by the LSTM is depicted in Fig. 3.2, where

- x_t—cell input data in t timestep.
- h_{t-1}, h_t—cell output in $t-1$ and t timesteps.
- C_{t-1}, C_t—cell state in $t-1$ and t timesteps.

Cell operation and output value can be described by the transition of cell states. The input values of each cell are: the cell state in the previous step (C_{t-1}), the output in the previous step (h_{t-1}) and a batch of input data (x_t). The whole operation process of the cells can be unfolded as follows.

- Define a variation of the input data and the cell output of the previous step.
- Flow the data through the forget gate.
- Determine whether the input value is retained using the input gate.
- Calculate the cell state of the actual time input.
- Define whether the current cell state is retained using output gate.
- Stipulate the new cell state in the context of forget gate output and in relation to current cell state and input gate.
- Determine the output value considering the output gate result.

A forget gate aims to decide regarding the new input value whether the previous cell state should be kept. While the 0 result means a complete forget decision, 1 means a complete retention of the past cell state. Values between the two extremes represent a transition of the states. This step is depicted by Fig. 3.3A. The mathematical representation is the following:

$$f_t = \sigma\left(W_f[y_{t-1}; X_t] + b_f\right) \tag{3.5}$$

where

- f_t—forget gate output $f_t \in [0, 1]$;
- W_f—cell weights of the corresponding forget cell state.
- $[h_{t-1}; X_t]$—matrix composed of the output of the previous step and the current input.
- b_f—forget gate bias term.
- σ—denotes a neural layer with sigmoid activation.

In the next step, a variation of two expressions is defined. The input gate determines whether the new input vector is retained as follows:

$$i_t = \sigma(W_t[y_{t-1}; X_t] + b_i) \tag{3.6}$$

where the expressions can be deduced from the forget gate equation. In parallel, the new cell state of the actual input is calculated:

$$C'_t = \tanh(W_c[y_{t-1}; X_t] + b_c) \tag{3.7}$$

where the tanh expression pushes the result to be in $[-1, 1]$ interval (see Fig. 3.3B). Then the combination of these two values will be added to the cell state (see Fig. 3.3C). To summarize the cell state transition from C_{t-1} to C_t, the discussed gate outputs can be used in the following equation:

$$C_t = C_{t-1} * f_t + C_t * i_t \tag{3.8}$$

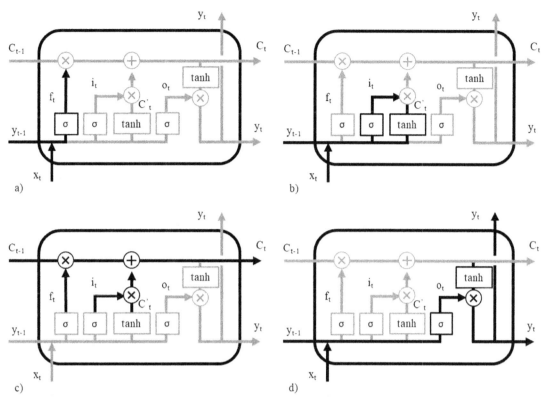

FIG. 3.3 Operation of an LSTM cell step-by-step: (A) denotes the forget gate, (B) describes the new cell state input values, (C) defines the new cell state, (D) shows the result of output gate.

It is clearly visible that the forget gate variable determines the importance of past cell state in the present, and the influence of a new input vector and the calculated state (mapped by C'_t and i_t) are simply added to the cell state. In the equation * means elementwise multiplication operation. While the forget gate determined the influence of the past cell state to next one, the output gate calculates whether the new cell state C_t determines the cell output value y_t (see Fig. 3.3D). An identical process with sigmoid activation is used as it was seen by the forget gate:

$$o_t = \sigma(W_o[y_{t-1}; X_t] + b_o) \tag{3.9}$$

Finally, the cell output value is defined by the new cell state and the result of the output gate:

$$y_t = \tanh(C_t) * o_t \tag{3.10}$$

The mathematical deduction of the LSTM networks clearly identifies the additional features against conventional feed-forward neural networks. The mapping capability of long-term dependencies traces the pathway for forecasting applications of LSTMs. It the next chapter an LSTM-based day-ahead load forecast model is presented, and its performance is evaluated against TSOs methodologies.

4   Short-term load forecast using LSTM network

In this section an LSTM-based neural network model is proposed using historical electricity load time series. Due to the proliferation of non-metered residential photovoltaic plants, it is assumed that the daily load curve is noticeably affected by these entities. The goal of the investigation is to confirm and measure the importance of this trend. For this reason, the introduced LSTM load predictor was applied to TSO frequency control areas with various load scales and renewable penetration. The time horizon of the prediction was day-ahead (24 h), the persistent prediction was implemented using a sliding time window method.

4.1 Input dataset

The prediction model uses only an electricity load time series dataset from the source of the ENTSO-E Transparency platform. For better transparency, the European TSOs are obliged to publish their day-ahead load predictions and the certified load measurements. The time granularity of the data is varied, both 15, 30 min and 1 h are used by the TSOs. Due to the limited expedience in this investigation, those regional load forecasts were chosen which publish data in 15-min resolution. In the context of this consideration, four countries were chosen with different features: Germany, Hungary, Austria and Netherlands.

For network training, the historical load dataset of 2015 was used, and it was tested on the summer dataset of 2017 and 2019.

4.2 Data preprocessing, standardization

Fortunately, ENTSO-E Transparency platform provides reliable data about the historical load and day-ahead forecasts, despite that some erroneous, missing and outlier data exists in the datasets. The synchronization to daylight saving time is also handled differently by the different TSOs.

Before running the LSTM network, the training dataset went through a min-max normalization. This method makes it possible to keep input data in a standard range, resulting in a faster learning process. The data was rescaled linearly between [0,1], using the following equation:

$$X_{std} = \frac{x - x_{min}}{x_{max} - x_{min}} \tag{3.11}$$

where

- X_{std}—normalized value.
- x—sample data before normalization.
- x_{max}; x_{min}—maximum and minimum value of the normalized dataset.

The introduced normalization method is highly sensitive to outliers; thus, it was investigated seriously in the data preprocessing stage. The benefit of the applied rescale equation is that it retains the original distribution of scores.

4.3 LSTM model specification

In this section, detailed features and results of the proposed electricity load forecast model are introduced. The algorithm was implemented in Python environment using the LSTM cell as a base unit of the network. The goal of the investigation was to develop an efficient time series load forecast model which outperforms national load forecast methodologies.

It was supposed that large scale renewable energy producers all have real time metering, the intermittent behavior of such entities affects only the scheduling of power plants. Meanwhile, non-metered small-scale energy producers may cause sudden changes or distorted periods of load due to the lack of real-time metering device (net metering).

Table 3.2 depicts the MAPE and MSE indicators of national load forecasts to demonstrate the state-of-the-art load forecast performance of each country. There are noticeable fluctuations in annual values, but there is a forecasting performance decay from 2017 to 2019.

For this reason, the neural network was trained with the historical load dataset of 2015 in different combinations. 2015 is the first consistent year of loads published by ENTSO-E Transparency portal. In this year, renewable penetration was moderate compared to 2019. In the testing phase, environmental variables were also considered in the training session, but the huge additional computational cost did not result in noticeable forecast improvement. Finally, two scenarios were tested:

predict daily load of 2017 July using the annual historical load dataset from 2015.
predict daily load of 2019 July using the annual historical load dataset from 2015.

The input datasets for each country were pre-processed and managed separately. The time dependent features of the electricity loads were extracted using One Hot Encoding. For the reproducibility of the simulations, a random seed was initialized. The dataset in each situation was divided into training, validation and test sets using 80%–10%–10% ratios, respectively. The training set was randomly shuffled for better learning performance.

TABLE 3.2 Transition of day-ahead load forecast performance (MAPE, MSE) from 2015 to 2019 in Hungary (HU), Austria (AT), Netherlands (NL) and Germany (DE).

MAPE	HU	AT	NL	DE
2015	3.85	7.90	19.57	3.05
2016	3.92	4.46	7.71	3.61
2017	3.85	4.80	7.42	2.56
2018	3.83	5.47	6.59	2.80
2019	4.21	4.56	12.25	3.54
MSE				
2015	42141	445302	5167751	5095805
2016	42661	160228	1462034	6822435
2017	45343	188555	1401678	3322359
2018	46092	253919	1250858	4072892
2019	62313	193105	3376333	6203953

The training set span the year of 2015, validation and test sets cover June and July months of 2017 and 2019, respectively. A fixed network structure was used with two hidden layers, and dropout was set to 0.2. The dropout algorithm randomly deactivates network units in the training phase. It is a powerful tool to avoid overfitting and virtually train multiple net structures at the same time. This results in more training iterations but less computational cost for each epoch. Besides dropout, early stopping was also applied in the model. Mean squared error was used as a cost indicator with rmsprop optimizer algorithm. In addition, the number of units in each hidden layer and batch size parameters were tuned using different running scenarios.

4.4 Result evaluation

At least five simulations were carried out for each scenario, and the three most promising training results of each are shown by Table 3.3. In general, the increase of hidden layer nodes over 16 units in each layer resulted in a performance drop.

For this reason, the best test MSE results were reached using 4–16 LSTM cells. In Table 3.3, the performance of national TSO's load forecast was also introduced in the period of the LSTM network test set.

It is clearly seen that the proposed model significantly outperforms the national TSO's load forecasting methods comparing the corresponding MSE values. A graphical representation of the test sets is depicted by the Fig. 3.4. The plotted time series span the period of 1–10th July and follow the logical structure of Table 3.3: Hungarian, Austrian, Dutch and German results are shown in 2017 and 2019, respectively. As a conclusion, the following observations can be taken:

- The Hungarian load forecast accuracy stagnated in the previous years, but in 2019 a noticeable drop can be seen in terms of accuracy. In addition, the Hungarian load prediction accuracy was among the best, but the less adaptive forecasting method and the noticeable increase of photovoltaic system capacities (1500 MW/5 years) may result in an emerging prediction error.
- The Austrian TSO estimations in the context of noticeable residential photovoltaic capacities are excellent; the forecast method may have been revised in 2016 (see the significant improvement in Table 3.3).
- The Dutch load is the most stochastic one, it is a great challenge to improve accuracy. It is seen that the deviation of forecast accuracy is high due to high load uncertainty.
- Despite of high penetration of intermittent renewable sources, German load forecast accuracy is notably more accurate than the Dutch one.

For a better understanding of the load prediction accuracy trends, and to highlight potential effects of non-metered electricity generation, a statistical comparison is discussed.

TABLE 3.3 Load forecasting model parameter set, and comparison of prediction accuracy.

	Layer 1 dim.	Layer 2 dim.	Batch size	Loss	Val. MSE	Test MSE	TSO load forecast MSE
HU 2017							
	4	4	64	0.0366	0.004	0.004	0.0472
	4	4	16	0.0328	0.0027	0.004	0.0472
	8	8	16	0.019	0.0019	0.002	0.0472
HU 2019							
	4	4	16	0.0359	0.0043	0.005	0.0477
	8	8	32	0.0195	0.002	0.003	0.0477
	16	16	128	0.0113	0.0018	0.002	0.0477
AT 2017							
	4	4	32	0.1719	0.0416	0.025	0.1222
	8	8	16	0.0906	0.0258	0.006	0.1222
	16	16	16	0.0607	0.0168	0.008	0.1222
AT 2019							
	16	16	16	0.0604	0.0171	0.006	0.0523
	4	4	16	0.1574	0.0251	0.029	0.0523
	8	8	32	0.0916	0.0215	0.019	0.0523
NL 2017							
	4	4	32	0.4102	0.0396	0.067	2.2795
	8	8	32	0.2212	0.0216	0.076	2.2795
	16	16	32	0.1372	0.0226	0.033	2.2795
NL 2019							
	16	16	32	0.1137	0.0097	0.01	1.2940
	4	4	16	0.3841	0.0401	0.055	1.2940
	8	8	32	0.2201	0.0166	0.031	1.2940
DE 2017							
	4	4	16	6.9153	0.7584	0.856	1.5971
	8	8	32	3.8938	0.41	0.578	1.5971
	16	16	32	2.0377	0.1979	0.158	1.5971
DE 2019							
	4	4	32	8.7443	1.9356	1.744	1.9315
	8	8	32	3.9597	0.4590	0.41	1.9315
	32	32	32	1.4175	0.2922	0.444	1.9315

5 Discussion on the correlation of non-metered generation and daily loads

As it was discussed above, the authors have chosen the example of four countries, Austria, Germany, Hungary and the Netherlands. They were selected considering their peak load, the nature of the daily load curve, the penetration of variable renewable energy sources and the high temporal resolution of available data. Forecasted and actual loads of the countries were collected from the ENTSO-E Transparency Platform for years 2015–19, in 15-min resolution.

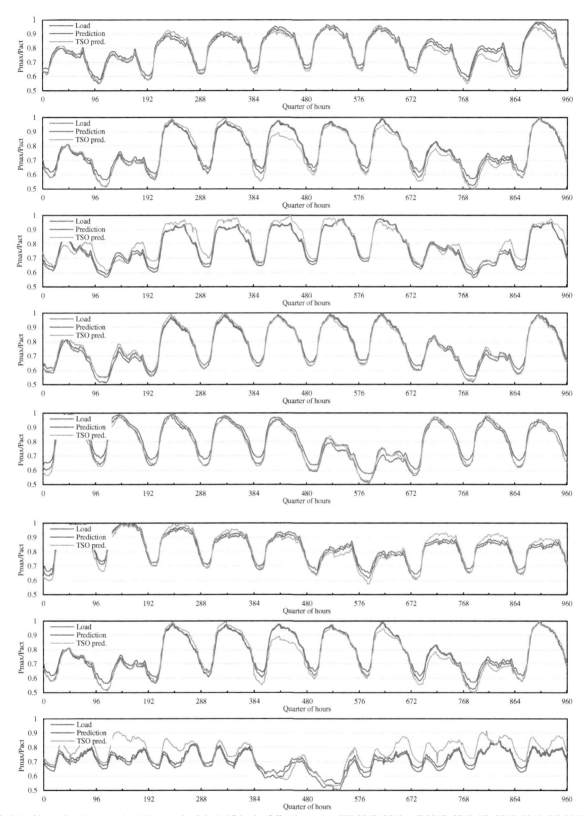

FIG. 3.4 Normalized test set simulation results July 1–10 in the following order: HU 2017, 2019, AT 2017, 2019, NL 2017, 2019, DE 2017, 2019; published reference daily load (*solid blue line*; *light gray* in print version), proposed prediction model results (*solid red line*; *dark gray* in print version) and TSO day-ahead prediction (*solid gray*; *gray* in print version).

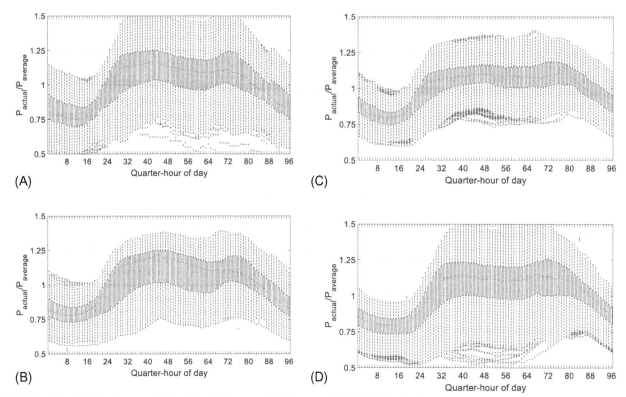

FIG. 3.5 Normalized load curves: (A) Austria, (B) Germany, (C) Hungary, and (D) the Netherlands.

For a better comparison, load values of each country were normalized to the average actual load of the country, recorded in the 5-year period, which was 7123, 55,854, 4866 and 12,515 MW for Austria, Germany, Hungary and the Netherlands, respectively. Fig. 3.5 shows the comparison of the actual load curves of the countries. (In each box, the central mark indicates the median, and the bottom and top edges of the box indicate the 25th and 75th percentiles, respectively. The whiskers extend to the most extreme data points not considered as outliers, and the outliers are plotted individually using the red "+" symbol.)

The curves show that on average the smallest difference between daily peaks and valleys is measured in Hungary. Austria and the Netherlands show similarly high variation despite having a significantly different power plant portfolio. It also can be stated that all load curves show the signs of the presence of non-metered photovoltaic generation, especially in early afternoon hours. It must be noted that all four countries are in the same time zone, although the temporal difference between solar zenith in Hungary and the Netherlands is approximately 1 h.

For the discussion, the authors have extended the error metric calculation shown in Table 3.2. Austria and Germany tend to over-forecast system loads (average errors are 0.0021 and 0.0177, respectively), while Hungary and the Netherlands show under-forecast (−0.0379 and −0.0399, respectively). However, these values only indicate the general tendencies, and reflect the accuracy of forecasts to a minor extent. The MSE of three countries is similar (0.0049, 0.0039 and 0.0031 for Austria, Germany and Hungary, respectively), while the metric of the Netherlands is approximately four times higher (0.0162), as shown in Fig. 3.6. Higher daytime errors in the figure also confirm the effect of non-metered generation, which issue is analyzed in more detail below.

For this test, the average error of the daily load curves is plotted for each year between 2015 and 2019 in Fig. 3.7. In the case of Austria, the error of forecasts was significantly higher during peak solar generation hours in 2015, 2018 and 2019, although the sign of the error was different. The years 2016 and 2017 show curves of different nature. This, and the change of the sign of the error suggest a change in forecast methodology; however, no such evidence was found by the authors. As for Germany, 2016 can be considered as an outlier, while all other years show similar curves and a reliable forecast. Forecast error curves of Hungary are also rather consistent, showing the highest errors during morning rush hours. Errors tend to increase somewhat tendentiously between 2015 and 2019. The biggest differences are clearly presented by the case of the Netherlands, where all curves show higher errors during peak solar generation hours, while the absolute error has also changed its sign.

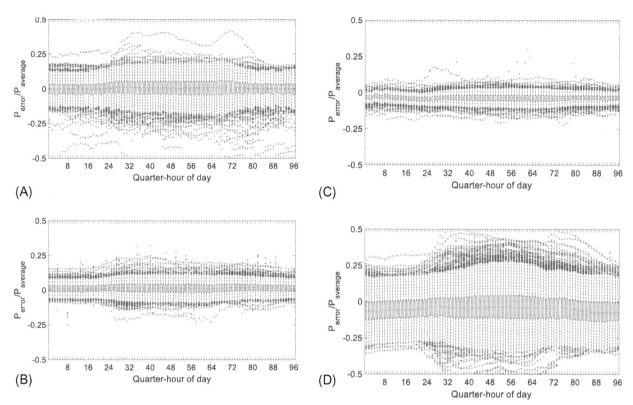

FIG. 3.6 Normalized error of load forecasts: (A) Austria, (B) Germany, (C) Hungary, and (D) the Netherlands.

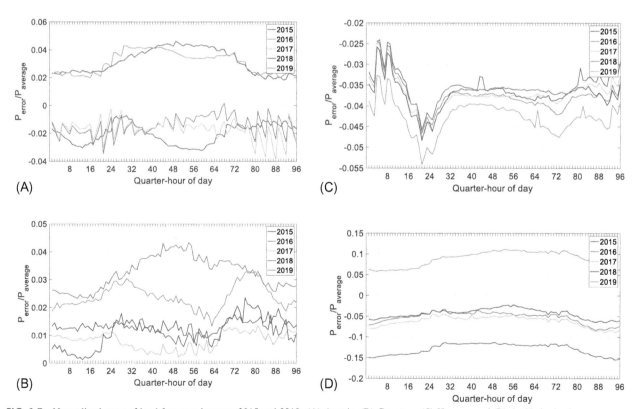

FIG. 3.7 Normalized error of load forecasts between 2015 and 2019; (A) Austria, (B) Germany, (C) Hungary and (D) the Netherlands.

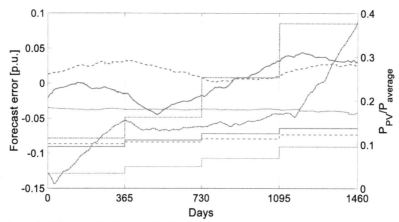

FIG. 3.8 365-Year moving average of the normalized error of load forecasts and installed non-metered solar photovoltaic capacity between 2015 and 2019; Austria *(solid line)*, Germany *(dashed line)*, Hungary *(dotted line)*, the Netherlands *(dash-dotted line)*.

For a better understanding of the potential correlation between changes in load forecast errors and the power generated by non-metered residential solar photovoltaic units, the authors have further processed the data. Daily forecast errors were calculated, and a 365-year moving average was applied to them to show possible tendencies. Also, installed non-metered photovoltaic capacity of each country was assessed. In the case of Hungary, capacity values are published annually by the regulator (Hungarian Energy and Public Utility Regulatory Authority, 2020) for non-metered units separately. In the other three countries, only total photovoltaic capacities were found. The share of non-metered units was approximated using an earlier deliverable of the PVP4Grid project from 2018, according to which this share was 62%, 14% and 70% in Austria, Germany and the Netherlands, respectively (TU Wien and Fundacion Tecnalia Research & Innovation, 2018). These capacities were once again normalized to the average load of each country, to have the same base values as the forecast errors.

The results of this assessment are shown in Fig. 3.8. It can be observed that forecast errors of Germany show very little correlation to installed capacities (−0.1384). Correlations of Austria and Hungary are moderate (0.7087 and −0.668, respectively). The Austrian numbers and curves show that while there might be some tendencies in the underlying data, the moving average of the forecast errors was not always monotonously increasing. In the case of Hungary, the moving average shows a small but monotonous increase in errors. The highest correlation of forecast errors and installed capacities were calculated for the Netherlands (0.8001), which once again supports the hypothesis that at least a part of the forecast error is caused by the increasing number of non-metered units.

6 Conclusions

In this chapter various aspects of load forecasting challenges were discussed, and it highlighted the effect of non-metered residential photovoltaic systems. Firstly, a detailed comparison of load forecasting methodologies was introduced in the context of the forecast horizon. As it was clearly shown, neural networks outperformed other forecasting techniques, setting the course for the introduced forecast model. Besides the literature review, practical load forecasting techniques were discussed applied by TSOs.

Then a detailed mathematical background of RNNs was presented, starting from the basic theory of neural networks. Finally, basic principles of the LSTM cells were introduced. This established the background for the proposed LSTM-based load forecasting model. The prediction results outperformed the precision of state-of-the-art TSO load forecast techniques for summer periods in 2017 and 2019. The load predictor was validated on the Austrian, German, Hungarian and the Dutch electricity loads. The mathematical section, the detailed parameter set, and the result evaluation prove the overall precise reproducibility of the introduced prediction method. For a better understanding of different residential electricity trends in each country, a statistical investigation was also given. The results also proved the hypothesis that residential photovoltaic entities play an important role in the characteristics of the daily load curves and the performance of TSO load forecasts. The publication results set out two directions of future work. Although the significant performance of the load prediction model was validated in a certain time interval, outlier- and national holidays should also be considered in the prediction algorithm. Moreover, prediction results give scope for address non-metered energy production patterns in daily load curves in context of different PV penetration levels.

References

Alzahrani, A., Kimball, J.W., Dagli, C., 2014. Predicting solar irradiance using time series neural networks. Procedia Comput. Sci. 36 (C), 623–628. https://doi.org/10.1016/j.procs.2014.09.065. Elsevier Masson SAS.

Austrain Power Grid, 2020. Day-Ahead Forecasts. Available from: https://www.apg.at/en/markt/Markttransparenz/load/load-forecast. (Accessed 11 May 2020).

Australian Energy Market Operator, 2017. Power System Operating Procedure – Load Forecasting.

Bashir, Z.A., El-Hawary, M.E., 2009. Applying wavelets to short-term load forecasting using PSO-based neural networks. IEEE Trans. Power Syst. 24 (1), 20–27. https://doi.org/10.1109/TPWRS.2008.2008606.

Cui, J., Gao, Q., Li, D., 2019. Improved long short-term memory network based short term load forecasting. In: Proceedings—2019 Chinese Automation Congress, CAC 2019, pp. 4428–4433, https://doi.org/10.1109/CAC48633.2019.8996379.

Dehalwar, V., et al., 2017. Electricity load forecasting for urban area using weather forecast information. In: 2016 IEEE International Conference on Power and Renewable Energy, ICPRE 2016, pp. 355–359, https://doi.org/10.1109/ICPRE.2016.7871231.

Gesino, A.J., Market Design Renewable Energy and TenneT, 2013. RES forecasting from a TSO perspective. In: EWEA Technology Workshop.

He, Y., Deng, J., Li, H., 2017. Short-term power load forecasting with deep belief network and copula models. In: Proceedings—9th International Conference on Intelligent Human-Machine Systems and Cybernetics, IHMSC 2017. vol. 1, pp. 191–194, https://doi.org/10.1109/IHMSC.2017.50.

Hochreiter, S., Schmidhuber, J., 1997. Long short-term memory. Neural Comput. 9, 1735–1780.

Hungarian Energy and Public Utility Regulatory Authority, 2020. Annual Data for Non-Metered Photovoltaic Generation. Available from: http://www.mekh.hu/nem-engedelykoteles-kiseromuvek-es-haztartasi-meretu-kiseromuvek-adatai-2019. (Accessed 11 May 2020).

Imani, M., 2019. Long short-term memory network and support vector regression for electrical load forecasting. In: 5th International Conference on Power Generation Systems and Renewable Energy Technologies, PGSRET 2019. IEEE, pp. 1–6, https://doi.org/10.1109/PGSRET.2019.8882730.

Jiang, Q., et al., 2018. Electricity power load forecast via long short-term memory recurrent neural networks. In: Proceedings—2018 4th Annual International Conference on Network and Information Systems for Computers, ICNISC 2018. IEEE, pp. 265–268, https://doi.org/10.1109/ICNISC.2018.00060.

Khuntia, S.R., Rueda, J.L., Van Der Meijden, M.A.M.M., 2016. Neural network-based load forecasting and error implication for short-term horizon. In: Proceedings of the International Joint Conference on Neural Networks, 2016 October (608540), pp. 4970–4975, https://doi.org/10.1109/IJCNN.2016.7727854.

Kostylev, V., Pavlovski, A., 2011. Solar power forecasting performance – towards industry standards. In: 1st International Workshop on the Integration of Solar Power into Power Systems, Aarhus, Denmark, pp. 1–8.

Lang, C., et al., 2019. Electricity Load Forecasting—an Evaluation of Simple 1D-CNN Network Structures. Available from: http://arxiv.org/abs/1911.11536.

Liao, Z., Pan, H., Zeng, Q., Fan, X., Zhang, Y., Yu, S., 2019. Short-Term Load Forecasting With Dense Average Network. arxiv.org, pp. 1–8. https://arxiv.org/pdf/1912.03668.pdf. (Accessed 29 May 2020).

Liu, C., et al., 2017. Short-term load forecasting using a long short-term memory network. In: 2017 IEEE PES Innovative Smart Grid Technologies Conference Europe, ISGT-Europe 2017—Proceedings, 2018 January, pp. 1–6, https://doi.org/10.1109/ISGTEurope.2017.8260110.

Lu, J., et al., 2019. A hybrid model based on convolutional neural network and long short-term memory for short-term load forecasting. In: IEEE Power and Energy Society General Meeting, 2019 August., https://doi.org/10.1109/PESGM40551.2019.8973549.

Ma, Y., et al., 2019. Short term load forecasting based on iForest-LSTM. In: 2019 14th IEEE Conference on Industrial Electronics and Applications (ICIEA). IEEE.

Massaoudi, M., et al., 2019. A Novel Approach Based Deep RNN Using Hybrid NARX-LSTM Model for Solar Power Forecasting. pp. 1–9. Available from: http://arxiv.org/abs/1910.10064.

Mayer, D., et al., 2008. Performance prediction of grid-connected photovoltaic systems using remote sensing. Report IEA-PVPS T2-07:2008. Available from: http://halshs.archives-ouvertes.fr/docs/00/46/68/25/PDF/7BAE9F5Bd01.pdf.

Mishra, S., Palanisamy, P., 2019. An Integrated Multi-Time-Scale Modeling for Solar Irradiance Forecasting Using Deep Learning. Available from: http://arxiv.org/abs/1905.02616.

Mukhoty, B.P., Maurya, V., Shukla, S.K., 2019. Sequence to sequence deep learning models for solar irradiation forecasting. In: 2019 IEEE Milan PowerTech, PowerTech 2019., https://doi.org/10.1109/PTC.2019.8810645.

Narayan, A., Hipely, K.W., 2017. Long short term memory networks for short-term electric load forecasting. In: 2017 IEEE International Conference on Systems, Man, and Cybernetics, SMC 2017, 2017 January, pp. 2573–2578, https://doi.org/10.1109/SMC.2017.8123012.

Nicolao, G.D., Pozzi, M., Soda, E., Stori, M., 2014. Short-term load forecasting: a power-regression approach. 2014 International Conference on Probabilistic Methods Applied to Power Systems (PMAPS), Durham, pp. 1–6. https://doi.org/10.1109/PMAPS.2014.6960648.

Ray, P., Mishra, D.P., Lenka, R.K., 2016. Short term load forecasting by artificial neural network. In: 2016 International Conference on Next Generation Intelligent Systems (ICNGIS).

Reikard, G., Hansen, C., 2019. Forecasting solar irradiance at short horizons: frequency and time domain models. Renew. Energy, 1270–1290. https://doi.org/10.1016/j.renene.2018.08.081. Elsevier Ltd.

Réseau de transport d'électricité, 2014. Consommation francaise d'électricité: Caractéristiques et méthode de prévision. pp. 1–4.

Rodrigues, F., Cardeira, C., Calado, J.M.F., 2014. The daily and hourly energy consumption and load forecasting using artificial neural network method: a case study using a set of 93 households in Portugal. Energy Procedia 62, 220–229. https://doi.org/10.1016/j.egypro.2014.12.383. Elsevier B.V.

Singh, S., Hussain, S., Bazaz, M.A., 2017. Short-term load forecasting with artificial neural network. In: 2017 Fourth International Conference on Image Information Processing., https://doi.org/10.1109/RTEICT42901.2018.9012625.

Sinkovics, B., Hartmann, B., 2018. Analysing effect of solar photovoltaic production on load curves and their forecasting. Renew. Energy Power Qual. J. 1 (16), 760–765. https://doi.org/10.24084/repqj16.462.

Srivastava, A.K., Pandey, A.S., Singh, D., 2016. Short-term load forecasting methods: a review. In: International Conference on Emerging Trends in Electrical, Electronics and Sustainable Energy Systems, ICETEESES 2016, pp. 130–138, https://doi.org/10.1109/ICETEESES.2016.7581373.

Sun, W., Lu, J., He, Y., 2005. Information entropy based neural network model for short-term load forecasting. In: Proceedings of the IEEE Power Engineering Society Transmission and Distribution Conference, 2005, pp. 1–5, https://doi.org/10.1109/TDC.2005.1546989.

Transpower New Zealand, 2016. GL-SD-204 Load Forecast Methodology and Processes.

TU Wien and Fundacion Tecnalia Research & Innovation, 2018. D2.1: Existing and Future PV Prosumer Concepts. *PVP4Grid project* (764786), pp. 1–123. Available from: https://www.pvp4grid.eu/wp-content/uploads/2018/08/D2.1_Existing-future-prosumer-concepts_PVP4Grid_FV.pdf.

Ulbricht, R., et al., 2013. First steps towards a systematical optimized strategy for solar energy supply forecasting. In: ECML/PKDD 2013, 1st International Workshop on Data Analytics for Renewable Energy Integration (DARE), pp. 14–25.

Wang, F., et al., 2012. Short-term solar irradiance forecasting model based on artificial neural network using statistical feature parameters. Energies 5 (5), 1355–1370. https://doi.org/10.3390/en5051355.

Webberley, A., Gao, D.W., 2013. Study of artificial neural network based short term load forecasting. In: IEEE Power and Energy Society General Meeting, pp. 7–10, https://doi.org/10.1109/PESMG.2013.6673036.

Xie, J., et al., 2015. Combining load forecasts from independent experts. In: 2015 North American Power Symposium, NAPS 2015., https://doi.org/10.1109/NAPS.2015.7335138.

Chapter 4

Forecasting week-ahead hourly electricity prices in Belgium with statistical and machine learning methods

Evangelos Spiliotis[a], Haris Doukas[a], Vassilios Assimakopoulos[a], and Fotios Petropoulos[b]

[a]*School of Electrical and Computer Engineering, National Technical University of Athens, Athens, Greece,* [b]*School of Management, University of Bath, Bath, United Kingdom*

Acronyms

AI	artificial intelligence
AMSE	absolute mean scaled error
ARIMA	autoregressive integrated moving average—SARIMA stands for seasonal ARIMA; ARIMAX stands for ARIMA with external variables
BNN	Bayesian neural network
CI	computational intelligence
Comb	combination of forecasting methods—sComb is the average of sNaive, SARIMA, MAPA.D, and MLR.A; mlComb is the average of MLP.A and RF.A; Comb is the average of the above-mentioned six methods
DES	seasonally adjusted exponential smoothing
DSES	seasonally adjusted simple exponential smoothing
ES	exponential smoothing
GRNN	generalized regression neural network
MAPA	Multiple Aggregation Prediction Algorithm—MAPA.D applies MAPA using DSES; MAPA.W applies MAPA by combining the components of the forecasts using a more aggressive weighting scheme to mitigate seasonal shrinkage
MASE	mean absolute scaled error
MCB	multiple comparisons with the best
ML	machine learning
MLP	multi-layer perceptron—MLP.A considers explanatory variables, while MLP.B does not
MLR	multiple linear regression—MLR.A considers explanatory variables, while MLR.B does not
MTA	multiple temporal aggregation
NN	neural network
RBF	radial basis function
RF	random forest—RF.A considers explanatory variables, while RF.B does not
RNN	recurrent neural network
RT	regression tree
SES	simple exponential smoothing
sNaive	seasonal naïve
SVM	support vector machine

1 Introduction

During the last decades, electricity markets have been deregulated, thus becoming more competitive when compared to their government-controlled ancestors. However, although electricity is still sold under the special rules and contracts that each market defines, its price typically displays notable volatility, mainly due to the numerous variables it is affected by (Kaminski, 2013). For example, given that electricity consumption is characterized by various seasonal patterns, identified at daily, weekly, and annual levels, electricity price tends to exhibit relative complex dynamics. Accordingly, since

Mathematical Modelling of Contemporary Electricity Markets. https://doi.org/10.1016/B978-0-12-821838-9.00005-0

electricity cannot be stored at a large scale and production is not always optimally balanced to the consumption, electricity price is respectively affected. Other external variables, such as weather conditions, fuel prices, holidays, and special events, further increase the uncertainty about the future electricity consumption and, therefore, the actual electricity price.

These unique characteristics that electricity prices display have significant implications for the operation and management of energy companies (Shahidehpour et al., 2002). Over- or under-contracting, a process that significantly affects the balancing of the market, leads to high costs that may result in notable financial losses and deteriorate the profitability of the companies. On the other hand, accurately predicting the price of electricity for the following hours or days, introduces vast opportunities for the energy companies, enhancing their competitive advantage and allowing for better short- and mid-term planning.

To that end, various forecasting approaches have been proposed in the literature to forecasts electricity prices (Weron, 2014), including, among others, statistical and Machine Learning (ML) methods that dominated the field over the years. The performance reported for these approaches varies across different studies, either due to the data and criteria used for their evaluation, or the tools and techniques utilized for their implementation. The inconclusiveness of the literature with regards to the superiority of the one approach over the other has led to confusion, which is partially driven by the replication crisis that the field of forecasting is caught up (Makridakis et al., 2018a). Moreover, while the inclusion of external variables is beneficial for energy forecasting tasks (Makridakis et al., 2020a), we are not sure if the benefits are consistent across families of models.

In this chapter, we provide an overview of the most popular and widely used statistical and ML methods, discussing their main advantages and limitations. Then, we consider the electricity market of Belgium and evaluate the performance of some representative methods of each category, including two ML and six statistical ones. We also examine the relative benefits from including predictor variables. We test the statistical significance of our results, both in terms of accuracy and bias, and conclude by suggesting avenues for future research.

2 Statistical and machine learning methods in electricity price forecasting

2.1 Overview of forecasting methods

By reviewing the literature, it becomes evident that there is no commonly accepted classification of the various forecasting approaches that have been developed for forecasting electricity prices (Weron, 2014). Each study offers its own classification, depending on the criteria used by the authors for performing this task and their academic background. However, most of the studies agree that forecasting approaches can be classified into three main categories, namely (i) simulation methods, (ii) statistical methods, and (iii) ML methods (Hong, 2014).

The first class of methods is based on mathematical models that simulate the way the electricity market works, considering information about the market rules, the market players, the bits, and the expected electricity consumption. Although these methods can provide valuable insights about the general dynamics of the market, they require a deep knowledge about its structure, detailed information about the involved stakeholders and their strategy, as well as continuous theoretical and empirical calibrations. Thus, when it comes to providing short-term forecasts, ranging from a few hours to a few days ahead, simulation methods offer limited advantages.

On the other hand, statistical methods are specifically designed so that they automatically capture the distinctive characteristics of electricity prices, both long- and short-term ones (Weron, 2006). This is done by utilizing mathematical models that relate future electricity prices with past ones (e.g., same hour of the previous day or week) and potentially external variables (e.g., weather conditions, holidays, fuel prices, and special events). If the input of the forecasting model is limited to past values of electricity prices, then it is typically called an "auto-regression model," while, if it considers a relatively significant number of external variables, it is labeled as a "regression model." In cases where no regression takes place (e.g., forecasting through moving averages or exponential smoothing), the model is called a "time series forecasting model." The main advantage of statistical methods is that they capture the particularities of the electricity prices, such as multiple seasonal cycles and trends. Also, statistical methods are computationally cheap. Finally, they are easy to interpret, thus allowing interested parties to understand the behavior of the prices and the market. Their main drawback is that they usually assume linear dependencies among the examined variables, thus providing sub-optimal results in cases where non-linear behaviors of electricity prices and explanatory variables are present.

The third class of forecasting approaches refers to methods that build on ML models (Díaz et al., 2019), i.e., algorithms that do not prescribe the data generating process but learn from data relationships. This class of methods is also met under other names, such as computational intelligence (CI), artificial intelligence (AI), and neural networks (NNs), with the latter being, in fact, a special case of ML methods. ML involves a variety of non-linear, unstructured regression models, including

NNs, regression trees (RTs), and support vector machines (SVMs). Depending on the architecture and the nature of the models, further classification is possible. For example, NNs can be classified into multi-layer perceptrons (MLPs), Bayesian neural networks (BNNs), generalized regression neural networks (GRNNs), radial basis functions (RBFs), as well as recurrent NNs (RNNs) that, in contrast to the previous NNs classes, have a memory and allow for patters to be learned in a chronologically way. The main advantage of ML methods is that they can identify, capture, and learn complex non-linear relationships. Thus, in contrast to statistical methods, they usually handle peaks and extreme values more effectively. Moreover, since these relations are learned and not assumed a-priory, the learning process becomes more flexible and dynamic. However, ML methods do come with some disadvantages. Due to their flexibility, ML methods are vulnerable to over-fitting and require lots of historical data to be adequately trained (Makridakis et al., 2018b). Also, in contrast to statistical methods, ML methods must be fine-tuned by hand, a task that requires lots of experience and engineering background to be properly accomplished. Even today, that many software providers (e.g., Python and R) offer advanced, yet easy to implement and customize ML algorithms, building accurate ML forecasting methods is considered more like art (Barker, 2020). Finally, the complexity of these methods makes them difficult to interpret, also leading to computationally expensive solutions.

Note that the classification used in this study is based solely on the way the different forecasting methods learn. Given other criteria, related to the way the data is handled (global vs. local models), the type of forecasts produced (point vs. probabilistic forecasts), the computational cost, the linearity of the models, or even subjective criteria, different classifications are possible (Januschowski et al., 2020). We adopt this classification given that it is the one most considered in the literature, while also allowing no loss of generality. Besides, this classification helps us better distinguish, discuss, and compare the two types of methods (i.e., statistical and ML methods) that are most widely used by academics and practitioners for generating short-term electricity prices forecasts and supporting decisions related with electricity spot price.

Also note that the claims made above are based on the conclusions drawn by most of the studies done in the field. This is important given that some studies do report significantly different results than others, thus leading to controversy. For example, having reviewed numerous statistical and ML papers, Aggarwal et al. (2009a) conclude that there is no systematic, consistent evidence of the outperformance of one method over the other. Weron (2014) claims that this can be partially explained by the differences observed between the educational training of engineers and statisticians, as "statistical" papers usually show that statistical methods outperform ML methods, and vice versa, meaning that the accuracy of the methods considered, both statistical and ML, may strongly depend on the expertise of the person training them. Limited evaluation periods consisting of a few days or weeks (Aggarwal et al., 2009b), inappropriate accuracy measures (Hyndman and Koehler, 2006), lack of replicability (Makridakis et al., 2018a), and short time series lengths (Weron, 2014) may also contribute to this issue. The inconclusiveness of the literature with regards to the superiority of the statistical methods over the ML ones is a hot topic of research within the forecasting community, ranging from high-frequency electricity prices data to low-frequency (e.g., yearly, quarterly, and monthly) micro, macro, industry, and demographic data (Makridakis et al., 2018b). The M4 forecasting competition (Makridakis et al., 2020b) shed some light in that direction by showing that ML methods can lead to superior accuracy, provided that both global and local dynamics of the series are considered. Forecasting competitions specifically designed to promote the research in electricity price forecasting, also contribute in that direction (Hong et al., 2016). In any case, more objective evidence is still required for making reliable conclusions and generalizations. In this study, we provide such evidence by considering some indicative statistical and ML methods, as described below.

2.2 Statistical methods

The first class of forecasting approaches used for predicting electricity prices, and probably the most popular one, refers to the statistical methods. Weron (2014) distinguishes them further into six (6) sub-classes: (i) similar-day and exponential smoothing methods, (ii) regression models, (iii) AR-type time series models, (iv) ARX-type time series models, (v) threshold autoregressive models, and (vi) heteroscedasticity and GARCH-type models. Although there is a large body of literature on all the sub-classes listed above, researches have focused on the first three sub-classes. In this study, we consider some indicative cases of such statistical methods, as well as some of their variants. We also consider the fourth sub-class, which can be seen as a mix of regression and AR models, i.e., auto-regressive models with external variables.

2.2.1 Seasonal naïve (sNaive)

According to this method, the forecast of the target period is equal to the last known observation of the same period. Depending on the frequency considered (e.g., 24 or 168 h), the forecasts of sNaive differ. Given that electricity prices are characterized by various seasonal patterns, identified at both daily and weekly level, we assume a frequency of 168 (24 h across 7 days of the week). Please, note that this method is different from the Naïve 2 method (Makridakis et al., 2020b), which is the naïve forecasting method on the seasonally adjusted data.

2.2.2 Exponential smoothing (ES)

This method was proposed in the late 1950s and, since then, has motivated some of the most successful forecasting methods in the field (Hyndman et al., 2008). In brief, ES involves a variety of models that produce forecasts by averaging the values of past observations using weights that exponentially decrease as observations get older. ES, although quite simple, provides reliable forecasts for many different forecast profiles. It is particularly useful for fast-moving data. In general, ES models extrapolate the series by estimating their level, trend, and seasonal components. After optimizing the smoothing parameters of each model, the most appropriate one can be selected using information criteria, which is the likelihood of a model penalized by its complexity. In this study, we implement ES using the "smooth" package for R (Svetunkov, 2019) as it allows handling series of high frequency. While extensions of exponential smoothing models to include external regressors have been proposed (Hyndman et al., 2008), we do not consider these models here as they often lead to estimation difficulties.

2.2.3 Seasonally adjusted simple exponential smoothing (DSES)

The simple exponential smoothing (SES) model is a case of the ES method, which produces non-seasonal and non-trended forecasts (Gardner, 1985). Thus, SES forecasts are based exclusively on the estimate of the running level of the series. Given that for short-term forecasting horizons electricity prices do not display significant trends, SES becomes a reasonable simplification to ES. Yet, given that electricity prices exhibit strong seasonal patterns, for SES to provide accurate results, the series must first be seasonally adjusted. We do so by using the classical, multiplicative decomposition by moving averages (Kendall and Stuart, 1983). After forecasting the seasonally adjusted series with SES, the forecasts are re-seasonalized. DSES, apart from being much simpler and faster to compute than ES, differs from seasonal ES models in a sense that the seasonal component of the series is deterministically estimated once across the whole series and it is not updated based on the most recent observations, thus capturing its global seasonal dynamics. In this regard, it is interesting to see whether a simplified model like DSES can outperform more complicated models like ES.

2.2.4 Seasonally adjusted exponential smoothing (DES)

This model applies ES, but instead of allowing the model to directly capture the seasonal dynamics of the series, seasonality is modeled externally using seasonal adjustments, exactly as done by DSES. We consider this variant of ES along with DSES in order to see whether capturing possible local trends is beneficial in terms of forecasting accuracy.

2.2.5 Multiple Aggregation Prediction Algorithm (MAPA)

Forecasters must deal with lots of modelling challenges related to sampling, parameter, and model uncertainties (Petropoulos et al., 2018). For instance, limited samples may lead to sub-optimal parameter estimations, especially if the data are complex or is characterized by significant volatility. Even worse, sub-optimal models may be selected for producing the forecasts, thus deteriorating forecasting accuracy. This is particularly relevant in electricity prices forecasting, where many different forecasting methods can be potentially used for performing this task. For example, even if we are sure that ES is an appropriate method for predicting the electricity prices of a market, the uncertainty present may lead the model selection algorithm used to a sub-optimal choice, being also potentially sub-optimally parameterized. Multiple temporal aggregation (MTA) can be used to mitigate the need to identify a single "correct" model or rely on a unique estimation of parameters (Silvestrini and Veredas, 2008). The approach is based on temporally aggregating the time series at multiple levels, which transforms the original data to lower time frequencies, highlighting different aspects of the series (Athanasopoulos et al., 2017). Thus, forecasts produced at lower aggregation levels are useful for capturing the periodic components of the series, like seasonality, while forecasts delivered at higher aggregation levels are useful for revealing the long-term ones, such as trends. This process has a lot of potential for fast-moving data, such as electricity prices, where the high sampling frequency displays increased noise and introduces multiple seasonal patterns at the original sampling frequency that require complex data pre-processing to be effectively handled.

In this study, we consider a special implementation of MTA, called Multiple Aggregation Prediction Algorithm (MAPA). MAPA (Kourentzes et al., 2014) differs from other MTA approaches proposed in the literature in a sense that instead of combining the forecasts produced at different temporal levels, it combines their components (level, trend, and seasonality). Thus, after aggregating the data, MAPA uses ES to generate forecasts at each level and then combines their components using appropriate weights. In this work, we consider the median operator since it is less affected by poorly estimated components due to extreme values and other types of outliers, leading possibly to more robust forecasts. Moreover, given that MTA has the undesirable effect of seasonality shrinkage (Spiliotis et al., 2019), we also investigate the performance of two modifications of the algorithm that make it appropriate for handling high-frequency time series, as proposed by Spiliotis et al. (2020). The first modification, MAPA.D, applies MAPA on seasonally adjusted data using DSES. The second modification, MAPA.W, applies MAPA but combines the components of the forecasts using a weighting scheme, which is more aggressive in retaining the high-frequency aspects of the seasonal pattern. MTA has been effectively proposed in the literature as an alternative for producing accurate forecasts for the case of electricity load forecasting (Jeon et al., 2019; Spiliotis et al., 2020). However, to the best of our knowledge, it has not been tested before for the case of electricity prices, which typically display similar properties. In this regard, it would be interesting to see whether MTA improves the forecasting performance of ES and if the proposed modifications add any value. The MAPA algorithm is implemented using the "MAPA" package for R (Kourentzes and Petropoulos, 2018).

2.2.6 Multiple linear regression (MLR)

This method is one of the most widely used statistical approaches for forecasting electricity prices. The forecasts are produced by relating the target/dependent variable (electricity price) with explanatory/independent variables (e.g., previous observations of electricity prices and electricity consumption forecasts). The method builds on the least-squares technique according to which a linear model is fitted to the data so that the sum of squared errors, i.e., the differences between the target and the predicted values, is minimized. MLR is simple to use, computationally cheap, and relatively accurate. This makes it a competitive alternative over other more sophisticated methods proposed in the field. Moreover, MLR is flexible in the sense that it can consider multiple explanatory variables, including past observations of the examined series, like done by time series models, and external variables used to incorporate additional information to the model. The main limitation of MLR is that it is linear, thus inadequate for capturing non-linear dependencies between the variables (at least if not properly transformed), with its performance depending strongly on the variables used for performing the regression. In other words, MLR, and regression algorithms, are typically only as good as the explanatory variables used for predicting the target variable. Forecasting the dependent variable relies on accurate forecasts of the independent variables. If the explanatory variables are linearly related to the target variable and effectively explain its variations through time, then the forecasts produced by MLR will be accurate and vice versa. Several techniques have been proposed in the literature to optimally determine the most effective set of explanatory variables (e.g., Lasso, Ridge regression, and stepwise regression) with encouraging results.

In order to investigate the possible benefits of including external variables to MLR, in this study, we consider two different implementations of the method. The first implementation, basic MLR or *MLR.B*, produces forecasts by performing a regression between the electricity prices and several explanatory variables that derive directly from the examined time series, as follows:

- Year (as an indicator for the trend)
- Month, one-hot encoded as an 11-long vector (seasonal dummy indicator)
- Weekday, one-hot encoded as a 6-long vector (seasonal dummy indicator)
- Hour, one-hot encoded as a 23-long vector (seasonal dummy indicator)
- Electricity price recorded 168h before the period being forecasted (same hour, previous week; measuring autocorrelation effects)
- Electricity price recorded 336h before the period being forecasted (same hour, 2 week ago; measuring autocorrelation effects)

The first four variables allow the method to better incorporate possible long-term trends (over the years) and seasonal effects (at daily, weekly, and yearly level). The rest two explanatory variables allow the method to determine the running level of the price, also considering the variations present due to seasonal factors. Note that none of these six variables depend on the knowledge of additional information other than the past values of the series. In this sense, the performance of MLR.B is directly comparable to that of ES, DES, and DSES.

The second implementation, advanced MLR or MLR.A, includes the abovementioned explanatory variables, plus the external variables listed below:

- Holidays, provided as binary indicators.
- Electricity load forecasts, as provided by the operator of the system.
- Electricity generation forecasts (capacity), as provided by the operator of the system.

Given that electricity price is profoundly affected by imbalances reported between the production and the consumption, it is expected that MLR.A will outperform MLR.B, as well as the rest of the univariate statistical methods discussed above.

2.2.7 Autoregressive integrated moving average (ARIMA)

The ARIMA method, also known as the Box-Jenkins methodology, is a popular time series forecasting method that produces predictions by considering the time correlations and the random nature of the examined data (Box and Jenkins, 1970). The autoregressive (AR) part of the method allows the future values to be approximated as a function of the past values. On the other hand, the moving average (MA) part enables the method to consider the past errors produced by the method, thus effectively capturing the randomness present. Finally, the integration (I) part enables the method to differentiate the series so that it becomes stationary and, therefore, better handle possible trends and seasonality. In the latter case, the ARIMA method is usually called SARIMA, as it involves both non-seasonal and seasonal AR and MA parts. ARIMA models are essentially regression models, where the regressors are past values of the series (AR) and the past errors (MA) at various lags. In this work, we consider seasonal ARIMA models that are implemented using the "forecast" package for R (Hyndman and Khandakar, 2008). Like done for ES, an algorithm performs a search over several ARIMA models, and the most appropriate one is selected using information criteria. As regression models, ARIMA can be expanded to include external/exogenous variables (ARIMAX/SARIMAX). We evaluate the performance of both SARIMA and SARIMAX, with the latter including the external variables considered by MLR.A, namely holidays, electricity load forecasts, and electricity generation forecasts.

2.3 Machine learning methods

The second class of forecasting approaches used for predicting electricity prices, constantly gaining more ground, refers to the ML methods. Weron (2014) distinguishes them further into three sub-classes: (i) feed-forward NNs, (ii) RNNs, and (iii) SVMs. During the last few years, researches have focused on the first two sub-classes of methods, also introducing another one, namely RTs. Given that the latter approach is still on its infancy in forecasting related applications, in this study, we consider some indicative cases of MLPs, the simplest version of NNs, and random forests, a more advanced version of RTs.

2.3.1 Multi-layer perceptron (MLP)

This method is the simplest implementation of feed-forward NNs, yet the most popular and widely used in forecasting (Zhang et al., 1998). The NN, exploited to perform a nonlinear regression between the target and the explanatory variables, consists of neurons organized into layers that have unidirectional connections between them. More specifically, the MLP consists of an input layer, having as many nodes as the explanatory variables considered, a set of hidden layers, with the nodes of each layer being the same or different, and an output layer of a single node. The NN is typically trained using the backpropagation technique or one of its variants that applies the gradient descent method so that the weights of the network (connections between the nodes) are appropriately defined. Given that there is no standard way for determining the optimal architecture of an MLP and its hyper-parameters, we proceed by considering a simplified, yet indicative version of it, as described below.

We construct a single hidden layer MLP of N input nodes and 2N hidden nodes, following the practical guidelines suggested by Lippmann (1987) aimed at decreasing the computational time needed for constructing the NN. The scaled conjugate gradient method (Møller, 1993) is then used instead of standard backpropagation for estimating the optimal weights. The method, which is an alternative to the famous Levenberg-Marquardt algorithm, has been found to perform better in many applications and is considered more appropriate for weight optimization. The learning rate is selected between 0.1 and 1, using random initial weights for starting the training process with a maximum of 100 iterations. The activation function of all layers is the logistic one. The NN is constructed using the "RSNNS" package for R (Bergmeir and Benitez, 2012). Like done for the case of the MLR method, we consider two different implementations of the MLP, the first one (MLP.B) producing forecasts by performing a regression between the electricity prices and several explanatory variables that derive directly from the examined time series, and the second one (MLP.A) by considering also the available external variables presented earlier. We note that, due to the nonlinear activation functions used, the data is scaled between 0 and 1 (min-max scaling) to avoid computational problems, meet algorithm requirements, and facilitate faster network learning. Once all predictions are made, the forecasts are then rescaled back to the original scale.

2.3.2 Random forest (RF)

RFs are based on a tree-like recursive partitioning of the input space, specified by the training sample (Breiman, 1993). Space is divided into regions, called the terminal leaves. Then, a sequence of tests is applied to decision nodes to define which leaf node an object should be classified in, based on the input provided and the error achieved. The tests are applied serially from the root node to the leaves until a final decision is made. Although powerful and completely unstructured, RTs are ineffective in cases where complex dynamics are present, especially for noisy data and large samples. RF, which is a combination of multiple RTs, can be effectively used to solve these issues. Each RT is trained so that it depends on the values of a random vector sampled independently and with the same distribution (Breiman, 2001). The accuracy of the method depends on the size of the forest, as well as the strength and correlation of the individual trees. Given that RF averages the predictions of multiple RTs, it is more robust to noise and less likely to over-fit on the training data. We consider a total of 100 non-pruned trees and N/3 randomly sampled variables at each split. Bootstrap sampling is done with replacement. The method is implemented using the "randomForest" package for R (Liaw and Wiener, 2002). Once again, we consider two implementations of the method, namely RF.B and RF.A, with the latter including external explanatory variables.

2.4 Combinations

Although combining forecasts has been proven a very effective strategy for improving forecasting performance in various time series forecasting applications (Makridakis et al., 2020b), it is still of limited use in the field of electricity prices forecasting. On the other hand, many studies have commented on this issue, encouraging researchers and practitioners to combine the forecasts derived from different, diverse methods (Weron, 2014). In this study, we do so by considering three different combinations of methods. The first combination, to be named sComb, is the simple average (equal weights) of sNaive, MAPA.D, SARIMA, and MLR.A. In practice, it is a combination of statistical methods, each one representing a case of this kind of methods (Naïve, exponential smoothing, AR-type, and linear regression). The second combination, to be named mlComb, is the simple average of MLP.A and RF.A, i.e., the two ML methods we expect to perform best. Finally, the last combination, to be named Comb, is the simple average of all the methods considered for sComb and mlComb. We do not examine complex combination schemes for our results to be easier to interpret, also keeping in mind that simple combinations of methods often work better than more complex ones (Petropoulos and Svetunkov, 2020).

3 Empirical evaluation

3.1 Dataset

To evaluate the performance of the statistical and ML methods presented in the previous section, we consider the electricity market of Belgium. The examined dataset consists of the hourly electricity prices of the EPEX-Belgium exchanges, ranging from 01-01-2010 to 31-12-2016 (61,368 h/7 years). The time series representing the prices is visualized in Fig. 4.1. As seen, the series displays significant volatility, being also profoundly affected by seasonal factors.

To better explore the seasonal patterns observed in the series, we plot the electricity prices data against the seasonal periods considering two different seasonal cycles, one of 24 and one of 168 h. In the first case, it is assumed that seasonality is observed at the daily level, while in the second case both at the daily and weekly level. Plots with overlapping observations suggest strong, consistent seasonal patterns and vice versa. The plots are provided in Fig. 4.2, indicating that considering the latter scenario would lead to better estimates about the seasonal dynamics. In this regard, all the examined methods are built in such a way that modelling a seasonal cycle of 168 h is possible.

Apart from the electricity prices, the dataset includes forecasts about the grid load and generation capacity in Belgium and France that serve as external explanatory variables. These forecasts become available on the website of the system operators and, as already discussed, are expected to contribute to the enhancement of the predictions produced by the regression forecasting methods. Note that the level of integration across Belgian and French markets is particularly high, with the former sharing common dynamics with the latter (de Menezes and Houllier, 2016). Thus, we proceed by enriching the dataset of the examined market with variables related to its neighbor market. The importance of considering market integration is discussed in detail by Lago et al. (2018), stressing the need of developing forecasting methods that take the dependencies of electricity markets into account.

The dataset also includes two external variables that indicate in a binary form, whether the period to be forecasted is a public holiday in France and Belgium, respectively. These two variables are expected to help the methods identify patterns related to non-working days. Finally, as described in the previous section, the dataset is completed by creating 11 one-hot

FIG. 4.1 Electricity price of the Belgium market for the period of 01-01-2010 to 31-12-2016. The time series consists of 61,368 observations, having a duration of 7 years.

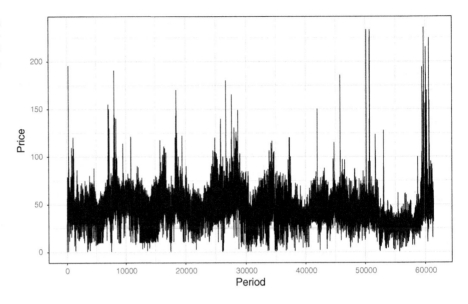

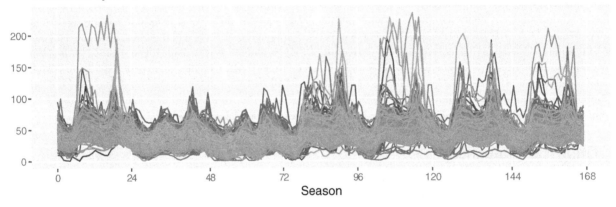

Seasonal cycle of 168 hours

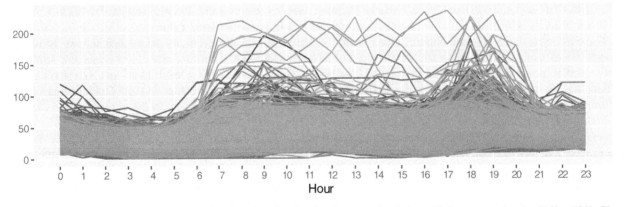

Seasonal cycle of 24 hours

FIG. 4.2 Distribution of the Belgium electricity prices data when plotted against the seasonal period, considering a seasonal cycle of 168 and 24 h. Given that in a non-tended time series with strong seasonality the observations will be overlapping, we anticipate low variance around the seasonal profile. This is evident for the weekly profile, in contrast to the daily profile, mainly due to the differences observed between the working days and the weekends.

encoded variables that indicate the month of the period to be forecasted, 6 one-hot encoded variables that indicate the weekday of the period to be forecasted, 23 one-hot encoded variables that indicate the hour of the period to be forecasted, as well as three more variables indicating the electricity price recorded 168 and 336 h before the period being forecasted, and the year of this period. These variables are used to enable the methods effectively handle the multiple, complex seasonal patterns present. Thus, we end up with a total of 49 explanatory variables for the MLR.A, MLP.A, and RF.A models, and a total of 43 explanatory variables for the MLR.B, MLP.B, and RF.B models. SARIMAX is built using as input along with the electricity prices time series, the forecasts about the grid load and generation capacity in Belgium and France, as well as the public holiday information described previously. Since the rest of the models (sNaive, ES, DES, DSES, MAPA, and SARIMA) are time series forecasting ones, they depend solely on the time series of the electricity price.

Note that, due to the spikes present, many researchers invest in advanced preprocessing techniques that allow even relatively simple forecasting approaches to effectively handle non-linear dependencies in the data. However, this study aims to compare the performance of different forecasting methods and highlight the strengths and weaknesses of each approach, including their effectiveness of dealing with spikes. So, we proceed by leaving the data mostly unprocessed. Our preprocessing is limited to replacing extreme outliers (the observations displaying the lowest and highest 0.1% values in the dataset) with more reasonable entries (average of the previous and next period).

3.2 Experimental set-up

Electricity prices display strong, multiple seasonal patterns at day, week, and year level. This means that, for a method to be properly evaluated, its performance has to be assessed for a period of at least one full calendar year (Aggarwal et al., 2009b). To that end, we split the dataset into multiple training and test sets, using the former sets for training the forecasting methods (estimating their parameters) and the latter sets for assessing their performances across a 5-year period.

More specifically, we consider a forecasting horizon of 1 week (168-step-ahead forecasts) and a training period of a fixed size equal to 2 years (17,520 h). We begin by using the sample ranging from 01-01-2010 to 31-12-2011 for training purposes, and the sample ranging from 01-01-2012 to 07-01-2012 for testing purposes. After generating our forecasts for the first week of January 2012, we repeat this experiment after 168 h by removing the first 168 observations of the training sample, adding the 168 observations of the test sample to the training sample, and forecasting the following week. This process is repeated 261 times, i.e., until the available dataset runs out of observations. The set-up used is rolling-origin evaluation (Tashman, 2000) of non-overlapping 168-h windows. The forecasting horizon was determined by the fact that energy companies utilize short-term electricity prices for their day-to-day market operations.

The forecasts are evaluated both in terms of forecasting accuracy (closeness of actual values and forecasts) and bias (consistent differences between actual values and generated forecasts). We use the mean absolute scaled error (MASE) (Hyndman and Koehler, 2006) for measuring the accuracy of the forecasts and the absolute value of the mean scaled error (AMSE) for measuring their bias. Both measures permit averaging forecasting performance across different scales, while also displaying better properties than other alternatives found in the literature, such as percentage errors (Weron, 2014). For both MASE and AMSE, lower values indicate better forecasts. MASE and AMSE are defined as

$$MASE = \frac{1}{h} \frac{\sum_{t=n+1}^{n+h} |y_t - f_t|}{\frac{1}{n-m} \sum_{i=m+1}^{n} |y_t - y_{t-m}|},$$

$$AMSE = \frac{1}{h} \frac{\left| \sum_{t=n+1}^{n+h} y_t - f_t \right|}{\frac{1}{n-m} \sum_{i=m+1}^{n} |y_t - y_{t-m}|}, \tag{4.1}$$

where y_t is the actual value of the predicted series at point t, f_t is the respective forecast of the method being evaluated, h is the forecasting horizon (168 h), n is the number of the data points available in the training set (17,520 h), and m is the data frequency (168 h).

3.3 Results

Table 4.1 summarizes the performances of the examined forecasting methods. The first column of the table presents the name of the method, the second column its type, while the last two columns the MASE and AMSE values, respectively. Entries in bold indicate the best forecasting approach per case.

TABLE 4.1 Comparison of statistical (S), machine learning (ML), and combination (C) forecasting methods in terms of accuracy (MASE) and bias (AMSE) for the test sample considered (5-year rolling origin evaluation).

Method	Type	MASE	AMSE
sNaive	S	1.053	0.573
ES	S	1.073	0.746
DES	S	1.091	0.768
DSES	S	1.089	0.765
MAPA	S	1.050	0.535
MAPA.W	S	0.929	0.542
MAPA.D	S	0.929	0.523
SARIMA	S	1.172	0.720
SARIMAX	S	0.964	0.634
MLR.B	S	0.983	0.664
MLR.A	S	0.856	0.537
MLP.B	ML	0.956	0.592
MLP.A	ML	0.866	0.553
RF.B	ML	0.964	0.563
RF.A	ML	0.821	0.455
sComb	C	0.858	0.484
mlComb	C	**0.769**	**0.425**
Comb	C	0.790	0.440

The best-performing method per measure is indicated using bold numbers.

Regarding the statistical methods used, we observe that sNaive, although the most straightforward approach, leads to more accurate and less biased forecasts than ES, DES, DSES, and SARIMA. Thus, we conclude that methods that depend on similar-day forecasting approaches may be proven difficult to beat in practice. It is also shown that ES and SARIMA lead to poor results, indicating that both methods fail to capture the complex dynamics of the predicted series. Moreover, we observe that ES outperforms DES and DSES both in terms of accuracy and bias, meaning that the two simplifications considered, i.e., the elimination of the local trends and the external seasonal adjustments, add value only in terms of computational efficiency, leading to slightly worse forecasts.

On the other hand, we find out that MTA is beneficial as it significantly improves the forecasting performance of traditional exponential smoothing methods applied to the original data. MAPA is about 2% more accurate and 28% less biased than ES, while MAPA.W and MAPA.D are about 13% more accurate and 30% less biased than ES. It is also more accurate than SARIMAX, which takes useful external variables into account. Thus, we conclude that MTA is an effective and cost-efficient approach for providing short-term electricity prices forecasts, especially when the undesirable effect of seasonality shrinkage is mitigated, and external information is not available. Fig. 4.3 visualizes the benefits of considering such MTA approaches (MAPA.W and MAPA.D) over traditional implementations of ES, highlighting that ES fails to effectively forecast the peak hours (08:00 to 20:00) of the day due to the limited information that the models it involves are capable of capturing, while MTA tends to smooth the series in such a way that night hours (00:00 to 06:00) are systematically over-shot and peak morning hours (07:00 to 11:00) are systematically under-shot.

We also observe that MLR, although performing better than traditional time series methods, is a suboptimal choice to MTA when external variables are not provided as inputs. Yet, as expected, introducing external explanatory variables does

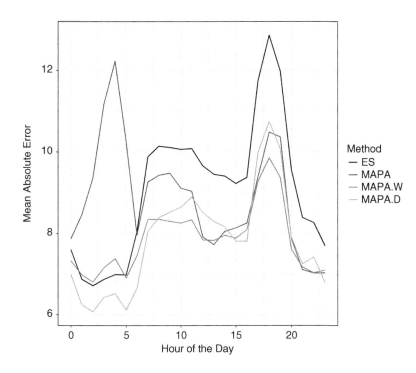

FIG. 4.3 The mean absolute forecast errors of the ES, MAPA, MAPA.W, and MAPA.D methods for each hour of the day. The results indicate that (i) ES fails to accurately forecast the peak hours of the day; (ii) MAPA over-shoots night hours and under-shoots peak morning hours; and (iii) MAPA.W and MAPA.D effectively capture the patterns of the series at all hours of the day.

improve the accuracy of MLR and SARIMA by about 18% and 13%, respectively, having a similar beneficial effect to bias. Interestingly, although simpler in nature, MLR.A does much better than SARIMAX, which considers the same external variables. In this regard, MLR.A is found to be the best statistical approach for predicting electricity prices.

Regarding the ML methods used, we find out that RF provides better results than all the statistical methods considered, at least when external variables are used as regressors. RF is the best performing method, being more accurate and less biased than both MLP and MLR. These results could indicate than RTs are better than NNs in capturing the complex dynamics identified in electricity prices data, in contrast to what the literature typically suggests. If compared to its statistical equivalent, i.e. MLR, RF is 2% more accurate and 15% less biased when external variables are omitted and 4% more accurate and 15% less biased when external variables are included. On the other hand, MLP does better than MLR only when external information is not provided. Similarly, to the statistical approaches, i.e., MLR and SARIMA, introducing external explanatory variables significantly improves the forecasting accuracy of MLP and RF by about 9% and 15%, respectively.

Fig. 4.4 demonstrates the benefits of including external explanatory variables to the forecasting methods considered in this study. As seen, the basic implementation of MLR, MLP, and RF methods is compared in terms of accuracy to that of the respective advanced ones for each hour of the day. In all cases, the improvements reported are substantial, especially for the peak hours. It is also interesting that, after including the external variables, the differences reported between the models are decreased, particularly for the first hours of the day (00:00 to 06:00).

As expected, according to MASE and AMSE, combining forecasts of different methods is proven as an effective strategy for improving forecasting performance and mitigating the uncertainty related to model selection. For example, sComb provides less biased forecasts than all the individual statistical methods used, being also the most accurate alternative (sComb is outperformed according to MASE only by MLR.A). Respectively, both mlComb and Comb improve the forecasting performance of the examined approaches, doing much better than the best performing individual method (RF. A). Yet, mlComb performs better than Comb, possibly because Comb involves some statistical methods, such as sNaive and SARIMA, that are significantly less accurate than the ML ones. This could indicate that the pool of methods used for constructing combinations plays a pivotal role in building high performing forecasting approaches, being a factor of greater importance than the increase of the diversity of the involved methods.

To further explore our results and validate the claims made, we proceed by applying the multiple comparisons with the best (MCB) test that compares whether the average ranking of a forecasting method is significantly different than the others

FIG. 4.4 Comparison of basic and advanced regression forecasting methods. The mean absolute forecast errors of the two different approaches of the MLR, MLP, and RF methods are displayed for each hour of the day.

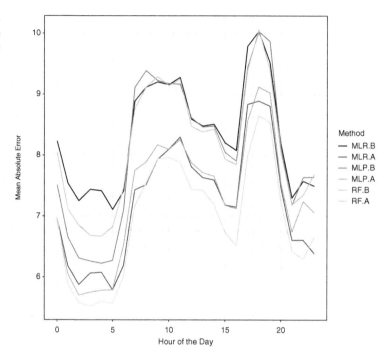

(Koning et al., 2005). If the confidence intervals of two methods overlap, their ranked performances are not statistically different, and vice versa. Weron (2014) discusses the importance of using such tests when comparing different forecasting approaches and strongly recommends their exploitation for drawing solid conclusions. Fig. 4.5 present the results of the MCB test, both in terms of accuracy and bias. In both cases, mlComb and Comb are ranked first, meaning that the results of Table 4.1 are indeed statistically significant. Moreover, it becomes evident that advanced regression forecasting methods do much better than simpler ones, thus highlighting the importance of considering external variables in the forecasting task discussed in this study. On the other hand, the differences observed between the various approaches are smaller for the case of AMSE, with sComb, RF.A, MAPA.D, and MAPA providing similarly biased forecasts to the best performing combination approach. In total, it is shown that combinations of methods are the best approach for forecasting electricity prices, if ML methods that consider external variables are included in the combination scheme.

An interesting insight can also be drawn regarding the performance of the forecasting methods considered for different forecasting horizons and days of the week. Fig. 4.6 help us draw such conclusions by presenting the mean absolute error of the best performing methods, namely MLR.A, MLP.A, and RF.A. We observe that, due to the particularities of the series and the relatively small length of the forecasting horizon used, forecasting performance does not deteriorate across the examined window. However, although in most of the days the methods display similar accuracy levels, this is not the case for Sundays where MLP.A provides clearly better forecasts than both RF.A, the best performing methods of the study, and MLR.A. Thus, we conclude that some methods may be better in handling particular seasonal dynamics and, therefore, that combinations of methods could be further improved by adjusting the weights of the combined methods based on the seasonal period they excel (e.g., hour, day, and month). In fact, this observation may partially explain why mlComb leads to better results than RFs.

Finally, given that computational cost is always relevant in forecasting tasks performed at a daily basis, we evaluate the efficiency of the examined methods by comparing their accuracy to the respective time required for achieving such a performance. Computational time was measured in seconds using a PC of the following characteristics: 4 cores, 8 GB RAM, 500 GB, HDD, and MS Windows 10. Our results are visualized in Fig. 4.7. As seen, apart from SARIMAX, statistical methods are generally faster to compute than ML ones. Yet, when advanced statistical methods are used, statistical approaches can be proven less efficient than ML ones. For example, RF and MLP are both faster than MAPA and SARIMA and similarly fast to ES. On the other hand, MLR is computed with almost zero cost, achieving comparable levels of accuracy to those of RF. In this regard, when the computational cost is not a constraint, ML methods and combinations of such methods can be probably considered, using simple statistical approaches otherwise.

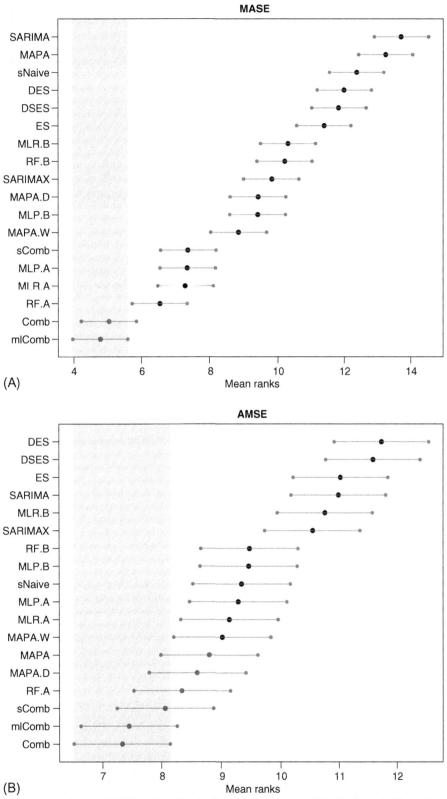

FIG. 4.5 MCB significance tests for the statistical, ML and combination forecasting methods considered in the study. The results are presented for both in terms of accuracy (MASE) and bias (AMSE).

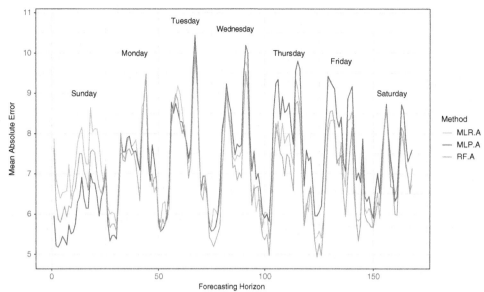

FIG. 4.6 Comparison of advanced statistical and ML methods. The mean absolute forecast errors of the MLR.A, MLP.A, and RF.A methods are displayed per forecasting horizon and day of the week.

FIG. 4.7 The accuracy achieved (MASE) by the examined methods vs. the computational time required for achieving such an accuracy. Results displayed for all 261 evaluation periods.

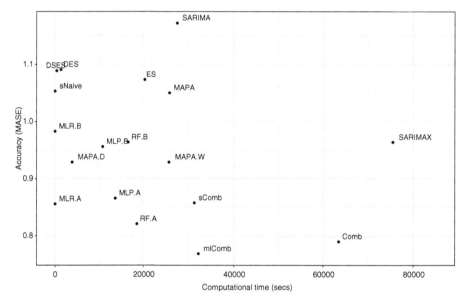

4 Conclusions

Providing accurate electricity price forecasts is mandatory for supporting decision making and short- to mid-term planning of energy companies, especially for their day-to-day market operations. However, electricity prices are characterized by high volatility and uncertainty as they are influenced by numerous variables, such as weather conditions, electricity consumption, and seasonal factors. To capture the complex dynamics of electricity prices and enhance forecasting performance, researchers and practitioners have proposed several statistical and ML methods, suggesting improvements over various benchmarks. Yet, the literature has been inconclusive about the superiority of the statistical methods over the ML ones, making it hard for the interested parties to draw reliable conclusions. Moreover, the value-added of explanatory variables in extrapolation tasks has not been separately assessed for statistical and ML methods.

This chapter provides an overview of the statistical and ML approaches commonly discussed in the literature and compares the performance of some of their representative forms, both simple and advanced ones, to shed some light in that direction. We consider a naïve benchmark, exponential smoothing, and some of its variants, the ARIMA method, two multiple linear regression models, two multi-layer perceptrons, and two implementations of random forest. When possible, we train the methods both by considering external explanatory variables and by just exploiting the historical observations of the series to be predicted so that the value added by the external variables, if any, to be assessed. We evaluate the performance of each approach, both in terms of accuracy and bias, using the case of the Belgium electricity market and test our results for statistical significance. In brief, we find out that:

- ML methods, and especially random forests, provide on average better forecasts than the statistical methods.
- Considering external variables, such as public holidays and projections about the expected load and power generation of the grid, significantly improves the performance of forecasting methods, both statistical and ML ones.
- Combining forecasts is beneficial, especially when the methods in the combination pool are highly accurate and diverse.
- Multiple temporal aggregation significantly improves the performance of traditional exponential smoothing methods, doing better than ARIMAX, which takes useful external variables into account.
- Although competitive, neural networks perform worse than random forests, leading to less accurate forecasts than some advanced statistical methods that exploit the same amount of information.

This study focused on comparing the forecasting performance of the various approaches. While the performance gains of using ML methods and combinations that involve such approaches were statistically significant, statistical approaches required in general less computational time. It would be interesting to further investigate if there is a positive trade-off between the achieved accuracy of ML methods and their computational cost. Also, in this study, we evaluated the performance of equal-weight combinations. Given that the quality of the combination approaches depends on the pools considered, we believe that investigating non-equal combination strategies might further improve the forecasting performance.

Acknowledgments

We would like to thank the editors for inviting us to contribute to this book, as well as for their comments that have helped us improve the quality of this study.

References

Aggarwal, S.K., Saini, L.M., Kumar, A., 2009a. Short term price forecasting in deregulated electricity markets. A review of statistical models and key issues. Int. J. Energy Sector Manage. 3 (4), 333–358.

Aggarwal, S.K., Saini, L.M., Kumar, A., 2009b. Electricity price forecasting in deregulated markets: a review and evaluation. Int. J. Electr. Power Energy Syst. 31, 13–22.

Athanasopoulos, G., Hyndman, R.J., Kourentzes, N., Petropoulos, F., 2017. Forecasting with temporal hierarchies. Eur. J. Oper. Res. 262 (1), 60–74.

Barker, J., 2020. Machine learning in M4: what makes a good unstructured model? Int. J. Forecast. 36 (1), 150–155.

Bergmeir, C., Benitez, J.M., 2012. Neural networks in R using the Stuttgart neural network simulator: RSNNS. J. Stat. Softw. 46 (7), 1–26.

Box, G., Jenkins, G., 1970. Time Series Analysis: Forecasting and Control. Holden-Day, San Francisco.

Breiman, L., 1993. Classification and Regression Trees. Chapman & Hall, Boca Raton, FL.

Breiman, L., 2001. Random forests. Mach. Learn. 45, 5–32.

de Menezes, L.M., Houllier, M.A., 2016. Reassessing the integration of European electricity markets: a fractional cointegration analysis. Energy Econ. 53, 132–150.

Díaz, G., Coto, J., Gómez-Aleixandre, J., 2019. Prediction and explanation of the formation of the Spanish day-ahead electricity price through machine learning regression. Appl. Energy 239, 610–625.

Gardner, E.S., 1985. Exponential smoothing: the state of the art. J. Forecast. 4 (1), 1–28.

Hong, T., 2014. Energy forecasting: past, present, and future. Foresight 2014 (Winter), 43–48.

Hong, T., Pinson, P., Fan, S., Zareipour, H., Troccoli, A., Hyndman, R.J., 2016. Probabilistic energy forecasting: Global Energy Forecasting Competition 2014 and beyond. Int. J. Forecast. 32 (3), 896–913.

Hyndman, R., Koehler, A.B., 2006. Another look at measures of forecast accuracy. Int. J. Forecast. 22, 679–688.

Hyndman, R., Khandakar, Y., 2008. Automatic time series forecasting: the forecast package for R. J. Stat. Softw. 27, 1–22.

Hyndman, R.J., Koehler, A.B., Ord, J.K., Snyder, R.D., 2008. Forecasting with Exponential Smoothing: The State Space Approach. Springer-Verlag, Berlin.

Januschowski, T., Gasthaus, J., Wang, Y., Salinas, D., Flunkert, V., Bohlke-Schneider, M., Callot, L., 2020. Criteria for classifying forecasting methods. Int. J. Forecast. 36 (1), 167–177.

Jeon, J., Panagiotelis, A., Petropoulos, F., 2019. Probabilistic forecast reconciliation with applications to wind power and electric load. Eur. J. Oper. Res. 279 (2), 364–379.

Kaminski, V., 2013. Energy Markets. Risk Books.

Kendall, M., Stuart, A., 1983. The Advanced Theory of Statistics. vol. 3 Griffin, pp. 410–414.

Koning, A.J., Franses, P.H., Hibon, M., Stekler, H.O., 2005. The M3 competition: statistical tests of the results. Int. J. Forecast. 21, 397–409.

Kourentzes, N., Petropoulos, F., Trapero, J.R., 2014. Improving forecasting by estimating time series structural components across multiple frequencies. Int. J. Forecast. 30 (2), 291–302.

Kourentzes, N., Petropoulos, F., 2018. MAPA: Multiple Aggregation Prediction Algorithm. R package version 2.0.4.

Lago, J., De Ridder, F., Vrancx, P., De Schutter, B., 2018. Forecasting day-ahead electricity prices in Europe: the importance of considering market integration. Appl. Energy 211, 890–903.

Liaw, A., Wiener, M., 2002. Classification and regression by random forest. R News 2, 18–22.

Lippmann, R.P., 1987. An introduction to computing with neural nets. IEEE ASSP Mag. 4 (2), 4–22.

Makridakis, S., Spiliotis, E., Assimakopoulos, V., 2018b. Statistical and Machine Learning forecasting methods: concerns and ways forward. PLoS One 13 (3), e0194889.

Makridakis, S., Assimakopoulos, V., Spiliotis, E., 2018a. Objectivity, reproducibility and replicability in forecasting research. Int. J. Forecast. 34 (4), 835–838.

Makridakis, S., Hyndman, R., Petropoulos, F., 2020a. Forecasting in social settings: the state of the art. Int. J. Forecast. 36 (1), 15–28.

Makridakis, S., Spiliotis, E., Assimakopoulos, V., 2020b. The M4 competition: 100,000 time series and 61 forecasting methods. Int. J. Forecast. 36 (1), 54–74.

Møller, M., 1993. A scaled conjugate gradient algorithm for fast supervised learning. Neural Netw. 6, 525–533.

Petropoulos, F., Hyndman, R.J., Bergmeir, C., 2018. Exploring the sources of uncertainty: why does bagging for time series forecasting work? Eur. J. Oper. Res. 268 (2), 545–554.

Petropoulos, F., Svetunkov, I., 2020. A simple combination of univariate models. Int. J. Forecast. 36 (1), 110–115.

Shahidehpour, M., Yamin, H., Li, Z., 2002. Market Operations in Electric Power Systems: Forecasting, Scheduling, and Risk Management. Wiley.

Silvestrini, A., Veredas, D., 2008. Temporal aggregation of univariate and multivariate time series models: a survey. J. Econ. Surv. 22 (3), 458–497.

Spiliotis, E., Petropoulos, F., Assimakopoulos, V., 2019. Improving the forecasting performance of temporal hierarchies. PLoS One 14 (10), 1–21.

Spiliotis, E., Petropoulos, F., Kourentzes, N., Assimakopoulos, V., 2020. Cross-temporal aggregation: improving the forecast accuracy of hierarchical electricity consumption. Appl. Energy 261, 114339. https://doi.org/10.1016/j.apenergy.2019.114339.

Svetunkov, I., 2019. smooth: Forecasting Using State Space Models. R Package Version 2.5.3.

Tashman, L.J., 2000. Out-of-sample tests of forecasting accuracy: an analysis and review. Int. J. Forecast. 16, 437–450.

Weron, R., 2006. Modeling and Forecasting Electricity Loads and Prices: A Statistical Approach. Wiley, Chichester.

Weron, R., 2014. Electricity price forecasting: a review of the state-of-the-art with a look into the future. Int. J. Forecast. 30 (4), 1030–1081.

Zhang, G., Eddy Patuwo, B., Hu, Y.M., 1998. Forecasting with artificial neural networks:: the state of the art. Int. J. Forecast. 14 (1), 35–62.

Chapter 5

Use probabilistic forecasting to model uncertainties in electricity markets—A wind power example

Yao Zhang[a] and Shutang You[b]

[a]*Shaanxi Province Key Laboratory of Smart Grid, Xi'an Jiaotong University, Xi'an, China,* [b]*Department of Electrical Engineering and Computer Science, The University of Tennessee, Knoxville, TN, United States*

1 Introduction

Renewable generation is often considered as non-dispatchable due to its randomness and intermittence. Thus, renewable generation has a large impact on power system stability, ancillary service and energy market. Renewable generation output forecast is an efficient tool to overcome these problems and increase renewable generation integration in power systems. Accurate forecasting of renewable generation can also provide technical support for trading renewable generation in electricity markets.

The conventional renewable generation forecasting (RGF), which gives the conditional expectation of renewable generation output, is referred to as deterministic or spot forecasting. Some recent research has been focusing on improving the accuracy of deterministic forecasting (Costa et al., 2008; Giebel et al., 2011). In fact, it is almost impossible to get the whole knowledge about future events, especially atmosphere changes. Therefore, every prediction has its inherent and irreducible uncertainty. Compared with deterministic forecasting, giving probabilistic information of future events may be a better choice. Recently, probabilistic forecasting has been a hot topic in the prediction theory (Abramson and Clemen, 1995), and it has been widely used in weather prediction (Palmer, 2002) and risk management in economics and finance (Timmermann, 2000).

Many studies have found that RGF is imprecise and its accuracy changes with time, indicating significant uncertainty in renewable generation forecasting. Probabilistic forecasting methods have been introduced to renewable generation and much literature on this topic has been published in the last decade. Conventional RGF usually gives a single value of future renewable generation output. In contrast, renewable generation probabilistic forecasting can provide uncertainty information, which is very useful for high renewable power systems. With the help of stochastic optimization, uncertainty information of renewable generation output has been applied in decision making, e.g., reserve requirement (Matos and Bessa, 2011), trading strategy of renewable generation (Pinson, 2007b), and unit commitment considering renewable generation uncertainty (Wang et al., 2008). These studies have shown that applying uncertainty forecasting into power system operation can significantly increase renewable generation penetration.

This chapter uses wind power generation as an example to present a framework of probabilistic forecasting for renewable energy generation. Firstly, the *k*-nearest neighbor algorithm is applied to find the days with similar weather conditions in historic dataset. Secondly, a novel kernel density estimator based on logarithmic transformation and boundary kernel is applied to derive the probability density of wind power generation from *k*-nearest neighbors. The main idea of KNN-KDE models is that similar situations lead to similar outcomes and then similar outcomes are used to predict the distribution. KNN-KDE contains two steps, i.e., the KNN step and the KDE step, which are visualized in Fig. 5.1. The advantage of this approach is that it could provide both point and probabilistic forecasts for wind power generation.

Mathematical Modelling of Contemporary Electricity Markets. https://doi.org/10.1016/B978-0-12-821838-9.00004-9

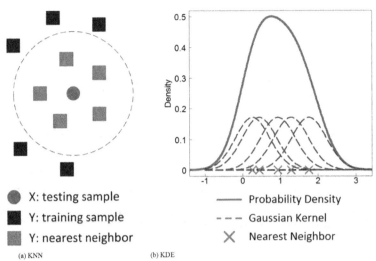

X: testing sample — Probability Density
Y: training sample - - - Gaussian Kernel
Y: nearest neighbor ✕ Nearest Neighbor

(a) KNN (b) KDE

FIG. 5.1 The principle of the KNN-KDE model used for short-term renewable power probabilistic forecasting.

2 Data source and data conditioning

2.1 Data source

All data sources in this probabilistic forecasting example come from the Global Energy Forecasting Competition 2014 (GEFCom2014) (Hong et al., 2014). These wind power data sources are divided into two parts: the first part is wind power measurements; the second one is weather forecasting information from Numerical Weather Prediction (NWP) output, i.e., (u, v)-wind at 10 and 100 m.

2.2 Data conditioning

2.2.1 Outlier detection

Outliers exist in the original data, primarily due to wind turbine maintenance. Then, the maintenance event detection criteria are defined as wind power output being zero in a successive 48 h. After detecting all maintenance events, impacted data are removed from the dataset.

2.2.2 Data preparation

Some raw dataset only provides the (u, v)-wind prediction, i.e., U10, V10 and U100, V100. Therefore, (u, v)-wind format data are converted into the wind speed w and wind direction ϕ format data. The conversion is realized by the following equations:

$$w = \sqrt{u^2 + v^2} \tag{5.1}$$

$$\phi = \begin{cases} \dfrac{180}{\pi} \times \text{atan2}(u, v) & \text{if atan2}(u, v) \geq 0 \\ \dfrac{180}{\pi} \times \text{atan2}(u, v) + 360 & \text{if atan2}(u, v) < 0 \end{cases} \tag{5.2}$$

Wind forecasts coming from NWP have a large impact on probabilistic wind power forecast. However, the NWP output is stochastic and may impair forecast accuracy. Therefore, m-order moving average is applied to condition the NWP output.

$$\bar{x}_t = \frac{1}{m} \sum_{j=-k}^{k} x_{t+j} \tag{5.3}$$

where x_{t+j} is the attributes in the input data and $m = 2k + 1$. $m = 5$ in this study. After the data condition process, all attributes in the dataset are listed in Table 5.1. As a typical hub height of modern wind turbines ranges from 40 to 120 m, the NWP output at 100 m is chosen as a candidate input. "WP100" is the spot prediction of wind power output based on multiple

TABLE 5.1 Summary of all attributes in the input data.

Name	Example	Meaning
YEAR	2012/2013/2014/...	Calendar year
MONTH	01/02/.../12	Calendar month
DAY	001/002/.../365 or 366	Day of a year
HOUR	00/01/.../23	Hour of a day
ZONEID	1/2/.../10	ID number of wind farm
TARGETVAR	0.05487912 p.u.	Wind power output (observation)
U100	−0.772611558 m/s	Zonal velocity component at 100 m
V100	3.160147739 m/s	Meridional velocity component at 100 m
WS100	4.669029962 m/s	Wind speed at 100 m
WD100	216.2552498 deg	Wind direction at 100 m
WP100	0.05487912 p.u.	Wind power output (spot prediction)

linear regressions, which will be elaborated more in Section 3.1. Attributes listed in Table 5.1 are all candidate inputs for the probabilistic forecasting model.

2.2.3 Distribution and correlation analysis

Fig. 5.2 shows the power output histogram of wind farm #1. It is found that wind power output apparently follows a distribution that is different from the Gaussian distribution, with a large amount of values clustered around the zero point. The same conclusion could be made from normal Q-Q plots, which is usually used as a check tool of the normal distribution hypothesis. Similar findings are observed when analyzing the power output of wind farm #2–10.

Another finding is the geographical dependence between wind farms. Fig. 5.3 gives the correlogram of wind power output at wind farms, using a graphical correlation matrix display developed in the R package "corrgram." All wind farms' names are plotted in the diagonal of correlogram, e.g., 'ZONE1_WP' represents the wind farm #1. Fig. 5.3 shows that positive correlation exists among wind farm #1–10. In addition, wind farm #1/#8/#9 and #4/#5/#6 have strong correlation within a subgroup.

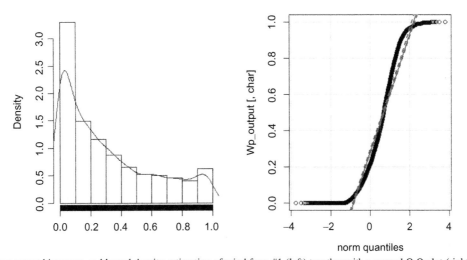

FIG. 5.2   The power output histogram and kernel density estimation of wind farm #1 (left) together with a normal Q-Q plot (right).

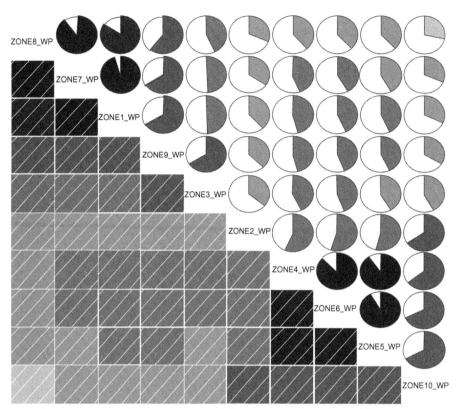

FIG. 5.3 The correlogram of wind power output between wind farms. A blue color and hashing that goes from lower left to upper right represents a positive correlation. The strength of the correlation is displayed by the size of the filled pie slice and the darkness of the blue color.

3 Forecasting methodology

3.1 Multiple linear regression

In this approach, probabilistic wind power forecasting (Pinson, 2006, 2013, Gneiting and Katzfuss, 2014) is based on k nearest neighbors. Point prediction of wind power generation is a necessary attribute that forms the weighted distance between two neighbors. Thus, multiple linear regression (MLR) was used to generate wind power point prediction, i.e., the attribute 'WP100' in Table 5.1.

Firstly, the range [0, 360] of wind direction "WD100" is split into several sub-intervals. For example, the interval [0, 360] could be divided into [0, 180] and [180, 360]. An interesting question is the optimal length of the sub-intervals. The cross-validation experiment shows that dividing the range [0, 360] into 12 groups yields the optimal point prediction of wind power generation. Secondly, the multiple linear regression model is fitted for each sub-interval. It takes the wind speed "WS100" and the time of a day "HOUR" as regressors. The fitting formulation is shown as follows.

$$\hat{p}_{t+k|t} = b_0 + b_1 \cdot w_{t+k|t} + b_2 \cdot w_{t+k|t}^2 + b_3 \cdot w_{t+k|t}^3 + b_4 \cdot \cos\left(\frac{2\pi}{24}d_{t+k|t}\right) + b_5 \cdot \sin\left(\frac{2\pi}{24}d_{t+k|t}\right) + b_6 \cdot \cos\left(\frac{4\pi}{24}d_{t+k|t}\right) + b_7$$
$$\cdot \sin\left(\frac{4\pi}{24}d_{t+k|t}\right)$$
(5.4)

where $wt+k|t$ is wind speed (i.e., "WS100" in Table 5.1) at time $t+k$ forecasted at time t. $dt+k$ is the time in hour (i.e., the "HOUR" in Table 5.1). For example, the time resolution of original dataset is 24 h, thus $dt+k$ takes value of 0, 1, 2, ..., 23. Eq. (5.4) uses Fourier series of the time of a day to model diurnal periodicity. In R language, if the wind direction "WD100" is treated as a factor variable, R could automatically fit all multiple linear regression models corresponding to 12 sub-intervals.

3.2 *k*-Nearest neighbors algorithm

k-Nearest neighbors (*k*-NN) is a non-parametric algorithm for classification and regression (Bishop, 2006). The basic principle of *k*-NN algorithm is to find its *k* nearest neighbors from the training data to predict a new point by taking the average ol its k nearest neighbors (Yesilbudak et al., 2013). Mangalova and Agafonov (2014) have proposed wind power point prediction using k-NN algorithm in GEFCom2012, and achieved the second place in the wind power track.

In this approach, the k-NN algorithm is used to search the proper training samples with similar wind condition in historical dataset. Then, based on the k nearest neighbors, a novel Kernel Density Estimator (KDE) is proposed to estimate wind power output probability density. The k-NN algorithm is realized by the following steps.

1. Calculate the distance between testing and training datasets.
2. Choose k-nearest neighbors from training examples that have smallest distances.
3. Predict wind power output using the weighted average value.
4. Predict wind power density using a novel KDE method.

In step 1, a distance needs to be defined to quantify the similarity of instances in the training and testing dataset. Euclidean, Mahalanobis, and Manhattan distances are some commonly used distances. In this method, the Manhattan distance is enhanced by adding weights.

$$D\left[X^{(i)}, X^{(j)}\right] = \sum_{n=1}^{r} w_n \left| x_n^{(i)} - x_n^{(j)} \right| \tag{5.5}$$

$$X^{(i)} = \left[x_1^{(i)}, ..., x_n^{(i)}, ..., x_r^{(i)} \right] \tag{5.6}$$

$$X^{(j)} = \left[x_1^{(j)}, ..., x_n^{(j)}, ..., x_r^{(j)} \right] \tag{5.7}$$

where $X^{(i)}$ and $X^{(j)}$ are instances; each instance X includes r attributions x_n ($n = 1, ..., r$) (e.g., the variables listed in Table 5.1), and w_n is weight, which equals to one in the original form of Manhattan distance, since it assumes each attribution has equal contribution to the distance. However, each attribution has different importance in wind power forecasting. For example, the weather variable 'wind speed' is high correlated to wind power generation. The weight w_n in the enhanced Manhattan distance can differentiate the contribution of each attribution. The value of weight w_n is optimized using the method described in the following subsection.

The k nearest neighbors are the instances who own k smallest distances. Let $X^1, X^2, ..., X^K$ denote the k nearest instances from training examples that are nearest to the testing instance X, and their wind power measurements are represented by p^1, $p^2, ..., p^K$. The distance between X and its nearest neighbors $X^1, X^2, ..., X^K$ follows an ascending order $d^1 \leq d^2 \leq ... \leq d^K$, where $d^k = D[X, X^k]$ ($k = 1, 2, ..., K$). Once k-nearest neighbors have been determined, wind power point prediction can be derived through an average weighted by an exponential function.

$$\hat{p} = \sum_{k=1}^{K} \delta^k p^k = \frac{\sum_{k=1}^{K} e^{-d^k} \cdot p^k}{\sum_{k=1}^{K} e^{-d^k}} \tag{5.8}$$

where p^k is the wind power output; d^k is the distance of the instance X^k. The weight δ^k assigned to the neighbor X^k equals to $\delta^k = e^{-d^k} / \sum_{k=1}^{K} e^{-d^k}$. Thus, the neighbor with a small d^k has a high weight, so that p^k has a larger impact on the wind power point prediction result $\hat{p}$.

3.3 Coordinate descent algorithm

The value of weight w_n in Eq. (5.5) is calculated by optimization. Use p^i represent wind power output measurement, and its prediction $\hat{p}^i$ is the average value of k-nearest neighbors (see Eq. 5.8). Then, the sum of square error (SSE) is used to quantify the point prediction accuracy due to its convenience for differential.

$$\text{SSE} = \sum_{i=1}^{m} \left(p^i - \hat{p}^i \right)^2 \tag{5.9}$$

According to Eqs. (5.5), (5.8), the prediction result $\hat{p}^i$ depends on $w_1, w_2, ..., w_r$. Thus, the determination of $w_1, w_2, ..., w_r$ is converted to minimizing (5.9).

$$\hat{w}_1, \hat{w}_2, \ldots, \hat{w}_r = \underset{w_1, w_2, \ldots, w_r}{\text{argmin}} \text{ SSE} = \underset{w_1, w_2, \ldots, w_r}{\text{argmin}} \sum_{i=1}^{m} \left[p^i - \hat{p}^i(w_1, w_2, \ldots, w_r) \right]^2 \tag{5.10}$$

The derivative of SSE of a specified weight w_n $(n = 1, \ldots, r)$ is

$$\frac{\partial SSE}{\partial w_n} = \sum_{i=1}^{m} 2 \left(\hat{p}^i - p^i \right) \frac{\partial \hat{p}^i}{\partial w_n} \tag{5.11}$$

$$= \sum_{i=1}^{m} 2 \left(p^i - \hat{p}^i \right) \frac{\sum_{k=1}^{K} p^{ik} e^{-d^{ik}} \sum_{k=1}^{K} e^{-d^{ik}} \left| x_n^{(i)} - x_n^{(k)} \right| - \sum_{k=1}^{K} e^{-d^{ik}} \sum_{k=1}^{K} p^{ik} e^{-d^{ik}} \left| x_n^{(i)} - x_n^{(k)} \right|}{\left(\sum_{k=1}^{K} e^{-d^{ik}} \right)^2}$$

where p^{ik} $(k = 1, 2, \ldots, K)$ are k-nearest neighbors to p^i, and d^{ik} is the distance assigned to the neighbor p^{ik}. $x_n^{(i)}$ and $x_n^{(k)}$ are the nth attribution of the testing example $X^{(i)}$ and its corresponding kth neighbor $X^{(k)}$.

Minimization of weights $w_1, w_2, \ldots, w_r$ is solved using the coordinate descent algorithm (Bertsekas, 1999). Table 5.2 provides some of the details of this algorithm. All weights are fixed in the innermost loop of this algorithm, except for a specified weight w_n to allow it to be optimized. The inner loop optimizes the weights $w_1, w_2, \ldots, w_r$ consecutively until the convergence condition is satisfied. Since individual optimization is unconstrained optimization problem, it can be solved efficiently using the derivative of SSE to a specified weight w_n Eq. (5.11) and a Newton-type algorithm.

A round of rolling optimization from w_1 to w_r is counted as one iteration. The convergence criterion is either one of the conditions below is satisfied.

- The percentage change of **w** of two consecutive iterations is less than ε.

$$\frac{\left\| w^{(k+1)} - w^{(k)} \right\|}{\left\| w^{(k)} \right\|} \leq \varepsilon \tag{5.12}$$

- The percentage change of SSE of two consecutive iterations is less than ε.

$$\frac{\left\| SSE^{(k+1)} - SSE^{(k)} \right\|}{\left\| SSE^{(k)} \right\|} \leq \varepsilon \tag{5.13}$$

TABLE 5.2 Coordinate descent algorithm for determining the optimal weight.

	Algorithm 1: Coordinate descent
1	Loop until convergence
2	For $n = 1, 2, \ldots, r$
3	$\hat{w}_n = \text{argmin}_{w_n} SSE(w_1, \ldots, w_{n-1}, w_n, w_{n+1}, \ldots w_r)$
4	End For
5	End Loop

3.4 Probabilistic forecasting based on KDE method

Once k nearest neighbors are determined, Eq. (5.8) gives the wind power point forecasting result. To further obtain probabilistic forecasting result (Zhang et al., 2014), a novel Kernel Density Estimator (KDE) was used to derive wind power probability density function (PDF). As a data-driven and non-parametric density function estimator, KDE is widely used in probabilistic wind power forecasting (Bessa et al., 2012a, b; Jeon and Taylor, 2012; Juban et al., 2007). However, some obstacles still exist in applying KDE in probabilistic wind power forecasting.

Statisticians found that KDE method only worked well for near-Gaussian distributions (Wand and Jones, 1994). However, the distribution of wind power output has a large portion around the zero point, which is far from Gaussian (Bludszuweit et al., 2008; Yang and Marron, 1999).

Accurate estimation of such a heavy-skewed distribution in the standard KDE method is difficult. This work proposed a logarithmic-transformation-based KDE approach to address the heavy-skewed wind power density (Marron and Ruppert, 1994; Yang and Marron, 1999; Karunamuni and Alberts, 2006).

$$\widetilde{p}^{i} = g_{\lambda}\left(p^{i}\right) = \begin{cases} \dfrac{1}{\lambda} \ln\left(1 + \lambda p^{i}\right) & \gamma_{P} > 0 \\[2mm] p^{i} & \gamma_{P} = 0 \quad (i = 1, 2, ..., K) \\[2mm] -\dfrac{1}{\lambda} \ln\left(1 - \lambda p^{i}\right) & \gamma_{P} < 0 \end{cases} \tag{5.14}$$

$$\gamma_{P} = \frac{\dfrac{1}{K}\sum\limits_{i=1}^{K}\left(p^{i} - \overline{p}\right)^{3}}{\left[\dfrac{1}{K-1}\sum\limits_{i=1}^{K}\left(p^{i} - \overline{p}\right)^{2}\right]^{\frac{3}{2}}} \tag{5.15}$$

where $p^1, p^2, ..., p^K$ are wind power measurements of k nearest neighbors and $\overline{p}$ is their mean value. $\widetilde{p}^1, \widetilde{p}^2, ..., \widetilde{p}^K$ are the transformed wind power output. γ_P is the skewness of the sample $p^1, p^2, ..., p^K$. If $\gamma_P > 0$, Eq. (5.14) handles with the right-skewed wind power density. If $\gamma_P < 0$, Eq. (5.14) handles with the left-skewed wind power density. If $\gamma_P = 0$, which represents the non-skewed distribution and no transformation is needed.

Parameter λ in Eq. (5.14) has a direct impact on the performance of logarithmic transformation. By automatically determining the value of parameter λ, the estimating error of the KDE model can be minimized. Wand and Jones (1994) proposed a quantitative indication L to evaluate the difficulty in using the KDE method to estimate the density. Using proposed transformation with λ, the function $L(\lambda)$ is defined as

$$L(\lambda) = \sigma_{\widetilde{p}} \int f_{\widetilde{p}}''\left(\widetilde{p}\right)^{2} d\widetilde{p} = \sigma_{\widetilde{p}} \int \left[\frac{1}{Kh^{3}}\sum_{i=1}^{K}G''\left(\frac{\widetilde{p} - \widetilde{p}^{i}}{h}\right)\right]^{2} d\widetilde{p} \tag{5.16}$$

where $\widetilde{p}$ is the transformed wind power output. $\sigma_{\widetilde{p}}$ is the standard deviation of the transformed samples $\widetilde{p}^1, \widetilde{p}^2, ..., \widetilde{p}^K$. The second derivative $f_{\widetilde{p}}''$ is estimated by the KDE model, $G''(.)$ is the second derivative of Gaussian kernel function $G(.)$. h is the bandwidth parameter estimated by the plug-in bandwidth selector (Wand and Jones, 1994).

A lower value of $L(\lambda)$ indicates that the transformed density $f_{\widetilde{p}}$ is less skewed, closer to Gaussian density, and more appropriate to apply the standard KDE tool. Therefore, parameter λ can be estimated by solving the minimization problem.

$$\hat{\lambda} = \underset{\lambda}{\arg\min} L(\lambda) \tag{5.17}$$

In this chapter, a search algorithm is proposed to automatically solve the optimal parameter $\hat{\lambda}$ in the nonlinear optimization (5.17), which is described in Table 5.3.

After the logarithmic transformation, the density estimation $\hat{f}_{\widetilde{P}}$ in the transformed scale can be constructed using the standard KDE tool. Then, by back transforming the density estimation, $\hat{f}_{P}$ in the original scale can be written as

$$\hat{f}_{P}(p) = \frac{1}{Kh} g_{\hat{\lambda}}'(p) \sum_{i=1}^{K} G\left[\frac{g_{\lambda}(p) - g_{\lambda}(p^{i})}{h}\right] \tag{5.18}$$

where $g_{\hat{\lambda}}'(.)$ is the derivative of logarithmic transformation; $G(.)$ is a kernel function.

TABLE 5.3 Coordinate descent algorithm for determining the optimal weight.

	Algorithm 2: Searching for the optimal $\hat{\lambda}$
1	Calculate the skewness γ_P of the original samples $p^1, p^2, \ldots, p^K$ via Eq. (5.15)
2	Select the appropriate type of logarithmic transformation $g_\lambda(p^i)$ via Eq. (5.14)
3	Let λ_i $(i=1,\ldots,n)$ be a finite grid in $\Lambda=(0,\lambda_M]$. These points are evenly distributed
4	For each λ_i in $\Lambda=(0,\lambda_M]$
5	Let $\tilde{p}^k = g_{\lambda_i}(p^k)$ $(k=1, 2, \ldots, K)$
6	Let $\sigma_{\tilde{p}}$ be the standard deviation of $\tilde{p}^1, \tilde{p}^2, \ldots, \tilde{p}^K$
7	Let h be the plug-in bandwidth (Wand and Jones, 1994)
8	Let $L(\lambda_i)$ be given by Eq. (5.16)
9	End For
10	Obtain the optimal parameter $\hat{\lambda}$ through searching the minimum point of $L(\lambda_i)$ over Λ

It is notable that the wind power variable is double-bounded and limited in the range [0,1]. Therefore, wind power density is restricted in a compact support, resulting in the boundary effect problem of the KDE method. Probabilistic wind power forecasts based on KDE method also suffers from the boundary effect problem. Fig. 5.4 presents an example of kernel density estimator. The KDE result is constructed using five observations with kernel function $G(.)$ chosen to be the $N(0,1)$ density $\phi(.)$. In Fig. 5.4, a large quantity of probability concentrates at the boundary $x=0$. It can be observed that Gaussian kernel function (the dashed line) falls outside the boundary $x=0$, resulting in the kernel density estimator (the solid line) being biased downward near the boundary $x=0$ and poor quality of probabilistic wind power forecast.

To solve the boundary effect issue, the boundary kernel method is applied. By redesigning the shape of kernel function $G(.)$ near the boundary, the boundary kernel method can eliminate the loss of probability density outside the wind power interval [0, 1]. More details about the boundary kernel method can be found in (Jones, 1993; Jones and Foster, 1996). Boundary kernel $G^B(z)$ is a linear combination of $\phi(z)$ and $z\phi(z)$, and takes the form of

$$G^B(z) = \frac{a_2 - a_1 z}{a_0 a_2 - a_1^2} \phi(z) \times \mathbf{1}_{x \in [0, 1]} \qquad (5.19)$$

$$a_i = \int_{(x-1)/h}^{(x-0)/h} w^i \phi(w) dw \quad i = 0, 1, 2 \qquad (5.20)$$

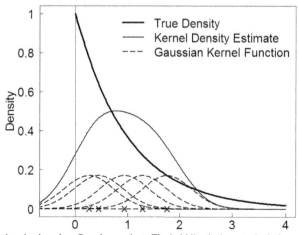

FIG. 5.4 Example of kernel density estimation based on five observations. The bold line is the actual wind power distribution. The solid line shows the kernel density estimator. Five observations $X_1, X_2, \ldots, X_5$ are denoted by the notation × at the bottom of this figure. The dashed line shows the corresponding Gaussian kernel $\phi[(x - X_i)/h]/5h$.

where x is the estimated point, h is the bandwidth parameter, $\phi(z)$ is the $N(0,1)$ density, and $\mathbf{1}_{x \in [0,1]}$ is the indicator function that takes value 1 for $x \in [0,1]$ and value 0 for $x \notin [0,1]$.

The proposed boundary kernel $G^B(.)$ is applied to replace the original kernel $G(.)$ in Eq. (5.18). Then, the KDE method based on logarithmic transformation and boundary kernel can be employed to construct the probability density of wind power output.

$$\hat{f}_P(p) = \frac{1}{Kh} g'_{\hat{\lambda}}(p) \sum_{i=1}^{K} G^B \left[\frac{g_{\hat{\lambda}}(p) - g_{\hat{\lambda}}(p^i)}{h} \right] \tag{5.21}$$

Then, the predictive density of wind power output is converted into 99 quantiles: $0.01, 0.02, \ldots, 0.99$, denoted by $q_1, q_2, \ldots, q_{99}$. Given the probability density of wind power output, the quantile q_a with a specified percentage a can be derived.

$$q_a = \hat{F}^{-1}\left(\frac{a}{100}\right) \tag{5.22}$$

where $\hat{F}^{-1}(.)$ is the inversion of the Cumulative Distribution Function (CDF). Quantiles can be used to construct the interval prediction (Pinson and Kariniotakis, 2010). For example, the predictive interval of wind power output with 95% confidence level is $[q_5, q_{95}]$.

3.5 Probabilistic forecasting based on KDE method

The proposed approach for probabilistic wind power forecasting has three main steps. Firstly, the new attribute "WP100" is added for each training sample using multiple linear regression. Secondly, k nearest neighbors with the first k smallest distances in training examples are selected. Finally, a novel KDE technique is utilized to generate wind power density. Fig. 5.5 illustrates the main process of this approach.

4 Model selection

The k value and the input variables have a large impact on prediction accuracy of k-NN algorithm. This work employed M-fold cross validation to determine the optimal k value and select the proper attributes. M is chosen as 7 in this study, i.e., 7-fold cross validation. The training dataset S was split into seven subsets $S_1, S_2, \ldots, S_7$. The subset S_1 is composed of the historical data on Monday; the subset S_2 for Tuesday; and so on. Such splitting strategy can reduce the effect of seasonal wind patterns on model selection. Fig. 5.6 shows the process of dataset splitting.

Assume that k value lies in the range $\Lambda = [100, 300]$. Let k_i $(i = 1, \ldots, n)$ be a finite grid in Λ, and these grid points are uniformly distributed. Thus, $k_1 = 100$, $k_2 = 110$, $\ldots$, $k_{21} = 300$. The algorithm of M-fold cross validation used in the determination of k value is shown in Table 5.4.

Another important step in model selection is choosing proper attributes as input variables. Possible attributes are shown in Table 5.2. They are "YEAR," "MONTH," "DAY," "HOUR," "U100," "V100," "WS100," "WD100," and "WP100." These 9 features will produce 2^9 possible attribute subsets, which are too many to evaluate and compare. In addition, only a small number of attributes is related to wind power output. If irrelevant variables are included in k-NN algorithm, over-fitting would be a potential problem. In this work, a heuristic attribute search procedure named forward search was utilized to find a proper attribute subset. Forward search procedure begins by finding the best subset with only one attribute. Then it finds the best subset with two components, including the first selected attribute and another one from the remaining attributes. Then, the third and fourth research finds the third and fourth attributes, respectively, and so on. The entire search procedure would stop until the prediction performance of the present stage is no better than that in the previous stage. The forward search algorithm is summarized in Table 5.5.

5 Results

5.1 Error measures

For the deterministic wind power forecast, RMSE is commonly used to evaluate the prediction performance (Hong et al., 2014).

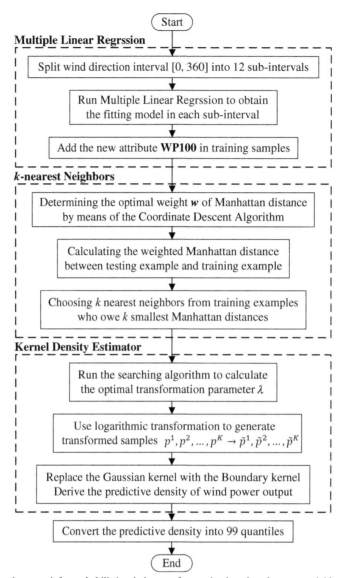

FIG. 5.5 Flowchart of the proposed approach for probabilistic wind power forecasting based on k-nearest neighbor algorithm and an enhanced kernel density estimator.

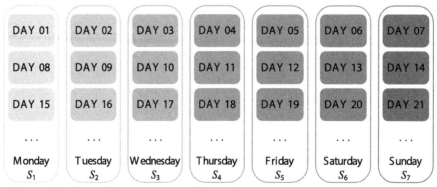

FIG. 5.6 Strategy of splitting training dataset S into seven subsets $S_1, S_2, \ldots, S_7$.

TABLE 5.4 M-fold cross validation algorithm for the determination of k value.

	Algorithm 3: Cross validation
1	For each k_i ($i=1,\dots,n$)
2	For $j=1, 2, \dots, M$
3	Train the prediction model with the value k_i on $S_1 \cup \dots \cup S_{j-1} \cup S_{j+1} \cup \dots \cup S_M$
4	Test the prediction model on S_j to get error measures $\hat{\varepsilon}_j$ (i.e., Quantile Score)
5	End For
6	The estimated error of prediction model with k_i is calculated as the average of $\hat{\varepsilon}_j$ over j
7	End For
8	Pick the prediction model corresponding to the parameter k_i with the lowest estimated error
9	Retrain the prediction model with the chosen k value on the entire training dataset S

TABLE 5.5 Forward search algorithm for attribute selection.

	Algorithm 4: Forward search
1	Initial the attribute subset $\mathcal{F} = \varnothing$
2	Repeat
3	For $i=1, 2\dots, l$
4	If the attribute $i \notin \mathcal{F}$
5	$\mathcal{F}_i = \mathcal{F} \cup \{i\}$, and use M-fold cross validation to evaluate the attribute subset $\mathcal{F}_i$
6	End If
7	End For
8	Set $\mathcal{F}$ to be the best attribute subset $\mathcal{F}_i$ found on step (3–7)
9	End Repeat
10	Select and output the best subset that was evaluated during the entire search procedure
11	Retrain the prediction model with the best attribute subset on the entire training dataset S

$$\text{RMSE} = \sqrt{\frac{1}{m}\sum_{i=1}^{m}\left(p^i - \hat{p}^i\right)^2} \tag{5.23}$$

where p^i and $\hat{p}^i$ are the wind power output observation and the prediction, respectively.

Evaluation measure employed in point prediction are based on the discrepancy between the observation and the prediction. However, for probabilistic forecasting, predictive information (e.g., probability density or a series of quantiles) can't be directly compared with the observation. In GEFCom2014, the full predictive densities composed by 99 quantile forecasts are to be evaluated by the quantile score calculated through the pinball loss function (Gneiting and Raftery, 2007; Pinson et al., 2007a). For the quantile forecast q_a with a specified percentage a, the quantile score is defined as

$$L\left(q_a, p^i\right) = \begin{cases} \left(1 - \dfrac{a}{100}\right)\left(q_a - p^i\right) \text{ if } p^i < q_a \\ \dfrac{a}{100}\left(p^i - q_a\right) \text{ if } p^i \geq q_a \end{cases} \tag{5.24}$$

where p^i is the observation and $a = 1, 2, \ldots, 99$. To evaluate 99 quantile forecasts, the quantile score is then averaged over all quantiles from 0.01 to 0.99.

$$L\left(p^i\right) = \sum_{a=1}^{99} L\left(q_a, p^i\right) \tag{5.25}$$

Finally, the quantile score is averaged for all observations in the required time period. A lower quantile score indicated better probabilistic forecast.

5.2 Model configuration

GEFCom2014 has 15 tasks. Each task's objective is to forecast wind power output for 1 month. Fig. 5.7 shows the numeric results of 7-fold cross validation to determine the optimal k value. This experiment is performed at wind farm #1, and the training dataset S spans a period of 9 months from January 1st, 2012 to September 30th, 2013 (i.e., the training dataset in Task 1). The Quantile Score is considered as the error measure to evaluate the effect of k value on probabilistic prediction performance. In Fig. 5.7, it could be found that Quantile Score tends to increase with the k value, especially when $k > 200$. The k value has little influence on Quantile Score in the interval $[100, 200]$. Considering a relatively large number of samples required for KDE method, the optimal k value is set at 200 for wind farm #1 in Task 1. Table 5.6 Forward search procedure of the best attribute subset at wind farm #1 in Task 1, while Table 5.7 Model configuration information for all wind farms.

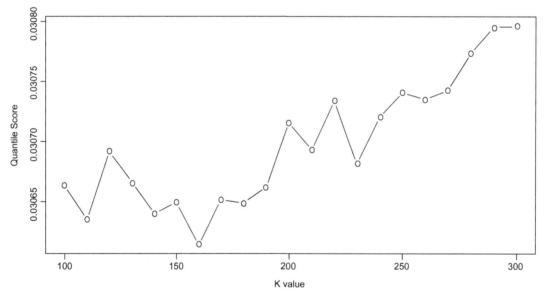

FIG. 5.7 Average quantile score of the predict model over seven subsets $S_1, S_2, \ldots, S_7$, as a function of k value for wind farm #1 in Task 1.

TABLE 5.6 Forward search procedure of the best attribute subset at wind farm #1 in Task 1.

Stage	Attribute subset	New added attribute	Quantile score
1	WP100/HOUR	HOUR	0.042279
2	WP100/HOUR/DAY	DAY	0.041755
3	WP100/HOUR/DAY/WS100	WS100	0.041600
4	WP100/HOUR/DAY/WS100/V100	V100	0.041682

TABLE 5.7 Model configuration information for all wind farms.

Farm	k	Attribute subset
#1	200	"DAY", "HOUR", "WS100", "WP100", "WS100_Nearby", "WP100_Nearby"
#2	200	"DAY", "HOUR", "WS100", "WP100"
#3	200	"DAY", "HOUR", "WS100", "WP100", "WS100_Nearby", "WP100_Nearby"
#4	200	"DAY", "HOUR", "WS100", "WP100"
#5	200	"DAY", "HOUR", "WS100", "WP100", "WS100_Nearby", "WP100_Nearby"
#6	200	"DAY", "HOUR", "WS100", "WP100", "WS100_Nearby", "WP100_Nearby"
#7	200	"DAY", "HOUR", "WS100", "WP100", "WS100_Nearby", "WP100_Nearby"
#8	200	"DAY", "HOUR", "WS100", "WP100"
#9	200	"DAY", "HOUR", "WS100", "WP100", "WS100_Nearby", "WP100_Nearby"
#10	200	"DAY", "HOUR", "WS100", "WP100", "WS100_Nearby", "WP100_Nearby"

Table 5.7 shows the entire procedure of the forward search algorithm at wind farm #1 in Task 1. Starting from the initial subset $\mathcal{F} = \{'\text{WP100}'\}$, the first stage of forward search algorithm is to seek the best subset consisting of two variables, and the search result was "WP100" and "HOUR." In the second and third stage, "DAY" and "WS100" were added into the attribute subset, respectively. In the fourth stage, "V100" was chosen as the candidate. It was found that Quantile Score in the fourth stage is a little worse than that in the third stage. Thus, the final feature subset is set as "DAY," "HOUR," "WS100," and "WP100."

In addition, a coordinate descent algorithm is designed to derive optimal weights of Manhattan distance. An illustration is made to validate the effectiveness of coordinate descent algorithm. Fig. 5.8 shows the decline of objective function SSE (see Eq. 5.9) in the procedure of coordinate descent algorithm. This algorithm re-optimizes every component of the weight vector w cyclically until satisfying the convergence condition. It started with a randomly chosen weight vector. In the first iteration, the objective function SSE decreased rapidly. In the following iterations, the decrease of objective function SSE becomes slow. Finally, the coordinate descent algorithm is terminated in the fourth iteration. For other wind farms, the configuration of k-NN algorithm is like that of wind farm #1. The similar model configuration may result from the geographical adjacency of 10 wind farms. Table 5.8 shows the model configuration information corresponding to each wind farm. Note that the attributes "WS100_Nearby" and "WP100_Nearby" come from the attributes "WS100" and "WP100" of the most correlated wind farm. The correlation between two wind farms is measured by Pearson Correlation, as shown in Fig. 5.3.

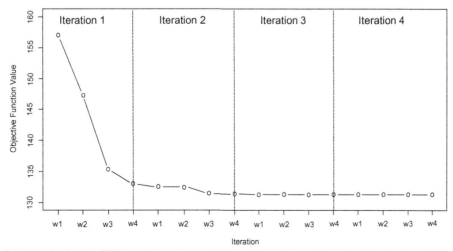

FIG. 5.8 Decrease of the objective function SSE in coordinate descent algorithm for Wind Farm #2. SSE optimization from the first weight to the last one is viewed as one iteration.

TABLE 5.8 Evaluation results in all 15 tasks of GEFCom2014.

Task (month)	Period	RMSE	Quantile score	Rank
1	Oct. 2012	0.1558162	0.03875	3
2	Nov. 2012	0.1650593	0.04133	4
3	Dec. 2012	0.1579582	0.03998	2
4	Jan. 2013	0.1465133	0.03792	4
5	Feb. 2013	0.1568895	0.04080	2
6	Mar. 2013	0.1574277	0.04014	3
7	Apr. 2013	0.1328434	0.03273	6
8	May. 2013	0.1580852	0.04018	5
9	Jun. 2013	0.1344665	0.03350	6
10	Jul. 2013	0.1533014	0.03824	6
11	Aug. 2013	0.1549925	0.03829	4
12	Sep. 2013	0.1658384	0.04014	4
13	Oct. 2013	0.1751401	0.04360	6
14	Nov. 2013	0.1618536	0.04176	7
15	Dec. 2013	0.1596625	0.04037	6
Average		0.1557230	0.03918	
Standard variance		0.0110230	0.00287	
Coefficient of variation[a]		0.0707840	0.07335	

[a]*Coefficient of variation equals to the standard variance divided by the average.*

5.3 Evaluation results

Based on Eq. (5.8), Fig. 5.9 displays parts of point prediction of wind farm #1'sgeneration in Task 1. Note that the time-stamp in Fig. 5.9 is the Universal Time Coordinated (UTC), instead of the local time. It could be found that the observed and predicted values match well. In order to visualize results of probabilistic wind power forecasting, 99 quantiles are converted into nine predictive intervals I_β ($\beta = 10, \ldots, 90$). Fig. 5.10 gives probabilistic forecasting of wind power output at wind farm #1 in the first week of Task 1, along with the corresponding measurements of wind power generation. A series of predictive

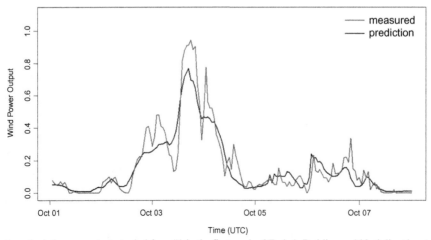

FIG. 5.9 Point forecasting of wind power output at wind farm #1 in the first week of Task 1. Red line and black line denote the wind power output measurement and prediction, respectively.

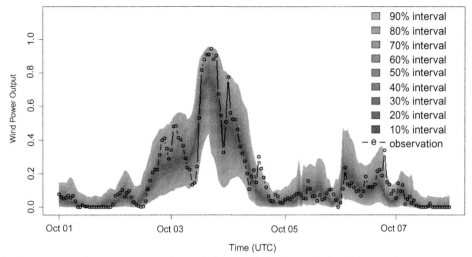

FIG. 5.10 Probabilistic forecasting of wind power generation at wind farm #1 in the first week of Task 1, shown by a series of predictive intervals with different nominal converge rates.

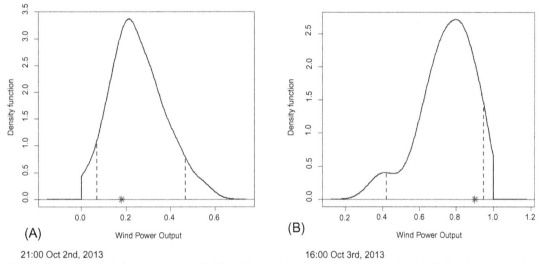

FIG. 5.11 Density forecasting of wind power output at wind farm #1 at two timestamps in Task 1 (i.e., October 2013). The solid line denotes the predictive density. Two vertical dotted lines denote the 90% predictive interval. The notation * denotes the actual wind power generation.

intervals is shown in the form of a fan chart, which gives a better visualization of predictive wind power distribution. Fig. 5.11, as a complement of Fig. 5.10, displays the shape of predictive wind power density at different timestamps, along with the actual wind power output. It can be found that prediction intervals are asymmetric around median forecasts. These results are understandable because the predictive density given by KDE approach is also asymmetric. These findings can also be observed in Fig. 5.10. It is also found that the width of predictive interval varies with the fluctuation of wind power generation. Predictive intervals tend to become wider when wind power generation fluctuates sharply.

To evaluate the accuracy of deterministic and probabilistic wind power forecasting, Table 5.8 gives evaluation results for all 15 months. RMSE and Quantile Score are error scores to evaluate the accuracy of point prediction and probabilistic prediction, respectively. The scores of the first three tasks come from the public leader board in "CrowdAnalytix," and the scores of the last 12 tasks are assessed and provided by GEFCom2014 organizers. In addition, both RMSE and Quantile Score are averaged over 10 wind farms. Table 5.8 illustrates that there is a little difference in RMSE or Quantile Score between different tasks. The performance of the proposed k-NN algorithm and KDE method was quite well in some tasks, such as Task 7 and 9, but a little poor in others, such as Task 2 and 14. These findings are understandable because the meteorological condition of wind power generation may be different between 2 months. In addition, maintenance events of wind turbine were carried out in some certain months, which also had an obvious impact on the prediction accuracy. The

TABLE 5.9 Evaluation results of 10 wind farms.

Farm	#1	#2	#3	#4	#5	#6	#7	#8	#9	#10
RMSE	0.13049	0.15482	0.14095	0.16680	0.16398	0.16921	0.12811	0.16169	0.15127	0.18238
QS	0.03246	0.03889	0.03772	0.04084	0.04196	0.04275	0.03267	0.03797	0.03703	0.04665

average, standard variance and coefficient of variation of RMSE and Quantile Score are also given in Table 5.9. The small coefficient of variation indicates the robustness of prediction performance of the proposed algorithm. Considering that all 15 tasks covers a period of more than 1 year, the combination of k-NN algorithm and KDE method could constantly provide good and reliable probabilistic forecasts of wind power generation in different weather conditions. Thus, the proposed approach has the potential for industrial application in future.

6 Error analysis

6.1 Geographical distribution

Evaluation results of probabilistic wind power forecasting for every wind farm are listed in Table 5.9. The performance of the proposed approach was quite well in wind farm #1 and #7, but quite poor in wind farm #6 and #10. The maximum difference of error score between two wind farms reached 0.05427 for RMSE and 0.01398 for Quantile Score (QS). Fig. 5.12 shows the empirical distribution of Quantile Score at 10 wind farms over 14 tasks. Fig. 5.12 also confirmed that wind farm #1 and # 7 were the easiest for probabilistic wind power forecasting, while wind farm #10 was the most difficult. The variation among all tasks was quite significant at wind farm #10. On the contrary, for wind farm #1, the performance of probabilistic wind power forecasts is very stable. The different topography among wind farms may be the main reason why the performance of wind power forecasting varied among 10 wind farms. In fact, some researchers (Giebel et al., 2011) have reported that the forecasting errors were generally higher for wind farms in more complex terrain. Therefore, the performance of probabilistic wind power forecasting is quite site-specific. The NWP model provides higher quality of weather forecasting in the simple terrain, which results in the better performance of wind power forecasting.

6.2 Error distribution

The performance of point and probabilistic wind power forecasting is re-evaluated in every day instead of in every task (i.e., every month). The error distributions of two wind farms are displayed, i.e., wind farm #1 representing the easiest one and wind farm #10 representing the most difficult one. Fig. 5.13 gives the histogram of Quantile Score at wind farm #1 and #10. In Fig. 5.13, the daily quantile score is mainly distributed in the range [0, 0.07] for wind farm #1 and in the range [0, 0.10] for wind farm #10, respectively. The variation of daily Quantile Score in wind farm #10 is more significant than that in wind

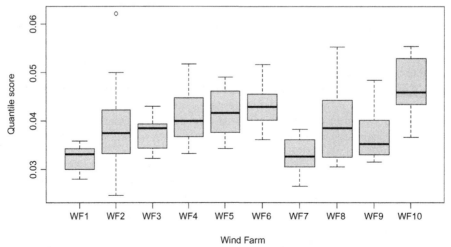

FIG. 5.12 Empirical distributions of Quantile Score at 10 wind farms. The boxplot gives the minimum and maximum of Quantile Scores of all 14 tasks (lower and upper tips), the first and third quartiles (box bounds), the median (central line) and the outlier (notation ∘).

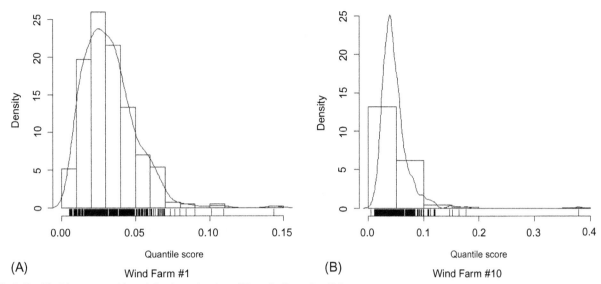

FIG. 5.13 The histogram and kernel density estimation of Quantile Score for all days.

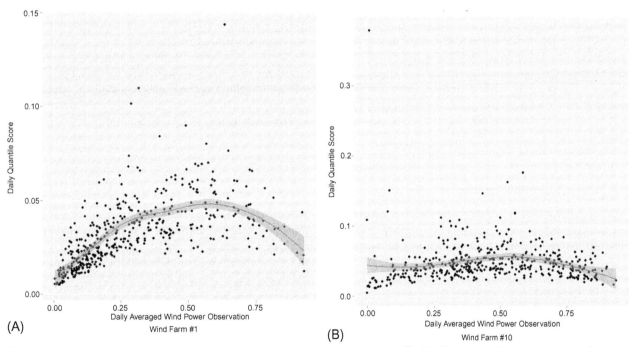

FIG. 5.14 Scatter plot of daily Quantile Score and daily averaged wind power measurement. The blue line denotes the smooth regression from wind power observation to Quantile Score.

farm #1. In addition, there was an outlier in Fig. 5.13B. Fig. 5.13 shows that the daily Quantile Score changes greatly at wind farms that has poor performance in probabilistic wind power forecasting.

The relationship between daily Quantile Score and daily averaged wind power measurement is shown in Fig. 5.14. It is observed that the probabilistic forecasting is less accurate when wind power observation was in the middle of the range [0, 1], especially for wind farm #1. In contrast, Quantile Score is smaller near the boundary $p = 0$ or 1, indicating a smaller error of probabilistic wind power forecasting.

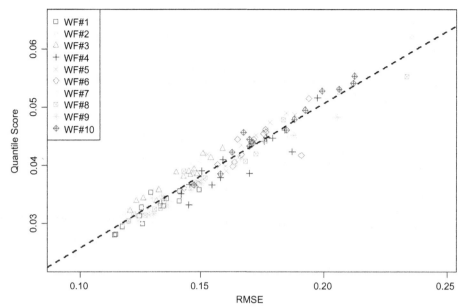

FIG. 5.15 Scatter plot of RMSE and Quantile Score at 10 wind farms. For each wind farm, RMSE and Quantile Score samples contain the evaluation results of 14 tasks. The dashed black line denotes the linear regression from RMSE to Quantile Score.

6.3 RMSE vs. quantile score

From Tables 5.8 and 5.9, it can be observed that the small RMSE generally corresponds to the small Quantile Score. Fig. 5.15 gives the scatter plot of RMSE and Quantile Score of 14 tasks of 10 wind farms. The result shows a strong positive correlation. The linear regression model from RMSE to Quantile Score is acceptable in practice although some outliers exist far from the regression line. In the prediction model, both point and probabilistic forecasting are based on k nearest neighbors found by the KNN algorithm. Point forecasts equals to the weighted average, and probabilistic forecasts are derived from the KDE method. Due to the similarity of approaches employed in point and probabilistic wind power forecasts, it is understandable that there exists a strong positive correlation between RMSE Score and Quantile Score (Fig. 5.15).

6.4 Impact of NWP quality

NWP model provides the weather forecasting information for the proposed approach. In this subsection, it is found that the error of NWP model was passed on to wind power forecast, resulting in the poor performance in some days. However, it is quite difficult to eliminate forecasting errors of weather variables issued by the NWP model.

When evaluating the proposed approach day by day, it is found that the performance (either RMSE or Quantile Score) was quite poor in some days. Two typical days are chosen, and their forecasting and evaluation results are shown in Fig. 5.16. Both RMSE and Quantile Score are very high in these 2 days. RMSE scores are above 0.4000 and Quantile Score are above 0.1300. In addition, for both point and probabilistic forecasting, a large deviation from the actual wind power output can be observed in Fig. 5.16. Then, further analysis was performed to discover the main reason causing the large error of the forecasting approach. Wind speed prediction at 100 m provided by NWP is the most relevant variable to wind power forecasting. In Fig. 5.16, the dashed black line denotes wind speed prediction issued by NWP. It is found that the trend of point and probabilistic forecasting was quite like that of wind speed prediction. When wind speed prediction goes upwards, the prediction of wind power output will be high.

However, any prediction approach has its inherent and irreducible uncertainty, including the NWP model. NWP model provides weather forecasting as input variables in the wind power forecast. Thus, the quality of the NWP model has a large impact on the forecasting accuracy. In two typical days shown in Fig. 5.16, the quality of NWP model wasn't good enough to provide the accurate weather forecasting. In Fig. 5.16A, according to weather forecast produced by the NWP model, wind speed would go downwards from 13:00 to 24:00. In fact, the actual wind power output went upwards during this period. Such mismatch of the trend between NWP model and actual wind power observation is also found in the period from 04:00 to 12:00. In Fig. 5.16B, the value of wind speed prediction ranges from 2 to 6 m/s. This low wind speed was insufficient to generate wind power. However, at 1:00, 6:00 and 20:00, the actual wind power output almost reached the nominal capacity.

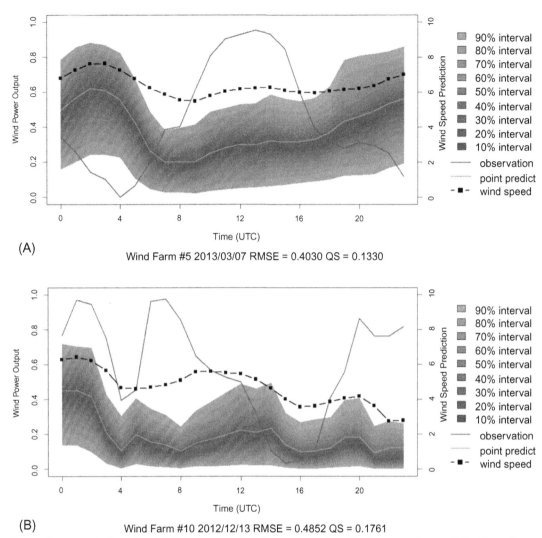

(A) Wind Farm #5 2013/03/07 RMSE = 0.4030 QS = 0.1330

(B) Wind Farm #10 2012/12/13 RMSE = 0.4852 QS = 0.1761

FIG. 5.16 Poor performance of point and probabilistic forecasts of wind power output issued by the proposed approach. Red line and green line denote the observation and point prediction of wind power output, respectively. The dashed black line denotes wind speed prediction provided by NWP.

7   Conclusions

In this work, the combination of *k*-NN algorithm and KDE method is proposed for probabilistic wind power forecasting. The effectiveness and accuracy of the approach is validated using the 12 weeks of data. Advantages of this approach include:

- A large evaluation dataset spanning a period of 1 year was used in the 12 evaluation weeks. Such a marathon-type validation verifies that this approach could provide probabilistic wind power forecasts with high quality and high reliability.
- This approach can provide point forecasting and probabilistic forecasting simultaneously with satisfactory accuracy. Both the *k*-NN algorithm and the KDE method are practical and easy-implementation methods for renewable power forecasting in industrial applications.
- As a general framework of probabilistic forecasting for renewable energy generation, this work is applicable not only to probabilistic wind power forecasting, but also to probabilistic solar power forecasting.

References

Abramson, B., Clemen, R., 1995. Probability forecasting. Int. J. Forecast. 11, 1–4.

Bertsekas, D.P., 1999. Nonlinear Programming, second ed. Athena Scientific, Belmont, MA.

Bessa, R., Miranda, V., Botterud, A., Wang, J., Constantinescu, E., 2012a. Time adaptive conditional kernel density estimation for wind power forecasting. IEEE Trans. Sust. Energy 3, 660–669.

Bessa, R., Miranda, V., Botterud, A., Zhou, Z., Wang, J., 2012b. Time-adaptive quantile-copula for wind power probabilistic forecasting. Renew. Energy 40, 29–39.

Bishop, C.M., 2006. Pattern Recognition and Machine Learning. vol. 1 Springer New York.

Bludszuweit, H., Dominguez-Navarro, J.A., Llombart, A., 2008. Statistical analysis of wind power forecast error. IEEE Trans. Power Syst. 23, 983–991.

Costa, A., Crespo, A., Navarro, J., Lizcano, G., Madsen, H., Feitosa, E., 2008. A review on the young history of the wind power short-term prediction. Renew. Sust. Energy Rev. 12, 1725–1744.

Giebel, G., Brownsword, R., Kariniotakis, G., 2011. The State-Of-The-Art in Short-Term Prediction of Wind Power: A Literature Overview, Technical Report, Anemos Project Deliverable Report D1.1. Available from: http://anemos.cma.fr/.

Gneiting, T., Raftery, A.E., 2007. Strictly proper scoring rules, prediction, and estimation. J. Am. Stat. Assoc. 102, 359–378.

Gneiting, T., Katzfuss, M., 2014. Probabilistic forecasting. Annu. Rev. Stat. Appl. 1, 125–151.

Hong, T., Pinson, P., Fan, S., 2014. Global energy forecasting competition 2012. Int. J. Forecast. 30, 357–363.

Jeon, J., Taylor, J.W., 2012. Using conditional kernel density estimation for wind power density forecasting. J. Am. Stat. Assoc. 107, 66–79.

Jones, M., Foster, P., 1996. A simple nonnegative boundary correction method for kernel density estimation. Stat. Sin. 6, 1005–1013.

Jones, M., 1993. Simple boundary correction for kernel density estimation. Stat. Comput. 3, 135–146.

Juban, J., Fugon, L., Kariniotakis, G., 2007. Probabilistic short-term wind power forecasting based on kernel density estimators. In: Proceedings of the European Wind Energy Conference, Milan, Italy. vol. 2007, pp. 1–11.

Karunamuni, R., Alberts, T., 2006. A locally adaptive transformation method of boundary correction in kernel density estimation. J. Stat. Plann. Inference 136, 2936–2960.

Mangalova, Agafonov, E., 2014. Wind power forecasting using the k-nearest neighbors algorithm. Int. J. Forecast. 30, 402–406.

Marron, J.S., Ruppert, D., 1994. Transformations to reduce boundary bias in kernel density estimation. J. R. Stat. Soc. Ser. B Methodol. 56, 653–671.

Matos, M.A., Bessa, R.J., 2011. Setting the operating reserve using probabilistic wind power forecasts. IEEE Trans. Power Syst. 26, 594–603.

Palmer, T.N., 2002. The economic value of ensemble forecasts as a tool for risk assessment: from days to decades. Q. J. R. Meteorol. Soc. 128, 747–774.

Pinson, P., Chevallier, C., Kariniotakis, G.N., 2007a. Trading wind generation from short-term probabilistic forecasts of wind power. IEEE Trans. Power Syst. 22, 1148–1156.

Pinson, P., 2013. Wind energy: forecasting challenges for its operational management. Stat. Sci. 28, 564–585.

Pinson, P., Kariniotakis, G., 2010. Conditional prediction intervals of wind power generation. IEEE Trans. Power Syst. 25, 1845–1856.

Pinson, P., 2006. Estimation of the Uncertainty in Wind Power Forecasting (Ph.D. Thesis). Center of Energy and Processes, Ecole des Mines de Paris, Paris, France.

Pinson, P., Nielsen, H., Moller, J., Madsen, H., Kariniotakis, G., 2007b. Non-parametric probabilistic forecasts of wind power: required properties and evaluation. Wind Energy 10, 497–516.

Timmermann, A., 2000. Density forecasting in economics and finance. J. Forecast. 19, 231–234.

Wand, P., Jones, C., 1994. Kernel Smoothing. Chapman&Hall, London.

Wang, J., Shahidehpour, M., Li, Z., 2008. Security-constrained unit commitment with volatile wind power generation. IEEE Trans. Power Syst. 23, 1319–1327.

Yang, L., Marron, J.S., 1999. Iterated transformation-kernel density estimation. J. Am. Stat. Assoc. 94, 580–589.

Yesilbudak, M., Sagiroglu, S., Colak, I., 2013. A new approach to very short term wind speed prediction using k-nearest neighbor classification. Energy Convers. Manag. 69, 77–86.

Zhang, Y., Wang, J., Wang, X., 2014. Review on probabilistic forecasting of wind power generation. Renew. Sust. Energ. Rev. 32, 255–270.

Chapter 6

Modelling interlinked commodities' prices: The case of natural gas

Konstantinos Tasiopoulos

Energy and Environmental Policy Laboratory, University of Piraeus, Piraeus, Greece

1 Introduction

Recently, a study from IEA concerning natural gas, highlighted that the demand for that commodity grew 4.6% in 2018 and that was the fastest annual pace since 2010 IEA (2019). Also, the study continues by assessing that the demand is expected to rise by more than 10% over the next 5 years and reach approximately 4.3 trillion cubic meters (tcm) in 2024. In our contemporary society, natural gas has aided in the reduction of air pollutant emission and limit the rise of CO_2 emissions by gradually dislocating coal and oil in power generation, heating and industrial uses. Of all the usages mentioned, power generation remains the largest consumer of natural gas, notwithstanding the slower growth due to the competition from renewables and coal. The growth in LNG export capacity is an indispensable parameter that allows international trade to play a growing role in the development of natural gas markets as they move towards greater globalization.

Specifically, according to ACER (2019) EU is progressively becoming more dependent on natural gas imports since domestic gas production continues to drop. As a matter of fact, for 2018 we had a reduction of 6.5% in comparison to the production of 2017. This reduction was offset by augmented imports of LNG (+10%) and increased pipeline imports from Russia. For 2018 ACER (2019) denoted that EU imported 77% of its consumed gas which accounts for +2.1% compared to 2017 while demand for natural gas decreased by 3.7% owing to weather conditions and lower gas-fired power generation.

In our analysis we will focus on the relationship between natural gas and electricity prices regarding the case of Netherlands. The reason is the fact that the Title Transfer Facility hub (TTF) is considered as not only euro (€) denominated gas benchmark but the European gas benchmark in general partly due to the fact that it surpassed the British National Balancing Point (NBP) during 2016 according to Heather (2019). TTF is a Virtual Trading Point (VTP) which means that it does not correspond to any physical entry or exit point which allows gas buyers and sellers to buy and sell gas without booking capacity and therefore the number of market participants is maximized Honore (2013). Heather (2019) evaluated European gas hubs according to five criteria such as market participation, traded products (that could be used for balancing or risk management), traded volumes, tradability index (bid and offer spread) and churn rates (the ratio of traded volume to actual physical throughput) and concluded that those criteria advocate to the fact that TTF is the largest and most liquid natural gas hub in Europe.

Most of the electricity produced in the Netherlands comes from fossil fuels. The fact that Netherlands after November 2015 implemented a policy of phasing out coal-fired power plants resulted to a declining rate in the production of coal-fired power plants making natural gas the leading provider with a proportion of approximately 44%. Thus, an analysis of these two interlinked markets with several econometric methods will provide useful insights to market participants and regulators with the latest data available.

The remainder of this paper is organized as follows: Section 2 describes briefly previous findings in the literature as far as natural gas is concerned, Section 3 describes the data and explains the adopted methodology, Section 4 presents the empirical results and finally Section 5 provides a summary of the findings and concluding remarks.

2 Literature review

There are many studies in the literature that examine the interaction of natural gas prices with other commodities with the usage of econometrical methods. Villar and Joutz (2006) proposed that a long run relationship between natural gas and crude oil exists for the case of Henry Hub and WTI. Also, Lin and Li (2015) suggested that the European and Japanese gas prices are cointegrated with Brent crude oil prices and that this long run relationship does not apply for the US market. They also extended their analysis by suggesting that although oil and gas prices for the case of United States are decoupled, oil price changes could spill over to gas prices. Furthermore, Perifanis and Dagoumas (2018) by examining time-varying price and volatility transmission between US natural gas and crude oil wholesale markets, provided further evidence that those two markets are decoupled.

Specifically, since natural gas has gained a progressively important role in electricity generation a variety of studies focus in modelling those two commodities. Jong and Schneider (2009) implemented cointegration methodology to examine the joint dynamics of multiple energy spot prices in the United Kingdom, Belgium and the Netherlands. They concluded that gas prices are strongly cointegrated, but this long run relationship of gas and power prices is only evident in the long run and for forward price levels. Efimova and Serletis (2014) investigated the volatilities of the oil, natural gas, and electricity markets for United States by implementing a trivariate BEKK parallel with DCC GARCH and examined volatility spillovers among the energy and electricity markets where they found evidence of volatility spillovers from one variable to another. Hulshof et al. (2016) in order to evaluate the efficiency of the gas market in Netherlands, they analyzed day-ahead spot price of TTF for 2011–14 where they found small positive impact of oil to the natural gas price and concluded that day ahead gas prices are determined by gas market fundamentals. Furio and Poblacion (2018) studied the Spanish electricity and National Balancing Point (NBP) natural gas forward prices with the implementation of different factor models and found evidence that those markets are cointegrated and what is more they are sharing common long term dynamics.

As far as causality between the two markets is concerned, Woo et al. (2006) and Emery and Liu (2002) by examining gas and electricity prices suggested a causal relationship among the two markets and that past natural gas prices could provide evidence on future electricity prices. Uribe et al. (2018) identified a bidirectional causality between gas and electricity markets which increases proportionally as their corresponding market prices increase. Alexopoulos (2017) with the application of a one step ahead rolling forecast argued that the cost of natural gas could be used as a predictor for retail electricity prices for the case of United States while Xia et al. (2020) identified a nonlinear causality among electricity and fuel source returns based on a multi-scale framework. Moreover, Nakajima and Hamori (2013) tested for Granger causal relationships among wholesale electricity, natural gas and crude oil prices in mean and variance. Their results suggested that gas prices Granger cause electricity prices in mean whereas no evidence of causality found in variance.

For the case of volatility, Chang et al. (2018) calculated spillover effects for natural gas spot, futures and ETF markets with the implementation of a multivariate conditional volatility diagonal BEKK model. Their empirical results indicated spillover effects between those markets for the cases of United States and United Kingdom. Likewise, Nakajima and Toyoshima (2020) studied spillovers among Henry Hub, National Balancing Point, Title Transfer Facility and Japan Korea Marker. They observed the existence of spillover effects among natural gas futures, from natural gas futures returns to natural gas spot returns, from natural gas spot returns to electricity spot returns and from natural gas futures returns to electricity futures returns.

As a part of EU's climate policy goals and Dutch's government decision in 2017 to phase out coal-fired power generation entirely by 2030 it is plausible educe that natural gas has an increasingly important role in the proportion of the wholesale electricity mix of Netherlands. Also, due to the fact that the wholesale electricity price is set by the marginal generating unit that could satisfy the quantity demanded for a given time and because that marginal generating unit is higher for the case of fossil fuels, the production from those fossil fuels (natural gas in our case) will eventually determine the final price. Hence, the analysis of those interlinked markets is of pivotal interest.

In our empirical analysis we augment those previous works by combining econometric methodologies to examine the price transmission mechanism and volatility spillover in a concise structure. For that reason, we used daily data for electricity day ahead prices and natural gas spot prices from corresponding Dutch markets.

3 Data and methodology

3.1 Data

The main concern of this study is the examination of interactions between electricity day ahead prices and the natural gas Title Transfer Facility (TTF) spot price with several econometric techniques. For this purpose, daily data were collected from European Network of Transmission System Operators for Electricity (ENTSOE) transparency platform for the former and from European Energy Exchange (EEX) for the latter. In the case of electricity prices hourly data were collected and transformed into daily averages. The data span is from 1/06/2015 to 6/18/2019 which gives a total of 1161 observation. Also, our observations were transformed to natural logarithms. As it is obvious from the Jarque-Bera test the sample data does not resemble a normal distribution neither in level form nor in first differences which is augmented by a

TABLE 6.1 Descriptive statistics.

	Δ(ELC)	Δ(TTF)	ELC	TTF
Observations	1160	1160	1161	1161
Mean	0.0018	−0.0483	3.7331	2.8765
Median	−0.2050	−0.1375	3.7221	2.8959
Maximum	47.6667	25.9081	4.2542	3.3393
Minimum	−45.5809	−17.8248	3.2276	2.3702
Std. dev.	10.2132	2.4981	0.2326	0.2199
Skewness	0.0593	0.8503	0.1323	−0.2511
Kurtosis	5.1861	16.7868	2.5387	2.3201
Jarque-Bera	231.6657	9326.739	13.6781	34.5563
Probability	0.0000[a]	0.0000[a]	0.0011	0.0000

[a]*Indicates significance at all levels (1%, 5%, 10 %).*

factor of 100. Likewise, the first difference of our variables advocates to an asymmetric distribution with excess kurtosis especially in the case of natural gas. As far as standard deviation is concerned, electricity returns are more volatile in comparison to natural gas. The reason is that electricity prices are more susceptible to hourly fluctuation caused from market dynamics of supply and demand. Descripted statistics are provided in Table 6.1 for both level form and at first differences. Throughout the analysis we use the abbreviations ELC for day ahead electricity prices and TTF which stands for natural gas spot price.

In Fig. 6.1 the time series that we study are depicted in their level form. It is evident that electricity day ahead prices are experiencing more fluctuating (volatile) movements in comparison to natural gas prices. Due to the fact that the distributions of both markets are influenced by some limited extreme movements (outliers) we set a 99% threshold which means that all data below the 1st percentile set to the 1st percentile while data above the 99th percentile set to the 99th percentile. This method allows us to have more robust results with a minimum loss of information.

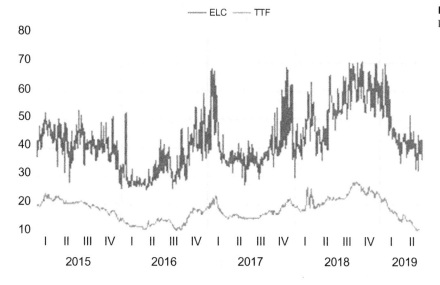

FIG. 6.1 Prices of electricity and natural gas in levels in (€/MWh).

3.2 Methodology

In the present study we examine the relationship of both electricity and natural gas markets by applying several econometric methods. In the first place, we test for possible structural breaks in our time series with the use of Bai and Perron (1998, 2003) multiple structural break approach. Then we study the price transmission mechanism both in the short and long run by accounting for asymmetric effects as denoted in Enders and Siklos (2001) between the aforementioned variables. Finally, we analyze volatility spillovers with the use of a multivariate conditional volatility model Diagonal BEKK (1995) and proceed with the interpretation of partial co-volatility spillovers as proposed in Chang et al. (2018).

3.2.1 Structural breaks

Due to the fact that our sample includes a wide range of data collection, it is plausible to examine the possibility of structural breaks in our variables. Structural changes may harm the stability of our calculated coefficients during the period that we are interested in. The benefit of this method is that it selects break dates endogenously. The tests are based upon the following standard linear regression model:

$$y_t = \delta_j z_t' + \beta x_t' + u_i, j = 1, ..., m+1 \text{ and } t = T_{j-1} + 1, ..., T_j \tag{6.1}$$

where y_t is an endogenous variable, z_t' is a vector of explanatory variables whose parameters are specified for each regime while x_t' is a vector of explanatory variables that are stable across regimes and u_i is the error term. Also, the convention that $T_0 = 0$ and $T_{m+1} = T$ is used as in Bai and Perron (1998). Finally, $(T_1, T_2, ..., T_m)$ denotes the break dates which are endogenously determined with a finite set of observations included in each regime. The coefficients δ_j and β in Eq. (6.1) are estimated with OLS. Thus, the parameters enclosed in δ_j and β matrices are the ones that minimize the sum of squared errors. In a more rigorous interpretation this minimization is given from the following objective function:

$$S(\beta, \delta | \{T\}) = \sum_{j=0}^{m} \sum_{t=T_j}^{j+1} {}^{-1} \left\{ y_t - \delta_j z_t' - \beta x_t' \right\} 2 \tag{6.2}$$

where S represents the sum of squared residuals in each m regime. The break point estimates given from $(\hat{T}_1, ..., \hat{T}_m)$ are the ones that minimize the total sum of squared residuals S so that the following relationship holds:

$$(\hat{T}_1, ..., \hat{T}_m) = argmin T_1, T_2, ... , T_m S_T(T_1, T_2, ..., T_m) \tag{6.3}$$

with the constraint that the breakpoints $(T_1, T_2, ..., T_m)$ are subjected to $T_i - T_{i-1} \geq q$ with q denoting the number of parameters.

The hypothesis that we test in order to estimate the number of break dates is based on Bai and Perron (1998) and is an F type test with the null of H0: $m = l$ against the alternative Ha: $m = l+1$. A statistically significant result signifies the inclusion of an additional break to the testing procedure whereas a failure of rejecting the null hypothesis denotes that a further inclusion of a structural break would not result in a better econometrical fit. Thus, the application of $l+1$ test have the interpretation of no structural change against the alternative that a single structural break has occurred. The implementation is conducted for each regime and contains $\hat{T}_{j-1} + 1$ to T_j observations for $j = 1, ..., m$ and $T_0 = 0$ and $T_{l+1} = T$ as aforementioned. The alternative hypothesis holds if the aggregate minimal value of the sum of squared residuals in all regimes with the addition break included $(l+1)$ is substantially minor compare to the value derived from the sum of squared residuals of l structural breaks model. Hence the selection of the break date is related with this global minimum. In a mathematical sense the $F_T(l+1 | l)$ statistic could be defined as:

$$F_T(l+1 | l) = \frac{\left\{ S_T(\hat{T}_1, ..., \hat{T}_l) - \min_{1 \leq i \leq l+1} \inf_{\tau \in \Lambda_{i,\eta}} S_T(\hat{T}_1, ..., \hat{T}_{i-1}, \tau, \hat{T}_i, ..., \hat{T}_l) \right\}}{\hat{\sigma}^2} \tag{6.4}$$

where $\Lambda_{i,\eta}$ is defined as:

$$\Lambda_{i,\eta} = \left\{ \tau; \hat{T}_{i-1} + (\hat{T}_i - \hat{T}_{i-1})\eta \leq \tau \leq \hat{T}_i - (\hat{T}_i - \hat{T}_{i-1})\eta \right\} \tag{6.5}$$

and $\hat{\sigma}^2$ is a consistent estimate of residual variance σ^2 under the null hypothesis of l breaks. Also, according to Bai and Perron (1998) for $i = 1$ the sum of squared residuals derived from the OLS estimation from each m regime $(T_1, T_2, ..., T_m)$ we have that $S_T(\hat{T}_1, ..., \hat{T}_{i-1}, \tau, \hat{T}_i, ..., \hat{T}_l)$ is interpreted as $S_T(\tau, \hat{T}_i, ..., \hat{T}_l)$ because of the convention that $T_0 = 0$ and for $i = l+1$ as $S_T(\hat{T}_1, ..., \hat{T}_l, \tau)$. The critical values are obtained through simulations for 5% level of significance.

3.2.2 Price transmission

The conventional way of examining price transmission mechanism between the variables of interest is by studying their short and long term behavior. This could be conducted through cointegration testing as proposed by Engle and Granger (1987), Johansen (1988), Johansen and Juselius (1990). Implicitly, those tests assume a symmetric pattern in the adjustment of the error correction term towards the long run equilibrium. Thus, there is no distinction between adjustments occurring above or below a specific threshold value (τ). Those different adjustments denoting the asymmetric response of the error correction term to positive and negative shocks accordingly.

For that reason, Enders and Siklos (2001) developed two nonlinear cointegration models that accounts for possible asymmetric error correction effects. Specifically, those models are a generalization of Enders and Granger (1998) threshold autoregressive (TAR) and momentum threshold autoregressive (MTAR) tests for unit roots into a multivariate setting. It is worth noting that through this procedure the Engle and Granger test appears as a special case. Prior to cointegration, we examined the stationarity properties of our two variables through unit root tests. For that reason, we used the Augmented Dickey-Fuller test (1979), the Kwiatkowski–Phillips–Schmidt–Shin (1992) and Zivot–Andrews (1992) test which considers the presence of a structural break in the data generating process. Once we assure that our variables are stationary in their differences I(1) we proceed with the cointegration testing.

In the present study Enders and Siklos (2001) procedure is used with the first step being the estimation of the long run model between day ahead price of electricity and the spot price of title transfer facility natural gas with the use of dynamic ordinary least squares (DOLS) as proposed in Stock and Watson (1993):

$$P_t^{elc} = C + P_t^{ttf} + \varepsilon_t \tag{6.6}$$

where P_t^{elc} is the logarithmic price of electricity and P_t^{ttf} is the logarithmic price of natural gas at time t. From Eq. (6.6) we derived the error term which is the spread between the two above mentioned variables and used them in the estimation of TAR and MTAR cointegration models. The two models are given from the following equation:

$$\Delta\hat{\varepsilon}_t = I_t\rho_1\hat{\varepsilon}_{t-1} + (1 - I_t)\rho_2\hat{\varepsilon}_{t-1} + \sum_{i=1}^{p-1} \gamma_i \ \Delta\varepsilon_{t-1} + u_t \tag{6.7}$$

where $\hat{\varepsilon}_t$ are the residuals from Eq. (6.6), $\Delta\hat{\varepsilon}_{t-1}$ are the lagged terms of residuals which are used to account for serial correlation and $u_t \sim i.\,i.\,d(0, \sigma^2)$. The coefficients ρ_1 and ρ_2 represents the asymmetric speed of adjustment towards the long run equilibrium and are expected to be negative as an indication of error correction. The term I_t is the Heaviside indicator function and for the TAR model is specified as:

$$I_t = \begin{cases} 1 & if \ \hat{\varepsilon}_{t-1} \geq \tau \\ 0 & if \ \hat{\varepsilon}_{t-1} < \tau \end{cases} \tag{6.8}$$

Providing that $\hat{\varepsilon}_{t-1}$ or the change in the spread between electricity and natural gas price is equal or greater than the threshold (τ), then Eq. (6.8) indicates a positive phase of the long run disequilibrium and as a result the spread is widening therefore the adjustment is given from $\rho_1\hat{\varepsilon}_{t-1}$. On the other hand, when $\hat{\varepsilon}_{t-1}$ is below the threshold value we have a negative phase and this signifies that the spread between the two variables is narrowing, thus the speed of adjustment is given from $\rho_2\hat{\varepsilon}_{t-1}$.

Concerning the case of MTAR model the Heaviside indicator function is given from the subsequent representation:

$$I_t = \begin{cases} 1 & if \ \Delta\hat{\varepsilon}_{t-1} \geq \tau \\ 0 & if \ \Delta\hat{\varepsilon}_{t-1} < \tau \end{cases} \tag{6.9}$$

The difference is that MTAR model depends on the differences of previous period error term, given from $\Delta\hat{\varepsilon}_{t-1}$. Hence, the asymmetric adjustment exhibits more momentum in one direction compare to the other. In order to specify the threshold value (τ) correctly, we used Chan's (1993) procedure which yields a super consistent estimate that minimizes the sum of squared errors of the fitted model.

Consequently, for both TAR and MTAR models we conduct Enders and Granger (1998) test to examine the null hypothesis that ρ_1 and ρ_2 are simultaneously equal to zero ($\rho_1 = \rho_1 = 0$) random walks. Thus, in case F-statistic is statistically significant then a symmetric cointegration test could be formulate with the null hypothesis that the two coefficients ρ_1 and ρ_2 are equal ($\rho_1 = \rho_2$). In case the alternative hypothesis holds then the two variables are cointegrated with an asymmetric adjustment mechanism.

3.2.3 Multivariate conditional volatility

Due to the examination of the second moments of our variables, we implement a diagonal BEKK model to test for co-volatility spillovers as proposed in Chang (2019). The main reason for the selection of such a multivariate conditional volatility model, is its proper regularity conditions and asymptotic properties of the quasi maximum likelihood estimators (QMLE) of the related parameters in the conditional means and variances as examined by McAleer (2005) and McAleer et al. (2008).

As a first step in estimating such a model is to derive the standardized residuals from a univariate conditional mean setting. In our case we used a generalized autoregressive conditional heteroscedasticity model (GARCH). For a univariate case let us assume that the conditional mean of our returns is expressed from the following equation:

$$y_t = E(y_t | I_{t-1}) + \varepsilon_t \tag{6.10}$$

where $y_t = \Delta \log P_t * 100$ symbolizes the log returns of a given variable in the univariate case, I_{t-1} is the information set available at time $t-1$ and ε_t represents the conditionally heteroscedastic returns shock. An ARCH(p) model as introduced by Engle (1982) can be presented as:

$$\sigma_t^2 = \omega + \alpha_1 \varepsilon_{t-1}^2 + \ldots + \alpha_p \varepsilon_{t-p}^2 \tag{6.11}$$

$$\varepsilon_t = \sigma_t z_t$$

$$z_t \overset{iid}{\sim} N(0, 1)$$

where σ_t^2 is the conditional variance which is time varying and depends on lagged squared terms of the returns shock ε_t. The generalized autoregressive conditional heteroscedasticity model (GARCH) introduced by Bollerslev (1986) is an improved specification of the initial ARCH(p) due to the fact that it reduces the parameters by including (q) lags of the conditional variance ($\sigma_{t-1}^2, \ldots, \sigma_{t-q}^2$). Thus, a GARCH($p,q$) process is defined as:

$$\sigma_t^2 = \omega + \sum_{i=1}^{p} \alpha_i \varepsilon_{p-1}^2 + \sum_{j=1}^{q} \beta_j \sigma_{t-q}^2 \tag{6.12}$$

The requirements for covariance stationarity in the case of a GARCH(p,q) framework is that $\sum_{i=1}^{p} \alpha_i + \sum_{j=1}^{q} \beta_i < 1$ and the unconditional variance of residuals is given from: $\sigma^2 = \dfrac{\omega_0}{1 - \left(\sum_{i=1}^{p} \alpha_i + \sum_{j=1}^{q} \beta_j \right)}$.

A multivariate extension of a univariate GARCH(p,q) could be presented from a full BEKK(p,q) model as proposed in Engle and Kroner (1995) that guarantees the positive definiteness of variance-covariance matrix. Also, BEKK model allows for the interaction of conditional variance and covariance of the variables of interest. The conditional covariance matrix of a general BEKK model H_t is given as:

$$H_t = CC' + \sum_{i=1}^{q} \left(A_i \varepsilon_{t-i} \varepsilon_{t-i}' A_i' \right) + \sum_{j=1}^{p} \left(B_j H_{t-j} B_j' \right) \tag{6.13}$$

where A_i and B_j matrices contain n^2 parameters each and C is a lower triangular matrix with $n(n+1)/2$ parameters. The positive definiteness of H_t matrix is guaranteed under the condition that CC' is also positive definite. The model entails the estimation of $n(n+1)/2 + n^2(p+q)$ parameters. Also, the error term in the multivariate setting is given as $\varepsilon_t = H_t^{1/2} z_t$, where z_t is an $(n \times 1)$ vector process of i.i.d. with $E(z) = 0$ and $E(z_t z_t') = I$.

In the simplest form which includes two variables the model could be presented as follows:

$$\begin{pmatrix} h_{11,t} & h_{12,t} \\ h_{21,t} & h_{22,t} \end{pmatrix} = CC' + \begin{pmatrix} \alpha_{11} & \alpha_{12} \\ \alpha_{21} & \alpha_{22} \end{pmatrix} \begin{pmatrix} \varepsilon_{1,t-1}^2 & \varepsilon_{2,t-1} \, \varepsilon_{1,t-1} \\ \varepsilon_{1,t-1} \, \varepsilon_{2,t-1} & \varepsilon_{2,t-1}^2 \end{pmatrix} \begin{pmatrix} \alpha_{11} & \alpha_{12} \\ \alpha_{21} & \alpha_{22} \end{pmatrix}$$

$$+ \begin{pmatrix} \beta_{11} & \beta_{12} \\ \beta_{21} & \beta_{22} \end{pmatrix} \begin{pmatrix} h_{11,t-1} & h_{12,t-1} \\ h_{21,t-1} & h_{22,t-1} \end{pmatrix} \begin{pmatrix} \beta_{11} & \beta_{12} \\ \beta_{21} & \beta_{22} \end{pmatrix} \tag{6.14}$$

The spillover effects are possible to be examined under the above specification of a Full BEKK model nevertheless the QMLE have no known asymptotic properties and as a result there is an issue with the determination of likelihood functions. Another drawback is the extensive number of parameters that arises under full BEKK. Accordingly, we restrict the full BEKK model into a diagonal BEKK which consists only of the diagonal parameters of A and B matrices and requires the estimation of $n(n+1)/2 + n(p+q)$ parameters:

$$\begin{pmatrix} h_{11,t} & h_{12,t} \\ h_{21,t} & h_{22,t} \end{pmatrix} = CC' + \begin{pmatrix} \alpha_{11} & 0 \\ 0 & \alpha_{22} \end{pmatrix} \begin{pmatrix} \varepsilon_{1,t-1} \\ \varepsilon_{2,t-1} \end{pmatrix} \begin{pmatrix} \varepsilon_{1,t-1} \\ \varepsilon_{2,t-1} \end{pmatrix}' \begin{pmatrix} \alpha_{11} & 0 \\ 0 & \alpha_{22} \end{pmatrix}' + \begin{pmatrix} \beta_{11} & 0 \\ 0 & \beta_{22} \end{pmatrix} \begin{pmatrix} h_{11,t-1} & h_{12,t-1} \\ h_{21,t-1} & h_{22,t-1} \end{pmatrix} \begin{pmatrix} \beta_{11} & 0 \\ 0 & \beta_{22} \end{pmatrix}' \tag{6.15}$$

As showed in McAleer et al. (2008) for diagonal BEKK the QMLE of the parameters are consistent and asymptotically normal in a way that standard inference on hypothesis testing is feasible. Furthermore, as shown in Chang (2019) for the bivariate case a partial co-volatility spillover examination could be examined. Those spillovers are defined as the effect of a shock in one variable at time $t-1$ on the consequent co-volatility of both variables of interest at time t. This could represent in a partial derivative notation as:

$$\frac{\partial H_{ijt}}{\partial \varepsilon_{it-1}} = a_{ii} \times a_{jj} \times \varepsilon_{jt-1}, \quad \text{where } i \neq j \tag{6.16}$$

where the coefficients a_i and a_{jj} are the diagonal elements of A matrix and ε_{jt-1} is the return shock of the variable i at time $t-1$. If both coefficients are statistically different from zero then there is a spillover effect from one variable's lagged shock to the co-volatility of the two variables. Due to the fact that every lagged shock of each variable would have a different impact in co-volatility spillover, the mean return shocks is used as in Chang (2019) in order to provide a general view as far as spillover is concerned.

4 Empirical results

4.1 Structural breaks

We initiate the analysis of our two variables ELC and TTF by conducting unit root tests in order to determine the order of integration that the data are committed to. Conventional ADF (1979) test with the null hypothesis of unit root parallel with the KPSS (1992) test with the null hypothesis of stationarity were conducted. Furthermore, because of the fact that unit root tests might provide inconsistent results when structural breaks are present, we further our examination by applying Zivot and Andrews (1992) unit root test which accounts for a single presence of a structural break in the data generating process. As it is evident in Table 6.2, all the above mentioned tests complied that both variables are integrated of order one I(1).

Consequently, in an effort to designate the exact number of structural breaks in our time series we implement Bai and Perron (1998, 2003) test for structural breaks. The advantage of this test is that there is no need for a prior knowledge of structural breaks in the data. On the contrary, structural changes are endogenously determined. As mentioned, it is necessary to study if the estimated coefficients remain stable during the testing period or if there is a possibility of a structural change in time series which has to be handled properly. Thus, we test the null of l breaks against the alternative of $l+1$ for each variable until there is no longer feasible for the F-statistic to reject the null hypothesis as defined in Eq. (6.4). The results are presented in Table 6.3 with the numbers in parenthesis of the F-statistic denoting the null against the alternative hypothesis and Break stands for the break dates.

For the Bai and Perron test we allowed parameters to have at most five breaks since the test requires a minimum segment size of observations which is determined by the trimming parameter. In our case the trimming percentage was chosen to be 15%. Therefore, the above process concludes that ELC has three structural breaks since the null hypothesis that there are three structural breaks against four cannot be rejected while TTF has two structural breaks due to the fact that the null hypothesis of two against three breaks cannot be rejected.

TABLE 6.2 Unit root tests.

	Level				First differences		
	ADF	KPPS	ZA		ADF	KPPS	ZA
	Intercept						
ELC	−2.2563	1.6543[a]	−3.188	Δ(ELC)	−11.8363[a]	0.0821	−11.35[a]
TTF	−1.6447	0.6403[b]	−2.193	Δ(TTF)	−7.7783[a]	0.1786	−8.311[a]
	Intercept and trend						
ELC	−2.5971	0.3867[a]	−3.577	Δ(ELC)	−11.8306[a]	0.0799	−11.48[a]
TTF	−1.5338	0.4196[a]	−2.601	Δ(TTF)	−7.8067[a]	0.1540	−8.305[a]

[a]*Indicates significance at all levels (1%, 5%, 10%).*
[b]*Indicates significance at all 5% and 10%.*

TABLE 6.3 Bai and Perron results.

Variables	F-stat (0vs1)	Break (1)	F-stat (1vs2)	Break (2)	F-stat (2vs3)	Break (3)	F-stat (3vs4)
LELC	19.9493[a]	1/22/2016	18.7761[a]	2/10/2017	15.4505[a]	8/20/2018	2.9604
LTTF	6.4173[a]	2/07/2017	11.1435[a]	8/16/2018	5.2946	–	–

[a]*Indicates significance at all levels (1%, 5%, 10%).*

Considering the above results, we notice that the second and the third break of ELC are very similar to the first and second break date of TTF with the break dates of TTF precede those of ELC. Hence, results advocate that we have four regimes in the case of ELC and three regimes for the case of TTF. For that reason, we construct three dummy variables for ELC and two for the case of TTF.

4.2 Price transmission

In order to examine the price transmission mechanism of our two variables we applied Enders and Siklos (2001) procedure which is basically an extension of the two-step symmetric method of Engle and Granger (1987) because it allows for asymmetric adjustments towards the long run equilibrium. For that reason, in our first step we calculate the long run relationship of our variables which augments the basic model given in Eq. (6.6) by accounting for structural breaks. Thus, three dummy variables plus a deterministic trend were added to the model. The estimation was conducted with OLS as dynamic OLS introduced by Stock and Watson (1993) did not provide any extra lead or lag parameter with the use of Akaike information criterion (AIC). Hence, the regression for the long run is given from:

$$P_t^{elc} = \hat{\beta}_0 + \hat{\beta}_1 P_t^{ttf} + \hat{\beta}_2 D_1 + \hat{\beta}_3 D_2 + \hat{\beta}_4 D_3 + \hat{\beta}_5 T + \varepsilon_{1,t} \tag{6.17}$$

$$P_t^{ttf} = \hat{\gamma}_0 + \hat{\gamma}_1 P_t^{elc} + \hat{\gamma}_2 D_4 + \hat{\gamma}_3 D_5 + \hat{\gamma}_4 T + \varepsilon_{2,t} \tag{6.18}$$

where P_t^{elc} and P_t^{ttf} are logarithmic values of ELC and TTF at time t, D_1, D_2, D_3, D_4, D_5 are dummy variables, T is the deterministic term and $\varepsilon_{1,t}$ with $\varepsilon_{2,t}$ are the residuals which could be expressed as the spread between the two variables.

Subsequently, the residuals obtained from Eqs. (6.17) and 6.18 were decomposed as in Eq. (6.8) for TAR model and as in Eq. (6.9) for MTAR model to test for cointegration and the type of asymmetry in both TAR and MTAR specifications. Monte Carlo experiments were conducted in order to obtain critical values for 5% level of significance for testing the null hypothesis of a random walk against the alternative of a TAR and MTAR model. The number of simulations used was 10.000. For the case of TAR model as presented in Eqs. (6.7) and (6.8) and for MTAR as given in Eqs. (6.7) and (6.9), F-statistics (φ) were calculated and given in Table 6.4.

The threshold value was calculated using Chan's method (1993) by arranging the values of $\hat{\varepsilon}_{t-1}$ and $\Delta\hat{\varepsilon}_{t-1}$ respectively in ascending order and excludes a trimming of 15% of the largest and smallest observations. Thus, a threshold parameter (τ) that minimizes the residual sum of squares over the remaining observations was chosen. The lag selection proposed by Akaike information criterion to remove serial correlation from the residuals. The dummy variables where also used in the calculation procedure as deterministic exogenous variables in order to have more robust results. Both TAR and MTAR models validated that there is a cointegration relationship when ELC is the dependent variable because ρ_1^+ and ρ_2^- parameters are nonzero and what is more this cointegration relationship is asymmetric.

In contrast, when TTF was inserted as the dependent variable the results for ρ_1^+ and ρ_2^- where not statistically significant neither in the symmetric nor in the asymmetric case and for that reason were omitted from the analysis. From the above depicted results in Table 6.4 we might conclude that the long run causality runs from TTF to ELC as the long run parameters of ELC represented by ρ_1^+ and ρ_2^- are statistically significant while those of TTF were not. The following results in Table 6.5 presenting the estimated coefficients of our two asymmetric error correction terms for both TAR and MTAR models. The estimated models are:

$$\Delta LELC_t = C + I_t \rho_1 \hat{\varepsilon}_{t-1} + (1 - I_t)\rho_2 \hat{\varepsilon}_{t-1} + \sum_{i=1}^{n} \alpha_i \ \Delta LELC_{t-1} + \sum_{i=1}^{n} \beta_i \Delta \ LTTF_{t-1} + u_t \tag{6.19}$$

with the TAR and MTAR specifications from Eq. (6.8) and Eq. (6.9) and in order to examine short run causality:

TABLE 6.4 Cointegration and symmetry testing.

	TAR	MTAR
τ	0.086393	0.086510
$\rho_1^+ = \rho_2^- = 0$	15.7128[a]	15.6037[a]
$\rho_1^+ = \rho_2^-$	4.3276[a]	4.1144[a]
ρ_1^+	−5.8788[a]	−4.1941[a]
ρ_2^-	−6.2596[a]	−7.2388[a]
Lags	15	15

[a]Indicates significance at 5% and 10%. The numbers are representing the corresponding t-statistics.

$$\Delta LTTF_t = C + I_t \rho_1 \hat{\varepsilon}_{t-1} + (1 - I_t)\rho_2 \hat{\varepsilon}_{t-1} + \sum_{i=1}^{n} \alpha_i \ \Delta LELC_{t-1} + \sum_{i=1}^{n} \beta_i \ \Delta LTTF_{t-1} + u_t \qquad (6.20)$$

Both TAR and MTAR models for the ELC case have statistically significant asymmetric error correction parameters for all levels of significance while TTF did not provide significant results as mentioned and for that reason are not depicted. Also, the rest of the lagged independent variables (30 in total) are not given but used in order to implement a Wald test to examine the short run causality. The sign of ρ_1^+ and ρ_2^- in both models are negative which indicates a path of correction towards the long run equilibrium. The speed of adjustment is very similar in the case of TAR with negative changes decaying slightly faster than the positive ones. In contrast, MTAR model provides a different rhetoric with negative shocks correcting faster than positive with a correction of 35% which makes positive changes to persist more than their negative counterparts. As the two information criteria discern the most appropriate model is MTAR. Also, no serial correlation is present in the residuals as indicated from the Ljung-Box Q-statistic.

Hence, we conduct a Wald test (Wald, 1945) to the first logarithmic differences of our lagged terms in order to find the direction of the short run causality. As it attested in the Table 6.6 in the short run we have a unidirectional causality from natural gas prices TTF to electricity prices ELC as we reject the null hypothesis that there is no causality from $\Delta LTTF_t$ to $\Delta LELC_t$ while in the opposite case we cannot reject the null that $\Delta LELC_t$ does not cause $\Delta LTTF_t$.

So, we conclude that both long and short term the causality runs from TTF to ELC which could be understood as a price transmission mechanism from the natural gas spot price side spillover to the day ahead electricity prices. Moreover, the analysis indicates that there is a threshold cointegration only from TTF to ELC and that there is a negative asymmetric price transmission as negative shocks tend to decay much faster towards the "attractor" rather that positive changes making the model to exhibit more "momentum" in one direction than the other.

TABLE 6.5 Presentation of TAR and MTAR models for LELC.

	TAR ($n = 15$)	MTAR ($n = 15$)
ρ_1^+	−0.3346[a]	−0.2872[a]
ρ_2^-	−0.3476[a]	−0.3542[a]
Adj. R^2	0.2667	0.2667
Q(36)	0.462	0.469
AIC	−1.9987	−1.9997
BIC	−1.8533	−1.9448

[a]Indicates significance at all levels (1%, 5%, 10%).

TABLE 6.6 Wald test for short run causality for the MTAR model.

Wald test with H_0:No causality	F-statistic	p-value
$\Delta LELC_t \rightarrow \Delta LTTF_t$		
$H_0 := \beta_1 = \ldots = \beta_n = 0$	1.0964	0.3736
$\Delta LTTF_t \rightarrow \Delta LELC_t$		
$H_0 := \alpha_1 = \ldots = \alpha_n = 0$	4.5014[a]	0.000

[a]*Indicates significance at all levels (1%, 5%, 10%).*

4.3 Multivariate conditional volatility

After examining the price transmission mechanism of our two variables, we continue the analysis by testing the co-volatility spillovers with an interpretation that was proposed in Chang et al. (2019). Both variables are converted to log-arithmic differences and multiplied by a factor of one hundred ($100 * \ln(P_t/P_{t-1})$). We initiate the analysis of volatility with a bivariate VAR(14) in first differences for the conditional mean equation, as shown in Table 6.7. In order to account for serial correlation issues in residuals we used the lag length proposed from Akaike information criterion (AIC). Although serial correlation is not an issue for the model, it is evident from the ARCH LM test that there is volatility clustering in the residuals. Volatility clustering is observed as noted in Mandelbrot (1963) *when large changes tend to be followed by large changes, of either sign and small changes tend to be followed by small changes.* For that reason, we will use a bivariate diagonal BEKK-GARCH model as proposed by Engle and Kroner (1995) to model this multivariate conditional volatility.

Having estimated the conditional mean of ELC and TTF we proceed with the bivariate diagonal BEKK(1,1) in order to correct for heteroscedasticity. If we proceed by solving the matrix of the Eq. (6.15) we derive the following equations of multivariate variance and covariance:

$$h_{11,t} = c_{11}^2 + a_{11}^2 \varepsilon_{1,t-1}^2 + \beta_{11}^2 h_{11,t-1} \tag{6.21}$$

$$h_{12,t} = c_{11}c_{21} + a_{11}a_{22}\varepsilon_{1,t-1}\varepsilon_{2,t-1} + \beta_{11}\beta_{22}h_{12,t-1} \tag{6.22}$$

$$h_{22,t} = c_{21}^2 + c_{22}^2 + a_{22}^2 \varepsilon_{2,t-1}^2 + \beta_{22}^2 h_{22,t-1} \tag{6.23}$$

From the equations above, the coefficients of A matrix represent the weights of lagged shocks and B the weights of the previous period covariance. We proceed with the results of diagonal BEKK(1,1). The parameters were estimated with Bollerslev and Wooldridge, (1992) quasi maximum likelihood (QML) due to the fact that the assumption of normality in standardized residuals is violated but in case the model is correctly specified in mean and variance then asymptotic properties of QML and standard errors could be derived validly. Thus, for the diagonal BEKK regularity conditions such as invertibility and asymptotical properties of QML estimators hold as noted in McAleer (2005) and McAleer et al. (2008). For our analysis the convergence of QML achieved after 34 iterations for a total set of 65 parameters in mean and variance. The results of BEKK(1,1) are given in Table 6.8.

The stationarity conditions for the BEKK(1,1) holds as $a_{11}a_{22} + \beta_{11}\beta_{22} < 1$. Also, GARCH effects which could be interpreted as the long run volatility in both cases are more persistent than the ARCH which represents the short run effects. The examination of standardized residuals showed that there is no serial correlation or heteroscedasticity remained. All the parameters are statistically significant for all levels of significance except the constant term of covariance. The weight of TTF in matrix A is larger in comparison with that of ELC therefore contributing more in the covariance equation and make diagonal BEKK representation appropriate due to the fact that other representations such as scalar BEKK exists. Implicitly, the case of scalar BEKK assumes that the weight of matrix A between our two variables have the same weight.

Because of the fact that the weights or multipliers of A matrix are statistically significant with a_{11} representing the weight of ELC and a_{22} is the weight of TTF, we continue by examining the co-volatility spillovers between the variables in the covariance equation as given in Eq. (6.22) which after the estimation could be interpreted as:

$$h_{12,t} = 0.2778 + 0.1021\varepsilon_{1,t-1}\varepsilon_{2,t-1} + 0.8632h_{12,t-1} \tag{6.24}$$

TABLE 6.7 Bivariate VAR(14) model.

Variables	ΔELC_t	Std. error	ΔTTF_t	Std. error
C	0.002665	0.002331	−0.000374	0.000552
ΔELC_{t-1}	−0.475703[a]	0.035539	−0.020133[a]	0.007115
ΔELC_{t-2}	−0.398043[a]	0.038728	−0.013343[b]	0.007328
ΔELC_{t-3}	−0.365648[a]	0.038129	−0.005462	0.007858
ΔELC_{t-4}	−0.317201[a]	0.037982	−0.002998	0.008485
ΔELC_{t-5}	−0.278490[a]	0.039987	−0.010099	0.008679
ΔELC_{t-6}	−0.230618[a]	0.040502	0.006293	0.008707
ΔELC_{t-7}	−0.121612[a]	0.038418	0.002624	0.007944
ΔELC_{t-8}	−0.168787[a]	0.037379	0.002309	0.008209
ΔELC_{t-9}	−0.208064[a]	0.035250	0.002008	0.007914
ΔELC_{t-10}	−0.174373[a]	0.037994	0.001679	0.008191
ΔELC_{t-11}	−0.165197[a]	0.038456	−0.003779	0.007967
ΔELC_{t-12}	−0.150047[a]	0.036199	0.008290	0.007324
ΔELC_{t-13}	−0.124348[a]	0.032586	0.005209	0.006593
ΔELC_{t-14}	−0.123011[a]	0.028587	−0.003857	0.005902
ΔTTF_{t-1}	0.734190[a]	0.100266	−0.041873	0.040662
ΔTTF_{t-2}	0.395417[a]	0.100541	0.014020	0.037474
ΔTTF_{t-3}	0.159461[b]	0.093324	0.008053	0.033048
ΔTTF_{t-4}	0.282509[a]	0.109143	0.025167	0.034186
ΔTTF_{t-5}	0.305517[a]	0.100516	0.034764	0.032832
ΔTTF_{t-6}	0.355158[a]	0.096379	−0.036845	0.035456
ΔTTF_{t-7}	0.327105[a]	0.099621	0.037691	0.037050
ΔTTF_{t-8}	0.181798[c]	0.092956	−0.004917	0.041395
ΔTTF_{t-9}	0.063496	0.098091	0.095032[a]	0.033116
ΔTTF_{t-10}	0.219410[c]	0.091476	0.062630[c]	0.030850
ΔTTF_{t-11}	0.129326	0.104482	0.007993	0.030915
ΔTTF_{t-12}	0.228677[c]	0.094469	−0.006317	0.029919
ΔTTF_{t-13}	0.109056	0.106033	0.010353	0.029606
ΔTTF_{t-14}	0.187586[c]	0.092067	0.045046	0.030046
Adj. R^2	0.2324		0.0115	
Multivariate normality test	0.0000			
Q (20)	0.5902			
ARCH—LM	0.0000			

[a]Indicates significance at all levels (1%, 5%, 10%).
[b]Indicates significance at 10%.
[c]Indicates significance at all 5% and 10%.

TABLE 6.8 Bivariate BEKK(1,1) model.

Variables	C		A	B
Δ(ELC)	3.3555[a]		0.2788[a]	0.9389[a]
	(1.207)		(0.0318)	(0.0146)
Δ(TFF)	0.1730[a]	0.0828	0.3661[a]	0.9193[a]
	(0.0624)	(0.0651)	(0.0310)	(0.0118)
Q(30)r	0.9467			
Q(30)r^2	0.1289			

[a]Indicates significance at all levels (1%, 5%, 10%).

We use matrix A in order to test for partial co-volatility spillover between our variables by differentiate the covariance equation Eq. (6.24) with respect to the returns' shocks $\varepsilon_{1,\,t-1}$ and $\varepsilon_{2,\,t-1}$. As mentioned in Chang et al. (2019) the weights of matrix A do not necessarily represent the volatility spillover effects because they have not been multiplied with a return shock or by the weight of the other variable in our bivariate case. Subsequently, we have to calculate the mean return shock for each variable and then interpret the results through the use of partial derivatives. More explicitly the partial co-volatility spillover is calculated from the Eq. (6.16).

Fig. 6.2 plot shows the calculated conditional covariance of Δ(ELC) and Δ(TTF) parallel with the conditional variances of each variable. The mean return shocks in Table 6.9 show that ELC has a negative value while TTF has a positive value. Also, regardless of sign TTF has the largest return shock.

If we want to analyze the spillover effect of ELC on the TTF then we have to use Eq. (6.16). which could be given as:

$$\frac{\partial H_{12t}}{\partial \varepsilon_{ELC,t-1}} = 0.2788 \times 0.3661 \times 0.0110 = 0.0011 \tag{6.25}$$

and for the spillover effect of TTF on the ELC we have:

$$\frac{\partial H_{12t}}{\partial \varepsilon_{TTF,t-1}} = 0.3661 \times 0.2788 \times (-0.0071) = -0.0007 \tag{6.26}$$

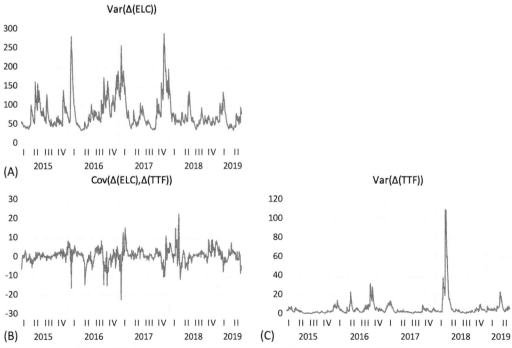

FIG. 6.2 (A) The variance of Δ(ELC); (B) the co-variance of Δ(ELC) and Δ(TTF); (C) the variance of Δ(TTF).

TABLE 6.9 Mean return shocks and A matrix from BEKK(1,1) model.

Variables	A_{ii}	$\bar{\varepsilon}_i$
ELC	0.2788	−0.0071
TTF	0.3661	0.0110

From the above estimated results, we could infer that there is a volatility spillover between our variables. The different signs from the above estimated co-volatility spillovers are determined by the sign of the return shock in the previous period. In our case we have an asymmetry in the estimated signs. Hence, we deduce that the spillover effects of our two variables are moving towards different directions. This might be reflected as a hedging portfolio for investors. A more holistic approach might be the estimation of mean spillover effects by accounting for each return shock separately and not in average as in our case.

5 Conclusions

The main purpose of the present analysis is to unravel the underlying dynamics among the variables understudy, namely electricity day ahead and natural gas spot prices in daily frequency for a total of 1161 observations from 1/06/2015 to 6/18/2019. The analysis was conducted for the case of Netherlands due to the fact that the Title Transfer Facility natural gas hub is considered as a benchmark for Europe and its contribution to Dutch electricity market is of outmost importance. Firstly, we examined for endogenous structural breaks in our variables in order to account for instability of coefficients throughout the period under study. Consequently, we carry on our analysis with the examination of the price transmission mechanism both in the long and in the short run with the usage of asymmetric cointegration approach. The model that fits the data suitably was the momentum threshold autoregressive (MTAR) with ELC as a dependent variable. The asymmetric cointegrating relationship suggested that TTF price decreases cause faster adjustments to ELC prices than increases. Hence, there is a unidirectional causality in the long run from gas to electricity. In addition, Wald test indicates that in the short run we have the same outcome as the natural gas prices are causing electricity prices. Then we examined the volatility spillovers effects with the implementation of a diagonal BEKK multivariate conditional volatility model. This method was preferred among others due to its regularity conditions such as invertibility and asymptotical properties of QML estimators. The analysis showed that indeed there is a volatility spillovers as both variables have statistically significant weights which were represented in A matrix. Consequently, after calculating the mean return shocks for each variable we represented the partial co-volatility spillovers of the conditional covariance equation derived from diagonal BEKK. Hence, the present analysis provides insights both in the price and volatility spillovers as well as in the structural breaks of the time series which might be useful for market participants and regulators.

References

ACER/CEER, 2019. ACER Market Monitoring Report 2018—Gas Wholesale Market Volume. Agency for the Cooperation of Energy Regulators and the Council of European Energy Regulators, Brussels.

Alexopoulos, T., 2017. The growing importance of natural gas as a predictor for retail electricity prices in US. Energy 137. https://doi.org/10.1016/j.energy.2017.07.002.

Bai, J., Perron, P., 1998. Estimating and testing linear models with multiple structural changes. Econometrica 66, 47–78.

Bai, J., Perron, P., 2003. Computation and analysis of multiple structural change models. J. Appl. Economet. 18 (1), 1–22.

Bollerslev, T., 1986. Generalized autoregressive conditional heteroskedasticity. J. Econ. 31 (3), 307–327.

Bollerslev, T., Wooldridge, J.M., 1992. Quasi-maximum likelihood estimation and inference in dynamic models with time varying covariances. Econom. Rev. 11, 143–172.

Chan, K., 1993. Consistency and limiting distribution of the least squares' estimator of a threshold autoregressive model. Ann. Stat. 21, 520–533.

Chang, C.L., McAleer, M., Wang, Y., 2018. Testing co-volatility spillovers for natural gas spot, futures and ETF spot using dynamic conditional covariances. Energy 151, 984–997. 10.1016.

Chang, C.L., Liu, C.P., McAleer, M., 2019. Volatility spillovers for spot, futures, and ETF prices in agriculture and energy. Energy Econ. 81 (C), 779–792. Elsevier.

Dickey, D.A., Fuller, W.A., 1979. Distribution of the estimators for autoregressive time series with a unit root. J. Am. Stat. Assoc. 74 (366), 427–431.

Efimova, O., Serletis, A., 2014. Energy markets volatility modelling using GARCH. Energy Econ. 43, 264–273. Elsevier.

Emery, G.W., Liu, Q., 2002. An analysis of the relationship between electricity and natural gas futures prices. J. Futures Mark. 22, 95–122.

Enders, W., Granger, C.W.J., 1998. Unit-root tests and asymmetric adjustment with an example using the term structure of interest rates. J. Bus. Econ. Stat. 16, 304–311.

Enders, W., Siklos, P., 2001. Cointegration and threshold adjustment. J. Bus. Econ. Stat. 19, 166–176. https://doi.org/10.1198/073500101316970395.

Engle, R., 1982. Autoregressive conditional heteroscedasticity with estimates of the variance of United Kingdom inflation. Econometrica 50 (4), 987–1007.

Engle, R.F., Granger, C., 1987. Co-integration and error correction: representation, estimation, and testing. Econometrica 55 (2), 251–276. Econometric Society.

Engle, R.F., Kroner, K.F., 1995. Multivariate simultaneous generalized ARCH. Econ. Theory 11, 122–150.

Furio, D., Poblacion, J., 2018. Electricity and natural gas prices sharing the long-term trend: some evidence from the Spanish market. Int. J. Energy Econ. Policy 8 (5), 173–180. Econjournals.

Heather, P., 2019. European Traded Gas Hubs: A Decade of Change. The Oxford Institute for Energy Studies, Oxford, p. 2019.

Honore, A., 2013. The Italian Gas Market: Challenges and Opportunities. OIES, Oxford.

Hulshof, D., Maat, J.P., Mulder, M., 2016. Market fundamentals, competition and natural-gas prices. Energy Policy 94. https://doi.org/10.1016/j.enpol.2015.12.016.

IEA, 2019. Gas 2019. IEA, Paris.

Johansen, S., 1988. Statistical analysis of cointegration vectors. J. Econ. Dyn. Control 12 (2), 231–254.

Johansen, S., Juselius, K., 1990. Maximum likelihood estimation and inference on cointegration—with applications to the demand for money. Oxf. Bull. Econ. Stat. 52 (2), 169–210.

Jong, C., Schneider, S., 2009. Cointegration between gas and power spot prices. J. Energy Markets 2. https://doi.org/10.21314/JEM.2009.023.

Kwiatkowski, D., Phillips, P.C.B., Schmidt, P., Shin, Y., 1992. Testing the null hypothesis of stationarity against the alternative of a unit root. J. Econ. 54 (1–3), 159–178.

Lin, B., Li, J., 2015. The spillover effects across natural gas and oil markets: based on the VEC-MGARCH framework. Appl. Energy 155, 229–241.

Mandelbrot, B.B., 1963. The variation of certain speculative prices. J. Bus. 36 (4), 394–419.

McAleer, M., 2005. Automated inference and learning in modeling financial volatility. Economet. Theor. 21 (1), 232–261.

McAleer, M., Chan, F., Hoti, S., Lieberman, O., 2008. Generalized autoregressive conditional correlation. Economet. Theor. 24 (6), 1554–1583.

Nakajima, T., Hamori, S., 2013. Testing causal relationships between wholesale electricity prices and primary energy prices. Energy Policy 62 (C), 869–877. Elsevier.

Nakajima, T., Toyoshima, Y., 2020. Examination of the spillover effects among natural gas and wholesale electricity markets using their futures with different maturities and spot prices. Energies 13, 1533. 10.3390.

Perifanis, T., Dagoumas, A., 2018. Price and volatility spillovers between the US crude oil and natural gas wholesale markets. Energies 11 (10). https://doi.org/10.3390/en11102757.

Stock, J., Watson, M., 1993. A simple estimator of cointegrating vectors in higher order integrated systems. Econometrica 61 (4), 783–820.

Uribe, J.M., Guillen, M., Mosquera-López, S., 2018. Uncovering the nonlinear predictive causality between natural gas and electricity prices. Energy Econ. 74, 904–916.

Villar, J.A., Joutz, F.L., 2006. The relationship between crude oil and natural gas prices. Energy Information Administration, Office of Oil and Gas, pp. 1–43.

Wald, A., 1945. Sequential tests of statistical hypotheses. Ann. Math. Stat. 16 (2), 117–186.

Woo, C.K., Olson, A., Horowitz, I., Luk, S., 2006. Bi-directional causality in California's electricity and natural-gas markets. Energy Policy 34, 2060–2070.

Xia, T., Ji, Q., Geng, J., 2020. Nonlinear dependence and information spillover between electricity and fuel source markets: new evidence from a multi-scale analysis. Physica A: Stat. Mech. Appl. 537. https://doi.org/10.1016/j.physa.2019.122298. Elsevier.

Zivot, E., Andrews, D., 1992. Further evidence on the great crash, the oil-Price shock, and the unit-root hypothesis. J. Bus. Econ. Stat. 10 (3), 251–270.

Part II

Modelling electricity markets

Chapter 7

An optimization model for the economic dispatch problem in power exchanges

Nikolaos E. Koltsaklis

Energy and Environmental Policy Laboratory, School of Economics, Business and International Studies, University of Piraeus, Piraeus, Greece

Nomenclature

h	set of hydroelectric units
a	set of total supply entities (thermal, hydroelectric units, renewables, and interconnections-imports)
bl	set of blocks (block orders)
dm	set of load entities
dt	set of representative days
fh	set of segments of the energy offer function of each hydroelectric unit (simple hourly offers)
fd	set of segments of the energy consumption function of each load entity (simple hourly offers)
fi	set of segments of the energy offer (consumption) function of each interconnection—imports (exports) (simple hourly offers)
ft	set of segments of the energy offer function of each thermal unit (simple hourly offers)
in	set of interconnections
res	set of renewable energy units (technologies)
$st \subseteq th$	set of specific thermal units (lignite, natural gas combined cycle)
t	set of time periods
th	set of thermal units (lignite, natural gas combined cycle, natural gas open cycle)

Parameters

$C^{sup}_{h, fh, t, dt}$	cost of each segment fh of the energy offer function of each hydroelectric unit h in each time period t and representative day dt (€/MW)
$CON^{MAR}_{st, dt}$	parameter denoting if block orders submitted by each thermal unit st during representative day dt is energy-inflexible or not (if yes: 1, otherwise: 0)
$CON^{VAR-t}_{st, dt}$	parameter denoting if block orders submitted by each thermal unit st during representative day dt is time-flexible or not (if yes: 1, otherwise: 0)
$CON^{blc}_{st, dt}$	parameter denoting if block orders submitted by each thermal unit st during representative day dt is price-inflexible or not (if yes: 1, otherwise: 0)
$CONt^{MAR-t}_{st, dt}$	parameter denoting if block orders submitted by each thermal unit st during representative day dt is energy-flexible or not (if yes: 1, otherwise: 0)
$CONt^{blc-t}_{st, dt}$	parameter denoting if block orders submitted by each thermal unit st during representative day dt is price-flexible or not (if yes: 1, otherwise: 0)
$C^{dem}_{dm, fd, t, dt}$	bid price of each segment fd of the energy consumption function of each load entity dm in each time period t and representative day dt (€/MW)
$C^{exp}_{in, fi, t, dt}$	bid price of each segment fi of the energy consumption function of each interconnection in (exports) in each time period t and representative day dt (€/MW)
$C^{imp}_{in, fi, t, dt}$	cost of each segment fi of the energy offer function of each interconnection in (imports) in each time period t and representative day dt (€/MW)
$C^{res}_{res, t, dt}$	energy supply cost of each renewable energy technology res in each time period t and representative day dt (€/MW)
$C^{bl}_{st, bl, dt}$	energy supply cost of each block order bl of thermal unit st in each representative day dt (€/MW)
$C^{sup}_{th, ft, t, dt}$	cost of each segment ft of the energy offer function of each thermal unit th in each time period t and representative day dt (€/MW)

$Ct^{bl}_{st, bl, t, dt}$ energy supply cost of each block order bl of thermal unit st in each time period t and representative day dt (€/MW)

$NF_{a, t, dt}$ net energy injection losses coefficient applied in each energy supply entity a in time period t and representative day dt (p.u.)

$Q^{sup}_{h, fh, t, dt}$ total amount of available energy of each hydroelectric unit h in segment fh of its energy offer function in time period t and representative day dt (MW)

$Q^{dem}_{dm, fd, t, dt}$ total amount of required energy of each load entity dm in segment fd of its energy consumption function in time period t and representative day dt (MW)

$Q^{exp}_{in, fi, t, dt}$ total amount of requited energy of each interconnection in (exports) in segment fi of its energy consumption function in time period t and representative day dt (MW)

$Q^{imp}_{in, fi, t, dt}$ total amount of available energy of each interconnection in (imports) in segment fi of its energy offer function in time period t and representative day dt (MW)

$Q^{mnd}_{res, t, dt}$ total amount of available energy of each renewable energy technology res in time period t and representative day dt (MW)

$Q^{bo}_{st, bl, t, dt}$ total amount of available energy of each thermal unit st in each block bl (block order) in time period t and representative day dt (MW)

$Q^{sup}_{th, ft, t, dt}$ total amount of available energy of each thermal unit th in segment ft of its energy offer function in time period t and representative day dt (MW)

$RC^{max}_{st, bl, dt}$ maximum value of the minimum acceptance ratio of each thermal unit st in each submitted block bl during representative day dt (p.u.) (uniform minimum acceptance ratio)

$RC^{min}_{st, bl, dt}$ minimum value of the minimum acceptance ratio of each thermal unit st in each submitted block bl during representative day dt (p.u.) (uniform minimum acceptance ratio)

$RCt^{max}_{st, bl, t, dt}$ maximum value of the minimum acceptance ratio of each thermal unit st in each submitted block bl during time period t and representative day dt (p.u.) (variable minimum acceptance ratio)

$RCt^{min}_{st, bl, t, dt}$ minimum value of the minimum acceptance ratio of each thermal unit st in each submitted block bl during time period t and representative day dt (p.u.) (variable minimum acceptance ratio)

UPT_{st} minimum operational/up time of each thermal unit st (h)

$U^{max-st}_{st, bl, t, dt}$ maximum desired value of the start-up period of block order bl of each thermal unit st in time period t and representative day dt (between 1 and 24, integer values) (time-flexible block orders)

$U^{min-st}_{st, bl, t, dt}$ minimum desired value of the start-up period of block order bl of each thermal unit st in time period t and representative day dt (between 1 and 24, integer values) (time-flexible block orders)

Continuous variables

$x^{sup}_{th, ft, t, dt}$ cleared energy supply of each thermal unit th in segment ft of its energy offer function in time period t and representative day dt (MW)

$x^{sup}_{h, fh, t, dt}$ cleared energy supply of each hydroelectric unit h in segment fh of its energy offer function in time period t and representative day dt (MW)

$x^{res}_{res, t, dt}$ cleared energy supply of each renewable energy unit res in time period t and representative day dt (MW)

$x^{dem}_{dm, fd, t, dt}$ cleared energy consumption of each load entity dm in segment fd of its energy consumption function in time period t and representative day dt (MW)

$x^{imp}_{in, fi, t, dt}$ cleared energy supply of each interconnection in (imports) in segment fi of its energy offer function in time period t and representative day dt (MW)

$x^{exp}_{in, fi, t, dt}$ cleared energy consumption of each interconnection in (exports) in segment fi of its energy consumption function in time period t and representative day dt (MW)

$b_{st, bl, t, dt}$ cleared energy supply of each block order bl of each thermal unit st in time period t and representative day dt (MW)

$x^{blc}_{st, bl, dt}$ cleared minimum acceptance ratio of each thermal unit st in each submitted block order bl during representative day dt (p.u.) (uniform minimum acceptance ratio)

$x^{blc}_{st, bl, t, dt}$ cleared minimum acceptance ratio of each thermal unit st in each submitted block order bl during time period t and representative day dt (p.u.) (variable minimum acceptance ratio)

Integer variables

$T^{st}_{st, bl, dt}$ value of the start-up period of block order bl of each thermal unit st in time period t and representative day dt (h)

$T^{end}_{st, bl, dt}$ value of the shut-down period of block order bl of each thermal unit st in time period t and representative day dt (h)

Binary variables

$u^{blc}_{st, bl, dt}$ 1, if block order bl of each thermal unit st is active during representative day dt;0, otherwise

$u^{blc}_{st, bl, t, dt}$ 1, if block order bl of each thermal unit st is active during time period t and representative day dt; 0, otherwise

$xt^{st}_{st, bl, t, dt}$ 1, if block order bl of each thermal unit st starts-up during time period t and representative day dt (time-flexible block order); 0, otherwise

$xt^{sd}_{st, bl, t, dt}$ 1, if block order bl of each thermal unit st shuts-down during time period t and representative day dt (time-flexible block order); 0, otherwise

1   Introduction

The European power system is facing significant transformation over the last years. The transition towards a low-carbon economy implies an increasing penetration of renewable energy into the system, higher values of energy efficiency, as well as the electrification of transport and other sectors (Koltsaklis et al., 2013). Moreover, it involves the process of providing consumers a more meaningful role, converting them into active market participants by enabling them to manage their demand actively, produce electricity for self-consumption and sell the excess amounts back to the grid. In that frame of reference, power markets regulations and technical infrastructures need to adapt to a decentralized market framework, where large utilities undergo rapid transformation, facing simultaneously strong competition and shrinking revenues in the wholesale markets. In addition, markets need to be redesigned in such a way as to enhance investments in low-carbon technologies, while at the same time guaranteeing security of supply and maintaining costs for both households and industries at affordable levels (Erbach, 2016).

In that context and for that purpose, a well-functioning and interconnected Internal Energy Market (IEM) is of utmost importance for maintaining security of energy supply, enhancing, and guaranteeing that all consumers can purchase energy at affordable prices. At this stage, a single price coupling algorithm under the title EUPHEMIA (acronym of Pan-European Hybrid Electricity Market Integration Algorithm) is applied in the energy markets of the countries that participate in the Price Coupling of Regions (PCR) project. This algorithm calculates the day-ahead electricity prices across Europe and allocates cross border transmission capacity on a day-ahead basis. The creation of the European Single Electricity Market stands out as a basic pillar of the European Union (EU) with the aim of promoting efficient cross-border electricity trading. The framework for the EU internal market is incorporated in the 3rd Energy Package, being put into place in March 2011, accompanied with a full set of directives formulated to implement this objective. As a consequence of the above, all EU member states are expected to conform to the European Target Model for power trading (Di Cosmo and Lynch, 2015).

In 2017, the electricity trading on the EEX Power Derivatives Market amounted to 2822 TWh, compared with 3920 TWh in 2016, i.e., a decrease of 28%, as a response of market participants to a series of events, including the unscheduled non-operation of around one third of French nuclear power fleet in the autumn and winter of 2016 that did not continue in 2017, as well as the regulatory uncertainty arising from the pending division of the German-Austrian bidding zone. Also, in 2017, 543 TWh were traded on the Power Spot business field, compared with 535 TWh in 2016, i.e., an increase of 2% (EEX, 2017).

There have been presented several works in the literature modelling EUPHEMIA aspects, in an attempt to draw conclusions from its implementation in both algorithmic (technical) and economic aspects. In a market clearing problem with non-convexities such as block orders, and complex orders, most of the time no market equilibrium exists. In that context, Madani and Van Vyve (2017) developed a mixed integer programming framework for day-ahead power auctions with uniform prices, including complex orders, namely the minimum income condition order, highlighting the trade-off relationship between a series of different objectives such as maximization of the total welfare, maximization of the volume to be traded, as well as minimization of paradoxically rejected block bids' opportunity costs. In addition, Sleisz et al. (2014) provided an analysis of the non-convexities of EUPHEMIA algorithm, incorporating two market products, namely minimum income conditions and unified purchase prices (PUN), which inject non-convexity into the problem by introducing the product of two variables on the optimization problem. Thus, a non-convex MIQCP (mixed integer quadratic constrained program) model is created and several algorithmic solution approaches can be utilized to deal with the non-convexities arising from these new aspects of the market. Moreover, Sleisz et al. (2015) investigated the deficiencies and possibilities of complex orders (minimum income, scheduled stop, and load gradient conditions), highlighting key modelling problems and proposing modelling variants from a variety of aspects including market theory, technical feasibility and mathematical programming. Furthermore, Meeus et al. (2009) investigated the effects that the size, type, and the number of blocks have on the day-ahead auctions organized by power exchanges, and more specifically on the total computational time and on the likelihood of paradoxically rejected block orders.

In an effort to widen the market products provided by EUPHEMIA and bridge the gap between economic dispatch problems and traditional unit commitment problems (Koltsaklis and Georgiadis, 2015; Koltsaklis et al., 2018). Sőrés et al. (2015) proposed new day-ahead market structures involving the integrated co-optimization of energy with ancillary services in power exchanges, while Herrero et al. (2015) investigated the extent to which long-term investment incentives can be influenced by the pricing rule adopted and the subsequent market remuneration. Bichpuriya and Soman (2010) provided a review of power exchanges analyzing electricity trading aspects, design issues of a power exchange in terms of bid types, block products, execution and validity conditions and bid matching, while international experiences on power exchanges are also studied. In the same context, Mazzi et al. (2015) provided an overview of European wholesale electricity markets, analyzing power auctions rules in the EU and provided a comparison among them to underline the most effective framework. Boffa et al. (2010) assessed the welfare achieved, in terms of savings to end-users, from increasing market interconnections in the Italian electricity spot market, highlighting that savings do not have a linear relationship with the amount of new transmission capacity additions, since even a minor increase in the amount of the transmission capacity is proved to significantly mitigate end users' expenses.

Following the first part of the research work focused on the hourly orders (Koltsaklis and Dagoumas, 2018), the present work proposes a new methodological approach that builds upon the EUPHEMIA algorithm by enhancing the block orders options, providing the market participants with additional products for the efficient and effective management of their portfolios. The optimization model developed is formulated as a mixed integer linear programming (MILP) model and used for the solution of the economic dispatch problem, considering all the current hourly, block and complex orders being available in the European Power Exchanges, which have been adopted by the EUPHEMIA algorithm, and additionally, incorporates new proposed, market block order-based products. The objective of the proposed optimization approach concerns the minimization of the power system's total daily net cost (total supply cost minus the total load utility) and subject to a series of constraints, including energy demand balance and all the ones arising from the hourly orders, block orders, and complex orders, including the proposed new types of blocks orders. The main contributions and the salient features of the proposed methodological framework are summarized as follows: In addition to the current EUPHEMIA options with uniform minimum acceptance ratio (energy-inflexible block orders), price offer (price inflexible block orders), and block order time limits (time-inflexible block orders), the proposed approach provide the market participants with corresponding variable options, namely the minimum acceptance ratio can be variable (within specific bounds) in each time period (energy-flexible block orders), the price offers can be variable in each time period (price-flexible block orders), as well as the block order time limits can be converted into decision variables (within a specific time horizon), subject also to the constraint that the block order duration to be at least equal to the thermal unit's minimum up/operation time (time-flexible block orders).

The remainder of the paper is structured according to the following: Section 2 provides the model's mathematical formulation, as well as Section 3 introduces the description of the case study employed. Section 4 provides a critical discussion of the results obtained from the model implementation, and finally, Section 5 draws upon some concluding remarks.

2 Mathematical model

2.1 Objective function

The objective function to be optimized concerns the minimization of the total daily net cost, namely the total supply cost minus the total load utility. The supply cost components include:

✓ Thermal units, with simple hourly offers and/or block orders,
✓ Hydroelectric units (simple hourly offers),
✓ Renewable energy units (simple hourly offers),
✓ Electricity imports (simple hourly offers).

The total load revenues emanate from:

✓ Electricity exports, with simple hourly offers and/or block orders,
✓ Load entities, with simple hourly offers and/or block orders.

Min Cost^{daily}

energy supply cost from thermal units (simple hourly offers)

energy supply cost from hydroelectric units (simple hourly offers)

$$\overbrace{\sum_{th}\sum_{ft}\sum_{t}\sum_{dt}x^{sup}_{th,ft,t,dt}\cdot C^{sup}_{th,ft,t,dt}} \quad + \quad \overbrace{\sum_{h}\sum_{fh}\sum_{t}\sum_{dt}x^{sup}_{h,fh,t,dt}\cdot C^{sup}_{h,fh,t,dt}}$$

energy supply cost from renewables (simple hourly offers)

$$+ \quad \overbrace{\sum_{res}\sum_{t}\sum_{dt}x^{res}_{res,t,dt}\cdot C^{sup}_{res,t,dt}} \quad +$$

energy supply cost from imports (simple hourly offers)

$$\overbrace{\sum_{in}\sum_{fi}\sum_{t}\sum_{dt}x^{imp}_{in,fi,t,dt}\cdot C^{imp}_{in,fi,t,dt}} \quad +$$

energy supply cost from thermal units (price − inflexible block orders)

energy supply cost from thermal units (price − flexible block orders)

$$\overbrace{\sum_{st}\sum_{bl}\sum_{t}\sum_{dt}b_{st,bl,t,dt}\cdot C^{bl}_{st,bl,dt}} \quad + \quad \overbrace{\sum_{st}\sum_{bl}\sum_{t}\sum_{dt}b_{st,bl,t,dt}\cdot Ct^{bl}_{st,bl,t,dt}} \quad -$$

energy consumption revenues from electricity exports (simple hourly offers)

$$\overbrace{\sum_{in}\sum_{fi}\sum_{t}\sum_{dt}x^{exp}_{in,fi,t,dt}\cdot C^{exp}_{in,fi,t,dt}} \quad -$$

energy consumption revenues from load entities (simple hourly offers)

$$\overbrace{\sum_{dm}\sum_{fd}\sum_{t}\sum_{dt}x^{dem}_{dm,fd,t,dt}\cdot C^{dem}_{dm,fd,t,dt}} \tag{7.1}$$

2.2 Model constraints

2.2.1 Energy supply limits

Constraints (7.2)–(7.5) describe the upper bounds for the generation output of thermal units, renewables, hydroelectric units, and electricity imports, when submitting simple hourly orders.

$$x^{sup}_{th,ft,t,dt} \le Q^{sup}_{th,ft,t,dt} \; \forall th,ft,t,dt \tag{7.2}$$

$$x^{res}_{res,t,dt} \le Q^{rnnd}_{res,t,dt} \; \forall res,t,dt \tag{7.3}$$

$$x^{sup}_{h,fh,t,dt} \le Q^{sup}_{h,fh,t,dt} \; \forall h,fh,t,dt \tag{7.4}$$

$$x^{imp}_{in,fi,t,dt} \le Q^{imp}_{in,fi,t,dt} \; \forall in,fi,t,dt \tag{7.5}$$

2.2.2 Energy consumption limits

Constraints (7.6) and (7.7) set the upper bounds for the energy consumption of load entities and electricity exports respectively, when submitting simple hourly orders.

$$x^{dem}_{dm,fd,t,dt} \leq Q^{dem}_{dm,fd,t,dt} \quad \forall dm,fd,t,dt \tag{7.6}$$

$$x^{exp}_{in,fi,t,dt} \leq Q^{exp}_{in,fi,t,dt} \quad \forall in,fi,t,dt \tag{7.7}$$

2.2.3 Energy exchange limits

Constraints (7.8) and (7.9) define the maximum bounds for net electricity imports and exports, correspondingly.

$$\sum_{fi} \left(x^{imp}_{in,fi,t,dt} - x^{exp}_{in,fi,t,dt} \right) \leq \sum_{fi} Q^{imp}_{in,fi,t,dt} \quad \forall in,t,dt \tag{7.8}$$

$$\sum_{fi} \left(x^{exp}_{in,fi,t,dt} - x^{imp}_{in,fi,t,dt} \right) \leq \sum_{fi} Q^{exp}_{in,fi,t,dt} \quad \forall in,t,dt \tag{7.9}$$

2.2.4 Block orders—Acceptance ratio

Constraints (7.10) and (7.11) set the operating conditions, namely minimum and maximum allowable minimum acceptance ratio values, for energy-inflexible block orders, while Constraints (7.12) and (7.13) define the same conditions for energy-flexible and time-inflexible block orders, namely for block orders with variable hourly acceptance ratio between the minimum and maximum desired values, as well as fixed block time limits, submitted by the market participants. Finally, Constraints (7.14) and (7.15) describe the relevant conditions for energy-flexible and time-flexible block orders, namely for block orders with variable hourly acceptance ratio between the minimum and maximum desired values, as well as variable block time limits, to be determined by the optimization solution.

$$x^{blc}_{st,bl,dt} \leq MAR^{max}_{st,bl,dt} \cdot y^{blc}_{st,bl,dt} \quad \forall st,bl,dt, \text{ if } CON^{MAR}_{st,dt} = 1 \tag{7.10}$$

$$x^{blc}_{st,bl,dt} \geq MAR^{min}_{st,bl,dt} \cdot y^{blc}_{st,bl,dt} \quad \forall st,bl,dt, \text{ if } CON^{MAR}_{st,dt} = 1 \tag{7.11}$$

$$xt^{blc}_{st,bl,t,dt} \leq MARt^{max}_{st,bl,t,dt} \cdot yt^{blc}_{st,bl,t,dt} \quad \forall st,bl,dt, \text{ if } CON^{MAR}_{st,dt} = 1 \text{ and } CONt^{Var-t}_{st,dt} = 0 \tag{7.12}$$

$$xt^{blc}_{st,bl,t,dt} \geq MARt^{min}_{st,bl,t,dt} \cdot yt^{blc}_{st,bl,t,dt} \quad \forall st,bl,dt, \text{ if } CON^{MAR}_{st,dt} = 1 \text{ and } CONt^{Var-t}_{st,dt} = 0 \tag{7.13}$$

$$xt^{blc}_{st,bl,t,dt} \leq MARt^{max}_{st,bl,t,dt} \cdot yt^{blc}_{st,bl,t,dt} \quad \forall st,bl,dt, \text{ if } CON^{MAR}_{st,dt} = 1 \text{ and } CONt^{Var-t}_{st,dt} = 1 \tag{7.14}$$

$$xt^{blc}_{st,bl,t,dt} \geq MARt^{min}_{st,bl,t,dt} \cdot yt^{blc}_{st,bl,t,dt} \quad \forall st,bl,dt, \text{ if } CON^{MAR}_{st,dt} = 1 \text{ and } CONt^{Var-t}_{st,dt} = 1 \tag{7.15}$$

2.2.5 Block orders energy generation

Eqs. (7.16) and (7.17) define the generation output from energy-inflexible and energy-flexible block orders, respectively.

$$b_{st,bl,t,dt} = Q^{blc}_{st,bl,t,dt} \cdot x^{blc}_{st,bl,dt} \quad \forall st,bl,t,dt, \text{ if } CON^{MAR}_{st,dt} = 1 \tag{7.16}$$

$$b_{st,bl,t,dt} = Q^{blc}_{st,bl,t,dt} \cdot xt^{blc}_{st,bl,t,dt} \quad \forall st,bl,t,dt, \text{ if } CONt^{MAR}_{st,dt} = 1 \tag{7.17}$$

2.2.6 Time-flexible block orders

Constraints (7.18)–(7.25) set all the relevant constraints for time-flexible block orders. In particular, constraints (7.18) state that the duration of each block order, if it is to be activated, has to be greater than or equal to the thermal unit's minimum operational/up time, while constraints (7.19) define their specific time limits. Constraints (7.20) set that shut-down time period has to be greater than or equal to the start-up time period, while constraints (7.21) and (7.22) provide the desired time intervals bounds for the start-up period of each time-flexible block order. Constraints (7.23) state that the start-up decision of each time-flexible block order is to be taken once for the studied period, while constraints (7.24) describe the same for the shut-down decision of each time-flexible block order. Eq. (7.25) constitute a logical relationship, correlating the start-up, shut-down, and operational decisions for each time-flexible block order.

$$T^{end}_{st,bl,dt} - T^{st}_{st,bl,dt} + \sum_t xt^{st}_{st,bl,t,dt} \geq UPT_{st} \cdot \sum_t xt^{st}_{st,bl,t,dt} \quad \forall st,bl,dt, if \ CON^{VAR-t}_{st,dt} = 1 \tag{7.18}$$

$$\sum_t ut^{blc}_{st,bl,t,dt} = T^{end}_{st,bl,dt} - T^{st}_{st,bl,dt} + \sum_t xt^{st}_{st,bl,t,dt} \cdot CON^{VAR-t}_{st,dt} \quad \forall st,bl,dt, if \ CON^{VAR-t}_{st,dt} = 1 \tag{7.19}$$

$$T^{end}_{st,bl,dt} \geq T^{st}_{st,bl,dt} \quad \forall st,bl,t,dt, if \ CON^{VAR-t}_{st,dt} = 1 \tag{7.20}$$

$$T^{st}_{st,bl,dt} \geq \sum_{t \geq U^{min-st}_{st,bl,dt}} xt^{st}_{st,bl,t,dt} \cdot t \quad \forall st,bl,dt, if \ CON^{VAR-t}_{st,dt} = 1 \tag{7.21}$$

$$T^{st}_{st,bl,dt} \leq \sum_{t \leq U^{max-st}_{st,bl,dt}} xt^{st}_{st,bl,t,dt} \cdot t \quad \forall st,bl,d\mathrm{t}, if \ CON^{VAR-t}_{st,dt} = 1 \tag{7.22}$$

$$\sum_t xt^{st}_{st,bl,t,dt} \leq 1 \quad \forall st,bl,dt, if \ CON^{VAR-t}_{st,dt} = 1 \tag{7.23}$$

$$\sum_t xt^{sd}_{st,bl,t,dt} \leq 1 \quad \forall st,bl,dt, if \ CON^{VAR-t}_{st,dt} = 1 \tag{7.24}$$

$$ut^{blc}_{st,bl,t,dt} - ut^{blc}_{st,bl,t,dt} = xt^{st}_{st,bl,t,dt} - xt^{sd}_{st,bl,t,dt} \quad \forall st,bl,t,dt, if \ CON^{VAR-t}_{st,dt} = 1 \tag{7.25}$$

2.2.7 Demand balance

Finally, Eq. (7.26) formulate the demand balance of the studied power system. In particular, the net, considering energy injection losses, energy supply from thermal units (simple hourly offers and block orders), hydroelectric (priced and non-priced) and renewables ones, and electricity imports should satisfy in each time period of each examined representative day the required electricity exports and electrical load.

$$
\overbrace{\sum_h Q^{mnd}_{h,t,dt} \cdot NF_{h,t,dt}}^{\substack{net\,hydro\,non-priced \\ energy\,supply \\ (simple\,hourly\,offers)}} + \overbrace{\sum_h \sum_{fh} x^{sup}_{h,fh,t,dt} \cdot NF_{h,t,dt}}^{\substack{net\,hydro \\ priced\,energy\,supply \\ (simple\,hourly\,offers)}} + \overbrace{\sum_{th} \sum_{ft} x^{sup}_{th,ft,t,dt} \cdot NF_{th,t,dt}}^{\substack{net\,thermal\,priced \\ energy\,supply \\ (simple\,hourly\,offers)}} + \overbrace{\sum_{res} x^{res}_{res,t,dt} \cdot NF_{res,t,dt}}^{\substack{net\,renewables\,priced \\ energy\,supply \\ (simple\,hourly\,offers)}}
$$

$$
+ \overbrace{\sum_{in} \sum_{fi} x^{imp}_{in,fi,t,dt} \cdot NF_{in,t,dt}}^{\substack{net\,priced \\ energy\,imports \\ (simple\,hourly\,offers)}} + \overbrace{\sum_{st} \sum_{bl} b_{st,bl,t,dt} \cdot NF_{st,t,dt}}^{\substack{net\,thermal \\ priced\,energy\,supply \\ (block\,orders)}}
$$

$$
= \overbrace{\sum_{dm} \sum_{fd} x^{dem}_{dm,fd,t,dt}}^{\substack{priced\,load\,consumption \\ (simple\,hourly\,offers)}} + \overbrace{\sum_{in} \sum_{fi} x^{exp}_{in,fi,t,dt}}^{\substack{priced\,energy\,exports \\ (simple\,hourly\,offers)}} \quad \forall t,dt \tag{7.26}
$$

The overall problem is formulated as a MILP (mixed-integer linear programming) problem, involving the cost minimization objective function (7.1), and subject to the Constraints (7.2)–(7.26).

3 Case study description

The Greek interconnected power system has been employed to test the applicability of the proposed methodological framework, the key characteristics of which are presented below. Eight representative day types (DT1–DT8) have been selected (24-h profile), including a weekday (a typical Wednesday) and a weekend day (a typical Sunday) for each of the four seasons (Winter, Spring, Summer, Autumn), as follows:

✓ DT1: a typical winter Wednesday

FIG. 7.1 Minimum average variable cost of each thermal unit during all the examined representative days (€/MWh).

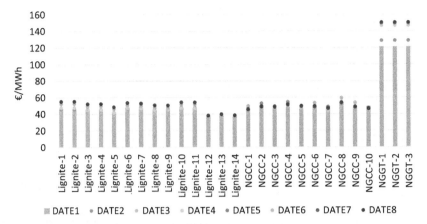

FIG. 7.2 Nominal and available power capacity of each thermal unit during all the examined representative days (MW).

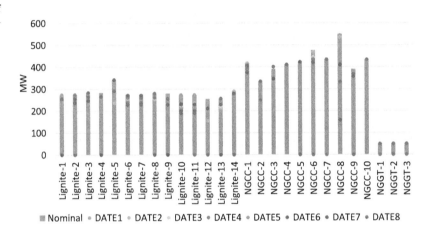

✓ DT2: a typical winter Sunday
✓ DT3: a typical spring Wednesday
✓ DT4: a typical spring Sunday
✓ DT5: a typical summer Wednesday
✓ DT6: a typical summer Sunday
✓ DT7: a typical autumn Wednesday
✓ DT8: a typical autumn Sunday

Fig. 7.1 depicts the minimum average variable cost (MAVC) of each thermal unit during all the examined representative days. As can be seen, three lignite-fired units comprise the most competitive ones, in terms of minimum average variable cost, while the other lignite-fired and natural gas combined cycle (NGCC) units are comparable among them, in terms of economic competitiveness. Natural gas open cycle units are characterized by the higher variable costs, and they typically operate a limited amount of time during the day, if required (Koltsaklis and Nazos, 2017).

Fig. 7.2 portrays the nominal and the available power capacity of each thermal unit during all the examined representative days. As can be observed, some of the units are off during specific dates (zero available capacity), due to their scheduled maintenance. Apart from this, the available capacity of many of them during several day types does not equal their nominal capacity, which can be attributed to several factors including fuel quality, as well as various malfunctions and damages (Koltsaklis et al., 2015). The total nominal thermal capacity amounts to around 8.3 GW, while the actual availability ranges from around 65% and 84% of the total, according to the examined representative day.

TABLE 7.1 Electricity demand per hourly time interval and representative day (MW).

Time interval (h)	DATE1	DATE2	DATE3	DATE4	DATE5	DATE6	DATE7	DATE8
1	6561	5875	4863	4789	7163	6530	4712	4448
2	6007	5354	4483	4423	6616	6164	4429	4188
3	5881	5309	4318	4202	6239	5883	4286	3986
4	5554	4990	4257	4118	6042	5664	4195	3868
5	5547	4797	4242	4030	5914	5525	4182	3830
6	5654	4757	4312	3935	5876	5423	4283	3855
7	6108	4886	4525	3949	5886	5187	4620	3956
8	7015	5239	5151	4205	6479	5269	5104	4039
9	7637	5572	5645	4575	7230	5611	5545	4287
10	8291	6087	6008	4930	7920	5943	5798	4722
11	8761	6552	6178	5362	8391	6325	5982	5108
12	8934	6889	6275	5623	8782	6716	6064	5456
13	9059	7020	6300	5717	9174	6926	6082	5568
14	9067	6866	6214	5489	9384	6999	5979	5438
15	8781	6397	5888	5068	9351	6891	5682	5031
16	8826	6465	5622	4711	9193	6738	5422	4698
17	8759	6577	5375	4605	8924	6673	5278	4596
18	8807	6707	5368	4701	8847	6630	5337	4728
19	9151	7408	5472	5045	8727	6563	5561	4936
20	9199	7596	5678	5284	8563	6578	6165	5628
21	9034	7562	6058	5594	8400	6608	6350	5795
22	8521	7222	6245	6012	8472	7054	5931	5552
23	7740	6698	5637	5698	8196	7034	5396	5131
24	7240	6323	5286	5278	7877	6804	4996	4777
Total	186,133	149,148	129,398	117,342	187,646	151,738	127,377	113,622

Table 7.1 presents the electricity demand per hourly time interval and representative day. As can be observed, the highest load requirements occur in the weekday of winter, while the lowest ones during the weekend of autumn. Not surprisingly, the electricity demand during the weekends is significantly lower than that of the weekdays in all seasons.

Table 7.2 presents the maximum availability of non-priced and priced hydro energy offers per representative day. As can be shown, the non-priced, mandatory hydro energy generation is a small percentage of the total hydro availability, ranging from 3.4% to 17% of the total, according to the examined representative day.

Fig. 7.3 portrays the total renewables' availability per hourly time period and representative day, including wind and solar power, biomass-fired, small hydroelectric and high-efficiency combined heat and power units. The total output is strongly dependent on the meteorological conditions, especially when referring to wind and solar power whose output is highly variable and intermittent.

Based on the analysis presented in Section 2, Table 7.3 presents all the scenarios employed in the examined case study along with their main characteristics based on the selected block order type, their technical characteristics, and the strategy type adopted. Note that each scenario is implemented for all the selected representative days.

TABLE 7.2 Maximum availability of non-priced (NPR) and priced (PR) energy offers per representative day (MW).

DT	Type	1	2	3	4	5	6	7	8	9	10	11	12	13	14	15	16	17	18	19	20	21	22	23	24
DT1	NPR	0	0	0	0	0	0	26	76	80	0	0	25	65	61	26	0	94	313	434	540	315	145	26	0
	PR	2747	2747	2747	2747	2747	2747	2721	2671	2667	2747	2747	2722	2682	2686	2721	2747	2653	2434	2313	2207	2432	2602	2721	2747
DT2	NPR	0	0	0	0	0	0	26	76	80	0	0	25	65	61	26	0	0	30	299	692	667	188	26	0
	PR	2723	2723	2723	2723	2723	2723	2697	2647	2643	2723	2723	2698	2658	2662	2697	2723	2723	2693	2424	2031	2056	2535	2697	2723
DT3	NPR	30	31	38	38	38	38	51	114	534	1010	905	634	113	48	51	64	38	68	38	93	397	922	76	40
	PR	2621	2620	2613	2613	2613	2613	2600	2537	2117	1641	1746	2017	2538	2603	2600	2587	2613	2583	2613	2558	2254	1729	2575	2611
DT4	NPR	649	38	38	38	38	38	64	197	201	121	121	166	166	119	122	103	58	88	68	113	910	1721	1002	208
	PR	2055	2666	2666	2666	2666	2666	2640	2507	2473	2553	2553	2508	2538	2585	2582	2601	2646	2616	2636	2591	1794	983	1702	2496
DT5	NPR	96	96	70	70	70	96	96	261	286	276	257	414	485	708	559	494	610	551	711	915	1171	1115	1100	935
	PR	2809	2809	2835	2835	2835	2809	2809	2644	2619	2629	2648	2491	2420	2197	2346	2411	2295	2354	2194	1990	1734	1790	1805	1970
DT6	NPR	543	543	114	114	114	140	140	267	272	262	222	345	450	470	349	304	320	485	650	934	1164	1495	1465	794
	PR	2394	2394	2823	2823	2823	2797	2797	2670	2665	2675	2715	2592	2487	2467	2588	2633	2617	2452	2287	2003	1773	1442	1472	2143
DT7	NPR	0	0	0	0	0	0	26	26	80	65	20	45	45	36	26	15	15	15	15	260	1220	661	101	0
	PR	2437	2437	2437	2437	2437	2437	2411	2411	2357	2372	2417	2392	2392	2401	2411	2422	2422	2422	2422	2142	1217	1776	2336	2437
DT8	NPR	160	120	0	0	20	20	46	61	125	85	35	45	45	56	46	20	20	84	179	352	880	614	126	0
	PR	2661	2701	2821	2821	2801	2801	2775	2760	2696	2736	2786	2776	2776	2765	2775	2801	2801	2737	2642	2469	1941	2207	2695	2821

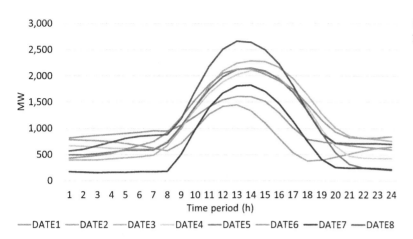

FIG. 7.3 Total renewables' availability per hourly time period and representative day (MW).

TABLE 7.3 Scenarios employed in the examined case study along with their main characteristics based on the selected block order type, their technical characteristics, and the strategy type adopted.

Scenario	Block order type	Identification— energy	Identification— price	Identification— time	Strategy type
1	Independent	Inflexible	Inflexible	Inflexible	*1 block for 1–24 h* Technical maximum at MAVC (€/MWh) 1–24 h
2	Independent	Inflexible	Inflexible	Inflexible	*3 blocks for 1–24 h* 1. Technical minimum: 0 (€/MWh) 2. (Technical maximum-Technical minimum)/2: MAVC +1 (€/MWh) 3. (Technical maximum-Technical minimum)/2: MAVC +2 (€/MWh)
3	Independent	Flexible	Inflexible	Inflexible	*1 block for 1–24 h* Technical maximum at MAVC (€/MWh) 1–24 h
4	Independent	Flexible	Flexible	Inflexible	*1 block for 2 time periods* Technical maximum: 0 (€/MWh) 1–8 h Technical maximum: MAVC (€/MWh) 9–24 h
5	Independent	Flexible	Flexible	Flexible	*1 block for 2 time periods* Technical maximum: 0 (€/MWh) 1–8 h Technical maximum: MAVC (€/MWh) 9–24 h

4 Results and discussion

This section provides the results derived from the model execution for a series of examined scenarios and for the different representative day-types. The problem has been solved to global optimality making use of the ILOG CPLEX 12.6.0.0 solver incorporated in the General Algebraic Modelling System (GAMS) tool (GAMS, 2017). An integrality gap of 0% has been achieved in all cases. With the objective of studying the effects of a range of aspects influencing the power market clearing procedure, and as a consequence the power system operation, several scenarios, 17 in total, have been identified. The cases have been structured so as to examine technical and economic factors influencing the resulting power mix, as well as the system's marginal price and the subsequent remuneration of market participants.

TABLE 7.4 Daily average system's marginal price in each representative day and scenario (€/MWh).

Scenario	DT1	DT2	DT3	DT4	DT5	DT6	DT7	DT8
1	66.128	55.320	48.246	48.246	57.362	50.753	54.264	50.680
2	66.128	54.435	48.376	39.765	58.436	49.162	52.716	40.701
3	78.779	56.104	49.188	45.619	58.756	51.397	55.110	50.019
4	66.128	40.211	33.031	30.640	50.857	35.736	39.340	33.218
5	66.128	40.334	33.516	30.003	50.857	37.126	39.591	32.323

4.1 Power system's marginal price

Table 7.4 presents the daily average system's marginal price in each representative day and scenario. Scenarios 1–5 refer to independent block orders under different operating aspects and adopted market strategy among them.

As can be observed in Table 7.4, there is noticeable variation in the resulting system's marginal price, according to the examined scenario and the selected day. As expected, the higher the required demand, the higher the resulting marginal prices. As a consequence, dates 1 and 2 (winter), as well as dates 5 and 6 (summer) report the higher values. The prices are higher in the winter than in the summer, due to the interaction with the neighboring systems, where prices are quite high during these dates, and thus the examined power system is converted into a net electricity exporter, exerting upward pressure on the prices.

Another interesting observation is that in the scenario combining energy flexibility (variable minimum acceptance ratio), price-flexibility (variable hourly price offers), and price offers lower than the minimum average variable cost (MAVC) of each unit, namely in scenarios 4 and 5, a significant reduction in the resulting prices is reported. It is also worth mentioning that the time-flexibility option (variable block time limits) in Scenario 4 can also exert significant downward pressures in the final marginal price.

4.2 Electricity trading

Table 7.5 presents the daily average electricity trading (net electricity imports, namely electricity imports minus electricity exports) in each representative day and scenario. The direction of electricity flows (+ for net electricity imports and − for net electricity exports) is determined based on the price differences of the interconnected power systems.

In general, electricity exports are positively correlated with low system's marginal prices. In the scenarios characterized by the highest provided flexibility (4, 5), significant electricity exports are reported for Greece's interconnected power systems, with the exception of some weekend day-types, where the dispatch of some thermal units is not considered profitable for both domestic consumption satisfaction and electricity exports, and thus net electricity imports contribute to the domestic load satisfaction.

Another generic conclusion is that electricity exports implementation is in line with the operation of domestic thermal units, which face significant competition from flexible electricity imports, creating unfavorable operating conditions for both thermal units and electricity exports during days with low demand. However, even during day-types when electricity imports are unavoidable, incorporation of energy-, price-, and time-flexibility provision from thermal units in the market

TABLE 7.5 Daily average electricity trading (net electricity imports) in each representative day and scenario (MWh).

Scenario	DT1	DT2	DT3	DT4	DT5	DT6	DT7	DT8
1	−14,034	−6801	16,019	24,353	1660	29,761	−4332	15,091
2	−14,034	−7178	16,397	21,295	2700	28,836	−6638	8838
3	−10,622	−6831	15,493	38,073	9114	33,103	−256	20,645
4	−14,034	−15,717	−5353	14,013	−5482	9678	−16,852	6032
5	−14,034	−15,585	−4045	14,639	−5482	11,777	−16,385	5324

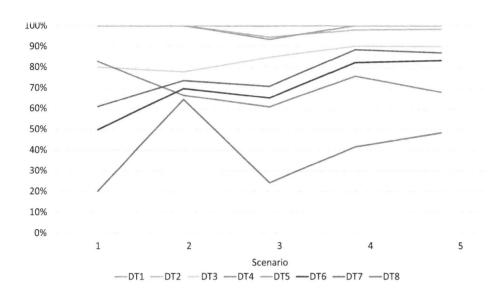

FIG. 7.4 Daily average utilization factor of lignite-fired units in each representative day and scenario (%).

operation can alleviate the negative impacts for these units' operation. All these aspects have to be systematically studied and taken into consideration in order to guarantee the economic feasibility of potential new power investments.

4.3 Thermal units' operation

Fig. 7.4 presents the daily average utilization factor of lignite-fired units in each representative day and scenario. It can be observed that the combined effects of low-demand periods (weekends in autumn and spring) have as a direct consequence a significant underutilization of lignite-fired units. It is worth mentioning that the utilization factor of lignite-fired units in day-type 8 is between 20% and 64% in all scenarios.

Fig. 7.5 presents the daily average utilization factor of natural gas-fired combined cycle units in each representative day and scenario. From the comparison of these figures, we can highlight that during dates of high demand, both technology types operate at peak levels, utilizing almost fully their available capacity. On the other hand, when demand levels are medium and/or even low, there is a clear trade-off between them in their resulting share in the power mix, influenced by their relevant economic competitiveness difference. Degrees of freedom, in terms of block orders' flexibility options, turns out to be beneficial for both technology types.

Table 7.6 shows the total daily revenues of a representative competitive lignite-fired unit in each scenario and selected day-type, while Table 7.7 contains the same type of information for a representative competitive natural gas-fired combined cycle unit in each scenario and selected day-type. Not surprisingly, the higher the system's marginal price, the higher the

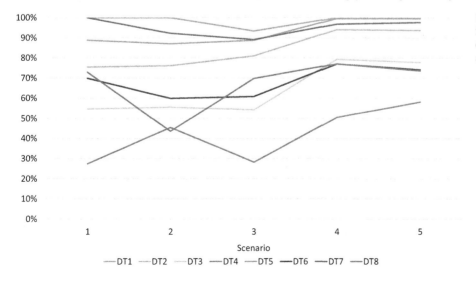

FIG. 7.5 Daily average utilization factor of natural gas-fired combined cycle units in each representative day and scenario (%).

TABLE 7.6 Total daily revenues of a representative lignite-fired unit in each scenario and selected day-type (€).

Scenario	DT1	DT2	DT3	DT4	DT5	DT6	DT7	DT8
1	141,914 €	75,012 €	52,200 €	52,206 €	83,300 €	40,404 €	41,229 €	16,115 €
2	330,154 €	258,508 €	236,713 €	179,420 €	293,789 €	228,589 €	244,931 €	183,642 €
3	216,911 €	79,487 €	59,554 €	35,337 €	93,371 €	44,400 €	45,736 €	12,666 €
4	225,278 €	67,429 €	41,918 €	39,244 €	146,666 €	45,242 €	50,161 €	24,121 €
5	225,278 €	69,739 €	45,896 €	32,541 €	146,666 €	56,206 €	51,419 €	19,744 €

TABLE 7.7 Total daily revenues of a representative natural gas-fired combined cycle unit in each scenario and selected day-type (€).

Scenario	DT1	DT2	DT3	DT4	DT5	DT6	DT7	DT8
1	202,568 €	94,408 €	8831 €	8792 €	69,107 €	12,901 €	85,892 €	44,699 €
2	394,555 €	277,537 €	211,413 €	173,694 €	288,035 €	214,741 €	261,298 €	177,781 €
3	329,182 €	101,346 €	19,345 €	8651 €	77,726 €	19,140 €	91,893 €	40,235 €
4	355,647 €	96,269 €	14,949 €	36,158 €	156,581 €	46,193 €	88,171 €	43,350 €
5	355,647 €	93,273 €	22,988 €	23,824 €	156,581 €	50,727 €	90,620 €	40,795 €

derived revenues for each unit. With regard to the lignite-fired unit, its highest revenues amount to less than 330,000 € during date1 in scenario 2, while its minimum daily revenues equal less than 13,000 € (date 8, scenario 3). Similarly, for the natural gas-fired combined cycle unit, its maximum net revenues are around 400,000 € (date 1, scenario 2), while its minimal revenues are less than 9000 € (date 4, scenario 3).

Fig. 7.6 depicts the total daily generation of natural gas-fired open cycle units in each representative day and scenario. As can be observed, they are operational only during days with high demand (dates 1 and 2), when, in additional, there is significant amount of exports to other neighboring countries, and thus, the power system operates close to its maximum limits.

Fig. 7.7 depicts the number of required iterations for the final solution execution due to the presence of paradoxically accepted/rejected block orders and/or violations of minimum income conditions. As can be seen, in some scenarios the model reaches its final solution in one execution, while in some other iterations are required, the maximum of which

FIG. 7.6 Total daily generation of natural gas-fired open cycle units in each representative day and scenario (MWh).

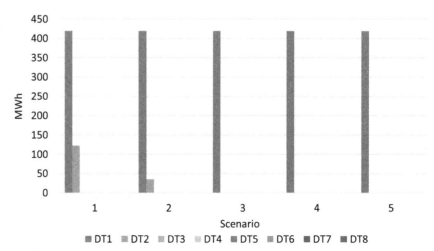

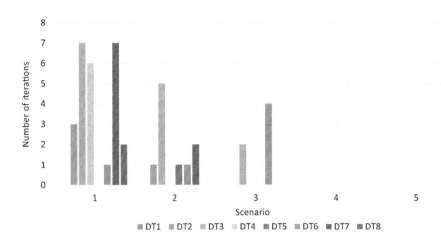

FIG. 7.7 Number of required iterations for the final solution execution due to the presence of paradoxically accepted/rejected block orders and/or violations of minimum income conditions.

are 7 (date 7, scenario 1). It is clear that in scenarios with high degrees of flexibility, e.g., scenarios 4 and 5, no iterations are required to reach the final solution.

5 Conclusions

The EU Pan-European Hybrid Electricity Market Integration Algorithm (EUPHEMIA) constitutes an algorithm developed by the PCR project toward a single internal EU electricity market. All power exchanges receive offers and bids from market participants and send them to a central location where through the utilization of EUPHEMIA, the algorithm determines which orders are accepted and at which price, with the objective of maximizing social benefit of power producers and consumers.

The first stable version of EUPHEMIA meeting the requirements of all markets taking part in PCR initiative was delivered in July 2012. Since then the work on continuous improvement and development of the algorithm is made to deal with the increasing market requirements, to facilitate the market coupling process and the creation of the internal European market, as well as for the further improvement of the available market products.

In this work, a new optimization approach has been developed that builds upon the EUPHEMIA algorithm by proposing additional block orders options, enhancing in this way the flexibility of market participants toward a robust and efficient management of their resources. The optimization framework developed is formulated as a mixed integer linear programming (MILP) model and applied for the solution of the economic dispatch problem in power exchanges. The proposed approach incorporates flexibility in three main aspects, namely minimum acceptance ratio, price offer, and block time limits.

Based on the above, a series of scenarios have been investigated to quantify the impacts of new products on a series of technical and economic factors. The results show that block orders, constructed in a way to provide a more realistic operation of thermal units that are unable to start-up and shut-down in short time periods, lead to lower daily average prices, with significant variations according to the products utilized and the strategy adopted. The shrinking power prices can create significant problems in the operation of thermal units, which have to recover both variable costs, as well as potential shutdown costs. On the other hand, the results show that the existence of flexibility options in the main aspects of block orders structure create more favorable conditions for increased utilization of thermal units. All these have to be considered and investigated in a detailed way from policy makers, market operators and regulators in the development of market design, and in the incentives provided for new investments in the power sector, both in the supply and the demand side, as well as in the transmission system, internal and cross-border.

References

Bichpuriya, Y.K., Soman, S.A., 2010. Electric power exchanges: a review. In: 16th National Power Systems Conference, 15–17 December, 2010. Available from: http://www.iitk.ac.in/npsc/Papers/NPSC2010/6146.pdf. (Accessed 6 May 2018).

Boffa, F., Pingali, V., Vannoni, D., 2010. Increasing market interconnection: an analysis of the Italian electricity spot market. Int. J. Ind. Organ. 28, 311–322.

Di Cosmo, V., Lynch, M.A., 2015. Competition and the single electricity market: which lessons for Ireland? Working Paper No. 497. Available from: https://www.esri.ie/pubs/WP497.pdf. (Accessed 6 May 2018).

Erbach, G., 2016. European Parliamentary Research Service (EPRS). Understanding Electricity Markets in the EU. Available from: http://www.europarl.europa.eu/RegData/etudes/BRIE/2016/593519/EPRS_BRI(2016)593519_EN.pdf. (Accessed 6 May 2018).

GAMS, 2017. GAMS—A User's Guide. Washington, DC https://www.gams.com/24.8/docs/userguides/GAMSUsersGuide.pdf. (Accessed 17 April 2018).

Herrero, I., Rodilla, P., Batlle, C., 2015. Electricity market-clearing prices and investment incentives: the role of pricing rules. Energy Econ. 47, 42–51.

Koltsaklis, N.E., Dagoumas, A.S., 2018. Incorporating unit commitment aspects to the European electricity markets algorithm: an optimization model for the joint clearing of energy and reserve markets. Appl. Energy 231, 235–258.

Koltsaklis, N.E., Dagoumas, A.S., Kopanos, G.M., Pistikopoulos, E.N., Georgiadis, M.C., 2013. A mathematical programming approach to the optimal long-term national energy planning. Chemical Engineering Transactions 35, 625–630. https://doi.org/10.3303/CET1335104.

Koltsaklis, N.E., Georgiadis, M.C., 2015. A multi-period, multi-regional generation expansion planning model incorporating unit commitment constraints. Appl. Energy 158, 310–331.

Koltsaklis, N.E., Nazos, K., 2017. A stochastic MILP energy planning model incorporating power market dynamics. Appl. Energy 205, 1364–1383.

Koltsaklis, N.E., Liu, P., Georgiadis, M.C., 2015. An integrated stochastic multi-regional long-term energy planning model incorporating autonomous power systems and demand response. Energy 82, 865–888.

Koltsaklis, N.E., Gioulekas, I., Georgiadis, M.C., 2018. Optimal scheduling of interconnected power systems. Comput. Chem. Eng. 111, 164–182.

Madani, M., Van Vyve, M., 2017. A MIP framework for non-convex uniform price day-ahead electricity auctions. EURO J. Comb. Optim. 5, 263–284.

Mazzi, N., Lorenzoni, A., Rech, S., Lazzaretto, A., 2015. Electricity auctions: a European view on markets and practices. In: International Conference on the European Energy Market, EEM2015.

Meeus, L., Verhaegen, K., Belmans, R., 2009. Block order restrictions in combinatorial electric energy auctions. Eur. J. Oper. Res. 196, 1202–1206.

Sleisz, A., Sorés, P., Raisz, D., 2014. Algorithmic properties of the all-European day-ahead electricity market. In: International Conference on the European Energy Market, EEM2014.

Sleisz, A., Divényi, D., Polgári, B., Sorés, P., Raisz, D., 2015. Challenges in the formulation of complex orders on European power exchanges. In: International Conference on the European Energy Market, EEM2015.

Sorés, P., Divényi, D., Polgári, B., Raisz, D., Sleisz, A., 2015. Day-ahead market structures for co-optimized energy and reserve allocation. In: International Conference on the European Energy Market, EEM2015.

EEX, 2017. EEX Group. Annual Report 2017, Local Expertise in Global Commodity Markets. Available from: http://www.eex.com/blob/81436/f4b65333492b59f0077243cbd21172ac/eexgroup-annual-report-2017b-eng-data.pdf. (Accessed 6 May 2018).

Chapter 8

Power system flexibility: A methodological analytical framework based on unit commitment and economic dispatch modelling

Stamatios Chondrogiannis[a], Marta Poncela-Blanco[a], Antonios Marinopoulos[b], Ilias Marneris[c], Andreas Ntomaris[c], Pandelis Biskas[c], and Anastasios Bakirtzis[c]

[a]*European Commission, Joint Research Centre (JRC), Ispra, Italy,* [b]*European Commission, Joint Research Centre (JRC), Petten, The Netherlands,* [c]*Department of Electrical and Computer Engineering, Aristotle University of Thessaloniki (AUTH), Thessaloniki, Greece*

Acronyms

aFRR	automatic Frequency Restoration Reserve
BM	Balancing Market
CHP	Combined Heat and Power
CPP	Critical Peak Pricing
DAM	Day-Ahead Market
DR	Demand Response
EENS	Expected Energy Not Served
ENS	Energy Not Served
ERNS	Expected Reserve Not Served
EVs	Electric Vehicles
FB	Flow-Based (market coupling)
FCR	Frequency Containment Reserve
IDM	Intra-Day Market
LOLE	Loss of Load Expectation
mFRR	manual Frequency Restoration Reserve
MILP	Mixed Integer Linear Programming
NTC	Net Transfer Capacity
PHEVs	Plug-in Hybrid Electric Vehicles
RES	Renewable Energy Sources
RR	Replacement Reserve
RTP	Real-Time Pricing
TOU	Time-Of-Use (pricing)
TSO	Transmission System Operator
UCED	Unit Commitment and Economic Dispatch
vRES	variable Renewable Energy Sources

1 Introduction

The profound transformation of the power system in the last decades is increasing the need of flexibility. All power systems had always a certain degree of flexibility to cope with unexpected outages, load variation and load forecast errors. The increased need of flexibility is related to the integration of large amounts of variable Renewable Energy Sources (vRES),

Mathematical Modelling of Contemporary Electricity Markets. https://doi.org/10.1016/B978-0-12-821838-9.00008-6

which introduces more uncertainty and variability, to the increased volumes of distributed energy resources, and the electrification of different energy uses (mainly heating and transport).

Although there is not a standard definition of flexibility, the International Energy Agency-International Smart Grids Action Network (IEA-ISGAN) proposes the following: "flexibility is the ability of the power system to manage changes" (Hillberg et al., 2019). This definition aims for a wide scope rather than focusing only to the balance of demand and supply. Following this approach, flexibility can be studied from very different perspectives all of them interlinked (see Fig. 8.1).

Flexibility has gained a lot of research attention but there is no standard procedure to analyze flexibility in power systems. Setting up a complete quantitative flexibility evaluation method is essential to identify flexibility needs, sources and the system capacity to deliver it. Assessments of flexibility are in general based on a step-wise approach, starting from the identification of the flexibility needs, followed by an identification of the technical flexibility of resources, the operational flexibility and finally the commercial (market) analysis of how the flexible resources are effectively utilized (Cochran et al., 2014; Poncela et al., 2018; Jaraite-Kazukauske et al., 2019).

Oree and Sayed Hassen design a composite metric to assess the flexibility of conventional generators (Oree and Sayed Hassen, 2016). Heydarian-Forushani and Golshan propose a new flexibility metric to determine the flexibility provided by various demand response programs (DRPs), tariff-based, incentive-based and combinational DR programs, in the day-ahead market clearing procedure (Heydarian-Forushani and Golshan, n.d.). Li et al. review various flexibility metrics differentiating indexes for power system planning and operational metrics focusing on the grid flexibility aspect (Li et al., 2018). Flexibility cannot be assessed through a single indicator, as different technical aspects should be considered. Heggarty et al. provide a non-exhaustive list of flexibility metrics for long-term planning purposes and the authors apply a new methodology to evaluate flexibility needs at annual, week and daily time horizon based on frequency spectrum analysis to the French power system (Heggarty et al., 2019). In the same way, Andrey et al. assess the flexibility needs over a day or a week. In both cases, the lack of flexibility and adequacy in operational reserves is not considered (Andrey et al., 2016).

This work presents a flexibility assessment considering the use of the different resources such as conventional generation fleet, interconnection capacity, storage, and demand response for an "energy-only" market considering the different types of operating reserves. To do so, the test case considers the different short-term market timeframes (day-ahead,

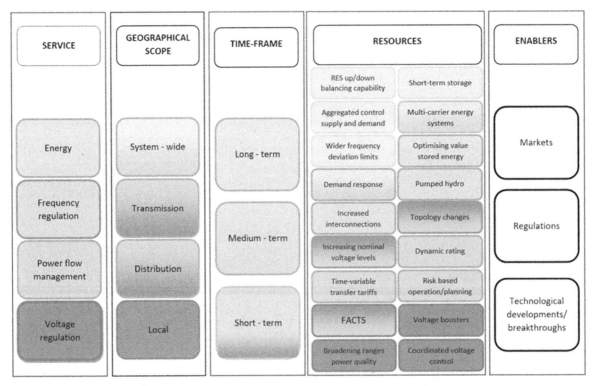

FIG. 8.1 Different perspectives from which flexibility can be analyzed. Following IEA-ISGAN approach (Hillberg et al., 2019) there are four main services where flexibility is key: energy, frequency regulation, power flow management and voltage regulation. These four requirements could have different geographical scope, from local (i.e. voltage) to system-wide (i.e. frequency regulation). Very related with geographical scope and requirements is the timeframe: from fractions of second up to minutes (i.e. voltage regulation—local scope) to medium term (from hours to days) and long-term (years).

intraday and balancing markets), different competing flexibility resources and it is applied to 21 interconnected European countries. The developed model, called PHOEBE (Probabilistic Hourly Optimization-Based Evaluation of Bulk Electric System Adequacy) has been developed by Aristotle University of Thessaloniki for the Joint Research Centre—European Commission.

1.1 Structure

In Section 2 of this chapter a set of flexibility indicators is proposed based on a stepwise flexibility assessment. This is divided in three sequential steps:

(A) Preliminary evaluation of flexibility requirements
(B) Assessment of technical capability of resources to provide flexibility
(C) Detailed analysis of power system operational flexibility

The first two steps are modeled independently, without considering the operational status of the different resources and the market ability to effectively deploy the required flexibility. The last step is based on the results of a UCED model. The respective indicators examined consider the operational status of the different resources as well as the impact of the market architecture on the deployment of the required flexibility. Weight is given in this last step of the methodology. Critical issues regarding the UCED model are discussed including among others its structure, the importance of the approach for aggregating generating units, modelling considerations of various elements (forecast errors, reserves, contingencies, demand, demand response, storage), and calculation of schedules for maintenance and hydro reservoir management. Further, the need to go beyond the classical in generation adequacy studies indicators of LOLE and EENS is elaborated, and the additional indicators employed in this work are presented along with their purpose and scope in the context of the overall flexibility analysis.

In Section 3, the case study is presented, along with the results of the simulations. These are used as a basis for highlighting important points in flexibility assessments, such as the need to differentiate between non-availability of energy versus non-availability of adequate level of reserves or the lack of generating capacity versus the lack of flexibility resources. Following, areas of further improvement of the presented methodological framework are identified with a focus on the UCED formulation, and areas for future development are briefly elaborated in view of the further decarbonization and decentralization of the power system.

The chapter closes with the main conclusions of this work and its contribution on framing flexibility as an explicit attribute of power system resources adequacy.

2 Methodology

2.1 Preliminary evaluation of flexibility requirements

The first step of the proposed flexibility assessment methodology is to assess the flexibility requirements of the system under study, using indicators that are calculated based only on system characteristics and analysis of the input data, and without considering the operational status of the different assets, i.e. without running any model-based simulations. The scope of this step includes the analysis of potential vRES penetration levels (in terms of both load and energy), the risk for vRES curtailment, and the estimation of maximum residual load ramps. Using appropriate indicators for these three properties of the system one can estimate the probability that at some point during the period under study flexibility will be required. These non-modeled based indicators, however, might only provide rough or in some cases conflicting indications for the adequacy when compared to the respective probabilistic indicators, which are described in Section 2.4. Therefore, one should use them with caution. These indicators are described below:

RES Load Penetration Index (RLPI): Maximum hourly coverage of load by non-dispatchable renewable generation (wind and solar) for each meteorological scenario and country c (or node in the UCED model).

$$RLPI(sc) = \max_{t=1,2,3,...,8760} \left(\frac{W(s,c,t) + S(s,c,t)}{L(s,c,t)} \right) \tag{8.1}$$

where $W(s,c,t)$, $S(s,c,t)$ and $L(s,c,t)$ are the wind and solar generation potentials and the demand, respectively, at time t for country c and meteorological scenario s. Higher levels of vRES penetration could be an indicator for a stronger requirement for flexibility, due to the variable and intermittent nature of vRES.

RES Energy Penetration Index (REPI): It is the average value of demand covered by variable RES generation (wind and solar) in a year's time.

$$REPI(c) = \sum_{s \in S} \left[\frac{\sum_{t=1}^{8760} (W(s,c,t) + S(s,c,t))}{\sum_{t=1}^{8760} L(s,c,t)} \right] * \frac{100}{|S|} \tag{8.2}$$

where $|S|$ is the cardinality of the meteorological scenario set.

RES Curtailment Risk (RCR): Number of periods of time with high probability of vRES curtailment (estimated as number of hours with negative residual load values).

$$RCR(c) = \sum_{s \in S} \left[\frac{N(s,c)}{8760} \right] * \frac{100}{|S|} \tag{8.3}$$

where $N(s,c)$ is the number of hours in the year with negative residual load $RL(s,c,t)$. In this work, the residual load is defined as follows:

$$RL(s,c,t) = L(s,c,t) - W(s,c,t) - S(s,c,t) \tag{8.4}$$

In Eq. (8.3), RCR is expressed as a percentage. If multiplied by the total number of hours in a year, i.e. 8760, then it is expressed in hours/year. RCR can be computed in energy terms (MWh/year) as:

$$RCR(c) = \sum_{s \in S} \sum_{t=1}^{8760} (-1) * (RL(s,c,t) < 0) * \frac{1}{|S|} \tag{8.5}$$

Maximum Residual Load Ramps (MRLR): Maximum observed residual load ramp for each ramping horizon (from 1 to 24) and ramping direction (up or down).

$$MRLR(\Delta tc) = \begin{cases} \max_{s \in S} \left(\max_{t=1,\cdots,8760} (RL(s,c,t+\Delta t) - RL(s,c,t)) \right) for\ dir = up \\ \\ \max_{s \in S} \left(\max_{t=1,\cdots,8760} (RL(s,c,t) - RL(s,c,t+\Delta t)) \right) for\ dir = down \end{cases} \tag{8.6}$$

Analyzing the residual load ramps, it can be seen that negative and positive ramps are not symmetric, so ramp-up and ramp-down requirements are different, too (Poncela et al., 2018). For that reason, all indicators related to ramps are calculated independently for the two directions.

2.2 Assessment of technical capability of resources to provide flexibility

In the second step of the proposed flexibility assessment methodology, the technical characteristics of the flexibility resources are evaluated, based only on technical data, i.e. without any simulations. The goal is to provide information for better understanding the potential capabilities of the resource fleet in the system, without considering the operational status of each asset. Within the scope of this analysis, the below indicator is calculated:

Flexibility capacity ratio: Percentage of installed capacity of a resource type relative to the peak demand of a country.

$$FLEX(c,pt) = \frac{\sum_{i \in I^{c,pt}} P_{max}(i)}{L_{peak}(c)} \tag{8.7}$$

where $P_{max}(i)$ is the maximum stable generation capacity of power plant i; pt is the plant type and $L_{peak}(c)$ is the peak demand of country c. This indicator can be used in a "flexibility chart" to analyze and compare the variety of solutions in different countries/areas (Yasuda et al., 2013).

2.3 UCED model

2.3.1 Basic features of the UCED model

The purpose of the UCED model is to evaluate in detail the behavior of the system by simulating its dispatch for a target year. The mathematical formulation of the UCED as a MILP problem is well documented in the literature, e.g. see (Lin and

Magnago, 2017, Conejo and Baringo, 2017). Its usage, however, in mid-term adequacy studies is relatively new, exemplified in Europe with ENTSO-E's MAF studies. While most existing studies/tools employed in mid-term power system adequacy give more weight to execution speed, the developed model in this work (PHOEBE) gives special attention to modelling accuracy; the scope is to capture the intraday flexibility issues that may occur due to various system and resource operating limitations, especially due to the challenges imposed by high vRES penetration. One should also keep in mind that most UCED formulations simulate an ideal power market, i.e. one where all generating units bid according to their marginal cost. This is the approach followed also in this work, considering its longer-term applicability. The main points of the implemented UCED model are summarized in Table 8.1.

The implemented model assumes a zonal organization of the power market, which is the case in Europe. Interconnectors between zones are represented by their NTC. This is the available transfer capacity for cross-zonal trade, which includes also security limitations against grid element contingencies. A main difference is HVDC interconnectors, for which contingencies are modeled explicitly following the paradigm of established generation adequacy assessments (ENTSO-E, 2019).

The UCED model is formulated as a Mixed-Integer Linear Programming (MILP) problem, incorporating both continuous and discrete binary decision variables:

$$\text{Minimize} \sum_{i \in I} \sum_{t \in T} \left[y(i,t)^* C_{SU}(i) \right] + \sum_{i \in I} \sum_{t \in T} \left[p(i,t)^* C_{EN}(i) \right] + \sum_{c \in C} \sum_{t \in T} \left[d_{IL}(c,t)^* C_{IL}(c) \right] +$$

$$+ \sum_{i \in I} \sum_{t \in T} \left[r_{FCR}(i,t)^* C_{FCR}(i) + r_{aFRR}(i,t)^* C_{aFRR}(i) + r_{mFRR}(i,t)^* C_{mFRR}(i) + r_{RR}(i,t)^* C_{RR}(i) \right] + \tag{8.8}$$

$$+ \sum_{c \in C} \sum_{t \in T} \left[r^{DR}_{FCR}(c,t)^* C^{DR}_{FCR}(c) + r^{DR}_{aFRR}(c,t)^* C^{DR}_{aFRR}(c) + r^{DR}_{RR}(c,t)^* C^{DR}_{RR}(c) \right]$$

The objective of the optimization problem is to minimize over all hours of the given scheduling horizon (Day-Ahead Market, Intra-Day Market, Balancing Market) the following costs (the list is in order of appearance of the various terms in the objective function):

(a) the power plants' (i) commitment costs ($C_{SU}(i)$) whenever a start-up occurs ($y(i,t)=1$);
(b) the energy ($p(i,t)$) provision costs of all power plants based on their marginal costs ($C_{EN}(i)$);
(c) the energy ($d_{IL}(c,t)$) provision costs of interruptible loads based on associated DR activation costs ($C_{IL}(c)$) per country c;
(d) the reserve costs of all power plants and for all types of reserves $r_{XX}(i,t)$, based on associated reserve offers ($C_{XX}(i)$); and,
(e) the reserve costs of DR resources for all types of reserves $r^{DR}_{XX}(c,t)$, based on associated reserve offers ($C^{DR}_{XX}(c)$).

Note that in this work reserve offers are considered equal to zero. Even though the objective function minimizes only the commitment and energy costs, reserve provision has a shadow cost equal to the Lagrangian multiplier per each type of reserve, which is an output of the model. Additionally, the optimization seeks to minimize:

(f) the load curtailment costs associated with scarcity conditions;
(g) the wind and solar spillage costs associated with low demand periods, and;
(h) the reserve deficit costs associated with non-coverage of the countries' reserve requirements, for all types of reserves.

TABLE 8.1 Fundamental aspects of the implemented UCED model.

Modelling aspect	Modelling approach	Modelling aspect	Modelling approach
Market behavior	Ideal (perfect competition)	Network	Zonal market model—NTC
Market sessions	DAM, IDM, BM	Market granularity	1 h (for all sessions)
Unit constraints	Operating states Ramp rates Min. up and down times	System constraints	Explicit representation of Reserves

The UCED model includes two general categories of constraints: unit constraints and system constraints. Unit constraints include the technical constraints of thermal generating units, of storage and of demand response. For the former, a detailed representation of their successive operating states is followed, namely the synchronization, soak, dispatchable and de-synchronization state (Marneris et al., 2017). In addition, their ramp rate limitations, minimum stable generation level, maximum capacity, and minimum up and down times are also modeled. Aggregation of generating units is made on power plant level. System constraints include the power balance in each zone, grid constraints, in the form of maximum flows between nodes (market zones) as defined by the NTC values, and reserve requirements.

A significant feature of the employed UCED formulation is the cascading representation of the Day-Ahead Market, the Intraday Market and the Balancing Market. In contrast to the classic paradigm where only the Day-Ahead Market is modeled, e.g. see ENTSO-E (2019), simulating the actual temporal sequence of market operations and respective dispatch outcomes is considered crucial for assessing flexibility. A particular reason is that contingencies are modeled when they "actually" happen, i.e. in the "real-time" balancing market, imposing their full stress on the modeled power system. In contrast, when only the Day-Ahead market is modeled, contingencies are effectively pro-actively solved, i.e. the respective generators are considered ex-ante unavailable for all the next 24 h, leading to an optimistic assessment of the capability of the system to respond to sudden power imbalances.

The sequence of the modeled market sessions is depicted in Fig. 8.2. The optimization horizon for the DAM is the 24 h of day D, and it is assumed to be cleared at 16:00 at D-1. Hence, all forecasts for variable RES and load have a lead-time of 8–32 h ahead. The Intraday Market is modeled as three sessions with an optimization horizon of 8 h each, during day D. Each session is cleared 1 h before the start of the optimization horizon resulting in forecast errors having a lead-time of 1–9 h ahead. Finally, the Balancing Market consists of 24-hourly sessions and its outcome is the real dispatch of the system.

The sequential structure of the UCED formulation determines the initial conditions of each optimization problem. For example, given that the DAM is supposed to be cleared 8 h before the day of delivery, it takes its initial conditions from the last hour of the third IDM session, which is supposed to take place 1 h before (see Fig. 8.2). IDM sessions take their initial conditions from the BM hourly results before execution, while each BM session takes its initial conditions from the immediately previous hourly BM session. A reverse order is followed for the commitment decision of power plants. Plants committed in the DAM will remain committed in the successive IDM and BM sessions, except if they experience a forced outage, and plants committed in an IDM session will remain committed in the respective BM sessions. Note that additional

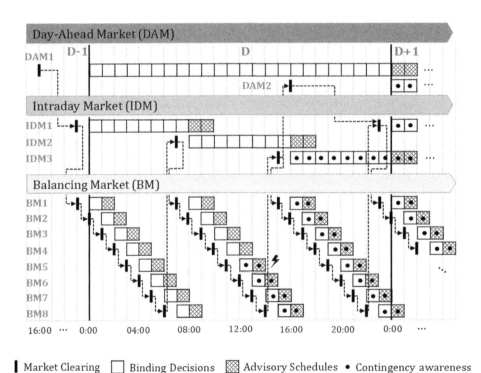

FIG. 8.2 Sequence of modeled market sessions.

plants are permitted to become committed in the IDM (medium-speed plants, e.g. gas CCGT/steam) or BM sessions (fast-start plants, e.g. hydro, gas OCGT).

Contingencies occur only in the BM. As a result, the unavailability of units experiencing forced outages is considered only in the optimization problem of the respective BM session and the successive sessions of all market segments (DAM, IDM and BM). In this way, the capability of the system to respond flexibly to such occurrences is much more realistically assessed.

The presented UCED model is employed in the context of a probabilistic Monte-Carlo framework. Several parameters of the real system are uncertain: load, hydro conditions, wind and solar generation as they are weather dependent, and unplanned outages of the different elements of the system (Billinton and Li, 1994). Different weather scenarios are considered to account for the variability and uncertainty of RES generation and demand. In addition, scenarios for forced outages of HVDC interconnectors and generators are also generated, using a two-state Markov component outage model. The combination of the different weather, hydro and forced outage scenarios, if considered stochastically independent, results in a high number of Monte Carlo scenarios to simulate. To prioritize some scenarios, i.e. the ones that can present more adequacy/flexibility issues, Monte Carlo scenarios are ranked first (i.e. prior to MC simulations) based on a severity index. This severity index consists of two terms, one accounting for capacity margin (available generating capacity versus peak net loads) and another accounting for ramping margin (available ramping capacity versus net load ramps). The higher the severity index, the more severe the specific Monte Carlo scenario is anticipated to be. In such way, the total number of Monte-Carlo scenarios actually simulated can be reduced by focusing on the most severe ones, i.e. with a higher expected probability that the examined power systems will experience adequacy/flexibility issues and assuring at the same time the convergence of the indicators.

2.3.2 Specific issues on the formulation of the UCED model

2.3.2.1 Modelling of Reserves

In many generation adequacy assessments Reserves, or Balancing Capacity, are modeled as an aggregate increase in demand, e.g. see ENTSO-E, (2019). This has two major disadvantages: First, the energy balance becomes distorted. Second, not all resources are able to offer all types of Reserves, leading to an optimistic evaluation of the capability of the system to operate in a secure way.

Dimensioning of reserves depends on the specific arrangements of the examined area. In general terms, reserves are used to cover imbalances in the system due to unexpected outages and forecast errors. The level of operating reserve needs to guarantee a safe and secure system operation. Recently, with the expansion of wind and solar generation, new techniques and models have been developed in the scientific literature to better estimate the amount of reserve required, to avoid unnecessary cost in case of oversizing reserves or the risk of load shedding in case of under-sizing reserves. Reserve sizing methods can be classified in (i) deterministic vs. probabilistic and (ii) static vs. dynamic. Deterministic methods are based on operator's experience and established assumptions and they are usually static, assuming the worst-case situation to fix the level of reserves for a long time period (typically 1 year). Probabilistic methods have been developed recently and they are based on the analysis of historical data of forecast errors (load, wind and solar generation day-ahead forecasts compared to actual realization of these variables). Depending on the type of forecasts (point forecast or probabilistic forecasts) the probabilistic reserve sizing can be less or more sophisticated. This type of reserve modelling is usually dynamic, i.e. the level of operating reserves is not constant during all hours of the day/year. Usually the empirical distribution function of solar, wind and load forecast errors are convoluted and the reserve need is determined in such a way that the forecast errors can be covered with a predefined probability (Bruninx et al., 2016). In respect to UCED implementations, static dimensioning of reserves is easier to implement. In dynamic dimensioning, the provisioned amount of reserves depends also on the dispatch of the system, i.e. the reserve volume is an output of the optimization algorithm, and not an ex-ante input to it. In this case, energy dispatch and reserve dimensioning are effectively co-optimized.

In this work the reserves' categorization followed in Europe is adopted (European Commission, 2017). Four types of Reserves are explicitly modeled, i.e. FCR, aFRR, mFRR, and RR corresponding to primary, secondary, and the last two categories tertiary reserve respectively. For FCR and aFRR a static dimensioning approach is followed, corresponding to the situation currently in Europe. The FCR amount is constant for all hours of the year for each modeled zone. aFRR aims at restoring frequency deviations, and power exchanges, caused by minute-to-minute variations of the net load. According to European Commission (2017), their dimensioning should be the outcome of a statistical analysis covering data from at least 1 year. However, due to lack of relevant data the former rule of the UCTE Code is followed and aFRR is dimensioned as a fixed percentage of the peak load (UCTE, 2004).

Reserve type mFRR is dimensioned in order to cover the loss of the largest infeed. This static approach inherently assumes annual dimensioning.

Reserve type RR aims at covering forecast errors, mainly from variable RES. It is noted that RR is not a specific Balancing Capacity product in certain control areas in Europe, especially where liquid intraday and balancing energy markets can cover such power deviations without TSO proactive intervention. Still, in the context of the proposed flexibility assessment framework it was opted to model such reserve requirement explicitly for all modeled zones, in order to have a better understanding of the capability of the examined power systems to respond to forecast errors. A simplified rule is followed for RR dimensioning corresponding to 2% of load forecast, plus 5% of wind forecast, plus 4% of PV forecast, which is a modification of the 3+5 rule proposed in National Renewable Energy Laboratory (NREL) (2010).

FCR and aFRR awards in the DAM are respected in all following markets segments, except when an awarded power plant experiences a forced outage. In such case the following market segment reallocates the respective awards. Given that FCR and aFRR are reserves with timeframes of seconds to minutes, and the resolution of the UCED model is hourly, the respective available capacity headroom is never "activated" by the algorithm, even when there is an energy shortage, i.e. they are assumed to be fully replaced by mFRR and RR within the same hour they were activated. This is representative of actual operational procedures, given that a lack of these two frequency regulation reserves would seriously endanger the integrity of the power system in the case of a major contingency.

On the contrary, mFRR is activated by the optimization algorithm inside the Balancing Market session where a contingency occurs. In the following BM session, the required minimum mFRR balancing capacity is restored. RR is also released in the BM sessions to cover power imbalances. However, in contrast to mFRR, RR is "procured" as a reserved headroom only in the DAM and the IDM sessions, and is released in the Balancing Market to cover the potential forecast errors.

Finally, for each generation technology a specific provision capability is defined per reserve type. The dispatched power output plus the cumulative upward reserve capacity awarded should be less than or equal to the rated capacity, while the dispatched power output minus the cumulative downward reserve capacity awarded should be larger than or equal to the minimum stable generation level for each unit, hour, and market segment.

2.3.2.2 Modelling of storage and DR

Following the requirements of the recent legislative package on Clean Energy for all Europeans (Clean Energy Package, CEP), most notably Regulation 2019/943 and recast Directive 2019/944, one of the future challenges to better complement the European resource adequacy assessment is to develop methodologies for modelling storage and demand response (ENTSO-E, 2019).

Modelling of large hydro pumped storage connected to the transmission grid has been included already since many years in UCED studies. However, explicit modelling of more recent energy storage technologies is quite challenging, especially since most of them, e.g. battery energy storage systems (BESS), are mainly connected to the distribution grid. Modelling an energy storage unit explicitly in such low level for resource adequacy assessment is almost impossible, unless one aggregates many such units and assume that they can be operated in coordination as one large energy storage. Currently, most of the BESS connected in the system are either residential/commercial units coupled with small distributed vRES, larger industrial units mostly for back-up purposes, or units as integral part of large vRES power plants. Regarding residential BESS, these are included in the modelling of implicit demand response, described in the following paragraphs. Industrial back-up energy storage does not contribute to resource adequacy of the whole system, whereas BESS integrated in vRES power plants operate with the goal to optimize the revenues of the plant. On the other hand, technologies such as thermal energy storage and power-to-gas that can be bulk enough to operate autonomously directly connected to the transmission grid are still not widely used. A popular way to model storage in general is to assume that they can operate like a pumped-hydro plant using appropriate power up and down ramp rates and energy constraints, without however any hydrological constraints related to climate conditions or dependence on upstream or downstream water reservoirs.

There are two general categories of Demand Response (DR): implicit (or price-based) and explicit (or incentive-based). Implicit DR refers to a situation when consumers choose to be exposed to time-varying electricity prices (and/or grid tariffs), which reflect the value and cost of electricity (and/or transportation, respectively), in different time periods (EURELECTRIC, 2015; European Commission, 2016). Having this information on dynamic pricing, consumers can decide whether to react, for example by shifting their consumption or storing their excess vRES-produced energy. These dynamic prices are offered by electricity suppliers and can range from a simple two-tariff scheme for day and night, up to very dynamic hourly or even sub-hourly prices. There are three main options for implicit DR, mostly applied for electricity prices, but in some cases also for distribution grid tariffs: (a) time-of-use (TOU) pricing, (b) critical peak pricing (CPP), and (c) real-time pricing (RTP). At the moment, TOU is used across Europe, and has been so since the 1970s and 1980s, so that the actual impact of this scheme can be sometimes considered embedded in the measured demand. CPP and RTP is implemented in just few EU countries, e.g. Spain, Estonia, Nordic countries (Ecofys, 2018; EURELECTRIC, 2017; Smart Energy Demand Coalition, 2017), due to lack of available signals from the suppliers but also due to lack of technical capabilities from the consumers. The ongoing rollout of smart meters aims at increasing the potential of implicit DR.

The main impact of implicit DR is load shifting and peak shaving (or peak clipping). In the former, the demand is reduced during peak hours and increased proportionally during off-peak hours of the same day, whereas in the latter, the consumption is reduced below an upper limit of power consumption. Since it is widely accepted that implicit DR leads mainly to load shifting and much less to peak clipping, the calculated DR potential in each country was split 90–10%, so that 90% was attributed to load shifting and 10% to peak clipping.

Modelling of Load Shifting in this work is done as a centralized decision-making process in the DAM, following the same schedule in IDM and BM. Pre-defined thresholds limit the maximum shifted load in positive and negative direction for each country and each time interval of the DAM. For the latter, the implicit DR potential may vary a lot during the day, thus it should be weighted accordingly. Therefore, in our model we assume that the demand reduction potential follows the trend of the load curve profile, by applying a normalization factor. This factor is not static for all days, but it is calculated dynamically for each model node, based on the respective estimated load curve for each day. With proper constraints in our model we also ensure that load deviations due to load shifting are balanced during the day, i.e. the load-shifting potential acts as a virtual storage unit that at the beginning and the end of each day must have no stored energy. A final constraint is applied for the maximum daily energy that can be shifted in each country.

Modelling of Peak Clipping is also done as a centralized decision-making process in the DAM and following similar constraints, however, there is obviously a threshold only for downward direction. At this point, it must be noted that a key assumption for the peak clipping in the future is that the peaks are kept constant, since they are based on the same sensitivity of load to temperature. The temperature dependence of load is analyzed in Section 2.3.2.5, where it is mentioned that the main reason for this dependence is heating and cooling. However, continuous improvements in energy efficiency will lead to better insulated buildings in the future, and thus in lower load sensitivity to temperature. In that sense, the modelling assumptions of peak clipping should be re-examined in the future.

Explicit DR refers to a situation when consumers or DR aggregators are participating and providing DR resources on the wholesale energy, reserves/balancing, and/or capacity markets (European Commission, 2016). In principle, consumers are offered dedicated incentives (fixed or time-varying) separate or in addition to their electricity rate. Their participation is usually enabled through dedicated control systems in response to signals sent by the TSO or energy supplier or to market conditions. These incentive-based DR schemes are usually implemented by industrial and large commercial customers. In this work the impact of explicit DR is evaluated with four mechanisms: (a) interruptible loads, (b) DR participation in Frequency Containment Reserves (FCR), (c) DR Participation in automatic Frequency Restoration Reserves (aFRR), and (d) DR Participation in Replacement Reserves (RR).

Large industrial facilities can participate currently in dedicated Interruptibility programmes offered by TSOs, by signing contracts, usually yearly ones, for load curtailment obligation during critical days of the year. These contracts usually include an availability price (€/MW/year) as a reward for availability, and an activation price (€/MWh) granted only when a curtailment is requested (accompanied with penalties for non-compliance). In our model, we assume yearly auctions for the Interruptibility contracts. For each country, constraints are applied for the maximum (contracted) Interruptibility potential and other contract specifications, like the maximum duration for load interruption within a day or the maximum frequency of interruptions in the course of a year. In order to determine the most critical days and avoid over-utilization of Interruptibility programmes, a data pre-process specifies the days of each MC year with the highest anticipated peak net load (i.e. load minus vRES production) per country, and these days are flagged as candidates for load interruption during the main UCED simulations. Curtailment is requested in advance of time by the TSOs; thus, the activation of load interruption is modeled as a centralized decision-making process embedded in the DAM of the pre-determined critical days. The DAM scheduling mechanism determines whether the load will be curtailed, based on the contracted activation cost of interruptible loads (assumed the same for all loads) in conjunction with other DAM input parameters. Once a load is selected for interruption based on the DAM results, it follows the curtailment programme in IDM and BM, as well.

DR resources in general can participate in Reserves provision at least in the upward direction, i.e. by load curtailment. In this work DR is modeled having the capability to offer upward FCR, aFRR, and RR. Provision of mFRR was not considered for reliability reasons, since mFRR activated for compensating imbalances due to contingencies may need to remain so for prolonged periods. For each type of Reserve and zone, a maximum provision capability by DR is introduced as a constraint to the optimization algorithm.

2.3.2.3 Modelling of maintenance operations and hydro operation

Before running the UCED model, maintenance schedules and hydro availability targets are optimized. Maintenance requirements of power plants have a cyclical pattern. The maintenance optimization problem places programmed shutdown of generation units along the year to guarantee the same level of available capacity reserve for all weeks of the year within a region (group of countries). The objective function to be minimized in this reliability-oriented problem is as follows (for various formulations with reliability objectives in maintenance scheduling the interested reader is referred to Dalah and McDonald (1997), Yare and Venayagamoorthy (2010), Suresh and Kumarappan (2013), Perez-Canto and Rubio-Romero (2013):

$$\text{Minimize} \sum_{w \in W} \left| \sum_{c \in C^g} (r_{Maint}(c, w)) - \frac{1}{52} * \left(\sum_{w' \in W} \sum_{c \in C^g} (r_{Maint}(c, w')) \right) \right| \forall g \in G \tag{8.9}$$

where $r_{Maint}(c, w)$ is the available excess capacity over weekly (w) peak load of country c, and g is the relevant region.

At this stage, non-dispatchable generation technologies do not contribute to the available capacity, while run-of river and reservoir and pumped hydro power plants contribute with a fixed-amount capacity credit. Additionally, each modeled country can import/export reserve capacity from/to other countries belonging to the same region. Nevertheless, capacity exchanges for the purpose of maintenance are limited to a pre-defined percentage (e.g. 20%) of the respective NTC. As to the mathematical formulation, a MILP problem is constructed given the employment of maintenance binary variables. Constraints in this problem include a limit to the number of power plants scheduled for maintenance simultaneously in each country, the number of periods that a generating unit is not available because of maintenance (set to one), and the length of the maintenance period (being equal to a technology specific duration).

Hydro units are aggregated into three main categories per country, "Hydro Pumped Storage," "Hydro Water Reservoir" and "Hydro Run-of-river" (RoR). Three distinctive hydro conditions are considered for each country: "dry," "normal" and "wet," along with their associated probabilities of occurrence. The pan-European perimeter is divided in two regions—the Nordic region and the rest of the countries—considering that dry/normal/wet hydro conditions are correlated among the countries within each region. Thereby, the probabilistic assessment considers an overall composition of nine hydro conditions (ENTSO-E, 2016). For each climatic-hydrologic scenario, a hydro mid-term scheduler provides a priori the daily hydro production/pumping availabilities. The main motivation for the hydro model used is twofold: (a) to perform an efficient hydro-thermal coordination in a longer (monthly) scheduling horizon prior to the detailed UCED simulations; and (b) to use directly accessible data for the majority of European countries (i.e. monthly hydro MWh), instead of other historic hydrologic data which are not often available for such a large case study.

The following historical data are obtained from ENTSO-E Data Portal (ENTSO-E, 2020) and UN Data (United Nations, 2020) for each type of condition (dry, normal and wet):

- monthly total hydro production (MWh);
- monthly hydro RoR production (MWh);
- monthly hydro pumped storage consumption (pumping in MWh);
- total hydro net generating capacity (installed capacity in MW);
- hydro RoR net generating capacity (installed capacity in MW);
- hydro pumped storage net generating capacity (installed capacity in MW).

Projections for the reference year are done by scaling the historical monthly production of hydro RoR and hydro water reservoir and pumping (consumption) of the pumped storage plants, according to the change on the installed capacity between the historical year and the target year. The hydro-thermal optimal coordination is then executed sequentially for each month of each scenario, as a linear relaxation of the UCED model described in Section 2.3.1. Its scope is to optimally allocate to each day of the month the monthly hydro production and pumped storage consumption quantities projected for the reference year, while considering several thermal power plant and reserve contribution restrictions. The resulting daily hydro production/pumping availabilities (in terms of MWh) are then used as maximum daily limits during the main Monte Carlo simulations (UCED model).

It is noted that these daily limits can be exceeded, if this overutilization is caused by the activation of RR or mFRR reserves in the Balancing Market. The excess is recovered on equal portions during the following 7 days of simulation.

2.3.2.4 Representation of non-explicitly modeled countries

Power exchanges with non-explicitly modeled countries are modeled ex-ante based on historical data. This is the approach followed also in ENTSO-E (2019). In addition, to avoid cases when a modeled country with scarcity conditions in a given hour (e.g. load curtailment) is exporting energy to a non-explicitly modeled country, due to a predefined exchange imposed to the interconnection, a certain level of flexibility is introduced allowing for an appropriate calibration of the pre-defined exchange. The calibration is associated with a given cost, which is lower than the load curtailment cost but higher than the resources' marginal costs, thus it only takes place in order to avoid load curtailment.

It is noted that the reduced number of countries modeled in detail in the presented example provides pessimistic results especially for nodes weakly interconnected with other explicitly modeled countries.

2.3.2.5 Modelling of demand

For an appropriate adequacy assessment, modelling of the demand is an important aspect. It is necessary to develop a methodology to model accurately the dependence of demand on temperature, especially in the current years of the energy transition and toward an increased electrification. This is mainly due to the increasing use of electric heating and cooling, which partially explains the surge in demand observed during cold spells in winter and/or heat waves in summer. Thus, the widespread use of electric heating and cooling combined with the observed hotter summers and harsher winters (attributed among others to climate change) might lead to higher demand fluctuations from 1 year to the other. Based on the above, a correct simulation of weather (temperature) changes is deemed necessary, in order to estimate the respective changes of the behavior of the electricity demand.

In our methodology, we use a simple linear model, where all possible temperatures are divided into three zones, a "heating zone," a "comfort zone" and a "cooling zone," with a different temperature gradient dP/dT for each one. The rationale behind this model is that for every temperature zone the (average) reaction of people toward temperature changes is different. For the "heating zone" dP/dT is negative, i.e. the power consumption increases while temperature is decreasing. For the "cooling zone" dP/dT is positive, i.e. the power consumption increases while temperature is increasing. For the intermediate "comfort zone" dP/dT is assumed to be zero, i.e. no significant change in the power consumption is observed for changes in the temperature. The same is valid for the "saturation zones," i.e. very low and very high temperatures. It is obvious that the actual temperature values that define the above zones and the respective dP/dT are different for each country and can be calculated using historical data for temperature and demand.

After defining the above parameters, historical data for the daily average temperatures and the hourly load demand for each country can be used to create hourly demand time-series for different climatic scenarios, adjusted with the load-temperature model. The above methodology is like the one that ENTSO-e uses in the MAF (ENTSO-E, 2019). In our model, we use the MERRA-2 model from NASA for the daily average temperatures for 30 historical years (1985–2014). The data are correlated with the Renewables. Ninja database, which we have used for the wind and solar power production.

2.4 Examined indicators for the detailed analysis of power system operational flexibility

In adequacy (reliability) studies, it is important to assess if there will be enough resource capacity to supply all the requested demand. Loss of Load Expectation (LOLE) and Expected Energy Not Served (EENS) are the most common indicators to estimate the risks of not supplying all customers. LOLE represents the number of hours per year in which it is statistically expected that the supply will not meet demand while EENS is the expected energy not supplied by the resources of the system in periods of loss of load. These are average values along all the simulated years, so the real values could differ depending on the specific circumstances of every year. Stress system periods can occur not only at periods of peak demand. The increased penetration of renewable energy generation in the system requires steeper ramps, deeper turndowns of conventional generators and shorter peaks in system operations. On the other hand, periods of low demand combined with high renewable generation are increasing and could result in tight situations due to local congestions, low inertia and inadequate sources for frequency and voltage regulation. It is important to assess the system, not only at peak demand periods but also at any time. For the same reason, calculation of LOLE and EENS is not enough to assess fully the flexibility needs of the system. In this work, we propose a set of flexibility indicators to analyze the different aspects of power system flexibility such as ramping, frequency control, inertia, etc. The probabilistic non-modeled based indicators to assess flexibility requirements and technical capabilities of resources have been already described in Sections 2.1 and 2.2, respectively. Following, the rest of the indicators, which are based on simulation results to consider for the operational status of the different assets, are presented in more detail. Thus, the value of flexibility resources can be fully analyzed, while assessing the impact of policy, market, technical and operational arrangements, such as reserve dimensioning, planned and unplanned outages, transmission congestions and active participation of demand response and RES into markets.

Loss of Load Expectation (LOLE): Expected number of hours in a given period (year) in which load curtailment occurs

$$LOLE(c) = \frac{\sum_{s=1}^{S}\left(N^{LOLD}(s,c)\cdot pr_s\right)}{\sum_{s=1}^{S} pr_s} \tag{8.10}$$

where $LOLE(c)$ is the loss of load expectation in country c; $N^{LOLD}(s,c)$ is the loss of load duration associated with the s-th Monte Carlo scenario simulation for country c and pr_s is the probability of occurrence associated with the s-th Monte Carlo scenario. It is important to notice that the denominator, $\sum_{s=1}^{S} pr_s$ could be minor than one, owing to the fact that simulated scenarios could be a subset of the scenario space.

Expected Energy Not Served Energy (EENS): Expected unserved energy by the resources of the system due to system capacity or flexibility limitations, EENS_cap and EENS_flex respectively.

$$EENS(c) = \frac{\sum_{s=1}^{S}\left(\sum_{t=1}^{8760} ENS(s,c,t)\right)\cdot pr_s)}{\sum_{s=1}^{S} pr_s} = EENS\_cap_c + EENS\_flex_c$$

$$= \frac{\sum_{s=1}^{S}\left(\sum_{t=1}^{8760} ENS\_CAP(s,c,t)\right)\cdot pr_s)}{\sum_{s=1}^{S} pr_s} + \frac{\sum_{s=1}^{S}\left(\sum_{t=1}^{8760} ENS\_FLEX(s,c,t)\right)\cdot pr_s)}{\sum_{s=1}^{S} pr_s} \tag{8.11}$$

where $\left(\left(\sum_{t=1}^{8760} ENS(s,c,t)\right)\right.$ is the energy not served associated with the s-th Monte Carlo scenario simulation in country c and pr_s is the probability of occurrence associated with the s-th Monte Carlo scenario. $\sum_{t=1}^{8760} ENS_C AP(s,c,t)$ and $\sum_{t=1}^{8760} ENS_F LEX(s,c,t)$ are the energy not served due to capacity and flexibility issues respectively associated with the s-th Monte Carlo scenario. The procedure to distinguish between these two values and compute the indicators is as follows: (i) identify hours with load curtailment, t; (ii) for these specific hours compute, for each online power plant i, the maximum power output increase $P_i^{max}(t) - p_i(t) - r_i^{FCR_{Up}}(t) - r_i^{aFRR_{Up}}(t) - r_i^{mRR}(t)$; (iii) if the maximum power output increase of all online power plants is higher than the load curtailment during hour t, the load curtailment is attributed solely to flexibility issues; i.e. theoretically, there is enough online capacity to cover the load, so $ENS\_CAP(s,c,t) = 0$ and $ENS\_FLEX(s,c,t) =$ load curtailment at time t. Otherwise, $ENS\_CAP(s,c,t)$ is equal to the excess of the load curtailment over the total maximum power output increase of all online power plants and the remaining amount of load curtailment is attributed to $ENS\_FLEX(s,c,t)$.

Renewable Energy Curtailments Expectation (RECE): Expected number of hours in a given period (year) in which renewable generation curtailment occurs.

$$RECE(c) = \frac{\sum_{s=1}^{S}\left(N^{REC}(s,c)\cdot pr_s\right)}{\sum_{s=1}^{S} pr_s} \tag{8.12}$$

where $RECE(c)$ is the renewable energy curtailments expectation in country c; $N^{REC}(s,c)$ is the renewable energy curtailments duration associated with the s-th Monte Carlo scenario simulation; pr_s is the probability of occurrence associated with the s-th Monte Carlo scenario.

Expected Renewable Energy Curtailments (EREC): Expected energy curtailment of renewable generation due to system flexibility issues.

$$EREC(c) = \frac{\sum_{s=1}^{S}\left(REC(s,c) \cdot pr_s\right)}{\sum_{s=1}^{S} pr_s} \tag{8.13}$$

where $EREC(c)$ is the expected renewable energy curtailment of country c; $REC(s,c)$ is the total curtailment of renewable generation due to system flexibility issues associated with the s-th Monte Carlo simulation.

Loss of Reserve Expectation (LORE): LORE is the expected number of hours in a given period (year) in which reserve curtailment occurs due to system capacity or flexibility limitations. It is estimated for each type of reserve and direction (upward and downward).

$$LORE\_XX_c = \frac{\sum_{s=1}^{S}\left(N\_XX_{sc}^{LOR} \cdot pr_s\right)}{\sum_{s=1}^{S} pr_s} \tag{8.14}$$

where $N\_XX_{sc}^{LOR}$ is the duration of the loss of the type of reserve analyzed (XX) associated with the s-th Monte Carlo scenario and pr_s is the Monte Carlo s-scenario probability.

Expected Reserve Not Served (ERNS): ERNS is the expected reserve not served due to system capacity or flexibility limitations. ERNS is calculated for each type of reserve and direction.

$$ERNS\_XX_c = \frac{\sum_{s=1}^{S}\left(RNS\_XX_{sc} \cdot pr_s\right)}{\sum_{s=1}^{S} pr_s} \tag{8.15}$$

where RNS_XX_{sc} varies depending on the reserve type analyzed (XX) associated with the s-th Monte Carlo simulation respectively.

Non-Synchronous Penetration Ratio (SNSP): An additional concern in the transition to a low carbon system is the evolution of system inertia which is an important element of frequency stability.

$$SNSP(s,c,t) = \frac{\sum P(s,c,t)_{in_{inverter}}}{\sum P(s,c,t)_{out}} = \frac{W(s,c,t) + PV(s,c,t) + HVDC(s,c,t)_{import}}{L(s,c,t) + P(s,c,t)_{export}} \tag{8.16}$$

where $W(s,c,t)$ and $PV(s,c,t)$ refers to wind and photovoltaic power generation, $L(s,c,t)$ is the system demand, and $HVDC(s,c,t)_{import}$ is the imported power through high voltage direct current (HVDC) interconnections, while $P(s,c,t)_{export}$ is the exported power, all of them at time step t. It is worth mentioning that inverters can emulate system inertia, so when this capability will be implemented, the numerator should be reduced accordingly (the emulation is different depending on the system the inverter is connected to: wind, PV or HVDC interconnection). For example, since 2006 Hydro Quebec Transénergie has required system inertia emulation from wind farms with rated output greater than 10 MW (Hydro-Québec TransÉnergie, 2009).

Along with the above indicators, which focus on the operational flexibility of the power system, two more are also included focusing on market aspects. These are the Negative Market Prices Expectation (NMPE) and the Expected Market Prices Volatility (EMPV).

Negative Market Prices Expectation (NMPE): NMPE is the expected number of hours in a given period (year) in which negative market prices occur.

$$NMPE_c = \frac{\sum_{s=1}^{S}\left(N_{sc}^{NMP} \cdot pr_s\right)}{\sum_{s=1}^{S} pr_s} \tag{8.17}$$

where *NMPEc* is the negative price expectation in country c; N_{sc}^{NMP} is the number of hours with negative prices in country c and s-th Monte Carlo scenario.

Expected Market Prices Volatility (EMPV): EMPV is the expected standard deviation of market clearing prices in a given year measured in €/MWh

$$EMPV_c = \frac{\sum_{s=1}^{S}\left(MPV_{sc} \cdot pr_s\right)}{\sum_{s=1}^{S}pr_s} \tag{8.18}$$

where MPV_{sc} is the standard deviation of market clearing prices associated with the s-th Monte Carlo simulation.

3 Methodology application

3.1 Case study

In this chapter, we apply the proposed methodology to a European case study for year 2025. The following 21 European countries are modeled explicitly: Austria (AT), Belgium (BE), Switzerland (CH), Czechia (CZ), Germany (DE), Spain (ES), Finland (FI), France (FR), Great Britain (GB), Greece (GR), Hungary (HU), Ireland (IE), Italy (IT), Luxembourg (LU), Netherlands (NL), Norway (NO), Poland (PL), Portugal (PT), Sweden (SE), Slovenia (SI), and Slovakia (SK). The selection was based on data availability, but also considered relevant particularities, such as high RES generation (e.g. DE, ES), flexible (e.g. AT, CH, NO, SE) or inflexible (FR) generation portfolios, foreseen future deficits in generation capacity (e.g. GR due to the withdrawal of several lignite generating units), weak interconnections (ES, GB, IE), and DR opportunities (BE, FI, FR, NL). The map of the network is presented in Fig. 8.3, while the publicly available sources for the data used for the modelling are shown in Table 8.2.

4 Results

This section contains results of the test case performed with PHOEBE. The results are comparatively presented for two cases, with and without demand response, to investigate the added value of active consumers in the energy transition. The results are also presented following the different steps of the methodology.

4.1 Preliminary evaluation of flexibility requirements

Fig. 8.4 shows the results of RLPI and REPI for the different meteorological years. The box plots provide a compact view of the main characteristics of these indicators. REPI which represents the average fraction of demand covered by wind and solar energy along the year, shows a more symmetric distribution than the RLPI which collects the highest hourly value for each year. Based on these indices, vRES curtailments are preliminary expected in DE, ES, GB, IE, NL and PT.

4.2 Assessment of technical capability of resources to provide flexibility

Following the preliminary estimation of the flexibility system requirements, the next step is to analyze the technical capacity present in the system based on the Flexibility Capacity Ratio of each flexibility resource. Fig. 8.5 shows the flexibility chart for six different countries. It is important to see the flexibility resource diversification (which flexible resources coexist in the different countries) and the installed capacity of each of them in relation with the peak demand. Regarding DR, although it seems not playing an important role, we will see later that its impact on the value of the different indicators, which is not negligible.

4.3 Detailed analysis of power system operational flexibility

The EENS indicator as well as its decomposition into capacity and flexibility parts are presented in Fig. 8.6. While for IE and NO most or all the EENS is attributed to capacity deficits, for ES, GB and PT a significant part of EENS is attributed to flexibility issues. Such differentiation is important for the design of policy instruments (e.g. capacity mechanisms) and/or

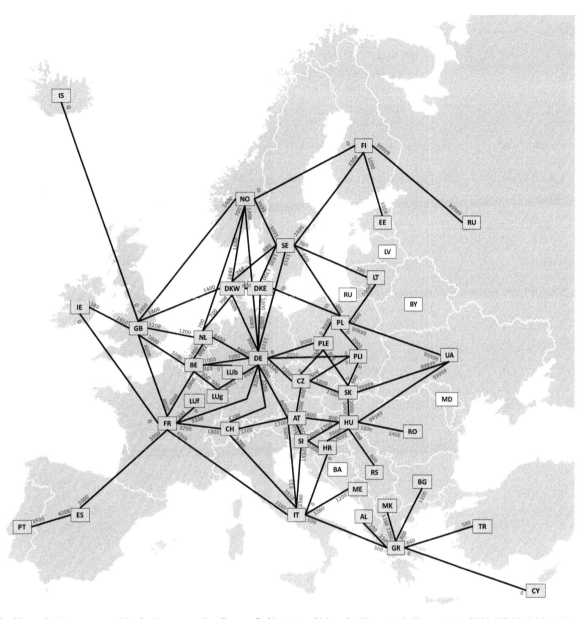

FIG. 8.3 Network adequacy capacities for the case study. *(Source: Bakirtzis, A., Biskas, P., Marneris, I., Ntomaris, A., 2018. DR Model for Adequacy Procedure. Final Report (D5). (Dissemination Internal to European Commission). European Commission.)*

TABLE 8.2 Data sources used in the case study.

Category	Input data	Source(s)
Network	Net Transfer Capacities (NTC) and pre-defined commercial exchanges for 2025	ENTSO-E, Mid-Term Adequacy Forecast (MAF) 2016[a]
Load related data	2-m daily average temperatures for each cell of the global grid	MERRA-2 database (NASA source)[b]
Load related data	Load-temperature sensitivity parameters for the 21 explicitly modeled countries	ENTSO-E, Winter Outlook Report 2016/2017 and Summer Review 2016[c]
Load related data	Population of cities/countries	City Population[d]
Load related data	Hourly load under normal climatic conditions for 2025	ENTSO-E, Mid-Term Adequacy Forecast (MAF) 2016

Continued

TABLE 8.2 Data sources used in the case study—cont'd

Category	Input data	Source(s)
Wind and solar	30 historical years (1985–2014) of hourly correlated wind and PV solar data	Renewables.Ninja database[e]
Wind and solar	National wind and solar installed capacity projections for 2025	ENTSO-E, Mid-Term Adequacy Forecast (MAF) 2016
Power plants related	List of generating units and installed capacities per unit (for 2015)	ENTSO-E Transparency Platform[f]
Power plants related	Unit and plant capacities, plant aggregation	Global Energy Observatory,[g] Open Power System Data[h]
Power plants related	Fuel and CO_2 prices	ENTSO-E, Mid-Term Adequacy Forecast (MAF) 2016, ENTSO-E, Ten-Year Network Development Plan (TYNDP) 2016
DR potential	DR potential for EU member states	Smart Energy Demand Coalition (2017), Bertoldi et al. (2016)
DR potential	Evolution of Implicit DR potential for Business as Usual (BAU) and three Policy scenarios for 2020, 2025, and 2030	EU DG Energy, "Impact assessment study on downstream flexibility, price flexibility, DR & smart metering (European Commission, 2016)
DR potential	Techno-economic data for Interruptible Loads (theoretic potential, activation cost, frequency and duration of interruption)	EU DG Energy, "Impact assessment study on downstream flexibility, price flexibility, DR & smart metering (European Commission, 2016; Gils, 2014)
Hydro related	Hydrological years (dry, wet, normal)	ENTSO-E, Mid-Term Adequacy Forecast (MAF) 2016
Hydro related	Monthly total hydro production (MWh); Monthly hydro RoR production (MWh); Monthly hydro pumped storage consumption (pumping in MWh); Total hydro net generating capacity (installed capacity in MW); Hydro RoR net generating capacity (installed capacity in MW); Hydro pumped storage net generating capacity (installed capacity in MW)	ENTSO-E Data Portal,[i] UN Data[j]
Forced outages and maintenance schedules	Forced Outage Rates (FOR)	ENTSO-E Winter Outlook Report 2016/2017
Forced outages and maintenance schedules	Unavailability rate for each HVDC interconnector (6%)	ENTSO-E, Mid-Term Adequacy Forecast (MAF) 2016
Predefined commercial exchanges in the borders with non-explicitly modeled countries	Real hourly commercial exchanges	ENTSO-E Transparency Platform

[a]*https://www.entsoe.eu/Documents/SDC%20documents/MAF/ENSTOE_MAF_2016.pdf.*
[b]*http://disc.sci.gsfc.nasa.gov/daac-bin/FTPSubset2.pl.*
[c]*https://www.entsoe.eu/Documents/Publications/SDC/2016-wor_report.pdf.*
[d]*https://www.citypopulation.de/Europe.html.*
[e]*https://www.renewables.ninja/downloads.*
[f]*https://transparency.entsoe.eu/generation/r2/installedCapacityPerProductionUnit/show.*
[g]*http://www.globalenergyobservatory.org/select.php?tgl=Edit.*
[h]*http://www.open-power-system-data.org/.*
[i]*https://www.entsoe.eu/data/data-portal/production/Pages/default.aspx.*
[j]*http://data.un.org/Data.aspx?d=EDATA&f=cmID%3AEC.*

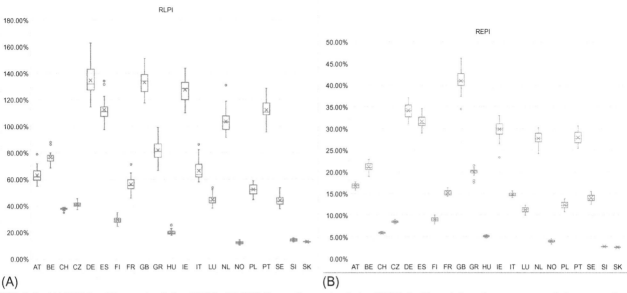

FIG. 8.4 (A) RES Load Penetration Index (RLPI). (B) RES Energy Penetration Index (REPI). Inside each box, there are two symbols representing: average (x point) and median (line). Outliers are represented as individual points.

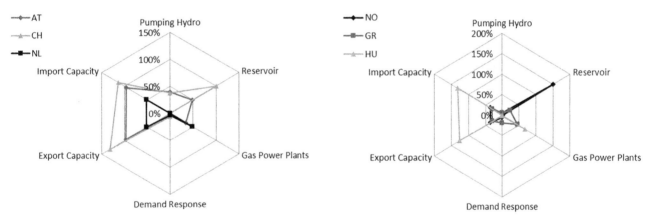

FIG. 8.5 Flexibility chart for different countries. The percentage represents the ratio between the capacity of a specific flexible resource and the peak demand. Demand response accounts only for explicit demand response.

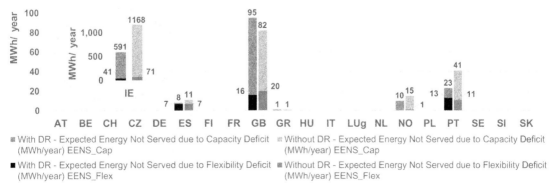

FIG. 8.6 Decomposition of Expected Energy Not Served, with and without DR.

regulatory/market interventions (e.g. introduction of flexibility products), and for finding an optimum balance between them.

Similar to EENS, ERNS indicate the expected deficits in upward or downward reserves, in MWh/year. The total deficits per country for all types of upward (positive values) and downward (negative values) reserves modeled by PHOEBE are recorded in Fig. 8.7. The results indicate a significant adequacy issue for upward reserves for IE (further disaggregated for the case with DR into 0.112, 2.034 and 11.996 GWh/year of FCR, aFRR and mFRR respectively). A great improvement in upward reserve adequacy can be noted for GB when considering the participation of DR, since the potential of DR in this country is significant. Currently in GB almost all balancing services are open to demand response.

An interesting result of our test case is that the expected total reserve not served in downward direction is larger with demand response than without demand response. Considering implicit and explicit demand response in the model impacts on the number of generators committed. This factor reduces the availability of downward regulation from generators in real time. This observation highlights the importance of modelling the temporal sequence of electricity markets and not only the Day-Ahead timeframe, and the need of careful design of DR participation in electricity markets, such as the potential necessity to offer downward regulation services too.

The LOLE indicator in hours/year is presented in Fig. 8.8. Accordingly, the LORE metric in hours/year is presented in Fig. 8.9 for the total upward reserves and in Fig. 8.10 for the total downward reserves in each country. The obtained patterns are like that of EENS and ERNS, respectively.

In most of the countries the EENS/ERNS obtained are, in general, low and this is attributed mainly to the following reasons:

(a) The three-market operation scheme (Day-Ahead Market, Intraday Market, Balancing Market) modeled by PHOEBE, follows a pragmatic approach in which the system is gradually adapted to changing conditions on load, wind and solar power production. Specifically, the Balancing Market assumes perfect load, wind and solar forecasts. However, the Day-Ahead and Intraday Market models use load, wind and solar power forecasts with associated forecast errors that are a function of the forecast lead time and the standard deviation of historical forecast error values. This adaptation (e.g. commitment of additional plants in the Intraday Market whenever needed) is a positive factor in adequacy assessment.

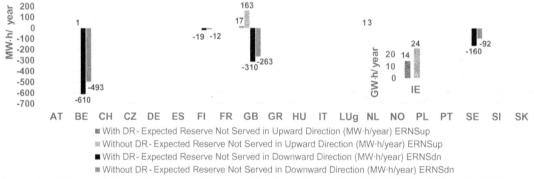

FIG. 8.7 Expected total Reserve Not Served in upward and downward direction, with and without DR. (Note: For IE the unit is GWh/year, while for all the other countries is MWh/year.)

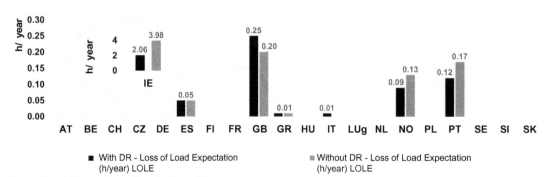

FIG. 8.8 Loss of Load Expectation, with and without DR.

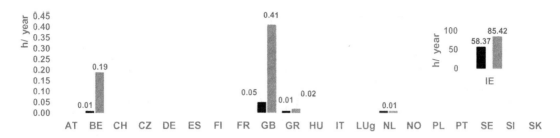

FIG. 8.9 Loss of Reserve Expectation in upward direction, with and without DR.

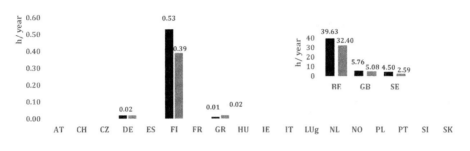

FIG. 8.10 Loss of Reserve Expectation in downward direction, with and without DR.

(b) The scheduling of different types of reserves (FCR, aFRR, mFRR, RR), and mainly the activation in the Balancing Market of (a) RR in a continuous (hour-by-hour) manner, and (b) mFRR whenever a contingency occurs, is another crucial factor for the low EENS obtained.

(c) The amount of reserves secured in the scheduling levels (Day-Ahead Market, Intraday Market) plays also a crucial role, since it determines the number of committed plants in the scheduling phase, and thus the reaction of the system in the real-time Balancing Market phase. This case study considers a rather safe-side operation in terms of scheduled reserves for all countries.

(d) The flexibility provided regarding the daily energy limits of reservoir and pumped hydro discussed in Section 2.3.2.3 helps the system to avoid energy deficits in hours with scarcity conditions.

(e) The introduction of a certain level of flexibility in the interconnections with non-explicitly modeled countries, which allows for a calibration of the pre-defined exchanges whenever these exchanges are in the wrong direction.

Fig. 8.11 presents the expected curtailment of renewable generation (wind and solar generation) per country due to system flexibility issues, while Fig. 8.12 presents the average number of hours that such curtailments are expected. The results imply some systematic flexibility problems for GB, IE and NO, while vRES curtailments are either non-existent or rather insignificant for the rest of the countries. Regarding the case of NO, it is emphasized that although it contains a hydro dominated power fleet (which is a flexible capacity source), the model detects possible renewable energy production curtailment. This counter-intuitive result is further discussed in Section 5.2.3.

Table 8.3 compares the Expected Renewable Energy Curtailments (with and without DR) with the initial assessment of the renewable energy risk curtailment (RCR) for the countries with positive values. The added value of the interconnection capacity, pumping hydro and the single market can be seen for DE, GB and ES where the risk of curtailment is reduced significantly. On the other hand, the UCED results indicate a small risk of vRES curtailments in countries where the non-modeled based indicators do not, e.g. GR and LU. An explanation for that is that the UCED optimization algorithm penalizes more reserve curtailment, including for downward reserves, than vRES curtailment.

Directly associated with EREC, NMPE provides the expected number of hours in a given period (year) in which negative market prices occur. During these hours, the market is not able to accommodate the excess energy generated coming from inflexible power plants and variable renewable energy production. Thus, in Fig. 8.13 the same pattern is obtained with the case of EREC presented earlier, while the positive effect of DR is also apparent in this case.

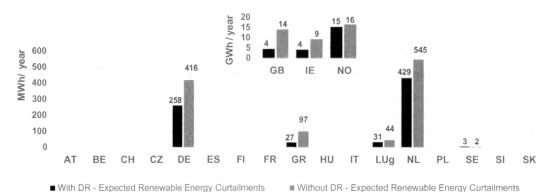

FIG. 8.11 Expected Renewable Energy Curtailments (EREC), with and without DR. (Note: For GB, IE and NO the unit is GWh/year, while for all the other countries is MWh/year.)

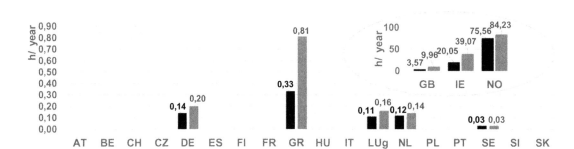

FIG. 8.12 Renewable Energy Curtailments Expectation (RECE), with and without DR.

TABLE 8.3 Comparison of Renewable energy Risk Curtailment (RCR), and Expected Renewable Energy curtailment (EREC) with and without demand response.

Country	Renewable Curtailment Risk (MWh/year)	Without DR—Expected Renewable Energy Curtailments (MWh/year)	With DR—Expected Renewable Energy Curtailments (MWh/year)
	RCR	EREC	EREC
DE	390,325 (0.206%)	416 (0.000%)	258 (0.000%)
ES	31,224 (0.034%)	0 (0.000%)	0 (0.000%)
GB	338,342 (0.239%)	13,953 (0.010%)	4340 (0.003%)
GR	0 (0.000%)	97 (0.001%)	27 (0.000%)
IE	21,970 (0.171%)	9190 (0.072%)	4052 (0.032%)
LU	0 (0.000%)	44 (0.007%)	31 (0.005%)
NL	2328 (0.007%)	545 (0.002%)	429 (0.001%)
NO	0 (0.000%)	16,445 (0.299%)	15,246 (0.278%)
PT	4487 (0.029%)	0 (0.000%)	0 (0.000%)

In parenthesis their percentage in respect to the vRES (wind and solar) average annual production potential.

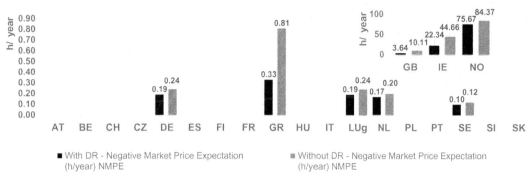

FIG. 8.13 Negative Market Price Expectation, with and without DR.

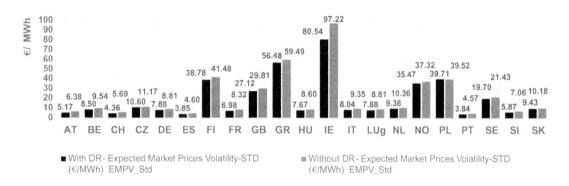

FIG. 8.14 Expected Market Price Standard Deviation, with and without DR.

An additional important indicator regarding market prices is the EMPV which provides the expected standard deviation of market clearing prices in the course of the year. The EMPV obtained for all countries is presented in Fig. 8.14, where the positive effect of DR is recorded once again: reduction of EMPV as a result of the participation of DR. A high volatility is noted in countries with more frequent load/reserve curtailments or renewable energy spillage (e.g. IE, GB, NO). High volatility is also noted in modeled countries which are connected with neighboring non-explicitly modeled countries, as for example FI, GR, and PL. This is partially expected, since these countries are radially interconnected with inner countries of the case study area, but it is also incurred due to modelling assumptions (changing the pre-defined exchanges in these interconnections whenever flows are in the wrong direction is associated with a higher penalty cost).

4.4 Convergence of the Monte Carlo simulations

To cope with the uncertainty and variability of generation and demand, the proposed methodology uses a Monte Carlo based method, running multiple scenarios. To reduce the number of scenarios, a severity index is proposed to identify ex-ante the scenarios that could present adequacy/flexibility issues.

The convergence of the ENS among the first 2000 scenarios executed in this case study is shown in Fig. 8.15. The trend of the moving average against the total number of Monte Carlo (N) simulations provides a good indication of the convergence of the simulations. When N is sufficiently large (i.e. when the Strong Law of Large Numbers and the Central Limit Theorem apply), the error between the expected value and the average of the sample has a normal (Gaussian) distribution, and its upper limit can be calculated from the following formula with 95% probability:

$$|\varepsilon_n| \leq 1,96 \cdot \frac{\sigma}{\sqrt{n}}$$

where ε_n is the error at n repetitions, and σ is the standard deviation.

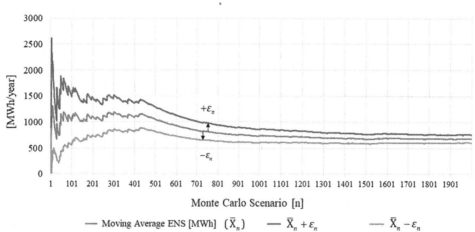

FIG. 8.15 ENS convergence for the 2000 Monte Carlo scenarios.

The respective confidence interval can be calculated using below limits, where $\overline{X}_n$ is the average value of the sample:

$$\left[\overline{X}_n - 1,96 \cdot \frac{\sigma}{\sqrt{n}}, \overline{X}_n + 1,96 \cdot \frac{\sigma}{\sqrt{n}} \right]$$

The moving average of the ENS (of the 21 countries in total) converged to around 680 MWh/year, and the error converged to approximately 78 MWh/year, confirming the execution of a sufficient number of scenarios. Additionally, Fig. 8.15 provides evidence on the application of the severity index (used to rank the scenarios prior to the simulations); the most severe scenarios are listed first, i.e. the scenarios on the left side of the graph in most cases experience higher ENS.

5 Discussion

5.1 Critical points

5.1.1 Non-availability of energy versus the non-availability of adequate level of reserve

Thanks to the model structure, non-availability of energy, expressed in EENS, is clearly differentiated from non-availability of adequate level of reserves, expressed in respective ERNSs. In the typical approach where upward reserves are aggregated as additional energy demand, the non-availability of adequate level of reserves is erroneously shown as energy not served. There is the position that for adequacy studies this is a valid approach, since the main interest is the examination of the capability of the power system not just serving demand, but serving it in a secure way. While this is true, explicit modelling of reserve requirements and clear identification of probable future structural deficiencies in their provision is important from a planning perspective. In such cases, efforts should be given in driving investments capable of providing the required missing Balancing Capacity, rather than simply offering energy. Thus, this is an important issue when designing corrective measures, such as capacity mechanisms.

Finally, detailed modelling of downward reserve requirements and systematic examination of probable deficiencies in their provision is important for assessing the flexibility of the power system in direct view of an increasing penetration of variable renewables. A systematic lack of downward Balancing Capacity demonstrates an increased probability of (forced) vRES curtailment.

5.1.2 Relation between flexibility characteristics and expected market outcomes

The expected number of hours with negative market prices occurrence is shown for each examined market zone in Fig. 8.13. There is a clear relation between these results and the expected vRES curtailment. Negative prices are an acknowledged sign of an inflexible supply side in real electricity markets (Baringa Partners LLP, 2015; Crampes and Ambec, 2017). They occur when inflexible conventional generation offers negative bids under conditions of low net demand in order to remain committed. UCED models can reveal such situations, which are of significant importance to market regulators, as long as a realistic modelling of the flexibility characteristics of the generation fleet is followed. On this, the aggregation level of conventional generation, representation of its technical constraints, especially the minimum up and down times, and a MILP formulation of the mathematical problem are all critical to detect such circumstances.

Another useful indicator regarding the expected market behavior of the system is the expected market prices volatility, measured in this work by the standard deviation of market clearing prices and shown in Fig. 8.14. In these results, countries with higher market volatility can be distinguished in two categories: First, those with identified flexibility problems as indicated by higher expectation of unserved energy, instances of inadequate level of reserves or vRES curtailment, e.g. GB and IE. Second, zones weakly interconnected with other explicitly modeled zones, e.g. Greece or Poland; in the case of Greece, this is due to the reduced number of interconnected countries modeled explicitly in this work; for the case of Poland due to the relatively low interconnection capacity with other countries. On the other hand, strengthened interconnections and increased opportunities for cross-border trade do indeed facilitate market convergence and reduced market volatility and vice versa (ACER, 2019).

Finally, it is noted again that UCED formulations, like the one presented here, model the behavior of an ideal market, and thus are inherently incapable of representing the behavior of actual market players, such as strategic bidding etc. On the other hand, they can provide useful insights to policy makers and market regulators, since their results are based on the market fundamentals revealing issues that can be considered structural.

5.1.3 Impact of demand response

In most of the countries where adequacy problems are found (e.g. ES, GB, IE, GR, NL, NO, PT), the consideration of the various DR mechanisms has a positive effect. The positive effect on the EENS/ERNS can be calculated based on two alternative modes:

$$(a) \sum_{c \in C} \frac{(EENS\&ERNS\_UP)_c^{WithoutDR} - (EENS\&ERNS\_UP)_c^{WithDR}}{(EENS\&ERNS\_UP)_c^{WithoutDR}} \tag{8.19}$$

$$(b) \sum_{c \in C} \left[\frac{(EENS\&ERNS\_UP)_c^{WithoutDR} - (EENS\&ERNS\_UP)_c^{WithDR}}{(EENS\&ERNS\_UP)_c^{WithoutDR}} \cdot \frac{YearConsumption_c}{\sum_{c \in C} YearConsumption_c} \right] \tag{8.20}$$

Calculation (a) provides the average EENS/ERNS improvement over the 21 countries, which results in 15% improvement as compared to the case that completely disregards the contribution of (Implicit and Explicit) DR. Calculation (b) provides the consumption-weighted average improvement over the 21 countries, which results in 14% improvement. These considerable improvements highlight the importance of a detailed consideration of Demand Response in generation adequacy and flexibility studies.

5.2 Identification of areas for further improvement

5.2.1 Representation of non-explicitly modeled countries

Any UCED study concentrates on a specific area. This is a necessary simplification for reasons of computational efficiency, data availability, but also organizational arrangements, e.g. European TSOs and market operators have set a high level of cooperation following to a significant degree the same operational rules and market arrangements under binding legal provisions. Thus, market interactions with non-explicitly modeled countries are a structural issue for any adequacy and flexibility assessment.

The employed UCED model work (PHOEBE) goes a step further than the simplified, yet widespread, approach where power exchanges with non-explicitly modeled countries are defined ex-ante for every hour of the target year based on historical data. Ex-ante power exports to non-explicitly modeled countries are modeled as a fictitious peak clipping demand response potential with a very high cost, being effectively the marginal cost unit, in order to avoid exports in scarcity hours. Despite this improvement, some issues still remain: it is important to notice that the future power exchanges may not follow the exact pattern as in the past, especially given the profound transformations that many power systems will experience due to decarbonization policies, especially when the examined Target Years are further in the future. Moreover, one should keep in mind that power exports to third countries may not actually be curtailed in the case of long-term contracts or other bilateral arrangements.

An obvious alternative approach is not considering at all power exchanges with non-explicitly modeled countries, thus considering the studied area as an isolated system. This decision could be considered particularly relevant for adequacy studies, but may give unrealistically pessimistic results, especially for zones that are traditionally net importers from third countries, e.g. Finland in Europe.

Finally, probably the most sophisticated approach is the representation of the countries beyond the studied area as a simplified generation fleet and an energy demand. This is effectively the approach followed by the market regulator in Ireland (Economic Consulting Associates (ECA), 2020). However, this is also the most difficult to implement method, since different configurations for the simplified resources portfolio of the non-explicitly modeled zones must be tested and evaluated, requiring extensive effort and considerable data.

5.2.2 Network modelling

The way the network is modeled depends fundamentally on the specific market arrangements in the studied area. Since the focus of this work is Europe, the zonal system has been considered. The studied area is divided into bidding zones which are assumed to behave as copper plates, i.e. internally the grid is considered to have effectively an infinite capacity. The only part of the network considered is interconnectors, which are modeled as maximum trade capacities (NTCs) between zones.

A more sophisticated, but still rather simplified, approach is modelling network constraints by the so-called Flow-Based (FB) market coupling, which is intended to become the preferred option in Europe, always in the context of zonal market arrangements (European Commission, 2015). This is based on a simplified representation of the internal network of each zone, where only certain Critical Network Elements (CNE) are considered. An even larger level of simplification is introduced by the fact that aggregation of nodal power injections and withdrawals into zones results in: first, the flows in each CNE to be expressed as a function of the net position of each zone by the so-called zonal Power Transfer Distribution Factors (PTDFs), and not as a function of the nodal net injections and withdrawals resulting in nodal PTDFs as dictated by the actual physics of the network, expressed by the Kirchhoff laws. Second, the available capacity for cross-border trade in each CNE, called Available Margin (AM), to depend on an estimation of the impact of a simplified list of contingencies (both in generation assets and network elements). Finally, the most important point is that PTDFs and AMs are an input to the market clearing algorithm, and thus are based on an estimation of TSOs of its outcome leading to a chicken-and-egg problem. The end result is that Flow-Based market coupling is incapable of avoiding dispatches that lead to grid congestions, especially caused by loop-flows, even if it is an improvement in comparison to the NTC approach (Schittekatte et al., 2019). In modelling terms, incorporation of the FB market coupling in a UCED model can be rather straightforward, with the incorporation of a DC power flow based on the PTDF matrix and the AMs of the CNEs (Boury et al., 2016).

The above discussion highlights the importance that flexibility assessments model existing market arrangements as accurately as possible, since these have a significant impact on the capability of the power system to operate in a secure way. In Europe, a fundamental aspect in the overall operation of the system is counter-trading/re-dispatching actions in which TSOs effectively change the dispatch with respect to the outcome of the "energy-only" markets in order to solve anticipated or real-time congestions in the grid. These actions have increased in economic volume the last years reaching more than €2 billion in 2017 (ACER (Agency for the Cooperation of Energy Regulators), 2018). Their systematic modelling in flexibility studies is important in order to examine in detail the constraints introduced by the finite capacity of the network, and respective additional costs. This is a necessary step moving from a resource adequacy methodological framework, as in this work or in ENTSO-E (2019), to a system adequacy including also power transmission grid adequacy.

To conclude, there are two main areas for improvement regarding the consideration of the grid in the context of the flexibility assessment methodological framework presented in this chapter. First, a more close-to-reality representation of market coupling between zones. This for the studied area means modelling the flow-based market coupling already implemented in Central-West Europe. Unfortunately, there is lack of publicly available data in order to permit such an effort, such as identification of CNEs, and assumed PDTFs and AMs.

Second, modelling re-dispatching actions. However, this would require extensive data gathering, since a nodal representation at least of the transmission system of the examined area is necessary. Even if the problem of data availability could be solved, there is a significant disparity of the operational procedures regarding countertrading/re-dispatching actions currently in Europe. From a modelling point of view, the critical issue is the notification period for providing re-dispatching services, since this will determine the place of the "re-dispatching market" in the chronological sequence of the modeled energy markets. A first approximation could be the assumption that such costly Remedial Actions would take place as close as possible to real-time. In such a case, the balancing market session presented above would also be the "re-dispatching market" and should transform into a Security Constrained UCED (SC UCED) problem where the optimum solution should be feasible against a predefined list of contingencies.

5.2.3 Mid-term/short-term hydro scheduling coordination

The results of the UCED model for Norway could be seen counter-intuitive at first sight: the MC simulations showed that load curtailment is expected (although rather small), as well as the largest vRES curtailment among all explicitly examined countries (although it accounts for just 0.299% of the average wind energy generation of the country for the case without

DR). Still, Norway has a very flexible generation fleet based on reservoir hydro, with an installed capacity considerably higher than the peak demand (see Fig. 8.5). On the other hand, it rather lacks on other flexibility resources.

The above counter-intuitive results could be attributed to a limitation of the modelling regarding the coordination of the mid-term (yearly) hydro scheduling with the rolling daily UCED simulations, explained in the following. As already discussed, the mid-term hydro scheduling algorithm optimally allocates given monthly hydro production quantities to each day of the respective month, and these daily hydro MWh quantities are subsequently imposed as binding targets during the main UCED simulations. Notably, the UCED model provides for the relaxation of the daily hydro production targets imposed by the mid-term hydro scheduling to overcome scarcity conditions or over-generation conditions (in hours of low load demand and high wind generation) in the Balancing Market. However, this flexibility is limited only to the upward/downward reserves awarded day-ahead or intra-day in the hydro units (cf. thermal units are usually able to provide more balancing energy in real-time than the one reserved, i.e. up to their technical maximum/minimum limitation). Additional deviations from the daily hydro production targets are penalized more than RES curtailment (priority is given to respecting the mid-term hydro production patterns). This results in vRES curtailment in hydro-dominated countries. This mid-term/short-term hydro scheduling coordination could be improved by prioritizing vRES production over hydro production (penalizing vRES curtailment at a higher price than hydro production curtailment) and correcting any additional deviations from the daily hydro production targets over the course of the next e.g. 7 days. Nevertheless, one should keep in mind that without detailed knowledge of water management constraints, which usually fall beyond the scope of large case studies such as pan-European adequacy assessments, relaxation of historic production patterns should be made with due prudence. Similarly, for load curtailment the model assumes that all hydro units can provide upward balancing energy only to the extent of the reserve awarded day-ahead/intra-day, thereby reducing upward real-time flexibility in this hydro-dominated country. Nevertheless, other authors have recently found risk of renewable energy curtailment for the Nordic power system for the same target year, i.e. 2025—see Nycander et al. (2020).

5.2.4 Better representation of the Intraday Market

In this work, Intraday Market is modeled as three distinctive market sessions. This is a simplification, since continuous trading is the organizational standard for the IDM in the examined area (European Commission, 2015). In this respect, a more realistic choice would be to model 24 IDM sessions per day with the obvious disadvantage of adding in computational burden.

Still, the IDM structure in Europe is going to evolve into a hybrid structure where continuous trading will co-exist with three auction sessions per trading day Agency for the Cooperation of Energy Regulators (ACER), 2019. Thus, the level of simplification introduced by the modelling assumption followed in this work could be considered low.

5.2.5 Better representation of the Balancing Market

In this work, the BM is assumed to have an hourly market time unit. Currently, the balancing markets in Europe, still organized in national control areas, have different time granularities varying from 15 min to 1 h with the direction of harmonizing it to the shortest aforementioned duration in the near future (Schittekatte et al., 2019).

From a flexibility assessment point of view, averaging net load variations into larger time periods, e.g. 1 h, leads to an optimistic view of the short-term net load variations to which the power system must be able to respond to. Overall, the choice of the modeled time granularity of the real-time market, where the adequacy and flexibility deficits are measured, is a trade-off between accuracy and invested computational effort, with the market arrangements of the studied area also being a decision criterion. In this respect, the presented model, applied for Europe, should upgrade to a 15 min market time unit for the BM in a next version.

5.2.6 Representation of thermal efficiency of conventional power plants

In this work, a simplified approach has been followed regarding the thermal efficiency of conventional thermal plants, considering a single value for their whole operating range. A random parameterization was imposed on top of that, leading to differences on the marginal cost of power plants of the same technology in the range of 0–1.5 €/MWh. This was to create artificially a merit order between plants of the same technology,[a] and it does not change the fundamental fact of assuming a flat efficiency curve.

---

a. It is noted that intra-national specificities, such as different fuel prices or the existence of Capacity Remuneration Mechanisms, have a significant impact on the real-life bidding behavior of market players, affecting in certain cases significantly the "commercial" merit order between conventional plants on pan-European level. However, such considerations are usually left out of adequacy and flexibility assessments, since they pertain more to market analyses (e.g. impact on fair competition).

Obviously, the above assumption leads to approximations regarding the dispatch calculated by the UCED algorithm that have an impact especially on the results regarding the expected market outcomes, such as clearing prices. A more sophisticated approach would be to approximate the efficiency curve of each plant with a stepwise function—effectively discretizing the efficiency curve. However, this would increase the computational burden since it would transform the size of the mixed integer linear problem to be solved.

Overall, one could argue that from an adequacy and flexibility assessment point of view, the approximation of a flat thermal efficiency curve is reasonable given that a more sophisticated representation would increase the necessary computational effort in an already heavy and time-consuming problem, without affecting the main outcomes regarding the capability of the system to supply demand. However, this may well not be so if of interest is the evaluation of market developments or a detailed analysis of greenhouse emissions under different policy scenarios.

5.3 Future challenges

The climate change abatement policies implemented throughout the world will drive further a profound change in modern energy systems. Already, one can discern the main trends characterizing this transformation in decarbonization, electrification, decentralization, sectoral integration[b] and digitalization. A brief discussion follows on the challenges they introduce in adequacy and flexibility assessments of power systems.

Further decarbonization of the power system most probably will continue to be based on increased penetration of variable RES, which are interfaced with the grid through power electronic converters. This poses challenges on the dynamic stability of power systems regarding inertia provision, voltage regulation and fault current contribution. Most probably, any thorough assessment of operational security of power systems in the future will have to include necessarily examination of these issues too. Due to the very different nature of the mathematical problems involved it is rather impossible to hard-link dynamic security analyses with adequacy and flexibility assessments (e.g. UCED models are based on a MILP formulation, dynamic and transient stability studies require solving a large set of algebraic-differential equations, while voltage stability is usually examined with small-signal eigenvalue analysis). Thus, soft-linking is the only solution, in which an iterative process is followed: First, a UCED analysis is made. Then, a set of characteristic "snapshots," i.e. dispatches, is chosen upon which dynamic, voltage and transient stability studies ensue. The final aim is to deduce from the latter certain rules-of-thumb, such as must-run generators or maximum Non-Synchronous Penetration Ratio, which can be incorporated as additional constraints into the UCED formulation. The interested reader can find a good example of this methodology in EirGrid, SONI (n.d.).

Electrification of sectors employing currently different forms of energy carriers, such as transport or heating, is at the core of the transition into a decarbonized energy system. This introduces significant uncertainties regarding power system adequacy and flexibility assessments, especially regarding projections on electricity demand annual growth and temporal behavior. On the former, a sensitivity analysis considering different scenarios on the evolution of electrification is a sound approach. However, estimating the seasonal and intraday variation of electricity demand in the future is more challenging. Consumption by EVs and PHEVs will mainly be determined by the level of proliferation of these technologies, prevailing guiding patterns, but also the implemented charging schemes. Significant data gathering effort on all these is needed in order to start making realistic assumptions. Regarding the heating sector, the temperature dependence of load may change considerably in the future with the proliferation of heat pumps. Another significant factor of uncertainty here is the impact of climate change on annual temperature variations, wind and irradiance patterns. The fundamental assumption behind the employment of the Monte-Carlo probabilistic approach based on past meteorological years, namely that these represent the totality of possible climatic variations in the future, may not hold true, especially if climate abatement policies prove relatively unsuccessful. Even though climate models are constantly improving, they are not yet on the level to produce detailed hourly time-series with a good confidence interval for the weather variables of interest in power system flexibility assessments.

Closely linked to the electrification trend is sectoral integration, i.e. the coupling of different energy carrier networks (in very general terms electricity, gas, and heat). This in principle is not something new. The gas network already interacts with the power system through gas-fuelled generating plants, while CHP facilities are an established technology. The change comes from the emergence of new technologies that make these interactions bi-directional. Here, one has to note hydrogen production by electrolysis that could have multi-faceted applications ranging from seasonal storage for the power system, to

---

b. In this work, the term sector coupling is used for the bidirectional coupling between the electricity and gas system (by Power-to-Gas technologies), while the term sectoral integration is used for the coupling of various energy networks (electricity, gas, heat) and sectors of the economy (energy networks, transport, industry, buildings) through various technologies (electro-mobility, synthetic fuels, etc.).

injection into the gas network, either directly or after transformation to methane. Regarding the Heating & Cooling sector, proliferation of district heating and heat pumps along with the emergence of sophisticated Energy Management Systems could increase considerably the demand response potential, mainly by utilizing the thermal inertia of buildings, and by providing time-of-use tariffs to end consumers. A first step to address these interactions in power system adequacy and flexibility assessments is by a better representation of electricity DR and storage coming from these sectors in terms of potential, but also behavior. However, as sectoral integration moves forward the need to develop integrated energy system models will increase. It is noted that such efforts have already started being undertaken (European Commission, n.d.).

Decentralization in power systems is an increasing trend with the proliferation of Distributed Energy Resources (DERs) ranging from PVs and micro-CHPs to small battery storage and EVs. A first challenge introduced to power system adequacy and flexibility assessments is estimation of future capacities of such resources, especially if grid adequacy is to be included in the analysis requiring growth projections on nodal level. Furthermore, the proliferation of DERs may necessitate in the future a finer spatial representation of the grid, getting down to the distribution level. Of equal significance may be the emergence of peer-to-peer energy transaction schemes or other forms of direct trading of electricity between active customers, such as energy communities. These challenge a fundamental assumption of methodologies based on UCED models, which is that all electricity is traded into a centralized auction-type spot market. A possible way forward could be the further development of agent-based UCED models, e.g. see Gallo (2016), complemented with a systematic behavioral analysis of customer direct trading schemes.

Finally, a critical point for future investigations is the development of a methodological framework for identification of optimum measures for flexibility provision, which can be broadly divided into two categories: investments and market reforms. The former necessitates the development of long-term (i.e. multi-year) optimization models with small temporal granularity (hourly or less). To the best of our knowledge this remains still an intractable problem from a computational point of view. Still, works have been presented in which a flexibility portfolio is optimized for a certain target year and under an external scenario coming from a long-term energy model, e.g. Bossavy et al. (2018). Regarding market reforms, market operators have taken certain steps the last years for providing necessary price signals for driving flexibility provision, such as smaller bidding intervals in Europe or introduction of ramping products in the United States. A comprehensive assessment of all measures presented in worldwide level is still lacking. Modelling studies could play a role on this as a tool for assessing ex-ante the impact of different market measures. However, such an effort would inadvertently face the issue of modelling realistically imperfect market competition.

6 Conclusions

This chapter presented a stepwise methodological framework for assessing power system flexibility, including the employment of both non-modeled based analysis and of a UCED Monte-Carlo probabilistic model. Important enhancements to the "status-quo" regarding the latter, such as detailed representation of Reserves requirements, Demand Response and the temporal sequence of short-term electricity markets, have been introduced and their implications to policy and regulatory decisions highlighted. At the same time, the initial steps of the presented methodological framework (preliminary evaluation of flexibility requirements and assessment of technical capability of resources to provide flexibility) facilitates the critical overview of the modelling results in order to identify the specific improvements needed, such as the hydro optimization for hydro-dominated countries. Finally, an overview has been provided regarding the future challenges that power system flexibility assessments face in front of wider developments in the energy system such as further decarbonization and decentralization, sectoral integration, proliferation of electro-mobility, and peer-to-peer transaction schemes.

Appendix: Further results

This Appendix provides further results, presented in Tables A.1–A.4, on the detailed analysis of power system operational flexibility.

Acknowledgments

The authors would like to thank Silvia Vitiello, Amanda Spisto, Gianluca Flego and Georgios Antonopoulos for their support on the development of the PHOEBE project, Igor Simonovski for his valuable support on the simulation phase using the JRC Petten High Performance Cluster facility, and Marcelo Masera for his comments. They would also like to acknowledge the previous contribution of Arturs Purvins on the development of the flexibility methodological framework presented in this work.

TABLE A.1 Expected Energy Not Served as a percentage of average annual demand (only countries with positive values are shown).

Country	Without DR		With DR	
	EENS (MWh/year)	EENS (% of average annual demand)	EENS (MWh/year)	EENS (% of average annual demand)
ES	11	0.000004	8	0.000003
GB	82	0.000024	95	0.000028
GR	1	0.000002	1	0.000002
IE	1168	0.002719	591	0.001376
NO	15	0.000011	10	0.000007
PT	41	0.000074	23	0.000041

TABLE A.2 Expected total Reserve Not Served in upward direction without DR (only countries with positive values are shown).

Country	FCR_up (MWh/year)	FCR_up (% of annual requirement)	aFRR_up (MWh/year)	aFRR_up (% of annual requirement)	mFRR_up (MWh/year)	mFRR_up (% of annual requirement)
BE	1	0.000112	0	0.000000	0	0.000000
GB	31	0.000687	41	0.001189	91	0.001731
IE	309	0.070548	4272	0.497169	19,907	0.206590
NL	0	0.000000	1	0.000043	2	0.000038

TABLE A.3 Expected total Reserve Not Served in upward direction with DR (only countries with positive values are shown).

Country	FCR_up (MWh/year)	FCR_up (% of annual requirement)	aFRR_up (MWh/year)	aFRR_up (% of annual requirement)	mFRR_up (MWh/year)	mFRR_up (% of annual requirement)
GB	0	0.000000	2	0.000058	15	0.000285
IE	112	0.025571	2034	0.236714	11,996	0.124491
NL	0	0.000000	0	0.000000	1	0.000019

TABLE A.4 Expected total Reserve Not Served in downward direction (only countries with positive values are shown). Deficits recorded only for downward FCR.

Country	Without DR		With DR	
	FCR_down (MWh/year)	FCR_down (% of annual requirement)	FCR_down (MWh/year)	FCR_down (% of annual requirement)
BE	493	0.055175	610	0.068269
FI	12	0.000623	19	0.000986
GB	263	0.005830	310	0.006871
SE	92	0.002549	160	0.004433

Finally, the financial support of European Commission, DG Energy B2 unit, under the contract ENER/B2/FV2014-742/SI2.702110 for the development of PHOEBE tool is duly recognized.

References

ACER, 2019. ACER Market Monitoring Report 2018 – Electricity Wholesale Markets Volume.

ACER (Agency for the Cooperation of Energy Regulators), 2018. Annual Report on the Results of Monitoring the Internal Electricity and Natural Gas Markets in 2017 – Electricity Wholesale Markets Volume.

ACER (Agency for the Cooperation of Energy Regulators), 2019. Decision No. 01/2019 of the Agency for the Cooperation of Energy Regulators of 24 January 2019 establishing a single methodology for pricing intraday cross-zonal capacity.

Andrey, C., Fournié, L., Gabay, M., de Sevin, H., 2016. The Role and Need of Flexibility in 2030: Focus on Energy Storage. European Commission, https://doi.org/10.2833/639890.

Baringa Partners LLP, 2015. Insights and News, Negative Pricing in the GB Electricity Market: Is the Outlook Positive? Available at: https://www.baringa.com/en/insights-news/blogs/july-2015/negative-pricing-in-the-gb-electricity-market/.

Bertoldi, P., Zancanella, P., Boza-Kisss, B., 2016. Demand Response Status in EU Member States. European Union.

Billinton, R., Li, W., 1994. Reliability Assessment of Electric Power Systems Using Monte Carlo Methods. Springer Science+Business Media, LLC.

Bossavy, A., Bossmann, T., Fournié, L., Humberset, L., Khallouf, P., 2018. Optimal Flexibility Portfolios for a High-RES 2050 Scenario. METIS Study S1. European Commission.

Boury, J., Van den Bergh, K., Delarue, E., 2016. The flow-based market coupling in Central Western Europe: concepts and definitions. Electr. J. 29 (1), 24–29.

Bruninx, K., Van den Bergh, K., Delarue, E., D'haeseleer, W., 2016. Optimization and allocation of spinning reserves in a low-cargon framework. IEEE Trans. Power Syst. 31 (2), 872–882.

Cochran, J., Miller, M., Zinaman, O., Milligan, M., Arent, D., Palmintier, B., O'Malley, M., Mueller, S., Lannoye, E., Tuohy, A., Kujala, B., Sommer, M., Holttinen, H., Kiviluoma, J., Soonee, S.K.Thu., 2014. Flexibility in 21st century power systems. United States. https://doi.org/10.2172/1130630.

Conejo, A.J., Baringo, L., 2017. Unit commitment and economic dispatch. In: Conejo, A.J., Baringo, L. (Eds.), Power System Operations. Springer, pp. 197–232.

Crampes, C., Ambec, S., 2017. Negative Prices for Electricity. Retrieved from Toulouse School of Economics: https://www.tse-fr.eu/negative-prices-electricity.

Dalah, K.P., McDonald, J.R., 1997. Generator maintenance scheduling of electric power systems using genetic algorithms with integer representation. In: Second International Conference on Genetic Algorithms in Engineering Systems.

Ecofys, 2018. Dynamic Electricity Prices. Brussels.

Economic Consulting Associates (ECA), 2020. SEM PLEXOS Model (2019–2025) Input Validation and Backcast Report. Retrieved from SEM Committee—The decision making authority for the Single Electricity Market on the island of Ireland: https://www.semcommittee.com/news-centre/sem-plexos-model-2019-2025-input-validation-and-backcast-report.

EirGrid, SONI. (n.d.). All Island TSO Facilitation of Renewables Studies. Retrieved from EIRGRID Group: http://www.eirgridgroup.com/site-files/library/EirGrid/Facilitation-of-Renewables-Report.pdf.

ENTSO-E, 2016. Mid-Term Adequacy Forecast. European Network of Transmission System Operators.

ENTSO-E, 2019. Mid-Term Adequacy Forecast, 2019 edition. Appendix 2. Methodology. entso-e.

ENTSO-E, 2020. Data Portal. Retrieved from: https://www.entsoe.eu/data/data-portal/production/Pages/default.aspx2020.

EURELECTRIC, 2015. Everything you always wanted to know about Demand Response, Dépôt légal D/2015/12.105/11. 29 May 2015 (Last updated: 20 March 2018). Available at: https://cdn.eurelectric.org/media/1940/demand-response-brochure-11-05-final-lr-2015-2501-0002-01-e-h-C783EC17.pdf.

EURELECTRIC, 2017. Dynamic pricing in electricity supply, A EURELECTRIC position paper. 16 February 2017 (Last updated: 19 March 2018). Available at: https://cdn.eurelectric.org/media/2113/dynamic_pricing_in_electricity_supply-2017-2520-0003-01-e-h-7FE49D01.pdf.

European Commission, 2015. COMMISSION REGULATION (EU) 2015/1222 Establishing a Guideline on Capacity Allocation and Congestion Management.

European Commission, 2016. Impact Assessment Study on Downstream Flexibility, Price Flexibility, Demand Response & Smart Metering.

European Commission, 2017. COMMISSION REGULATION (EU) 2017/1485 of 2 August 2017 establishing a guideline on electricity transmission system operation. Official Journal of the European Union.

European Commission. (n.d.). METIS. Retrieved from European Commission: https://ec.europa.eu/energy/data-analysis/energy-modelling/metis_en.

Gallo, G., 2016. Electricity market games: how agent-based modeling can help under high penetrations of variable generation. Electr. J. 29 (2), 39–46.

Gils, H.C., 2014. Assessment of the theoretical DR potential in Europe. Energy 67, 1–18.

Heggarty, T., Bourmaud, J.-Y., Girard, R., Kariniotakis, G., March 2019. Multi-temporal assessment of power system flexibility requirement. Appl. Energy 238, 1327–1336.

Heydarian-Forushani, E., & Golshan, M. E. (March 2020). Quantitative flexibility assessment of a comprehensive set of demand response programs. International Journal of Electrical Power & Energy Systems, Volume 116.

Hillberg, E., Herndler, B., Wong, S., Pompee, J., Bourmaud, J.-Y., Lehnhoff, S., et al., 2019. Flexibility Needs in the Future Power System. IEA Energy Technology Network, https://doi.org/10.13140/RG.2.2.22580.71047.

Hydro-Québec TransÉnergie, 2009. Transmission Provider Technical Requirements for the Connection of Power Plants to the Hydro Québec Transmission System. Retrieved April 15, 2020, from: http://www.hydroquebec.com/transenergie/fr/commerce/pdf/exigence_raccordement_fev_09_en.pdf.

Jaraite-Kazukauske, J., Kazukauskas, A., Brännlund, R., Krishnamurthy, C., Kriström, B., 2019. Intermittency and Pricing Flexibility in Electricity Markets. Energiforsk. Retrieved from: https://energiforsk.se/media/26463/intermittency-and-pricing-flexibility-in-electricity-markets-energiforskrapport-2019-588.pdf.

Li, J., Liu, F., Li, Z., Shao, C., Liu, X., 2018. Grid-side flexibility of power systems in integrating large-scale renewable generations: a critical review on concepts, formulations and solution approaches. Renew. Sustain. Energy Rev. 93, 272–284.

Lin, J., Magnago, F.H., 2017. Power system unit commitment. In: Lin, J., Magnago, F.H. (Eds.), Electricity Markets: Theories and Applications. Wiley-IEEE Press, pp. 97–117.

Marneris, I.G., Biskas, P.N., Bakirtzis, A.G., 2017. Stochastic and deterministic unit commitment considering uncertainty and variability reserves for high renewable integration. Energies 10 (1), 140.

National Renewable Energy Laboratory (NREL), 2010. GE Energy, Western Wind and Solar Integration Study, prepared for National Renewable Energy Laboratory (NREL). Available at: https://www.nrel.gov/grid/wwsis.html.

Nycander, E., Söder, L., Olauson, J., Eriksson, R., 2020. Curtailment analysis for the Nordic power system considering transmission capacity, inertia limits and generation flexibility. Renew. Energy 152, 942–960.

Oree, V., Sayed Hassen, S.Z., 2016. A composite metric for assessing flexibility available in conventional generators of power systems. Appl. Energy 177 (C), 683–691.

Perez-Canto, S., Rubio-Romero, J., 2013. A model for the preventive maintenance scheduling of power plantsincluding wind farms. Reliab. Eng. Syst. Safety 119, 67–75.

Poncela, M., Purvins, A., Chondrogiannis, S., 2018. Pan-European analysis on power system flexibility. Energies 11 (7), 1765. https://doi.org/10.3390/en11071765.

Schittekatte, T., Reif, V., Meeus, L., 2019. The EU Electricity Network Codes. FSR Technical report (2019 ed.).

Smart Energy Demand Coalition, 2017. Explicit Demand Response in Europe–Mapping the Markets 2017. Brussels.

Suresh, K., Kumarappan, N., 2013, April. Hybrid improved binary particle swarm optimization approach for generation maintenance scheduling problem. Swarm Evol. Comput. 9, 69–89.

UCTE, 2004. UCTE Operation Handbook. Appendix 1: Load Frequency Control and Performance.

United Nations, 2020. UN Data. Retrieved from: http://data.un.org/Data.aspx?d=EDATA&f=cmID%3AEC.

Yare, Y., Venayagamoorthy, G.K., 2010, September. Optimal maintenance scheduling of generators using multiple swarms-MDPSO framework. Eng. Appl. Artif. Intell., 895–910.

Yasuda, Y., Ardal, A., Carlini, E., Estanqueiro, A., Flynn, D., Gómez-Lázaro, E., Kondoh, J., 2013. Flexibility chart: Evaluation on diversity of flexibility in various areas. In: 12th International Workshop on Large-Scale Integration of Wind Power into Power Systems as well as on Transmission Networks for Offshore Wind Power Plants, London, UK.

Chapter 9

Retailer profit maximization with the assistance of price and load forecasting processes

Ioannis Panapakidis

Department of Electrical and Computer Engineering, University of Thessaly, Volos, Greece

1 Introduction

The European Union (EU), in a concerted effort, is promoting the creation of a single electricity market. At the same time, the goals of reducing greenhouse gas emissions are leading to radical transformation of the electrical system, so both the market and the electrical networks are in transition (Hyland, 2016). The Target Model for the single European market identifies the minimum required specifications to be followed by their individual national electricity markets Member States, to form a common architecture operation, which will then lead to the coupling of EU markets and competition to benefit to the end consumer (Newbery et al., 2016). The main goal of the restructuring of the electricity market is the reduction of energy costs both in wholesale and retailer sides and the strengthening of security of supply, through the gradual convergence of the wholesale price of electricity and expanding interconnections between Member States for the effective functioning of the market (Glachant and Ruester, 2014; Ringler et al., 2017). The maturation of energy markets has given energy to one additional feature. In addition to being traded, energy has been converted and subject to negotiation (Hawker et al., 2017; Mastropietro and Gómez-Elvira, 2014). Energy products enter one organized negotiation environment that forces them to become more standardized, but without affecting their nature, i.e. still bear the characteristics of the products of the natural energy market. The term standardization refers to the definition of packets or units of electricity based on criteria such as location or delivery method and timing period (Castagneto-Gissey, 2014).

The reduction in energy costs is expected to be driven by increased competition in the electricity generation, as well as in the field of electricity supply. Indicatively, in the period 2021–2030, a package of measures will be investigated to strengthen it competition in the wholesale electricity market, as a continuation of the measures already in place have been scheduled for the abolition of fees and taxes currently imposed on competitive power plants. At the same time, the existing mechanisms will be gradually replaced by the energy market financial products to achieve a smooth transition to the new market context and not to slow down the strengthening of competition. The liberalization of energy markets has led to an increase in their volume energy transactions (Le et al., 2019). The above results from the creation new dynamics of liquidity in energy markets, which were the result of the ability of the consumers to freely to choose their supplier among many that lead the monopoly of distribution companies to be abolished (Mastropietro et al., 2015).

In the new liberalized market landscape, the term load serving entity describes an agent that is responsible to cover the demand of a number of consumers (Defeuilley, 2009). The retailer has only rights for covering the demand and not purchase energy through interconnections and bid it in the wholesale market. The retailer acts as the intermediate agent between the generation and demand sides (Bae et al., 2014). The task of the retailer is twofold: (i) Select the appropriate mechanism for energy procurement and (ii) determine the appropriate selling price to its clients (Boroumand et al., 2015; Guo et al., 2019; Nojavan and Zare, 2018). The scope is to maximize the profitability, i.e., the ration of profit to income. This can be accomplished by minimizing the cost of electricity procurement and by maximizing the selling of electricity. It should be noted that the selling price should lead to increased revenue but simultaneously not be high enough in order not to motivate the consumers to select another retailer, i.e., the selling price should be competitive in the retail market. According to the literature, the procurement mechanisms are the pool market, forward contracts, call options and self-production (Hatami et al., 2009). Thus, the researchers face the profit maximization problem considering a hybrid model structure of the market, i.e. the market allows both for long-term contracts and short-term transactions in the day-ahead pool market (Corrgljé and De Vries, 2008).

Mathematical Modelling of Contemporary Electricity Markets. https://doi.org/10.1016/B978-0-12-821838-9.00010-4

The profit maximization problem has been the subject of a number of researches. Hatami et al. (2009) proposes a model built on mixed-integer stochastic programing to define the optimal electricity procurement mechanism and selling price. Pool market prices and retailer's load is treated as stochastic variables and are drawn through a set of scenarios each one using a GARCH model. The selling price is fixed with no variations between the periods. The retailer's policy towards risk is modeled using the Conditional Value-at-Risk (CVaR) measure. The authors check how the profit changes considering different combinations of procurement mechanisms. Carrión et al. (2007) examine two mechanisms, namely, pool market and forward contract and three types of consumers, namely, residential, commercial and industrial. Both pool prices and demand are extract through ARIMA models that provide a set of scenarios. The authors use a scenario reduction technique to decrease the number of scenarios. The consumers' response to the selling price is modeled via a linear price/demand function. Carrión et al. (2009) examine how the retailer's decisions related to the risk of pool prices influence the profit. As the retailer relies more on the pool market, the profits are increased. This is due to the fact that, in general, the forward contract prices are higher than the average price on the market. Gabriel et al. (2002) employ a Monte Carlo simulation to determine future loads in order to analyze a set of retailer strategies for balancing settlement risks. The study examines how different response of the consumers to selling price influence the profit. Gabriel et al. (2006) investigate the problem of contract design in respect to prices and quantities, both at supply and end-user levels. The authors developed a stochastic programming methodology that allows the retailer to make informed contractual decisions, particularly in respect to contract prices and quantities. Yusta et al. (2005), examine a variety of factors in the retailer problem such as price strategy, upper price limits, consumer elasticity on prices and other. It should be noted that all previous researches consider fixed selling price. Since consumers are encouraged to hold a more active role in power markets through self-production and Demand Response (DR), dynamic pricing becomes important. According to (Fallahi and Smith, 2017; Qadrdan et al., 2017) there is a variety of benefits of DR in power systems. Price-based DR programs refer to dynamic prices. The aim is motivating consumers to shift the demand from peak to valley hours or shave the peak demand completely. Real-Time Pricing (RTP) are the most accurate scheme to transfer generation costs to the end-consumers (Alipour et al., 2019). The latter are charged with a tariff that varies in hourly basis. Apart from the benefits for the utilities and system operators, the consumers can experience electricity bill savings. Yusta et al. (2007) regard a distribution test case system where a set of consumers is allocated. The scope is to derive the optimal selling price that varies per hour. The response to the prices is evaluated by five demand functions, namely the linear, hyperbolic, potential, logarithmic and exponential. Mahmoudi-Kohan et al. (2010b) perform clustering to group together consumer with similar consumption behavior. The load profile of each cluster is utilized in profit maximization. The objective function is solved separately for each cluster and corresponding selling price rates follow the chronological variation of the power demand. Mahmoudi-Kohan et al. (2010a) introduces an acceptance function that considers the number of consumers that accept to buy electricity from the retailer on a specific price. The clustering tool is used a number of consumers into groups. The acceptance function serves as constraint in the profit maximization and differs from the price/demand function. The RTP curves follow the patterns of the load profiles.

Based on the previous literature survey the main conclusions that can be drawn are: (i) All the papers treat pool prices and demand as stochastic variables and (ii) the topic of dynamic pricing has not received a considerable attention. In the present study, the focus is to replace the stochastic program approach using machine learning algorithms and specifically, neural networks. The latter are preferred in many forecasting problems over traditional time series models that are used in the related studies of the literature to formulate the set of scenarios (Hahn et al., 2009). In time series models, there is a need to define a priori the structure of the model through statistical tests. Neural networks refer to black box modelling, i.e., there is no a priori requirement for the structure of the model; it derived through the training procedure (Mjalli et al., 2007). In order to fully evaluate the neural network based approach, three different architectures are examined for load and price forecasting. The focus is to study the influence of the forecasting accuracy in the retailer's profit. Also, the proposed profit maximization model is formulated to generate RTP tariff schemes.

2 Methodology

2.1 Problem formulation

The decision making framework of the retailer is distinguished into two phases, i.e. medium-term and short-term actions. The time horizon may refer to 1 day, 1 week, etc. At the beginning of the time horizon, the retailer decides about the purchase amounts from Forwards Contracts (FCs). Next, while the information about the real System Marginal Price (SMP) is available, the selling price per hour is decided. The retailer serves one group of consumers with similar characteristics. The response of the consumers to the offered price is simulated by a linear price/demand function. It is regarded, that the consumers react rationally; while the selling price is high, the demand is decreased and vice-versa. In the case where the FC purchased amount cannot cover the demand, the difference is covered via the amount coming from the pool market. Due to the uncertainties present when dealing with the future pool prices and demand, a risk management mechanism is considered. This means that the retailer has no perfect knowledge of these quantities and therefore, forecasting tasks are required. The 24 h period is classified into five periods, as shown below:

- Period#1 = {01:00,02:00,03:00,04:00,05:00,06:00,07:00,08:00,09:00,10:00}
- Period#2 = {11:00,12:00,13:00,14:00}
- Period#3 = {15:00,16:00,17:00,18:00}
- Period#4 = {19:00, 20:00,21:00, 22:00}
- Period#5 = {23:00,24:00}

In particular, the periods refer to peak and off-peak hours. Period#2 and Period#4 correspond to peak hours while the others to off-peak hours. Based on these periods five FCs are regarded which differ within the day period and between the days of the week. Also, five periods are defined within the day. Each contract has five blocks that refer to each power amount that differ in the price. The block limits are 20, 40, 60, 80 and 100 kW. Let $f = 1, 2, ..., F$ be the number of FCs and $j = 1, 2, ..., N_j$ the number of blocks. The cost C_t^F that is related to the FCs in period t is given by:

$$C_t^F = \sum_{f \in F} \sum_{j=1}^{N_j} \lambda_{fjt}^F P_{fjt}^F, \forall t \tag{9.1}$$

$$0 \leq P_{fjt}^F \leq P_{fjt,\max}^F, \forall f, j, t \tag{9.2}$$

$$P_{ft}^F = \sum_{j=1}^{N_j} P_{ftj}^F, \forall f, t \tag{9.3}$$

where λ_{fjt}^F and P_{fjt}^F are the price and amount purchased from f-th contract and N_j-th block, respectively, at period $t = 1, 2, .., T$. Eq. (9.2) sets a limit of the amount to be purchased of each block. The term $P_{fjt,\max}^F$ refers to the maximum power offered by the specific FC, i.e., it refers to the block size. Eq. (9.3) refers to the total power of each contract P_{ft}^F which is given as the sum of the powers of each block.

Let λ_t^P be the price in the pool market at period $t = 1, 2, .., T$. The cost of energy purchased from the pool C_t^P is expressed as:

$$C_t^P = \lambda_t^P \cdot E_t^P, \forall t \tag{9.4}$$

where E_t^P is the energy purchased for the pool at period t.

Initially, the consumers are charged with a nominal selling price r_o at period $t = 1, 2, .., T$. Next, the retailer offers a new price after the solution of the profit maximization problem. The new prices are a decision variable to the problem. The retailer seeks to find the optimal prices at period t that maximize the profit. Let $r(t)$ be a random selling price at period $t = 1, 2, .., T$ after the solution of the problem. Due to the nominal price r_o the consumers' nominal demand is indicated as d_o. The DR of the consumers to the selling price $r(t)$ is indicated as $d(t)$. The relationship among these parameters is modeled through the following price/demand function:

$$d(r(t)) = d_o \left\{ 1 + \frac{\beta(t)[r(t) - r_o]}{r_o} \right\} \tag{9.5}$$

Eq. (9.5) refers to a linear analogy between the offered price and the responsive demand. If the selling price $r(t)$ is higher than r_o, demand $d(t)$ becomes lower than d_o. The parameter that controls the level of the analogy is the elasticity $\beta(t)$ at period $t = 1, 2, .., T$. The nominal demand d_o is obtained via load forecasting. Fig. 9.1 shows a linear price/demand function. The elasticity parameter defines the slope of the line.

To reach out into a feasible solution to the problem, an energy balance constraint should be imposed. For each time instant t the demand of the consumers E_t^D should be covered by two procurement mechanisms:

$$E_t^D = E_t^P + \sum_{f \in F} P_{ft}^F, \forall t \tag{9.6}$$

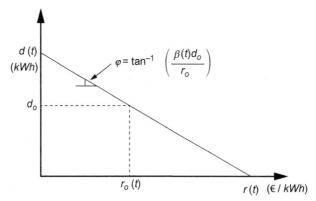

FIG. 9.1 Linear price/demand function.

To correspond to formulation of the problem, Eq. (9.5) is rewritten as:

$$E_t^D = E_{ot}^D \left\{ 1 + \frac{\beta(t)\left(\lambda_t^D - \lambda_{ot}^D\right)}{\lambda_{ot}^D} \right\}, \forall t \tag{9.7}$$

where E_{ot}^D is the nominal demand, λ_{ot}^D is the nominal selling price and λ_t^D is the selling price at period $t = 1, 2, \ldots, T$.

Theoretically, the higher the offered price the higher will be the profits. In order to for the retailer to become competitive and follow the rules of the market set by the regulatory authorities, a price limitation is needed. If the consumers elasticity would be extremely low, without price limitation the selling price would be correspond to unrealistic high values. The price limitation is given by the following equation:

$$\sum_{t=1}^{T} E_t^D \lambda_t^D \leq \lambda_{max}^D \sum_{\tau=1}^{T} E_t^D \tag{9.8}$$

where λ_{max}^D is the upper limit of the selling price.

The expect profit is obtained by the difference between the revenues and the costs. The revenues R_t refer to the product between the selling price and the consumers load:

$$R_t = \lambda_t^D E_t^D, \forall t \tag{9.9}$$

Apart from the costs related with the electricity procurement, the retailer is charged with transmission and distribution system access tariffs C^N:

$$C^N = \sum_t \left(\lambda_{et} E_t^D + \lambda_{pt} P_t \right) \tag{9.10}$$

where λ_{et} and λ_{pt} are the energy and power elements of the network access tariff, respectively and P_t is the contracted power.

The retailer's profit RP is expressed as:

$$RP = \sum_t \left(R_t - C_t^P \right) - \sum_t C_t^F - C^N = \sum_t \left[\left(\lambda_t^D E_t^D - \lambda_t^P E_t^P - \lambda_{et} E_t^D - \lambda_{pt} P_t \right) - \sum_{f \in F} \sum_{j=1}^{N_j} \lambda_{fjt}^F P_{fjt}^F \right] \tag{9.11}$$

For the purpose of eliminating the possibility of manifesting low or negative profits, an additional term is included in the objective function that expresses the profit. As a risk management mechanism, the CVaR (Conditional Value-at-Risk) measure is considered. For a given confidence interval $\alpha \in (0, 1)$, the CVaR is defined as expected value of the profit smaller than the $(1 - \alpha)-$ quantile of the profit distribution. It is:

$$\text{Maximize}_{\xi, \eta(\omega)} \ \xi - \frac{1}{1-\alpha} \sum_{\omega \in \Omega} \pi(\omega)\eta(\omega)$$

subject to:

$$-\left\{ \sum_t \left(R_{ct\omega} - C_{t\omega}^P - C_t^F \right) - C^N \right\} + \xi - \eta(\omega) \leq 0, \forall \omega \tag{9.12}$$

$$\eta(\omega) \geq 0, \forall \omega$$

where ξ and $\eta(\omega)$ are auxiliary variables. The optimal value of ξ refers to the highest value of the profit not exceeding by any profit outcome with a probability less to $(1-\alpha)$. The term $\eta(\omega)$ is the difference between the optimal ξ and the profit of scenario ω. Note that Eq. (9.12) gives the general form of the CVaR measure where probabilities scenarios are considered.

Finally, the profit maximization problem of the retailer is formulated as:

$$\text{Maximize}_{P_{fjt}^F, \lambda_t^D, E_t^P, \xi, \eta}$$

$$\sum_{t=1}^{N_T}\left[\left(\lambda_t^D E_t^D - \lambda_t^P E_t^P - \lambda_{et} E_t^D - \lambda_{pt} P_t\right) - \sum_{f\in F}\sum_{j=1}^{N_j}\lambda_{fjt}^F P_{fjt}^F\right] + \gamma\left(\xi - \frac{1}{1-\alpha}\eta\right) \tag{9.13}$$

Subject to: (9.2), (9.6), (9.8), (9.12) and (9.11).

The weight factor γ is used to control the balance between the risk and the profit. As γ increases the retailer adopts a more conservative policy towards risk. A risk taker retailer chooses low γ values. This means that the expected profits are increased but the variations of the actual profits are more intense. The profit maximization problem is formulated as a mixed integer nonlinear problem and is solved by commercial software (Brooke et al., 1998).

2.2 Test case

A test case with a retailer serving 84 residential consumers is examined. The test period is 1 day of September 2007, namely the 04/09/2007. The System Marginal Price (SMP) of the Greek electricity market is regarded. Fig. 9.2 displays the annual time series of the load and SMP for the year 2007. The load series refer to the aggregated load of the consumers. The network access tariffs correspond to the ones of the Greek system. The nominal electricity selling tariff λ_{ot}^D is obtained by the sum of the forecasted SMP, transmission and distribution network access tariffs increased by 10%. With this approach, the retailer charges the consumers an amount of 10% higher than the nominal (initial) costs related to the pool market.

For the SMP and load forecasting, three different models are applied separately, namely a Feed-Forward Neural Network (FFNN), an Elman Neural Network (ENN) and a General Regression Neural Network (GRNN) (Hippert et al., 2001; Liu, 2018; Nose-Filho et al., 2011). The scope is to compare how different forecasting models influence the profit.

Both the FFNN and ENN have one hidden layer. For hidden and output layers the linear activation function is selected. The training algorithm is the Resilient Backpropagation (Igel and Hüsken, 2003). In order to select the most suitable

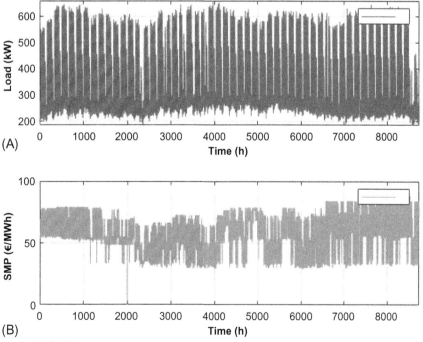

FIG. 9.2 (A) Load time series (B) SMP time series.

historical values as inputs for the models, a correlation analysis is held. Fig. 9.3 shows the Pearson correlation curve for load and SMP (Xu and Wunsch, 2006). The correlation is applied in the year of 2007 and seeks to extract the relationship of the current hourly value and those that precede it up to 9 days in the past (i.e., 216 hourly values). Tables 9.1 and 9.2 present the most correlated values for load and SMP, respectively. It can observe that the load shows the highest correlation with the values 1 week before. This fact implies a strong weekly periodicity of the total load of the 84 residential consumers. On the other hand, SMP presents high correlation with the values of the previous day. Since, the SMP present more volatiles compared to the load, the highest correlation is 0.8859 lower than the threshold of 0.90. For the load forecasting, the lagged values 167 and 168 are selected. For the price forecasting, the lagged values 25 and 168 are selected. It should mention that values 1,2, …,24 cannot be selected since we refer to day-ahead forecasting processes. The test day is 04/07/2007. The training set involves the period 01/01/2007–03/09/2007, i.e., all the days prior to the test day are used for training.

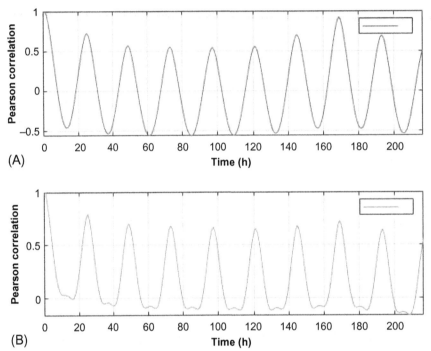

FIG. 9.3 Correlation coefficient curves for (A) load (B) SMP.

TABLE 9.1 Highest correlation values for the load.

Pearson correlation	Lag
0.9573	1
0.9176	168
0.8789	167
0.8788	169
0.8523	2
0.7794	166
0.7788	170

TABLE 9.2 Highest correlation values for the SMP.

Pearson correlation	Lag
0.8859	1
0.7940	24
0.7647	2
0.7474	23
0.7423	25
0.7285	168
0.7054	48

The prediction accuracy will be evaluated with a set of validity indicators. Let P_m^a and P_m^f are the actual and predicted variable of the m-th day of the test set, $m = 1, 2, \ldots, M$, respectively. The Absolute Error (AE) is defined as (Wang et al., 2017):

$$AE = \sum_{m=1}^{M} \left| P_m^a - P_m^f \right| \tag{9.14}$$

The Mean Absolute Error (MAE) is the sum all AEs (Wang et al., 2017):

$$MAE = \frac{1}{M} \sum_{m=1}^{M} \left| P_m^a - P_m^f \right| \tag{9.15}$$

The Mean Absolute Percentage Error (MAPE) is given by (Wang et al., 2017):

$$MAPE = \frac{1}{M} \sum_{m=1}^{M} \frac{\left| P_m^a - P_m^f \right|}{P_m^a} \times 100 \tag{9.16}$$

The Root Mean Squared Error (RMSE), is expressed as (Wang et al., 2017):

$$RMSE = \frac{1}{M} \sqrt{\sum_{m=1}^{M} \left(P_m^a - P_m^f \right)^2} \tag{9.17}$$

The Mean Absolute Range Normalized Error (MARNE) is the absolute difference between the actual and forecast variable, normalized to the maximum value (Soldo et al., 2014):

$$MARNE = \frac{1}{M} \sum_{m=1}^{M} \frac{\left| P_m^a - P_m^f \right|}{\max \left(P_m^a \right)} \times 100 \tag{9.18}$$

No external parameters are considered as inputs to the models.

3 Results

The three algorithms are applied separately on the load and price forecasting tasks. Tables 9.3 and 9.4 present the scores of the algorithms on the metrics. In both variables, the FFNN leads to lower errors followed by the ENN. Figs. 9.4 and 9.5 illustrate the demand and market price of the test day and the respective forecasts, respectively.

From Fig. 9.4 it can be concluded that the highest errors are met in noon peak hours. In the SMP forecasting case, high errors are observed in the early morning hours and at midnight. The forecasts serve as the nominal demand and nominal SMP for the test case. FFNN and ENN are executed for variable number of neurons in the hidden layer during training. The

TABLE 9.3 Algorithms comparison for the load forecasting process.

MAE (MW)	RMSE (MW)	MAPE (%)	MARNE (%)	Model
7.822	10.414	1.904	1.320	FFNN
8.653	11.111	2.138	1.461	ENN
13.078	15.448	3.546	2.208	GRNN

TABLE 9.4 Algorithms comparison for the SMP forecasting process.

MAE (€/kWh)	RMSE (€/kWh)	MAPE (%)	MARNE (%)	Model
0.005	0.010	12.141	7.201	FFNN
0.005	0.010	12.349	7.131	ENN
0.006	0.011	16.658	8.415	GRNN

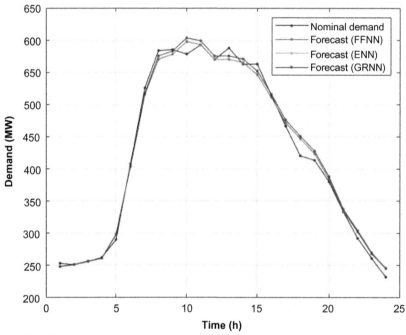

FIG. 9.4 Nominal demand and load forecasts.

configuration that refers to the lowest training error is chosen to perform the forecasts of the test day variables, namely load and SMP. The optimal number of neurons in the hidden layer may differ for the load and SMP forecasting.

Various combinations of load and SMP forecasting are investigated. The retailer's model is executed for $\beta = -1$ and $\gamma = 1$. The network access tariff correspond to the general residential tariff of Greek electric sector. Table 9.5 presents the profit and profitability of the various combinations of load and SMP forecasting. There are 9 combinations in total, thus, the objective function is solved for these combinations. Recall that there are no scenarios for load and SMP, only one forecast per parameter. The highest profit is obtained by the ENN/GRNN combinations followed by the FFNN/GRNN. This fact implies that when GRNN is used for the SMP forecasting, the retailer can expect the higher profits. Since GRNN corresponds to the higher prediction errors, it can be concluded that the higher the deviation from the real values leads to the higher economic benefits. This is also visible in the case of FFNN for SMP forecasting. Low profits are expected when high

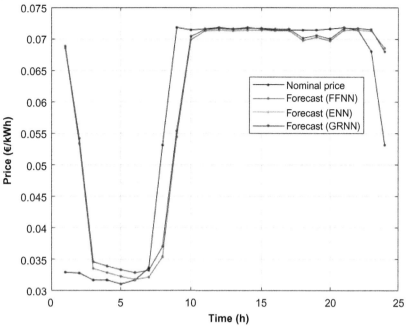

FIG. 9.5 Nominal price and price forecasts.

TABLE 9.5 Profit and profitability for the various combinations of load and SMP forecasting.

Profit (€)	Profitability	Load	SMP
352.010	0.421	FFNN	FFNN
355.804	0.422	ENN	ENN
367.167	0.425	GRNN	GRNN
355.231	0.422	FFNN	ENN
370.327	0.426	FFNN	GRNN
352.581	0.421	ENN	FFNN
370.872	0.426	ENN	GRNN
348.753	0.421	GRNN	FFNN
351.945	0.422	GRNN	ENN

prediction accuracy is gained. However, this conclusion is drawn from the specific conditions of β and γ. In all cases, the profitability is relatively identical. This indicator provides information on the relationship between the revenues and actual profit. Since the upper threshold of selling price to the consumers is limited from market regulation for the purpose of keeping the retail market competition robust, in order to increase the profitability ration, the retailer should seek for more auspicious FC with the generation companies.

To further investigate the above finding, the deviations between the nominal (real) value of load and SMP and the forecasts are shown in Figs. 9.6 and 9.7, respectively. The deviation is actually the difference between the real and forecasted value. Positive deviations refer to cases where the forecast is lower than the real value. For load forecasting, the GRNN leads to higher values than expected in the first morning hours. This is also the case for the SMP; GRNN overestimates the values of the two parameters.

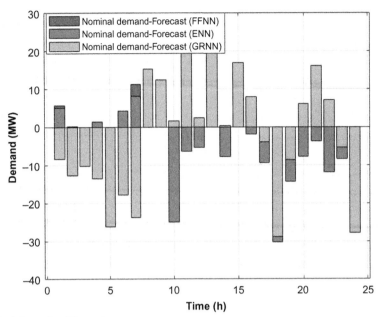

FIG. 9.6 Errors between actual demand and forecasts.

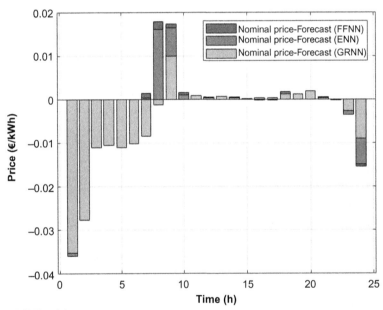

FIG. 9.7 Errors between actual SMP and forecasts.

In the case of load, there are 10, 8, and 12 instances with positive deviations for the FFNN, ENN, and GRNN forecasts, respectively. More specifically, the FFNN results in positive deviations at hours 1, 2, 4, 6, 7, 8, 9, 13, 15, and 16, the ENN at hours 1, 4, 6, 7, 8, 9, 13, and 15 and the GRNN at hours 8, 9, 10, 11, 12, 13, 14, 15, 16, 20, 21, and 22. The highest deviation is met at hours 15, 13, and 13 for the FFNN, ENN and GRNN, respectively. For the specific hours, the absolute percentage errors are 2.955%, 2.078%, and 3.545% for FFNN, ENN and GRNN, respectively. For negative deviations the highest are met at hour 18 for all algorithms. The absolute percentage errors are 6.239%, 7.199%, and 6.871% for the FFNN, ENN, and GRNN, respectively. In the case of price, there are 16, 12, and 13 instances with positive deviations. The highest deviation is met at hours 8, 9, and 9 for the FFNN, ENN, and GRNN, respectively. For the specific hours, the absolute percentage errors are 33.835%, 22.846%, and 13.904% for FFNN, ENN, and GRNN, respectively. For negative deviations the highest are met at hour 1 for all algorithms. The absolute percentage errors are above 50% for all algorithms.

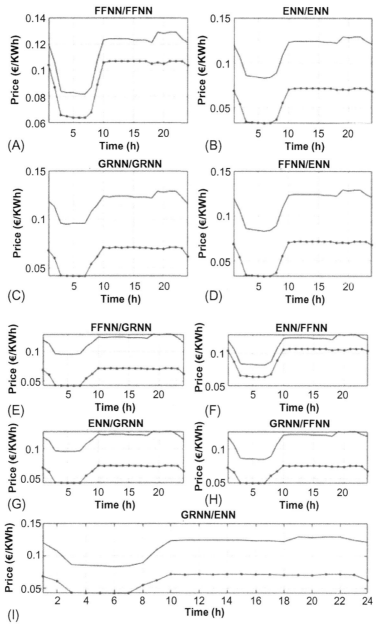

FIG. 9.8 Initial *(blue (gray in print version) line)* and final RTPs *(blue (gray in print version) line)* for: (A) FFNN/FFNN (B) ENN/ENN (C) GRNN/ GRNN (D) FFNN/ENN (E) FFNN/GRNN (F) ENN/FFNN (G) ENN/GRNN (H) GRNN/FFNN (I) GRNN/ENN.

Through dynamic pricing schemes it is feasible to transfer the cost of generated electricity to the end consumers. Thus, dynamic pricing acts as the link between the generation and demand sides. In the present study, the dynamic price is manifested as RTP. The selling price differs per hour. Fig. 9.8 shows the initial and final RTPs for the various forecasting combinations. Fig. 9.9 presents the initial and final demands for the various forecasting combinations. Finally, Fig. 9.10 depicts the contributions of the two procurement mechanisms for the various combinations. Tables 9.6 and 9.7 present the contributions of each mechanism in physical values and percentages, respectively.

According to the retailer's problem formulation, both the initial and final RTPs follow the trends of the hourly generation cost as expressed by the SMP. The initial RTP (nominal price) is based on the SMP forecasting plus on the network access tariffs. Therefore, SMP forecasting is used to set the initial RTP of the consumers. In the case of the linear demand function, the selling price increase is accompanied with a demand increase. The initial (nominal) demand is based on the forecasts while the final demand is calculated as the DR of the consumers the selling price. For simplicity, it is assumed that all consumers are characterized by the same elasticity value. It can be noticed that selling price follow the trend of the nominal RTP. The deviations from the nominal price depend on the procurement mechanism and the selling price

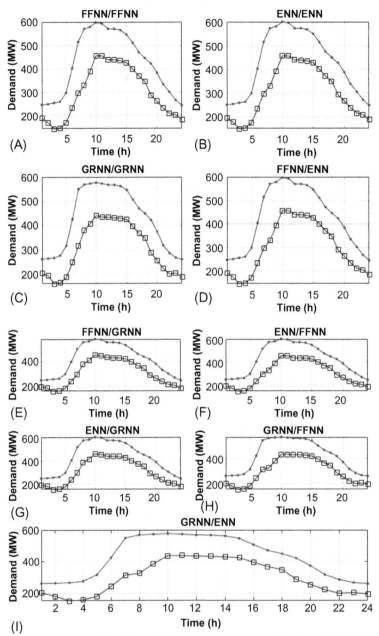

FIG. 9.9 Initial *(blue (gray in print version) line)* and final demands *(blue (gray in print version) line)* for: (A) FFNN/FFNN (B) ENN/ENN (C) GRNN/GRNN (D) FFNN/ENN (E) FFNN/GRNN (F) ENN/FFNN (G) ENN/GRNN (H) GRNN/FFNN (I) GRNN/ENN.

limitation. Since, the retailer has no influence on the market price (i.e., the SMP) and the upper limit of the price limitation, the only parameter for open negotiation is the FCs, which refer to bilateral agreements between the retailer and one or more generation companies. Another parameter that influence the profit is the elasticity of the consumers. Since many parameters in the profit maximization problem are controllable by the retailer, a forecasting process can serve as the basis for minimizing the economic risk.

The trade-off between the procurement mechanisms is showed in Tables 9.6 and 9.7. It can be observed that are cases with zero contribution from the pool market. In all cases, the majority of electricity is purchased from FCs. The type of forecasting algorithm influences the magnitude of the mechanism contributions.

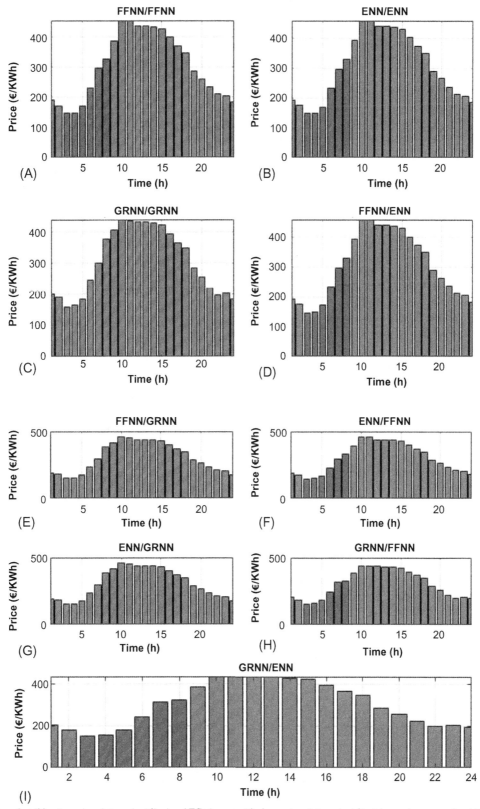

FIG. 9.10 Pool market *(blue (gray in print version) line)* and FCs *(orange (dark gray in print version) line)* demand coverage for: (A) FFNN/FFNN (B) ENN/ENN (C) GRNN/GRNN (D) FFNN/ENN (E) FFNN/GRNN (F) ENN/FFNN (G) ENN/GRNN (H) GRNN/FFNN (I) GRNN/ENN.

TABLE 9.6 Contribution of the two procurement mechanisms in MWh.

Pool market (MWh)	FCs (MWh)	Total energy (MWh)	Load	SMP
1327.925	5910.796	7238.721	FFNN	FFNN
1323.795	5938.22	7262.015	ENN	ENN
14.311	7292.52	7306.831	GRNN	GRNN
1327.724	5925.58	7253.304	FFNN	ENN
0	7349.642	7349.642	FFNN	GRNN
1323.996	5922.778	7246.774	ENN	FFNN
0	7357.159	7357.159	ENN	GRNN
1375.33	5827.424	7202.754	GRNN	FFNN
1375.129	5842.578	7217.707	GRNN	ENN

TABLE 9.7 Contribution of the two procurement mechanisms in percentage.

Pool market (%)	FCs (%)	Total energy (%)	Load	SMP
18.34	81.66	100	FFNN	FFNN
18.23	81.77	100	ENN	ENN
0.20	99.80	100	GRNN	GRNN
18.31	81.69	100	FFNN	ENN
0	100	100	FFNN	GRNN
18.27	81.73	100	ENN	FFNN
0	100	100	ENN	GRNN
19.09	80.91	100	GRNN	FFNN
19.05	80.95	100	GRNN	ENN

4 Conclusions

In modern day electricity market, the retailer faces two main issues, the selection of the procurement mechanism and the selling price to the consumers. The maximization of the retailer's profit depends on these issues and is formulated as an optimization task. The scope of the FCs is to minimize the economic risk associated with the volatilities of the market prices. Also, the risk can be minimized by an accurate price forecasting process. Apart from forecasting accuracy, the complexity of the profit maximization problem is decreased; stochastic based simulations are omitted. This is also the case for the demand of the consumers. In the day-ahead transactions, the retailer bids an estimated demand. Again, a day-ahead load forecasting process can aid on the efficient strategic actions' framework by the retailer.

In this study, a profit maximization model is presented. The model builds on load and price forecasting and optimally selects the procurement mechanism and defines the selling price, Contrary to the majority of the literature, the selling price is not fixed by changes in the daily period. The results showed that the selection of the forecasting algorithm for load and market price influence the results. The higher the deviation from the real price, higher profits can be accomplished. This finding is based only on a predefined value of the elasticity parameter and of the weight factor that determines the trade-off among pool market. Future expansions of the model will regard eternal variables in the forecasting processes. Also, different price/demand functions can be tested. Finally, a parametric analysis will be implemented for various crucial parameters that influence the profit.

References

Alipour, M., Zare, K., Seyedi, H., Jalali, M., 2019. Real-time price-based demand response model for combined heat and power systems. Energy 1681, 1119–1127.

Bae, M., Kim, H., Kim, E., Chung, A.Y., Kim, H., Roh, J.H., 2014. Toward electricity retail competition: survey and case study on technical infrastructure for advanced electricity market system. Appl. Energy 133, 252–273.

Boroumand, R.H., Goutte, S., Porcher, S., Porcher, T., 2015. Hedging strategies in energy markets: the case of electricity retailers. Energy Econ. 51, 503–509.

Brooke, A., Kendrick, D., Meeraus, A., Raman, R., 1998. GAMS: A User's Guide. GAMS Development Corporation, Washington, DC.

Carrión, M., Conejo, A.J., Arroyo, J.M., 2007. Forward contracting and selling price determination for a retailer. IEEE Trans. Power Syst. 22 (4), 2105–2114.

Carrión, M., Arroyo, J.M., Conejo, A.J., 2009. A bilevel stochastic programming approach for retailer futures market trading. IEEE Trans. Power Syst. 24 (3), 1446–1456.

Castagneto-Gissey, G., 2014. How competitive are EU electricity markets? An assessment of ETS phase II. Energy Policy 73 (2014), 278–297.

Correljé, A.F., De Vries, L.J., 2008. Competitive Electricity Markets Design, Implementation, Performance. Elsevier Global Energy Policy and Economics Series.

Defeuilley, C., 2009. Retail competition in electricity markets. Energy Policy 37 (2), 377–386.

Fallahi, Z., Smith, A.D., 2017. Economic and emission-saving benefits of utilizing demand response and distributed renewables in microgrids. Electr. J. 30 (9), 42–49.

Gabriel, S.A., Genc, M.F., Balakrishnan, S., 2002. A simulation approach to balancing annual risk and reward in retail electrical power markets. IEEE Trans. Power Syst. 17 (4), 1050–1057.

Gabriel, S.A., Conejo, A.J., Plazas, A.M., Balakrishnan, S., 2006. Optimal price and quantity determination for retail electric power contracts. IEEE Trans. Power Syst. 21 (1), 180–187.

Glachant, J.-M., Ruester, S., 2014. The EU internal electricity market: done forever? Util. Policy 30, 1–7.

Guo, Y., Shao, P., Wang, J., Dou, X., Zhao, W., 2019. Purchase strategies for power retailers considering load deviation and CVaR. Energy Procedia 158 (2019), 6658–6663.

Hahn, H., Meyer-Nieberg, S., Pickl, S., 2009. Electric load forecasting methods: tools for decision making. Eur. J. Oper. Res. 199 (3), 902–907.

Hatami, A.R., Seifi, H., Sheikh-El-Eslami, M.K., 2009. Optimal selling price and energy procurement strategies for a retailer in an electricity market. Electr. Power Syst. Res. 79 (1), 246–254.

Hawker, G., Bell, K., Gill, S., 2017. Electricity security in the European Union—the conflict between national capacity mechanisms and the single market. Energy Res. Soc. Sci. 24, 51–58.

Hippert, H.S., Pedreira, C.E., Souza, R.C., 2001. Neural networks for short-term load forecasting: a review and evaluation. IEEE Trans. Power Syst. 16 (1), 44–55.

Hyland, M., 2016. Restructuring European electricity markets—a panel data analysis. Util. Policy 30, 33–42.

Igel, C., Hüsken, M., 2003. Empirical evaluation of the improved Rprop learning algorithms. Neurocomputing 50, 105–123.

Le, H.L., Ilea, V., Bovo, C., 2019. Integrated European intra-day electricity market: rules, modeling and analysis. Appl. Energy 23815, 258–273.

Liu, B., 2018. Short-term load forecasting of distributed energy supply system based on Elman neural network. In: Proceedings of the 2018 China International Conference on Electricity Distribution, pp. 2175–2178.

Mahmoudi-Kohan, N., Parsa Moghaddam, M., Sheikh-El-Eslami, M.K., 2010a. An annual framework for clustering-based pricing for an electricity retailer. Electr. Power Syst. Res. 80 (9), 1042–1048.

Mahmoudi-Kohan, N., Parsa Moghaddam, M., Sheikh-El-Eslami, M.K., Shayesteh, E., 2010b. A three-stage strategy for optimal price offering by a retailer based on clustering techniques. Int. J. Electr. Power Energy Syst. 32 (10), 1135–1142.

Mastropietro, C.B.P., Gómez-Elvira, R., 2014. Toward a fuller integration of the EU electricity market: physical or financial transmission rights? Electr. J. 27 (1), 8–17.

Mastropietro, P., Rodilla, P., Batlle, C., 2015. National capacity mechanisms in the European internal energy market: opening the doors to neighbors. Energy Policy 82, 38–47.

Mjalli, F.S., Al-Asheh, S., Alfadala, H.E., 2007. Use of artificial neural network black-box modeling for the prediction of wastewater treatment plants performance. J. Environ. Manag. 83 (3), 329–338.

Newbery, D., Strbac, G., Viehoff, I., 2016. The benefits of integrating European electricity markets. Energy Policy 94, 253–263.

Nojavan, S., Zare, K., 2018. Optimal energy pricing for consumers by electricity retailer. Int. J. Electr. Power Energy Syst. 102, 401–412.

Nose-Filho, K., Plasencia Lotufo, A.D., Minussi, C.R., 2011. Short-term multinodal load forecasting using a modified general regression neural network. IEEE Trans. Power Delivery 26 (4), 2862.

Qadrdan, M., Cheng, M., Wu, J., Jenkins, N., 2017. Benefits of demand-side response in combined gas and electricity networks. Appl. Energy 19215, 360–369.

Ringler, P., Keles, D., Fichtner, W., 2017. How to benefit from a common European electricity market design. Energy Policy 101, 629–643.

Soldo, B., Potočnik, P., Šimunović, G., Šarić, T., Govekar, E., 2014. Improving the residential natural gas consumption forecasting models by using solar radiation. Energy Build. 69 (2014), 498–506.

Wang, H., Yi, H., Peng, J., Wang, G., Liu, Y., Jiang, H., Liu, W., 2017. Deterministic and probabilistic forecasting of photovoltaic power based on deep convolutional neural network. Energy Convers. Manag. 153, 409–422.

Xu, R., Wunsch, D., 2006. Clustering. John Wiley & Sons, Inc.

Yusta, J.M., Rosado, I.J.R., Navarro, J.A.D., Vidal, J.M.P., 2005. Optimal electricity price calculation model for retailers in a deregulated market. Electr. Power Syst. Res. 27 (5–6), 437–447.

Yusta, J.M., Khodr, H.M., Urdaneta, A.J., 2007. Optimal pricing of default customers in electrical distribution systems: effect behavior performance of demand response models. Electr. Power Syst. Res. 77 (5–6), 548–558.

Chapter 10

Modelling cross-border interactions of EU balancing markets: A focus on scarcity pricing

Anthony Papavasiliou

UCLouvain, Louvain la Neuve, Belgium

Acronyms

ATC	available transfer capacity
BE	Belgium
BRP	balancing responsible party
BSP	balancing service provider
CEP	clean energy package
EBGL	electricity balancing guideline
NL	Netherlands
ORDC	operating reserve demand curve
TSO	transmission system operator

Nomenclature

Sets

K	set of zonal model links
G	set of generators
L	set of loads
Z	set of zones
RL	set of reserve loads

Parameters

ATC_k^+, ATC_k^-	ATC capacity in upward and downward direction
P_g^+	capacity of generator g
R_g^+	ramp limit of generator g
D_l^+	capacity of consumer l
C_g	marginal cost of generator g
V_l	valuation of load l
V_l^R	valuation of reserve slice l
$D_l^{R,\,+}$	capacity of reserve slice l
α_g	risk aversion coefficient of agent g
P_ω	probability of scenario ω
$\rho_{z\omega}^{RT,\,*}$	equilibrium real-time energy price in zone z in scenario ω
$\rho_\omega^{R,\,RT,\,*}$	equilibrium real-time reserve price in Belgium in scenario ω
$\rho_z^{DA,\,*}$	equilibrium day-ahead energy price in zone z
$\rho_z^{R,\,DA,\,*}$	equilibrium day-ahead reserve price in zone z
$d_{l\omega}^{R,\,RT,\,*}$	real-time reserve demand of Belgian TSO in scenario ω for reserve segment l

Mathematical Modelling of Contemporary Electricity Markets. https://doi.org/10.1016/B978-0-12-821838-9.00009-8

Primal variables

e_k transported power along zonal link k
p_g production of generator g
d_l demand of consumer l
d_l^R reserve demand of slice l

Dual variables

λ_k^+, λ_k^- flow gate capacity limit dual variables
$\rho_{z,\omega}^{RT}$ real-time energy price in zone z in scenario ω
ρ_z^R reserve price in zone z
ρ_z energy price in zone z
$\mu 1_g$ dual of generator g capacity constraint
$\mu 2_g$ dual of generator g ramp constraint
ν_l dual of consumer l capacity constraint
μ_l^R dual of reserve slice l capacity constraint
$q_{g\omega}$ risk-adjusted probability of scenario ω for agent g

1   Introduction

Although the US and EU electricity market designs differ considerably, both systems share a need for a market design that is capable of signaling a need for investment in "flexible" resources. Flexible resources, in the context of this chapter, are resources that are capable of offering balancing services in the form of reserves. Scarcity pricing is a market design that has been proposed for addressing this need. The design becomes especially relevant in a regime of large-scale renewable energy and distributed resource integration, where the system should become increasingly capable to adapt to the highly variable, largely unpredictable, and largely uncontrollable fluctuations of net demand.

The transposition of the scarcity pricing design from the US to the EU market requires a careful consideration of the commonalities and differences among the two market architectures. The common points and differences of these markets are analyzed in detail by Papavasiliou et al. (2019) and are not repeated here. Instead, the appendix of the present chapter, which is sourced from Papavasiliou et al. (2019), provides a glossary of market design terms that are related to the Belgian and Texas markets, as representative market design models of a typical EU and US design, respectively. The remainder of this chapter focuses on the specific topic of neighboring market interactions in the case of a unilateral implementation of scarcity pricing.

1.1   Scarcity pricing in US markets

Scarcity pricing (Hogan, 2005; Stoft, 2002) is a market mechanism for improving the valuation of reserve capacity. In US parlance, the mechanism corresponds to the introduction of an elastic demand curve in real-time markets that trade energy and reserves. This demand curve reflects the incremental value of reserve capacity in terms of improving system security. This demand curve is referred to as an operating reserve demand curve, abbreviated as ORDC. The mechanism becomes especially valuable in reflecting the real-time value of reserve capacity in regimes of large-scale renewable energy integration and serves to attract various forms of "flexible" capacity to the system. The term flexible here refers to resources that can offer operating reserve, and includes demand response, combined cycle gas turbines, and other technologies that can respond rapidly to abrupt and unpredictable variations in system conditions.

The effect of introducing this demand curve in real-time market clearing is the emergence of a price signal, or ORDC adder, which is effectively a price for real-time reserve capacity, as well as an adder to the system lambda, i.e., an add-on to the real-time energy price. Although an ideal implementation of the mechanism would entail a real-time co-optimization of energy and reserves, in which case the adder would emerge automatically by virtue of the presence of the ORDC, the mechanism can also be implemented by an ex-post computation of the adder as a function of remaining reserve capacity in the system. Therefore, the real-time co-optimization of energy and reserves is not essential to the implementation of the mechanism (although the presence of a real-time market for reserve capacity is essential, as we discuss subsequently). Through appropriate market design, this real-time adder is back-propagated to forward (e.g., day-ahead) markets for reserve capacity. This back-propagation may rely on virtual trading, a day-ahead co-optimization of energy and reserves, or an internalization of opportunity costs (Papavasiliou et al., 2019).

1.2 Scarcity pricing in EU markets

In EU parlance, scarcity pricing amounts to (i) an introduction of the scarcity adder to the imbalance price, which affects the settlement of balancing responsible parties, and (ii) an introduction of the scarcity adder for settling the availability of real-time reserve capacity, which affects balancing service providers.

Scarcity pricing has recently gained traction among EU market design stakeholders. This is reflected in two important EU legal articles, the European Commission Electricity Balancing Guideline (EBGL), and the European Parliament Clean Energy Package (CEP). Concretely, article 44(3) of the EBGL and article 20(3) of the CEP refer to a *shortage pricing function*, as a mechanism that individual EU transmission system operators may decide to implement unilaterally.

The implementation of scarcity pricing in Belgium has been studied by Papavasiliou and Smeers (2017), Papavasiliou et al. (2018), and Papavasiliou et al. (2019). These investigations led to an ex-post simulation, by the Belgian transmission system operator ELIA, of the scarcity prices that would have transpired in Belgium in 2017 assuming the scarcity pricing mechanism had been in place for that year (ELIA, 2018). Since October 2019, the Belgian TSO publishes scarcity prices publicly online for information purposes, one day after real-time operations.

One important complication for the implementation of scarcity pricing in EU market design is that the EU lacks a real-time market for reserve capacity. This means that reserve imbalances are not settled in real time (for example, free bids are not remunerated in real time for the sake of being simply present and protecting the system). Reserve capacity is traded in forward (typically day-ahead) reserve capacity auctions, but not in real time. This creates serious, if not insurmountable, difficulties with the back-propagation of scarcity prices, since balancing service providers who sell reserve capacity in forward reserve markets are not liable for buying back that capacity against a real-time price if that reserve capacity is activated for providing balancing energy. Article 44.3 of the EBGL offers a possible way out by allowing a scarcity pricing function which can be decided unilaterally by TSOs. Such a scarcity pricing function can be designed in such a way as to emulate the effects of a real-time market for reserve capacity. This is not the focus of the present chapter, but it is an important institutional consideration related to the implementation of scarcity pricing.

1.3 Cross-border considerations

In light of the fact that article 44.3 of the EBGL allows for a unilateral implementation of scarcity pricing, the Belgian regulatory authority has raised questions about the cross-border effects of scarcity pricing. Concretely, suppose that Belgium implements the mechanism, whereas neighboring zones do not. How should the settlement exactly work out? And what could one expect in terms of balancing energy prices and day-ahead energy and reserve prices in neighboring zones?

We address these questions in the present chapter using a stochastic equilibrium model which is based on previous work by Papavasiliou et al. (2019). The origins of the stochastic equilibrium model draw from Ralph and Smeers (2015). Stochastic equilibrium has been applied in a context of capacity expansion planning in previous research, see Ehrenmann and Smeers (2011) for related applications.

Note that the stochastic equilibrium model that we present in this chapter does not require risk averse agents in order to provide useful insights. It can also provide useful insights in the case were all agents are risk neutral, because it explains the mechanism by which agents arbitrage real-time prices against day-ahead prices. Thus, the stochastic equilibrium framework provides a quantitative approach to explaining the back-propagation of energy and reserve prices in forward (e.g., day-ahead) markets when a change is introduced to the real-time market design (e.g., via the introduction of a scarcity adder). Further note that the stochastic equilibrium framework is, in a sense, required. The market model that we consider in this chapter features a missing market: the Dutch TSO does not trade reserve capacity in real time. The representation of this market incompleteness is impossible via an equivalent optimization model (Harker, 1993).

1.4 Structure of the chapter

In the following section we present the stochastic equilibrium model that we employ. In Section 3 we apply the model to a simple two-zone example which attempts to emulate, in rough strokes, the interaction of Belgium with the Netherlands. The model is purely conceptual and is used for understanding concepts as opposed to providing a realistic market simulation. Nevertheless, the model provides interesting insights. These insights and their institutional implications are discussed in Section 4. Section 5 concludes the chapter and indicates promising areas of further analysis.

2 The stochastic equilibrium model

In order to understand the basic principles of a unilateral implementation of scarcity pricing, we present in this section a transmission constrained stochastic equilibrium model. We will specifically assume (i) a uniform pricing of energy for BSPs and BRPs (both in Belgium as well as abroad), and (ii) a pricing of reserve capacity for BSPs (only in Belgium). Although the uniform pricing of energy for BSPs and BRPs in this stylized model deviates from actual practice in EU balancing market design, it is the first step in understanding the general principles. We proceed with the description of the model.

2.1 Real time

2.1.1 Real-time balancing platform

We represent the function of the real-time platform (e.g., MARI) as a maximization of the value of available capacity. We use an ATC model between the two zones, so the only variable decided by the platform is the transportation of power from the Belgian zone to the Dutch zone. We assume an ATC model for the platform.

$$\max_e \sum_{k=(m,n)\in K} (\rho_n - \rho_m) \bullet e_k$$

$$\left(\lambda_k^+\right) : e_k \leq ATC_k^+, k \in K$$

$$\left(\lambda_k^-\right) : -e_k \leq -ATC_k^-, k \in K$$

The KKT conditions are described as follows:

$$\rho_m - \rho_n + \lambda_k^+ - \lambda_k^- = 0, k = (m,n) \in K$$

$$0 \leq \lambda_k^+ \perp ATC_k^+ - e_k \geq 0, k \in K$$

$$0 \leq \lambda_k^- \perp e_k - ATC_k^- \geq 0, k \in K$$

The formulation is indicating that, if there is congestion in the m-to-n direction, then the price in location n is higher than the price in location m.

2.1.2 Generators in the Netherlands

Generators solve the following profit maximization, for every $g \in G_{NL}$:

$$\max_p \left(\rho_{n(g)} - C_g\right) \bullet p_g$$

$$\left(\mu 1_g\right) : p_g \leq P_g^+$$

$$p_g \geq 0$$

The KKT conditions are given as follows:

$$0 \leq \mu 1_g \perp P_g^+ - p_g \geq 0$$

$$0 \leq p_g \perp C_g - \rho_{n(g)} + \mu 1_g \geq 0$$

The notation $n(g)$ indicates the zone at which resource g is located.

2.1.3 Generators in Belgium

Generators in Belgium solve the following profit maximization, for every $g \in G_{BE}$:

$$\max_{p,r} \left(\rho_{n(g)} - C_g\right) \bullet p_g + \rho_{n(g)}^R \bullet r_g$$

$$\left(\mu 1_g\right) : p_g + r_g \leq P_g^+, k \in K$$

$$\left(\mu 2_g\right) : r_g \leq R_g$$

$$p_g, r_g \geq 0$$

The KKT conditions are given as follows:

$$0 \leq \mu 1_g \perp P_g^+ - p_g - r_g \geq 0$$

$$0 \leq \mu 2_g \perp R_g - r_g \geq 0$$

$$0 \leq p_g \perp C_g - \rho_{n(g)} + \mu 1_g \geq 0$$

$$0 \leq r_g \perp - \rho_{n(g)}^R + \mu 1_g + \mu 2_g \geq 0$$

2.1.4 Loads

Loads solve the following profit maximization, for every $l \in L$:

$$\max{}_d \left(V_l - \rho_{n(l)}\right) \bullet d_l$$

$$(v_l) : d_l \leq D_{l\omega}^+$$

$$d_l \geq 0$$

The KKT conditions are given as follows:

$$0 \leq v_l \perp D_{l\omega}^+ - d_l \geq 0$$

$$0 \leq d_l \perp - V_l + \rho_{n(l)} + v_l \geq 0$$

It is straightforward to offer reserve provision to the load model but does not affect the insights of the model.

2.1.5 Belgian network operator

The Belgian network operator is interested in reliability, procured in the form of reserve capacity through a demand curve.

$$\max{}_{d^R} \sum_{l \in RL_{BE}} \left(V_l^R - \rho_{n(l)}^R\right) \bullet d_l^R$$

$$\left(\mu_l^R\right) : d_l^R \leq D_l^{R,+}, l \in RL_{BE}$$

$$d_l^R \geq 0, l \in RL_{BE}$$

where RL_{BE} is the set of ORDC segments of the Belgian TSO.

The KKT conditions are given as follows:

$$0 \leq \mu_l^R \perp D_l^{R,+} - d_l^R \geq 0$$

$$0 \leq d_l^R \perp - V_l^R + \rho_{n(l)}^R + \mu_l^R \geq 0$$

2.1.6 Market clearing

The energy market clearing conditions are described as follows for every $z \in Z$:

$$\sum_{l \in L_z} d_l + \sum_{k=(z,\bullet)} e_k - \sum_{g \in G_z} p_g - \sum_{k=(\bullet,z)} e_k = 0$$

Note that there are no explicit market clearing conditions for transmission rights.

The reserve market clearing condition for Belgium is described as follows:

$$\sum_{l \in RL_{BE}} d_l^R - \sum_{g \in G_{BE}} r_g = 0$$

2.2 Day ahead

2.2.1 Day-ahead market clearing platform

The day-ahead market clearing platform (EUPHEMIA) maximizes the day-ahead value of the network by solving the following optimization (analogous to the balancing platform in real time):

$$\max_e \sum_{k=(m,n)\in K} (\rho_n - \rho_m)^\bullet e_k$$

$$\left(\lambda_k^+\right): e_k \leq ATC_k^+, k\in K$$

$$\left(\lambda_k^-\right): -e_k \leq -ATC_k^-, k\in K$$

The KKT conditions are described as follows:

$$\rho_m - \rho_n + \lambda_k^+ - \lambda_k^- = 0, k=(m,n)\in K$$

$$0 \leq \lambda_k^+ \perp ATC_k^+ - e_k \geq 0, k\in K$$

$$0 \leq \lambda_k^- \perp e_k - ATC_k^- \geq 0, k\in K$$

2.2.2 Generators in Belgium

The real-time profit is used for formulating the day-ahead generator profit maximization. This parameter is computed once the real-time model has been solved. The real-time profit is expressed as follows for each $g \in G_{BE}$:

$$\Pi_{g\omega}^{RT} = \left(\rho_{BE,\omega}^{RT,*} - C_g\right)^\bullet p_{g\omega}^* + \rho_\omega^{R,RT,*} \bullet r_{g\omega}^*,$$

where $p_{g\omega}^*$ and $r_{g\omega}^*$ are the optimal solutions of the real-time model, and where $\rho_{z,\omega}^{RT,*}$ and $\rho^{R,RT,*}$ is the equilibrium real-time energy price and real-time reserve price respectively.

Each generator $g \in G_{BE}$ solves the following problem:

$$\max_{p,r,VaR,u} \rho_{n(g)}^\bullet p_g + \rho_{n(g)}^R \bullet r_g + VaR_g - \frac{1}{\alpha_g}\sum_{\omega\in\Omega} P_\omega^\bullet u_{g\omega}$$

$$\left(q_{g\omega}\right): u_{g\omega} \geq VaR_g - \left(\Pi_{g\omega}^{RT} - \rho_{n(g),\omega}^{RT,*} \bullet p_g - \rho_\omega^{R,RT,*} \bullet r_g\right)$$

$$\left(\mu 2_g\right): r_g \leq R_g$$

$$u_{g\omega} \geq 0$$

The KKT conditions can be expressed as follows for every $g \in G_{BE}$:

$$0 \leq u_{g\omega} \perp \frac{P_\omega}{\alpha_g} - q_{g\omega} \geq 0, \omega\in\Omega$$

$$\left(p_g\right): \sum_{\omega\in\Omega} q_{g\omega}^\bullet \rho_{n(g),\omega}^{RT,*} - \rho_{n(g)} = 0$$

$$0 \leq r_g \perp \sum_{\omega\in\Omega} q_{g\omega}^\bullet \rho_{n(g),\omega}^{RT,*} - \rho_{n(g)}^R + \mu 2_g \geq 0$$

$$\left(VaR_g\right): \sum_{\omega\in\Omega} q_{g\omega} = 1$$

$$0 \leq q_{g\omega} \perp u_{g\omega} - VaR_g + \Pi_{g\omega}^{RT} - \rho_{n(g),\omega}^{RT,*} \bullet p_g - \rho_\omega^{R,RT,*} \bullet r_g \geq 0, \omega\in\Omega$$

$$0 \leq \mu 2_g \perp R_g - r_g \geq 0$$

Note that we allow for virtual trading of energy, but not of reserves, since we introduce a ramp rate constraint for units, which limits the amount of day-ahead reserve capacity that they can trade.

2.2.3 Generators in the Netherlands

Dutch generators $g \in G_{NL}$ only access the energy market in real time:

$$\Pi_{g\omega}^{RT} = \left(\rho_{NL,\omega}^{RT,*} - C_g \right) \bullet p_{g\omega}^*.$$

The day-ahead optimization of Dutch generators is expressed as follows, for every $g \in G_{NL}$:

$$\max_{p,r,VaR,u} \rho_{n(g)} \bullet p_g + \rho_{n(g)}^R \bullet r_g + VaR_g - \frac{1}{\alpha_g} \sum_{\omega \in \Omega} P_\omega \bullet u_{g\omega}$$

$$\left(q_{g\omega} \right) : u_{g\omega} \geq VaR_g - \left(\Pi_{g\omega}^{RT} - \rho_{n(g),\omega}^{RT,*} \bullet p_g \right)$$

$$\left(\mu 2_g \right) : r_g \leq R_g$$

$$u_{g\omega} \geq 0$$

The KKT conditions can be expressed as follows for every $g \in G_{NL}$:

$$0 \leq u_{g\omega} \perp \frac{P_\omega}{\alpha_g} - q_{g\omega} \geq 0, \omega \subset \Omega$$

$$\left(p_g \right) : \sum_{\omega \in \Omega} q_{g\omega} \bullet \rho_{n(g),\omega}^{RT,*} - \rho_{n(g)} = 0$$

$$0 \leq r_g \perp -\rho_{n(g)}^R + \mu 2_g \geq 0$$

$$\left(VaR_g \right) : \sum_{\omega \in \Omega} q_{g\omega} = 1$$

$$0 \leq q_{g\omega} \perp u_{g\omega} - VaR_g + \Pi_{g\omega}^{RT} - \rho_{n(g),\omega}^{RT,*} \bullet p_g \geq 0, \omega \in \Omega$$

$$0 \leq \mu 2_g \perp R_g - r_g \geq 0$$

2.2.4 Loads

As in the case of generators, we need to first compute real-time profits for all $l \in L$, $\omega \in \Omega$:

$$\Pi_{l\omega}^{RT} = \left(V_l - \rho_{n(l),\omega}^{RT,*} \right) \bullet d_{l\omega}^*.$$

Loads solve the following profit maximization in all zones, i.e., for all $l \in L$:

$$\max_{d,VaR,u} -\rho_{n(l)} \bullet d_l + VaR_l - \frac{1}{\alpha_l} \sum_{\omega \in \Omega} P_\omega \bullet u_{l\omega}$$

$$\left(q_{l\omega} \right) : u_{l\omega} \geq VaR_l - \left(\Pi_{l\omega}^{RT} + \rho_{n(l),\omega}^{RT,*} \bullet d_l \right)$$

$$u_{l\omega} \geq 0$$

The KKT conditions are expressed as follows for all $l \in L$:

$$0 \leq u_{l\omega} \perp \frac{P_\omega}{\alpha_l} - q_{l\omega} \geq 0, \omega \in \Omega$$

$$\left(d_l \right) : \rho_{n(l)} - \sum_{\omega \in \Omega} q_{l\omega} \bullet \rho_{n(l),\omega}^{RT,*} = 0$$

$$0 \leq r_g \perp -\rho_{n(g)}^R + \mu 2_g \geq 0$$

$$(VaR_l) : \sum_{\omega \in \Omega} q_{l\omega} = 1$$

$$0 \leq q_{l\omega} \perp u_{l\omega} - VaR_l + \Pi^{RT}_{l\omega} + \rho^{RT,*}_{n(l),\omega} \cdot d_l \geq 0, \omega \in \Omega$$

It is straightforward to offer reserve provision to the load model, but does not affect the insights of the model.

2.2.5 Network operator

The network operator of each zone $z \in Z$ solves the following for procuring day-ahead reserve capacity:

$$\max_{d^R} \sum_{l \in RL_z} \left(V^R_l - \rho^R_{n(l)} \right) \cdot d^R_l$$

$$(\mu^R_l) : d^R_l \leq D^{R,+}_l, l \in RL_z$$

$$d^R_l \geq 0, l \in RL_z$$

where RL_{BE} is the set of ORDC segments of the Belgian TSO.

The KKT conditions are given as follows:

$$0 \leq \mu^R_l \perp D^{R,+}_l - d^R_l \geq 0$$

$$0 \leq d^R_l \perp - V^R_l + \rho^R_{n(l)} + \mu^R_l \geq 0$$

Note that the behavior of the network operator is notably different from that of the market agents. The network operator is represented in the day-ahead market with a day-ahead demand curve, which is fundamentally different from the producers and consumers, who do not incur any physical cost or benefit in the day ahead, but rather engage in a purely financial position.

2.2.6 Market clearing

The following day-ahead energy market clearing condition c

$$\sum_{l \in L_z} d_l + \sum_{k=(z,\bullet)} e_k - \sum_{g \in G_z} p_g - \sum_{k=(\bullet,z)} e_k = 0$$

Transmission rights are not traded explicitly, but rather implicitly within the day-ahead market clearing platform, so we represent this implicit trading through the maximization of network value in the day-ahead platform.

We also have the following market clearing condition for day-ahead reserve capacity for every zone $z \in Z$:

$$\sum_{l \in RL_z} d^R_l - \sum_{g \in G_z} r_g = 0$$

3 Application on a two-zone system

We consider a stylized two-zone example, with the two zones connected by a link of limited capacity. We limit our analysis to a two-zone model in order to understand the effects that are at play. The model is depicted in the following Fig. 10.1. The available transfer capacity of the link in both directions is assumed to be equal to 1000 MW.

The system consists of the capacities described in Table 10.1.[a] The valuation of the consumers in each zone is assumed equal to 8300 €/MWh, which is the estimate of the Belgian Federal Bureau for the value of lost load in Belgium (Papavasiliou et al., 2018). We assume a demand of 13.1 GW for the Netherlands, and a demand of 8.2 GW for Belgium in the base scenario.

---

a. Dutch gas units are assumed to be newer and more efficient than Belgian gas units.

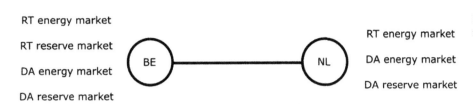

FIG. 10.1 The two-zone test system that is analyzed in Section 3.

RT energy market

RT reserve market

DA energy market

DA reserve market

RT energy market

DA energy market

DA reserve market

TABLE 10.1 Generation resources in the example of Section 3.

Name	Capacity (MW)	Marginal cost (€/MWh)	Zone
CoalNL	3400	35	NL
GasNL	5400	65	NL
RenewableNL	5000	0	NL
NucBE	5000	7	BE
OtherBE	3000	40	BE
GasBE	1000	70	BE

We introduce uncertainty into the model by considering two different scenarios:

1. A scenario where neither system is experiencing scarcity.
2. A scenario where the Belgian system is experiencing scarcity, and the Dutch one is not. We want this scenario to correspond to a situation where Belgium uses Dutch reserves, and we want to understand how these activated reserves should be paid for. We consider a case in which the link is not congested in our numerical simulations, although the model is general enough to also represent the case of a congested link.

We will assume that scarcity originates from variations in net demand, as opposed to loss of generation capacity. We present net demand scenarios in Table 10.2. These scenarios cover cases 1 and 2 above.

In the following sections, we build the model incrementally, and analyze the equilibrium outcomes by adding one feature at a time. This allows us to understand the effect of each market design component. Specifically, in Section 3.1 we consider a market that only trades energy in real time. In Section 3.2 we introduce a market for real-time reserve capacity **only** in Belgium. In Section 3.3 we introduce a day-ahead energy market and analyze the back-propagation of energy prices. In Section 3.4, we introduce a day-ahead reserve market, and analyze the formation of day-ahead reserve prices. In Section 3.5 we consider a scenario of scarcity which captures the focus of our analysis: what happens when the Belgian system is so tight that it needs to rely on neighboring balancing energy to the extent of depleting the neighboring markets' resources?

3.1 Market for real-time energy in both zones

We first consider the equilibrium in each of the scenarios of Table 10.2. The results of the market clearing are presented in Table 10.3.

TABLE 10.2 Scenarios in the stochastic model.

Scenario	Demand BE (MW)	Demand NL (MW)	Probability
Base	8200	13,100	0.99
Scarcity	9100	13,100	0.01
Scarcity (Section 3.5)	8900	13,700	0.01

TABLE 10.3 Market clearing results for the model of Section 3.1.

	Base	Scarcity	Scarcity (Section 3.5)
Energy price NL (€/MWh)	65	70	70
Energy price BE (€/MWh)	65	70	70
CoalNL prod (MW)	3400	3400	3400
GasNL prod (MW)	4900	5400	5400
RenewableNL prod (MW)	5000	5000	5000
NucBE prod (MW)	5000	5000	5000
OtherBE prod (MW)	3000	3000	3000
GasBE prod (MW)	0	400	800
Flow NL-BE (MW)	200	700	100

In the base scenario, the equilibrium energy price is 65 €/MWh in both zones. The flow is 200 MW along the interconnector, from NL to BE, however the link is not congested, and this explains the equal prices. The marginal resource is gas in the Netherlands. In the scarcity scenario, the equilibrium energy price is 70 €/MWh in both zones. The flow is 700 MW along the interconnector, from NL to BE, however the link is not congested, and this explains the equal prices. The marginal resource is gas in Belgium. In the scarcity scenario of Section 3.5, the equilibrium energy price is again 70 €/MWh. The marginal resource is gas in Belgium, and the import of power from the Netherlands is 100 MW, since this scenario involves higher demand in the Netherlands and lower demand in Belgium, relative to the scarcity scenario of the third column of Table 10.3. The scarcity scenario of Section 3.5 exhibits similar behavior, with Dutch gas units being marginal, and with less imports from the Netherlands to Belgium.

3.2 Market for real-time reserve capacity in Belgium but not in the Netherlands

We introduce next a real-time ORDC for Belgium, but not for the Netherlands. We construct this ORDC by using three segments, which we present in Table 10.4. Note that the valuation for reserve capacity beyond RL3 is 0 €/MWh.

The results of the market clearing are presented in Table 10.5.

The energy price is consistent with the reserve price in Belgium. Note that the reserve price is non-zero, and equal to 8 €/MWh in both scenarios. The non-zero reserve price can be understood from the point of view of the gas units in Belgium, which are offering both reserve and energy. On the reserve service, the Belgian gas unit is earning a positive profit, and is indeed limiting its supply of reserve due to its ramp limit. The unit is indifferent about how much energy to offer in the energy market, since the profit margin of the energy market is zero, which is consistent with the fact that the Belgian gas unit is producing a non-zero quantity. Effectively, the reserve price is set from the ORDC, since at 350 MW we are in the interior of the third segment of the ORDC, which is valued at 8 €/MWh.

Note that we assume that the Dutch market does not have a market for real-time reserve capacity, hence the Table 10.5 does not have a "Reserve NL" row. On the other hand, the Belgian market can source real-time energy from the Netherlands.

TABLE 10.4 Reserve demand curve (ORDC) for the Belgian real-time reserve market.

ORDC segment	Width (MW)	Valuation (€/MWh)
RL1	200	8000
RL2	100	20
RL3	100	8

TABLE 10.5 Market clearing results for the model of Section 3.2.

	Base scenario	Scarcity scenario
Energy price NL (€/MWh)	65	70
Energy price BE (€/MWh)	65	70
Reserve price BE (€/MWh)	8	8
CoalNL prod (MW)	3400	3400
GasNL prod (MW)	4900	5400
RenewableNL prod (MW)	5000	5000
NucBE prod (MW)	5000	5000
OtherBE prod (MW)	3000	3000
GasBE prod (MW)	0	400
Flow NL-BE (MW)	200	700
Reserve BE (MW)	350	350

3.3 Day-ahead energy market

Having introduced real-time markets for energy for both zones and a real-time market for reserve in Belgium, we now introduce virtual trading and a day-ahead energy market in both zones. For this purpose, we rely on a risk measure for agents. We use Conditional Value at Risk (CVaR), for which risk neutrality is a special case (whereby the risk coefficient α_g is equal to 1 for all agents, and the risk-neutral probability $q_{g\omega}$ is equal to the physical probability measure P_ω for all scenarios and all agents). The formulation is explained in Section 2. The results of the model are presented in Table 10.6.

The result of the equilibrium is a day-ahead energy price of 65.05 €/MWh for both zones, which is the weighted average of the real-time energy prices. Note that we have assumed virtual trading implicitly in our model, in the sense that the day-ahead production/demand of producers/consumers is not limited by physical limitations related to the maximum production or consumption capacity of these resources. Mathematically, this is represented by the fact that the day-ahead generator model of the Belgian generators does not include a constraint of the type $p_g + r_g \leq P_g^+$. Note, however, that Belgian generators are not allowed to trade reserve capacity virtually, which means mathematically that we impose the constraint

TABLE 10.6 Market clearing results for the model of Section 3.3.

	Base scenario real time	Scarcity scenario real time	Day-ahead
Energy price NL (€/MWh)	65	70	65.05
Energy price BE (€/MWh)	65	70	65.05
Reserve price BE (€/MWh)	8	8	N/A
CoalNL prod (MW)	3400	3400	3284.9
GasNL prod (MW)	4900	5400	5317.4
RenewableNL prod (MW)	5000	5000	4917.2
NucBE prod (MW)	5000	5000	3683.1
OtherBE prod (MW)	3000	3000	376.8
GasBE prod (MW)	0	400	22.1
Flow NL-BE (MW)	200	700	304.7
Reserve BE (MW)	350	350	N/A

$r_g \leq R_g$ in the day-ahead model of the Belgian generators. We have observed in previous work (Papavasiliou et al., 2019) that the virtual trading assumption has minor implications for the equilibrium outcome in the risk-neutral case.

3.4 Day-ahead reserve market

We now proceed to introduce a day-ahead market for reserve capacity to the model. Note that we now have a different reserve market for each zone. We assume that the day-ahead reserve capacity auctions are conducted simultaneously with the day-ahead energy auctions. In practice, reserve capacity auctions precede the auctioning of energy in the Belgian market. We have shown in previous analysis (Papavasiliou et al., 2019) that the sequential and simultaneous clearing produce similar outcomes in risk-neutral models.

All operating reserve demand curves in this model (day-ahead reserve demand curve of Belgium and Netherlands, as well as real-time reserve demand curve of Belgium) are assumed to follow the specifications of Table 10.4. The results of the model are presented in Table 10.7. In practice, the existing day-ahead reserve demand curves in Belgium are essentially inelastic (in the sense that the Belgian TSO sets hard reserve requirements). The model can be easily adapted to handle inelastic day-ahead reserve requirements by adapting the parameters of Table 10.4 accordingly.

Note that there is no "transportation" of reserve capacity, which means that each zone can only satisfy its local reserve requirements with its local reserve resources. We comment on this assumption in the sequel. The results of the model are presented in Table 10.7.

The Belgian and Dutch day-ahead reserve price becomes 8 €/MWh. There are 326.1 MW of reserve sourced from Belgium, and 350 MW of reserve sourced from the Netherlands. The day-ahead equilibrium of the Belgian reserve capacity market is illustrated in Fig. 10.2. The situation is identical for the Dutch market.

The non-zero reserve price is driving the reserve supply to 350 MW in the Netherlands, which is the ramp rate of the gas units in the Dutch system. From the point of view of Dutch resources, this is consistent with generator incentives, because every MW offered in the day-ahead reserve market represents a posit profit margin for Dutch units. The reserve supply in Belgium is 326.1 MW, which is consistent with Belgian gas units' incentives, since Belgian reserve providers are indifferent between selling the reserve capacity in the day-ahead reserve price, or in the average real-time reserve price. Note that we assume, in this model, that Dutch generators which offer reserves are not held accountable for holding this capacity available in real time. We have shown in previous work (Papavasiliou et al., 2019) that this can lead to a significant undervaluation of reserves in the Netherlands (compared to a scarcity pricing mechanism or compared to the obligation of carrying this reserve capacity in real time).

TABLE 10.7 Market clearing results for the model of Section 3.4.

	Base scenario real time	Scarcity scenario real time	Day-ahead
Energy price NL (€/MWh)	65	70	65.05
Energy price BE (€/MWh)	65	70	65.05
Reserve price BE (€/MWh)	8	8	8
Reserve price NL (€/MWh)	N/A	N/A	8
CoalNL prod (MW)	3400	3400	3284.9
GasNL prod (MW)	4900	5400	5317.4
RenewableNL prod (MW)	5000	5000	4917.2
NucBE prod (MW)	5000	5000	3683.1
OtherBE prod (MW)	3000	3000	376.8
GasBE prod (MW)	0	400	22.1
Flow NL-BE (MW)	200	700	304.7
Reserve BE (MW)	350	350	326.1
Reserve NL (MW)	N/A	N/A	350

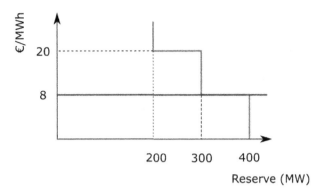

FIG. 10.2 The day-ahead reserve market equilibrium for the Belgian market (identical for the Dutch market). The *red (dark gray in print version) curve* represents the demand curve of the TSO for reserve capacity. The *blue (light gray in print version) curve* represents the supply curve of BSPs for reserve capacity. Due to quantity indeterminacy, any clearing quantity between 300 and 400 MW is a valid day-ahead equilibrium.

3.5 Leaning on Dutch resources

We proceed to analyze a situation in which the Dutch system is tight to the point of having leftover capacity which is less than its day-ahead reserve requirement. We specifically consider a case where the demand in the scarcity scenario is 8900 MW in Belgium and 13,700 MW in the Netherlands, as shown in Table 10.2. The reason that this choice of values is interesting is that (i) it avoids the unrealistic case where Belgian capacity is exceeded by Belgian demand, while (ii) leaving only 100 MW of reserve available in the Netherlands and 100 MW in Belgium. This implies that we expect tension between the provision of reserve in Belgium, and the Netherlands, and we are interested in understanding where the market equilibrates under such conditions. The results of the model are presented in Table 10.8.

We obtain the following results from the model: a real-time energy price of 65 €/MWh in the base scenario, for both zones; a real-time energy price of 90.3 €/MWh in the scarcity scenario, for both zones; and a day-ahead reserve price of

TABLE 10.8 Market clearing results for the model of Section 3.5.

	Base scenario real time	Scarcity scenario real time (model)	Scarcity scenario real time (platform)	Day-ahead
Energy price NL (€/MWh)	65	90.3	70	65.25
Energy price BE (€/MWh)	65	90.3	70	65.25
Reserve price BE (€/MWh)	8	20.3	N/A	8.12
Reserve price NL (€/MWh)	8	N/A	N/A	8
CoalNL prod (MW)	3400	3400	3400	6756.5
GasNL prod (MW)	4900	5400	5400	7334.8
RenewableNL prod (MW)	5000	5000	5000	6990.4
NucBE prod (MW)	5000	5000	5000	8444.1
OtherBE prod (MW)	3000	3000	3000	7057
GasBE prod (MW)	0	800	800	5774.6
Flow NL-BE (MW)	200	100	100	59.6
Reserve BE (MW)	350	200	N/A	300
Reserve NL (MW)	N/A	N/A	N/A	350

8 €/MWh in the Netherlands and 8.12 €/MWh in Belgium. The 20.3 €/MWh price for real-time reserve capacity in Belgium under the scarcity scenario is compatible with the leftover reserve capacity in Belgium. Concretely, since 200 MW of reserve remain available in Belgium, any reserve price between 20 €/MWh and 8000 €/MWh is compatible with the Belgian real-time operating reserve demand curve.

The effect of the tighter situation, therefore, is to lift reserve prices slightly in the day-ahead market for Belgium, whereas the price in the Netherlands is not affected. Note that the remainder of real-time reserve capacity in the Netherlands is zero (since all of its balancing capacity is used to cover the needs of Belgium), but this is anyways consistent with the loose definition of reserve as capacity that is only sold in the day ahead without any real-time obligation to keep any of it available after activation. It is also interesting to note that any excess capacity that remains in the system is available in Belgium, *not* the Netherlands: the Belgian gas units keep 200 MW of reserve available in real time. Thus, Belgium is relying on foreign resources to cover its real-time energy needs, and the 200 MW of excess reserve that are available throughout the entire system are actually reserved for Belgium.

In column 4 of Table 10.8, we have repeated the results of column 4 of Table 10.3. We now label these results as "Scarcity scenario real time (platform)". These are the results that would have been produced by a balancing platform (e.g., PICASSO or MARI) under truthful bidding. Since such platforms do not co-optimize energy and reserves, the prices that emerge may not be consistent with a co-optimization of energy and reserve. In Section 4.1 we discuss how articles 18.4 (d) and 44.3 of the EBGL could be invoked to remedy this effect.

We compare the equilibrium solution to what would occur in a business-as-usual case in which Belgium does not operate a real-time market for reserve capacity. The results are presented in Table 10.9.

In this case, the day-ahead reserve capacity price amounts to 8 €/MWh for both Belgium and the Netherlands.

4 Discussion

4.1 Equilibrium model solutions versus actual platform outcomes

The equilibrium model that we present in this chapter assumes a co-optimization of reserve and energy in Belgium in real time. In practice, a balancing platform will receive bids from BSPs and dispatch on the basis of these bids without performing such an endogenous co-optimization. This can be represented in our model by using the results of the platform as hard constraints in the real-time equilibrium. Concretely, we would need to enforce that, for the models which include

TABLE 10.9 Business-as-usual results for the model of Section 3.5.

	Base scenario real time	Scarcity scenario real time	Day-ahead
Energy price NL (€/MWh)	65	70	65.05
Energy price BE (€/MWh)	65	70	65.05
Reserve price BE (€/MWh)	N/A	N/A	8
Reserve price NL (€/MWh)	N/A	N/A	8
CoalNL prod (MW)	3400	3400	2954
GasNL prod (MW)	4900	5400	4659.2
RenewableNL prod (MW)	5000	5000	4317.8
NucBE prod (MW)	5000	5000	4603.5
OtherBE prod (MW)	3000	3000	2773.6
GasBE prod (MW)	0	800	346.4
Flow NL-BE (MW)	200	100	−27.6
Reserve BE (MW)	N/A	N/A	350
Reserve NL (MW)	N/A	N/A	350

reserve capacity in real time (Sections 3.2–3.5) that the real-time production and market clearing prices should obey the results of the model of Section 3.1. This can be enforced as a hard constraint in principle, and we can observe from the results of Sections 3.1–3.4 that it holds anyway for our specific instance.

In the general case, this additional requirement may result in an infeasible equilibrium model, in the sense that the outcome of the balancing platform may be incompatible with a real-time co-optimization of energy and reserves. This is the case, for example, in Table 10.8, where we observe that the real-time energy price in Belgium and the Netherlands in the model is 90.3 €/MWh, whereas the balancing platform would produce a price of 70 €/MWh. Forcing the price in the stochastic equilibrium model to 70 €/MWh is infeasible.

Even if a balancing platform which does not trade energy cannot reproduce the result of a co-optimization of energy and reserve, scarcity pricing can be emulated indirectly, by an ex post settlement. Concretely, article 18.4(d) of the EBGL attributes a BSP to an associated BRP, and article 44.3 of the EBGL allows the possibility of introducing an additional settlement mechanism separate from imbalance settlement. Scarcity pricing can therefore be implemented by (i) introducing the scarcity adder to the imbalance settlement (see article 52.2(d) of the EBGL), payable by BRPs, (ii) keeping the platform settlement price for activated energy, and (iii) introducing two terms, related to the real-time value of balancing energy and to reserve capacity imbalance, as foreseen by article 44.3 of the EBGL.

4.2 Institutional considerations

An underlying institutional concern of this analysis has been to understand how the proposed mechanism should interact with neighboring BSPs and BRPs. Note that this is in fact not a concern, according to the design considered in our model. The balancing platforms will produce a local zonal energy price for each BSP in the market. Zones which apply scarcity pricing settle their BRPs (and the associated BSPs of each BRP) according to the standard scarcity pricing formulas (Papavasiliou et al., 2019), whereas zones which do not apply scarcity pricing are not affected. Concretely, Dutch resources will pay the Dutch zonal price, and therefore they are not directly affected by the adder settlements (even if the adder may have an effect on the equilibrium outcome of the balancing platform). The fact that Dutch resources are being activated in order to address a Belgian scarcity incident is not at odds with the fact that these Dutch resources are supplying their balancing energy in the Dutch zone, and the balancing platforms produce a price for this balancing energy.

There is no need for violating the merit order of the balancing platform in order to arrive to the equilibrium outcome of Section 3.5. It is indeed true that, with a marginal cost of 70 €/MWh for Belgian gas units, one would expect that a balancing price of 90.4 €/MWh would result in an activation of these units. Instead, these units are kept as spare reserve capacity. Nevertheless, this can happen if the Belgian gas units incorporate the opportunity cost of using up their real-time reserve capacity into their balancing offer to the balancing platform, which is effectively what the equilibrium model is capturing. If neighboring Dutch BSPs are not exposed to real-time markets for reserve capacity in the Netherlands, they anyways would not internalize the cost of delivering this reserve in real time to their day-ahead reserve capacity auction bids.

This discussion underscores the importance of applying scarcity pricing for reserve imbalance settlements (equivalently, putting in place a real-time market for reserve capacity), and not limiting the application of the adder as an add-on to imbalance charges. Indeed, if scarcity adders would only be limited to add-ons on the imbalance price, then one could envision that Belgian BSPs might lower their marginal price so that they would be selected at the expense of imported bids from foreign BSPs. This would raise a concern among foreign NRAs as a violation of the (common) merit order: if the scarcity adder is applicable if the import potential is not fully used, then the perception is that Belgian BSPs push away foreign BSPs. By contrast, the application of scarcity pricing, as it is intended, for settling not only real-time energy but also real-time reserve capacity, would eliminate the interest for Belgian BSPs to mark down their bids, since whatever Belgian BSPs gain on the margin from providing balancing energy is balanced off from using up reserve capacity during activation. What remains is the incentive for Belgian BSPs to internalize the real-time adders in their day-ahead reserve capacity bids, which would serve towards back-propagating real-time scarcity adders to day-ahead reserve prices in Belgium.

5 Conclusions and perspectives

We can draw the following conclusions from our analysis of the simplified model:

- A unilateral implementation of ORDC in Belgium does not affect the day-ahead reserve price of the Netherlands.
- A unilateral implementation of ORDC in Belgium increases the day-ahead reserve price in Belgium.
- A unilateral implementation of ORDC in Belgium increases the real-time energy price in the Netherlands under conditions of scarcity.

- The approach appears to be compatible with the provisions of the EBGL:
  - ○ Only Belgian resources are affected by the settlement, therefore there is no application of an adder on foreign balancing resources.
  - ○ The merit order of the balancing platform (e.g., MARI) is respected, opportunity costs can be incorporated by Belgian resources in their balancing offers.

For the moment, it is not possible for Belgium to procure reserve capacity in the day-ahead time frame from neighboring zones, e.g., the Netherlands. It will be possible to procure reserve capacity in the future from neighbors (though there is no hard date yet) according to article 33 of the EBGL by joining a balancing cooperation region. Joining a balancing cooperation region requires using one of the techniques that are described in articles 40–43 of the EBGL, which amounts to either (i) a so-called co-optimized allocation of cross-zonal capacity or (ii) a so-called market-based allocation. Either of the two aforementioned techniques will determine what part of cross-zonal capacity in the day ahead will be reserved for exchanging balancing capacity. This allocation of balancing capacity and cross-zonal transmission capacity would take place before the day-ahead energy market in case of market-based allocation; in case of co-optimized allocation it will take place during the day-ahead energy market. In future work, therefore, we are interested in developing equilibrium models that inform how settlements should be arranged when Dutch generators can sell reserve capacity to Belgium in the day ahead. This includes a clarification of the roles and responsibilities related to the procurement of transmission rights for delivering the reserve capacity.

Appendix: Glossary

The following glossary provides short definitions of specific terms that are used in the Texas and Belgium market, and points out correspondences whenever relevant.

Adjustment period (Texas) a process following the day-ahead market and before reliability unit commitment in Texas day-ahead operations, where schedules of individual generators are adjusted in order to allow for self-commitment and outages.

Automatic frequency restoration reserve/aFRR (Belgium) Synonym, and most recent terminology for, secondary reserve.

Available regulation capacity/ARC (Belgium) A function operated by ELIA which computes the amount of capacity which can be made available for responding in the upward and downward direction within 15 min.

Balancing responsible party/BRP (Belgium) Entity in the Belgian market which is responsible for arriving to real time with a forward financial position that exactly matches its net physical position.

Balancing service provider/BSP (Belgium) Entity in the Belgian market that offers secondary and/or tertiary reserves.

Base point deviations (Texas) These are deviations of resources during their real-time dispatch from the energy and ancillary services set-points that have been instructed by the system operator.

Continuous intraday market (Belgium) An energy market that operates after the day-ahead auction and until 45 min before real time, with a continuous matching of bids on a bilateral first-come-first-serve basis.

Current operating plan/COP (Texas) The hourly on/off, technical minimum, technical maximum, and ancillary service obligation schedule of individual generators in the Texas day-ahead market. This is the analogue of nominations in the Belgian market.

Coordination of the Injection of Production Units/CIPU contract (Belgium) A legacy classification of conventional units (as opposed to newer renewable or demand-side resources) in the Belgian system, along with an associated set of rules that govern the operation of these units.

Day-ahead reliability unit commitment/DRUC (Texas) The day-ahead process that includes TSA and RUC.

EUPHEMIA (Belgium) The algorithm that is used for clearing the European day-ahead power exchange.

Energy bids (Texas) Demand-side bids in the ERCOT day-ahead market that are submitted by QSEs for buying energy.

Energy-only offers (Texas) Supply-side bids in the ERCOT day-ahead market that are submitted by QSEs for selling energy.

Free bids (Belgium) Bids for upward and downward regulation which are submitted to the Belgian real-time market by resources that have not pre-committed their capacity as reserve.

Frequency control reserve/FCR (Belgium) Synonym, and most recent terminology for, primary reserve.

Independent system operator/ISO (Texas) ERCOT, the entity which operates the electric power system and electricity market of Texas, including the day-ahead and real-time reserve and energy markets.

Intraday price coupling of regions/IDPCR (Belgium) A continuous auction that trades energy after the day-ahead market and before real time.

Load frequency control/LFC (Texas) Automatic control that is sent every 4 s to resources that are providing regulation in the Texas market, triggered by frequency deviations. This is the analogue of primary reserve in the Belgian system.

Locational marginal prices/LMP (Texas) Marginal value of locational power balance constraint in the SCED.

Manual frequency restoration reserve/mFRR (Belgium) Synonym, and most recent terminology for, tertiary reserve.

Minimum contingency level/MCL (Texas) The minimum amount of reserve capacity, below which the ORDC adder produces a real-time price equal to VOLL.

Market information system/MIS (Texas) The information technology platform that is used in the ERCOT market in order to map postings related to market operations.

Net regulation volume/NRV (Belgium) The energy that ELIA dispatches in order to cope with system imbalance.

Nomination (Belgium) The day-ahead procedure whereby the set-point, technical maximum and quantity of offered reserve of individual resources are declared by the owners to the system operator.

Paradoxically rejected bids/PRB (Belgium) Bids in the day-ahead power exchange which may be rejected, even if activating them would result in a profit for these resources.

Pool (Texas) The organization of the day-ahead market in Texas whereby the non-convex costs and operating constraints of generators are represented explicitly in the day-ahead market bids.

Portfolio bidding (Belgium) The practice whereby market participants enter the day-ahead power exchange with a bid representing a portfolio of resources, as opposed to an individual generator or load.

Power exchange (Belgium) EPEX Spot, the entity which operates the Belgian day-ahead energy market, and the actual operation of trading energy in the day-ahead time frame.

Primary reserve/R1 (Belgium) Reserve in the Belgian market that needs to react within 3 s. This is the analogue of regulation in the Texas market.

Proactive balancing (Europe) The notion that BRPs freeze their schedules hours in advance of real time, with the TSO taking over balancing of the system from that point onwards.

Qualified scheduling entities/QSE (Texas) Market entities that manage generation resources and load resources.

Reactive balancing (Europe) The notion that BRPs should be responsible for balancing their perimeter right up to real time operations, with the TSO providing advance indicators that can help BRPs balance their perimeter, and with the TSO only handling any remaining imbalances.

Reliability unit commitment (Texas) A process which is executed in the day-ahead time frame after the Texas day-ahead market in order to commit additional units beyond those committed by the day-ahead market, in case the ISO assesses that this is needed in order to ensure reliable operations.

Reserve price adders (Texas) The adder computed by the ORDC methodology. This corresponds to the Belgian scarcity adder.

Real-time online reserve price adder/RTORPA (Texas) The amount of reserve capacity that can be made available in a horizon of 30 min, as measured every 5 min by the results of a SCED run.

Real-time offline reserve price adder/RTOFFPA (Texas) The amount of reserve capacity that can be made available in a horizon of 60 min, as measured every 5 min by the results of a SCED run.

Real-time reserve price for online reserve/RTRSVPOR (Texas) The average of RTORPA over a 15-min interval, used for settlement purposes.

Real-time reserve price for offline reserve/RTRSVPOFF (Texas) The average of RTRSVPOFF over a 15-min interval, used for settlement purposes.

Real-time settlement point prices (Texas) The result of combining locational marginal prices with reserve price adders, which is used for paying activated reserves.

Reliability must run/RMR units (Texas) Resources that are required to run in real time for reliability reasons, independently of the outcome of the day-ahead market.

Reservation (Belgium) The procurement of reserve capacity by the TSO in auctions that take place before the day-ahead energy market.

Responsive reserve service/RRS (Texas) Reserve that needs to be made available within 30 min in the Texas market. This is the analogue of tertiary reserve in the Belgian market, in the sense that it is the slowest type of operating reserve.

R3 flexible (Belgium) A type of tertiary reserve product offered in the Belgian market which has less stringent delivery conditions than standard tertiary reserve.

R3 standard (Belgium) The reference tertiary reserve product that is offered in the Belgian market.

Secondary reserve/R2 (Belgium) Reserves that need to be activated within 7.5 min in the Belgian market. This is like responsive reserves in the Texas market, in these sense that this is the fastest operating reserve.

Security constrained economic dispatch/SCED (Texas) A real-time dispatch model that is run in the Texas market every 5 min.

Self-commitment (Texas) The decision to commit a unit independently of the result of the day-ahead market. Self-commitment typically takes place in the adjustment period after the day-ahead market, and resources that are self-committed are not guaranteed a make-whole payment for their fixed and start-up costs.

Shift factor (Texas) Output produced by the network security analysis function of ERCOT, which is added to the system lambda in order to determine the LMP.

Strategic reserve (Belgium) An emergency measure used in Belgium for keeping units that are intended to be mothballed as available backup capacity in order to overcome adequacy issues during winter months.

System imbalance The discrepancy between injections and offtakes of power which produce deviations from reference frequency.

Tertiary reserve/R3 (Belgium) Reserves that need to be activated within 15 min in the Belgian market. This is similar to the Texas non-spinning reserve, in the sense that it is the slowest operating reserve.

Three-part supply offers (Texas) Supply-side bids in the ERCOT day-ahead market that are submitted by QSEs for selling energy and are associated to individual generators.

Transmission security analysis/TSA (Texas) Part of the DRUC process which generates input for RUC by screening contingencies.

Transmission service provider/TSP (Texas) TSPs are responsible for operating and monitoring transmission resources (lines, transformers, buses).

Transmission system operator/TSO (Belgium) ELIA, the entity which operates the Belgian electric power system.

Two-settlement system (Texas) An accounting system for treating day-ahead financial transactions followed by physical real-time injections/withdrawals of power. The two-settlement system can be viewed in two identical ways. (i) Agents buy out their *entire* financial position at the real-time price, and are also paid the real-time price for their entire physical production/withdrawal. (ii) Equivalently, agents are paid the real-time price for the difference between their physical injection/withdrawal and their position in the forward day-ahead market.

Acknowledgments

The author wishes to acknowledge Marijn Maenhoudt and Alain Marien of the Belgian Regulatory Commission for Electricity and Gas (CREG) for helpful exchanges.

References

Ehrenmann, A., Smeers, Y., 2011. Stochastic Equilibrium Models for Generation Capacity Expansion. Vol. 163 of Stochastic Optimization Methods in Finance and Energy, International Series in Operations Research and Management Science, Part 2. Springer, pp. 273–310.

ELIA, 2018. Study Report on Scarcity Pricing in the Context of the 2018 Discretionary Incentives. December 20,.

Harker, P.T., 1993. Lectures on Computation of Equilibria with Equation-Based Methods. CORE, Université Catholique de Louvain.

Hogan, W.W., September 2005. On an 'energy only' electricity market design for resource adequacy. Tech. rep. Center for Business and Government, JFK School of Government, Harvard University.

Papavasiliou, A., Smeers, Y., 2017. Remuneration of flexibility under conditions of scarcity: a case study of Belgium. Energy J. 38 (6), 105–135.

Papavasiliou, A., Smeers, Y., Bertrand, G., 2018. An extended analysis on the remuneration of capacity under scarcity conditions. Econ. Energy Environ. Policy 7 (2).

Papavasiliou, A., Smeers, Y., de Maere d'Aertrycke, G., June 6, 2019. Study on the general design of a mechanism for the remuneration of reserves in scarcity situations.

Ralph, D., Smeers, Y., 2015. Risk trading and endogenous probabilities in investment equilibria. SIAM J. Optim. 25 (4), 2589–2611.

Stoft, S., 2002. Power System Economics. IEEE Press and Wiley Interscience.

Chapter 11

Electricity portfolio optimization: Cost minimization using MILP

Agis Koumentakos

Energy & Environmental Policy Laboratory, School of Economics, Business and International Studies, University of Piraeus, Piraeus, Greece

Nomenclature

e_b^{DR}	the contribution of the total energy curtailed in the specific segment b
μ_b	an indicator of the DR zonal prices
$C_i^{4HPL} C_j^{2HPL}, C_k^H$	are the quarterly cost of each flexible PLC and the hourly product, respectively
t	quarter time slice
$\gamma_i, \gamma_j, \gamma_t$	respectively in MWs
C_b^{DR}	the accumulated cost up to segment b
$P(t)$	the curve of power demand
P_t	the day ahead demand in quarterly frame
D_{act}^{PP}	the duration of each power level measured in quarters
P_{max}^{PP}	the maximum power output of the power plant
α, β	the number of BLCs and 12-h PLCs respectively in MWs
p_t^{PP}	the output capacity of power in MW of the power plant at time period t
p_t^{SM}	the power curve of the quarterly power from the spot market
$C^{SM} C^{BL} C^{12HPL}$	the quarterly cost of each flexible PLC and the hourly product, respectively
T	the set of quarter-hour time slices per day
c^{total}	the total cost beared by the provider in order to meet the demand
C^{SM}	the total cost the provider pays for buying power from the SM
e^{total}	the total daily energy provided in MWh
N^B	the total number of distinct price zones/segments
P_t^{total}	the total power provided at time slice t
c_{ER}^{DR}	total cost for the day ahead DR
c_F	total cost of "Flexible PLCs"
c_I	total cost of "Fully Integrated"
c_p	total cost of "poutil"
$\gamma_i, \gamma_j, \gamma_t$	the number of 4-h PLCs, 2-h PLCs and hourly products
12-h PLC	peak load contract of 12-h duration
2-h PLC	peak load contract off 2-h duration
4-h PLC	peak load contract of 4-h duration
b	the segment indicator
BLC	base load contract
CPP	critical peak pricing
DAM	day ahead market
DLC	direct load control
DR	demand response
DSO	distribution system operator
EPEX Spot	European Power Exchange
EUPHEMIA	algorithm solving the coupling of the day-ahead power markets in the PCR region
HUPX	Hungarian Power Exchange
I	dyadic indicators of specific time periods

Mathematical Modelling of Contemporary Electricity Markets. https://doi.org/10.1016/B978-0-12-821838-9.00011-6

LFC	load following contract
PLC	peak load contract
RES	renewable energy sources
RTP	real time pricing
SM	spot market
P_b^{DR}	the zonal price
TSO	transmission system operator
Z_1, Z_2, Z_3	zonal pricing borders for the DR

1   Introduction

A vital characteristic of modern developed societies is electrification. The electricity demand is constantly growing as a direct result of the respective energy demand growth. At the same time societies around the world already face the environmental impact of this situation, highlighting the need of efficiency and viability. Main industries such as: maritime, automobile etc. are turning to electricity. The liberalization of the electricity sector has opened the door to many new market stakeholders from the production side all the way to the retail. Therefore, the importance of power markets, their structures and mechanisms for their proper operation, are growing. In this context the present research focuses in the transitioning role of electricity providers. This transition is mostly shaped by the constantly growing Renewable Energy Sources (RES) production as well as the market competitiveness. A vital part of an electricity market is the Day Ahead Market (DAM). The DAM has a specific structure and way of operating that has not changed significantly the last years. The review of DAM will orbit around the standardized products available in the markets. This focus is important for the present research, as the major part of the developments refer to such products. Focusing on European energy markets, there exist more than a couple of different products concerning the DAM. The most common, in almost every modern market, are hourly and block orders (Nord, EPEX, IPEX, HEnEx, etc.) (Bichpuriya and Soman, 2010; EPEX SPOT, 2020; Nord Pool, 2019).

Hourly products are bids for sell/buy referring to a specific only hour of DAM. They are separated to Hourly Step Orders and Hourly Linear Piecewise Orders. In general, hourly step orders refer to a specific amount of energy and a certain price limit. A buy step order will refer to a specific volume and an upper price limit that the buyer is willing to pay. Relatively, a sell step order refers to a specific volume and a lower price limit that the seller is willing to sell the energy. Hourly Linear Piecewise orders differ from step, as they do not bid specific price and volume of energy. Specifically, they do bid a volume of energy that starts to be accepted after a specific price po until fully accepted at price p1. These bids are called linear, as they do have a steady ratio between volume/price, therefore forming a linear order with a slope equal to that ratio. An order is characterized as block order when it consists of a fixed amount and price of energy, referring to the same day and more than one time periods. However, block orders vary, providing different capabilities that suit different occasions of trading. According to one of the two largest spot markets in Europe, there exist four distinct types of block orders: Regular, Profile, Curtailable and Linked (Koltsaklis and Dagoumas, 2018).

Generally, the idea of block orders suits greatly the needs of power producers such as those of thermal powerplants that face significant start/stop costs. Specifically, without block orders, the optimal solution of any algorithm solving the electricity market, would result in unrealistic dispatch of thermal units. Research developed around EUPHEMIA's algorithm of the European electricity exchange, states that block orders indeed succeed in avoiding shut down of powerplants and realistic dispatch results (Koltsaklis and Dagoumas, 2018). The significance of the start-up costs, and their implications in bidding in the SM, has attracted great attention among researchers and the industrial sector, resulting to detailed modelling in order to face the problem. Block order, and certain modelling constraints, can provide a solution to the problem. Also, the linked blocks provide the ability to bid a higher priced parent block, covering the start-up costs, and a lower priced child block reflecting the lower operating expenses of the unit. The distributor's portfolio does include a natural gas powerplant. However, the bidding strategy in the DAM is not in the scope of the present research. The different block orders and hourly products are presented to justify the available standardized products, which are also included in the energy portfolio. It is important from the distributor's point of view, which products would be available to him in the DAM, as the variety, flexibility and price of those directly affects the optimal solution.

Additional to the DAM products, the present research deals with demand response (DR). Fig. 11.1 provides a classification of the DR programs. DR is any method or program that tries to control the demand of electricity, from the consumer side, in order to optimize the system. Along with Distributed Generation, DR has great potential in altering the operation and increasing the efficiency of the electricity system. The means to implement DR be of economical nature, such as incentivizing consumers to increase their load in off peak hours and curtail it in peak hours. Moreover, it can optimize the

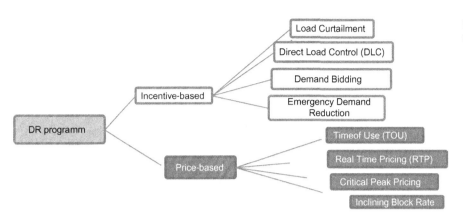

FIG. 11.1 Classification of DR programs (Jordehi, 2019).

dispatch of the power generation units, thus reducing their environmental impact. There are numerous different DR programs that can be superficially presented below (Parrish et al., 2019; Mohsenian-Rad and Leon-Garcia, 2010).

Following the first part of the research work focused on the SM and DR options of the provider. The present work bases its methodological approach upon an open source algorithm named "poutil," available through the GAMS library. Our research integrates additional capabilities to the model, such as hourly products of the SM and realistic constrains regarding the DR. Additionally we develop and propose new flexible SM products that will reduce further the overall cost of the provider. The optimization models developed are formulated as mixed integer linear programming (MILP) models and used for the solution of the optimal electricity portfolio management of the provider, in order to meet the entire demand. The objective of the proposed optimization approach concerns the minimization of the provider's total daily cost and subject to a series of constraints, including energy demand balance and all the ones arising from the hourly orders, block orders, DR including the proposed new types of blocks orders referred to as peak load contracts (PLCs). The remainder of the paper is structured according to the following: Section 2 provides the model's mathematical formulation beginning with the objective function and the different modelling packages that each of the three models involves. Later in Section 2 the major equation's modelling is presented in detail, along with the exact case scenario. Section 3 provides a critical discussion of the results obtained from the model implementation, and finally, Section 4 draws upon some concluding remarks

2 Mathematical model

The present section represents the mathematical modelling of the research. At first we present the objective function of the problem and the different equation sets for each of the three models, the original and two developed.

2.1 Objective function

The objective function to be optimized concerns the minimization of the total daily net cost. This cost consists of the respective cost the provider bears for utilizing each of the three different options in order to meet the demand and include:

- Power generation from the natural gas powerplant, with specific operational stages, startup/shut down costs and block orders.
- Spot market (base load contracts, peak load contracts, hourly products).
- Demand response program, curtailing part of the demand in quarter resolution.

$$\text{Min } c^{total}$$

$$c^{total} = C^{PP} + C^{SM} + c_{ER}^{DR}$$

c^{total} is the total cost beared by the provider in order to meet the demand; C^{PP} is the cost for producing power at the own powerplant; C^{SM} is the total cost the provider pays for buying power from the SM; c_{ER}^{DR} is total cost for the day ahead DR.

Poutil: $P_t^{total} = P_t^{PP} + P_t^{SM} + P_t^{DR}$, $c^{total} = C^{PP} + C^{SM} + c_{ER}^{DR}$

Power from the powerplant	$P_t^{PP} = 0.1 \cdot (a_s + 2) P_{max}^{PP}, \forall t, a_s \in \{2,3,4,5,6,8\}$
Power from the spot market	$P_t^{SM} = \alpha + I_t^{12HPL} \cdot \beta$
Power from the demand response	P_t^{DR}
Cost of the powerplant	$C^{PP} = c^{PP} \cdot P_t^{PP}$
Cost of the spot market	$C^{SM} = C^{BL} \cdot \alpha + C^{12HPL}$
Cost the demand response	$c_{ER}^{DR} = \sum_{b=1}^{N^B} (C_b^{DR} \cdot \mu_b + P_b^{DR} \cdot e_b^{DR})$

Flexible PLCs: $P_t^{total} = P_t^{PP} + P_t^{SM} + P_t^{DR}$, $c^{total} = C^{PP} + C^{SM} + c_{ER}^{DR}$

Power from the powerplant	$P_t^{PP} = 0.1 \cdot (a_s + 2) P_{max}^{PP}, \forall t, a_s \in \{2,3,4,5,6,8\}$
Power from the spot market	$P_t^{SM} = \alpha + I_t^{12HPL} \cdot \beta + I_{it}^{4HPL} \cdot \gamma_i + I_{jt}^{2HPL} \cdot \gamma_j$
Power from the demand response	P_t^{DR}
Cost of the powerplant	$C^{PP} = c^{PP} \cdot P_t^{PP}$
Cost of the spot market	$C^{SM} = C^{BL} \cdot \alpha + C^{12HPL} + \sum_t C_i^{4HPL} \cdot \gamma_i + \sum_t C_j^{2HPL} \cdot \gamma_j$
Cost of the demand response	$c_{ER}^{DR} = \sum_{b=1}^{N^B} (C_b^{DR} \bullet \mu_b + P_b^{DR} \bullet e_b^{DR})$

Fully integrated: $P_t^{total} = P_t^{PP} + P_t^{SM} + P_t^{DR}$, $c^{total} = C^{PP} + C^{SM} + c_{ER}^{DR}$

Power from the powerplant	$P_t^{PP} = 0.1 \cdot (a_s + 2) P_{max}^{PP}, \forall t, a_s \in \{2,3,4,5,6,8\}$
Power from the spot market	$P_t^{SM} = \alpha + I_t^{12HPL} \cdot \beta + I_{it}^{4HPL} \cdot \gamma_i + I_{jt}^{2HPL} \cdot \gamma_j + I_k^H \bullet \gamma_t$
Power from the demand response	P_t^{DR}
Cost of the powerplant	$C^{PP} = c^{PP} \cdot P_t^{PP}$
Cost of the spot market	$C^{SM} = C^{BL} \cdot \alpha + C^{12HPL} + \sum_t C_i^{4HPL} \cdot \gamma_i + \sum_t C_j^{2HPL} \cdot \gamma_j + \sum_t C_k^H \bullet \gamma_t$
Cost the demand response	$c_{ER}^{DR} = \sum_{b=1}^{N^B} (C_b^{DR} \bullet \mu_b + P_b^{DR} \bullet e_b^{DR})$
Additional constrains	$\gamma_i \le 100$ MW $P_t^{DR} \le 150$ MW

2.2 Case description and modelling

In this chapter, we describe the problem and the modelling of it. Since our model is based on the original (Rebennack et al., 2010), it was considered appropriate to present the problem in the same way and maintain the same variables, so that the differentiation and evolution of the present model was evident. This way the reader-researcher will be able to compare the new models more easily with the original one. The case scenario refers to an electricity provider, referred as "distributor" in the original model, responsible for meeting the demand of its customers. It is hypothesized that the distributor knows the specific energy demand of the Day Ahead ($D+1$). The demand forecast is a table of quarterly forecasted demand in MWs for the next 24 h and consists of a continuous function.

$$P(t), \quad 0 \le t \le 24 \tag{11.1}$$

where $P(t)$ is given in MW and represents the curve of power demand and t symbolizes the hour of the day.

The original case separates the day ahead demand from hourly to quarterly resolution, mentioning that such a frame constitutes a common standard in many electricity systems. Therefore:

$$T := \{1, \ldots, N^T = 96\} \tag{11.2}$$

$$P_t, t = 1, \ldots, N^T \tag{11.3}$$

where T is the set of quarter-hour time slices per day, P_t is given in MW and represents the day ahead demand in quarterly frame, and t symbolizes from now on the quarters of the day ahead.

The present research's scope does not include the methods, or the technical means required in forecasting the Day Ahead demand. However, such a forecast is not difficult, because it refers to a specific consumer portfolio. The specific group of consumers whether industrial, commercial or residential, constitute a specific energy demand curve. This demand can be accurately forecasted through historical data, considering any existing seasonality, trends and "events." Knowing the $D+1$ electricity demand, P_t the provider must provide all the electricity asked, leaving none of the demanded capacities unmet. This means the model considers 100% demand coverage as a prerequisite and constitutes one of the initial constraints. To do this, the distributor has more than one means in its disposal. The first option is a natural gas powerplant in distributor's possession. The powerplant does operate however the distributor decides, always under the technical constraints such as start and stop times etc., and will be presented in detail in Section 2.2.1. The decision of this kind of powerplant was taken due to two different reasons. Firstly, the same unit was considered in the original model, and therefore helps to preserve the comparability between the original model and the new one developed in this research. Secondly, natural gas fired powerplants are a technology that is expected to continue to operate for the next years, having a pivotal role along with RES in the gradual removal of lignite powerplants. The second option in the distributor's disposal is obtaining the required energy from the Electricity Market. The case refers only to short term operations of the distributor, therefore any activities in the market regarding the spot market (SM), and specifically the products of DAM. This means that long term products such as forwards or bilateral etc. are disregarded, focusing only on a $D+1$ optimization model. The specific products available, and the capabilities of the distributor in regarding the SM, will be thoroughly discussed. The third and last option is controlling the demand. This option is used when the energy obtained from the other two, powerplant and SM, is incapable of meeting completely the demand. Incapable of meeting the demand does not mean actual physical incapability, but economic preferability. To clarify this, covering the demand in peak hours using only the first two options, might be more expensive for the distributor than making use of the third option as well, to cover part of the demand. Controlling the demand is known as demand response (DR) and can be executed in different ways. This option can be very helpful, especially in peak hours or in "events," by curtailing the excess in demand or shifting the load to other time periods. Such capabilities can also be used for avoiding extreme price peaks or downs, thus increasing the markets stability by decreasing volatility. However, this option does have the drawback of preventing the use of energy for specific types of use and specific time periods, reducing the consumer's freedom. The interaction required between the distributor or any other responsible for the DR and the final consumer raises, numerous challenges. The purpose of the research is to provide the distributor with the optimum scenario. The solution is optimizing of the mixture of the three options in order to meet the demand with the minimum cost.

2.2.1 Modelling the power-plant

As stated in the introductory part of this section, the distributor has the ability to produce power from a natural-gas fired powerplant.

Let the maximum power output of the power plant equal to 300 MW.

$$P_{max}^{PP} = 300 \text{ MW} \tag{11.4}$$

During normal operation the powerplant should not be operated at less than 40% of the maximum capacity. Therefore:

$$p_t^{PP} \geq 0.4 P_{max}^{PP}, \quad \forall t \tag{11.5}$$

where p_t^{PP} represents the output capacity of power in MW of the power plant at time period t.

In case the powerplant is not used, then $p_t^{PP} = 0$. Moreover, the powerplant must operate in specific steps meaning that its power output does not follow a continuous curve but is rather a step equation. Specifically, it can operate in eight, including idle stage, different stages, as shown in Table 11.1.

This is mathematically translated to the following equation substituting Eq. (11.5):

TABLE 11.1 Natural gas powerplant operating stages.

Operating stage	Output capacity (MW)
1. Idle	0
2. 40% of max. capacity	120
3. 50% of max. capacity	150
4. 60% of max. capacity	180
5. 70% of max. capacity	210
6. 80% of max. capacity	240
7. 90% of max. capacity	270
8. 100% of max. capacity	300

$$p_t^{PP} = 0.1(a_s + 2)P_{max}^{PP}, \quad \forall t \tag{11.6}$$

where $a_s \in \{2,3,4,5,6,8.\}$.

Apart from the power output steps, the powerplant does have another techno-economical constraint. As stated before, the startup/shut down cost of thermal units plays a significant role in their operating expenses. Therefore, it cannot be excluded from the model. To integrate this technical constraint would require a specific minimum operation period of the powerplant. However, such a constraint is incomplete, because it allows the powerplant to change power constantly from one step to the other. To avoid this, we follow the original modelling of "poutil" by constraining each power output level to operate a minimum period of 2h before changing. This is modeled as:

$$D_{act}^{PP} = 8 \tag{11.7}$$

where: D_{act}^{PP} is the duration of each power level measured in quarters

Now we can add the constraint regarding the minimum idle time of the powerplant to be at least 4h, such as

$$p_j^{PP} = p_{j+1}^{PP} = \ldots = p_{j+m}^{PP}, \quad \text{with } m \geq 15 \tag{11.8}$$

where j is a time interval containing an idle time.

Most of the modelling of the powerplant can be found in the original article (Rebennack et al., 2010), therefore the rest of the modelling section will present only the additional modelling that was made to create the two new models, "Flexible PLCs" and "Fully Integrated."

2.2.2 Modelling the spot market

The distributor can not only produce power through the power plant, but also buy from the spot market (SM). In the original model, the SM does provide two different standardized products, Base Load and Peak Load Contracts, BLCs and PLCs respectively. The BLC is the purchase of a specific amount of power (MW) for a duration of 24h. The total amount of energy bought from a BLC is the product of power bought (MW) multiplied by 24h, which is the BLC duration. A PLC is the purchase of power referring only to peak hours (08:00–20:00). The new model integrates the ability of the provider to participate more actively in the SM, being able to purchase two additional PLCs of smaller duration, as well as hourly products that are available in every electricity market these days.

2.2.2.1 Improving the peak load contracts

The spot market of the initial model does provide one 12-h PLC from 08:00–20:00 and a 24-h base block product. The price of PLC is obviously higher than the BLC, as it refers to a smaller time period of greater demand when more expensive power units are called in order to satisfy the demand. However, these two block products from the SM do not optimize the flexibility of the market. For example, in order to meet the peaks of the demand at the Peak Zone, the distributor can only buy 12-h PLCs, and cover any incapability of energy delivery through load following contracts (LFCs). LFC is mostly known as demand response and is the most expensive choice. From the demand side, for an average day of the year, there exist specific periods where power demand is greater than the rest of the day. These periods known as peak-hours, could raise the power demand even by 188% in the present case of the model. However, this growth is not gradual, neither the demand remains constant after reaching an upper maximum. The continuous fluctuations of the demand, especially during the Peak Zones, underline the absence of smaller, hence more flexible, PLCs. The above problem can be perceived from the supply side through the DR, which are increasing dramatically whenever the demand rapidly rises, and are presented in detail in Section 3. For example, the additional demand in peak hours would be covered by LFCs and not PLCs, because the marginal cost of an additional MW through a 12-h PLC would be greater. Reminding at this point that the distributor is incapable of producing additional power from the natural gas plant as it is already running at maximum capacity. Based on the above, having the ability to buy smaller-flexible PLCs, a distributor might reduce the amount of MW "bought" from LFCs, which are paid to the final customers for reducing their consumption.

2.2.2.2 Pricing the different PLCs

The original model that our research is based, does not integrate the ability of buying all the standardized products of the SM. Without such a product, any hourly demand peak cannot be efficiently satisfied by the original BLC and PLCs, not even from our flexible PLCs. In the original model, any demand peak of such is covered through demand response, having none constraint over the maximum energy or power that can be curtailed. Therefore, the PLCs therefore emerge as a mean ot reducing the overall cost by substituting part of the expensive LFCs. For this reason, pricing the new PLCs is of great significance, as it directly affects the optimal solution. Further explaining this correlation between PLCs and demand response (DR), if the PLC price approaches that of a DR, then the distributor will not have enough motive to buy power from a PLC instead of the more flexible LFC. On the other hand, if a PLC is cheaper than an LFC, to counterweight being less flexible, then a distributor would choose the first, not constraining the natural demand of the final customers through LFC. This section of the research does present the pricing the new PLCs. This happens by re-pricing all the products (including the BLC and PLC of the original model), based on the new hourly day ahead prices that we integrate. The latest addition of hourly products, as in any Day Ahead market, cannot be dealt respectively to the flexible PLCs. Inserting the capability of hourly power purchase in the Day Ahead requires also the price curve. The distributor in our model has to operate as any other player of the Day Ahead market, and forecast the DA price. The differences between the forecasted and the real price are of no concern in our model, as they are covered either through Intraday or balancing markets. Following on from the above, the distributor does bid in the Day Ahead Market quantities that remain to be satisfied and cannot be covered by the powerplant production, or are more economic than the block products of the SM. Pricing based on the new hourly products, is a robust way and reassures the integrity of our numerical results. In the present subsection, we present the pricing of all the SM products based on the new hourly prices, and not on the original prices of the model "poutil." As explained above, this is the method used in the optimization model, as it provides trustworthy results. To price the products based on the hourly prices, we must first choose which hourly prices to integrate. The present research uses hourly prices of the Hungarian Energy Exchange, HUPX. HUPX is the most developed energy exchange in SEE, and constitutes the Spot Price for many countries such as Serbia, Albania, F.Y.R.O.M. and others. Specifically, the prices belong to a random week-day of March 2020 and are presented in the next chapter. The whole 24 h constitute the Baseload. The 12 h 8 AM to 8 PM constitute the Peak Load. Respectively, the pricing of the new flexible PLCs of 4&2 h, is actually the average price of the respective hourly prices. Fig. 11.2 helps in understanding the relations between the SM products and the Hourly Prices.

The products of the above figure are priced as the numerical averages of the respective hourly prices. It is important to notice that in contrast to the BLC and 12-h PLC, the 4 and 2-h PLC do not constitute a single contract, but three and six respectively. These contracts have also different prices. This means that these products do introduce two new characteristics-options in our model. Firstly the smaller PLCs, as stated, provide greater flexibility to the distributor, giving him a greater resolution to its energy bought from the SM. Secondly, having mentioned the price difference between same products of different time periods, the model integrates the logic that pricing is affected, not only by the duration of the product, but also of the specific time that this product is used. This is exactly the reality of the markets and the reason we integrate an hourly product to the model. Although the scope of the present research excludes the consideration of any trading-bidding strategy for the energy bought through the SM, a provider of the modern electricity market should be able to participate more actively in the spot market. Therefore, without getting into trading details and modelling, the integrated model includes hourly products, as well as flexible PLCs that share the same pricing philosophy. Based on the above, having concluded in the integration of all the products (hourly, 2-h PLC, 4-h PLC, 12-h PLC and BLC), we hereby present the mathematical modelling. Starting with the power from the SM, we move directly to the new additional equations of the new models.

$$p_t^{SM} = \alpha + I_t^{12HPL} \cdot \beta + I_{it}^{4HPL} \cdot \gamma_i + I_{jt}^{2HPL} \cdot \gamma_j + I_k^H \cdot \gamma_t \tag{11.9}$$

where $i \in \{1,2,3\}$, $j \in \{1,2,3,4,5,6\}$, $k \in [1,24]$.

p_t^{SM} is the power curve of the quarterly power from the spot market, α, β are the number of BLCs and 12-h PLCs respectively in MWs, γ_i, γ_j, γ_t are the number of 4-h PLCs, 2-h PLCs and hourly products, respectively, in MWs, I are dyadic indicators of specific time periods, and k is an integer.

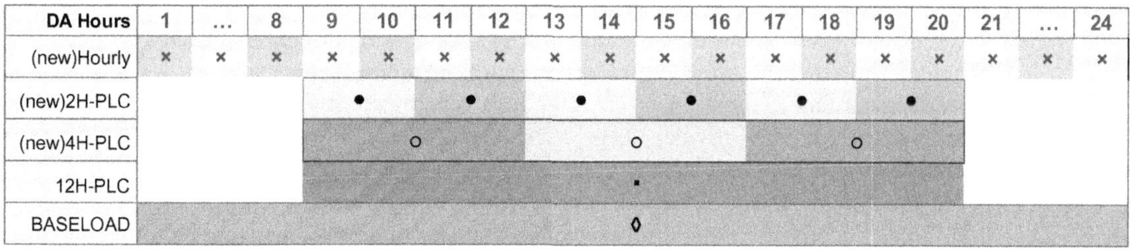

DA Hours	1	...	8	9	10	11	12	13	14	15	16	17	18	19	20	21	...	24
(new)Hourly	×	×	×	×	×	×	×	×	×	×	×	×	×	×	×	×	×	×
(new)2H-PLC				•		•		•		•		•		•				
(new)4H-PLC				○				○				○						
12H-PLC								▪										
BASELOAD								◊										

FIG. 11.2   All the products of the SM in the "Fully Integrated" model.

The above equation represents the power coming from the SM each quarter. It is equal to the notional amount of power coming from each product of the SM. Starting with the power from BLCs, as they refer to the entire 24 h of the day ahead, the power is fix for any time slice, t. The 12-h PLC is also providing fixed amount of power for the entire peak load period. However, the model must know when we enter the peak load time period when the PLCs are available. Therefore, the dyadic indicator I_t^{12HPL} indicates when the time slice t belongs in the peak zone by changing its value to 1, and equals 0 when outside of the peak load time period. The same situation exists for the 4 and 2 h PLCs. The only difference compared to the 12-h PLC, is that the flexible PLCs do not have fixed power throughout the peak load time period. The flexible PLCs can have different power volumes, as there are three and six different 4-h PLCs and 2-h PLCs, respectively. Therefore, exist different variables of power γ for each of the 12 distinct flexible PLCs (three 4-h PLCs and six 2-h PLCs). The same goes for the dyadic indicators I, which state if the time slice belongs in the specific flexible PLC or not. For example:

$$I_{1t}^{2HPL} \cdot \gamma_1$$

Gives the quarterly power coming from the first 2-h PLC, and the dyadic indicator will equal 1 for the respective time period of the first, out of the six, 2-h PLCs. Moreover, the dyadic indicator I_k^H indicates at which specific hour the t belongs. The same logic is followed for creating the respective cost equation of the SM. Specifically, the cost is equal to the amount of power from the SM, multiplied by the respective power price. The original model "poutil" does not provide a quarterly distribution of the cost of the power from the SM, but only the total cost for the day ahead. Therefore, the total cost of the "Fully integrated" model, is calculated based on the below equation:

$$C^{SM} = C^{BL} \cdot \alpha + C^{12HPL} \cdot \beta + \sum_t C_i^{4HPL} \cdot \gamma_i + \sum_t C_j^{2HPL} \cdot \gamma_j + \sum_t C_k^H \cdot \gamma_t \tag{11.10}$$

where C^{SM} is the total cost the provider pays for buying power from the SM, C^{BL}, C^{12HPL} are the costs for one MW (contract) of the BLC and the 12-h PLC, respectively, and C_i^{4HPL}, C_j^{2HPL}, C_k^H are the quarterly cost of each flexible PLC and the hourly product, respectively.

The present research does also calculate the total SM cost of the two new models considered and compares it with the original. However, the quarterly cost curve is created and presented in Section 3 as it shows in detail the cost minimization achieved by our models compared to the original.

2.2.3 Modelling the demand response

Demand response has attracted a lot of attention, as said in the introduction of the thesis. A clustering of the many different DR programs available in the modern markets takes part in the literature review section. An important factor, that directly affects the success of any DR program, is the rate of response from the consumers. The response rate differs strongly among the numerous DR programs, with DLC and TOU being the most efficient. The two new models, "Flexible PLCs" and "Fully Integrated," integrate the same DR program as the original model "poutil." However, the nature of DR is such, that a short presentation of its modelling is helpful. The DR presentation serves also the integration of a new constraint regarding the DR, which is explained below after the modelling of the DR price zones.

2.2.3.1 Pricing the DR program

It should be clear by now that DR, and specifically the power curtailment through LFCs, is in general the most expensive mean of meeting the demand. Regardless of the specific additional cost in €/MWh, DR should be the most expensive mean, in order to incentivize the distributors of further optimizing their operations, and secure consumer welfare through other means and not by curtailment. Another logical explanation is that due to its quarterly resolution, LFC is the most flexible compared to the rest available means of the distributor (powerplant, SM), for meeting the demand. The quarterly resolution is visible in most figures in the results chapter. The initial LFC implemented in "poutil" belongs in the DLC category of DR programs and remains an efficient way of controlling the demand in peak hours. The suitability of this program is based on the need of simpler DR programs in order to achieve greater consumer engagement (Parrish et al., 2019). The price of the DR is not fixed, but changes according to the level of curtailability. Specifically, the pricing is divided in three distinct zones of aggregated curtailed energy. The provider keeps track of the curtailed amount of energy of the entire year, and follows an annually based priced system, with the aforementioned zones. The prices are the incentives paid to the consumers, hence they are equal to the cost the provider bears for the curtailment.

Let Z_1, Z_2, Z_3 be the volume boundaries of the three annual price zones in MWh. Then, the below figure presents the exact values forming the respective zones. However, the model is working on a day ahead basis, therefore the annually

TABLE 11.2 From annual to daily DR cost zonal pricing (Rebennack et al., 2010).

DR zonal price (€/MWh)	Annual zonal borders (MWh)	Daily zonal borders (MWh)
80	54,750	150
65	182,500	500
52	Max	Max

based price system is improper. As in "poutil," to overcome this, we transform the annual zones to daily ones. This can be easily done by diving the zone values Z_1, Z_2, Z_3 by the number of days constituting a year.

$$Z_1^d = Z_1 / 365, \quad Z_2^d = Z_2 / 365, \quad Z_3^d = Z_3 / 365 \tag{11.11}$$

where Z_1^d, Z_2^d, Z_3^d are the respective daily zonal borders in MWh.

Table 11.2 represents both the annual zonal borders and the daily zonal borders with the respective prices.

The cost of the curtailed energy that the provider must bear is calculated by the following equation:

$$c_{ER}^{DR} = \sum_{b=1}^{N^B} \left(C_b^{DR} \cdot \mu_b + P_b^{DR} \cdot e_b^{DR} \right) \tag{11.12}$$

where c_{ER}^{DR} is the total cost for the day ahead DR, C_b^{DR} is the accumulated cost up to segment b, μ_b is an indicator of the DR zonal prices, P_b^{DR} is the zonal price, e_b^{DR} is the contribution of the total energy curtailed in the specific segment b, b is the segment indicator, and N^B is the total number of distinct price zones/segments.

From the above equation, we get that the total cost of the DR is equal to the accumulated cost up to the segment that the total curtailed energy belongs, plus the cost of the excess energy. Specifically, the total curtailed energy will belong in one of the three different segments, N^B. In the model there exist three segments, $N^B = 3$. However, we keep the variable N^B, so that the model remains generic and customizable. As stated, the curtailed energy belongs in the segment b. Therefore, the sum of the products $C_b^{DR} \cdot \mu_b$ from 1 to b, equals to the total accumulated cost of all the segments up to b. The rest of the energy that belongs in the last segment b, has a cost that equals to the product of the remaining energy and the respective price per MWh of segment b.

2.3 Summing up the different models

Based on all of the above in the present research, there are numerous different models created. The research uses the research, continually referenced throughout the text as a modelling base. This model named "poutil," is publicly available through the GAMS Library (Rebennack et al., 2010), and is used as a reference. The original model, "poutil" has as an input a volatile demand. It does equip the provider with the following capabilities, as mentioned above:

- Power production from the natural gas fired powerplant.
- Energy received from the SM, through BLCs and 12 h PLCs
- The ability of demand response (DR) in quarterly resolution.

Solving the case, using the model "poutil," gives a specific cost. This cost refers to the total cost that the energy provider will have to bear, in order to meet the demand. The aim of this research is reminded here, as creating a model aiming to the development of the capabilities of the provider, the integration of more options, as well as the modernization to meet the current situation of the electricity sector. Therefore, we created two new models, the "Flexible PLCs" and the "Fully Integrated." Starting with the "Flexible PLCs," this model does provide the energy provider with all the abilities of the "poutil" and adds the following:

- Additional energy received from the SM through 4-h PLCs and 2-h PLCs.

The "Flexible PLCs" model works as a transitional model from "poutil" to the "Fully Integrated." It is useful in order to present the importance of the smaller flexible PLCs proposed. Finally, the "Fully Integrated" model is presented, which includes all options of the above two models and the additional: *Day Ahead Hourly Products*. As explained above, these hourly products of the SM are priced based on HUPX. It is also important to mention again, that in order to preserve the comparability of the new models, "Flexible PLCs" and "Fully Integrated," with the model "poutil," the initial prices of the

TABLE 11.3 SM product prices in the "Fully Integrated" model.

DA hours	Hourly (€/MWh)	2-h PLC (€/MWh)	4-h PLC (€/MWh)	12-h PLC (€/MWh)	BLC (€/MWh)
1	30.73				37.6
2	26.78				
3	26.07				
4	26.78				
5	29.06				
6	33.85				
7	42.78				
8	46.42				
9	44.24	41	44.3	40.2	
10	37.78				
11	33.22	33.1			
12	32.86				
13	30.72	29.9	31.6		
14	29.28				
15	31.27	33.1			
16	34.88				
17	38.84	42.2	52.2		
18	45.46				
19	61.29	62.2			
20	63.03				
21	51.2				
22	40.62				
23	34.95				
24	30.75				

latter have been altered. Specifically, all prices are based on the hourly prices of HUPX, hence the new prices of all the SM products can be seen in Table 11.3.

Since the 'Fully Integrated" model integrates all the above capabilities, it is reasonable to present in this last part, before the Results chapter, the final equations for power and cost. The total power of the provider must meet the demand, and is equal to the sum of the power produced in the powerplant, the SM, as well as the curtailed power through DR. Therefore:

$$P_t^{total} = P_t^{PP} + P_t^{SM} + P_t^{DR} \tag{11.13}$$

where P^{total} is the total power provided at time slice t.

Based on the above equation, we get that the total energy provided is the sum of all the power at each time slice.

$$e^{total} = \frac{1}{4} \cdot \sum_t P_t^{PP} + P_t^{SM} + P_t^{DR} \tag{11.14}$$

where e^{total} is the total daily energy provided in MWh.

The e^{total} is the sum of all the power provided during each time slice t, divided by four. Dividing by four is necessary in order to provide the energy volume in MWh. This happens because the model has a quarterly resolution, not an hourly.

Moreover, the objective of the model is the minimization of the total cost beared by the provider in order to meet the demand. Therefore, it is calculated through the following equation:

$$c^{total} = C^{PP} + C^{SM} + c^{DR}_{ER} \tag{11.15}$$

This cost is equal to the cost of providing the respective energy e^{total}. As stated before, the model code is based on the code of "poutil," and all the required information and explanations of such modelling are included in (Rebennack et al., 2010). There is no reason to represent and explain the entire model in the present research, but only the additional code and model capabilities that are developed. Therefore, the last modelling development was the integration of two additional constraints to the already existing ones. However, as stated before, the cost equation refers to the total, not to the quarterly curve. The quarterly cost distribution is created after the model solution, using spreadsheet software. The cost and power quarterly distribution were created in the present research and are presented and discussed in Section 3.

The first constraint refers to the DR program and is actually a transformation of the existing constraint in the original model. All three means, that are in the disposal of the provider to meet the demand, have upper constraints. In the original model, the powerplant can produce up to 300 MW, and the power from the SM and DR can both have a maximum value equal to the maximum power demanded. As far as the DR is concerned, such an upper constraint means that the model can have a solution where in some quarters the entire demand would be curtailed. Such an assumption is not realistic and could as well provide unrealistic solutions. In addition it is clear that a complete engagement of the consumers in DR programs is far from reality. Therefore, even if the scenario of a full curtailment of the entire demand for a specific time period was realistic, and not jeopardizing the systems goal, even then, it would be impossible to achieve. It is so, because that would require the entire demand side (consumers) to be participants in the DR program, translating to a 100% engagement. Therefore, the "Fully Integrated" model constrains the amount that can be curtailed to 150 MW, when the maximum quarterly demand is around 500 MW, or 33.3% maximum curtailment. The second constrain refers to the Hourly products. These products belong to the SM, where the power from the SM in the original model has no upper constrains. The same logic was followed to the additional flexible PLCs. However, the hourly products are constrained to a maximum of 100 MW. This constrain keeps the model generic, in cases that the Spot Price reaches zero, or very low prices. In such an occasion, the model would choose to meet the entire demand through the hourly product, which is again nonrealistic. An electricity provider cannot base its entire consumer portfolio in just one product, as it greatly increases the risk. The rest of the constraints can be found in the code of the "Fully Integrated" and the original "poutil."

3   Results and discussion

In this section the numerical results of all three models are presented and compared. Starting with original model "poutil" we inserted the BLC and 12 h PLC prices and the required constraints mentioned above. Solving the model resulted in a total cost of

$$c_p = 289,092.3 €$$

Solving the same problem with new models "Flexible PLCs" and "Fully Integrated" resulted in the below costs:

$$c_F = 272,092.0 €, \quad c_I = 263,871.3 €$$

where c_p, c_F, c_I are the total costs for meeting the day ahead demand of the model "poutil," "Flexible PLCs" and "Fully Integrated," respectively.

From the above it is observed that both of the new models did reduce significantly the daily cost of the energy provider. In fact, the precise cost optimization is presented below after the production results. In order to properly compare the results of the three models, we start with a detailed analysis of the original model "poutil." The quarterly power contribution of the energy provider is presented in Fig. 11.3.

Fig. 11.3 consists of four different elements P^{PP}_t, P^{SM}_t, P^{DR}_t and electricity cost. The first three are not other than the three options, the provider has, in order to meet the demand and the line represents the electricity cost. In detail, the orange area represents the quarterly power production of the providers' natural gas fired powerplant. The cyan area represents the amount of power bought from the SM and the purple columns represent the DR through load curtailment. The figure visualizes optimal solution of "poutil." The quarterly resolution of the figure shows the extent to which the provider utilizes each of the three power options every quarter. Reminding that, the model has a 100% demand satisfaction as a prerequisite, means that the aggregated quarterly power of all three options equals the quarterly demand. Having said that, it is observed that the demand is greater during peak hours, time slices [33, 80]. Thus, the power load of all options (P^{PP}_t, P^{SM}_t, P^{DR}_t)

FIG. 11.3 Quarterly power distribution, solved with "poutil."

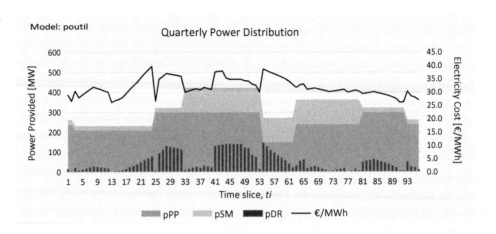

increase respectively. It should be pointed out that an increase in the curtailed power through DR leads to an increased cost, as it is the most expensive among all means of meeting the demand. This is observed at time slices [13, 24], when the increase of DR creates an equivalent increase at the quarterly cost. After time slice *t25*, the increase of electricity cost is interrupted, as the production of the powerplant and the energy from SM increase too. This happens to control the amount of power coming from the expensive DR program. Generally, most of the expenses occur during the peak hours as the demand is greater that time, forcing the model to utilize more DR, while also balancing the purchased amount of BLCs and 12h PLCs. Noticeably, the demand during peak hours is not only higher but also significantly volatile, as it reaches a minimum volume of 262 MW and a maximum load of 563 MW, in less than 5 h. At this point, the model has to optimize the amount of power among all options, while the powerplant is already at its maximum capacity of 300 MW leaving the rest demand to be met by the SM and the DR. The SM, although cheaper in €/MWh compared to the DR, does have the drawback of smaller resolution, providing only 24 h BLCs and 12-h PLCs. Thus, the fluctuations of the demand cannot be covered from the SM. The original SM of 'poutil," will reserve each MW for minimum of 12 h, when it is actually needed for two or less hours. This lack of greater resolution, in the SM products of the "poutil," leaves all this volatile demand to be met by the DR program. The greater DR utilization the greater the cost, but this is unavoidable when facing volatile demand, as it is the only option with a quarterly resolution. Apart from the economic aspect of this situation, there also exists the realistic. The "poutil" model, that we solve, has an upper constraint regarding the power from DR, equal to 150 MW. In the original research (Rebennack et al., 2010), the "poutil" model is solved with a DR constraint equal to the maximum energy demand. This means that if it is more economical, the model would solve the problem by meeting even the whole demand through DR. Such a scenario is not realistic, as it destroys the consumer's welfare, as well as the operation of the system. That is why, as explained above in the present research, the "poutil" model is solved with an upper constraint regarding the power from DR. The upper constraint serves also the purpose of integrating the consumer engagement aspect. As already mentioned, the literature suggests that it is very difficult to achieve complete consumer engagement in DR programs.

The two models created in the present research, do share the same constraints and options with "poutil." The "Flexible PLCs" model has the below solution.

Fig. 11.4 provides Quarterly power distribution, solved with "Flexible PLCs," where three things are of main interest. Firstly, the power received from the SM increases, especially during the peak hours and it is more flexible having a higher resolution. This is the result of integrating the 4-h and 2-h PLCs into the model. Secondly, concerning the power plant generation, the unit's production reaches the maximum capacity for an extended period compared to that of model "poutil." Finally yet importantly, the power from DR is considerably reduced, especially during the first peak hours, where in model "poutil" was reaching its highest values. These results underline the importance of the flexible PLCs, which manage to meet most of the demand initially met by DR. Thus, the flexibility of the products plays a pivotal role in optimizing the costs of the provider. However, the PLCs exist only during the peak hours, whereas the hourly products found in every energy market, refer to the whole day. Moving to the second model developed in the present research, the "Fully Integrated" constitutes the optimum model integrating every option of the previous two models, adding also the hourly products of the SM. Fig. 11.5 provides the model's quarterly power contribution, solved with the "Fully Integrated" model.

The integration of hourly spot products is noticeably altering the amount of power received from each of the three options. The powerplant is operating even closer to it's maximum capacity than in the previous models, as well as the power

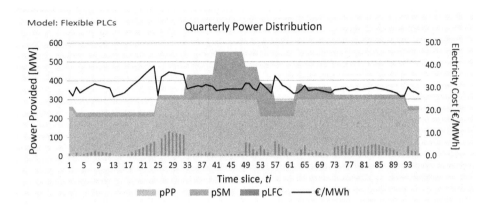

FIG. 11.4 Quarterly power distribution, solved with "Flexible PLCs."

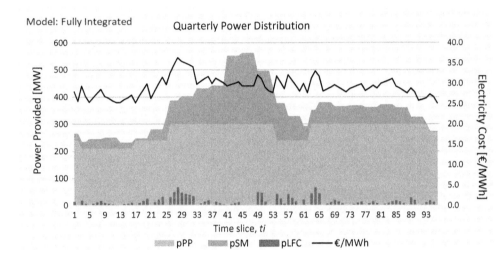

FIG. 11.5 Quarterly power distribution, solved with "Fully Integrated."

from the SM is increased. Those two factors, along with the increased resolution of the hourly spot product of the SM, constitute an optimization model that utilizes the capabilities of DR, only for meeting the excess demand of quarter resolution. Therefore, the power from DR program is reduced to minimum. In Figs. 11.3–11.5, the black curve represents the total quarterly cost in €/MWh, that is shaped by the respective power from each of the three options. This way we can observe the effect of the power mixture has on the final cost of the provider. Following the same logic, the below figures present the quarterly distribution of the cost of each of the three options. The orange area, the blue area and the purple columns, this time, represent the respective quarterly cost of the power production of the power plant, the power bought from the SM and the curtailed power through the DR, respectively.

Figs. 11.6–11.8 present in detail the solution of each model and its optimization decisions, for each quarter of the day. The optimal solution emerges from the "Fully Integrated" model that maximizes the power production from the power-plant. In addition, it "prefers" the utilization of power from the SM instead of the more expensive DR program. It does so until the point that the resolution of the SM products can meet the demand, leaving the rest of demand to be met by the DR. It is of importance to remind the constraint regarding the maximum curtailment of 150 MW from the DR, that ensures customers well-fare. This constrain prevents also model from curtailing unrealistically big parts of the demand. Table 11.4 compares the two new models to the original, revealing the key factors of reducing the cost of the energy provider.

Observing Figs. 11.6–11.8 on the cost distribution, it is shown that reducing the amount of power covered through DR and satisfying it by the other two options, reduces the overall cost. This can be also properly visualized in Fig. 11.9, where we present the power mixture of every different model along with its total cost.

Another significant comparison is that of the final quarterly cost per MWh that the provider has to cover in order to meet the demand. The visual comparison of this curve, between the three different optimization models, follows in Fig. 11.10.

FIG. 11.6 Quarterly cost distribution, solved with "poutil."

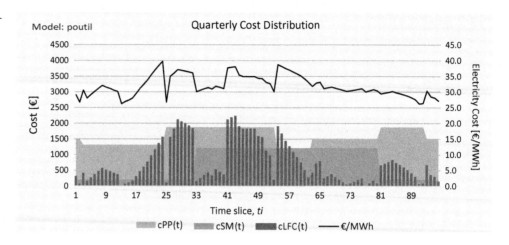

FIG. 11.7 Quarterly cost distribution, solved with "Flexible PLCs."

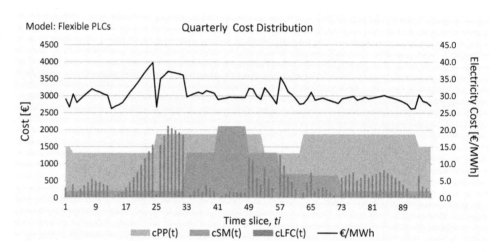

FIG. 11.8 Quarterly cost distribution, solved with "Fully Integrated."

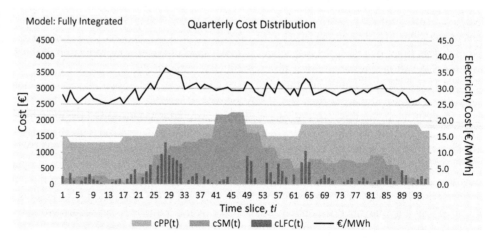

TABLE 11.4 The values of key variables α of each model.

Model	pPP	pSM	pDR	Total energy (MWh)	cPP	cSM	cDR	Total cost €	Avg. power cost €/MWh
Fully Integrated	26,250	8228	1238	35,716	164,062.5	77,441.34	22,367.5	263,871.3	29.2
2-4h PLC	25,560	6848	3308	35,716	159,750	60,588	51,754	272,092.0	30.4
Poutil	24,030	6912	4774	35,716	150,187.5	68,092.8	70,812	289,092.3	32.0

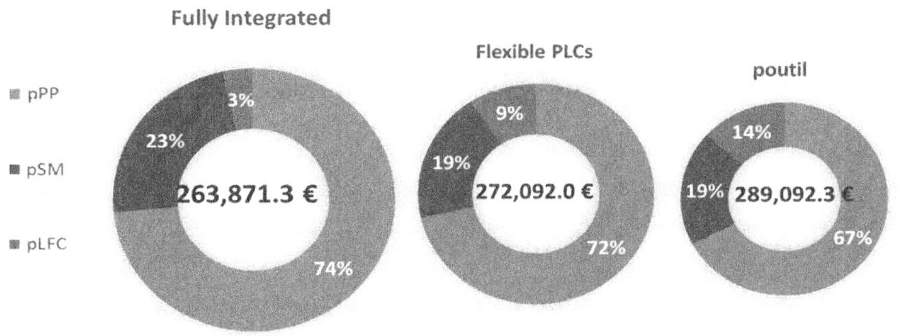

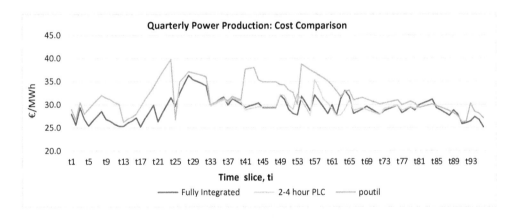

FIG. 11.9 The different power mixtures of the optimal solution of the three different models.

FIG. 11.10 Comparing the optimal quarterly cost distributions of the three models.

4 Conclusions

The present chapter concludes our research and includes all the main points and results, as well as its conclusions. It also sets some guidelines for future research and development of the model. In the present work, two new models were created, the "Flexible PLCs" and the "Fully Integrated," with "Fully Integrated" being the final form of the proposed model. A significant reduction in the total cost of the electricity provider was achieved compared to the resolution of the original model. Specifically, the total cost for meeting the daily demand amounts to *289,092.3* € based on the original model "poutil," and *263,871.3* € based on the "Fully Integrated." This additional cost reduction equals to *25,221.0* € or *8.7%* of the total daily cost. This significant cost reduction is due to two factors. The first is the creation of new short-term products of the SM, during the volatile demand. The second is the hourly product of the day ahead SM. Both of these additions enabled the supplier to cope with more abrupt changes in demand, by purchasing these products, instead of curtailing the demand. This means that there will be a significant reduction in costs, as the DR is the most expensive option to meet the demand. It is clarified that the significant cost reduction achieved, is not due to the introduction of new lower prices in the market products of the new model, while retaining the old more expensive prices to the original model. Specifically, in the original model "poutil," which as far as the SM products are concerned, has only BLC and 12-h PLC, the costs of these two products were redefined based on the hourly prices integrated by the "Fully Integrated" model. The solution of "poutil" was calculated with the new prices and not with the original ones. That way the comparability between "poutil" and "Fully Integrated" is preserved.

Moreover, the new model integrates a significant constraint regarding the DR. This constraint puts an upper limit to the amount of power that can be curtailed quarterly. It is also very important because, as it is mentioned in the literature review, most of the research around DR does not take the consumers' engagement into account. Therefore, the DR upper constraint takes into account the partial engagement of the consumer portfolio, to nearly one third of the total portfolio. This constraint serves also another purpose, as it restricts the optimal solution of curtailing the entire demand for a specific quarter or time period of the day. Those two changes make the model more realistic, considering not only the cost minimization, but also the consumers welfare and system's reliability. The reason that DR is the most expensive among the three options that the provider has, is to avoid the extensive curtailment of demand. Finally, it is worth mentioning that this model is generic, therefore it considers any electricity demand or market prices. However, in order to present specific results, only one daily price distribution of demand and one of day ahead hourly prices was used. This means that, although in the present solution some of the PLCs were not utilized, or that the DR did not reach the upper constraint, this could easily occur in another scenario.

References

Bichpuriya, Y.K., Soman, S.A., 2010. Electric power exchanges: a review. In: 16th National Power Systems.

EPEX SPOT, 2020. Trading Product. Available from: https://www.epexspot.com/en/tradingproducts. (Accessed February 2020).

Jordehi, A.R., 2019. Optimisation of demand response in electric power systems, a review. Renew. Sust. Energy Rev. 103, 308–319.

Koltsaklis, N., Dagoumas, A., 2018. Policy implications of power exchanges on operational scheduling: evaluating EUPHEMIA's market products in case of Greece. Energies 11 (10).

Mohsenian-Rad, A., Leon-Garcia, A., 2010. Optimal residential load control with price prediction in real-time electricity pricing environments. IEEE Trans. Smart Grid. 1 (2), 120–133. https://doi.org/10.1109/TSG.2010.2055903.

Nord Pool, 2019. Nord Pool AS, Order Types. Available from: https://www.nordpoolgroup.com/trading/Day-ahead-trading/Order-types/. (Accessed 23 February 2020).

Parrish, B., Gross, R., Heptonstall, P., 2019. On demand: can demand response live up to expectations in managing electricity systems? Energy Res. Soc. Sci. 51, 107–118.

Rebennack, S., Kallrath, J., Pardalos, P.M., 2010. Energy portfolio optimization for electric utilities: case study for Germany. In: Bjorndal, E., Bjorndal, M., Pardalos, P.M., Ronnqvist, M. (Eds.), Energy, Natural Resources and Environmental Economics. Springer, pp. 221–246. Available from: https://www.gams.com/latest/gamslib_ml/libhtml/gamslib_poutil.html. (Accessed 2020).

Part III

Modelling technology challenges in electricity market

Chapter 12

Business opportunities in the day ahead markets by storage integration: An application to the German case

Ángel Arcos-Vargas, David Canca, and Fernando Núñez

School of Engineering, Department of Industrial Engineering and Management Science, University of Seville, Seville, Spain

1 Introduction

Without a doubt, the two main concerns of society today are climate change and poverty eradication (COP21) and, in both cases, electricity production plays a key role. On the one hand, electricity production is the source of almost 25% of greenhouse gas emissions (International Energy Agency, 2019), while on the other hand, the fact that it is a universal, low-cost and safe primary resource, contributes to the economic growth of countries and thus to the poverty reduction.

Recent technological advances (Sussams and Leaton, 2017) have made electricity production from renewable sources compatible with both objectives. Currently, electricity from renewable sources has comparable costs to other conventional technologies but has the disadvantage of being unmanageable.

As the demand for electricity can undergo significant changes depending on the economic activity, holidays, temperature or time of day, among others, power plants have to be matched with those requirements of the market. This adjustment can be done in a planned manner, or by leaving it to market forces (as is the case in most Western countries). This balance is achieved through market mechanisms, among which we can highlight the daily market (day ahead market) in which companies offer at their short term marginal costs (in the hypothesis that the market works in a perfectly competitive way), obtaining hourly prices, which once adjusted by technical restrictions (network capacity), ensure the proper functioning of the system. These variations in demand lead to significant price variations, which are the basis of the business model proposed in this chapter.

The German case is particularly interesting due to the important contribution of renewable energy production in its energy mix (which leads to significant variations in production, which are not manageable), and a significant industrial consumption, which means that if renewable production increases at times of low activity, an excess of supply appears, leading to electricity prices at very low levels, or even negative.

In this context, electricity arbitrage may make more sense than in the Spanish case studied by Arcos, Canca and Nuñez (Arcos-Vargas et al., 2020), using Li-Ion batteries to transfer energy over time. Electricity trading or arbitrage consists of taking advantage of the price differences that appear in the market to buy it when it is cheap, storing it in batteries, and offering it again in the market, when the mathematical model predicts that the price will be higher. In fact, it is not pure arbitrage, if we refer to the definition found in the Oxford Dictionary, it is understood as arbitrage "the simultaneous purchase and sale of securities, currencies or commodities in different markets or in derived forms to take advantage of different prices for the same asset."

The model developed in this paper performs the above explained arbitrage. These price differences should be enough to justify the investments, losses in the charging and discharging process and operation and maintenance expenses. A similar business model was developed by Hakim et al. 2009 and subsequently patented. In our analysis, it has been assumed that the impact of these potential arbitrage agents will not affect the market price, due to their small size in relation to the total energy exchanged.

The electricity arbitrage issue has been dealt with in several research projects, in which generation and storage technology is analyzed, applying it to real cases in different countries or used into theoretical models. A comprehensive review has been carried out in Arcos-Vargas et al. (2020) and is here depicted in Table 12.1.

Mathematical Modelling of Contemporary Electricity Markets. https://doi.org/10.1016/B978-0-12-821838-9.00012-8

TABLE 12.1 Research on electricity arbitration in recent years.

References	Market	Technology	Contribution
Adebayo et al. (2018)	Alberta—Canada	Non-specified	Impact on benefits and battery design of access tarifs
Berrada et al. (2016)	NYISO market	CAES, PHS	Arbitrage benefits in day a head, intraday and ancillary services
Bradbury et al. (2014)	U.S. markets	PHS, CAES, ZEBRA, EDLC, LA, Li-Ion	Maximum TIR configuration (hours) for each technology
Connolly et al. (2011)	11 different countries	PHS	Optimal configuration and operational strategies
Daggett et al. (2017)	United Kingdom	Li-Ion	Arbitrage and renewable penetration
Das et al. (2015)	California ISO	CAES	Grid benefits, Wind penetration and Pay back
Hou (2017)	Denmark	Hidrogene	Wind optimization
Jannesar et al. (2018)	Iran	Vanadium Redox Battery (VRB)	Optimal sizing for improving distribution network performance
Kazempour et al. (2009)	Alberta—Canada	NaS, PHS	PHS technology has a clear advantage over SNa batteries
Krishnamurthy et al. (2018)	California ISO	Batteries	Optimal bidding strategies
Metz and Saraiva (2018)	Germany	Non-specified	Arbitrage profitability and sustainability conditions
Nasrolahpour et al. (2016)	Alberta—Canada	PHS	Optimal sizing and strategies for maximum benefit
Sioshansi et al. (2009)	Australia	PHS	Parameter influence on profitability
Terlouw et al. (2019)	Switzerland	Li-Ion PHS, CAES, NaS, LA, VRB	Best technology
Walawalkar et al. (2007)	New York	NaS and Flywheel	Relevant factors in profitability
Wu and Lin (2018)	China	Non-specified	Optimal sizing for a non-competitive market
Yucekaya (2013)	Turkey	CAES	Optimal arbitrage
Zakeri and Syri (2014)	Finland	PHS, CAES, NaS, LA, VRB	Optimal sizing

Source: Arcos-Vargas, A., Canca, D., Núñez, F., 2020. Impact of battery technological progress on electricity arbitrage: an application to the Iberian market. Appl. Energy260, 114273.

Subsequently, some papers have been published that are interesting to frame this work, or to define possible future lines of research, such as Khastieva et al. (2019), in which they carry out an interesting analysis on the value of energy storage for transmission investment, analyzing how different incentive schemes can improve the economic welfare (in this research we limit ourselves to the day ahead electricity market, being the network services and the ancillary services, as seen below, a possible source of additional income).

The contribution of Brijs et al. (2019) is also particularly relevant, in which they quantify the opportunities for electricity arbitrage in both the intraday and short-term markets, analyzing a real case for Belgium. Baumgarte et al. (2019), on the other hand, analyze a variety of business models for energy storage, based on different technologies, although we miss an underlying mathematical model.

This chapter develops a mathematical model that serves to determine the buying and selling positions in the market, considering the energy losses in the battery charging and discharging processes and the deterioration of its useful life. For our purposes, the Li-Ion storage technology has been selected as well as the wholesale market of the next day of electricity in Germany as a sample market, due to, as mentioned before, its important volatility, associated to the renewable generation and its high industrial consumption.

Costs, features and round-trip efficiency of Li-Ion battery devices have improved significantly during the recent decades as a result of technological advances. In this context, it has been observed a cost reduction by around 90%–about this fact, see the contribution of Sussams and Leaton (2017). This development has been made possible by its implementation in the EV; indeed, Tesla announced at its previous annual conference that the cost of its battery will be $100 per kWh later this year. This quick change would demand a revision of many of the aforementioned researches, since the relative costs of the technologies have drastically changed in favor of Li-Ion, currently presenting lower values than those considered in previous works.

In order to include the new performance values of Li-Ion batteries, a mixed-integer linear programming optimization model has been developed to analyze what would be the optimal arbitrage operation to be applied in the German wholesale daily market (using real hourly values) for which different battery/converter configurations (Energy/Power) are evaluated. Once the optimal operation is defined for each of the selected configurations, a financial analysis is performed to define the optimal solution from an economic point of view.

The mathematical model is applied using the real 2018 hourly prices for the EPEX SPOT, which presents daily price differences that, in comparison with other markets with less volatility, could compensate the investment, operation and maintenance costs of the equipment.

An Energy Storage System (ESS) is defined by the quantity of energy and power it is capable of storing (MWh and MW). Such values depend on the number of connected cells (MWh) and the inverter capacity (MW). The investment of each composition will be assessed by the addition of these two components (battery and inverters). In the present study, given that the agents have a price to be taken, the really relevant issue is the relationship between both components (battery/inverter size), which provide the number of hours that the energy storage system can supply the nominal capacity of the inverter.

To provide conservative results, only the income derived from participation in the daily market is considered, not including additional incomes associated with the provision of ancillary services; participation in the intraday market; congestion resolution services to the distributor, as well as the support to the system operator in the management of restrictions. However, the assessment of such impacts would also involve a technical network study, which is beyond the scope of this investigation.

The suggested optimization method can be implemented for any wholesale electricity market and any configuration of battery characteristics. The results achieved will be of interest to both industry and academia, as they illustrate the impact of the improvements in battery technology (cost, lifetime and effectiveness—round trip efficiency) on the economics of the trading business.

The remaining of the chapter is organized as follows: following this introduction, Section 2 presents the mathematical formulation of the trading mathematical model (including the time—hours—for selling and buying electricity as well as the optimal amounts) for different configurations (battery/inverter). Section 3 describes the study case, including some information about the German market, a quick comparative analysis with the Spanish market and the technical characteristics of the Li-Ion battery that has been selected for the analysis. The obtained findings are included in Section 4, where the economic analysis of each configuration undertaken is carried out, determining the most appropriate inverter size. In addition, it also includes an assessment of how the financial results might change if the technology progress cuts the batteries' costs, makes them more efficient in round-trip efficiency or extends their lifetime, for which Panel Data techniques have been applied. The chapter finishes with a collection of conclusions and recommendations for energy policy.

2 Trading mathematical model

The objective of the trading energy model consists in the maximization of profits obtained from energy purchase and sale operations during a certain planning interval. To this end, the model considers hour-by-hour electricity prices. Since the purchase and sale of electricity per hour depends on the inverter conversion rate, the optimal trading strategy will be obtained by varying the inverter size, using the hourly prices of the electricity as an input. The model parameters and the definition of variables are provided below:

Parameters

T	Set of periods (hours)
ρ_t	Electricity price at hour $t \in T$
C_o	Defines the initial battery capacity (10 MWh in our experiments)
C_{max}	Represents the conversion rate of the converter, i.e. the capacity used by the converter to transform the energy stored in the battery into electricity
C_d	Deterioration of the battery capacity per charge/discharge cycle
r	Defines the loss of energy due to the conversion process. This parameter is measured as a percentage of the battery charge state

Variables

x_t	Binary variable. x_t takes value 1 if the battery is charged at period (hour) $t \in T$. 0 otherwise
y_t	Binary variable. y_t takes value 1 if the battery is discharged at period $t \in T$. 0 otherwise
α_t	Binary variable. α_t takes value 1 if the battery has finished a charge/discharge cycle at period $t \in T$. 0 otherwise
	Binary variable. β_t takes value 1 if prior to period $t \in T$, the last performed operation was a charge and 0 if it was a discharge
P_t	Represents the amount of electricity purchased and stored in the battery during period $t \in T$
S_t	Measures the amount of energy discharged from the battery during period $t \in T$. This energy is transformed into electricity and sold at the same period
N_t	Measures the cumulated number of charging/discharging cycles that has been done just until period $t \in T$
C_t	Represents the remaining capacity of the battery at the end of period $t \in T$
B_t	Measures the level of energy in the battery at the end of period $t \in T$

As shown, the parameters needed for the model are determined by the battery and the inverter technology, specifically we consider: the round-trip efficiency in the charge/discharge process, the capacity of battery and inverter and the useful life of the battery (i.e., the number of charging/discharging cycles until the effective battery capacity decreases to a 20% of the initial one). It is assumed that the battery capacity diminishes in a proportional way with the number of charging/discharging cycles. We also suppose that the operation and maintenance battery costs are negligible (1%) and proportional to the equipment value.

The mathematical formulation is as follows:

$$Max \sum_{t \in T} \rho_t (S_t - P_t) \tag{12.1}$$

$$P_t \le (C_{t-1} - B_{t-1})/(1-r), \quad t \in T \tag{12.2}$$

$$S_t \le B_{t-1}(1-r), \quad t \in T \tag{12.3}$$

$$P_t \le C_{max} x_t, \quad t \in T \tag{12.4}$$

$$S_t \le C_{max} y_t, \quad t \in T \tag{12.5}$$

$$x_t + y_t \le 1, \quad t \in T \tag{12.6}$$

$$B_{t-1} + P_t(1-r) - S_t/(1-r) = B_t, \quad t \in T \tag{12.7}$$

$$C_t = C_{t-1} - C_d \cdot C_o \cdot \alpha_{t-1}, \quad t \in T \tag{12.8}$$

$$\beta_1 = 0 \tag{12.9}$$

$$\beta_{t-1} - \beta_t \le \alpha_t, \quad t \in T \setminus \{1\} \tag{12.10}$$

$$x_t \le \beta_t, \quad t \in T \tag{12.11}$$

$$y_t \le 1 - \beta_t, \quad t \in T \tag{12.12}$$

$$\beta_{t-1} - y_t - x_t \leq \beta_t, \quad t \in T \setminus \{1\} \tag{12.13}$$

$$\beta_{t-1} + y_t + x_t \geq \beta_t, \quad t \in T \setminus \{1\} \tag{12.14}$$

$$x_t, y_t, \alpha_t, \beta_t \in \{0, 1\}, \quad t \in T$$

$$P_t, S_t, C_t, B_t \geq 0, \quad t \in T \tag{12.15}$$

$$N_t \in \mathbb{N}^+, \quad t \in T.$$

The objective function (12.1) aims to maximizing the cash-flows obtained from the battery operation during the planning horizon.

At each period t, the amount of electricity purchased, represented by P_t, must be less or equal to the available battery capacity (12.2), which is unknown and measurable by the term $(C_{t-1} - B_{t-1})/(1 - r)$. Here, r, as previously mentioned, measures the loss of energy as consequence of the conversion process which takes place at the converter. This parameter is measured as a percentage of the current battery energy level, then $(1 - r)$ stands for the roundtrip efficiency of the electricity conversion process. With respect to the discharge process, constraints (12.3) bound the electricity that can be discharged and sold at period t, S_t. This variable must be less or equal to the level of charge of the battery affected by the loss of energy in the conversion process. Then, at each period t, the maximum possible discharge is $B_{t-1}(1 - r)$. Moreover, hourly purchase and electricity sales are also bounded by the inverter capacity trough constraint sets (12.4) and (12.5) respectively. These constraints incorporate binary variables x_t and y_t into the righ hand side. When ay purchase is done at period t, the corresponding variable x_t must take value 1. Similarly, if a sale of electricity is done at period t, the corresponding y_t variable must be set to 1. Binary variables x_t and y_t are used with the objective of measuring the charging and discharging operations. Since, charge and discharge operations cannot be performed at the same period, constraints set (12.6) are incorporated into the model.

Constraints set (12.7) model the temporal evolution of the battery level (B_t) depending on whether a purchase or sale of electricity has been done at period $t - 1$. Then, for each period t, the battery level is obtained by adding or subtracting to the previous battery level B_{t-1} the charge or discharge of energy, respectively. Nota that Li Ion batteries have a slight temporal self-discharge, but, for our purposes we won' consider this effect, since, in general, the normal operation will imply daily charges and discharges and, as consequence, the self-discharge effect is negligible.

Constraints (12.8) model the decrement of the battery capacity (due to the increment in the number of charging/discharging cycles) with time. The battery capacity at period t can me modeled by decreasing the capacity in C_d if a new charge/discharge cycle takes place at period $t - 1$, which is controlled by the binary variable α_{t-1}.

Modelling the behavior of variables α_t (which are in charge of computing the occurrence of new charge/discharge cycles) is the most difficult part of the formulation. In order to deal with this issue, a new set of binary variables is needed. Variables β_t (binary step state variables) represents the last battery operation performed prior to period t. Suppose, for instance, that the battery was charged at period $t = 2$ and no other battery operation occurs until period $t = 5$, where a discharge operation takes place. In this illustration $\beta_2 = 1$ (a charge), $\beta_3 = 1$, $\beta_4 = 1$ (no operation has been done at periods 3 and 4) and $\beta_5 = 0$ (since a discharge has taken place); since at this moment a new charging/discharging cycle must be computed, the variable α_5 must be set to 1 and the battery capacity must be decreased in C_d.

Constrains set (12.9)–(12.14) are used to model in a general way this behavior. Initially, the state variable is set to cero (12.9). For the rest of periods, as stated in Eq. (12.10), if $\beta_{t-1} = 1$ (the last battery operation prior to t was a charge one) and $\beta_t = 0$ (the battery has been discharged at period t), the variable α_t must be set to 1. The state variables are also related to the binary charging/discharging variables, x_t and y_t respectively. If $x_t = 1$, a charging operation has been done at period t, then α_t must be one, as enforced by constraints (12.11). By contrary, if a discharge operation has been done at period t, $y_t = 1$, the battery state variable β_t must be set to cero, which is imposed by constraints (12.12). If the last performed battery operation at time $t - 1$ was a charge ($\beta_{t-1} = 1$) and no charge or discharge has been done at time t, β_t must be 1, which is enforced by constraint set (12.13). Finally, when at time $t - 1$ the last performed battery operation was a discharge ($\beta_{t-1} = 0$) and no charge or discharge operation has been done at period t, the variable β_t must be equal cero, as imposed by constraints (12.14).

Constraints set (12.15) are used to specify the domain of the model variables.

2.1 Practical implementation issues

Note that, at a first glance de size of the planning horizon is unknown since it represents the number of periods (hours) until the battery capacity reach a low enough residual value for which the battery operation is not worth, which cannot be determined prior to run the optimization model. Since we deal with hourly prices, there are 8670 time periods per year (24 h per day times 365 days per year). Then, working with complete years, the length of T will be an unknown multiple of 8670 time periods. Concerning the model dimensions, if we consider only 1 year (8760 periods of 1 h), the model size rises 100,765 constraints, 30,654 continuous variables and 35,033 binary variables. As consequence of both issues, the a priori unknown length of T and the difficulty to optimally solve such a big model, we decide the use of a sequential strategy to solve the problem. Moreover, even if the time horizon was known, by its nature, there is an uncertain component regarding the future electricity prices. Consequently, we opt for solving the problem in a sequential way, year by year, beginning each year the battery operation from the residual capacity of the previous year, until exhausting the battery capacity. Without loss of generality, we fix an initial value initially of to 10 MWh for the capacity of the battery. Note that this does not affect the validity of results, since the problem is scalable to any other battery size (the battery size does not influence the market's operation). For this battery size, we solve the problem by varying the inverter size from 1 to 10 MW. Summarizing, the analysis of one scenario involves the resolution of 10 (different inverter sizes) times N (unknown number of years) optimization problems. The value of N depends on the battery deterioration, which also depends on the inverter size.

From the results of the sequential resolution of the trading model, we perform an economic analysis considering the results obtained for each inverter size.

3   Data description

The information on electricity prices used in this study comes from the transparency platform ENTSO-E, which collects a publishes data on generation, transmission and demand for the pan-European market. ENTSO-E collects data from information providers such as TSOs, power exchanges or other qualified third parties. Next, we analyze the German daily prices, but comparing them with those of the Spanish electricity market to get a relative perspective. Fig. 12.1 shows the distribution of the hourly electricity price in Germany (and Spain) in year 2019. Compared to the Spanish case, prices in Germany are, on average, 10 €/MWh cheaper and show a standard deviation 4.6 €/MWh greater (15.52 vs 10.88 €/MWh); this greater volatility in German hourly prices should favor the profitability of the trading business with storage. In addition, the German market sometimes shows negative prices which can be even lower than −50 €/MWh at certain hours; this is due to the important presence of not managed generation (mainly windfarms) and to the high industrial component of its demand. The most extreme cases are reached when large amounts of renewable energy are incorporated into the grid in periods of low industrial activity.

Fig. 12.2 depicts two graphs on the evolution of the electricity price in Germany and Spain during 2019. Graph (A) represents the daily average of the hourly prices (in € per MWh). These average prices have tended to fall during the year 2019 in both countries, although in the German case they generally present lower values and a larger variance. In graph (B), the distance between maximum and minimum hourly prices (maximum daily margin) for each day is shown for both

FIG. 12.1   Distribution of the hourly prices in Germany and Spain, Year 2019.

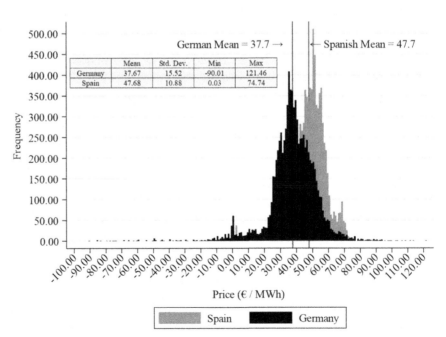

	Mean	Std. Dev.	Min	Max
Germany	37.67	15.52	-90.01	121.46
Spain	47.68	10.88	0.03	74.74

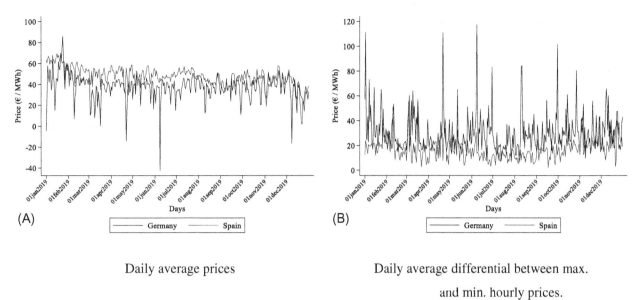

Daily average prices

Daily average differential between max.
and min. hourly prices.

FIG. 12.2 Electricity price evolution in Germany and Spain, Year 2019.

TABLE 12.2 Main features of Li-Ion batteries.

	Li-Ion
Specific energy (Wh/kg)	130–147
Energy density (Wh/L)	250–730
Specific power (W/kg)	250–340
Nominal voltage (V)	3.6
Charge/discharge cycles	5000
Monthly self-discharge (%)	3%
Round-trip efficiency (%)	92%
CAPEX (€/kWh)	100

countries. It is observed that the gap between extreme prices within the day is much more pronounced in the German case, where it exceeds 100 €/MWh some days.

As stated in the introduction, Li-Ion batteries have been selected as the storage technology due to their better performance and recent technological advancement. An analysis of the different storage technologies considered can be found in Arcos-Vargas et al. (2020). Table 12.2 shows the technical specifications of LI-Ion batteries, which have been obtained from different sources—Gomez-Expósito et al. (2017), Segui Pedro (2018), Bardo Cáceres (2010), Hernández Romero (2016), Battery University (2019), Jofemar Energy (2016), Vélez Moreno (2012), Clean Technica (2017) and IRENA (2017).

The current performance of this type of storage technology has been significantly improved in recent years. In particular, the cost has been reduced by an average of 20% per year during the period 2010–19 and given the intensity of research focused on this field, it is foreseeable that the trend will continue. If the cost reduction continues at this rate, costs would be halved in 3.5 years.

4 Results and discussion

This section estimates the physical evolution of the battery and the financial return of implementing battery arbitrage in Germany. The base case analyzed in this section consists of a 10 MWh battery valued at 2 million € (200,000 € per MWh of capacity) with a round-trip efficiency of 92% and 5000 charge cycles until it reaches 20% of total capacity. The inverter size is a parameter to set and can vary from 1 to 10 MW, costing each additional MW 30,000 €. The operating strategy developed in Section 2 aims to maximize the profit of the storage owner. The accounting conditions of the investment are presented in Table 12.3.

Battery amortization is linked to its loss of capacity every operating year. In order to make comparisons with the results obtained by Arcos-Vargas et al. (2020) for the Spanish case, the different alternatives have been valued until year 11 of operation, except in the case of inverters of size 1 or 2 MW, which operate till year 10—in any case, the residual value of each business alternative will depend on the battery capacity at the end of the last operating year. For its part, each inverter is amortized in 15 years, and their residual value will be given by the pending book value (net value).

4.1 Technical analysis of the trading model with BESS

The material evolution of the battery during the investment period is represented in Fig. 12.3. Specifically, Fig. 12.3 shows the relationship, during the investment duration and considering different sizes for the inverter (from 1 to 10 MW), between the "annual average of daily battery cycles" and the "battery capacity at the beginning of each year (MWh)." As depicted, in the first operational years, the batteries with both, largest and smallest inverters, show fewer daily cycles than the storage units with medium-size inverters. Moreover, the battery with the smallest inverter (1 MW) maintains a relatively stable annual average of daily cycles until year 8 of operation—just over 1.6 daily cycles—(something relatively similar happens

TABLE 12.3 Investment conditions.

Battery operation period	10 or 11 years
Inverter amortization period	15 years
Maintenance costs	1% over investment
Discount rate	6.5%
Corporation tax	25%

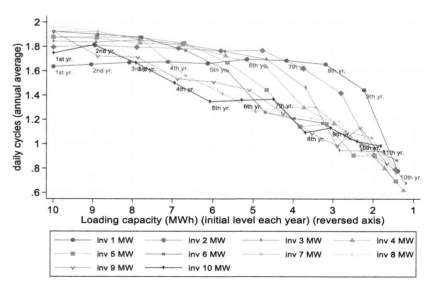

FIG. 12.3 Annual evolution of charging capacity and battery cycles by inverter.

with the 2 MW inverter), while batteries that work with larger inverters show a more pronounced temporary fall in the number of cycles, thus experiencing a lower rate of battery consumption (usable capacity degradation).

4.2 Financial analysis of the trading model with BESS

The optimization model presented in Section 2 has determined the BESS trading strategy for each possible inverter (from 1 to 10 MW). Based on this information, we are able to analyze the economic results of these optimal buying/selling operations. To this end, Fig. 12.4 represents those hours in which the battery (e.g., the one with a 4 MW inverter) is either selling electricity (1900 h, 21.7% of the total hours of the year), buying electricity (1942 h, 22.2%) or doing nothing (4917 h, 56.1%) during the year 2019. In a complete year, and taking into account the battery capacity level at every hour, the battery tends to purchase (charge) in the hours where price electricity is low or even negative (brown markers) and to vend (discharge) in the hours where price electricity is higher (green markers); moreover, there are intermediate prices (black markers) where the battery stands inactive (neither charge nor discharge).

Fig. 12.5 looks into the trading operation of a certain day (e.g., August 1, 2019). The figure considers different inverter sizes, from 1 to 10 MW, for the 10 MWh battery, and represents three graphs: hourly costs of purchased energy (Fig. 12.5A), hourly revenues of sold energy (Fig. 12.5B), and the corresponding accumulated pre-tax cash-flow throughout the day (Fig. 12.5C). As observed, the hourly periods of battery charge (demanding electricity) and discharge (offering electricity) are longer for smaller inverter sizes but, as we might expect, hourly costs and revenues are smaller for those inverters (due to their lower capacity to get or provide electricity). For its part, Fig. 12.5C shows that, at the end of the chosen day, larger inverters allow a pre-tax cash-flow close to 300 €, while smaller inverters, such as those of 2 or 3 MW, generate cash-flows somewhat higher than 200 €—remember that the 10 MW inverter costs 300,000 € in our simulation while the 2 MW inverter would cost 60,000 euros.

The hourly cash-flow generated by the optimal trading with storage in the German electricity market allows us to perform a financial return analysis. We propose three financial indicators: Net Present Value (*NPV*), Net Present Value per € invested ($\frac{NPV}{I}$) and Internal Rate of Return (*IRR*). In order to get them, we derive the cash inflows and outflows due to the investment in an annual basis and, subsequently, obtain the annual cash flows as the difference between those two flows. A reasonable discount rate of 6.5% has been adopted, although it will really depend on the characteristics and leverage of each investor.

Fig. 12.6 shows the financial indicators *NPV* (left axis) and $\frac{NPV}{I}$ and *IRR* (right axis) for the different sizes of inverter considered. The best inverter in terms of *NPV* is the one of size 2 MW, which shows the least negative *NPV*: −1.78 M€. As can be observed in Fig. 12.5C, the daily cash-flow grows significantly when we jump from the 1 MW inverter to the 2 MW inverter; that is, the 10 MWh battery with a 2 MW inverter gets results which are relatively near to the higher daily cash-flows provided by the largest inverters, but requiring, yes, a relatively low investment in inverter.

For its part, the $\frac{NPV}{I}$ and *IRR* indicators grow slightly (taking fewer negative values in absolute terms) with the inverter size until reaching values close to −0.8 (−80%) and −0.1 (−80%), respectively. This is, in the best case (10 MW inverter),

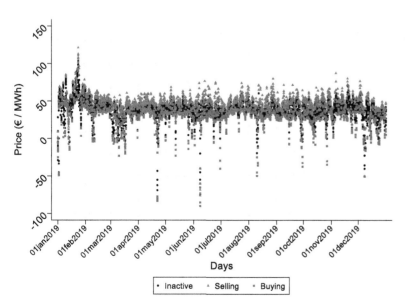

FIG. 12.4 Intra-year operation of 10 MWh battery and 4 MW inverter, Germany, Year 2019.

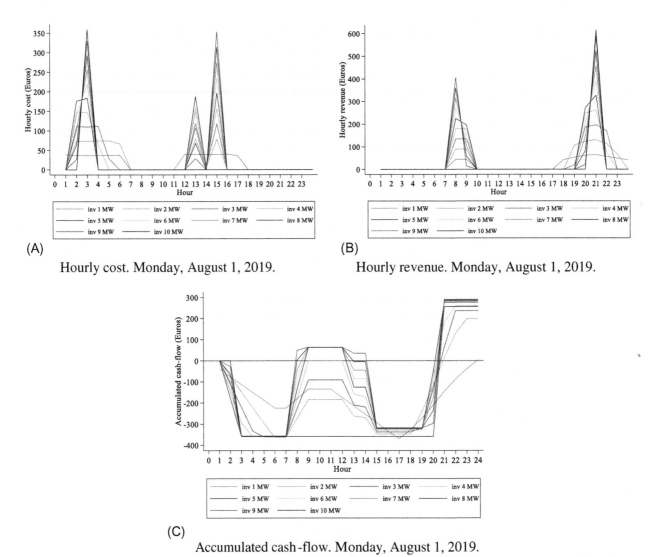

(A)

Hourly cost. Monday, August 1, 2019.

(B)

Hourly revenue. Monday, August 1, 2019.

(C)

Accumulated cash-flow. Monday, August 1, 2019.

FIG. 12.5 Daily profit from the energy trading by inverter size, Germany, August 1, 2019.

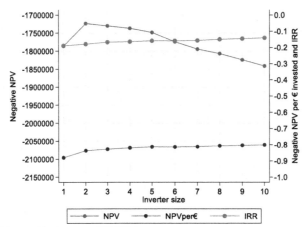

FIG. 12.6 IRR, NPV and NPV per € invested by inverters, 10 MWh battery.

we recover approximately the 20% of the total investment. For its part, the negative *IRR* indicates that the non-discounted cash flows add up to a value which is less than the total investment; the investment is losing money at the rate of the negative *IRR*.

4.3 Econometric analysis

In the previous development, the optimal BESS strategy for a 10 MWh battery with 92% of round-trip efficiency and an expected life of 5000 cycles has been described as base case, for each inverter size (from size 1 to 10 MW). In that case, the optimal configuration, in terms of IRR and $\frac{NPV}{I}$, points out to the use of the largest inverters.

In this section, we wonder to what extent the optimal trading strategy depends on technical improvements in the storage system, improvements which are expected to occur in the next years. In particular, envisaged improvements will be directed to reduce the battery cost and increase both the round-trip efficiency and the number of battery cycles. The current negative financial returns give more interest, if possible, to the measure of the impact of these technological advances on the trading business; moreover, the results of this economic analysis might guide technical contributions coming from research institutions.

To evaluate the causal effects of technological improvements in BESS on the arbitrage business with storage, we consider:

- three possible values of round-trip efficiency: 92% (base case), 93% and 94%,
- three different number of cycles: 5000 (base case), 6000 and 7000,
- and four different battery costs: 50,000, 100,000, 150,000 and 200,000 (base case) €/MWh.

To estimate the financial effect of each of these changes, three multiple regression models have been proposed which differ only in the endogenous variable: *NPV* for the 1st model, $\frac{NPV}{I}$ for the 2nd one, and *IRR* for the 3rd model. The estimated models are as follows:

$$NPV\left(or\ \frac{NPV}{I}\ or\ IRR\right) = \hat{\beta}_0 + \hat{\beta}_{11}C_{1.5} + \hat{\beta}_{12}C_1 + \hat{\beta}_{13}C_{0.5} + \hat{\beta}_{21}L_{6000} + \hat{\beta}_{22}L_{7000} + \hat{\beta}_{31}E_{93\%} + \hat{\beta}_{32}E_{94\%} + \hat{\beta}_{41}I_1 + \hat{\beta}_{42}I_2 + \ldots$$
$$+ \hat{\beta}_{410}I_{10} + \hat{\varepsilon}$$

(12.16)

where,

$C_{1.5}$: "1" if battery price 1.5 M€, "0" in another case.
C_1: "1" if battery price 1 M€, "0" in another case.
$C_{0.5}$: "1" if battery price 0.5 M€, "0" in another case.
L_{6000}: "1" if battery has 6000 cycles, "0" in another case.
L_{7000}: "1" if battery has 7000 cycles, "0" in another case.
$E_{93\%}$: "1" if battery round-trip efficiency is 93%, "0" in another case.
$E_{94\%}$: "1" if battery round-trip efficiency is 94%, "0" in another case.
I_1: "1" if inverter size is 1 MW, "0" in another case.
I_2: "1" if inverter size is 2 MW, "0" in another case.
...
I_{10}: "1" if inverter size is 10 MW, "0" in another case.

Table 12.4 shows the results of the three multivariate regression models.

The reference case in the estimations is given by the 4 MW inverter (cost: 0.12 M€) and the 10 MWh battery (cost: 2 M€) with 92% round-trip efficiency and 5000 charge cycles. The regression models have 360 observations each one, corresponding to the different technological configurations, this is, all possible combinations of: 4 different battery costs {2 M€, 1.5 M€, 1 M€, 0.5 M€}, 3 different cycle of expected life levels {5000, 6000, 7000}, 3 round-trip efficiency levels {92%, 93%, 94%}, and 10 possible inverters {1 MW, 2 MW, ..., 10 MW}. The goodness-of-fit for the three regressions is high, with an adjusted R^2 coefficient higher than 97% in the three models. The respective predicted errors are zero mean and follow Gaussian distributions.

The most significant indicator used to measure the technological improvement of BESS is the cost of the battery. As it is expected to fall down in the next years, the regression analysis has considered three possible costs for the 10 MWh battery which are lower than the base price of 2 M€; namely, 1.5, 1 and 0.5 M€.

As for the battery expected life, some experts predict that 7000 cycles can be reached in the coming years. Therefore, we introduce two dummy variables in the estimates which represent the cases of 6000 and 7000 cycles, being 5000 cycles the reference case. As with the battery cost, the obtained coefficients are significant (p-values <0.01) and positive. Thus, an increment of 1000 cycles in the 10 MWh storage unit increases the NPV around 76,000 € and the $\frac{NPV}{I}$ and IRR indicators around 0.06 and 0.03 percentage points, respectively.

The third technical attribute of the battery analyzed is the round-trip efficiency, which is 92% in the base case (this is, 8% of the energy is lost each charge-discharge). To study this feature, two dummy variables have been included in the regression models, representing efficiencies of 93% and 94% respectively. According to our results, an improvement of 1% in round-trip efficiency improves NPV just over 6000 € and indicators $\frac{NPV}{I}$ and IRR by 0.005 and 0.001 percentage points, respectively.

Regarding the inverter size, the results obtained depend on the financial indicator used as endogenous variable. Thus, the best inverters are those of size 3 and 4 MW in NPV terms, 4–8 MW in $\frac{NPV}{I}$ terms—note that the dummy coefficients of inverters from 5 to 8 MW do not differ significantly from zero— and 8 to 10 MW in terms of IRR indicator. Valuing all this information together and considering the theoretical nature of IRR indicator, we indicate the inverter size 4 MW as the best alternative.

Table 12.4 illustrates that the NPV value in the base case amounts to −1,705,562 €, which tells us that, at the end of the period, almost 88% of the initial investment (2,120,000 €) will be lost. Using the values proposed above, an expected improvement the round-trip efficiency by 1%, will provide an increase of about 6000 € of NPV; the increase of 1000 life cycles (20%) will provide an annual increase of more than 75,000 € of NPV, while the reduction of any amount of the cost of the battery will directly increase the NPV.

TABLE 12.4 Regression models for NPV, NPV/I and IRR.

	Endog. variable →	NPV	NPV/investment	IRR
10MWh-Battery cost (base category: 2,000,000 €)	500,000	1457168.40***	0.455***	0.114***
		432.27	148.74	93.91
		0.00	0.00	0.00
	1000,000	994902.68***	0.192***	0.049***
		295.14	62.69	40.78
		0.00	0.00	0.00
	1,500,000	497574.67***	0.067***	0.017***
		147.61	21.93	14.41
		0.00	0.00	0.00
Cycles (base category: 5000 cycles)	6000	76301.60***	0.058***	0.032***
		26.14	21.92	30.72
		0.00	0.00	0.00
	7000	152579.29***	0.115***	0.058***
		52.26	43.28	55.03
		0.00	0.00	0.00
Round trip eff. (base category: 92%)	93%	6151.56**	0.005*	0.001
		2.11	1.93	0.54
		0.04	0.05	0.59
	94%	12576.66***	0.010***	0.002**
		4.31	3.76	1.99
		0.00	0.00	0.05

TABLE 12.4 Regression models for NPV, NPV/I and IRR—cont'd

	Endog. variable →	NPV	NPV/investment	IRR
Inverter (base category: 4MW inverter)	1	−87158.03***	−0.120***	−0.031***
		−16.35	−24.93	−16.40
		0.00	0.00	0.00
	2	−18068.50***	−0.039***	−0.015***
		−3.39	−8.16	−7.86
		0.00	0.00	0.00
	3	−198.07	−0.011**	−0.005**
		−0.04	−2.36	−2.47
		0.97	0.02	0.01
	5	−13389.70**	0.000	0.001
		−2.51	0.08	0.55
		0.01	0.93	0.58
	6	−30937.62***	−0.003	0.001
		−5.80	−0.53	0.77
		0.00	0.60	0.44
	7	−47780.32***	−0.005	0.003
		−8.96	−1.01	1.58
		0.00	0.31	0.11
	8	−63519.81***	−0.007	0.005***
		−11.92	−1.35	2.86
		0.00	0.18	0.00
	9	−85045.43***	−0.012**	0.005***
		−15.96	−2.40	2.83
		0.00	0.02	0.01
	10	−105318.79***	−0.016***	0.006***
		−19.76	−3.25	3.36
		0.00	0.00	0.00
Constant		−1705561.93***	−0.813***	−0.154***
		−347.08	−182.45	−87.55
		0.00	0.00	0.00
Number of observations		360	360	360
Log likelihood		−4111.57	897.28	1230.72
Residual sum of squares		1.75E+11	0.14	0.02
R-squared		99.0%	99.0%	98.0%
Adjusted R-squared		99.0%	99.0%	97.0%
AIC		8257.2	−1760.6	−2427.4
BIC		8323.2	−1694.5	−2361.4

Note: Coefficient, t statistic and *p-value* shown for each variable. Significance levels: * $p < .1$; ** $p < .05$; *** $p < .01$.

Considering a 20% improvement in the three parameters considered (1000 life cycles, 2% round trip efficiency, and 400,000 € reduction in battery cost), it would provide an increase in NPV rounding up to 500,000 €, being the most significant contribution (80%) the reduction of battery cost. If technological progress continues along the same path (20% annually), the business model based on arbitrage of electricity using Li-Ion batteries will have a positive NPV by 2024.

5 Conclusions and policy implications

This chapter proposes a mathematical model for the analysis of the business model of energy arbitrage in the next day's wholesale market and presents an application to the German case. The study combines three mathematical methodologies: optimization, financial analysis and econometric analysis; the output of each methodology is used as the input for the following. The MIP optimization model provides as output the optimal arbitrage (in the German electricity market) of a 10 MWh battery which can be combined with inverters of different sizes and to which different capabilities (in terms of cycles and round-trip efficiency) can be assumed. The proposed optimization model simulates the behavior of the charging/discharging process of a Li-Ion battery, selecting the optimal purchase/sale of electricity for each hour during a full year with the aim of maximizing the revenue. At each period, the model updates the real capacity of the battery by decreasing the total capacity as a function of the number of charging/discharging cycles. This can be done thanks to the inclusion of state variables, representing the last performed operation. Since the purchase and sale of electricity depend on the inverter transformation capacity, we run the model iteratively by varying the inverter transformation rate, from 1 to the initial size of the battery. Note that the conversion loss is also incorporated in the model, ensuring the purchase of electricity is a bit higher than the residual capacity at each period and that the real sale of electricity in a period is a bit lower that the discharged energy.

Our study defines as 10 MWh battery of reference the one costing 2 M€, with 92% round-trip efficiency and 5000 charge cycles. By combining this battery with 10 possible inverter sizes (from 1 to 10 MW), we generate 10 storage system configurations which optimal arbitrages in the electricity market can be seen as alternative business opportunities. The optimal arbitrage of each business opportunity is simulated for more than 10 years, which allows us to generate annual time series of their respective cash-flows. From these annual cash-flows, we calculate three dynamic financial indicators in order to measure the goodness of each possible investment or storage system configuration; namely, net present value (NPV), net present value per € invested ($\frac{NPV}{I}$) and Internal Rate of Return (IRR). The optimal configuration (in Germany) for the reference battery is given by the 10 MW inverter if we attend to $\frac{NPV}{I}$ and IRR indicators; 2 MW inverter if we look at the NPV indicator.

In the last part of the study, the calculation of the three financial indicators mentioned is extended to 360 possible storage configurations in order to control for the possible technological and economic evolution of storage systems in the coming years. The different combinations come from considering: 4 different 10 MWh battery costs {2 M€, 1.5 M€, 1 M€, 0.5 M€}, 3 different cycle levels for that battery {5000, 6000, 7000}, 3 round-trip efficiency levels for that battery {92%, 93%, 94%}, and 10 possible inverter sizes {1 MW, 2 MW, ..., 10 MW}. The three financial indicators for each scenario are inserted as endogenous variables in respective econometric models which allow us to analyze the effect on the arbitrage business' profitability of changes in the price of the battery, in its useful life and round-trip efficiency, and in the size of the inverter. Ceteris paribus, a 10 MWh battery which is 0.5 M€ cheaper, has 1000 more cycles and a round-trip efficiency 1% higher, improves the business NPV approximately 0.49 M€, 0.076 M€ and 0.006 M€, respectively. As for the inverter size, the results obtained depend on the financial indicator used as endogenous variable: the best inverters are those of size 3 and 4 MW in NPV terms, 4–8 MW in $\frac{NPV}{I}$ terms, and 8–10 MW in terms of IRR indicator.

The results are conservative, since they only consider the income derived from the participation in the next day market, not including other possible income such as those derived from the market of auxiliary services, or in the flexibility markets, recently regulated in Europe in the Directive (EU) 2019/944 of the European Parliament on common rules for the internal market for electricity.

Both the mathematical model, as well as the results obtained in the German case, can be useful both to companies (which must prepare their structures to participate in these markets in the coming years) and to research centers, which will be able to focus their work on those aspects that are most profitable for the business. The mathematical model is adaptable to any wholesale electricity market. As further research, a comparison of the market performances of different countries could be carried out, analyzing in which of them the participation would be more interesting, and when.

References

Adebayo, A.I., Zamani-Dehkordi, P., Zareipour, H., Knight, A.M., 2018. Impacts of transmission tariff on price arbitrage operation of energy storage system in Alberta electricity market. Util. Policy 52, 1–12.

Arcos-Vargas, A., Canca, D., Núñez, F., 2020. Impact of battery technological progress on electricity arbitrage: an application to the Iberian market. Appl. Energy 260, 114273.

Bardo Cáceres, S., 2010. Almacenamiento distribuido en viviendas para alisar la curva de demanda de energía eléctrica. Trabajo final de carrera, Universitat Politècnica de Catalunya (UPC).

Battery University, 2019. Learn About Batteries. Available from: https://batteryuniversity.com/learn/.

Baumgarte, F., Glenk, G., Rieger, A., 2019. Business Models and Profitability of Energy Storage. Available from SSRN 3421370.

Berrada, A., Loudiyi, K., Zorkani, I., 2016. Valuation of energy storage in energy and regulation markets. Energy 115, 1109–1118.

Bradbury, K., Pratson, L., Patiño-Echeverri, D., 2014. Economic viability of energy storage systems based on price arbitrage potential in real-time U.S. electricity markets. Appl. Energy 114, 512–519.

Brijs, T., Geth, F., De Jonghe, C., Belmans, R., 2019. Quantifying electricity storage arbitrage opportunities in short-term electricity markets in the CWE region. J. Energy Storage 25, 100899.

Clean Technica, 2017. Batteries Keep on Getting Cheaper. Available from: https://cleantechnica.com/2017/12/11/batteries-keep-getting-cheaper/.

Connolly, D., Lund, H., Finn, P., Mathiesen, B.V., Leahy, M., 2011. Practical operation strategies for pumped hydroelectric energy storage (PHES) utilizing electricity price arbitrage. Energy Policy 39, 4189–4196.

Daggett, A., Qadrdan, M., Jenkins, N., 2017. Feasibility of a battery storage system for a renewable energy park operating with price arbitrage. In: 2017 IEEE PES Innovative Smart Grid Technologies Conference Europe (ISGT-Europe). IEEE, pp. 1–6.

Das, T., Krishnan, V., McCalley, J.D., 2015. Assessing the benefits and economics of bulk energy storage technologies in the power grid. Appl. Energy 139, 104–118.

Gomez-Expósito, A., Sudria, A., Alvarez, E., Díaz, J.L., Pérez-Arriaga, J.I., Arcos-Vargas, A., Pérez de Vargas, J., 2017. El almacenamiento de energía en la distribución eléctrica del futuro. Real Academia de la Ingeniería, Madrid.

Hakim, D.B., Danley, D.R., Caplan, M., 2009. Energy Arbitrage by Load Shifting. U.S. Patent No. 7,590,472, U.S. Patent and Trademark Office, Washington, DC.

Hernández Romero, A., 2016. Análisis económico de un sistema de almacenamiento para la disminución de desvíos de producción en un parque eólico. Trabajo Final de Máster, Escuela Técnica Superior de Ingeniería, Universidad de Sevilla (US).

Hou, P., Enevoldsen, P., Eichman, J., Hu, W., Jacobson, M.Z., Chen, Z., 2017. Optimizing investments in coupled offshore wind-electrolytic hydrogen storage systems in Denmark. J. Power Sources 359, 186–197.

International Energy Agency, 2019. World Energy Outlook. Paris, France, International Energy Agency.

IRENA, 2017. Accelerating the Global Energy Transformation. International Renewable Energy Agency, Abu Dhabi.

Jannesar, M.R., Sedighi, A., Savaghebi, M., Guerrero, J.M., 2018. Optimal placement, sizing, and daily charge/discharge of battery energy storage in low voltage distribution network with high photovoltaic penetration. Appl. Energy 226, 957–966.

Jofemar Energy, 2016. Almacenamiento electroquímico con baterías de flujo. Available from: http://www.f2e.es/uploads/doc/20160704075330.f2e_jofemar.pdf.

Kazempour, S.J., Moghaddam, M.P., Haghifam, M.R., Yousefi, G.R., 2009. Electric energy storage systems in a market-based economy: comparison of emerging and traditional technologies. Renew. Energy 34 (12), 2630–2639.

Khastieva, D., Hesamzadeh, M.R., Vogelsang, I., Rosellón, J., Amelin, M., 2019. Value of energy storage for transmission investments. Energy Strategy Rev. 24, 94–110.

Krishnamurthy, D., Zhou, Z., Thimmapuram, P.R., Botterud, A., 2018. Energy storage arbitrage under day ahead and real time price uncertaintly. IEEE Trans. Power Syst. 33, 84–93.

Metz, D., Saraiva, J.T., 2018. Use of battery storage systems for price arbitrage operations in the 15-and 60-min German intraday markets. Electr. Power Syst. Res. 160, 27–36.

Nasrolahpour, E., Kazempour, S.J., Zareipour, H., Rosehart, W.D., 2016. Strategic sizing of energy storage facilities in electricity markets. IEEE Trans. Sustain. Energy 7 (4), 1462–1472.

Segui Pedro, C., 2018. Todo sobre baterías y almacenamiento de energía. Available from: https://www.barriolapinada.es/baterias-almacenamiento-energia/.

Sioshansi, R., Denholm, P., Jenkin, T., Weiss, J., 2009. Estimating the value of electricity storage in PJM: arbitrage and some welfare effects. Energy Econ. 31 (2), 269–277.

Sussams, L., Leaton, J., 2017. Expect the Unexpected: The Disruptive Power of Low-Carbon Technology. Carbon Tracker Initiative (CTI), London, United Kingdom.

Terlouw, T., AlSkaifa, T., Bauerb, C., van Sarka, W., 2019. Multi-objective optimization of energy arbitrage in community energy storage systems using different battery technologies. Appl. Energy 239, 356–372.

Vélez Moreno, S., 2012. Estudio de un sistema de almacenamiento de energía eólica por medio de baterías. Trabajo final de carrera, Escuela Técnica Superior de Ingenieros de Minas, Universidad Politécnica de Madrid (UPM).

Walawalkar, R., Apt, J., Mancini, R., 2007. Economics of electric energy storage for energy arbitrage and regulation in New York. Energy Policy 35, 2558–2568.

Wu, W., Lin, B., 2018. Application value of energy storage in power grid: a special case of China electricity market. Energy 165, 1191–1199.

Yucekaya, A., 2013. The operational economics of compressed air energy storage systems under uncertaintly. Renew. Sust. Energy Rev. 22, 298–305.

Zakeri, B., Syri, S., 2014, May. Economy of electricity storage in the Nordic electricity market: the case for Finland. In: 11th International Conference on the European Energy Market (EEM14). IEEE, pp. 1–6.

Chapter 13

The integration of dynamic demand in electricity markets: Blockchain 3.0 as an enabler of microgrid energy exchange, demand response and storage

Stavros Lazarou[a] and Evangelos Kotsakis[b]

[a]*Department of Electrical and Electronic Engineering Educators, School of Pedagogical and Technological Education (ASPETE), Heraklion Attikis, Athens, Greece,* [b]*European Commission—Joint Research Centre, Ispra, VA, Italy*

1 Introduction

Despite its computational requirements, blockchain is a promising ledger technology for the energy market in the era of smart infrastructure, distributed generation from renewable energy sources, storage, demand response and electric vehicles (EV). It offers the capability of clearing energy market transactions without the need of a trusted authority. It potentially reduces costs and there is not a single point of failure since the information is stored across all nodes. However, it could suffer privacy issues.

Wang et al. (2019a) support the opinion that distributed energy trading is able to offer additional flexibility and that previous drawbacks of blockchain technology have been overcome at its newest versions. Additionally, several contemporary blockchain implementations facilitate climate friendly causes. This is an issue of paramount importance, since it is able to mobilize the communities toward a noble reason toward improving technology penetration to the society and the capability to offer better services through the collective, open source, contribution from software and hardware developers. Andoni et al. (2019) point out in their conclusions the importance of empowering the society from a different point of view. The blockchain technology is able to increase the participation of the prosumers in the energy market. All transactions are cleared through the transparent exchange of information and data across all nodes of the blockchain system. The contribution of every node is similar in nature with respect to the required computational power and its trading limitations. Every transaction is stored on every node in a transparent manner providing the ability to all the participants to double check the whole process and better understand how the market found an equilibrium at any specific trading moment.

As explained by Wu and Tran (2018), the operational characteristics of blockchain enhance trust between market participants and provide more flexible arrangements for the operation of new renewable energy sources configurations. Blockchain microgrid configuration could theoretically be more flexible to accommodate the special needs of the emerging and futuristic energy production from renewable energy sources. This is due to by the default enhanced flexibility of blockchain, but also due to the fact that minor changes to accommodate the specificities of new or evolving systems could be more difficult to implement from a centrally organized market or a large aggregator. The futuristic potential of blockchain is part of the experts' perception in the energy market.

This is also depicted on the survey conducted by Brilliantova and Wolfgang Thurnerb (2019). They explain the disruptive potential of the technology but they also connect its penetration to regulators' capability to accommodate the special status of blockchain compared to aggregator type models and provide the appropriate legal framework for its effective, safe operation that respects the privacy of individuals and blocks the market participation to malicious dishonest participants.

Another important issue described in the survey of Zheng et al. (2019) is the capability of the business community to create business models for blockchain. Up to now, the existing models are heavily based on crypto-currency patterns. Although the nature of blockchain is currency related, it is important for its business models to effectively meet the special business requirements of energy related processes. On this pattern, Ul Hassan et al. (2019) explain that the existing currency focused blockchain open source platforms need to be properly adjusted to accommodate the needs of the energy market. They also propose to create modular capabilities to easily modify its characteristics if needed.

On smart grids level, Kim and Huh (2018) give emphasis to the fact that the electricity system is mostly interconnected and a potential threat from several improvised blockchain powered micro-grids could potentially deteriorate the operational safety of the system. Having this said, cyber security precautions served at the regulator, network operator and prosumer level shall be exhaustively exercised. Alladi et al. (2019) critically address the issue of wider cooperation across all stakeholders, including the industry and the research community to meet all the requirements and deal with the future challenges.

All the above are issues that are further elaborated in this chapter. In Section 2, Peer-to-peer (P2P) energy trading, the existing scientific work on peer-to-peer trading is provided and commented. Section 3, Demand response, Storage, Electric Vehicles and Blockchain explains the specificities of blockchain with respect to demand response, storage and the connection to electric vehicles. Section 4, Implementation level investigates the pilot projects across several levels and the lessons learned are presented. Section 5, Technical issues on blockchain, demand response and storage, describes the technological advancements to meet all the above requirements in an effective manner. Section 6, Social dimension gives attention to the potential social benefits of the technology. Finally, conclusions from the bibliography and proposals for future engagement on the subject are proposed.

2 Demand response, storage, electric vehicles and peer-to-peer (P2P) blockchain energy trading

2.1 Peer-to-peer (P2P) energy trading

Micro grids peer-to-peer (P2P) energy trading is a promising application of blockchain technology. In this case, the blockchain ledger needs to tackle limitations imposed by the market but also and more importantly, from the technical operation of the system, which is a specificity of the energy market. Every node is connected through the power system and the P2P trading system (Fig. 13.1). The balance between consumption and production shall be always respected and especially for the isolated of weakly connected micro-grids additional provisions shall be taken to safeguard their dynamic performance during faults. Blockchain shall be also capable to further improve efficiency and reduce emissions. This can be achieved through being able to perform demand response routines and taking advantage of the available connected storage facilities.

To tackle this issue, Hayesa et al. (2020) propose the co-simulation of the distribution networks and the peer-to-peer trading schemes for the participants of the market that are connected to the same network. Power flow simulations are run for the P2P market to avoid any potential voltage violations. Their findings indicate the moderate penetration of intermittent

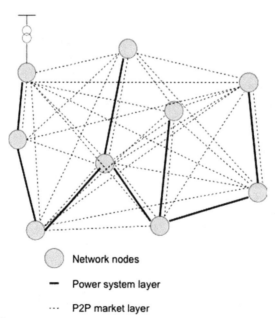

FIG. 13.1 Network nodes connection points.

distributed generators that participate to P2P trading do not substantially affect distribution grid voltage. However, as long as the penetration of pronsumers that participate to P2P trading is increasing, the strain imposed to the grid is also being affected. Guerrero et al. (2019) developed a methodology to safeguard that P2P transactions so that not to violate low voltage network constraints. They use three factors. The Voltage Sensitivity Coefficients express the voltage changes due to the connection of the distributed generators. The Power Transfer Distribution Factors describe the power alterations across the network due to the new injections. The Loss Sensitivity Factors depict changes of network losses due to P2P trading. The combination of the above meets energy trading requirements without stressing the network.

Another important issue in microgrid P2P trading is the inter-micro grid trading capabilities and/or trading across different voltage levels. This is necessary due to the nature of the clients needed to be served by the P2P trading scheme that include mobile assets such as electric vehicles (EV), but also to improve efficiency taking advantage of potential lower energy prices and carbon emissions at other parts of the networks. Abdella and Shuaib (2018) review the bibliography on the subject. Li et al. (2019c) and describe the specifications to achieve interoperability between transactive microgrids. According to their vision, blockchain technologies have to be able to cooperate with each other and provide the capability to clear transactions and smart contracts even between microgrids.

2.2 Demand response, storage, electric vehicles and blockchain

Flexibility of blockchain systems facilitate electric vehicles to participate to the market in a safe and beneficial manner for the network and the user. EVs are also able to provide storage ancillary services to the grid and organize their charging based on demand management. Several blockchain implementations propose the relevant procedure. A concrete example of EVs providing voltage stability ancillary services and contribute to grid resilience is proposed by Liu et al. (2018). They demonstrate that blockchain-based optimization techniques are able to over perform genetic algorithms for meeting the same objective. This is an additional benefit when this technology is compared to centralized solutions for market clearing operations. Hou et al. (2019) developed a blockchain based procedure for administering storage giving priority to local loads. The storage facilities at their study seek first to satisfy the loads that are near them and then they are participating to the market. In this manner, the energy transportation cost and the computational burden to solve the dispatch problem is being reduced. Silva et al. (2019) implemented a blockchain-based electric vehicle energy trading platform for a campus parking lot. Their system was able to improve the load factor of the nearby university buildings and provide transparency for the transactions conducted. Wang et al. (2020) provide a holistic approach for optimizing electric vehicle charging energy transactions against internal and external factors. This solutions shows adequate performance and it will soon be able to accommodate vehicle to grid operations.

Providing EVs and storage cyber safe charging operations is the research subject of several works. According to Mhaisen et al. (2019), storage is more vulnerable to attacks due to its potential to create disruption to the system. Based on this, they propose a methodology based on blockchain that enhances security. They also compare their approach to the traditional way of conducting similar operations. Chen and Zhang (2019) propose a secure charging trading scheme that alleviates the burden of the communication layer. Their methodology enhances the will of EVs to participate to the market and contribute to demand management initiatives. However, this could potentially increase the attempts of malicious vehicles that are willing to lose their benefits in order to harm the system. It is generally accepted that at least most of the participants to the market are honest players. Kim et al. (2019) tackle the problem of denial of service and privileged insider attacks in the case of loss of the aggregator in an electric vehicle charging service. Their application could be used either for charging or for vehicle to grid operations. They claim that they provide enhanced security even compared to other blockchain based solutions. Chaudhary et al. (2019) have developed a blockchain energy trading system optimized for electric vehicles. Their system uses energy coins to be consumed by the vehicles. Their findings demonstrate the proof-of-concept and that this solution remains computationally and communication wise inexpensive.

3 Implementation level

Pilot blockchain projects were developed or visioned to include several levels of complexity. On system level it includes countries, at local level it includes cities and at entities level industrial users. Buth et al. (2019) investigate the potential of using blockchain nationwide for the energy system of the Netherlands. According to their opinion, even if new procedures will be adopted and several central need to be formed or dissoluted, the impact of the new technology is not major. They form an interesting table were they observe that the influence of pronsumers and market operators will be increased, and transmission and distribution system operators will be enhanced even marginally due to the expected decrease of the energy transferred. Aggregators, as expected, will have a diminishing position. Ahl et al. (2020) consider blockchain as a natural continuation of the energy system evolvement in Japan and globally, however, they believe that living labs and regulator sandboxes will contribute to understand in detail its more effective implementation. Both of these two slightly different approaches show that blockchain, even having to face important challenges, could be useful in the digitization of nationwide energy systems.

Shen and Pena-Mora (2018) collected the available bibliography of their time for implementing blockchain at city level. Their findings point out the infancy state of blockchain at the time of this publication. Mengelkamp et al. (2018) evaluate the performance of blockchain against seven attributes, as it was deployed to Brooklyn microgrid project. These are the microgrid setup, grid connection, information system, market mechanism, pricing mechanism, energy management trading system and regulation. Their findings demonstrate a satisfactory penetration of the technology and their future proposed work is revolving around its social acceptance and regulation. Van Cutsem et al. (2020) investigate blockchain potential for smart-buildings. At their approach they consider a community of smart buildings as market participants, which are willing to optimize their performance against several factors such as energy cost and carbon emissions. The open source implementation they adopt is capable to control up to 100 buildings. Park et al. (2018) propose a blockchain system for clearing energy market between prosumers and consumers at smart homes. They seek to create a long run, sustainable market that will provide incentives to the stakeholders to participate in a sustainable manner.

Dang et al. (2019) propose an already available blockchain solution for organizing the energy trading demand management activities of an industrial user. This work, as a proof-of-work concept for one large market participant, shows adequate performance for industrial use and the potential for more than one user. Jean Bürer et al. (2019) support the opinion that on energy industry level, blockchain technology is not expected to have significant impact. They believe that the endogenous complexity of the electricity system is difficult to be adequately served by this technology. However, they understand that blockchain will stimulate the creation of new business models and it will lead the way toward a more artificial intelligence oriented electricity system.

4 Technical issues on blockchain, demand response and storage

4.1 Blockchain implementations applicable to energy systems

As indicated at Table 13.1, several blockchain implementations are available, which are mostly open source, downloadable from Github. The work of the majority of the researchers on the field is based mostly on these. Di Silvestre et al. (2018) performed an experiment for the use of blockchain in clearing the energy market. They observe that the lack of offering of ancillary services substantially affect the capability of the system to transfer energy and consequently fulfill the obligations agreed by the market. To overcome the issue of power losses, two indices are adopted. According to O'Donovan and O'Sullivan (2019), the main challenges for the real world blockchain energy systems are revolving around "Infrastructure and environment", "Technical transparency" and "Project innovation velocity." They recognize the accelerating appearance rate of new blockchains for energy, however, the appropriate lessons learned from the previous cases need to be better organized in order to have more impact. Musleh et al. (2019) among others, investigate the degree of blockchain adoption in the energy market. Their findings show that the energy industry is increasingly adopting the new technology, having to demonstrate numerous implementation examples. Nevertheless, there are challenges which are expected to be covered in near future.

Access to the blockchain trading platform at several early implementations does not provide permissions, however, for smart grid energy trading it is expected that permission based blockchains could support safer operation. Belotti et al. (2019) investigate this transition. They describe five types of consensus and the routines to support them. It is of paramount importance that safety considerations are taken into account. Zheng et al. (2020) describe the potential of smart contracting, which could be potentially applicable to energy trading. They identify the existence of potential bugs and the lack of experts that will be capable to advance the technology of smart contracting across all fields. Li et al., (2019) provided a solution for limiting communication and computational blockchain requirements without undermining the quality of the market. They consider the energy trading process as a Stackelberg game. This approach worked adequately for a microgrid, however, it remains to be scaled up to more complex environments such as inter-microgrid energy trade and to further improve security.

As far as the computational requirements are concerned, Toor et al. (2019) point out the applicability of fog computing to blockchain energy trading applications. Their approach is able to improve computational footprint without undermining the quality of the application. Sittón-Candanedo et al. (2020) investigate Edge computing as a technological advancement that could be beneficial for smart grids. One of the applications are blockchain energy trading. They support the opinion that the whole process is able to improve the total quality of service through increasing overall efficiency.

TABLE 13.1 Blockchain implementations.

	Github site
Bitcoin (https://bitcoin.org/)	N/A
Ethereum (https://ethereum.org)	https://github.com/ethereum
Hyperledger (https://www.hyperledger.org)	https://github.com/hyperledger/hyperledger
Fabric (http://fabfile.org)	https://github.com/fabric
Burrow (https://www.hyperledger.org)	https://hyperledger.github.io/burrow
Besu (https://www.hyperledger.org)	https://github.com/hyperledger/besu
Indy (https://www.hyperledger.org)	https://github.com/hyperledger
Iroha (https://www.hyperledger.org)	https://github.com/hyperledger/iroha
Sawtooth (https://www.hyperledger.org)	https://github.com/hyperledger/sawtooth-core
Corda (https://www.corda.net/)	https://github.com/corda/corda
Tendermint	https://github.com/tendermint/tendermint
ChainCore	https://github.com/CryptoWorldChain/chaincore
HydraChain	https://github.com/hydrachain/
EnerChain (https://enerchain.ponton.de)	N/A
Monax (https://monax.io/)	https://github.com/monax
Iota (http://iota.org/)	https://github.com/iotaledger
Stellar (https://www.stellar.org)	N/A
Roodstock (https://www.rsk.co)	N/A
EOS (https://eos.io)	N/A
Quorum (https://www.goquorum.com)	N/A

4.2 Ancillary services market (demand response—voltage support/reactive energy)

The impact of ancillary services becomes apparent in an isolated microgrid, without which its operation is not possible. Nevertheless, it is also beneficial for the interconnected system if prosumers are able to offer these services. It improves system performance and reduces total costs. Di Silvestre et al. (2018) include the remuneration procedure for reactive power balancing from distributed generators to the blockchain. Using a test network, they are able to demonstrate the improvement in terms of voltage stability offered by their approach. Yang et al. (2020) propose a methodology to cover the supply-demand balance with load shifting capabilities, vehicle to grid support and storage. In this way, the benefits of blockchain are combined with additional flexibility being able to offer a secure trading environment for energy local networks.

Noor et al. (2018) also develop a demand management platform based among others on blockchain. This proof-of-concept case uses game theory to balance the existing situation but also the new demand and supply. Results show that peak shaving is being achieved maximizing the benefits for the users and the utility. Xu et al. (2019) use an ant colony optimization method on a blockchain energy trading system. In this case, a microgrid group transaction is solved. Their model is also improves market quality safeguarding that high income and low cost phenomena are excluded from the transaction process. Their findings emphasize on the competency factor between market participants.

Zahid et al. (2020) propose a blockchain energy trading platform. Their simulations show that their model has adequate performance and the capability to inform the authenticated participants for their trading history. They prefer using blockchain because of its transparency and traceability. Blockchain and continuous double auction mechanism is used by Wang et al. (2017). The benefits of their approach include the dynamic alteration of production and consumption of the parties based on market signals. They consider the situation where a production or consumption will not be able to honor its contract and how this needs to be mitigated by the system. Zhao et al. (2018) provide an integrated energy trading blockchain system for a combined electricity and gas market. The Ethereum platform they used proved the concept and provided low-cost transaction capabilities to the participants.

Devine and Cuffe (2019) propose the demurrage mechanism to incentivize energy market demand management. At their implementation, energy tokens' value reduces across time. For rational, non-malicious actors, demurraging will cover the need of supply-demand balancing, but system stability needs to be further safeguarded against special events or cyberattacks. Liu et al. (2019) created a blockchain energy trading system based on the proof-of-benefit pattern. In this manner, the consumers are incentivized to provide demand management ancillary services. The authors used a real dataset prove their methodology, however, the dynamic performance of the system when the behavioral patterns of market participants remains to be taken into account.

Khajeh et al. (2020) investigate how flexibility of the power system across different stakeholders including the transmission, distribution system operator and the prosumer could be supported by blockchain. According to their findings, blockchain contribution could be on securing data and enhancing transparency across market participants. Khatoon et al. (2019) investigate the potential of blockchain in incentivizing energy efficiency. They propose the utilization of this technology to trade energy efficiency certificates. Their findings demonstrate the effectiveness of the proposed implementation.

5 Blockchain demand management considerations and power system operation

5.1 Algorithmic representation of blockchain

Bibliography offers a plethora of different algorithmic implementations for energy trading blockchain solutions, which abide to the same basic principles of shared contribution in calculating each trading step and the common storage of all data. Every trading snapshot is stored in blockchain blocks (Fig. 13.2) and shared with all market participants. The previous and the following group of blocks are bound with each other for authentication purposes. For energy trading applications, each block contains information on the consumed/produced energy at every node, the price and any other relevant information is required to clear the market and operate the system. The model to calculate these values varies for every solution. It certainly includes limitations for every node related to its capacity but the way of clearing the market could be different in every case. Some solutions proposed in the bibliography take into consideration limitations imposed by the power system such as system losses and lines loading. Other solutions are able to calculate the flexibility of the system nodes, for example the cost of not providing maximum energy at a given market step.

An interesting approach is elaborated by Thakur and Breslin (2018). They propose a blockchain for micro-grids that is scalable, secure and trustful offering asynchronous and distributed execution. Their algorithm starts describing the coalition formation for microgrid's energy exchange and then the distributed consensus is established and communicated across all nodes. The demand response constraints are inserted to the system at the initial stage.

Wang et al. (2019b) use a blockchain system to solve the demand response problem at a microgrid. They use three distinct load profiles that correspond to residential, industrial and commercial users. Each one of them has a degree of flexibility in terms of consumption, possible capability of energy production and storage. As a generalization, every prosumer could be modeled as:

$$load^t = \sum_0^{24} Consumption + \sum_0^{24} BatteryStorage - \sum_0^{24} DistributedGeneration \qquad (13.1)$$

where daily load is expressed as the hourly consumption, the power requirements for storage at this node and its energy production usually from renewable energy sources. The next step is to calculate the energy balance in a common pool. Foti and Vavalis (2019) present a uniform price, double action blockchain system for clearing energy market. In this case, all market participants are paying and are being paid in a market defined price for each solution market step. Each participant

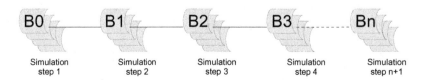

FIG. 13.2 Blockchain.

for every market step proposes a price for selling energy. The producers that offer lower prices start first up to the point that the load is fully covered.

Noor et al. (2018) implement the demand side management part of their blockchain using a discomfort cost element. According to their approach, a constant that varies based on the flexibility of the customer is multiplied with the expected loss of power. A large constant for inflexible loads disincentivizes the equilibrium for an optimal solution that offers a potential large reduction of power for a solution step for this customer, compared with the power requested from the load. A relevant representation is proposed at Eq. (13.2) that applies to every simulation step.

$$D_l^t = \left(W_l^t\right) * \left[\left(l_r^t\right) - \left(l_a^t\right)\right] \tag{13.2}$$

where D corresponds to the factor that expresses the potential customers' discomfort due to loss of requested power. W is connected to the willingness of the customer to have her/is load cut, l is the actual load eventually the customer receives from the system and r the requested load before clearing the demand management energy market.

Tan et al. (2019) give emphasis to privacy-preserving when energy service company do their scheduling. Even if it is not clear which is the exact procedure of enhancing privacy, the authors use a blockchain system to solve their problem. They put each market solution in blocks, the relationship between the nodes is defined by the smart contract and the goods, in this case the energy, is paid in cryprocurrency. Each node, at each market step can be a seller, a buyer or remain idle. The blockchain system, coming initially from the financial industry, also provides the capability of using virtual currencies to clear the market.

Van Leeuwen et al. (2020) develop a blockchain system that uses real prosumer data and takes into consideration electricity network constraints in line with the energy market optimization problem itself. To optimize the energy trading problem, they use the alternating direction method of multipliers method. Several other optimization methods could have been used such as iterative or heuristics. However, it is of paramount importance that they are solved without substantial computational effort from the participation nodes and consequently they do not limit the applicability of the solution. At this point, it has to be mentioned that the energy market is not calculated continuously but in half an hour steps. This is adequate time to calculate next step without substantial calculation requirements. Li et al. (2019b) split consumption in several patterns and provide to their system in a separate manner the production from renewables. They demonstrate that at their blockchain privacy and the whole system security could be enhanced without substantial burden to the overall operation.

The proposed algorithm is summarized in Fig. 13.3. The process begins loading the required data. This includes the description of the system, the nature and potential limitations in the operation of the nodes. This information is combined with the pre-calculated output of the distributed generators that produce energy from intermittent sources. An optimization routine calculates the operation of the battery energy storage systems and the demand management requirements and calculates the energy market. The next step is to confirm that the solution does not violate network constraints. Finally the smart contracts are established, the information is shared with all market participants, the market is cleared and the process restarts for the next market step.

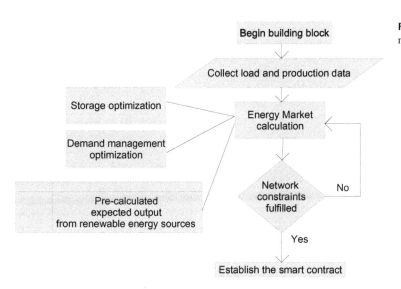

FIG. 13.3 A Flowchart for creating a block at an energy market blockchain.

5.2 Steady state and dynamic network constraints

Network constraints refer to the need of operating the system in a safe manner. To achieve this, it has to observe predefined current and voltage limits as well as dynamic stability requirements. These considerations become more important for isolated microgrids, where the grid is not available to offer the services but it is relevant to connected microgrids that participate to the ancillary services market. Maximum current at all branches are limited by lines' thermal capacity. Power flow analysis or the steady state estimation is the main procedure to calculate, among others, energy flows, voltages, currents and overall losses. In power flow a node is considered as the reference, which has pu voltage 1 and angle 0. A generator bus is able to provide the power needed for the circuit to balance. The rest of the buses have a predefined load or production. Distributed generators from renewable energy intermittent sources could be considered as negative loads. El-Hawari (1995) describes the load flow equations based on voltages V_{bus} and currents I_{bus} nX1 vectors. The admittances are dimensioned as nXm matrixes as follows:

$$Y_{ii} = Y_{ii} = -Y_{Lii} \tag{13.3}$$

$$Y_{ii} = \sum_{j=0}^{n} Y_{Lij} \tag{13.4}$$

Power of each bus is connected to voltage and current as:

$$I_i = \frac{S_i}{V_i} \tag{13.5}$$

then, for every bus:

$$\frac{P_i - jQ_i}{V_i} = \sum_{j=1}^{n} Y_{ij} V_j \\ i = 1, \dots, n \tag{13.6}$$

in other form:

$$P_i - jQ_i = V_i \sum_{j=1}^{n} Y_{ij} V_j \\ i = 1, \dots, n \tag{13.7}$$

the bus voltages are expressed in polar form:

$$V_i = |V_I| e^{j\theta} i = |V_I| < \theta_i \tag{13.8}$$

or rectangular form:

$$V_i = e_i + jf_i \tag{13.9}$$

then, for the rectangular form we have:

$$Y_{ij} = G_{ij} + jB_{ij} \tag{13.10}$$

$$P_i = e_i \left(\sum_{j=1}^{n} \left(G_{ij} e_j - B_{ij} f_j \right) \right) + f_i \left(\sum_{j=1}^{n} \left(G_{ij} f_j - B_{ij} e_j \right) \right) \tag{13.11}$$

$$Q_i = f_i \left(\sum_{j=1}^{n} \left(G_{ij} e_j - B_{ij} f_j \right) \right) + e_i \left(\sum_{j=1}^{n} \left(G_{ij} f_j - B_{ij} e_j \right) \right) \tag{13.12}$$

for the polar form it applies:

$$Y_{ij} = |Y_{ij}| < \psi_{ij} \tag{13.13}$$

$$P_i = |V_i| \sum_{j=1}^{n} |Y_{ij}| |V_j| \cos \left(\theta_i - \theta_j - \psi_{ij} \right) \tag{13.14}$$

$$P_i = \left| V_i \left| \sum_{j=1}^{n} \left| Y_{ij} \right| \right| V_j \right| \sin\left(\theta_i - \theta_j - \psi_{ij}\right)$$ (13.15)

or in the hybrid form we have:

$$Y_{ij} = \left| Y_{ij} \right| \left(\cos\psi_{ij} + j\sin\psi_{ij} \right) = G_{ij} + jB_{ij}$$ (13.16)

and

$$G_{ij} = \left| Y_{ij} \right| \cos\psi_{ij}$$ (13.17)

$$B_{ij} = \left| Y_{ij} \right| \sin\psi_{ij}$$ (13.18)

for

$$P_i = \left| V_i \left| \sum_{j=1}^{n} \left| Y_{ij} \right| \right| V_j \right| \left[\cos\left(\theta_i - \theta_j\right)\cos\psi_{ij} + \sin\left(\theta_i - \theta_j\right)\sin\psi_{ij} \right]$$ (13.19)

$$Q_i = \left| V_i \left| \sum_{j=1}^{n} \left| Y_{ij} \right| \right| V_j \right| \left[\sin\left(\theta_i - \theta_j\right)\cos\psi_{ij} + \cos\left(\theta_i - \theta_j\right)\sin\psi_{ij} \right]$$ (13.20)

we have:

$$P_i = \left| V_i \left| \sum_{j=1}^{n} \right| V_j \right| \left[G_{ij}\cos\left(\theta_i - \theta_j\right)B_{ij}\sin\left(\theta_i - \theta_j\right) \right]$$ (13.21)

$$Q_i = \left| V_i \left| \sum_{j=1}^{n} \right| V_j \right| \left[G_{ij}\sin\left(\theta_i - \theta_j\right)B_{ij}\cos\left(\theta_i - \theta_j\right) \right]$$ (13.22)

As far as microgrid's transient behavior is concerned, it is mostly characterized by the participation of relatively enhanced production from renewable sources. They are mostly connected through power electronics but it possible to have synchronous or asynchronous electric machines for hydro, wind and biomass micro plants. Consequently, an isolated microgrid has low inertia, potentially affecting its ability to deliver power with adequate quality. Based on this, it is beneficial to consider the dynamic performance of electric machines participating in the blockchain-based market. Eremia and Shahidehpour (2013) provide a wide analysis on the inertia problem in power systems. Initially the "second order model" is being considered:

$$\frac{d\omega_r}{dt} + \frac{D}{M}(\omega_r - \omega_0) = \frac{\omega_0}{MS_b}(P_m - P_e)$$
$$\frac{d\delta}{dt} = \omega_r - \omega_0$$ (13.23)

where P_m and P_e are the mechanical and electrical powers per unit referred to S_b, which is the apparent power, ω_r and ω_0 are the angular and nominal velocities of the rotor respectively, D is the damping co-efficient, δ is the rotor angle and M corresponds to the "mechanical starting time of the generator." When $D=0$ the Eq. (13.23) in absolute values writes as follows:

$$\dot{\delta}_\kappa = \omega_r - \omega_o$$
$$\dot{\omega}_r = \frac{\omega_0}{MS_b}(P_m - P_e)$$ (13.24)
$$k = 1,...,N$$

where N is the number of generators connected to the system in a given solution of the energy market. The linearization of these equations around the operational point gives:

$$[\dot{\Delta\delta}] = [\Delta\Omega]$$
$$[\dot{\Delta\Omega}] = [M]^{-1}\left\{[\Delta P_m] - [\Delta P_e]\right\}$$ (13.25)

knowing that:

$$P_e = f\{\delta_1, ..., \delta_N, E_1, ..., E_N\}$$
$$k = 1, ..., N \tag{13.26}$$

if E_N are the electromotive force and δ the generators' angle and:

$$[K] = \begin{bmatrix} K_{11} & \cdots & K_{1N} \\ \vdots & & \vdots \\ K_{Nl} & \cdots & K_{NN} \end{bmatrix} \tag{13.27}$$

$$K_{Ki} = \left(\frac{\partial P_e}{\partial \delta_i}\right)$$

$$[F] = \begin{bmatrix} K_{11} & \cdots & K_{1N} \\ \vdots & & \vdots \\ K_{Nl} & \cdots & K_{NN} \end{bmatrix} \tag{13.28}$$

$$F_{Ki} = \left(\frac{\partial P_e}{\partial E_i}\right)$$

$[K]$ is the matrix of "synchronizing power coefficients" that connects power with angle and $[F]$ is the matrix that connects power with electromotive force for each generator.

$$[\Delta P_e] = [K][\Delta\delta] + [F][\Delta E]$$

$$[M] = \text{diag}\{M_k\} = \text{diag}\left\{\frac{MS_b}{\omega_0}\right\} \tag{13.29}$$

and $[M]$ is the matrix of "inertia coefficients" or simply "inertias." Consequently frequency stability is connected to the installed capacity and the technical specifications of the generator.

6 Social dimension

The potential of blockchain to contribute in the transition of power systems will empower prosumer to participate proactively to a more vibrant energy market and will reduce microgrid transaction costs. Energy trading at microgrids level is simplified. All transactions are negotiated directly by the market participants without the need of a central clearing authority. This creates trust between the stakeholders and being able to have access to the negotiating process and its outcome at any trading moment enhances transparency. However, it needs to be mentioned, that being able to have access to the market data of all participants could potentially create privacy concerns. Samuel et al. (2020) investigate the threat of privacy bridges at the electric vehicle charging process. Their simulation shows that the risk can be mitigated.

Several developing countries face the challenge of electrification to improve the quality of life of their people and create more competitive small businesses. The cost of installing new transmission systems could not be easily afforded by the poor. In this case, the use of isolated microgrids is an effective solution. Blockchain technology is able to contribute in the procedure of clearing the local market without the need of a central authority, which dramatically reduces microgrid costs. However, as Ahl et al. (2019) point out the importance of creating the appropriate institutional foundations to be able to cherish the benefits of emerging technologies such as blockchain.

7 Conclusions and future work

This work has investigated the main opportunities from the adoption of blockchain at the energy market and the major issues arising. It appears to be a promising and disruptive technology, which practically means that its increased penetration is directly connected to the regulatory framework. Brilliantova and Wolfgang Thurnerb (2019) stress the importance of the regulators capability to provide the appropriate legal framework for its operation.

As far as the energy system is concerned, the connection of new innovative sources require specialized capabilities. Therefore, the development of modularity at the open source blockchain platforms for accommodating energy related needs will be beneficial for the microgrid community. On the other hand, operators and power system engineers have to update their network planning procedures in order to be able to consider P2P trading in microgrids.

The proliferation of different blockchain platforms require a standardization processes for interoperability. This is important for being able to clear transactions between microgrids that use different platforms. It is important to stress it out that due to the increasing use of electric instead of fossil fuel power vehicles, the total energy handled by the energy system will increase. Blockchain will help to manage this increase.

Moreover, varying energy prices at the customer level require the capability of all customers to be adequately educated in order to take advantage of the system. Consumption when prices are high could severely increase energy bills and potential lead to energy poverty if households are on the edge of being able to pay their energy. Several measures have to be taken to safeguard adequate access to electricity for everyone.

References

Abdella, J., Shuaib, K., 2018. Peer to peer distributed energy trading in smart grids: a survey. Energies 11, 1560.

Ahl, A., Yarime, M., Tanaka, K., Sagawa, D., 2019. Review of blockchain-based distributed energy: implications for institutional development. Renew. Sustain. Energy Rev. 107, 200–211.

Ahl, A., Yarime, M., Goto, M., Chopra, S., Manoj, K.N., Tanaka, K., Sagawa, D., 2020. Exploring blockchain for the energy transition: opportunities and challenges based on a case study in Japan. Renew. Sustain. Energy Rev. 117, 109488.

Alladi, T., Chamola, V., Rodrigues, J.J.P.C., Kozlov, S.A., 2019. Blockchain in smart grids: a review on different use cases. Sensors 19, 4862.

Andoni, M., Robu, V., Flynn, D., Abram, S., Geach, D., Jenkins, D., McCallum, P., Peacock, A., 2019. Blockchain technology in the energy sector: a systematic review of challenges and opportunities. Renew. Sustain. Energy Rev. 100, 143–174.

Belotti, M., Božic, N., Pujolle, G., Secci, S., 2019. A vademecum on blockchain technologies: when, which, and how. IEEE Commun. Surv. Tutorials 21 (4), 3796–3838.

Brilliantova, V., Wolfgang Thurnerb, T., 2019. Blockchain and the future of energy. Technol. Soc. 57, 38–45.

Buth, M.C.(.A.)., Wieczorek, A.J.(.A.)., Verbong, G.P.J.(.G.)., 2019. The promise of peer-to-peer trading? The potential impact of blockchain on the actor configuration in the Dutch electricity system. Energy Res. Soc. Sci. 53, 194–205.

Chaudhary, R., Jindal, A., Aujla, G.-S., Aggarwal, S., Kumar, N., Raymond Choo, K.-K., 2019. BEST: blockchain-based secure energy trading in SDN-enabled intelligent transportation system. Comput. Secur. 85, 288–299.

Chen, X., Zhang, X., 2019. Secure electricity trading and incentive contract model for electric vehicle based on energy blockchain. IEEE Access 7, 178763–178778.

Dang, C., Zhang, J., Kwong, C.-P., Li, L., 2019. Demand side load management for big industrial energy users under blockchain-based peer-to-peer electricity market. IEEE Trans. Smart Grid 10 (6), 178763–178778.

Devine, M., Cuffe, P., 2019. Blockchain electricity trading under demurrage. IEEE Trans. Smart Grid 10 (2), 2323–2325.

Di Silvestre, M.-L., Gallo, P., Ippolito, M.-G., Sanseverino, E.-R., Zizzo, G., 2018. A technical approach to the energy blockchain in microgrids. IEEE Trans. Ind. Inf. 14 (11), 4792–4803.

El-Hawari, M., 1995. Electrical Power Systems—Design and Analysis. Wiley-IEEE Press.

Eremia, M., Shahidehpour, M., 2013. Handbook of Electrical Power System Dynamics: Modeling, Stability, and Control. Wiley-IEEE Press.

Foti, M., Vavalis, M., 2019. Blockchain based uniform price double auctions for energy markets. Appl. Energy 254, 113604.

Guerrero, J., Chapman, A., Verbic, G., 2019. Decentralized P2P energy trading under network constraints in a low-voltage network. IEEE Trans. Smart Grid 10 (5), 5163–5173.

Hayesa, B.P., Thakurb, S., Breslinb, J.G., 2020. Co-simulation of electricity distribution networks and peer to peer energy trading platforms. Electr. Power Energy Syst. 115, 105419.

Hou, W., Guo, L., Ning, Z., 2019. Local electricity storage for blockchain-based energy trading in industrial Internet of Things. IEEE Trans. Ind. Inf. 15 (6), 3610–3619.

Jean Bürer, M., de Lapparent, M., Pallotta, V., Capezzali, M., Carpita, M., 2019. Use cases for Blockchain in the Energy Industry Opportunities of emerging business models and related risks. Comput. Ind. Eng. 137, 106002.

Khajeh, H., Laaksonen, H., Gazafroudi, A.S., Shafie-khah, M., 2020. Towards flexibility trading at TSO-DSO-customer levels: a review. Energies 13, 165.

Khatoon, A., Verma, P., Southernwood, J., Massey, B., Corcoran, P., 2019. Blockchain in energy efficiency: potential applications and benefits. Energies 12, 3317.

Kim, S.-K., Huh, J.-H., 2018. A study on the improvement of smart grid security performance and blockchain smart grid perspective. Energies 11, 1973.

Kim, M., Park, K., Yu, S., Lee, J., Park, Y., Lee, S.-W., Chung, B., 2019. A secure charging system for electric vehicles based on blockchain. Sensors 19, 3028.

Li, Y., Yang, W., He, P., Chen, C., Wang, X., 2019b. Design and management of a distributed hybrid energy system through smart contract and blockchain. Appl. Energy 248, 390–405.

Li, Z., Bahramirad, S., Paaso, A., Yan, M., Shahidehpour, M., 2019c. Blockchain for decentralized transactive energy management system in networked microgrids. Electr. J. 32, 58–72.

Liu, C., Keong Chai, K., Zhang, X., Tseng Lau, E., Chen, Y., 2018. Adaptive blockchain-based electric vehicle participation scheme in smart grid platform. IEEE Access 6, 25657–25665.

Li, J., Zhou, Z., Wu, J., Li, J., Mumtaz, S., Lin, X., Gacanin, H., Alotaibi, S., 2019. Decentralized on-demand energy supply for blockchain in Internet of Things: a microgrids approach. IEEE Trans Comput. Soc. Syst. 6 (6), 1395–1406.

Liu, C., Chai, K.K., Zhang, X., et al., 2019. Peer-to-peer electricity trading system: smart contracts based proof-of-benefit consensus protocol. Wirel. Netw. https://doi.org/10.1007/s11276-019-01949-0.

Mengelkamp, E., Gärttner, J., Rock, K., Kessler, S., Orsini, L., Weinhardt, C., 2018. Designing microgrid energy markets a case study: the Brooklyn microgrid. Appl. Energy 210, 870–880.

Mhaisen, N., Fetais, N., Massoud, A., 2019. Secure smart contract-enabled control of battery energy storage systems against cyber-attacks. Alex. Eng. J. 58, 1291–1300.

Musleh, A., Yao, G., Muyeen, S., 2019. Blockchain applications in smart grid—review and frameworks. IEEE Access 7, 86746–86757.

Noor, S., Yang, W., Guo, M., van Dam, K., Wang, X., 2018. Energy Demand Side Management within micro-grid networks enhanced by blockchain. Appl. Energy 228, 1385–1398.

O'Donovan, P., O'Sullivan, D.T.J., 2019. A systematic analysis of real-world energy blockchain initiatives. Future Internet 11, 174.

Park, L.W., Lee, S., Chang, H., 2018. A sustainable home energy prosumer-chain methodology with energy tags over the blockchain. Sustainability 10, 658.

Samuel, O., et al., 2020. Electric vehicles privacy preserving using blockchain in smart community. In: Barolli, L., Hellinckx, P., Enokido, T. (Eds.), Advances on Broad-Band Wireless Computing, Communication and Applications. BWCCA 2019. vol. 97. Springer, Cham. Lecture Notes in Networks and Systems.

Shen, C., Pena-Mora, F., 2018. Blockchain for cities—a systematic literature review. IEEE Access 6, 76787–76819.

Silva, F.C., Ahmed, M.A., Martínez, J.M., Kim, Y.-C., 2019. Design and implementation of a blockchain-based energy trading platform for electric vehicles in smart campus parking lots. Energies 12, 4814.

Sittón-Candanedo, I., Alonso, R.S., García, Ó., Gil, A.B., Rodríguez-González, S.A., 2020. Review on edge computing in smart energy by means of a systematic mapping study. Electronics 9, 48.

Tan, S., Wang, X., Jiang, C., 2019. Privacy-preserving energy scheduling for ESCOs based on energy blockchain network. Energies 12, 1530.

Thakur, S., Breslin, J.G., 2018. Peer to peer energy trade among microgrids using blockchain based distributed coalition formation method. Technol. Econ. Smart Grids Sustain. Energy 3, 5. https://doi.org/10.1007/s40866-018-0044-y.

Toor, A., ul Islam, S., Sohail, N., Akhunzada, A., Boudjadar, J., Ali Khattak, H., Ud Din, I.J.P.C., Rodrigues, J., 2019. Energy and performance aware fog computing: a case of DVFS and green renewable energy. Future Gener. Comput. Syst. 101, 1112–1121.

Ul Hassan, N., Yuen, C., Niyato, D., 2019. Blockchain technologies for smart energy systems: fundamentals, challenges, and solutions. IEEE Ind. Electron. Mag. 13 (4), 106–118.

Van Cutsem, O., Ho Dac, D., Boudou, P., Kayal, M., 2020. Cooperative energy management of a community of smart-buildings: a Blockchain approach. Electr. Power Energy Syst. 117, 105643.

Van Leeuwen, G., Al Skaif, T., Gibescu, G., van Sark, T., 2020. An integrated blockchain-based energy management platform with bilateral trading for microgrid communities. Appl. Energy 263, 114613.

Wang, J., Wang, Q., Zhou, N., Chi, Y., 2017. A novel electricity transaction mode of microgrids based on blockchain and continuous double auction. Energies 10, 1971.

Wang, N., Zhou, X., Lu, X., Guan, Z., Wu, L., Du, X., Guizani, M., 2019a. When energy trading meets blockchain in electrical power system: the state of the art. Appl. Sci. 9, 1561.

Wang, X., Yang, W., Noor, S., Chen, C., Guo, M., van Dam, K.H., 2019b. Blockchain-based smart contract for energy demand management. Energy Procedia 158, 2719–2724.

Wang, B., Liu, W., Wang, M., Shen, W., 2020. Research on bidding mechanism for power grid with electric vehicles based on smart contract technology. Energies 13, 390.

Wu, J., Tran, N.K., 2018. Application of blockchain technology in sustainable energy systems: an overview. Sustainability 10, 3067.

Xu, Z., Yang, D., Li, W., 2019. Microgrid group trading model and solving algorithm based on blockchain. Energies 12, 1292.

Yang, X., Wang, G., He, H., Lu, J., Zhang, Y., 2020. Automated demand response framework in ELNs: decentralized scheduling and smart contract. IEEE Trans. Syst, Man Cybern.: Syst. 50 (1), 58–72.

Zahid, M., Ali, I., Khan, R.J.U.H., Noshad, Z., Javaid, A., Javaid, N., 2020. Blockchain based balancing of electricity demand and supply. In: Barolli, L., Hellinckx, P., Enokido, T. (Eds.), Advances on Broad-Band Wireless Computing, Communication and Applications. BWCCA 2019. vol. 97. Springer, Cham. Lecture Notes in Networks and Systems.

Zhao, S., Wang, B., Li, Y., Li, Y., 2018. Integrated energy transaction mechanisms based on blockchain technology. Energies 11, 2412.

Zheng, X., Zhu, Y., Si, X., 2019. A survey on challenges and progresses in blockchain technologies: a performance and security perspective. Appl. Sci. 9, 4731.

Zheng, Z., Xie, S., Dai, H.-N., Chen, W., Chen, X., Weng, J., Imran, M., 2020. An overview on smart contracts: challenges, advances and platforms. Future Gener. Comput. Syst. 105, 475–491.

Chapter 14

Optimizing CHP operational planning for participating in day-ahead power markets: The case of a coal-fired CHP system with thermal energy storage

Pablo Benalcazar and Jacek Kamiński

Mineral and Energy Economy Research Institute of the Polish Academy of Sciences, Department of Policy and Strategic Research, Division of Energy Economics, Kraków, Poland

Acronyms

ADN	active distribution network
CHP	combined heat and power
EC-ST	extraction-condensing steam turbine
ED	economic dispatch
EES	electrical energy storage
GA	genetic algorithm
HOB	heat-only boiler
HWT	hot water tank
LP	linear programming
MILP	mixed-integer linear programming
MINLP	mixed-integer nonlinear programming
NLP	nonlinear programming
PSO	particle swarm optimization
PURPA	Public Utility Regulatory Policies Act
PWL	piecewise linear
SB	steam boiler
TES	thermal energy storage
UC	unit commitment

Nomenclature

h	discrete time periods (hours), $h \in H$
hob	heat-only boilers, $hob \in HOB$
i	characteristic points in the feasible operation region of the CHP plant equipped with an extraction-condensing unit, $i \in I$
j	piecewise linear approximation breakpoints of the heat-only boiler fueling function, $j \in J$
p	pollutant, $p \in P$
sb	pulverized coal-fired boilers, $sb \in SB$

Parameters

A^{TES}	total surface area of the tank
C_h^E	electricity price at hour h
C_h^{HOB}	heat-only boiler fueling cost
C_{SU}^{HOB}	start-up costs of heat-only boiler
C_{SU}^{SB}	start-up costs of pulverized coal-fired boiler (CHP plant)

Mathematical Modelling of Contemporary Electricity Markets. https://doi.org/10.1016/B978-0-12-821838-9.00014-1

C_{VOM}^{CHP-P} variable O&M cost related to electrical power production of the CHP plant

C_{VOM}^{HOB} variable O&M cost of heat-only boiler

C_{VOM}^{CHP-Q} variable O&M cost related to thermal power production by the CHP plant

C_i^{CHP} fueling cost at the CHP characteristic point i

C_p^{EM} emission cost of pollutant p

Cp_{water} specific heat capacity of water

D_h heat demand at hour h

E_p^{HOB} emission factor of pollutant p in the coal-fired heat-only boiler

E_p^{SB-P} emission factor of pollutant p in the coal-fired CHP unit (electrical output)

E_p^{SB-Q} emission factor of pollutant p in the coal-fired CHP unit (thermal output)

Fb_j cost function coefficient Fb in segment j

Fm_j cost function coefficient Fm in segment j

P_i^{CHP} electrical power generated at the CHP (extraction-condensing unit) characteristic point i

Q_{MAX}^{HOB} maximum capacity of heat-only boiler (HOB-U1 and HOB-U2)

Q_i^{CHP} thermal power generated at the CHP (extraction-condensing) characteristic point i

S^{MAX} maximum thermal energy storage capacity

$T_h^{outdoor}$ outdoor temperature at hour h

U^{TES} heat transfer coefficient

η_{CH} thermal energy storage charge efficiency

η_{DC} thermal energy storage discharge efficiency

θ_{MAX}^{CH} maximum charge rate of thermal energy storage (fraction of total capacity)

θ_{MAX}^{DC} maximum discharge rate of thermal energy storage (fraction of total capacity)

ρ_{water} density of water

ΔPQ_{MAX} maximum rate of change of combined output

ΔPQ_{MIN} minimum rate of change of combined output

L lower bound of electrical power generation for Big-M constraints

M sufficiently large constant for Big-M constraints

U upper bound of electrical power generation for Big-M constraints

V volume of the tank

Positive variables

c_h^{CHP} CHP (extraction-condensing turbogenerator) fueling costs at hour h

p_h^{CHP} electrical energy generated by the CHP plant (extraction-condensing unit) at hour h

$q_{h,hob}^{HOB}$ production of heat-only boiler hob at hour h

q_h^{CHP} thermal energy produced by the CHP plant (extraction-condensing unit) at hour h

q_h^{PUR} slack variable representing thermal energy purchased at hour h

s_h thermal energy storage level at hour h

s_h^{CH} thermal energy charged to storage at hour h

s_h^{DC} thermal energy discharged from storage at hour h

s_h^{loss} energy losses of the TES to the surroundings at hour h

t_h^{Water} water temperature of the fully mixed thermal energy storage at hour h

$\gamma_{h,hob}^{HOB}$ slack variable of piecewise linear approximation breakpoints of heat-only boiler hob fueling function at hour h

Binary variables

$k_{h,sb}$ auxiliary variable for Big-M constraint

$l_{h,sb}$ auxiliary variable for Big-M constraint

$x_{i,h}^{CHP}$ characteristic point i in the feasible operation region of the CHP plant as a convex combination at hour h

$y_{h,hob}^{HOB}$ binary variable associated with the commitment of the heat-only boiler hob. 1 if the boiler is operating in hour h and 0 otherwise

$y_{h,sb}^{SB}$ binary variable associated with the commitment of the coal-fired boiler sb supplying steam to the extraction-condensing steam turbine. 1 if the boiler is operating (up) in hour h and 0 otherwise

y_h^{CH} binary variable associated with charge state of TES. 1 if the TES is charged at hour h and 0 otherwise

y_h^{DC} binary variable associated with discharge state of TES. 1 if the TES is discharged at hour h and 0 otherwise

$z_{h,hob}^{HOB}$ binary variable associated with the start-up of the heat-only boiler hob. 1 if boiler is switched on at hour h and 0 otherwise

$z_{h,sb}^{SU-SB}$ binary variable associated with the start-up action of a coal-fired boiler sb supplying steam to the extraction-condensing steam turbine. 1 if the boiler is switched on in hour h and 0 otherwise

z_h^{CHP} binary variable associated with the operation state of the CHP plant. 1 if the CHP plant is operational at hour h and 0 otherwise

1 Introduction

Combined heat and power (CHP), or more commonly referred to as "cogeneration," has been internationally recognized as a low-carbon electricity technology that will transform the way future power systems operate. For over a century, the disposition of a wide range of CHP technologies in national and regional power systems have led to improvements in energy efficiency, enhancements in the reliability of local energy infrastructure, and higher competitiveness of energy-intensive sectors. In the last two decades, the technological advances in energy storage technologies have motivated the deployment of CHP plants coupled with thermal (TES) and electrical (EES) energy storage systems. A wide range of studies has reported on the crucial role that these types of systems will play in the reduction of the world's dependence on fossil fuels and on reaching the long-term power sector decarbonization targets. Moreover, in recent years, energy storage technologies have empowered CHP engineers and operators to identify new business opportunities in local electricity markets.

The operation of cogeneration systems has been actively studied in the disciplines of Operational Research, Energy Systems Engineering, Production and Power Engineering, Energy Economics, among other areas directly related to the electricity and heat sectors. A significant portion of the available literature associated with CHP systems has concentrated on the short-term and medium-term operation of these type of installations, i.e., Unit Commitment (UC) and Economic Dispatch (ED) (Salgado and Pedrero, 2008). The development of new methods and strategies in these disciplines have been inspired by the need of innovative solutions to reduce fuel consumption, lower greenhouse gas emissions, and increase economic returns during periods in which CHP systems face large fluctuations of electricity and heat demands as well as high volatility of energy prices (Bischi et al., 2016).

Mathematical optimization techniques have been applied successfully in the planning and operation of power systems since the late 1950s. The advent of digital computers and the possibility of solving at a reasonable amount of time analytical models for economic dispatch, and at the end of the 1960s models for unit commitment, revolutionized the energy sector (Delson and Shahidehpous, 1992). Mathematical optimization found its practical use into the area of planning and operation of cogeneration facilities in the late 1970s, partly prompted by the implementation of the Public Utility Regulatory Policies Act (PURPA) in the United States, which enabled small-scale generators to sell electricity into the power grid and required utilities to purchase power from non-utility generators with a capacity between 20 and 80 megawatts (Benalcazar and Kamiński, 2016; Doty and Turner, 2012; Kalam et al., 2012; Wickart and Madlener, 2007). Nowadays, mathematical programming methods, which are commonly categorized into heuristic (e.g., Particle Swarm Optimization, Simulated Annealing, Tabu search, etc.) and classic techniques (e.g., Linear and Quadratic Programming, Nonlinear Programming, Dynamic Programming, among others) are considered highly effective approaches for solving operation planning problems of advanced CHP systems (Bansal, 2005; Benalcazar and Kamiński, 2019; Irving and Song, 2000; Song and Irving, 2001; Soroudi, 2017).

Among the developed researches that focus on the optimal operation of cogeneration systems, several stand out because of their reasonable computational times and capability of finding global optimal solutions or close-to-optimal solutions. Lahdelma and Hakonen (2003) and Rong et al. (2003) solved the hourly multi-site CHP planning problem with a mixed-integer linear programming model and with the use of the "Power Simplex" algorithm, a specialized algorithm to solve efficiently convex CHP models. In Dvořák and Havel (2012) a two-stage framework for the operational optimization of a CHP plant located in the Czech Republic and connected to a medium-sized district heating network was presented. A mixed-integer programming approach was employed to model the mass and energy balance equations of the constituent components of the system. A novel contribution of their work was the use of piece-wise linear approximations to model the components of the thermodynamic cycle of a boiler, an extraction-condensing turbine, and a backpressure turbine. Furthermore, the objective function of the optimization problem was formulated for profit maximization from contracted power products. Along the same lines, Havel and Šimovič (2013) developed a MILP model implemented in MATLAB for the day-ahead production planning of two large-scale combined heat and power plants in Central Europe. Their model incorporated mass and energy balance equations, ramping constraints, minimum up and downtimes, as well as block models for plant components such as boiler, extraction-condensing turbine, reduction and cooling station, and heat exchangers. The non-linear characteristics of various components were modeled through a piecewise linearization method and the objective function aimed to maximize profits from electricity sales.

Gopalakrishnan (2014) and Gopalakrishnan and Kosanovic (2015) proposed a mathematical model for the short-term operational planning of combined heat and power plants connected to district heating systems. Due to the nonlinear equipment characteristics in cogeneration systems, the model was formulated as a mixed-integer nonlinear problem (MINLP) and solved with the use of a genetic algorithm method. The principal objective of the model was to minimize the total fuel consumption of the system. In Mohammadi-Ivatloo et al. (2013), a method comprised of an improved version of particle swarm optimization (PSO), referred to as "time varying acceleration coefficients" (TVAC-PSO), was proposed to solve the economic dispatch of combined heat and power plants. The method considered the non-linear and non-convex functions of unit fuel costs with valve-point effects and transmission losses. Their method was validated with five different test systems, consisting of several power-only units, heat-only units, and CHP units. The obtained results were compared with other heuristic methods, demonstrating that TVAC-PSO methods are able to converge to a solution in a shorter amount of time. Mitra et al. (2013) employed a mixed-integer linear programming formulation to address the operational optimization of an industrial CHP plant equipped with steam turbines, gas turbines with heat recovery steam generators, and boilers. Each one of the plant components was formulated independently and linked with the use of mass and energy balances. The feasible operating region (linear formulation) of gas and steam turbines allowed to determine the discrete modes of operation of each component at every time segment of the planning horizon. The main objective of their research work was to maximize profit from the sale of electricity surplus and steam. Their results showed that the employment of the proposed optimization framework could lead to an increase in profit of up to 5% during high utilization rates and approximately 20% during low utilization rates. Sadeghian and Ardehali (2016) used a mixed-integer nonlinear programming model with a double Benders decomposition approach to determine the optimal dispatch of a large-scale combined heat and power system. The system comprised thermal power generation units as well as integrated CHP units that sold heat and electricity simultaneously. The problem was formulated with a multi-objective function that: (1) maximized revenues from selling electricity in the energy and ancillary market and heat to the heat market; (2) minimized emissions by giving a monetary value to the environmental emissions. Results from their simulation showed that in multi-objective formulations, the economic profit was highly sensitive to the variation of electricity market spot prices. Mollenhauer et al. (2016) implemented a mixed-integer linear programming model to determine the optimal operation strategy of a combined heat and power plant with extraction-condensing steam turbines. The approach used in their study involved the development of a generic model built from basic parameters (that are often available during research and innovation projects), and several dynamic constraints generally found in a unit commitment problem formulation. In their model, two constraints are of considerable importance since they link the gap between boiler load and limits of production: (a) constraint related to the power loss coefficient and (b) constraint related to the maximum heat extraction. The results from the optimization model were validated with results from EBSILON Professional and demonstrated the efficacy of the generic model in describing the performance characteristics of a CHP system.

In a more recent work, Rong and Lahdelma (2017) proposed a linear programming approach to minimize the total production and power transmission costs of a hybrid system comprised of condensing power plants, heat-only boilers, solar- and wind-powered technologies, nuclear-powered technologies, while satisfying the local demand for heat and electricity. Power-only and heat-only plants are modeled as a convex combination of extreme points with a zero heat or electrical power component. The model formulation includes constraints related to power transmission capacity and power exchange (surplus/slack power), which help establish a cost-efficient production and transmission coordination in the system and among units. Zou et al. (2019) developed an innovative model to optimize the simultaneous generation of heat and power of 11 test cases with the implementation of an improved version of a genetic algorithm (GA). The proposed algorithm included the application of two new kinds of crossover operations and a novel mutation operation. The experimental results revealed that the improved algorithm also referred to as IGA-NCM (improved genetic algorithm with novel crossover and mutation) provided better results, in terms of cost minimization, and higher stability than other classical genetic algorithms. Reviews of research works related to the optimal operation of CHP systems can be found in Salgado and Pedrero (2008) and Wang et al. (2019b). The main existing methods and models reviewed in this section are summarized in Table 14.1.

In recent years, numerous studies have analyzed the role that energy storage plays on the optimal operation strategy and economic balances of combined heat and power systems. Typically, the integration of a thermal storage can lead to a considerable increase in performance by lowering the fuel consumption of conventional boilers and decreasing the amount of useful heat dissipated (Bischi et al., 2016). Moreover, some studies have shown that TESs increase the operational flexibility of the system by partially decoupling the thermal supply from the electricity generation (Streckiene et al., 2009). Consequently, several studies have investigated the impact of integrating thermal energy storage units into CHP systems with the use of computational methods (Smith et al., 2013) and a large portion of authors have proposed mathematical programming methods mostly based on classic techniques, particularly on mixed-integer linear programming approaches, to solve the operational planning problem of CHP systems with TES units. For instance, Koltsaklis et al. (2014) presented a MILP framework for the optimal design and operation planning of energy networks involving multiple generation technologies (e.g., internal combustion engine, Stirling engine, proton exchange membrane fuel cell and gas turbine), heat storages, and an external heat source (refinery). The objective function of the model minimized the annualized total system costs while considering capital costs, start-up costs, heat purchase costs, variable operating costs, electricity trade costs as well as revenues from electricity sales back to the power grid. To illustrate the effectiveness of the MILP framework, the

TABLE 14.1 Optimization methods for CHP systems.

References	Year	Optimization method							Optimization goal		CHP power generation technology		
		Heuristic			Classic				Profit maximization	Costs minimization	Steam turbine	Gas turbine	Other technologies
		GA	PSO	Other heuristic methods	LP	MILP	NLP	MINLP					
Lahdelma and Hakonen (2003)	2003					✓				✓	✓		✓
Dvořák and Havel (2012) zlvatloo et al. (2013)	2013		✓							✓	✓		✓
Mitra et al. (2013)	2013	✓				✓			✓		✓	✓	✓
Havel and Šimovič (2013)	2013					✓				✓	✓		
Gopalakrishnan and Kosanovic (2015)	2015							✓		✓	✓	✓	
Sadeghian and Ardehali (2016)	2016			✓					✓			✓	✓
Mollenhauer et al. (2016)	2016					✓				✓	✓		✓
Rong and Lahdelma (2017)	2017				✓					✓	✓		✓
Zou et al. (2019)	2019	✓						✓		✓	✓		✓

model was applied to two problem instances, a typical Mediterranean residential energy network and an urban energy network. Moreover, Monte Carlo analyses were performed to investigate the sensitivity of the system to variations in the heat demand. Short et al. (2017) considered the dispatch optimization for a decentralized CHP plant with a theoretical dual energy storage and assumed to have the possibility of interacting with a day-ahead market and an intra-day market. The work aimed to explore the economic sensitivity in a CHP plant to the accuracy of heat and electricity load predictions as well as cost function approximations. In their research, a short-term load prediction model was developed to estimate the demand for heat and electricity. Furthermore, the unit commitment horizon was set to be very long or very short to investigate the behavior of the model, which included open-source optimization components, and the accuracy of the results. Kia et al. (2017a) modeled the optimal day-ahead scheduling of CHP power units with a combination of electric storage and thermal storage systems as a two-stage stochastic mixed-integer linear programming problem. The authors determined in the first stage the optimal scheduling of boilers, energy storages, and electricity exchange with the aim of minimizing operation costs; whereas in the second stage, the stochastic elements in a wholesale electricity market were evaluated, including the determination load shedding costs. In a later work, Kia et al. (2017b) proposed a similar approach for the energy management of an active distribution network (ADN) with inter-zonal energy transactions and a load commitment program.

Kumbartzky et al. (2017) used a multi-stochastic mixed-integer linear programming approach to optimize the short-term operation of a gas-fired CHP unit with thermal storage. The model was developed as a decision-support tool for simulating the revenue potential from the participation of the unit in the German day-ahead spot market and the minute reserve. Various scenarios were adopted to investigate the impact of the participation of the unit in different electricity markets, the stochasticity of electricity prices, and evaluate the changes in the operation of the CHP-TES system. Fang and Lahdelma (2016) investigated the application of an hourly dynamic optimization model, multi-period linear programming, based on a sliding time window method to determine the dispatch strategy of the system. The model aimed to minimize the net operating costs of a CHP unit (back pressure turbine) with an auxiliary boiler and a thermal energy storage. A novelty of the study was the use of a 5-day sliding time window, where the model determined the heat and power production for the first day of the time window based on the energy prices of the 5-day model. To assess and validate their method, three different cases were developed using actual historical energy and price data from a CHP unit located in Espoo, Finland. Steen et al. (2015) presented a novel formulation for the thermal energy storage model of the Decision Support Tool for Decentralized Energy Systems (DER-CAM). DER-CAM, an optimization model originally developed by the US National Renewable Laboratory, formulated as a mixed-integer linear program. The objective function minimized the total annual costs or the CO_2 emissions from the operation of power technologies (i.e., Combined heat and power and conventional power units, solar photovoltaic, and other renewable technologies) in a microgrid. Their new energy storage formulation improved the accuracy of the thermal losses and decreased costs of operation, hence improving the competitiveness of the technology.

Romanchenko et al. (2018) pointed out the economic benefits of utilizing a hot water tank (HTW) or the thermal inertial of buildings (referred to as building inertial thermal energy storage, BITES) in the district heating system of Goteborg (Sweden), the second-largest DH in Sweden and which is supplied by 28 heat generation units (three of them being CHP plants). In their research, three scenarios were investigated to evaluate the different utilization parameters of the two thermal energy storages. The study employed a techno-economic optimization model formulated as a MILP and with the goal of minimizing the total operating costs of the district heating system. The mathematical model considered hourly electricity prices, carbon dioxide emissions, fuel costs and technical constraints related to minimum and maximum power output limits, minimum-up and down-times, among other operational elements. Their analysis showed that TES storages decrease the load variations up to a week and provide a more stable operation of thermal units, decreasing the wear in the constituent elements of the system.

The study carried out by Jiménez Navarro et al. (2018) demonstrated the positive effects of thermal energy storages on the overall economic performance and utilization of CHP plants. With the application of an improved and extended version of the Dispa-SET model—a unit commitment and dispatch model developed by the Joint Research Centre (JRC), Directorate for Energy, Transport and Climate of the European Commission—and by evaluating several scenarios, their analysis indicated that the deployment of thermal energy storages in small to mid-scale power systems increase flexibility and lead to the maximization of efficiencies in cogeneration plants. However, although thermal energy storages provide significant cost reductions, their operation can also result in low utilization of CHPs when they are competing with renewable energy systems.

Wang et al. (2019c) explored the application of a MILP model to optimize the hourly dispatch of a CHP plant connected to a thermal energy storage (also referred to as heat accumulator). A numerical example of a CHP unit located in Copenhagen, Denmark and participating in the local heat market as well as in the Elspot market (day-ahead market of Nord Pool) was used to evaluate the hourly operational planning and the flexibility of the system. The objective function of the proposed optimization model sought to minimize the total marginal heat cost of the system. Additionally, the study evaluated the flexibility of different types of steam turbines (backpressure, backpressure with bypass operation, backpressure without bypass operation, extraction with one power loss factor and extraction with two power loss factors) and the economic benefits of operating a heat accumulator during the winter and in the summer. Their investigation revealed that the operation modes of the prime movers and the integration of thermal energy storages significantly affect the optimal dispatch of the CHP units as well as the total heat costs of the system. In a more recent work, Wang et al. (2019a) studied the flexibility potential of a CHP plant that supplies heat to a Danish district heating system and provides real-time balancing services. A two-stage optimization model was proposed to compute a heat production plan and to determine the optimal hourly dispatch while minimizing the total system costs. Two case studies were conducted involving similar mathematical models with different prime movers; the first case study focused on the dispatch of the CHP system in a day-ahead heat market whereas the second case study focused on the redispatch for real-time wind power balancing. Their results suggested that thermal energy storages have a major impact on the flexibility of cogeneration systems and help reduce the hourly power imbalances.

Merkert et al. (2019) considered the optimal scheduling of a CHP unit connected to a district heating system and evaluated the possibility of using the thermal inertia of the network as energy storage. The scheduling problem was formulated as a mixed-integer linear programming model with the objective function of minimizing the overall costs of the system. The model was implemented in Julia with the JuMP package. The district heating dynamics were formulated as an outer approximation of the thermal inertia of the network and included the introduction of state-of-charge constraints, constraints related to the maximum and minimum possible supply temperature as well as classical unit commitment constraints. The computational results showed that operating a district heating network as an energy storage can provide higher flexibility and lead to savings of up to 4.6% of the total costs. Mollenhauer et al. (2017) analyzed the effects of heat pumps and thermal energy storages on the flexibility of CHP plants. The case study of a district heating system located in Germany was presented, where different CHP plant types equipped with backpressure and extraction condensing units supplied heat as well as electricity to the local market. In addition, the study described the main elements of a unit commitment and dispatch model formulated as a mixed-integer linear program. The economic operational benefit was investigated by comparing the increase in profits generated from integrating a thermal energy storage and heat pumps to the original system. This led to the analysis of four CHP plants with different characteristics. Their results indicated that thermal energy storages and heat pumps can be used to substitute heat-only boilers in a CHP system and their operation provides higher electricity sales. A summary of the main existing methods and models described above are presented in Table 14.2.

In this context, the focus of this chapter is to provide a mathematical framework for the co-optimization of heat and power and for solving the operation planning problem a coal-fired CHP system. In the rest of the chapter, we describe the characteristics of the model including its objective function and constraints. Later, we present an illustrative example based on a typical cogeneration system operating in Central and Eastern Europe to demonstrate the applicability of the proposed approach. Finally, the results obtained from the optimization process and the benefits of the mathematical framework are discussed.

2 Mathematical model

The optimization model employs a mixed-integer linear programming (MILP) formulation for the minimization of the hourly production costs of a cogeneration system. The cogeneration system considered for the development of the model comprises a CHP plant, two auxiliary boilers (also referred to as heat-only boilers) and a tank thermal energy storage. The formulation presented in this chapter optimizes the production plan of the system considering the thermal demand of a municipal district heating system and the potential revenues from the sales of electricity in the local power market. The mathematical model also contemplates the technical constraints related to the operation of the extraction-condensing steam turbine driven by two pulverized coal-fired boilers, and the relationship between the input fueling rates and loads of the auxiliary boilers. Fig. 14.1 presents an overview of the modelling approach proposed in this work. The heating network is not modeled; however, the proposed formulation may be further extended to consider flow temperatures in addition to mass and energy flows within the network. Moreover, the approach proposed by Romanchenko et al. (2018) is adopted to estimate the thermal losses of the energy storage. The key decisions determined by the model include the following:

i. The electrical p_h^{CHP} and thermal q_h^{CHP} power output of the CHP plant along with the power output of the heat-only boilers $q_{h,\,hob}^{HOB}$ at time period h.

ii. The operating status of the cogeneration system at time period h; including the on/off operation state of the CHP plant z_h^{CHP}, of the pulverized-coal fired boilers supplying high pressure steam to the turbine $y_{h,\,sb}^{SB}$, and of the heat-only boilers $y_{h,\,hob}^{HOB}$.

TABLE 14.2 Optimization methods for CHP systems with thermal energy storage.

References	Year	Optimization method Classic					Optimization goal		CHP power generation technology				Energy storage technology	
		LP	MILP	NLP	MINLP	Other classic methods	Profit maximization	Costs minimization	Steam turbine	Gas turbine	CCGT	Other technologies	Thermal energy storage	Electrical energy storage
Koltsaklis et al. (2014)	2014		✓					✓		✓		✓	✓	
Short et al. (2017)	2017		✓					✓	✓				✓	✓
Kia et al. (2017a)	2017		✓				✓					✓	✓	✓
Kia et al. (2017b)	2017		✓					✓				✓	✓	✓
Kumbartzky et al. (2017)	2017		✓					✓	✓	✓			✓	
Fang and Lahdelma (2016)	2016		✓					✓	✓				✓	
Steen et al. (2015)	2015		✓					✓	✓			✓	✓	✓
Romanchenko et al. (2018)	2018		✓					✓	✓			✓	✓	
Jiménez Navarro et al. (2018)	2018	✓	✓					✓	✓			✓	✓	
Wang et al. (2019c)	2019		✓					✓	✓			✓	✓	
Wang et al. (2019a)	2019		✓					✓	✓			✓	✓	
Merkert et al. (2019)	2019		✓					✓	✓				✓	
Mollenhauer et al. (2017)	2017		✓				✓		✓			✓	✓	

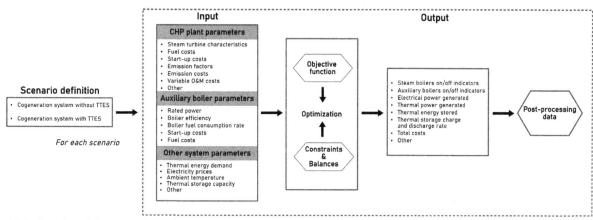

FIG. 14.1 Overview of the proposed modelling approach.

iii. The tank thermal energy storage level s_h and the energy inputs s_h^{DH} and outputs s_h^{CH} (due to charging and discharging) of the energy storage unit at time period h.

iv. The thermal energy storage operation mode at time period h. The energy storage may only operate either in a charging mode y_h^{CH} or discharging mode y_h^{DC}.

v. The temperature of the water inside the fully mixed tank storage t_h^{Water} and the storage losses s_h^{loss} related to the temperature differential between the storage medium and the outer wall (outdoor temperature).

vi. Total operating costs and total revenues from electricity sales.

2.1 Objective function

The objective function of the mathematical model minimizes the hourly operating costs of the system while taking into consideration the revenues generated from the sales of electricity in the local power market. This modelling approach is commonly used to simulate the operation strategy of CHP plants that can participate in the spot and balancing power markets. In Eq. (14.1), operating cost or operational expenditures correspond to the summation of fueling costs, emission costs, operation and maintenance costs, start-up costs of each constituent element of the system. The emission costs in the objective function include carbon emission costs (CO_2) and other fees related to the combustion of fossil fuels such as sulfur dioxide (SO_2), nitrogen oxides (NO_x), particulate matter (PM) among others. Moreover, the allocation of emissions in the CHP output is in accordance with the energy content method (WRI and WBCSD, 2006). Revenues are collected from trading electricity in the spot market. Note that in the objective function expenses related to the construction of fixed assets (capital costs) are excluded since the mathematical framework presented in this chapter is developed for the short-term operation planning of CHP systems.

$$\min \overbrace{\sum_h c_h^{CHP} + \sum_h \sum_{hob} C_h^{HOB} \cdot \gamma_{h,hob}^{HOB}}^{Hourly\ fueling\ costs}$$

$$+ \overbrace{\sum_h \sum_p \left(\left(p_h^{CHP} \cdot E_p^{SB-P} \cdot C_p^{EM} \right) + \left(q_h^{CHP} \cdot E_p^{SB-Q} \cdot C_p^{EM} \right) \right) + \sum_h \sum_{hob} \sum_p q_{h,hob}^{HOB} \cdot \left(E_p^{HOB} \cdot C_p^{EM} \right)}^{Hourly\ emission\ costs}$$

$$+ \overbrace{\sum_h \left(p_h^{CHP} \cdot C_{VOM}^{CHP-P} + q_h^{CHP} \cdot C_{VOM}^{CHP-Q} \right) + \sum_h \sum_{hob} q_{h,hob}^{HOB} \cdot C_{VOM}^{HOB}}^{Hourly\ VOM\ costs}$$

$$+ \overbrace{\sum_h \sum_{sb} z_{h,sb}^{SU-SB} \cdot C_{SU}^{SB} + \sum_h \sum_{hob} z_{h,hob}^{HOB} \cdot C_{SU}^{HOB}}^{Hourly\ start-up\ costs} - \overbrace{\sum_h p_h^{CHP} \cdot C_h^E}^{Hourly\ revenues-Electricity\ sales} \qquad (14.1)$$

2.2 Constraints

2.2.1 Feasible operation region

The feasible operation region of a CHP plant equipped with an extraction-condensing unit is modeled as the combination of convex points representing the gross electrical and thermal power generation (E, Q) possibility set of the CHP plant, also referred to as the characteristic area. The fueling costs C_i^{CHP} of the CHP plant are modeled as a convex function of the (E, Q) possibility set I forming a bounded polyhedron $(C_i^{CHP}, Q_i^{CHP}, P_i^{CHP})$ (Lancia and Serafini, 2018; Verbruggen et al., 2016). This modelling approach was presented in Lahdelma and Hakonen (2003) and Rong et al. (2003) and it has been extended for the investigation of steam plants, DHS, trigeneration plants, combined cooling, gas and steam turbines, hydropower (Kia et al., 2017b; Kumbartzky et al., 2017). Constraints (14.2)–(14.6) represent the power, heat, and cost components of the CHP production. The variable $x_{i,h}$ is time-dependent and allows a variation in the power output of the CHP plant based on the hourly thermal demand. The addition of a point $(0, 0, 0)$ to the feasible operation region gives the possibility of shutting down the system for scheduled and unscheduled shutdowns. Constraint (14.5) ensures that at most a single combination of characteristic points for each hour of the planning horizon. Moreover, this decision variable is restricted to non-negative values.

$$p_h^{CHP} = \sum_{i \in I} P_i^{CHP} x_{i,h} \quad \forall h \tag{14.2}$$

$$q_h^{CHP} = \sum_{i \in I} Q_i^{CHP} x_{i,h} \quad \forall h \tag{14.3}$$

$$c_h^{CHP} = \sum_{i \in I} C_i^{CHP} x_{i,h} \quad \forall h \tag{14.4}$$

$$\sum_{i \in I} x_{i,h} = 1 \quad \forall h \tag{14.5}$$

$$x_i \geq 0 \quad \forall i \tag{14.6}$$

2.2.2 Thermal energy balance

Constraint (14.7) reflects the overall thermal energy balance of the system (comprised of a CHP unit, a tank thermal energy storage, and a set of auxiliary boilers) in period h. It is the sum of the heat supplied by the thermal sources minus heat outputs. The thermal input sources are: (1) the heat supplied by the CHP unit (steam exiting turbine/condenser), (2) the heat supplied by the auxiliary boilers, and (4) the discharge of energy from the TES. Additionally, to prevent any infeasibility issues, (5) a slack variable (q_h^{PUR}) is added to the constraint which represents the purchase of additional heat with a high penalty cost. The heat output is represented by the thermal energy directed to the energy storage and the thermal demand (of the site or the DHS). An important implication of this inequality constraint is that it allows the system to generate an excess of heat at time periods with high electricity prices and when the revenues outweigh the rise in production costs.

$$q_h^{CHP} + \sum_{hob} q_{h,hob}^{HOB} + q_h^{PUR} + s_h^{DC} - s_h^{CH} \geq D_h \quad \forall h \tag{14.7}$$

2.2.3 Operation state of the CHP plant

Constraint (14.8) declares a transition variable that is forced to take a binary value depending on the operating status of the CHP plant. Operational if a characteristic point in the feasible operation region of the CHP plant is selected $(z_h^{CHP} = 1)$. Non-operational (shut-down state) if the point $(0, 0, 0)$ in the feasible operation is selected $(z_h^{CHP} = 0)$.

$$z_h^{CHP} = \sum_{i \in I} x_{i,h} \quad \forall h \tag{14.8}$$

2.2.4 Operation state of pulverized-coal fired boilers supplying steam to the extraction-condensing turbine

The relationship between the operating status of the pulverized-coal fired boilers supplying high pressure steam to the turbine and the feasible operation region of the extraction-condensing turbine is modeled by using Big-M constraints. Constraints (14.9)–(14.14) introduce several logical variables that are associated with the commitment status of each coal-fired

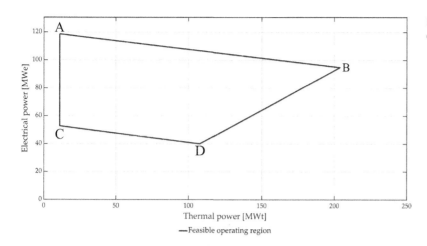

FIG. 14.2 Feasible operating area of the extraction-condensing steam turbine.

boiler in the CHP plant. Since the upper and lower bounds of electric power production in a CHP plant (line A-B and C-D) are related to maximum and minimum inlet steam flow of the turbine and the amount of fuel fed to the boilers, as depicted in Fig. 14.2, the logical state of each coal-fired boiler is found by introducing a set of bilinear constraints with auxiliary variables and two fixed bounds (M and N).

The linearization employed describes the following conditions: if the electrical power output of the CHP unit at the time period h is between some lower limit L and upper limit U, the operating status of the coal-fired boiler must be equal to 1 (the boiler powered ON). Otherwise, if the electrical power output is outside the two intervals (lower limit L and upper limit U) the coal-fired boiler status is equal to 0 (powered OFF). This modelling approach is implemented for both line segments of the feasible operation region (A-B and C-D). The characteristic points (Q_i^{CHP}, P_i^{CHP}) in the interval A-B are only attainable when the two coal-fired boilers are running, while the characteristic points (Q_i^{CHP}, P_i^{CHP}) in the interval (C-D) are attainable only when one boiler is generating steam. The Big-M constraints are modeled as follows:

$$p_h^{CHP} + M \cdot \left(1 - k_{h,sb}\right) \geq L \quad \forall h, sb \tag{14.9}$$

$$p_h^{CHP} - M \cdot k_{h,sb} \leq L \quad \forall h, sb \tag{14.10}$$

$$p_h^{CHP} + M \cdot l_{h,sb} \geq U \quad \forall h, sb \tag{14.11}$$

$$p_h^{CHP} - M \cdot \left(1 - l_{h,sb}\right) \leq U \quad \forall h, sb \tag{14.12}$$

$$k_{h,sb} + l_{h,sb} - 2 \cdot y_{h,sb}^{SB} \leq 1 \quad \forall h, sb \tag{14.13}$$

$$k_{h,sb} + l_{h,sb} - 2 \cdot y_{h,sb}^{SB} \geq 0 \quad \forall h, sb \tag{14.14}$$

where $k_{h,sb} \in \{0,1\}$ and $l_{h,sb} \in \{0,1\}$ are auxiliary variables. The binary variable $y_{h,sb}^{SB}$ describes the commitment status of the coal-fired boilers. This variable that has a value 1 if, and only if, the electrical power generation is between the upper and lower limit $L \leq \sum_{i \in I} P_i^{CHP} x_{i,h} \leq U$. The above-presented constraints can be extended to include two coal-fired boilers by using different upper and lower limits. Table 14.3 shows a summary how constraints (14.9)–(14.14) operate.

2.2.5 Start-up trajectory of pulverized coal-fired boilers supplying steam to the extraction-condensing turbine

Constraint (14.15) models the start-up trajectories of the pulverized coal-fired boilers supplying steam to the extraction-condensing turbine. $z_{h,sb}^{SU-SB} = 1$ if the boiler is switched on, otherwise $z_{h,sb}^{SU-SB} = 0$. Additionally, the start-up costs for each boiler are modeled in the objective function using the binary variable $z_{h,sb}^{SU-SB}$.

$$z_{h,sb}^{SU-SB} \geq y_{h,sb}^{SB} - y_{h-1,sb}^{SB} \quad \forall h, sb \tag{14.15}$$

2.2.6 Maximum and minimum limits of combined generation

Similar to (Short et al., 2017), constraints (14.16), (14.17) model the maximum (ΔPQ_{MAX}) and minimum (ΔPQ_{MIN}) rate of change of the combined power output of the CHP unit. These limits are given by endogenous technical characteristics of the turbogenerator and other key constituent equipment of the CHP plant. Moreover, they ensure a stable

TABLE 14.3 Relationship of Big-M constraints.

Constraint	Relationship
Constraints (14.9), (14.10)	$k_h=1$, if $p_h^{CHP} \leq L$
Constraints (14.11), (14.12)	$l_h=1$, if $p_h^{CHP} \leq U$
Constraints (14.13), (14.14)	$y_{h,sb}^{SB}=1$, if $L \leq p_h^{CHP} \leq U$

and efficient plant operation considering the limits of production (combined output of p_h^{CHP} and q_h^{CHP}) at each hour of operation.

$$\left(p_h^{CHP} + q_h^{CHP}\right) - \left(p_{h-1}^{CHP} + q_{h-1}^{CHP}\right) \leq \Delta PQ_{MAX} \quad \forall h \tag{14.16}$$

$$\left(p_h^{CHP} + q_h^{CHP}\right) - \left(p_{h-1}^{CHP} + q_{h-1}^{CHP}\right) \leq \Delta PQ_{MIN} \quad \forall h \tag{14.17}$$

2.2.7 Auxiliary boilers power output and fuel consumption

In accordance to Ahmadi et al. (2013), Magnani and Boyd (2009), and Short et al. (2017), constraint (14.18) models the relationships between the required input fueling rates and the load of the auxiliary boilers. The relationships have been modeled by means of convex piecewise linear (PWL) approximations of the fuel consumption functions. This linearization technique is a practical way of dealing with quadratic functions. Fm_j denote the slopes of the line segments j while Fb_j represent the intersections of each segment. The fueling costs of the auxiliary boilers are given in the objective function by multiplying the hourly fuel consumption ($\gamma_{h,hob}^{HOB}$) to the price of the fuel C_h^{HOB}.

$$\gamma_{h,hob}^{HOB} \geq Fb_j + \left(Fm_j \cdot q_{h,hob}^{HOB}\right) \quad \forall h, hob, j \tag{14.18}$$

2.2.8 Auxiliary boilers power output limits

Constraint (14.19) restricts the hourly thermal power output of the auxiliary boilers (also referred to as heat-only boilers) to stay below the maximum rated capacity of each unit. $y_{h,hob}^{HOB}$ links the thermal power output of the boilers to their operating status.

$$q_{h,hob}^{HOB} \leq y_{h,hob}^{HOB} \cdot Q_{MAX}^{HOB} \quad \forall h, hob \tag{14.19}$$

2.2.9 Must-run constraints of auxiliary boilers

Constraint (14.20), (14.21) state that the auxiliary boilers must enter operation when the heat demand exceeds the maximum thermal power output of the CHP plant (Q_{MAX}^{CHP}) or the combined capacity of the CHP plant and one heat-only boiler ($Q_{MAX}^{CHP} + Q_{MAX}^{HOB}$).

$$q_h^{CHP} \geq y_{h,hob}^{HOB} \cdot Q_{MAX}^{CHP} \quad \forall h, hob \tag{14.20}$$

$$q_h^{CHP} + q_{h,hob=HOB-U1}^{HOB} \geq y_{h,hob=HOB-U2}^{HOB} \cdot \left(Q_{MAX}^{CHP} + Q_{MAX}^{HOB}\right) \quad \forall h, hob \tag{14.21}$$

2.2.10 Start-up and shut-down trajectories of auxiliary boilers

Constraint (14.22), (14.23) model the start-up and shut-down trajectories of the heat-only boilers. The binary variable $z_{h,hob}^{HOB}$ indicates the change in state of each unit.

$$z_{h,hob}^{HOB} \geq y_{h,hob}^{HOB} - y_{h-1,hob}^{HOB} \quad \forall h, hob \tag{14.22}$$

$$z_{h,hob}^{HOB} \geq -y_{h,hob}^{HOB} + y_{h-1,hob}^{HOB} \quad \forall h, hob \tag{14.23}$$

2.2.11 Thermal energy storage inventory balance

Constraint (14.24) describes the thermal energy balance of the tank storage, which has been modeled as a sensible heat storage with hot water as the storage medium. It is assumed in this formulation that the energy storage is fully mixed and can only be charged by the technologies capable of providing hot water at a similar temperature and pressure conditions (Stadler et al., 2009; Steen et al., 2015). The energy stored at any given time step is equal to the energy state in the previous time step $(t-1)$, plus the thermal energy provided to the energy storage (directed from the CHP unit) and minus the thermal energy discharged to balance the thermal demand. This constraint considers energy losses of the TES to the surroundings (s_h^{loss}) and losses related to its charge and discharge efficiencies (η_{CH}, η_{DC}). The formulation of thermal losses developed by Romanchenko et al. (2018) is adopted to provide a more detailed representation of the operating conditions of the tank storage.

$$s_h = s_{h-1} + s_h^{CH} \cdot \eta_{CH} - \frac{s_h^{DC}}{\eta_{DC}} - s_h^{loss} \quad \forall h \tag{14.24}$$

2.2.12 Thermal energy storage capacity limit

Constraint (14.25) sets the upper limit of the amount of energy that can be stored in the TES. This limit is given by the actual physical capacity of the storage (S^{MAX}).

$$s_h \leq S^{MAX} \quad \forall h \tag{14.25}$$

2.2.13 Thermal energy storage charge and discharge limits

Constraint (14.26) specifies the maximum hourly charge rate of the TES. Likewise, constraint (14.27) specifies the maximum hourly discharge rate from the energy storage to accommodate the system's thermal demand. These are important technical constraint that should be studied in detail since they have a considerable impact on the temperature profile inside the tank and its thermal losses to the surroundings. Constraints (14.26), (14.27) introduce the binary variables y_h^{CH} and y_h^{DC} which work as indicator variables and describe the operation state of the energy storage. Similar to Kia et al. (2017a), constraints (14.28), (14.29) set the limits of maximal charge and discharge considering the state of charge of the TES (energy stored available) in the previous period.

$$s_h^{CH} \leq \left(S^{MAX} \cdot \theta_{MAX}^{CH}\right) \cdot y_h^{CH} \quad \forall h \tag{14.26}$$

$$s_h^{DC} \leq \left(S^{MAX} \cdot \theta_{MAX}^{DC}\right) \cdot y_h^{DC} \quad \forall h \tag{14.27}$$

$$s_h^{CH} + s_{h-1} \leq S^{MAX} \quad \forall h \tag{14.28}$$

$$s_h^{DH} - s_{h-1} \leq 0 \quad \forall h \tag{14.29}$$

2.2.14 Thermal energy storage operation mode

Constraint (14.30) specifies that the thank thermal energy storage may only operate either in a charging mode or discharging mode in time period h. This modelling approach is commonly used for tank thermal energy storage systems since it simplifies the dynamics of the overall system (Kia et al., 2017b; Nash et al., 2017).

$$y_h^{CH} + y_h^{DC} \leq 1 \quad \forall h \tag{14.30}$$

2.2.15 Storage thermal energy losses to the surroundings

The mathematical formulation of the energy losses from the tank storage to the surroundings presented in constraint (14.31) is similar to the one found in Romanchenko et al. (2018). This constraint represents the heat transfer between the storage medium (hot water) and the outer wall of the TES (outdoor temperature). The hourly losses (s_h^{loss}) are calculated in accordance to the temperature differential, the heat transfer coefficient and the total surface area of the tank.

$$s_h^{loss} = \left(t_h^{water} - T_h^{outdoor}\right) \cdot U^{TES} \cdot A^{TES} \quad \forall h \tag{14.31}$$

2.2.16 Uniform water temperature in the thermal energy storage

In accordance to Romanchenko et al. (2018), constraint (14.32) reflects the water temperature of the fully mixed thermal energy storage. This constraint relates the water temperature in the storage t_h^{Water} to the amount of energy being charged or discharged (heat losses and gains) as well as the energy stored in the previous time step $(t-1)$.

$$t_h^{Water} = t_{h-1}^{Water} + \left(\frac{s_h^{DH}/\eta_{DC}}{V \cdot Cp_{water} \cdot \rho_{water}} \right) - \left(\frac{s_h^{CH} \cdot \eta_{CH}}{V \cdot Cp_{water} \cdot \rho_{water}} \right) \quad \forall h \tag{14.32}$$

3 Illustrative example

The large-scale integration of energy systems and the urgent need to decarbonize the heating sector are two fundamental challenges in contemporary power markets. In the European Union, energy vector coupling has become a crucial solution to reduce fossil fuel consumption and lowering greenhouse gas emissions. Furthermore, thermal energy storage technologies can make a key contribution to the decarbonization of the heating sector by bridging the energy supply-demand gap at almost no extra costs. Considering this, we demonstrate the general applicability of the proposed modelling approach (for the co-optimization of heat and power) with the use of an illustrative example based on a typical cogeneration system operating in Central and Eastern Europe. Further, for comparison purposes, we investigate the effects of integrating an energy storage unit into an existing cogeneration system. To limit the scope of this work to a particular technology of energy storage and to put this method into a practical context for contemporary heat and electricity markets, the term "energy storage" used throughout this section refers to a hot water tank thermal energy storage. Therefore, the illustrative example is evaluated under the two scenarios presented in Table 14.4.

In order to define the reference scenario, let us assume that the senior executives of a CHP plant operated by a municipal energy supply company are interested in evaluating the possibility of investing in the construction of a thermal energy storage, specifically in a centralized tank thermal energy storage. The mission of the investment decision is to improve the system's flexibility, increase the economic benefits of participating in the day-ahead electricity market, and reduce either fueling and/or carbon emission costs. Thus, in the reference scenario a CHP plant equipped with two pulverized coal-fired boilers and an extraction-condensing steam turbine is considered. In addition, the CHP system is supported by two coal-fired heat-only boilers.

Each one of the steam boilers (SB-U1 and SB-U2) have a heat power of 165 MW. Pulverized coal is burned in the boilers, where the generated heat is used to produce high-pressure steam. The steam flows to an extraction-considering steam turbine (EC-ST), where it passes through rotating blades and drives an electric generator (Woodruff et al., 2017). An advantage of this type of turbine is its flexibility, since it is possible to extract steam from the turbine at different pressure stages for industrial/heating purposes and to generate electricity (Mollenhauer et al., 2016). The maximum electrical power output from the condensing activity of the CHP plant is 120 MWe and the unit can supply a maximum of 205 MWt of useful heat to the district heating system. The lower and upper limits of the feasible operating area represent the modes of operation of one or two steam boilers.

In addition, the two heat-only boilers (HOB-U1 and HOB-U2), each one with a thermal power of 80 MW and fueled by coal supply hot water to a district heating system. The total thermal power of the CHP system is 365 MWt (turbo generator set and two auxiliary boilers) and the electrical power output reaches 120 MWe. A key requirement of the CHP system is that it must always meet the thermal demand of the district heating system and its industrial customers. Furthermore, the CHP system is 100% self-sufficient, it can cover the electrical consumption of its constituent equipment (pumps, compressors, among other auxiliary equipment) and it can supply its electricity surplus to the spot market.

TABLE 14.4 Scenario description.

Scenario	Description
Reference scenario	Conventional CHP system (two pulverized coal-fired boilers, an extraction-condensing steam tribune and two heat-only boilers)
Alternative scenario	Conventional CHP system with thermal energy storage

TABLE 14.5 Key technical characteristics of the CHP system.

Parameter	Q_{MAX}^{CHP}	P_{MAX}^{CHP}	Q_{MAX}^{HOB}	ΔPQ_{MAX}
Value	205 MW$_t$	120 MW$_e$	80 MW$_t$	120 MW

Tables 14.5 and 14.6 summarize the key technical characteristics of the CHP system and the economic parameters used in the optimization model.

As it was mentioned previously, although there is a wide range of thermal energy storage systems, to narrow down the focus of the alternative scenario, a water-based storage tank was selected to demonstrate the usefulness of the proposed modelling approach. This type of energy storage technology is a well-established concept, it has acquired a high level of technical maturity in Europe, and can be found in numerous CHP systems in Scandinavian countries and Central and Easter Europe (Mollenhauer et al., 2017). Furthermore, the non-toxicity of water, its high specific heat capacity, and relative low cost when compared to other materials including sand, iron or concrete, has made this storage medium one of the most common in TES.

Let us assume in the case of the alternative scenario that the municipal energy supply company selected a vertical cylindrical hot water tank for retrofitting the existing CHP plant. Similar to other studies that examined the mathematical modelling of thermal energy storages (Campos Celador et al., 2011; Romanchenko et al., 2018; Steen et al., 2015), in this chapter the hot water tank is assumed to be a fully mixed thermal energy storage. In reality, a hot water tank presents a temperature profile intermediate between an ideal stratified case and a fully mixed case (Campos Celador et al., 2011), but following a common approach used for modelling this type of energy storage system, and to keep the computational times within an acceptable range, the thermal losses implemented in the model are based on the temperature differential between the storage medium and the ambient temperature. Table 14.7 summarizes the key technical parameters of the TES.

4 Computational results

The MILP formulation was implemented in the modelling language GAMS 30.2.0, soft-linked to MATLAB 2019b, and solved using CPLEX 12.10. The model was employed for the analysis of the illustrative example with two scenarios. The outputs of both scenarios are summarized and used to assess the economic and operational impacts of the use of a tank storage for sector coupling.

In the first scenario, or reference scenario, a CHP plant (equipped with an extraction-condensing turbogenerator) and two auxiliary boilers supply hot water to a district heating network. Since the primary goal of this scenario is to exemplify the typical case of a coal-fired CHP system that does not have an energy storage unit, the results of this scenario act as the baseline. The results from the reference scenario show that 88% of the heat is generated by the CHP plant, 11% by the first heat-only boiler (HOB-U1) and less than 1% by the second boiler (HOB-U2). In contrast, in the alternative scenario, the integration of an energy storage with the CHP system leads to a considerable drop in the amount of thermal energy produced by the CHP and the auxiliary boilers. Roughly 83% of the heat generated originates from the CHP unit while the remaining 17% is produced by one of the auxiliary boilers (9%) and the thermal energy discharged from the tank thermal energy storage (8%). Fig. 14.3A shows the annual thermal production (in percentage) by each of the constituent elements of the CHP system. The use of a thermal energy storage—in this case a hot water tank storage with a capacity of 700 MWh—also has an impact on the operational hours of the constituent elements as well as on the costs and revenue streams of the system. Because of the lower amount of thermal energy supplied by the heat-only boilers and the ability of the energy storage to serve as a heat source to balance the energy demand and supply at little or no extra costs, the CHP system experiences a decline of 2% in the total system operating costs and a rise of 4% in net profits. Furthermore, approximately 5000 metric tons of CO_2, or 0.5% of the total annual greenhouse gas emissions, are avoided due to the lower fuel consumption of the auxiliary boilers.

TABLE 14.6 Key economic parameters.

Parameter	C_{SU}^{HOB}	C_{SU}^{CHP}	C_h^{HOB}	$C_{p=CO_2}^{EM}$	$C_{h(average)}^{E}$
Value	1850 €	2800 €	56 €/ton	16 €/ton	51 €/MWh

TABLE 14.7 Key technical parameters of the TES.

Parameter	S^{MAX}	A^{TES}	V	ρ_{water}	U^{TES}	$\theta_{MAX}^{CH\&DC}$
Value	700 MWh	2820 m²	1500 m³	996 kg/m³	0.12 W/m² °C	85 MWh/h

Fig. 14.3B presents the heat load duration curve and the heat production from the different sources when the CHP system includes a thank thermal energy storage. In a typical scenario where a CHP system does not include a TES, as it is the situation of the reference scenario, the heat production from the constituent elements should follow the load curve. This would ensure that the heat demand in each hour of the year is being met in a cost-effective manner. However, the usage of the energy storage throughout the year influences the operation of the heat sources in the CHP system. As it is shown in Fig. 14.3, the TES allows to displace thermal power output of the CHP by storing the excess of heat generated. The stored energy (depicted as the colored regions above the load curve) is later used for peak-load shifting and shaving. Moreover,

FIG. 14.3 (A) Annual thermal demand served per constituent element of the CHP system and (B) duration curve for heat demand.

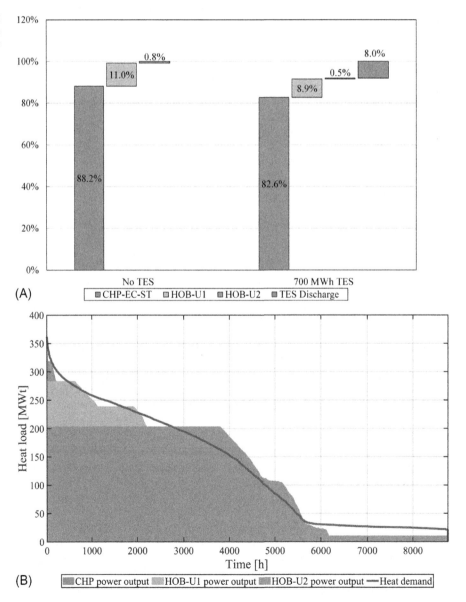

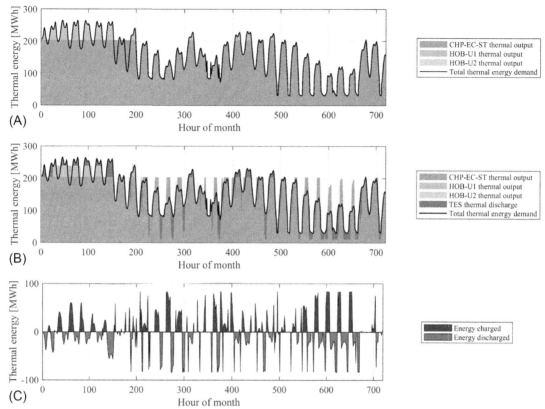

FIG. 14.4 Optimal operation of the CHP system (Spring). (A) Without TES; (B) with TES; and (C) storage charge/discharge schedule.

incorporating a TES into the CHP system results in longer operating hours of the CHP plant, reducing the mechanical wear and tear of the steam turbine.

As previously mentioned, the CHP plant considered in the illustrative example is equipped with an extraction-condensing steam turbine. Although this type of steam turbine provides high levels of operational flexibility when compared to back-pressure steam turbines, the cogeneration process of the CHP system is affected by a decrease in power production, commonly referred to as "power loss coefficient", which is caused by the substitution of heat for power generation (Urošević et al., 2013; Verbruggen et al., 2013, 2016). This is also explained by the technical characteristic of the extraction-condensing turbine, which generally includes one or more extraction points and allows the efficient extraction of steam at different temperatures for industrial applications. Furthermore, in the reference scenario, the thermal-load-following strategy imposed on the dispatch strategy of the CHP system and the lack of a storage diminishes the potential of reaching the maximum level of electricity production during periods of high thermal demand and high electricity prices.

Integrating a tank energy storage into the CHP system enables plant operators to optimally manage the thermal and electrical power production considering electricity prices and mitigate the impact of the power loss coefficient. This is reflected in the proposed approach by incorporating the revenues from power sales into the objective function. The minimization of the operating costs of the system considering the potential revenues from electricity sales modifies the control strategy of the TES. Cost reduction becomes the primary purpose of the thermal storage, either by supplying heat to the district heating system at relatively low cost (replacing existing heat-only boilers) or by allowing the CHP plant to operate at maximum electrical power at hours of high electricity prices, while at the same time, meeting the thermal demand.

Figs. 14.4–14.7 present the optimization results (monthly) of the scenarios considering two different seasonal conditions (Spring and Winter) and show a comparison of the charge and discharge strategies of the energy storage. During the spring months (Figs. 14.4 and 14.5), because of the relatively mild outdoor temperatures (average temperatures range between 3°C and 14°C), the heat fluxes of the tank storage are frequently used for peak shaving. This helps mitigate costs (e.g., operating and fueling costs) by partially or fully replacing one of the auxiliary boilers and ensure a stable supply of electric power (as shown in Fig. 14.4A and B). Moreover, when the TES is used for smoothening the variation of heat demand by load shifting and valley filling, the CHP plant is able to generate substantially higher amounts of electricity

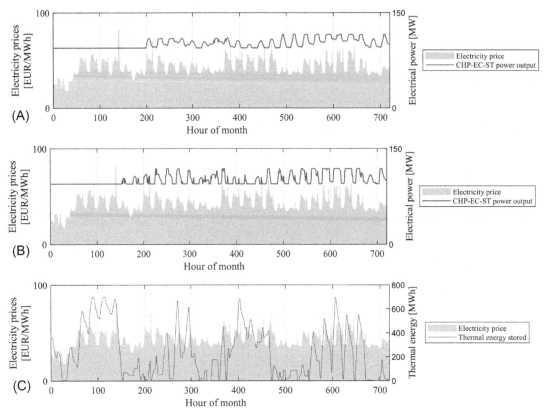

FIG. 14.5 Electrical power output of the CHP plant (Spring). (A) Without TES; (B) with TES; and (C) heat storage level.

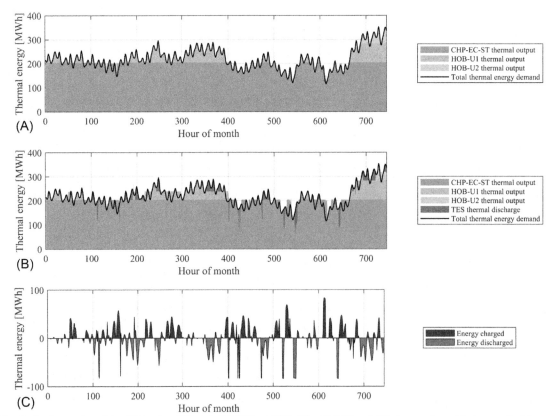

FIG. 14.6 Optimal operation of the CHP system (Winter). (A) Without TES; (B) with TES; and (C) storage charge/discharge schedule.

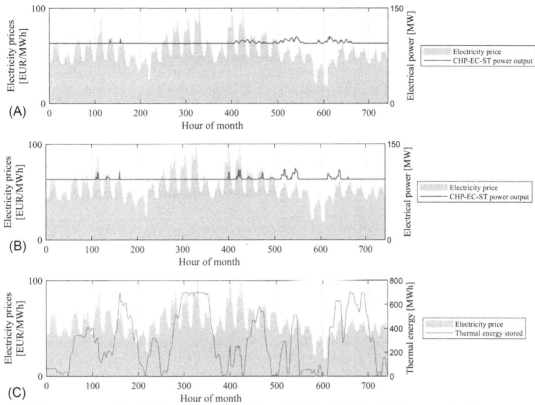

FIG. 14.7 Electrical power output of the CHP plant (Winter). (A) Without TES; (B) with TES; and (C) heat storage level.

at time periods with high market prices, when compared to the case of the CHP system without an energy storage (Fig. 14.5A and B).

Figs. 14.6 and 14.7 show the optimal operation of the CHP system during a winter month (average outdoor temperatures below freezing, ranging between $-4°C$ and $-1.2°C$). As the outdoor temperature drops, the demand for hot water in the district heating network peaks—due to the increasing need for space heating. This makes the auxiliary boilers particularly important in the CHP system (Fig. 14.6A). However, the use of a thermal energy storage changes the dynamics of the system in such a way that the operating costs of the system are minimized by using the heat stored in the tank to partially replace a heat-only boiler, as shown in Fig. 14.6B. The electricity generation profile of the CHP plant (Fig. 14.7B) exhibits significantly lower variations since most of the available power in the system is used to meet the thermal demand. Nonetheless, this demonstrates the reliability of the proposed framework for the simultaneous optimization of power generation and heat.

5   Conclusions

This chapter presents a mixed-integer linear programming (MILP) approach for solving the operation planning problem of a coal-fired CHP system. The system comprises a CHP plant (equipped with an extraction-condensing steam turbine driven by two pulverized coal-fired boilers), two auxiliary boilers and a tank thermal energy storage. The objective of the mathematical model is the minimization of the operating costs of the CHP system considering the heat demand of a district heating network and the potential revenues from the exchange of electricity with the local power market. An illustrative example based on a typical cogeneration system operating in Central and Eastern Europe has been used to demonstrate the applicability of the proposed approach. Two scenarios have been investigated to highlight the advantages of the model in dealing with the simultaneous optimization of thermal and electrical power (co-optimization of heat and power). The first scenario (called the reference scenario), which acts as the baseline for comparison, concerns the optimization of energy production of a CHP system without thermal energy storage. In the second scenario, a TES with a capacity of 700 MWh is integrated to the existing CHP system.

By comparing the results of the optimization procedures, we can investigate the economic and operational effects of the energy storage on the optimal operation of the CHP system. The results exhibit that the integration of an energy storage with the CHP system leads to a considerable drop in the amount of thermal energy produced by the CHP and the auxiliary boilers. Integrating a tank energy storage into the CHP system enables plant operators to optimally manage the thermal and electrical power production considering electricity prices and mitigate the impact of the power loss coefficient. Moreover, the findings suggest that the integration of an energy storage has a direct impact on the operational hours of the constituent elements as well as on the costs and revenue streams of the system.

The proposed model formulation may be extended to consider flow temperatures in addition to mass and energy flows within the network. Additionally, possible paths for future research may include extending the formulation for electrical energy storage, low-temperature district heating, and gas-fired power units.

Acknowledgments

The authors thank Przemysław Kaszyński and Adam Suski for useful discussions. This work was carried out as part of the statutory activity of the Mineral and Energy Economy Research Institute of the Polish Academy of Sciences.

References

Ahmadi, H., Marti, J.R., Moshref, A., 2013. Piecewise linear approximation of generators cost functions using max-affine functions. IEEE Power Energy Soc. Gen. Meet., 6–10. https://doi.org/10.1109/PESMG.2013.6672353.

Bansal, R.C., 2005. Optimization methods for electric power systems: an overview. Int. J. Emerg. Electr. Power Syst. 2. https://doi.org/10.2202/1553-779X.1021.

Benalcazar, P., Kamiński, J., 2016. Capacity markets and cogeneration facilities: recommendations for Poland. Polit. Energ. 19, 61–76.

Benalcazar, P., Kamiński, J., 2019. Short-term heat load forecasting in district heating systems using artificial neural networks. IOP Conf. Ser. Earth Environ. Sci. 214, 012023. https://doi.org/10.1088/1755-1315/214/1/012023.

Bischi, A., Pérez-Iribarren, E., Campanari, S., Manzolini, G., Martelli, E., Silva, P., Macchi, E., Sala-Lizarraga, J.M.P., 2016. Cogeneration systems optimization: comparison of multi-step and mixed integer linear programming approaches. Int. J. Green Energy 13, 781–792. https://doi.org/10.1080/15435075.2016.1161635.

Campos Celador, A., Odriozola, M., Sala, J.M., 2011. Implications of the modelling of stratified hot water storage tanks in the simulation of CHP plants. Energy Convers. Manag. 52, 3018–3026. https://doi.org/10.1016/j.enconman.2011.04.015.

Delson, J.K., Shahidehpous, S.M., 1992. Linear programming applications to power system economics, planning and operations. IEEE Trans. Power Syst. 7, 1155–1163. https://doi.org/10.1109/59.207329.

Doty, S., Turner, W.C., 2012. Energy Management Handbook, eighth ed. The Fairmont Press, Lilburn.

Dvořák, M., Havel, P., 2012. Combined heat and power production planning under liberalized market conditions. Appl. Therm. Eng. 43, 163–173. https://doi.org/10.1016/j.applthermaleng.2011.12.016.

Fang, T., Lahdelma, R., 2016. Optimization of combined heat and power production with heat storage based on sliding time window method. Appl. Energy 162, 723–732. https://doi.org/10.1016/j.apenergy.2015.10.135.

Gopalakrishnan, H., 2014. Operational Planning in Combined Heat and Power Systems. University of Massachusetts, Amherst.

Gopalakrishnan, H., Kosanovic, D., 2015. Operational planning of combined heat and power plants through genetic algorithms for mixed 0-1 nonlinear programming. Comput. Oper. Res. 56, 51–67. https://doi.org/10.1016/j.cor.2014.11.001.

Havel, P., Šimovič, T., 2013. Optimal planning of cogeneration production with provision of ancillary services. Electr. Power Syst. Res. 95, 47–55. https://doi.org/10.1016/j.epsr.2012.07.020.

Irving, M.R., Song, Y.-H., 2000. Optimisation techniques for electrical power systems. Part 1: mathematical optimisation methods. Power Eng. J. 14, 245–254. https://doi.org/10.1049/pe:20000509.

Jiménez Navarro, J.P., Kavvadias, K.C., Quoilin, S., Zucker, A., 2018. The joint effect of centralised cogeneration plants and thermal storage on the efficiency and cost of the power system. Energy 149, 535–549. https://doi.org/10.1016/j.energy.2018.02.025.

Kalam, A., King, A., Moret, E., Weerasinghe, U., 2012. Combined heat and power systems: economic and policy barriers to growth. Chem. Cent. J. 6, S3. https://doi.org/10.1186/1752-153x-6-s1-s3.

Kia, M., Nazar, M.S., Sepasian, M.S., Heidari, A., Siano, P., 2017a. Optimal day ahead scheduling of combined heat and power units with electrical and thermal storage considering security constraint of power system. Energy 120, 241–252. https://doi.org/10.1016/j.energy.2016.11.079.

Kia, M., Setayesh Nazar, M., Sepasian, M.S., Heidari, A., Siano, P., 2017b. An efficient linear model for optimal day ahead scheduling of CHP units in active distribution networks considering load commitment programs. Energy 139, 798–817. https://doi.org/10.1016/j.energy.2017.08.008.

Koltsaklis, N.E., Kopanos, G.M., Georgiadis, M.C., 2014. Design and operational planning of energy networks based on combined heat and power units. Ind. Eng. Chem. Res. 53, 16905–16923. https://doi.org/10.1021/ie404165c.

Kumbartzky, N., Schacht, M., Schulz, K., Werners, B., 2017. Optimal operation of a CHP plant participating in the German electricity balancing and day-ahead spot market. Eur. J. Oper. Res. 261, 390–404. https://doi.org/10.1016/j.ejor.2017.02.006.

Lahdelma, R., Hakonen, H., 2003. An efficient linear programming algorithm for combined heat and power production. Eur. J. Oper. Res. 148, 141–151. https://doi.org/10.1016/S0377-2217(02)00460-5.

Lancia, G., Serafini, P., 2018. Compact Extended Linear Programming Models, EURO Advanced Tutorials on Operational Research. Springer International Publishing, Cham, https://doi.org/10.1007/978-3-319-63976-5.

Magnani, A., Boyd, S.P., 2009. Convex piecewise-linear fitting. Optim. Eng. 10, 1–17. https://doi.org/10.1007/s11081-008-9045-3.

Merkert, L., Abdoul Haime, A., Hohmann, S., 2019. Optimal scheduling of combined heat and power generation units using the thermal inertia of the connected district heating grid as energy storage. Energies 12. https://doi.org/10.3390/en12020266.

Mitra, S., Sun, L., Grossmann, I.E., 2013. Optimal scheduling of industrial combined heat and power plants under time-sensitive electricity prices. Energy 54, 194 211. https://doi.org/10.1016/j.energy.2013.02.030.

Mohammadi-Ivatloo, B., Moradi-Dalvand, M., Rabiee, A., 2013. Combined heat and power economic dispatch problem solution using particle swarm optimization with time varying acceleration coefficients. Electr. Power Syst. Res. 95, 9–18. https://doi.org/10.1016/j.epsr.2012.08.005.

Mollenhauer, E., Christidis, A., Tsatsaronis, G., 2016. Evaluation of an energy- and exergy-based generic modeling approach of combined heat and power plants. Int. J. Energy Environ. Eng. 7, 167–176. https://doi.org/10.1007/s40095-016-0204-6.

Mollenhauer, E., Christidis, A., Tsatsaronis, G., 2017. Increasing the flexibility of combined heat and power plants with heat pumps and thermal energy storage. J. Energy Resour. Technol. 140, 020907. https://doi.org/10.1115/1.4038461.

Nash, A.L., Badithela, A., Jain, N., 2017. Dynamic modeling of a sensible thermal energy storage tank with an immersed coil heat exchanger under three operation modes. Appl. Energy 195, 877–889. https://doi.org/10.1016/j.apenergy.2017.03.092.

Romanchenko, D., Kensby, J., Odenberger, M., Johnsson, F., 2018. Thermal energy storage in district heating: centralised storage vs. storage in thermal inertia of buildings. Energy Convers. Manag. 162, 26–38. https://doi.org/10.1016/j.enconman.2018.01.068.

Rong, A., Lahdelma, R., 2017. An efficient model and algorithm for the transmission-constrained multi-site combined heat and power system. Eur. J. Oper. Res. 258, 1106–1117. https://doi.org/10.1016/j.ejor.2016.09.002.

Rong, A., Hakonen, H., Lahdelma, R., 2003. An efficient linear model and optimization algorithm for nation-wide combined heat and power production. Turku Centre for Computer Science, Turku. TUCS Technical Report No. 531.

Sadeghian, H.R., Ardehali, M.M., 2016. A novel approach for optimal economic dispatch scheduling of integrated combined heat and power systems for maximum economic profit and minimum environmental emissions based on Benders decomposition. Energy 102, 10–23. https://doi.org/10.1016/j.energy.2016.02.044.

Salgado, F., Pedrero, P., 2008. Short-term operation planning on cogeneration systems: a survey. Electr. Power Syst. Res. 78, 835–848. https://doi.org/10.1016/j.epsr.2007.06.001.

Short, M., Crosbie, T., Dawood, M., Dawood, N., 2017. Load forecasting and dispatch optimisation for decentralised co-generation plant with dual energy storage. Appl. Energy 186, 304–320. https://doi.org/10.1016/j.apenergy.2016.04.052.

Smith, A.D., Mago, P.J., Fumo, N., 2013. Benefits of thermal energy storage option combined with CHP system for different commercial building types. Sustainable Energy Technol. Assess. 1, 3–12. https://doi.org/10.1016/j.seta.2012.11.001.

Song, Y.H., Irving, M.R., 2001. Optimisation techniques for electrical power systems part 2 heuristic optimisation methods. Power Eng. J. 15, 151–160. https://doi.org/10.1049/pe:20010307.

Soroudi, A., 2017. Power System Optimization Modeling in GAMS, first ed. Springer International Publishing, https://doi.org/10.1007/978-3-319-62350-4.

Stadler, M., Marnay, C., Siddiqui, A., Lai, J., Coffey, B., Aki, H., 2009. Effect of Heat and Electricity Storage and Reliability on Microgrid Viability: A Study of Commercial Buildings in California and New York States. Ernest Orlando Lawrence Berkeley National Laboratory, Berkeley, CA. https://gridintegration.lbl.gov/publications/effect-heat-and-electricity-storage.

Steen, D., Stadler, M., Cardoso, G., Groissböck, M., DeForest, N., Marnay, C., 2015. Modeling of thermal storage systems in MILP distributed energy resource models. Appl. Energy 137, 782–792. https://doi.org/10.1016/j.apenergy.2014.07.036.

Streckiene, G., Martinaitis, V., Andersen, A.N., Katz, J., 2009. Feasibility of CHP-plants with thermal stores in the German spot market. Appl. Energy 86, 2308–2316. https://doi.org/10.1016/j.apenergy.2009.03.023.

Urošević, D., Gvozdenac, D., Grković, V., 2013. Calculation of the power loss coefficient of steam turbine as a part of the cogeneration plant. Energy 59, 642–651. https://doi.org/10.1016/j.energy.2013.07.010.

Verbruggen, A., Dewallef, P., Quoilin, S., Wiggin, M., 2013. Unveiling the mystery of Combined Heat & Power (cogeneration). Energy 61, 575–582. https://doi.org/10.1016/j.energy.2013.09.029.

Verbruggen, A., Klemeš, J.J., Rosen, M.A., 2016. Assessing cogeneration activity in extraction–condensing steam turbines: dissolving the issues by applied thermodynamics. J. Energy Resour. Technol. 138, 052005. https://doi.org/10.1115/1.4033424.

Wang, J., You, S., Zong, Y., Cai, H., Træholt, C., Dong, Z.Y., 2019a. Investigation of real-time flexibility of combined heat and power plants in district heating applications. Appl. Energy 237, 196–209. https://doi.org/10.1016/j.apenergy.2019.01.017.

Wang, J., You, S., Zong, Y., Træholt, C., Dong, Z.Y., Zhou, Y., 2019b. Flexibility of combined heat and power plants: a review of technologies and operation strategies. Appl. Energy 252, 113445. https://doi.org/10.1016/j.apenergy.2019.113445.

Wang, J., You, S., Zong, Y., Traeholt, C., Zhou, Y., Mu, S., 2019c. Optimal dispatch of combined heat and power plant in integrated energy system: a state of the art review and case study of Copenhagen. Energy Procedia 158, 2794–2799. https://doi.org/10.1016/j.egypro.2019.02.040.

Wickart, M., Madlener, R., 2007. Optimal technology choice and investment timing: a stochastic model of industrial cogeneration vs. heat-only production. Energy Econ. 29, 934–952. https://doi.org/10.1016/j.eneco.2006.12.003.

Woodruff, E., Lammers, H., Lammers, T., 2017. Steam Plant Operation, tenth ed. McGraw-Hill Education, New York.

WRI, WBCSD, World Resources Institute, World Business Council for Sustainable Development, 2006. Allocation of GHG Emissions From a Combined Heat and Power (CHP) Plant, Guide to Calculation Worksheets. World Resources Institute; World Business Council for Sustainable Development. https://ghgprotocol.org/sites/default/files/CHP_guidance_v1.0.pdf.

Zou, D., Li, S., Kong, X., Ouyang, H., Li, Z., 2019. Solving the combined heat and power economic dispatch problems by an improved genetic algorithm and a new constraint handling strategy. Appl. Energy 237, 646–670. https://doi.org/10.1016/j.apenergy.2019.01.056.

Chapter 15

Statistical analysis of power flows based on system marginal price differentials between two power systems

Eleftherios C. Venizelos

Energy & Environmental Policy Laboratory, School of Economics, Business and International Studies, University of Piraeus, Piraeus, Greece

Acronyms

FI	fitting indicator
MNC	maximum number criterion
PDF	probability density function
PTR	physical transmission rights
RES	renewable energy sources
SMP	system marginal price
SMPd	system marginal price differential
TSO	transmission system operator

Nomenclature

$count_{total}$	number of all historical data
r^i	record i of historical data
SMP_A^i	system marginal price of power system A
SMP_B^i	system marginal price of power system B
cap^i	interconnection capacity
pf^i	power flow
$SMPd^i$	system marginal price differential
$pf\%^i$	power flow as a percentage of the interconnection capacity
C_k	number of records in *classification* k
$range_k^{SMPd}$	range of *SMPd* values for *classification* k
$min_k^{SMPd}.\ max_k^{SMPd}$	minimum and maximum *SMPd* value of *classification* k
$min_k^{pf\%}.\ max_k^{pf\%}$	minimum and maximum *pf%* value of *classification* k
$step_k^{SMPd}$	length of *SMPd* subranges
$step_k^{pf\%}$	length of *pf%* flow states
μ_x	mean value of *SMPd* values included in spectrum$_x$
σ_x	standard deviation of *SMPd* values included in spectrum$_x$
$spectrum_k^{SMPd}$	length of spectrum of *SMPd* values of *classification* k
$spectrum_k^{pf\%}$	length of spectrum of *pf%* values of *classification* k
p	number of edge spectrums $\neq \varnothing$
$N_k.\ M_k$	number of *SMPd* subranges and *pf%* flow states, respectively
$range_{SMPd}^{n.\ k}$	*SMPd* subrange n of *classification* k
$state_{pf\%}^{m.\ k}$	flow state m of *classification* k
$c1_{SMPd}^{n.\ k}.\ c2_{SMPd}^{n.\ k}$	limits of *SMPd* subrange n of *classification* k
$c1_{pf\%}^{m.\ k}.\ c2_{pf\%}^{m.\ k}$	limits of flow state m of *classification* k
$count\_range_{SMPd}^{n.\ k}$	number of records included in *SMPd* subrange n of *classification* k
$count\_state_{pf\%}^{m.\ k}$	number of records included in flow state m of *classification* k
$count_k^{n.\ m}$	number of records included simultaneously in *SMPd* subrange n and flow state m of *classification* k

Mathematical Modelling of Contemporary Electricity Markets. https://doi.org/10.1016/B978-0-12-821838-9.00015-3

$prob_k^{n, m}$	probability of a random record simultaneously included in *SMPd* subrange *n* and flow state *m* of *classification k*
$rep\_prob_k^n$	probability of the representative flow state of *SMPd* subrange *n* of *classification k*
$count_{fit}^k$	number of records r^j that fit the proposed analysis
FI^k	fitting indicator regarding of data included in *classification k*
FI	overall fitting indicator of all the historical data under analysis

1 Introduction

In modern power markets, the effective forecast of renewable energy sources (RES) production, electricity prices, and cross-border power flows are directly connected to the profitability of the market players and therefore, the social welfare through the power trading activity. The accurate prediction of these parameters is also of high importance for the system operators (TSOs), since it allows them to implement more efficient scheduling of the production units and ultimately minimize the cost for the end customer. The development of novel methodologies and models is a crucial prerequisite to reach the highest performance of the power markets. Many studies and approaches are proposed toward this direction. In the present chapter, a statistical analysis of power flows considering system marginal price differentials is presented. However, it is worth presenting the relative literature about various data analysis approaches, some of them implemented in other concepts than power markets, in order to set a comprehensive prism for the presentation of the current study.

A statistical analysis is performed in (Bąk et al., 2019) for ranking Poland's voivodeship cities by the level of road traffic. The zero unitarization method is used as a method for data normalization, considering the arithmetic mean of normalized values for further classification of diagnostic features of the data. The standard statistical analysis is based on integral parameters that account for the main features of a dataset. Although the integral parameters give good results under basic unimodal conditions in a single peaked spectrum, they start to lose significantly their meaning when there are more than one spectra under study. For this reason, statistical analysis approaches are developed for better results, such as the Spectral Partitions Statistics (SPS) as presented in (Portilla-Yandún et al., 2019) where the case study of ocean wave directional spectra is analyzed. The SPS method in (Portilla-Yandún et al., 2015) is based on the principle of linear superposition of different wave trains inherent in the wave spectrum. Thus the integral parameters of the individual clusters that are formed are much more meaningful than those calculated for the whole spectrum, because the loss of consistency of total integral parameters in multimodal spectra arises from the fact that these correspond to vector means of all the individual components. The partitioning is based on an algorithm where the local peak values are defined as cluster's centrals and the rest of the data are concentrated around these centrals forming partitions. A statistical analysis approach on the surge phenomenon that occurs in a compressor is performed in (Bontempo et al., 2017). The application of the methodology lies on the analysis of the unsteady flow characteristics of a free spool centrifugal compressor operated under surge flow conditions. As a result, the analysis has allowed the identification of the instantaneous states with the highest probability in the unstable envelope.

A statistical analysis is utilized in (Katinas et al., 2017) for the estimation of wind power generation in Lithuania. Different Weibull probability density function methodologies were presented and evaluated for the study, considering as input the characteristics of wind in a specific location. Another paper that copes with the determination of the Weibull distribution parameters based on historical data is (Rocha et al., 2012). In this study, a statistical analysis is utilized for the estimation of the errors of the seven methodologies that presented, among which, the maximum likelihood method and the modified maximum likelihood method. An examination of the impact of RES production to the power markets is presented in (Gianfreda et al., 2016), considering the electricity-fuel nexus and the resulting electricity prices for various scenarios. The hourly data under analysis are formulated in time series as signals, where the outliers are considered as noise and handled accordingly in a preprocessing stage, by using weekly median prices. In paper (Unger et al., 2018) tree scenarios of price differentials are considered between four distinguished interconnections regarding western Denmark in the Nord Pool market, in order to estimate the effect of wind energy production on cross-border electricity pricing. The three scenarios are referring to positive, negative, or zero difference between the prices of an interconnection. The method of maximum likelihood is also considered in this analysis.

In (Petrella and Sapio, 2012) a statistical analysis on the Italian wholesale electricity prices is performed as a preliminary data analysis for assisting the baseline models, where the goal is to uncover the basic features of the prices quoted on the Italian power exchange. An Artificial Neural Network model (ANN) is implemented in (Dagoumas et al., 2017) for electricity price forecasting of a power system, where the ANN model incorporates clustering techniques for organizing time periods in different clusters identifying the time periods with high certainty of forecasting. A comparison of forecasting models for electricity prices is presented in (Gianfreda et al., 2020) considering RES penetration, where the results of the study show that models considering additionally to RES, the demand and fuels have much better performance than those without. In (Lago et al., 2018) deep learning algorithms are examined for their performance in electricity prices forecasting and a comparison of 27 common approaches for electricity price forecasting is performed. The paper (Lu et al., 2020) presents machine learning models for carbon trading volumes and price forecasting. The forecasting steps implemented in this paper are data collection, data decomposition, data normalization, data classification, prediction using machine learning models, predictive result superposition and denormalization and error analysis.

In paper (Elyas and Wang, 2016) the focus is on the statistical analysis of transmission line capacities. In the first part of the paper, the transmission line capacities are defined by a mathematical distribution and then the categorization of the line capacities into smaller intervals is proposed, in order to create more precise models. In publication (Chen et al., 2020), the potential economic impact of cross-border transmission capacity in Northwestern Europe is presented. In the scope of this study, the historical data are also modeled in time series considering four representative days, each for every season. A study of the efficient use of transmission capacity for cross-border trading is presented in (Plancke et al., 2016). In the scope of this study, a flow-based algorithm is developed considering the estimation of cross-border power flows in Central-Western Europe region for the day-ahead market. In (Pantos et al., 2003) a transmission price methodology is proposed which is based on power flow estimations. The results of power flow volumes are estimated by performing a statistical analysis on historical data of the generators' and loads' contribution on the transmission lines, considering a set of different operating states of the power system.

In the scope of the publication (Sulakov, 2017), a statistical approach is utilized on historical data of physical power flows, which pass through the Bulgarian transmission system. The correlation between net exports and transmission losses is also examined and the resulted value of this paper is that it shows the impact of the traded volumes on the transmission grid losses, within a power system, which are translated to a negative financial impact on the hosted TSO's revenues. A graphical solution of cross-border electricity flows of Germany is presented in (Kumar and Möst, 2017) considering also the RES capacity of the power system. Furthermore, the concept of clustering of the historical data is utilized also in this analysis, as well as correlation indicators between different parameters of the power system, such as net imports, net exports, RES generation, residual demand, and others. The paper gives a simplified theoretical analysis in the hypothesis of the increase of power flows due to an increase in renewable generation capacity, but further research is required for proving the robustness of this hypothesis. A methodology of cross-border annual power flows estimation is proposed in (Murray, 2019) based on nodal price differentials. It is proposed that the future flows can be estimated by converting the predicted set of price differentials into equivalent nodal voltages, with the highest voltage translated into the lowest price, and using the admittance matrix to translate these into flows. In (Schäfer et al., 2019) are presented the most important trading patterns of cross-border power flows in the European electricity markets. The estimation of the physical power flows is based on the flow tracing algorithm, considering the tracing of power flows through the network from the exporting countries to the importing ones.

Although there are numerous publications for statistical analysis methodologies and power flow estimations, there are quite a few of them considering the electricity trading between two power systems and more specifically between Italy and Greece. The proposed methodology is an attempt to fill this gap and produce valuable results assisting the electricity trading between two power systems. This methodology aims to define the power flows, as a percentage of the interconnection capacity, based on the system marginal price differentials (SMPd) of two power systems. More specifically, the output of the analysis is a probability density function (PDF) of power flow percentages and a representative power flow range is elected for a given SMPd value.

2 Methodology

The historical data are classified according to the interconnection capacity and the direction characterization of power flows (economical or noneconomical) forming four classifications. For every classification, the values of $SMPd$ are distributed within a certain spectrum which is defined by the analysis. Every $SMPd$ is classified in a unique subrange of the initial spectrum of the classification. For every subrange of $SMPds$ a PDF of power flow percentages is estimated, and a representative range of power flows is defined.

Every record i of the historical data is considered as a vector with the following elements:

$$r^i = \left(SMP_A^i, SMP_B^i, cap^i, pf^i, SMPd^i, pf\%^i\right) \tag{15.1}$$

where the system marginal price differential ($SMPd^i$) and the power flow as a percentage of the interconnection capacity ($pf\%^i$) are calculated as follows:

$$SMPd^i = SMP_B^i - SMP_A^i \tag{15.2}$$

$$pf\%^i = pf^i / cap^i \tag{15.3}$$

As a first step of the analysis, the historical data are classified into four groups according to the interconnection capacity (cap^i) and the system marginal price differential ($SMPd^i$) of every record r^i, as shown as follows:

$$if\ cap^i = 0 \rightarrow r^i \in classification \quad 1$$

$$if\ cap^i <> 0\ and\ SMPd^i < 0 \rightarrow r^i \in classification \quad 2$$

$$if\ cap^i <> 0\ and\ SMPd^i > 0 \rightarrow r^i \in classification \quad 3$$

$$if\ cap^i <> 0\ and\ SMPd^i = 0 \rightarrow r^i \in classification \quad 4$$

As a result, the number of records included in every *classification* is represented as follows, where $count_{total}$ is the total number of records of the historical data:

$$C_k = \sum_1^{count_{total}} r^i\ if\ r^i \in classification\ k \qquad k = 1,2,3,4 \tag{15.4}$$

Regarding *classification* 1, the interconnection capacity equal to zero means that the cable is out of service, so for every record r_1^i, it is expected to have as a result zero power flow percentage ($pf\%_1^i = 0$) for every value of $SMPd_1^i$.

For the analysis of *classifications* 2 and 3, where the interconnection capacity is greater than zero, the PDF of the power flows is defined by following certain steps. At first, the spectrum of system marginal price differentials ($SMPd$) is defined and is further divided into subranges by introducing a step of analysis ($step_k^{SMPd}$). Similarly, the spectrum of power flow percentages ($pf\%$) is defined and is further divided into subranges by introducing a step of analysis ($step_k^{pf\%}$). In the scope of this analysis, every subrange of power flow percentages is referred to as a flow state. A table of probabilities is formulated, where every column represents a subrange of $SMPd$ values and every row represents a flow state. Hence, for every subrange of $SMPd$ values, a PDF of power flows is estimated according to the table of probabilities.

The spectrum of the $SMPd$ values distribution is defined as follows, where the parameters max_k^{SMPd}, min_k^{SMPd} are the maximum and minimum $SMPd$ values of the spectrum, respectively.

$$spectrum_k^{SMPd} = max_k^{SMPd} - min_k^{SMPd} \tag{15.5}$$

For the outliers to be handled more efficiently, the initial $spectrum_k^{SMPd}$ is analyzed in certain stages. For this purpose, the maximum number criterion (MNC) is introduced, in order to define the minimum length of spectrum with the maximum number of records included (i.e., 99% of records should be included in a certain range of values). Also, it is assumed that the $SMPd$ values follow the Normal Distribution $N(\mu, \sigma^2)$. So, at the first stage of this procedure, the mean value μ_1 and the standard deviation σ_1 of the $spectrum_k^{SMPd}$, i.e., $[min_k^{SMPd}, max_k^{SMPd}]$, are calculated and the MNC is applied on the range of values $[\mu_1 - 3\sigma_1, \mu_1 + 3\sigma_1]$, i.e., spectrum$_1$, which is a subrange of $spectrum_k^{SMPd}$. At the second stage, the mean values μ_l, μ_g and the standard deviations σ_l, σ_g of the range $[min_k^{SMPd}, \mu_1 - 3\sigma_1]$, i.e., spectrum$_l$ and the range $[\mu_1 + 3\sigma_1, max_k^{SMPd}]$, i.e., spectrum$_g$, that include, respectively, lower and greater values from spectrum$_1$, are calculated and the MNC is applied on the range $[\mu_l - 3\sigma_l, \mu_g + 3\sigma_g]$, i.e., spectrum$_2$. The second stage is repeated until the MNC is satisfied. As a last stage of this procedure, the two remaining edge spectrums are defined as $[min_k^{SMPd}, \mu_l - 3\sigma_l]$, i.e., spectrum$_{le}$ and $[\mu_g + 3\sigma_g, max_k^{SMPd}]$, i.e., spectrum$_{ge}$. The parameter p is defined as the number of edge spectrums that include at least one record. As a result, the final spectrum of $SMPd$ values under the MNC is defined as follows:

$$spectrum_k^{SMPd} = \left(\mu_g + 3\sigma_g\right) - \left(\mu_l - 3\sigma_l\right) \tag{15.6}$$

It is noted that if the upper limit of the proposed range is greater than the maximum value of the initial spectrum of values, $(\mu_g + 3\sigma_g) > max_k^{SMPd}$, then the final spectrum under MNC is defined by Eq. (15.7):

$$spectrum_k^{SMPd} = max_k^{SMPd} - (\mu_l - 3\sigma_l) \tag{15.7}$$

Accordingly, if the lower limit of the proposed range is lower than the minimum value of the initial spectrum of values, $(\mu_l - 3\sigma_l) < min_k^{SMPd}$, then the final spectrum under MNC is defined by Eq. (15.8):

$$spectrum_k^{SMPd} = \left(\mu_g + 3\sigma_g\right) - min_k^{SMPd} \tag{15.8}$$

So, by defining a spectrum without outliers, fewer steps will be needed for the analysis of the *SMPd* values. The number of subranges of *SMPd* values, N_k, is calculated by rounding up the following deviation to the first integer and adding up the *p* parameter. The parameter $step_k^{SMPd}$ defines the step of analysis and it is equal to the length of every *SMPd* range of values.

$$N_k = \left\lceil spectrum_k^{SMPd} / step_k^{SMPd} \right\rceil + p \qquad p = 0 \ldots 2 \tag{15.9}$$

The subrange *n* of *SMPd* values of *classification k* is symbolized as follows:

$$range_{SMPd}^{n,k}, \quad n = 1 \ldots N_k \tag{15.10}$$

The limits of the range *n* of *SMPd* values of *classification k* are defined as follows:

$$c1_{SMPd}^{n,k} = (n-1) * step_k^{SMPd} \tag{15.11}$$

$$c2_{SMPd}^{n,k} = n * step_k^{SMPd} \tag{15.12}$$

In case of $p \neq 0$, the limits of the edge ranges are formulated considering the edge values of the initial spectrum, which are max_k^{SMPd} and min_k^{SMPd}, in order to include the whole spectrum of data values. It is also noted that the parameter $step_k^{SMPd}$ has the same sign as the *SMPd* values. So, for *classifications* 2 the parameter $step_k^{SMPd}$ is a negative value, whereas for *classifications* 3, the parameter $step_k^{SMPd}$ is a positive value.

The spectrum of the power flow percentages of *classification k* is defined as follows, where $max_k^{pf\%}$ and $min_k^{pf\%}$ are the maximum and minimum power flow percentages of the historical data, respectively:

$$spectrum_k^{pf\%} = max_k^{pf\%} - min_k^{pf\%} \tag{15.13}$$

The number of flow states, M_k, is calculated by rounding up the following deviation to the first integer as shown as follows, where $step_k^{pf\%}$ is an elected step of the analysis:

$$M_k = \left\lceil spectrum_k^{pf\%} / step_k^{pf\%} \right\rceil \tag{15.14}$$

The flow state *m* of *classificaion k* is symbolized as follows:

$$state_{pf\%}^{m,k}, \quad m = 1 \ldots M_k \tag{15.15}$$

The limits of flow state *m* of *classification k* are defined based on the following equations:

$$c1_{pf\%}^{m,k} = (m-1) * step_k^{pf\%} \tag{15.16}$$

$$c2_{pf\%}^{m,k} = m * step_k^{pf\%} \tag{15.17}$$

The number of records that are included in *SMPd* subrange *n* of *classification k*, regardless of the flow state, is calculated as follows:

$$count\_range_{SMPd}^{n,k} = \sum_1^{C_k} r_k^i \tag{15.18}$$

considering the constraint:

$$SMPd_k^i \in range_{SMPd}^{n,k} \tag{15.19}$$

The number of records included in flow state *m* of *classification k*, regardless of the *SMPd* subrange, is calculated as follows:

$$count\_state_{pf\%}^{m,k} = \sum_1^{C_k} r_k^i \tag{15.20}$$

considering the constraint:

$$pf\%_k^i \in state_{pf\%}^{m,k} \tag{15.21}$$

In order to define the table of probabilities per flow state of every *SMPd* subrange, the table of numerical count of records is formulated first, where the number of records that simultaneously belong to *SMPd* subrange n and flow state m of *classification* k is calculated as shown in Eq. (15.22):

$$count_k^{m,n} = \sum_1^{C_k} \sum_1^{N_k} \sum_1^{M_k} r_k^i \tag{15.22}$$

considering at the same time both of the following constraints:

$$SMPd_k^i \in range_{SMPd}^{n,k} \tag{15.23}$$

$$pf\%_k^i \in state_{pf\%}^{m,k} \tag{15.24}$$

The probability of occurrence of flow state m for a *SMPd* value that is included in subrange n is calculated as follows, where the number of records that simultaneously belong to *SMPd* subrange n and flow state m is divided by the total number of records of the *SMPd* subrange n, where all the flow states are considered.

$$prob_k^{m,n} = count_k^{m,n} / count\_range_{SMPd}^{n,k} \tag{15.25}$$

The probability density function (PDF) of flow states for the *SMPd* subrange n of *classification* k is formulated by applying Eq. (15.25) for all the flow states ($m = 1 \ldots M_k$).

The representative flow state of *SMPd* subrange n of *classification* k is symbolized as $repState_k^n$ and is elected as the one with the highest probability of occurrence, and the corresponding probability is defined as follows:

$$rep\_prob_k^n = \max\left(prob_k^{n,m}\right) \quad m = 1 \ldots M_k \tag{15.26}$$

2.1 Validation of the statistical analysis

In order to evaluate the robustness of the model and the precision on the forecasted power flows for a given *SMPd*, a fitting indicator (*FI*) is introduced as an index of accuracy for the estimated power flows. The robustness of the proposed model is greater as the fitting indicator increases. For the evaluation of the proposed methodology, the representative flow state of every *SMPd* subrange is used, as described before. The actual power flow percentages of the historical data are compared to the estimated flow states of the model. For every record of the historical data (r_i), if the power flow percentage is included in the estimated flow state, the record r_i is considered as a fit. For every *classification* k, the number of records that fit the model ($count_{fit}^k$) is divided by the total number of records of the historical data ($count_{total}$), formulating the relative fitting indicator (FI^k) as presented as follows with the corresponding equations.

$$count_{fit}^k = \sum_1^{C_k} r_{i,k} \tag{15.27}$$

considering at the same time both of the following constraints:

$$SMPd_k^i \in range_{SMPd}^{n,k} \tag{15.28}$$

$$pf\%_k^i \in repState_k^n \tag{15.29}$$

The relative fitting indicator (*FI*) of *classification* k is calculated as follows:

$$FI^k = count_{fit}^k / count_{total} \tag{15.30}$$

The final overall fitting indicator (*FI*) of the model is calculated as follows, where the total number of the records that fit the model is divided by the total number of records of the historical data:

$$FI = \frac{\sum_1^k count_{fit}^k}{count_{total}} \tag{15.31}$$

3   Methodology application

The application of the methodology is performed on the ex-post historical data of imports from Italy to Greece for a period of over 4 years [Henex (http://www.enexgroup.gr/nc/en/home/), GME (https://www.mercatoelettrico.org/En/Default. aspx), entso-e (https://transparency.entsoe.eu/), admie (http://www.admie.gr/nc/en/home/), terna (https://www.terna.it/en/)]. More specifically, the period examined is from 1-1-2015 to 30-9-2019 on an hourly resolution. The system marginal prices of Greece and Italy and the system marginal price differentials are presented in Fig. 15.1A and B, respectively. It is worth noticing that the distribution of the *SMPd*s in Fig. 15.1C is similar to the Normal distribution. In Fig. 15.1D the *SMPd*s are illustrated with the blue color and the SMP of Greece with the green one.

The power flows are presented in Fig. 15.2. The values of power flow percentages higher than 100%, refer to the usage of the interconnection capacity considering wrong direction energy flows, according to the trading schedule. Wrong direction power flows refer to noneconomic flows, where the direction of power flows is from the power system with the higher *SMP* to the one with the lower *SMP*. Thus the power flow percentages could be lying between 0%, where there are no power flows, and 200%, where there are scheduled wrong direction power flows at a percentage of 100% of the interconnection capacity additionally to 100% of normal direction of power flows.

The classifications of the historical data are presented in Table 15.1. The number of records per classification and the corresponding percentage, considering that the total number of records is $count_{total} = 41,620$, are presented as well.

Classification 2 is chosen to demonstrate the numerical data of the methodology, since it includes most of the records (56.65%) of the historical data under study. The distribution of *SMPd*s is presented in Fig. 15.3A. In Fig. 15.3B the *SMPd*s are illustrated compared to the *SMP* values of Greece.

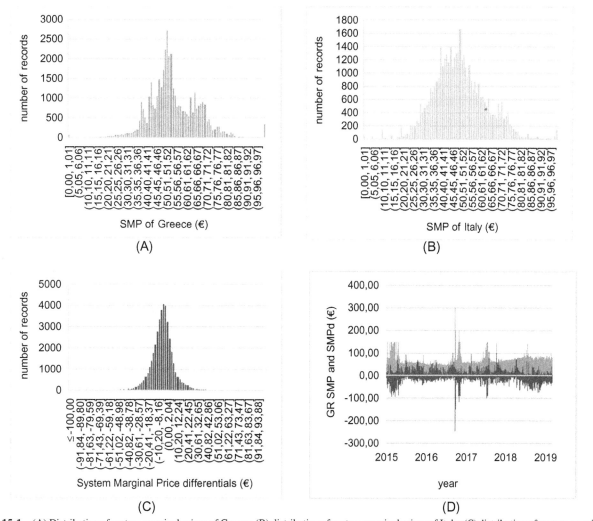

FIG. 15.1   (A) Distribution of system marginal prices of Greece; (B) distribution of system marginal prices of Italy; (C) distribution of system marginal price differentials; (D) system marginal prices of Greece compared to the system marginal price differentials.

FIG. 15.2 Power flows as a percentage of the interconnection capacity.

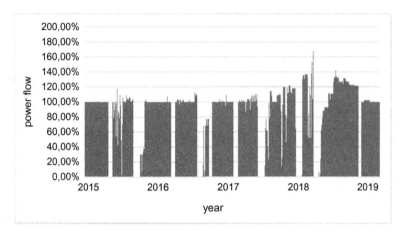

TABLE 15.1 Classification of the historical data under analysis.

Classification k	C_k	$C_k/count_{total}$
1	7988	19.19%
2	23,577	56.65%
3	9966	23.95%
4	89	0.21%

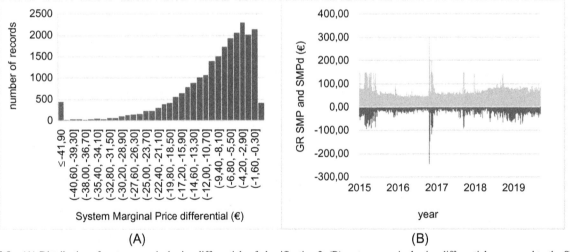

(A)   (B)

FIG. 15.3 (A) Distribution of system marginal price differentials of classification 2; (B) system marginal price differentials compared to the SMP of Greece.

The negative values of *SMPd* mean that the system marginal price of Greece is higher than the system marginal price of Italy as derived from Eq. (15.2), considering power system A as Greece and power system B as Italy. Since the historical data under study refer to power flow of imports, the positive values of *SMPd* mean that the *SMP* of Italy is lower than the *SMP* of Greece. So, for the records that *SMPd* is a positive value, the power flow is characterized as noneconomic (wrong direction). The power flow percentages of the historical data are shown in Fig. 15.4.

Following the procedure described before for the outliers to be handled more efficiently, the spectrum of the *SMPds* values is defined considering the maximum number criterion (MNC) and the results are presented in Table 15.2. For the MNC to be satisfied in this application of the methodology, the 99% of the values is required to be included in the proposed spectrum.

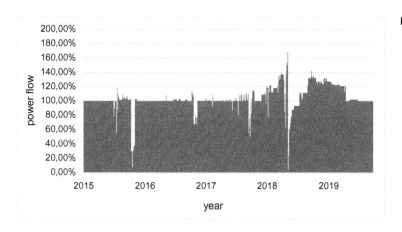

FIG. 15.4 Power flows of classification 2.

TABLE 15.2 Parameters of the spectrum analysis of classification 2.

Parameter	Result
max_2^{SMPd}	0.00
min_2^{SMPd}	−246.00
$spectrum_k^{SMPd}$	246.00
μ_1	−10.13
σ_1	10.59
$\mu_1 + 3\sigma_1$	21.65
$\mu_1 - 3\sigma_1$	−41.90
upper limit$_1$	0
lower limit$_1$	−41.90
spectrum$_1$	41.90
MNC_1	98.07%
μ_l	−60.86
σ_l	20.15
$\mu_l + 3\sigma_l$	−0.41
$\mu_l - 3\sigma_l$	−121.32
upper limit$_2$	0
lower limit$_2$	−121.32
spectrum$_2$	121.32
MNC_2	99.98%

The range of spectrum$_1$ is $[−41.90, 0]$, where $\mu_1 + 3\sigma_1 > max_2^{SMPd}$, so the *upper limit*$_1$ equals to zero instead of 21.65. The MNC for spectrum$_1$ is not satisfied, since only 98.07% of the historical data are included, so there is a large number of records out of spectrum$_1$, as shown also in Fig. 15.3A. Similarly, the range of spectrum$_2$ is $[−121.32, 0]$, where the 99.98% of the historical data are included and the MNC is satisfied, where $\mu_l + 3\sigma_l > max_2^{SMPd}$, so the *upper limit*$_2$ equals to zero instead of 20.15. Hence, the rest 0.02% of the data is included in the range of values $[min_2^{SMPd}, \mu_l − 3\sigma_l]$, because $\mu_l − 3\sigma_l > min_2^{SMPd}$ and $p = 1$. Considering a step of analysis as $step_2^{SMPd} = −1$, the number of *SMPd* subranges is $N_k = 123$ according to Eq. (15.9). The limits of each *SMPd* subrange and the number of values included in every subrange are calculated by using Eqs. (15.11), (15.12), and (15.18), respectively, and the results are demonstrated in Table 15.3.

TABLE 15.3 Limits and number of records per SMPd subrange.

n	$c1_{SMPd}^{n,\,2}$	$c1_{SMPd}^{n,\,2}$	$count\_range_{SMPd}^{n,\,2}$
1	0.00	−1.00	1582
2	−1.00	−2.00	1639
3	−2.00	−3.00	1585
4	−3.00	−4.00	1779
5	−4.00	−5.00	1610
6	−5.00	−6.00	1566
7	−6.00	−7.00	1458
8	−7.00	−8.00	1301
9	−8.00	−9.00	1212
10	−9.00	−10.00	1097
11	−10.00	−11.00	1009
12	−11.00	−12.00	810
13	−12.00	−13.00	780
14	−13.00	−14.00	725
15	−14.00	−15.00	630
16	−15.00	−16.00	626
17	−16.00	−17.00	477
18	−17.00	−18.00	445
19	−18.00	−19.00	388
20	−19.00	−20.00	318
21	−20.00	−21.00	308
22	−21.00	−22.00	251
23	−22.00	−23.00	199
24	−23.00	−24.00	183
25	−24.00	−25.00	182
26	−25.00	−26.00	132
27	−26.00	−27.00	112
28	−27.00	−28.00	120
29	−28.00	−29.00	98
30	−29.00	−30.00	79
31	−30.00	−31.00	69
32	−31.00	−32.00	49
33	−32.00	−33.00	42
34	−33.00	−34.00	33
35	−34.00	−35.00	42
36	−35.00	−36.00	41
...	...	...	...
123	−121.32	−246.00	4

As demonstrated in Fig. 15.5, when the *SMPd* values are low the count of records included in the corresponding sub-ranges is higher and vice versa. That means that the lower the system marginal price differentials were, the higher the number of executed trades would be.

The spectrum of power flow percentages is 0–200%, due to noneconomic direction of power flows as mentioned before. Considering a step of flow state analysis as $step_2^{pf\%} = 5\%$, the number of flow states is $M_2 = 40$ according to Eq. (15.14). The limits of each flow state and the count of values included are calculated by using Eqs. (15.16), (15.17), and (15.20), respectively. The results are demonstrated in Table 15.4.

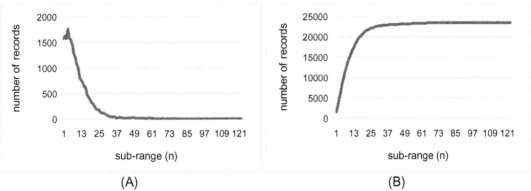

(A)   (B)

FIG. 15.5   (A) Number of records per SMPd subrange; (B) cumulative number of records per SMPd subrange.

TABLE 15.4 Limits and number of records per flow state of classification 2.

m	$c1_{pf\%}^{m,2}$	$c1_{pf\%}^{m,2}$	$count\_state_{pf\%}^{m,2}$
1	0%	5%	1210
2	5%	10%	473
3	10%	15%	335
4	15%	20%	359
5	20%	25%	327
6	25%	30%	401
7	30%	35%	362
8	35%	40%	449
9	40%	45%	427
10	45%	50%	399
11	50%	55%	432
12	55%	60%	468
13	60%	65%	454
14	65%	70%	500
15	70%	75%	563
16	75%	80%	685
17	80%	85%	713
18	85%	90%	824
19	90%	95%	998
20	95%	100%	7959
21	100%	105%	1991

Continued

TABLE 15.4 Limits and number of records per flow state of classification 2—cont'd

m	$c1_{pf\%}^{m,2}$	$c1_{pf\%}^{m,2}$	$count\_state_{pf\%}^{m,2}$
22	105%	110%	688
23	110%	115%	912
24	115%	120%	599
25	120%	125%	568
26	125%	130%	267
27	130%	135%	146
28	135%	140%	39
29	140%	145%	3
30	145%	150%	12
31	150%	155%	5
32	155%	160%	4
33	160%	165%	4
34	165%	170%	1
35	170%	175%	0
36	175%	180%	0
37	180%	185%	0
38	185%	190%	0
39	190%	195%	0
40	195%	200%	0

It is obvious that most of the records are concentrated around the power flow percentage of 100%. Quite lower, but worth mentioning, is the number of records concentrated around the power flow percentage of 0%.

For every $SMPd$ subrange the number of records included per flow state is calculated according to Eq. (15.22). The results are formulated in Table 15.5, where the number of records is defined per flow state in every $SMPd$ range. Fig. 15.6 provides the distribution of power flow states of classification. Applying Eq. (15.25) in Table 15.5, the matrix of probabilities is formulated as shown in Table 15.6.

The representative flow state of every $SMPd$ range is elected as the one with the highest probability of occurrence. As an example, for $range_{SMPd}^{1,2}$ the highest probability is $prob_k^{1,1} = 14.41\%$, and so $m = 1$ is the representative flow state for this subrange. So, for a given $SMPd$ value that is included in $range_{SMPd}^{1,2}$, the representative flow state (most probable to occur) is $state_{pf\%}^{1,2}$ with range of power flow percentages between 0% and 5%.

As another example, if the system marginal prices of Greece and Italy formulate a $SMPd$ that is included in subrange $n = 21$, i.e., $range_{SMPd}^{21,2}$, where $c1_{SMPd}^{21,2} = -20$ and $c2_{SMPd}^{21,2} = -21$, the power flow will be between 95% and 100% of the interconnection capacity with probability of occurrence at $prob_2^{20,21} = 49.03\%$, as the representative flow state of this case is $m = 20$, with limits $c1_{pf\%}^{20,2} = 95\%$ and $c2_{pf\%}^{20,2} = 100\%$. The probabilities of flow states for $range_{SMPd}^{21,2}$ are demonstrated in Table 15.7 and the corresponding formulated PDF is shown in Fig. 15.7.

The probability density functions of power flows for various subranges are illustrated in Fig. 15.8. In case of subrange 1, the representative flow state corresponds to 0–5% of power flows at a percentage of occurrence 14.41%, whereas the second probable percentage of occurrence is 11.50% and corresponds to power flows between 95% and 100%. In this case, since the probabilities of the most predominantly flow states are close to one another, further analysis can be implemented by splitting the subrange 1 into smaller subranges using a smaller step of analysis $step_k^{SMPd}$. Regarding subranges 2, 3, 4, 7, 10 and 21, as illustrated in Fig. 15.8, the representative flow state corresponds to power flows between 95% and 100% with

TABLE 15.5 Number of records per flow state of every SMPd subrange.

$c1^{m,2}_{p\%}$	$c2^{m,2}_{p\%}$	m \ n	1	2	3	4	5	6	7	8	9	10	…	19	20	21	…	123
		$c1^{n}_{SMPd}$	0	−1	−2	−3	−4	−5	−6	−7	−8	−9	…	−18	−19	−20	…	−121.32
		$c2^{n}_{SMPd}$	−1	−2	−3	−4	−5	−6	−7	−8	−9	−10	…	−19	−20	−21	…	−246
0%	5%	1	228	203	153	138	126	86	73	36	32	17	…	4	3	2	…	3
5%	10%	2	85	76	66	59	32	25	20	27	18	12	…	2	3	2	…	0
10%	15%	3	56	62	36	45	37	27	19	16	8	2	…	0	2	0	…	0
15%	20%	4	56	65	52	51	31	26	21	16	13	8	…	0	1	1	…	0
20%	25%	5	50	43	46	48	38	28	22	17	14	7	…	0	0	0	…	0
25%	30%	6	57	57	46	52	50	29	27	18	13	11	…	0	0	3	…	0
30%	35%	7	49	51	40	50	41	32	25	21	7	9	…	1	1	3	…	0
35%	40%	8	60	62	65	50	41	34	21	22	16	13	…	1	1	1	…	0
40%	45%	9	41	69	60	55	42	31	25	17	16	12	…	5	0	1	…	0
45%	50%	10	62	42	41	64	42	39	25	16	11	12	…	1	1	1	…	0
50%	55%	11	53	42	50	43	40	43	36	19	15	17	…	3	5	1	…	0
55%	60%	12	49	60	56	54	53	36	38	29	23	10	…	2	2	2	…	0
60%	65%	13	52	59	49	60	57	36	31	19	19	18	…	3	0	1	…	0
65%	70%	14	65	66	43	51	45	51	41	31	38	11	…	2	7	0	…	0
70%	75%	15	69	64	54	58	47	55	43	28	21	24	…	1	2	2	…	0
75%	80%	16	71	63	60	67	58	68	51	31	30	27	…	6	5	5	…	1
80%	85%	17	58	69	69	94	58	55	50	45	32	23	…	9	2	3	…	0
85%	90%	18	70	87	87	85	61	81	69	44	45	31	…	3	5	5	…	0
90%	95%	19	74	84	82	109	89	82	82	64	44	45	…	8	10	6	…	0
95%	100%	20	182	215	260	362	383	420	446	476	511	496	…	186	138	151	…	0
100%	105%	21	42	46	85	75	101	125	117	136	123	123	…	52	45	38	…	0
105%	110%	22	18	11	29	31	43	48	65	35	31	36	…	14	15	22	…	0
…	…	…	…	…	…	…	…	…	…	…	…	…	…	…	…	…	…	…
155%	160%	32	0	0	0	2	0	0	0	0	0	0	…	0	0	0	…	0
160%	165%	33	0	0	0	1	0	1	0	0	0	0	…	0	0	0	…	0
…	…	…	…	…	…	…	…	…	…	…	…	…	…	…	…	…	…	…
195%	200%	40	0	0	0	0	0	0	0	0	0	0	…	0	0	0	…	0

FIG. 15.6 Distribution of power flow states of classification.

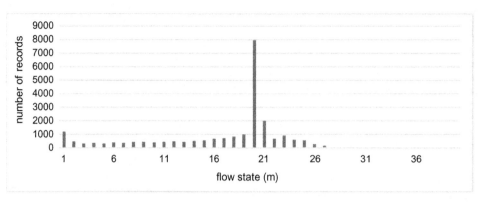

FIG. 15.6 Distribution of power flow states of classification.

more enhanced probability of occurrence as the system marginal price differential gets higher. Regarding subrange 123 the power flows are estimated between 0% and 5% with probability of occurrence at 75%. It is obvious that this case has the clearest results in terms of forecasted power flows for a given $SMPd$. The same accuracy of the forecasted power flows can be succeeded on every other subrange for a smaller step of analysis, whereas a result there would be fewer data included on every subrange, but with essentially enhanced probability of the representative flow state.

Regarding classification 1 where the interconnection capacity is zero, the resulted power flows will be zero independently of the system marginal price differentials. For classification 3 and 4 the same analysis is implemented as for classification 2. As a comment, the whole classification 4 constitutes one subrange as the $SMPd$ of all data is the same and equal to zero.

In order to evaluate the robustness of the model and the precision on the forecasted power flows for a given $SMPd$, the fitting indicator (FI) is calculated according to Eqs. (15.27)–(15.31) as an index of accuracy for the estimated power flow states, where different values of step of analysis are considered. The results of the relative fitting indicators, considering $step_k^{SMPd} = 1$ and $step_k^{pf\%} = 5\%$ are presented in Table 15.8, where the overall fitting indicator is $FI = 47.45\%$. For $step_k^{SMPd} = 0.001$ and $step_k^{pf\%} = 5\%$, the results of the relative fitting indicators are presented in Table 15.9, where the overall fitting indicator is $FI = 72.68\%$. In Table 15.10 the results of the relative fitting indicators are presented considering $step_k^{SMPd} = 0.001$ and $step_k^{pf\%} = 10\%$ and the overall fitting indicator is $FI = 74.77\%$. Table 15.11 provides the results of the fitting indicator considering different steps of analysis.

As presented in Tables 15.8–15.11, the fitting indicator is sensitive to the steps of analysis that will be chosen. More specifically, only the results of classifications 2 and 3 are affected by the values of $step_k^{SMPd}$ and $step_k^{pf\%}$ since the results of classifications 1 and 4 remain the same independently of the analysis steps as explained before. Considering the same $step_k^{pf\%} = 5\%$, the fitting indicator is improved from 47.45% to 47.96% when the length of $SMPd$ subranges gets from 1 to 0.1. It is also obvious that when the length of $SMPd$ subranges is $step_k^{SMPd} = 0.001$ the fitting indicator is improved dramatically to 72.68%. This happens because the historical data of system marginal price differentials are expressed to the third decimal number, so the most accurate allocation to subranges can be succeeded which leads to more enhanced probabilities of the corresponding flow states during the statistical analysis. So the smaller the length of the subranges the better the results will be. On the other hand, when the value of $step_k^{pf\%}$ is getting higher the fitting indicator is improved, but not as much as in the case of minimization of $step_k^{SMPd}$. The $step_k^{pf\%}$ is practically expressing the level of tolerance of the forecasted power flows. As it is presented in Table 15.11, the change of $step_k^{SMPd}$ from 10% to 5%, considering $step_k^{SMPd} = 0.001$, leads to a relatively small change of the fitting indicator from 74.77% to 72.68%. This shows that the model remains robust even if smaller level of tolerance of the forecasted power flows are chosen.

The present statistical analysis is implemented on ex-post historical data of imports. The same analysis can be performed on ex-post historical data of exports. The contribution of this methodology is to define the probability density function (PDF) of power flows, considering the system marginal prices on either side of the interconnection between two power systems. The resulted PDFs can be used for assisting the trading activity in terms of forecasting the power flows, for given system marginal price differentials. The consideration of Physical Transmission Rights (PTRs) of the interconnection is left for future study, since that could give an added value on the results of the present analysis for the recognition of the electricity trading patterns. Another aspect that could bring value to the results of the proposed methodology is the consideration of the seasonality of the historical data by using clustering and neural networks methods which are also left open for future research.

TABLE 15.6 Probability of occurrence per flow state of every SMPd subrange.

		n	1	2	3	4	5	6	7	8	9	10	...	19	20	21	...	123
		$c1^{n}_{SMPd}$	0	−1	−2	−3	−4	−5	−6	−7	−8	−9	...	−18	−19	−20	...	−121.32
		$c2^{n}_{SMPd}$	−1	−2	−3	−4	−5	−6	−7	−8	−9	−10	...	−19	−20	−21	...	−246
m	$c1^{m,2}_{p\%}$	$c1^{m,2}_{p\%}$																
1	0%	5%	14.41%	12.39%	9.65%	7.76%	7.83%	5.49%	5.01%	2.77%	2.64%	1.55%	...	1.03%	0.94%	0.65%	...	75.00%
2	5%	10%	5.37%	4.64%	4.16%	3.32%	1.99%	1.60%	1.37%	2.08%	1.49%	1.09%	...	0.52%	0.63%	0.00%	...	0.00%
3	10%	15%	3.54%	3.78%	2.27%	2.53%	2.30%	1.72%	1.30%	1.23%	0.66%	0.18%	...	0.00%	0.63%	0.32%	...	0.00%
4	15%	20%	3.54%	3.97%	3.28%	2.87%	1.93%	1.66%	1.44%	1.23%	1.07%	0.73%	...	0.00%	0.31%	0.00%	...	0.00%
5	20%	25%	3.16%	2.62%	2.90%	2.70%	2.36%	1.79%	1.51%	1.31%	1.16%	0.64%	...	0.00%	0.00%	0.00%	...	0.00%
6	25%	30%	3.60%	3.48%	2.90%	2.92%	3.11%	1.85%	1.85%	1.38%	1.07%	1.00%	...	0.00%	0.00%	0.97%	...	0.00%
7	30%	35%	3.10%	3.11%	2.52%	2.81%	2.55%	2.04%	1.71%	1.61%	0.58%	0.82%	...	0.26%	0.31%	0.97%	...	0.00%
8	35%	40%	3.79%	3.78%	4.10%	2.81%	2.55%	2.17%	1.44%	1.69%	1.32%	1.19%	...	0.26%	0.31%	0.32%	...	0.00%
9	40%	45%	2.59%	4.21%	3.79%	3.09%	2.61%	1.98%	1.71%	1.31%	1.32%	1.09%	...	1.29%	0.00%	0.32%	...	0.00%
10	45%	50%	3.92%	2.56%	2.59%	3.60%	2.61%	2.49%	1.71%	1.23%	0.91%	1.09%	...	0.26%	0.31%	0.32%	...	0.00%
11	50%	55%	3.35%	2.56%	3.15%	2.42%	2.48%	2.75%	2.47%	1.46%	1.24%	1.55%	...	0.77%	1.57%	0.32%	...	0.00%
12	55%	60%	3.10%	3.66%	3.53%	3.04%	3.29%	2.30%	2.61%	2.23%	1.90%	0.91%	...	0.52%	0.63%	0.65%	...	0.00%
13	60%	65%	3.29%	3.60%	3.09%	3.37%	3.54%	2.30%	2.13%	1.46%	1.57%	1.64%	...	0.77%	0.00%	0.32%	...	0.00%
14	65%	70%	4.11%	4.03%	2.71%	2.87%	2.80%	3.26%	2.81%	2.38%	3.14%	1.00%	...	0.52%	2.20%	0.00%	...	0.00%
15	70%	75%	4.36%	3.90%	3.41%	3.26%	2.92%	3.51%	2.95%	2.15%	1.73%	2.19%	...	0.26%	0.63%	0.65%	...	0.00%
16	75%	80%	4.49%	3.84%	3.79%	3.77%	3.60%	4.34%	3.50%	2.38%	2.48%	2.46%	...	1.55%	1.57%	1.62%	...	25.00%
17	80%	85%	3.67%	4.21%	4.35%	5.28%	3.60%	3.51%	3.43%	3.46%	2.64%	2.10%	...	2.32%	0.63%	0.97%	...	0.00%
18	85%	90%	4.42%	5.31%	5.49%	4.78%	3.79%	5.17%	4.73%	3.38%	3.71%	2.83%	...	0.77%	1.57%	1.62%	...	0.00%
19	90%	95%	4.68%	5.13%	5.17%	6.13%	5.53%	5.24%	5.62%	4.92%	3.63%	4.10%	...	2.06%	3.14%	1.95%	...	0.00%
20	95%	100%	11.50%	13.12%	16.40%	20.35%	23.79%	26.82%	30.59%	36.59%	42.16%	45.21%	...	47.94%	43.40%	49.03%	...	0.00%
21	100%	105%	2.65%	2.81%	5.36%	4.22%	6.27%	7.98%	8.02%	10.45%	10.15%	11.21%	...	13.40%	14.15%	12.34%	...	0.00%
22	105%	110%	1.14%	0.67%	1.83%	1.74%	2.67%	3.07%	4.46%	2.69%	2.56%	3.28%	...	3.61%	4.72%	7.14%	...	0.00%
...	...	...	...	...	...	...	...	...	...	...	...	...	...	...	...	...	...	...
32	155%	160%	0.00%	0.00%	0.00%	0.11%	0.00%	0.00%	0.00%	0.00%	0.00%	0.00%	...	0.00%	0.00%	0.00%	...	0.00%
33	160%	165%	0.00%	0.00%	0.00%	0.06%	0.00%	0.06%	0.00%	0.00%	0.00%	0.00%	...	0.00%	0.00%	0.00%	...	0.00%
...	...	...	...	...	...	...	...	...	...	...	...	...	...	...	...	...	...	...
40	195%	200%	0.00%	0.00%	0.00%	0.00%	0.00%	0.00%	0.00%	0.00%	0.00%	0.00%	...	0.00%	0.00%	0.00%	...	0.00%

TABLE 15.7 Probability density function of SMPd subrange 21.

m	$c1_{pf\%}^{m,\ 2}$	$c1_{pf\%}^{m,\ 2}$	$prob_2^{m,\ 21}$
1	0%	5%	0.65%
2	5%	10%	0.00%
3	10%	15%	0.32%
4	15%	20%	0.00%
5	20%	25%	0.00%
6	25%	30%	0.97%
7	30%	35%	0.97%
8	35%	40%	0.32%
9	40%	45%	0.32%
10	45%	50%	0.32%
11	50%	55%	0.32%
12	55%	60%	0.65%
13	60%	65%	0.32%
14	65%	70%	0.00%
15	70%	75%	0.65%
16	75%	80%	1.62%
17	80%	85%	0.97%
18	85%	90%	1.62%
19	90%	95%	1.95%
20	95%	100%	49.03%
21	100%	105%	12.34%
22	105%	110%	7.14%
23	110%	115%	6.82%
24	115%	120%	5.52%
25	120%	125%	5.84%
26	125%	130%	0.97%
27	130%	135%	0.32%
28	135%	140%	0.00%
29	140%	145%	0.00%
30	145%	150%	0.00%
31	150%	155%	0.00%
32	155%	160%	0.00%
33	160%	165%	0.00%
34	165%	170%	0.00%
35	170%	175%	0.00%
36	175%	180%	0.00%
37	180%	185%	0.00%
38	185%	190%	0.00%
39	190%	195%	0.00%
40	195%	200%	0.00%

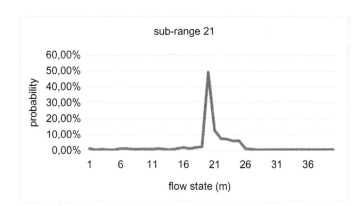

FIG. 15.7 Probability density function of SMPd subrange 21 of classification 2.

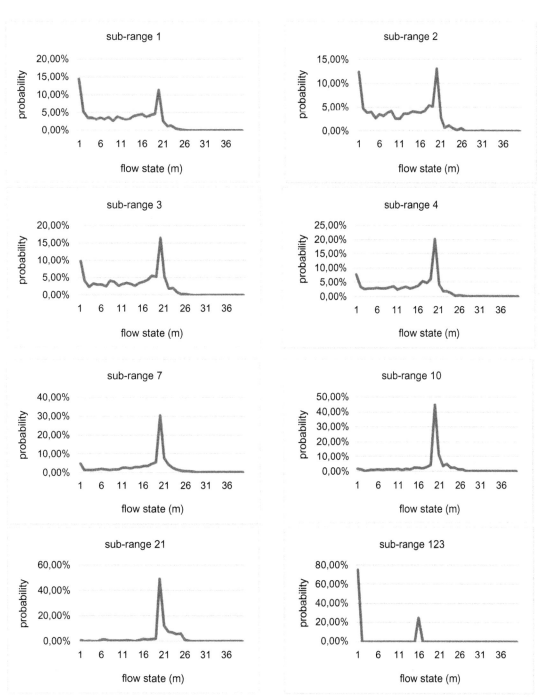

FIG. 15.8 Probability density functions of various subranges of SMPd values of classification 2.

TABLE 15.8 Relative fitting indicators considering length of subranges equal to 1 and length of flow states equal to 5%.

Classification k	Number of fit records	C_k	FI^k
1	7988	7988	100.00%
2	8025	23,577	34.04%
3	3722	9966	37.35%
4	14	89	15.73%

TABLE 15.9 Relative fitting indicators considering length of subranges equal to 0.001 and length of flow states equal to 5%.

Classification k	Number of fit records	C_k	FI^k
1	7988	7988	100.00%
2	15,276	23,577	64.79%
3	6972	9966	69.96%
4	14	89	15.73%

TABLE 15.10 Relative fitting indicators considering length of subranges equal to 0.001 and length of flow states equal to 10%.

Classification k	Number of fit records	C_k	FI^k
1	7988	7988	100.00%
2	15,890	23,577	67.40%
3	7227	9966	72.52%
4	14	89	15.73%

TABLE 15.11 Results of the fitting indicator considering different steps of analysis.

Scenario	$step^{SMPd}$	$step^{pf\%}$	FI
1	0.1	2%	44.70%
2	1	5%	47.45%
3	0.5	5%	47.48%
4	0.1	5%	47.96%
5	0.5	6%	50.99%
6	0.001	5%	72.68%
7	0.001	10%	74.77%

4   Conclusions

In this chapter a statistical analysis on ex-post historical data is introduced. At first, an overview of similar methodologies and problems is presented in order to define the gap in the related literature. The methodology is described in detail, and an application of the proposed methodology is performed for better demonstration of the potential advantages that are derived from this study. The statistical analysis is performed on ex-post historical data of power flows of imports from Italy to Greece for a period of over 4 years. The same analysis can be performed on power flows of exports. The main contribution of this study is the definition of a probability density function (PDF) of power flows considering the system marginal price differentials (*SMPds*) between two power systems. The definition of these PDFs of power flows can assist on the trading activity in terms of power flow forecasting and trading pattern recognition, both valuable to market players. It can also be utilized from system operators for contributing to the optimization of the capacity schedule of the power system and the usage of the interconnection.

In order to define the PDFs of power flows, the initial data are classified according to the interconnection capacity and the direction characterization of the power flows (economical or noneconomical). Then, for every classification, a further partitioning of the *SMPds* is performed and for every resulted subrange of the spectrum a representative flow state (i.e., range of power flow percentages) is defined. As a result, a matrix of probabilities is formulated. So, for a given value of *SMPd*, this model has as a result, a forecast of the power flow, since *SMPd* value belongs to a unique subrange of the initial spectrum, which in turn is represented from a defined flow state. The robustness of the methodology is evaluated by introducing a fitting indicator, which in certain cases is approaching a percentage of 75% of accuracy on the results, compared to the initial historical data. A drawback of this study lies on the fact that, there was no consideration of the Physical Transmission Rights (PTRs) of the interconnection, which is left for future research. For the implementation of the statistical analysis, the Matlab 2019a (https://www.mathworks.com/company/newsroom/mathworks-announces-release-2019a-of-matlab-and-simulink.html) is utilized and the figures are exported to MS Excel for better demonstration of the results.

References

Bąk, I., Chabe, K., Szczecińska, B., 2019. The statistical analysis of road traffic in cities of Poland. Green Cities 2018. Transp. Res. Proc. 39, 14–23.

Bontempo, R., Cardone, M., Manna, M., Vorraro, G., 2017. A statistical approach to the analysis of the surge phenomenon. Energy 124, 502–509.

Chen, Y.-K., Koduvere, H., Gunkel, P.A., Kirkerud, J.G., Skytte, K., Ravn, H., Bolkesjø, T.F., 2020. The role of cross-border power transmission in a renewable-rich power system—a model analysis for Northwestern Europe. J. Environ. Manag. 261, 110194.

Dagoumas, A.S., Koltsaklis, N.E., Panapakidis, I.P., 2017. An integrated model for risk management in electricity trade. Energy 124, 350–363.

Elyas, S.H., Wang, Z., 2016. Statistical analysis of transmission line capacities in electric power grids. In: 2016 IEEE Power & Energy Society Innovative Smart Grid Technologies Conference (ISGT), Minneapolis, MN, pp. 1–5.

Gianfreda, A., Parisio, L., Pelagatti, M., 2016. Revisiting long-run relations in power markets with high RES penetration. Energy Policy 94, 432–445.

Gianfreda, A., Ravazzolo, F., Rossini, L., 2020. Comparing the forecasting performances of linear models for electricity prices with high RES penetration. Int. J. Forecast 36 (3), 974–986, ISSN: 0169-2070, https://doi.org/10.1016/j.ijforecast.2019.11.002.

Katinas, V., Marčiukaitis, M., Gecevičius, G., Markevičius, A., 2017. Statistical analysis of wind characteristics based on Weibull methods for estimation of power generation in Lithuania. Renew. Energy 113, 190–201.

Kumar, S., Möst, D., 2017. Cross border commercial flow of electricity for Germany: what does market data tell us? In: 14th International Conference on the European Energy Market (EEM), Dresden, pp. 1–6.

Lago, J., Ridder, F., Schutter, B., 2018. Forecasting spot electricity prices: deep learning approaches and empirical comparison of traditional algorithms. Appl. Energy 221, 386–405.

Lu, H., Ma, X., Huang, K., Azimi, M., 2020. Carbon trading volume and price forecasting in China using multiple machine learning models. J. Clean. Prod. 249, 119386.

Murray, B., 2019. The development of cross border interconnection and trading. Glob. Energy Interconnect. 2 (3), 254–263.

Pantos, M., Grgic, D., Gubina, F., 2003. New transmission service pricing technique based on actual power flows. In: IEEE PowerTech Conference, Bologna, Italy.

Petrella, A., Sapio, A., 2012. Assessing the impact of forward trading, retail liberalization, and white certificates on the Italian wholesale electricity prices. Energy Policy 40, 307–317.

Plancke, G., Vos, K.D., Jonghe, C.D., Belmans, R., 2016. Efficient use of transmission capacity for cross-border trading: available transfer capacity versus flow-based approach. In: 2016 IEEE International Energy Conference (ENERGYCON), Leuven, pp. 1–5.

Portilla-Yandún, J., Cavaleri, L., Van Vledder, G.P., 2015. Wave spectra partitioning and long term statistical distribution. Ocean Model 96, 148–160.

Portilla-Yandún, J., Barbariol, F., Benetazzo, A., Cavaleri, L., 2019. On the statistical analysis of ocean wave directional spectra. Ocean Eng. 189.

Rocha, P.A.C., Sousa, R.C.d., Andrade, C.F.d., Silva, M.E.V.d., 2012. Comparison of seven numerical methods for determining Weibull parameters for wind energy generation in the northeast region of Brazil. Appl. Energy 89 (1), 395–400.

Schäfer, M., Hofmann, F., Khalek, H.A., Weidlich, A., 2019. Principal cross-border flow patterns in the European electricity markets. In: 16th International Conference on the European Energy Market (EEM), Ljubljana, Slovenia, pp. 1–6.

Sulakov, S.I., 2017. The cross-border trade impact on the transmission losses. In: 15th International Conference on Electrical Machines, Drives and Power Systems (ELMA), Sofia, pp. 115–118.

Unger, E.A., Ulfarsson, G.F., Gardarsson, S.M., Matthiasson, T., 2018. The effect of wind energy production on cross-border electricity pricing: the case of western Denmark in the Nord Pool market. Econ. Anal. Policy 58, 121–130.

Chapter 16

EW Flex: A decentralized flexibility marketplace fostering TSO-DSO cooperation

Sam Hartnett, Jesse Morris, and Ioannis Vlachos
Energy Web, Zug, Switzerland

Abbreviations

ADMS	advanced distribution management system
ADR	automated demand response
DER	distributed energy resource
DERMS	distributed energy resource management system
DID	decentralized identifier
DSO	distribution system operator
EV	electric vehicle
EW	energy web
EW-DOS	energy web decentralized operating system
EWNS	energy web name service
EWT	energy web token
IoT	internet of things
OEM	original equipment manufacturer
SCADA	supervisory control and data acquisition
TSO	transmission system operator
UFTP	USEF Flex trading protocol
USEF	Universal Smart Energy Framework

1 Introduction

Today, utility customers around the world spend roughly ~$140B (USD) on rooftop solar, storage, building controls, smart appliances, and electric vehicles. By 2030 that number is expected to increase tenfold to over $2 trillion (nearly three times greater than global utility investment in generation, transmission, and distribution assets). These naturally diverse assets have the technical potential to provide a range of grid services, but to date they are chronically underutilized (existing demand response and storage assets have about a 0.8% capacity factor) largely due to the costs and complexities associated with registering and managing millions of small-scale assets.

Meanwhile the speed and scale of the shift toward renewable and local power is forcing utilities, regulators, and wholesale markets to re-evaluate conventional paradigms. What happens when the majority of electricity is produced by zero-marginal-cost renewables, much of which is coming from the distribution grid rather than the bulk power system?

New energy market designs are coming fast. Along with them, so are shifts in roles and responsibilities across grid operators, retailers, and customers. There are growing trends toward dynamic retail tariffs, local electricity markets, exposing retail customers to wholesale markets, and even "peer-to-peer" or other types of transactive energy markets that clear from the bottom up. With this context, there is a clear and urgent need to transition customers—and their assets—from being a passive "end point" in a complex supply chain to becoming active participants in a dynamic energy system.

Mathematical Modelling of Contemporary Electricity Markets. https://doi.org/10.1016/B978-0-12-821838-9.00016-5

2 The TSO-DSO coordination issue

Currently there are a lot of discussions around grid architecture as a holistic discipline and especially around some of its discrete elements, such as the discord over electricity market reforms (Clark, 2017), rate design (Lo et al., 2019), and utility business models (Cross-Call et al., 2018). In many ways, these are arguments about the appropriate roles and responsibilities for TSOs, DSOs, retailers, aggregators, and "prosumers" themselves.

Should TSOs extend their current responsibilities down to the level of individual assets on the distribution grid? Should DSOs expand their role to become distribution market operators? Should customer-owned assets participate in wholesale and/or local markets directly, or only via aggregated pools? There is no universally "correct" answer to these questions. However as summarized by Roberts (2019), most answers can be categorized somewhere along this spectrum (Kristov et al., 2016):

1. *Top-down extension*: A top-down approach in which TSOs extend their current responsibilities to operate markets and balance the grid all the way to devices at the distribution level (either directly or via aggregators).
2. *Bottom-up growth*: A bottom-up approach featuring a recursive set of balancing responsibilities and/or markets nested below the transmission-distribution interface; in this approach balancing starts at the individual building (or microgrid) level via devices behind the meter, then buildings form the unit of measure for distribution-level balancing performed by the DSO, and the TSO is focused exclusively on the bulk power system.

The top-down approach more or less continues the pre-existing top-down architecture of our legacy grids, but dramatically expands the scope of the TSO's duties. The bottom-up model implies a more proactive role for distribution utilities (and other local-level stakeholders), requiring them to not only build and maintain the distribution grid but also perform many of the functions traditionally reserved for TSOs, including operating markets (or procuring services) for things like capacity, energy, and balancing.

There are valid arguments for both paths. TSOs have the tools and expertise required to administer markets and maintain system balance, so it seems natural to extend their purview to the distribution system. On the other hand, DSOs already operate the infrastructure (perhaps most significantly, metering) at the distribution level and in most cases have well-established systems for managing customer relationships, DER interconnection processes, and planning processes. Expanding their role can help both the DSO and TSO focus on what they each do best.

Thinking in terms of "maximal" or "minimal" TSO/DSO somewhat misses the point. In reality there are going to be many stakeholders beyond TSOs and DSOs who want to access DERs (not to mention electric vehicles (Miller and Potter, 2020) and charging infrastructure) for various purposes, including aggregators, retailers, OEMs (Energy Web, 2020), and prosumers themselves.

A better way to frame the grid architecture debate is: What is the most secure, efficient way to perform key market processes (from asset qualification, to registration, to activation, to settlement) for vast numbers of assets at the grid edge?

Regardless of which path takes hold in any given market, providing customers a stable supply of electricity as well as access to markets and services calls for the cooperation and coordination of TSOs and DSOs. In Europe, this need has been already identified by the vast majority of TSOs and DSOs (ENTSO-E, 2018) and prioritized by the European Commission as well as the Council of European Energy Regulators (CEER, 2016). In Australia and in Texas, TSOs have articulated an urgent need to "increase the visibility and controllability" (AEMO, 2019) of DER via improved coordination with DSOs. Even vertically integrated utilities must better integrate transmission and distribution system planning (Warren, 2019).

Putting the customer at the center of the grid architecture requires an entirely new set of capabilities for all market participants, no matter which entity acts as the "authority." In either case, there needs to be a secure, scalable way to identify customers and their devices, verify attributes about them (including operational capabilities and financial relationships), and manage permissions (e.g., the ability to participate in a given market) based on those attributes.

There's no way to perform these tasks centrally. It's not about more performant algorithms, more "transactions per second," or any computational performance issue. We already have super-performant technologies, but in many markets DERs remain underutilized (at best) or invisible. A customer- and DER-centric grid architecture requires collaborative governance, particularly distributing and delegating responsibilities traditionally reserved for TSOs or DSOs to a web of individual actors.

3 The Energy Web Decentralized Operating System

EW-DOS is a stack of software and standards, including the Energy Web Chain, that will enable market participants to digitally integrate and orchestrate the billions of low-carbon energy assets, buildings, and customers that will comprise the 21st-century grid. EW-DOS comprises three layers:

- *Trust*, which anchors self-sovereign decentralized digital identities (DIDs) and provides a way to timestamp immutable data-sets and the associated state transitions in smart contracts via the public Energy Web Chain;
- *Utility*, the "middleware" layer of the EW-DOS stack, which simplifies the experience of creating and using decentralized applications with dedicated solutions for high-volume messaging, user-experience tools, and back-end application services; and
- *Toolkit*, with open-source templates for constructing applications that facilitate renewable energy markets, e-mobility programs, and DER market participation.

3.1 Trust layer

The Trust Layer is a multi-party consensus and shared state on the EW Chain

- *EW Chain*: A public, proof-of-authority (PoA) blockchain operated by validator nodes from the EW member ecosystem that features a native token (EWT) and hosts decentralized digital identities, executes smart contracts, and provides proofs for verifying the state of data and events.

3.2 Utility layer

The Utility Layer is a middleware component that give developers tools to easily build user-facing applications that gain the advantages of decentralized digital infrastructure yet deliver familiar UX to customers. The EW-DOS Utility Layer services are provided by Utility nodes, a separate set of nodes hosted by members of the Energy Web community. These services are priced and paid in EWT, the native token of the EW Chain.

- *Energy Web Name Service (EWNS)*: Enables users to map human-readable names (e.g., name.ewc) to their DID address and create a sub-name for other resources, like an email address or smart contract (e.g., resource.name.ewc.). This is a deployment of the Ethereum Name Service on the Energy Web Chain.
- *Key Recovery*: A multi-signature wallet that governs ownership over a DID, solves the "password reset" problem, and prevents adversaries from unilaterally gaining control over a DID (itself a smart contract governed by a key pair) in the event that the identity owner loses access to their original key pair.
- *Transaction Relay*: A service enabling end-users to interact with the EW Chain without needing to hold or manage tokens. Delegated proxy nodes pay for transaction fees in EWT on behalf of users and applications.
- *Messaging*: A decentralized messaging service for high-volume, low-latency (e.g., machine-to- machine) communications that can be integrated with on-chain transactions and signatures.
- *Storage*: EW is developing decentralized storage solutions for content addressed data (those which must not be editable) and key-value data (which contains things that need to have a predictable key or an arbitrary key), but in many cases existing storage solutions (e.g., either private cloud or on-premise database) will be used for commercial applications and the messaging and other chain abstraction components will serve as a connective tissue to on-chain components.
- *Identity Directory*: Decentralized identifiers (DIDs) are a new type of identifier for verifiable, persistent, resolvable, and secure digital identities that are directly owned and controlled by end users. DIDs enable the controller of a DID to prove it has control over itself and to be implemented independently of any centralized registry, identity provider, or certificate authority. The Identity Directory is a smart contract that contains the universal list of DIDs and associated claims on the EW Chain.
- *Bridges*: Purpose-built smart contracts that enable the transfer of tokens, and eventually any arbitrary data or transaction, between different blockchains (e.g., EW Chain to public Ethereum). The first two production bridges are designed to transfer tokens between the EW Chain and the main Ethereum network; one enables users to transfer native EWT from the EW Chain to an ERC-20 representation on Ethereum and the other enables users to transfer DAI stablecoins from the Ethereum network to a bridged DAI on the EW Chain.
- *Oracles*: For use cases where it's beneficial to leverage multiple input sources (e.g., monitoring of local voltage for multi-party reconciliation, reporting of distributed solar for renewable portfolio standards accounting), we are building on top of emerging open-source protocols, particularly the Chainlink protocol, for establishing a network of independent nodes to provide event data to on-chain contracts.
- *Other Chain Abstraction*: In addition to EWNS and the Transaction Relay, we are continuing to develop application programming interfaces (APIs) that make it easier for applications and users to interact with the EW Chain.

3.3 Toolkit layer

The Toolkit Layer is a free, open-source templates that simplify and speed up the process of developing enterprise applications. It consists of the following components:

- *Application Registry*: Application registries act as an "authorization layer" for DIDs, and this reference architecture provides a standardized way to create bespoke registries with administrative features specific to a particular geography, market, or application.
- *EW Origin*: A series of customizable open-source software modules designed to support provenance and traceability use cases, including digital renewable energy marketplaces and demand-side management.
- *EW Flex*: An open-source software architecture for coordinating DER data and operations across organizational and technological boundaries, allowing millions of DERs to participate in wholesale electricity markets and demand-side management programs.
- *Other Toolkits*: We are continuing to develop additional toolkits as we gather additional requirements from our global network of members. In-development toolkits include functionality that enables digital identities to settle payment; automatically conduct evaluation, measurement, and verification (EM&V); post value in escrow; and engage in complex transactions (e.g., financial contracts).

4 EW Flex

EW Flex is an open-source software architecture for coordinating distributed energy resource (DER) data and operations across organizational and technological boundaries. Flex solves existing pain points in harmonizing transmission- and distribution-system operations, managing an ever-growing growing fleet of diverse distributed energy resources, and reconciling data among participants in wholesale markets or across information and operational technology systems within vertically integrated utilities.

Flex consists of a series of toolkits that address the full lifecycle of DER participation in wholesale markets and/or demand-side management programs, from prequalification through settlement. Flex was born out of requirements for integrating one million distribution-level, behind-the-meter batteries into a wholesale frequency regulation market, but can be applied in any regulatory or market context from utility "Bring Your Own Device" programs, to deregulated competitive markets, to emerging electric mobility programs.

4.1 EW Flex architecture

EW Flex makes end-to-end DER participation in electricity markets or demand-side management programs trusted by grid operators and as easy as online shopping for customers. Flex covers six distinct workflows in market operations.

- *Register Market Stakeholders*: The first step in improving data coordination among multiple parties within a given market or program is to register relevant stakeholders - such as the transmission system operator, distribution utilities, balancing responsible parties, aggregators, retailers, hardware manufacturers, and hardware installers - into a common architecture via a universal, secure digital identity. Flex DID allows the stakeholders to create decentralized identifiers (DIDs) and use them to sign messages, authenticate data, and establish permissions for data access or business processes.
- *Pre-qualify DER Types*: Conventional prequalification for large-scale assets typically involves physical commissioning and inspection. That approach doesn't scale to millions of customer-owned assets. Fortunately, those assets are mass-produced by manufacturers who can verify the physical attributes of each DER model. Based on these attributes, the relevant market stakeholders can define permission and/or eligibility criteria for certain DER types to participate in different markets, programs, or services. Flex DID and the EW-DOS Application Registry Reference Architecture combine to establish and enforce eligibility criteria for DER participation in markets based on its attributes. For example, a particular battery or inverter may be qualified to provide ancillary services whereas a smart thermostat may be qualified only for peak-shaving (capacity) services.
- *Register Customers and DERs*: Flex UI enables customers to manage their DIDs, which inform market participation based on their attributes. Customers enrich their DIDs through a process of verifiable claims, in which the customer presents pre-defined documentation or data to a delegated authority to validate each attribute. For example, a customer who owns a rooftop solar system may make a claim about the capacity or model number of their inverter; a hardware vendor or installer who has been authorized by the local grid operator would review the necessary information

(or validate in-person) before signing the claim with their digital identity. As attributes are validated, the underlying digital identity is automatically integrated into application registries that define the terms for market participation. Each DID is fully owned and controlled by its creator forever; in addition to application registries, DIDs can be used as a reference point for any number of applications, systems, and/or datasets. A customer's DID may be linked to a retailer's billing database, a grid operator's DER registry database, and an aggregator's offer management platform.

- *Manage DER Offers/Schedules*: The Flex Core protocol lets grid operators (and/or other market participants) implement bespoke DER offer (or operating schedule) lifecycles for different capacity, energy, or ancillary service products. Flex Core administers permissions for registered DERs in the offer management platform, integrates with existing operational systems (e.g., SCADA, ADMS) using IEC protocols, performs settlement at a granular level (high volumes of small-scale transactions), and enables designated third parties (e.g., aggregators, retailers) to aggregate DERs and provide services to DER owners for optimized pricing. The Flex IoT client implements a secure mechanism for low-compute devices (such as smart inverters, appliances, or controls systems) to submit offers to the Flex Core platform, respond to control signals for activation, calculate baselines for settlement purposes, and connect to other Flex nodes. Combined, these modules enable the customers or delegated third parties (e.g., aggregators) to translate human-readable preferences into machine-readable offer parameters or operational schedules, and use Flex IoT to send these offers to the grid operator and into the Flex Core platform, which can manage offers based on a security-constrained least-cost optimization.
- *Activate DERs*: Depending on the requirements of a given market or program, the activation of DER may be initiated via a price signal or direct command. Flex Core is designed to support high-volume, low-latency communication (as quickly as 500 milliseconds or less) to facilitate DER participation in ancillary services markets but can be customized for any capacity or energy service.
- *Settlement*: Using meter (or other operational) data along with offer data, Flex Core calculates event performance metrics for each activated DER based on market/program rules. Measurement and verification methodology can be customized to any baseline type, program design, or calculation framework. The performance metrics are assigned to each DER identity via Flex DID and can support financial settlement in a variety of ways including on-bill credits, conventional invoices, automated bank transfers, or on-chain transfer of funds.

5 Decentralized vs centralized flexibility marketplaces

EW Flex is unique in its usage of decentralized technology and offers functionality that is not possible in a centralized solution.

- The open Flex architecture enables utilities and grid operators to procure services from DER on an ongoing basis: Many DER initiatives are based on relatively static, long-term contracts. A typical program may define a specified quantity of DER capacity or energy over a multi-year period; this offers the benefit of certainty when it comes to resource adequacy but such contracts require prolonged procurement processes (months to years) and preclude flexibility in the face of changing grid conditions, regulatory paradigms, or business requirements. With Flex, utilities and grid operators can easily access both existing DER and new DER as they are deployed. Such dynamism will be increasingly valuable as customers continue to adopt DER for a wide variety of economic, operational, and environmental reasons. Flex enables continuous procurement of services that reflects the ever-changing DER portfolio within a particular service territory.
- The Decentralized Identity system creates trust while preserving privacy. DIDs and verifiable claims make it possible to prove certain attributes about a given user or DER to any authorized market participant or system without disclosing the underlying information. Accordingly, market stakeholders do not need to necessarily share all (or any) customer data with one another or the Flex Core in order to execute registration, activation, or settlement processes; the settlement and the transaction volume is only available to the parties in the transaction. This empowers all market participants to stay in control of their data and avoids the centralization of information.
- A decentralized architecture enhances resilience and performance. By design, a decentralized system has no single point of failure. Most conventional attack vectors are ineffective against a decentralized implementation of Flex Core, just as it is impossible to shut down all email or DNS built on decentralized protocols. The security and confidentiality of the data is guaranteed by end to end encryption and the encryption of the data at rest. Furthermore, in order to get access to a user's data, the private key of that specific user is required. This makes an attack on the full system much harder as each individual user must be hacked individually before an attacker can gain access to the entire system.

- An open protocol is inherently interoperable with all DER types, systems, and business models. Flex modules enable any DER, regardless of type, manufacturer, or contractual relationship, to establish a universal digital twin that all market participants can trust and rely on to perform market processes. Once the digital twin is established, any number of market participants can integrate DERs into multiple platforms for different services (e.g., wholesale energy vs. ancillary services vs. retailer-specific portfolio hedging) by referencing a common pool of digital identities. This architecture makes it easy to prevent double counting across programs or portfolios, and every user in the system can give and withdraw permission to third parties to act on their behalf, opening the possibilities of value-added services from multiple actors (e.g., aggregators competing to provide proprietary offer strategies or DER pooling). This openness allows for more innovation and greater customer choice.

Fig. 16.1 presents an example architecture for leveraging Flex to develop a DER/demand-side management platform.

5.1 EW Core

The EW Core performs messaging and data storage functions, as well as providing a shared state (i.e., consensus) for key data associated with DIDs for prosumers, market participants, and DER devices via EW's implementation of the W3C Decentralized Identifier standard. This component establishes a secure way to generate and manage key pairs for digital identities on the Energy Web Chain. It also provides methods for establishing and validating DID credentials via verifiable claims.

5.2 Application registry

EW's application registry reference architecture provides a standardized way to create bespoke registries with administrative features specific to a particular geography, market, or application. Utility application registries act as an "authorization" layer, setting the rules and roles for DIDs that wish to participate in a given market or program. EW's reference architecture includes a series of open-source smart contracts and dApps for managing changes and updates to the registry and creating an audit trail of all interactions between DIDs within the registry.

5.3 EW Flex platform

EW Flex follows a modular architecture includes four components, as shown in Fig. 16.2:

- *Flex Core*: The Flex Core module is responsible for the onboarding of digital assets and flexibility market participants, as well as for asset activation and settlement for the provisioned flexibility. Flex Core leverages the application registry reference architecture and the concept of DIDs. Flex Core enables grid operators to manage the full lifecycle of DER

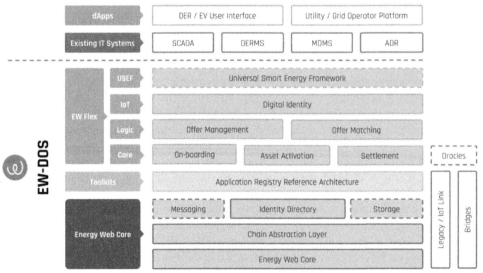

FIG. 16.1 Example architecture DER & EV solutions built on EW-DOS. *(From EWF, 2020. Energy Web Foundation, accessible at: https://www.energyweb.org/, last assessed: 15 June 2020).*

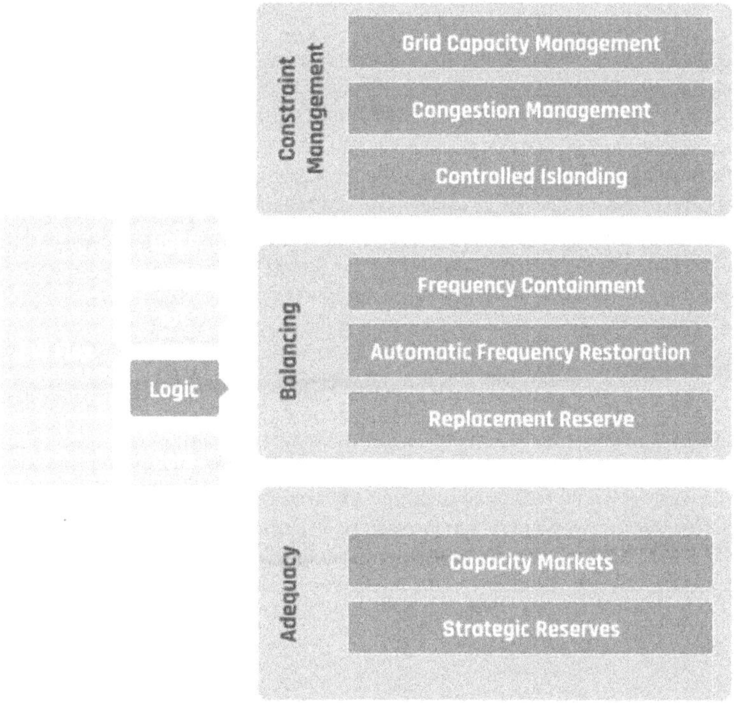

FIG. 16.2 Flex logic example services (derived from the Universal Smart Energy Framework—USEF).

participation in electricity markets, from onboarding, to offering/scheduling, to matching, to activation and settlement. Flex Core surfaces relevant attributes and operational information from qualified DER within their territory and allows the grid operator to set rules and criteria for prequalifying DER in specific markets/programs, establishing constraints and limitations that impact offer optimization, and monitoring DER behavior over time.

- *Flex Logic*: The Flex Logic module implements the business logic of the EW Flex platform. It is responsible for managing the lifecycle of flexibility offers, and also implements algorithms for optimizing the matching of flexibility offers and requests according to the specific use case and the related market rules. By varying the functionality of the Flex Logic module, a multitude of use cases for flexibility can be realized.
- *Flex IoT*: The Flex IoT module implements a Real-Time Operating System for embedded devices. It allows DER and EV/EVSE assets to have their own digital identity via the use of cryptographic chips and to participate automatically in flexibility markets by cryptographically signing flexibility offers and, at the same time, verifying incoming requests for flexibility.
- *Flex USEF*: Flex USEF is the higher layer of EW Flex that implements the Universal Smart Energy Framework (USEF). USEF delivers the market model for the trading and commoditization of energy flexibility, and the architecture, tools and rules to make it work effectively. By making EW Flex to be USEF-compliant we ensure that projects and technologies are connected at the lowest cost, thus guaranteeing interoperability with existing and future technologies. Moreover, Flex USEF implements the USEF Flex Trading Protocol (UFTP). UFTP is a subset of the USEF framework that describes the corresponding market interactions between the various actors to resolve grid constraints by applying congestion management or grid-capacity management. UFTP can be used as a standalone protocol for flexibility forecasting, offering, ordering, and settlement processes.

6 Conclusions

We have presented the EW-DOS and its toolkit, EW Flex, for implementing a flexibility marketplace. Based on the notion of DIDs it so possible that small-scale DERs, such as residential batteries, to participate in multiple markets driven by the TSO and the DSOs. The use of DIDs for building a digital registry of all energy assets will allow for both DSOs, TSOs, aggregators and other energy market stakeholders to exploit at its maximum the available flexibility of the energy assets of the residential users and make them the center and the key beneficiary of the energy transition.

References

AEMO, 2019. Maintaining Power System Security with High Penetrations of Wind and Solar Generation. Australian Enegry Market Operator. Accessible at: https://www.aemo.com.au/-/media/Files/Electricity/NEM/Security_and_Reliability/Future-Energy-Systems/2019/AEMO-RIS-International-Review-Oct-19.pdf. last assessed: 15 June 2020.

CEER, 2016. CEER Position Paper on the Future DSO and TSO Relationship. Council of European Energy Regulators. Accessible at: https://www.ceer.eu/documents/104400/3731907/C16-DS-26-04_DSO-TSO-relationship_PP_21-Sep-2016.pdf. last assessed: 15 June 2020.

Clark, T., 2017. Regulation and Markets: Ideas for Solving the Identity Crisis. Wilkinson Barker Knauer.

Cross-Call, D., Goldenberg, C., Guccione, L., Gold, R., O'Boyle, M., 2018. Navigating Utility Business Model Reform. Rocky Mountain Institute.

Energy Web, 2020. Sonnen Leverages Energy Web Chain, EW Origin for Virtual Power Plant That Saves Wind Energy, Reduces Grid Congestion. accessible at: https://medium.com/energy-web-insights/sonnen-leverages-energy-web-chain-ew-origin-for-virtual-power-plant-that-saves-wind-energy-862d54df4bed. last assessed: 15 June 2020.

ENTSO-E, 2018. TSOs-DSOs to Continue Cooperation for Smarter Electricity Grids. European Network of Transmission System Operators for Electricity. accessible at: https://www.entsoe.eu/news/2018/10/23/tsos-dsos-to-continue-cooperation-for-smarter-electricity-grids/. last assessed: 15 June 2020.

Kristov, L., De Martini, P., Taft, J.D., 2016. A tale of two visions: designing a decentralized transactive electric system. IEEE Power Energy Mag. 14, 63–69.

Lo, H., Blumsack, S., Hines, P., Meyn, S., 2019. Electricity rates for the zero marginal cost grid. Electr. J. 32, 39–43.

Miller, D., Potter, M., 2020. Electric Vehicles Are the Next Dominant Class of Renewable Energy Buyer. Accessible at: https://rmi.org/electric-vehicles-are-the-next-dominant-class-of-renewable-energy-buyers/. last assessed: 15 June 2020.

Roberts, D., 2019. Clean Energy Technologies Threaten to Overwhelm the Grid. Here's How It Can Adapt.

Warren, C., 2019. Distribution system planning gets a makeover - EPRI develops tools to help distribution planners navigate the complexity of a changing grid. EPRI J.

Further reading

EWF, 2020. Energy Web Foundation. accessible at: https://www.energyweb.org/. last assessed: 15 June 2020.

Part IV

Modelling policy challenges in electricity markets

Chapter 17

Forecasting electricity supply shocks: A Bayesian panel VAR analysis

Michael L. Polemis[a] and Nicholas Apergis[b]

[a]Department of Economics, University of Piraeus, Greece and Hellenic Competition Commission, Athens, Greece, [b]University of Derby, Derby, United Kingdom

1 Introduction

Although there is attention by policymakers and government officials on the impact of oil supply shocks on the main macroeconomic variables, such as the level of economic growth or the level of employment (Barsky and Kilian, 2002; Hamilton, 2003; Ramey and Vine, 2011; Kilian, 2008a, b, 2009a, b) little attention has been paid on the examination of the macroeconomic consequences of electricity supply shocks. This strand of literature is rapidly growing and calls for an in-depth examination either from a theoretical or an empirical standpoint.

Our approach deviates from the existing literature focusing solely on the examination of electricity supply interruptions within a microeconomic perspective (Reichl et al., 2013; Nooij et al., 2007; Balducci et al., 2002). Specifically, the study constitutes one of the very few attempts in modelling and estimating the determinants of possible electricity supply shocks on the macroeconomic performance of a large scaled economy, such as the US. More specifically, the empirical methodology adopted in this chapter makes use of modelling GDP per capita growth across US states as time variation in vector autoregression (VAR) models by allowing the coefficients to stochastically vary, while they are also free to vary as a deterministic function of observable economic characteristics, such as total electricity supply or other economic controls, typically, by pooling the data across US states and time in a panel VAR setup for that purpose.

The motivation of this chapter is to investigate the relationship and the possible spillovers between electricity supply shocks and US macroeconomic performance since there is considerable evidence that this relationship has been unstable over time. The analysis uses monthly regional data from the US states, spanning the period January 2001 to September 2016, combining a novel identification strategy for electricity supply shocks based on inequality constraints with the estimation of a time-varying Bayesian panel VAR model (TVBPVAR). This methodology makes use of a Bayesian shrinkage estimator for panel VAR models which, contrary to time series VAR modelling, allows the coefficients to vary as a stochastic function of observable characteristics (Wieladek, 2016). Moreover, it accounts for the presence of cross-section dependence, while it utilizes "*second-generation*" panel unit root tests, which is justified by the fact that traditional stationarity tests (known as "*first-generation*" tests) suffer from size distortions and the ignorance of cross-section dependence.

The contribution of this chapter is threefold. First and foremost, it is the first study that links electricity supply shocks decomposed by fuel mix (i.e., nuclear, coal, renewable energy sources, natural gas) with the US macroeconomic performance. In this way, we attempt to shed some light on the mechanism of electricity supply shocks and how these shocks have changed over time. Moreover, the empirical model allows for time-varying heteroskedasticity in the VAR innovations that accounts for changes in the magnitude of structural shocks and their immediate impact on the US macroeconomic performance. Second, it goes beyond the existing literature in that it uses a particularly long panel of 50 US states on a monthly basis over the period January 2001–September 2016. Third, in contrast to the existing empirical studies which assume that the variables are not correlated across the panel dimension (cross-sectional independence), we perform appropriate methods in order to deal with this issue. This is a common phenomenon appeared in macro-level data resulting in low power and size distortions of tests that assume cross-section independence (Pesaran, 2004). The latter may arise due to common unobserved effects generated by changes in the US states legislation (i.e., taxation, currency regulatory restrictions, import quotas).

Mathematical Modelling of Contemporary Electricity Markets. https://doi.org/10.1016/B978-0-12-821838-9.00017-7

2 Data and sample

The empirical analysis is based on a large panel dataset of 9450 monthly observations. Spanning the period from January 2001 to September 2016 ($N=50$ and $T=189$). The sample selection includes all the 50 US states.

The electricity supply variables are seasonally adjusted and include both total electricity generation (per capita), as well as power production by specific energy source (coal, nuclear, natural gas, oil, hydroelectric, biomass, wind, and solar). The reason for decomposing electricity generation by fuel is to investigate whether different patterns of electricity supply shocks prevail in the industry, thus, affecting the overall macroeconomic performance of the US economy. All the above variables are taken from the EIA and especially from the electricity data browser.[a] The level of economic growth is proxied by per capita real GDP across US states. Measured in 2009 USD. The latter which is drawn from the Regional Economic Accounts of the Bureau of Economic Analysis (BEA), provides the market value of goods and services produced by the labor and property located in a US state.[b] In other words, real GDP by state is an inflation-adjusted measure that is based on national prices for the goods and services produced within each state. Total employment (full-time and part-time) is used as a proxy for the labor force. The aforementioned variable, which is also taken from BEA, includes wage and salary jobs, sole proprietorships, but not unpaid family workers, nor volunteers per US state, over the sample period. School enrolment is used as a proxy for human capital and includes public elementary and secondary schools, by state and jurisdiction. This variable is drawn from the US Department of Education and especially from the National Center for Education Statistics. Gross fixed capital formation includes land improvements, plant, machinery, and equipment purchases, and the construction of roads, railways, and building, including schools, offices, hospitals, private residential dwellings, commercial and industrial buildings and finally net acquisitions of valuables. This indicator is measured in constant 2010 USD prices per US state and is extracted from the DataStream database. Finally, we use the public deficit variable, which is drawn from the US Census Bureau and especially from the Federal, State and Local Governments database of the US Department of Commerce.[c]

3 Empirical methodology

Let us assume the following time-varying coefficient panel VAR model:

$$Y_{c.} = X_{c.}B_{c.} + E_{c.} \quad \text{with} \quad E_{c.} \sim \left(0'_{c.\tau} \sum_c A_{c.\tau}\right) \tag{17.1}$$

where $Y_{c.t}$ is and $1xN$ matrix of N endogenous variables for state c at time t. contains the lags of $Y_{c.}$ and a constant term. The total number of lags is L. and $K=L+1$. The total number of states is $C(T)$. Moreover, it is assumed that $A_{c.}$ is a lower triangular matrix. Next, $y_{c.t} \equiv \text{vec}(Y_{c.t})$. $\beta_{c.\tau} \equiv \text{vec}(B_{c.\tau})$. $a_{c.\tau} \equiv \text{vec}(A_{c.\tau})$ and $e_{c.t} \equiv \text{vec}(E_{c.t})$. In addition, the time-varying characteristic of the coefficients $\beta_{c.}$ and $a_{c.}$ is considered. Based on the work by Wieladek (2016), it is assumed that these coefficients vary as a function of observables:

$$\beta_{c.}|y_{c.}.X_{c.t}.a_{c.\tau}.\sum_c \sim N(D_{c.\tau}\delta_B.\Lambda_{BC}) \tag{17.2}$$

$$a_{c.}|y_{c.}.X_{c.t}.\beta_{c.\tau}.\sum_c \sim N(D_{c.\tau}\delta_A.\Lambda_{AC}) \tag{17.3}$$

where δ_B. δA is a matrix of pooled coefficients across states. Which relate the weakly exogenous variables $D_{c.t}$ to the individual state coefficients $\beta_{c.\tau} A_{c.\tau}$. with the variances Λ_{BC}. Λ_{AC} determining the tightness of these priors. We parameterize $\Lambda_{BC} = \lambda_B L_{BC}$ and $\Lambda_{AC} = \lambda_A L_{AC}$. with λ_A and λ_B being shrinkage parameters, which are estimated from the data. For these parameters, the approach recommended by Jarociński (2010) is followed and which assumes an inverted Gamma density:

$$\lambda_B|y_{c.}.X_{c.t}.\beta_{c.\tau}.\sum_c \sim IG_2 \propto \lambda_B^{-(v+2)/2} \exp(-1/2s/\lambda_B) \tag{17.4}$$

$$\lambda_A|y_{c.}.X_{c.t}.\alpha_{c.\tau}.\sum_c \sim IG_2 \propto \lambda_A^{-(v+2)/2} \exp(-1/2s/\lambda_A) \tag{17.5}$$

---

a. https://www.eia.gov/electricity/data/browser/.
b. https://www.bea.gov/regional/index.htm.
c. https://www.census.gov/govs/.

The greater λ_B and λ_A are. The larger the degree to which the state-specific coefficients are allowed to differ from the common mean. If $\lambda_B \to \infty$ and $\lambda_A \to \infty$ this approach leads to state-by-state estimates. While $\lambda_B = 0$ and $\lambda_A = 0$ implies pooling across all states of the dynamic and contemporaneous coefficients, respectively.

The parameterization of Λ_{BC} and Λ_{AC} in this manner has the econometrically convenient property that it is necessary only to estimate two hyper-parameters, i.e., λ_B and λ_A. to determine the degree of heterogeneity in the lagged dependent variable and contemporaneous coefficients, respectively. However, there is one drawback: the coefficients in $\beta_{c.}$ and $a_{c.}$ may have different magnitudes. In specifying a single parameter that determines the degree of heterogeneity, there is therefore the risk that some coefficients can differ from the common mean by a small fraction of their own size, while others can differ by orders of magnitude. Following the approach proposed in Jarociński (2010) and a procedure analogous to the Litterman (1986) prior. L_{BC} is a matrix of scaling factors used to address this problem. In particular, $L_{BC}(k.n) = \sigma^2_{cn}/\sigma^2_{ck}$. where c denotes the state, n the equation and k the number of the variable regardless of lag. σ^2_{cn} is the estimated variance of the residuals of a univariate auto-regression of the endogenous variable in equation n, of the same order as the VAR, and is obtained pre-estimation. σ^2_{ck} is the corresponding variance for variable k and obtained in an identical manner. L_{AC} is obtained in a similar manner. To the extent that unexpected movements in variables reflect the difference in the size of VAR coefficients, scaling by this ratio of variances allows us to address this issue. Finally, $A'.$ is assumed to be lower triangular, with ones on the diagonal, following the approach in Primiceri (2005). As a result $|A_c'| = \prod a_c = 1$ and $|A'_{c.\,\tau} \sum_c A_{c.\,\tau}| = |\sum_c|$.

Previous works have adopted three different ways of estimating panel VAR models with the structure as set out in Eqs. (17.1)–(17.5). Abbritti and Weber (2010) and Towbin and Weber (2013) assume that $\lambda_B = 0$, implying that B_c is a deterministic function of the vector of weakly exogenous variables. $D_{C.}$. Eqs. (17.2) and (17.3) can be substituted back into Eq. (17.1) and the model can be easily estimated by OLS, equation by equation. If this is assumption is violated, as is likely to be the case with macroeconomic data, estimating the model with state fixed effects leads to dynamic heterogeneity bias (Pesaran and Smith, 1995). Pesaran et al., (1999) use the mean group estimator to address this problem. But to the extent that this approach requires estimation state-by-state, modelling variation in coefficients as a set of more than two exogenous variables is typically not feasible. Even in moderately sized VARs, due to the degrees of freedom considerations. Finally, the coefficients. $\beta_{c.}$ and a, vary with τ, as oppose to t. This mixed frequency structure is an advantage of this framework, since the state specific economic characteristics in $D_{c.\tau}$ may be available only at an annual, as opposed to quarterly frequency.

A completely non-informative prior with s and v set to 0 results in an improper posterior in this case. We, therefore, set both quantities to very small positive numbers, which is equivalent to assuming a weakly informative prior. But it is important to point out that λ is estimated from the total number of coefficients that this prior is applied to, namely the product of state (C), equations (N) and total number of coefficients in each equation (K). Given this large number of effective units, any weakly informative prior will be dominated by the data. Similarly, given that A_C is lower-triangular with ones on the diagonal, a_c^j. where j refers to the equation, can be drawn equation by equation from:

$$\left({}^{\mathrm{j}}_{c.}| \, \alpha'^{j}_{c..} \, E_c. \, \Lambda_{AC}\right) = \left(F_c^{-} \left(\sum_c{}^{-1} \otimes EJ'_{c.t}\right) e_{c.t} + L_{AC}{}^{-1} \lambda_A{}^{-1} \alpha'^{ij}_{c.t.} F_c{}^{-1}\right) \tag{17.6}$$

where $F_c = \sum_c{}^{-1} \otimes EJ'_{c.t} EJ_{c.t} + L_{AC}{}^{-1} \lambda_A{}^{-1} \cdot e_{c.t}$ is the error term of equation j and $EJ'_{c.t}$ contains all of the other relevant $e_{c.}$ "s" as explanatory variables for that equation. Given that $A_{c.\tau}$ is lower-triangular, this means that in the case of the second equation. $EJ'_{c.t}$ will consist of one other error term in the case of the third equation of two, etc. δ_A is drawn from:

$$\left(\delta_A| \, a_{c..} \, \Lambda_{AC}\right) = \left(\sum \sum D'_{c.} \Lambda_{AC}{}^{-1} D_{c.}\right)^{-1} \sum \sum D'_{c.\tau} \Lambda_{AC}{}^{-1} a_{c.\tau}. \left(\sum \sum D'_{c.} \Lambda_{BC}{}^{-1} D_{c.}\right)^{-1}) \tag{17.7}$$

λ_A is treated as a hyper parameter and drawn from the following inverse gamma 2 distribution:

$$p\left(\lambda_A| \, \alpha'_{c.\tau.} a_{c.\tau}\right) = IG_2\left(s + \sum \sum \left(a_{c.\tau} - \alpha'_{c.\tau.}\right)' L_{AC}{}^{-1} \left(a_{c.\tau} - \alpha'_{c.\tau.}\right) \gamma N(N-1)/2 + v\right) \tag{17.8}$$

Finally, the country-specific variance matrix of the residuals. Σ_c is drawn from an inverse-Wishart distribution:

$$\left(\sum_c| \, A_{c.\tau}{}^{-1} \cdot \beta_{c.\tau}\right) = IW\left(U'_c U_c. T_c\right) \tag{17.9}$$

where $U_C = [U_{c.1} \dots U_{c.T}]'$. $U_{c.t} = A_{c.\tau}^{-1} E_{c.t}$ and T_c is the number of observations for each state. For the purposes of our empirical analysis, we estimate this model by repeatedly drawing from the posteriors of the Gibbs sampling chain in (8)–(14) 150.000 times, discarding the first 50.000 draws as burn-in and retaining every 100th of the remaining draws for inference.

4 Results and discussion

Fig. 17.1 shows Impulse Responses Functions (IRFs) for GDP per capita growth to shocks in total electricity supply (bivariate model). at the 10th percentile of total electricity supply and at the 90th percentile. These results illustrate that GDP per capita growth increases following a positive electricity supply shock (across all three distributions), which is a result consistent with several time series and panel data studies in the literature (Narayan et al., 2010; Lorde et al., 2010; Bildirici et al., 2012; Solarin and Shahbaz, 2013; Jakovac and Vlahinic Lenz, 2016).

Fig. 17.1 also illustrates IRFs for GDP per capita growth to shocks in electricity generated by different fuel mix (i.e., coal, nuclear, natural gas, oil, hydro, biomass, solar, wind). The new empirical findings clearly support that decomposed electricity shocks exert a robust positive impact on GDP per capita growth, indicating that all sources of energy seem to be conducive to GDP per capita growth in the case of the US states. However, a closer inspection of Fig. 17.1 reveals several differences between the IRFs for each electricity fuel source.

Specifically, in the case of electricity generated from coal (see first row, second column of the diagram), it is emphasized that the innovations generated by a one standard deviation shock are positive, albeit statistically insignificant, within the first 10 years (125 months approximately) showing an increasing rate of return. Subsequently, the confidence bands become narrow, making the response of GDP per capita growth to electricity from coal shocks after this time period significant. This outcome reveals the low penetration of coal in the electricity generation in the US compared to other alternative fuels, such as nuclear and natural gas, where the confidence bands are much narrower from the beginning of the simulated time period.

It is also interesting to note that the speed of adjustment toward the long-run equilibrium portrays a slightly different pattern among the different categories of electricity supply shocks. To be more specific, in the case of electricity from oil, the innovations generated by a one standard deviation shock are strongly positive for the first 5 years after the initial shock

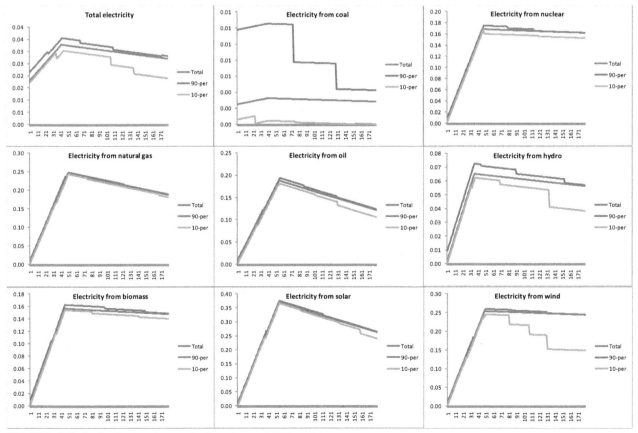

FIG. 17.1 IRFs for the bivariate time-varying Bayesian panel VAR model.

(approximately 55 months), turning into negative (but still statistically significant) thereafter. Similarly, the response of GDP/capita growth to an electricity shock in the Renewable Energy Sources (RES), such as biomass, solar and wind, turns to be negative after the first 5 (simulated) years. However, we must bear in mind that the negative effect is more elastic in the case of electricity generated by biomass, as compared to electricity from solar revealing that GDP/capita growth stabilizes at a faster pace than the latter response after the initial (positive) shock.

Contrary to the above findings, we argue that the response of GDP growth to a one standard deviation shock stemmed from the electricity generation from hydro is positive for the first 2.5 years (nearly 30 months) and negative across the rest of the period (10 years). confirming that the positive effect of GDP/growth to an electricity supply shock is evident only in the short run (short-lived).

5   Conclusions

The empirical findings clearly illustrated that the US macroeconomic performance improved following a positive electricity supply shock (regardless of the energy source it originated). These results could be important for policymakers, academic researchers, and government officials. More specifically, they call for the need to strengthen the effectiveness of energy generating agencies by ensuring systematic replacements of worn-out equipment and necessary tools in order to drastically reduce power losses. Any electricity outages are expected to have spillovers from distorted macroeconomic performance that affect both domestic and global welfare. Furthermore, to sustain economic growth across US states, the national energy policymakers should support two policy coordinates, one centered on capital use, and the other focused on electricity consumption. Tax facilities offered to capital owners and/or low interest rates are strong incentives for new investments, which are expected to stimulate and expand the electricity supply network. In terms of electricity supply, to promote economic growth, energy policies should focus on the price level of electricity or, directly, on its demand side. In this manner, low prices or a strong demand can lead to higher levels of economic growth.

Moreover, US energy policymakers should design and implement sustainable electricity conservation policies without adversely affecting economic growth. Such policies aim at reducing wastage of electricity, such as demand-side management and efficiency improvement measures. Therefore, to ensure the security of supply to meet the demand of electricity, it is important for them to emphasize primarily alternative sources of electricity, such as renewable energy sources that were also shown to exert a positive impact on economic growth. The findings further portray that given that US states seem to be electricity independent states, the performance of certain factors of production, i.e. labor and capital, is not expected to be determined by any enough supply of electricity.

The overall findings validate that electricity supply stimulates economic growth across US states. Intuitively, improvements in electricity supply are a necessity for the enhancement of the economy. It is, therefore, necessary to ensure secure, reliable, efficient, clean and sustainable electricity in the country. Hence, policymakers should put in place any necessary policies that could restructure the electricity supply industry. Restructuring could be done, if needed, by adopting retail competition policies which advocate more players to enter the electricity supply industry, resulting in more electricity being supplied, while keeping electricity prices low.

Acknowledgments

The authors need to express their deep gratitude to Lutz Kilian, Thanasis Stengos, and George Deltas for their valuable comments and suggestions that enhanced the value of this work. Needless to say, the usual disclaimer applies.

References

Abbritti, M., Weber, S., 2010. Labor Market Institutions and the Business Cycle—Unemployment Rigidities vs. Real Wage Rigidities. European Central Bank (Working Paper Series 1183).

Balducci, P.J., Roop, J.M., Schienbein, L.A., Desteese, J.G., Weimar, M.R., 2002. Electrical Power Interruption Cost Estimates for Individual Industries. Sectors and U.S. Economy. PNNL-13799. Pacific Northwest National Laboratory, U.S. Department of Energy.

Barsky, R.B., Kilian, L., 2002. Do we really know that oil caused the great stagflation? A monetary alternative. NBER chapters. In: NBER Macroeconomics Annual 2001, 16. National Bureau of Economic Research, pp. 137–198.

Bildirici, M.E., Bakirtas, T., Kayikci, F., 2012. Economic growth and electricity consumption: auto regressive distributed lag analysis. J. Energy South. Afr. 23, 29–45.

Hamilton, J.D., 2003. What is an oil shock? J. Econ. 113 (2), 363–398.

Jakovac, P., Vlahinic Lenz, N., 2016. Energy and Economy in the Republic of Croatia: Macroeconomic Effects of Electricity Generation and Consumption. University of Rijeka (Working Paper).

Jarociński, M., 2010. Responses to monetary policy shocks in the east and the west of Europe: a comparison. J. Appl. Econ. 25, 833–868.

Kilian, L., 2008a. Exogenous oil supply shocks: how big are they and how much do they matter for the US economy? Rev. Econ. Stat. 90 (2), 216–240.

Kilian, L., 2008b. A comparison of the effects of exogenous oil supply shocks on output and inflation in the G7 countries. J. Eur. Econ. Assoc. 6 (1), 78–121.

Kilian, L., 2009a. Comment on "Causes and Consequences of the Oil Shock of 2007–08" by James D. Hamilton. Brook. Pap. Econ. Act. 1, 267–278.

Kilian, L., 2009b. Not all oil price shocks are alike: disentangling demand and supply shocks in the crude oil market. Am. Econ. Rev. 99 (3), 1053–1069.

Litterman, R., 1986. Forecasting with Bayesian vector autoregressions-five years of experience. J. Bus. Econ. Stat. 4 (1), 25–38.

Lorde, T., Waithe, K., Francis, B., 2010. The importance of electrical energy for economic growth in Barbados. Energy Econ. 32, 1411–1420.

Narayan, K.P., Narayan, S., Stephan, P., 2010. Does electricity consumption panel granger cause GDP? A new global evidence. Appl. Energy 87, 215–238.

Nooij, M., Koopmans, C., Bijvoet, C., 2007. The value of supply security: the costs of power interruptions: economic input for damage reduction and investment in networks. Energy Econ. 29, 277–295.

Pesaran, M.H., 2004. General Diagnostic Tests for Cross Section Dependence in Panels. (Cambridge Working Papers in Economics. No. 435 and CESifo Working Paper. No. 1229).

Pesaran, M.H., Shin, Y., Smith, R.P., 1999. Pooled mean group estimation of dynamic heterogeneous panels. J. Am. Stat. Assoc. 94, 621–634.

Pesaran, M.H., Smith, R., 1995. Estimating long-run relationships from dynamic heterogeneous panels. J. Econ. 68, 79–113.

Primiceri, G., 2005. Time varying structural vector autoregressions and monetary policy. Rev. Econ. Stud. 72 (3), 821–852.

Ramey, V.A., Vine, D., 2011. Oil, automobiles, and the US economy: how much have things really changed? In: NBER Macroeconomics Annual 2010. vol. 25. University of Chicago Press, Chicago, pp. 333–367.

Reichl, J., Schmidthaler, M., Schneider, F., 2013. The value of supply security: the costs of power outages to Austrian households. Firms and the public sector. Energy Econ. 36, 256–261.

Solarin, S.A., Shahbaz, M., 2013. Trivariate causality between economic growth. Urbanization and electricity consumption in Angola: cointegration and causality analysis. Energy Policy 60, 876–884.

Towbin, P., Weber, S., 2013. Limits of floating exchange rates: the role of foreign currency debt and import structure. J. Dev. Econ. 101 (C), 179–194.

Wieladek, T., 2016. The Varying coefficient Bayesian Panel VAR Model. Bank of England (Staff Working Paper No. 578).

Chapter 18

Formulating and estimating an energy security index: A geopolitical review of quantitative approaches

John A. Paravantis

Department of International and European Studies, University of Piraeus, Piraeus, Greece

Without data, you're just another person with an opinion.

—W. Edwards Deming (1900–1993)

1 Introduction

Although energy has been crucial for economic development throughout human history, it is an ill-distributed economic good, subject to price fluctuations, with repercussions in many domains of life. Because of its size, technological scale, and monetary investment, energy has always been entwined with geopolitics, and intricately connected to governments and political contention.

Energy may be regarded as a geopolitical tool to pursue state goals, adding an element of hard power with overlapping military, political and economic dimensions (Morgenthau, 1985; Klare, 2008). The ability of a country to access the energy resources that it needs to maintain the current level of its national power without compromising its foreign policy, economic, social and environmental objectives, is referred to as energy security. Energy security is paramount to human security (Sovacool and Mukherjee, 2011) and has become an increasingly popular concept for policy makers, academics and entrepreneurs. The attention has been caused by the emergence of new giants of the world economy and their rising energy demand. Current energy security challenges relate to satisfying the energy demand of developing nations with rapidly rising income such as China and India. At the same time, peak oil concerns are not as relevant as they were before the shale revolution (Crooks, 2015), and there is more confidence about the physical availability of oil.

Yet, defining energy security more concretely brings to mind the parable of the three blind men and the elephant (Narula and Reddy, 2015). There is no universal definition of energy security (Kruyt et al., 2009; APERC, 2007), which Chester (2010) has aptly described as "*slippery*" and "*polysemic*". One may be lost in a multitude of dimensions, components and metrics. As a result, energy security has become an umbrella term for different policy goals (Winzer, 2012).

What issues does energy research address? Sovacool (2014) answered this question by carrying out a content analysis of 4444 papers from *Energy Policy*, *The Energy Journal* and *the Electricity Journal*, out of which 75 research questions were gleaned. It turns out that authors from various disciplines covered the following topics of energy research in the 15 years preceding Sovacool's paper: markets, supply and demand, behavior, climate change, pollution, land use, research and development, industry, politics (including energy security), pricing and prices, institutions, investment, public policy, and development. Energy security was among the topics that have demanded larger shares of author attention over time.

This chapter reviews and documents the research literature that defines energy security by proposing specific dimensions, components and corresponding metrics. It also discusses quantitative and qualitative methods that may be used to calculate a complex numerical index for energy security. In an assessment of energy security of 18 countries from 1990 to 2010, Sovacool (2013a), a world-class expert in the field, identified a number of shortcomings of energy security index studies, among which ignoring geopolitical relationships. Therefore, this chapter adopts a geopolitical perspective, focusing on research that addresses regional concerns and carries out cross-country comparisons.

The subject of quantitative methods for the computation of energy security indexes is vast. Månsson et al. (2014) provided an extensive review of commonly used methodologies for the quantitative evaluation of the supply dimension of

Mathematical Modelling of Contemporary Electricity Markets. https://doi.org/10.1016/B978-0-12-821838-9.00020-7

energy security. This chapter is not as comprehensive as their focused approach, but (a) reviews the concept and definitions of energy security, (b) addresses a wider spectrum of its dimensions reviewing quantitative and qualitative research, and (c) adopts a geopolitical perspective.

The rest of this chapter is structured as follows: The concept and formulation of energy security is examined, with a discussion of its dimensions and components (Section 2). Then energy security is linked to metrics and quantitative approaches for the estimation of an energy security index (Section 3), with details given on the role of energy markets (Section 3.1), the use of qualitative techniques (Section 3.2), weighting and aggregating (Section 3.3), using other indexes (Section 3.4), and forecasting (Section 3.5). The chapter is rounded up with the conclusions (Section 4).

2 Conceptualizing energy security

As pointed out by Cherp and Jewell (2014), a classic definition of energy security has been provided by Yergin (1988), who visualized energy security as the assurance of "*adequate, reliable supplies of energy at reasonable prices*", adding a geopolitical component by qualifying that this assurance must be provided "*in ways that do not jeopardize national values or objectives*".

Energy security means different things to different countries, depending on: their geographical location; their natural resource endowment; their economic disposition (Luft and Korin, 2009); their status as producer/exporter, consumer/importer or transit (Johansson, 2013), their vulnerability to energy supply disruptions; their political system; their ideological views and perceptions (Marquina, 2008); and the status of their international relations, e.g., reliance on Russian gas depends on historical experiences during the Cold War (Leonard and Popescu, 2007, as cited by Johansson, 2013). Examined over different historical time frames, the concept of energy security is dynamic and fluid, with evolving energy policy challenges (Månsson et al., 2014; Winzer, 2012).

Månsson et al. (2014) comment on the multiple, vague and often diverging meanings of energy security and its link to human security, and explain that energy security is difficult to define both because it represents multiple dimensions as well as because of the different perceptions of stakeholders. Countries may value the parameters of energy security differently depending on natural resources endowment, economic development, industrialization, and geopolitical realities. While some countries may strive to provide energy access to their poor population in rural or urban areas, others may prioritize their industry and service sectors.

Energy security is composed of a small number of dimensions; each dimension contains components; and each component may be measured by metrics, i.e., quantitative or qualitative indicators. When all metrics, components and dimensions are aggregated, an energy security index is obtained. To measure energy security, its dimensions, components and metrics must be defined and quantified based on available data. This section discusses how energy security is conceptualized with dimensions and components.

Dimensions and components may be combined in numerous ways. In a paper evaluating the energy security in the Asia Pacific, Sovacool (2011a) reported that were at least 45 different definitions of energy security that shared a great deal of similarity, and led to difficulties in terms of the operationality of the concept. Ang et al. (2015) identified 83 energy security definitions in the literature. Some of the most eminent will now be reviewed.

In an extension to the original International Energy Agency (IEA) definition of energy security, the Asia Pacific Energy Research Centre (APERC, 2007) highlighted the so-called four As of energy security: (1) availability of the supply of energy resources; (2) affordability of the price of energy resources so that economic performance is not affected adversely; (3) accessibility to all social actors; and (4) acceptability from a sustainability standpoint. The first two As (availability and affordability) constitute the classic approach to energy security (20th century), while the latter two (accessibility and acceptability) reflect certain contemporary concerns (21st century), e.g., fuel poverty and global climate change. Other definitions of energy security also use the term availability to imply stable and uninterrupted supply of energy (IEA, 2007; EC, 2000; Yergin, 2006), while some authors use the term reliability to refer to the role of energy infrastructure (Jun et al., 2009; WEC, 2016a). As for accessibility, it has been at the center of energy security debates and policy approaches into the 21st century (Kopp, 2014). Cherp and Jewell (2014) compared the four As to the five As of access to health care (availability, accessibility, accommodation, affordability and acceptability).

The four-A definition may be enhanced or expanded. For instance, it may be argued that different energy sources relate to the dimensions of energy security differently, e.g., with oil, physical and economic availability may be its preeminent aspect, while with shale oil and gas, environmental acceptability may be an important concern. Furthermore, Goldthau and Sovacool (2012) talked about the following three key energy challenges: energy security, energy justice, and a low carbon transition, highlighting the need to consider energy security as a democracy issue, equity as an important aspect of accessibility, and global climate change as an important aspect of acceptability. In a final example, in a 2013 speech in

Yale University, Daniel Yergin has argued (Yale University, 2013) that there are three new dimensions of energy security: (1) physical security in respect to threats like terrorism; (2) integrated energy shocks caused by natural disasters such as hurricanes and superstorms, in which electric power, fuel, emergency services, etc. are all down at the same time and entire regions are immobilized; and (3) cyberthreats that can affect large scale production and create global havoc.

A similar set of four dimensions of energy security has been proposed by Sovacool and Rafey (2011): (1) availability, i.e., diversifying fuels, preparing for disruption recovery, and minimizing dependence on foreign supplies; (2) affordability, i.e., providing affordable energy services, and minimizing price volatility; (3) efficiency and development, i.e., improving energy efficiency, altering consumer attitudes, and developing energy infrastructure; and (4) environmental and social stewardship, i.e., protecting the natural environment, communities and future generations.

In a paper examining the role of coal in energy security, Sovacool et al. (2011a) considered the following four criteria, which correspond to dimensions of energy security: (1) availability, i.e., fuel diversification and reduced dependence on foreign supplies; (2) affordability, i.e., affordable energy services and reduced price volatility; (3) efficiency, i.e., innovation, performance of energy equipment, and consumer behavior; and (4) stewardship, i.e., social and environmental sustainability.

Alhajji (2007) differentiated between six dimensions of energy security: economic, environmental, social, foreign policy, technical and security. Vivoda (2010) listed seven salient energy security dimensions: environment, technology, demand side management, socio-cultural or political factors, human security, international elements like geopolitics, and the formulation of energy security policy; and 44 attributes of energy security. In research on how hydrogen energy systems can enhance energy security, Ren et al. (2014) presented a six As definition of energy security: availability (i.e., geological existence), (geopolitical) accessibility, (economic) affordability, (environmental) acceptability, (technological) applicability, and adaptability (related to substitution).

In a paper surveying the attitudes of energy consumers towards energy security, Knox-Hayes et al. (2013) extracted the following dimensions of energy security: (1) availability, indicating security of supply and affordability; (2) welfare, indicating equity and environmental quality; (3) efficiency, representing various factors including low energy intensity and small-scale energy (with some overlap with welfare); (4) affordability, indicating (among other factors) price affordability and small-scale energy; (5) environment, appearing to be very similar to welfare; (6) transparency, standing for equity, transparency and education; (7) climate, connected to global climate change and having significant overlap with welfare and environment; and (8) equity, overlapping with other dimensions.

Goldthau and Sovacool (2012) suggested that energy is characterized by stronger vertical complexity (cutting through technological systems), more pronounced horizontal complexity (involving many actors across geographical scales), higher entailed costs (such as capital intensity and externalities), and stronger path dependency and inertia (with obvious socio-technical lock-in effects). Energy security, energy justice and low carbon transition were discussed as constituting challenges to an effective global governance.

In a paper assessing five different energy security policy packages, Sovacool and Saunders (2014) discussed the complexity of energy security by citing Drexel Kleber, the Director of the Strategic Operations Power Surety Task Force of the US Department of Defense, who argued that energy security is an amalgamation of the following five Ss: (1) *surety*, i.e., certainty of access to energy and fuel sources; (2) *survivability*, i.e., resilience and durability against potential damage; (3) *supply*, i.e., physical availability of energy resources; (4) *sufficiency*, i.e., adequacy of supply from various sources; and (5) *sustainability*, i.e., prolongation of supply with mitigation of environmental impacts. The authors conceptualized energy security as having the following dimensions: (1) *availability* of energy fuels and services, which they call the bedrock of energy security; (2) *affordability*, i.e., stable and affordable costs for current and future generations (encompassing a sense of sustainability also included in the fourth component); (3) *safety* and technological resilience; (4) *environmental*, social and economic sustainability; and (5) *governance*, i.e., quality, transparency and accountability. Finally, the authors explored five energy security policy packages, targeting: (1) oil self-sufficiency, i.e., lessening dependence on foreign fuels; (2) energy affordability, i.e., maintaining cheap prices; (3) energy access, i.e., providing universal access to grids and services for heating and cooking; (4) climate change mitigation by reducing greenhouse gas emissions and lowering the carbon footprint of the energy sector; and (5) water availability, i.e., promoting forms of energy production that can operate in areas of water stress and scarcity.

In a paper on the energy security in Asia Pacific, Sovacool (2011a) presented more dimensions of energy security identified by experts: availability, i.e., self-sufficiency; dependency, i.e., being energy independent; diversification, referring to variety and disparity; decentralization, i.e., small-scale energy; innovation, i.e., research and development; investment and employment; trade, encompassing geopolitics and interconnectedness; production, i.e., economic growth, reliability; price stability, including predictability; affordability, i.e., low cost, competition, subsidization, profitability; governance, including the concepts of transparency, accountability, legitimacy as well as resource curse; access, i.e., equity and energy poverty; reliability, i.e., safety; literacy, referring to education and quality of knowledge; resilience, i.e., stockpiling and adaptation; land use management; water quality and availability; ambient and indoor pollution and human health; energy efficiency, including conservation; and mitigation of greenhouse gas emissions. Regarding energy independence, self-sufficiency may be a more pragmatic target since even a producer/exporter country cannot really extricate itself from the global energy markets and their vulnerabilities (Zhao, 2019).

In a paper synthesizing a framework for energy security, Sovacool and Mukherjee (2011) presented the following dimensions with corresponding components: (1) availability, i.e., security of supply and production, dependency and diversification; (2) affordability, i.e., price stability, access and equity, decentralization and affordability; (3) technology development and efficiency, i.e., innovation and research, safety and reliability, resilience and adaptive capacity, efficiency and energy intensity, and investment and employment; (4) environmental and social sustainability, i.e., land use, water, climate change, and pollution; and (5) regulation and governance, i.e., governance, trade and regional interconnectivity, competition and markets, and knowledge and access to information. These authors also presented a comprehensive list of simple, intermediate and complex indicators of different aspects of energy security.

How are the dimensions of energy security covered by the research literature? In a paper examining 40 years of energy security trends, Brown et al. (2014) found that 91 peer-reviewed academic articles covered the dimensions of energy security differently. In particular, availability was covered by 82% of the examined articles; affordability by 51% of the articles; energy and economic efficiency by 34% of the articles; and environmental stewardship by 26% of the articles.

3   Estimating energy security

Månsson et al. (2014) used literature material of 2011–2013 to review commonly used methodologies (rather than individual papers) for the quantitative evaluation of the supply dimension of energy security. The authors argue that a secure supply chain is a vital requirement for the provision of energy services, e.g., crude oil may be extracted in a remote country, transported by sea or pipeline to a refinery, and distributed by road to gasoline stations.

Månsson et al. (2014) argue that although the term energy security is widely used, there is less interest in developing methodologies for evaluating energy security. They found a great variety of methodologies, which they attributed to the diversity of the background of researchers involved in energy security research (e.g., political science, economics, engineering, natural sciences) and the different aspects of energy security. They noted that:

- *Economic* methodologies are used to monetize effects, predict the future, and study market efficiency.
- *Engineering* methodologies target empirical data and include multi-criteria analysis and optimization to study reliability, weigh threats to supply security, and compare the security of different energy systems.
- Geological depletion, resource potential and diversity are examined in *natural science* approaches that target physical availability.
- *Political science* provides perspectives on how international relations and energy security interact, and use quantitative methods (such as game theory) to analyze interdependence, distribution of power, and incentives to use energy as a weapon.
- *Systems* studies combine engineering and economics, and use models to examine scenarios and generate forecasts at different levels of detail. The authors pointed out that the aggregation of indicators into indexes can disguise the vulnerability of specific sectors, such as transportation.
- Finally, *complexity* studies examine system interaction and feedback mechanisms.

Månsson et al. (2014) classified the reviewed methodologies into the following groups:

1. *Primary energy supply*: availability of resources; geographic concentration of resources; forecasts and scenarios of energy export; and average production cost and cost fluctuations.
2. *Upstream markets and imports*: systematic and specific risk; reliability of suppliers and supply routes; dependence, independence and interdependence among states.
3. *Domestic markets and infrastructure*: reliability, resilience and robustness of infrastructure.
4. *Economic vulnerability*: welfare loss from high or volatile prices; economic consequences of resource scarcity; outage cost from power disruptions.
5. *Integrated perspectives*: holistic supply chain security and security of energy services; spatial and temporal security comparisons.

They note that methods may be used to study threats and hazards (such as an extreme weather event or war), disturbances (such as a supply shortage or a price spike), and consequences of impacts or strains (such as welfare effects) to the energy supply system.

On the geopolitics of energy security, Månsson et al. (2014) note that the geographical concentration of energy resources may increase over time, as fewer countries are producers. They discuss political stability and investments in exploration and extraction activities as related indicators, and mention that the historic level of political instability in producer countries is used in assessing the future reliability of a country. They argue that the domestic demand is a function of political, economic and demographic factors. They suggest political stability and the investment climate in producer countries as indicators that may affect supply. Finally, they frame domestic renewables as a substitute for imported fossil fuels, thus impacting energy dependence favorably.

Månsson et al. (2014) mention that complexity approaches such as Agent-Based Modelling (ABM) may be used to represent how individuals or organizations interact in a socio-technical system. Market decentralization and the impact of policies on incentives may be studied with ABM. The application of complexity approaches including ABD in global politics has been reviewed by Paravantis (2016).

Indicators that have been used to assess the exposure to high energy prices include the energy use by a nation or sector, spending on energy, and the energy use per capita. Price shock may be analyzed with historical price data, and its risk may be mitigated by switching suppliers and supply routes, guided by an import risk analysis. Månsson et al., 2014 mention that the direct and indirect cost of a power supply interruption for end users may be measured with the Value of Lost Load (VoLL). Finally, the authors wrote that the optimal level of reliability may be measured with: (1) surveys and interviews, e.g., willingness to pay to avoid an outage; (2) lost production and leisure time during an outage; (3) market behavior; and (4) case studies.

The part of Månsson et al. (2014) work that reviews the integrated perspectives is the most interesting for this chapter. The authors argue that integrating different aspects of energy security calls for prioritization. Indexes of energy security may be calculated by using (1) a scoring/ranking system for each indicator and (2) a weighting scheme to aggregate several indicators into a single value. The authors make the point that the choice of indicators and weighting factors is usually not transparent nor well explained. Some indexes rely on expert opinions to set weighting factors, introducing a qualitative aspect into what is essentially quantitative research. Such aggregation may make detailed assessment of strengths and weaknesses difficult. Cost-benefit and multicriteria analysis are other method of prioritizing, often requiring significant probability and magnitude or severity inputs. Finally, real options theory (which helps decide whether to invest now or wait) may be used to analyze how energy companies respond to incomplete knowledge and uncertain situations. The authors write that such research perspectives may include cross-national (i.e., spatial) comparisons, following developments and trends over time, and evaluating alternative scenarios. Finally, the authors warn that perceptions and preferences of what energy security is and how it should be valued may differ among countries and time periods, so it may not be appropriate to use the same index to analyze heterogeneous countries at different times.

Kisel et al. (2016) discuss short and long-term methods related to the assessment of energy security. The authors point out that the definition of energy security is widely disputed in the literature. They compare the World Energy Council's (WEC) energy sustainability index to the World Energy Forum's (WEF) energy triangle. The WEC's energy sustainability index contains the following indicators: diversity of electricity generation (Shannon index); ratio of total energy production to consumption; distribution losses (as percentage of generation); five-year compound aggregate growth rate of the ration of the Total Primary Energy Consumption (TPEC) to GDP; days of oil and oil product stocks (as fuel export merchandise value as percentage of GDP for exporters, and net fuel imports as percentage of GDP for importers). The WEF energy triangle contains the following indicators: diversity of total primary energy supply (Herfindahl index); electrification ration; quality of electricity supply (obtained by survey); percentage of population using solid fuels for cooking; import dependence; and diversification of import counterparts. The authors present a variety of indicators for technical energy security, organized in operational resilience, technical resilience, and technical vulnerability sections. They also discuss indicators for economic energy dependence, including the economic energy dependence of the power sector; the merchandise value of imports of the power sector; the merchandise value of exports of the power sector; and the GDP of a country. Finally, they also discuss the difficulties in assessing numerically the political affectability of energy security, mentioning political stability and corruption. The authors close their work by organizing all these indicators into an energy security matrix.

Adopting an international perspective, Sovacool and Brown (2009) researched the interaction among dimensions of energy security in 22 industrialized countries (including the US) from 1970 to 2005. Conflicts were presented among the following dimensions of energy security: energy availability, energy affordability, energy and economic efficiency, and environmental stewardship. The following 10 metrics were grouped in four dimensions: (1) availability, measured by oil import dependence, natural gas import dependence, and availability of alternative fuels; (2) affordability, measured by electricity and gasoline retail prices; (3) energy and economic efficiency, measured by energy intensity, energy use per capita, and average on-road fuel economy for passenger vehicles; and (4) environmental stewardship, measured by sulfur dioxide and carbon dioxide emissions. These were evaluated without aggregation into an energy security index. Of the countries, only Belgium, Denmark, Japan and the UK were found to have made progress on multiple dimensions of energy security. These metrics recur in later research by Sovacool.

Sovacool and Rafey (2011) examined a coal fired-power plant project in South Africa, arguing that different aspects of energy security may conflict with one another. They wrote of the following dimensions of energy security: availability, affordability, efficiency and development, and environmental and social stewardship. They also mentioned the following metrics: electricity prices, (motivation to) invest in renewable energy, green jobs, rich-poor gap, export orientation of the economy, greenhouse has emissions, environmental degradation associated with mining and combustion of coal.

Bambawale and Sovacool (2011a) examined China's energy security from the perspective of energy users. A review of the academic literature resulted in the formulation of seven hypotheses related to the security of supply, self sufficiency and trade, climate change, decentralization, energy efficiency, research and innovation, and geopolitics. The geopolitical hypothesis questioned whether China would emphasize military and geopolitical security given that its energy demand were likely to lead to conflicting interests with other large energy consuming nations. An online survey collected 312 responses (at a response rate of 78%). The survey did not contain direct questions on the geopolitical hypothesis, so references to it were inferred from other items. The security of supply emerged as the most important dimension, supporting the author's hypothesis about the importance of geopolitical security.

In a similar work, Bambawale and Sovacool (2011b) sampled the perspective of government, business, civil society, and academic stakeholders in India. A survey (administered both online and offline) was completed by 172 respondents. Seven hypotheses were distilled from the literature review, related to: security of supply, equitable access, research and development, energy efficiency, self sufficiency and trade, nuclear energy, and the energy-water nexus. The security of supply was ranked as first or second in importance by 40% of respondents, the highest such percentage of the previous hypotheses.

It has become evident that there is a multitude of energy security indicators. In the aforementioned paper by Sovacool and Mukherjee (2011), the authors suggest that energy security is a multidimensional concept. Five dimensions and 20 components were examined, and an impressive total of 320 simple and 52 complex indicators and metrics were tabulated. Turning to components and metrics, energy reserves and stockpiles, fuel mixes and diversification, price stability and affordability, justice and equity, technology development, energy efficiency, resilience, investment, environmental quality, governance, and regulation were considered to influence and thus form part of contemporary national energy security issues. The concept of an integrated composite index was proposed without computational details as to the aggregation method. The authors warn that collecting data for energy security metrics is not an easy task.

Sovacool and Brown (2009) considered energy security to be defined according to the following criteria (i.e., dimensions), which may be measured with corresponding metrics:

1. *Availability*, measured by: oil and natural gas import dependence; availability of alternative fuels.
2. *Affordability*, measured by: retail electricity, gasoline and petrol prices.
3. *Energy and economic efficiency*, measured by: energy intensity; electricity use per capita; average fuel economy of passenger vehicles.
4. *Environmental stewardship*, measured by sulfur dioxide (SO_2) and carbon dioxide (CO_2) emissions.

In a paper evaluating the energy security performance of 18 countries from 1990 to 2010, Sovacool et al. (2011b) presented a more detailed list of dimensions, components and corresponding metrics:

1. *Availability* is related to the total primary energy supply per capita (in thousand tons of oil equivalent); average reserve to production ratio for fossil fuel sources (as remaining years of production); self sufficiency (as percent energy demand produced domestically); and share of renewable energy in total primary energy supply (in percent of supply).
2. *Affordability* is related to the stability of electricity prices (in percent change); percent population with high quality connections to the electricity grid (in percent of electrification); households dependent on traditional fuels (as percent of population using solid fuels); and the average retail price of gasoline (in US$ in purchasing power parities for 100 liters of regular gasoline).
3. *Technology development and efficiency* is related to research intensity (as percent of total government expenditures devoted to research and development); energy intensity (as energy consumption per dollar of GDP); grid efficiency (as percent electricity transmission and distribution losses); and energy resources and stockpiles (as years of energy reserves left).
4. *Environmental sustainability* is related to the forest cover (in percent of land area); water availability (as percent of population with access to improved water); per capita carbon dioxide emissions (in metric tons of carbon dioxide per capita); and per capita sulfur dioxide emissions (in metric tons of carbon dioxide per capita).

5. Finally, *regulation and governance* is related to the worldwide governance ratings (as a score); annual energy exports (in 2009 US$ in purchasing power parities); per capita energy subsidies (in 2009 US$ in purchasing power parities); and the quality of energy information (as percent complete data).

In a paper responding to critique, Sovacool (2012) tabulated the same list of five dimensions with components and metrics.

In the aforementioned paper assessing the energy security performance of 18 countries in Asia Pacific from 1990 to 2010 (Sovacool, 2013a), the following dimensions and components were listed (with 20 metrics mentioned as in previous research): (1) *availability*, with the components of security of supply, production, dependency and diversification; (2) *affordability*, with the components of stability, access, equity and affordability; (3) *technology development and efficiency*, with the components of innovation and research, energy efficiency, safety and reliability, and resilience; (4) *environmental sustainability*, with the components of land use, water, climate change, and pollution; and (5) *regulation and governance*, with the components of governance, trade and connectivity, competition, and information. The following shortcomings of energy security index studies were identified: (a) topical focus, either on industrial countries of the EU, OECD and North America or geared towards sustainable development and energy poverty; (b) scope and coverage, with many index studies being sector specific (e.g., electricity, oil, fossil fuels), ignoring geopolitical considerations, and using unbalanced or limited metrics; (c) transparency, i.e., hiding underlying assumptions, dynamics and weights, so that indexes play the role of "*Trojan horses … dressed a certain way to get inside the gates of energy policymaking*"; and (d) continuity, i.e., being snapshots rather than covering a number of years. A great disparity was found among countries and trade-offs among energy security components were established.

Sovacool (2013b) carried out an analysis of 19 countries and two case studies in the Asia Pacific from 1990 to 2010. His research involved interviews, surveys, and an international workshop. The energy security dimensions and metrics used were as in Sovacool (2012). It was found that Malaysia showed the most improvement and Myanmar the least improvement of energy security over time.

In a study of Denmark, Sovacool (2013c) found it to be the most energy secure country. The core of Denmark's success is a commitment to energy efficiency; prolonged taxes on energy fuels, electricity, and carbon dioxide; and incentives for combined heat and power and wind turbines. The author argues that social opposition to larger wind turbines and consolidation of wind farms which exclude farmers and local cooperatives. Recent development included the Danish Society of Engineers Energy Plan, which was based on reducing energy demand, improving energy efficiency, expanding renewable energy, and promoting intelligent energy system (a component that has not received much coverage in the literature), all of which hint at energy security dimensions. Denmark sought to obtain 30% of their total energy supply from renewable sources by 2025.

In a cross-national survey of attitudes towards energy security, Knox-Hayes et al. (2013) analyzed mostly data from online and print version of the survey from 10 countries. The questionnaire was structured so that energy security attitudes were measured in multiple dimensions. Factor and Correlate Analysis rendered the following (partially overlapping) dimensions of energy security, each a function of relevant questionnaire items:

1. *availability*, a function of secure oil, trade, depletion, price signal, and affordable price,
2. *welfare*, a function of equity, land, water, pollution, climate change, and emissions,
3. *efficiency*, a function of trade, small scale, low energy, research and development, equity, transparency, and education,
4. *affordability*, a function of price signal, affordable price, small scale, research and development, and equity,
5. *environment*, a function of land, water, pollution, climate change, and emissions,
6. *transparency*, a function of equity, transparency, and education,
7. *climate*, a function of climate change, and emissions,
8. *equity*, a function of equity, transparency, education, land, and water.

Multiple regression models were estimated with the energy security factors as dependent variables and sociodemographic and regional predictors as independent variables. This research represents an original method of establishing both the dimensions of energy security and their dependence on socioeconomic and regional characteristics.

In the aforementioned research striving to determine meaningful dimensions, components and metrics, Ren and Sovacool (2014) presented one of the most detailed definitions of energy security, involving the following dimensions, components and metrics:

1. *Availability*, measured by: security of supply, equal to $\frac{\text{total production energy}}{\text{total consumed energy}}$; self-sufficiency, equal to $\frac{\text{imported energy}}{\text{total consumed energy}}$; diversification, measured by a diversity index such as the Shannon-Wiener; renewable energy, equal to $\frac{\text{renewable energy}}{\text{total consumed energy}}$; and technological maturity, a qualitative metric.

2. *Affordability*, measured by: price stability, equal to the deviations of price about a global mean value; dependency, equal to $\frac{\text{total imported energy}}{\text{population}}$; market liquidity, a qualitative metric; decentralization, equal to $\frac{\text{total energy by distributed and small scale generation}}{\text{total energy production}}$; electrification, equal to the percentage of population with reliable access to grid; and equity, equal to the percentage of households depending on wood, straw, etc. for cooking and heating.
3. *Acceptability*, measured by the following qualitative metrics: environment, a composite of several "*micro aspects*" that are "*measured individually*"; social satisfaction, national governance, international governance, transparency, and investment and employment.
4. *Accessibility*, measured by the following qualitative metrics: import stability, trade, political stability, military power, and safety and reliability, all qualitative metrics.

Sovacool (2015) pointed out that, further to being a national or geopolitical concern, energy security also has a household dimension (i.e., fuel poverty), which has been under-examined in energy research.

Ren and Sovacool (2015) examined China's energy security and used a multicriteria decision making technique (the Analytic Hierarchy Process, AHP) to prioritize hydroelectricity, wind energy, solar energy, biomass, and nuclear energy. The dimension of availability was represented by the metrics of current and future installed capacity, and current and future electricity generation. The dimension of affordability was represented by the metric of electricity price. The dimension of accessibility was represented by the metrics of technology maturity, and resource reliability. Finally, the dimension of acceptability was represented by the metrics of carbon dioxide mitigation, social acceptability, and governmental support. Hydroelectricity and wind power were found to be the most promising, and nuclear and solar power the least promising in terms of enhancing energy security.

In a paper analyzing 11,000 technological accidents from 1874 to 2014, Sovacool et al. (2015) argued that the assessment of accident risk is a key component of energy security. They also mention that the International Energy Agency (IEA) considers that small modular biomass, geothermal and solar devices can deliver energy security benefits more rapidly and comprehensively than larger systems.

In a survey of 2495 respondents in 11 countries (including Denmark and the US), Sovacool and Tambo (2016) used two focus groups to develop the following 16 dimensions of energy security described in detail: securing a supply of fossil fuels and uranium; bolstering trade in energy fuels and commodities; minimizing the depletion of domestically available fuels; providing predictable and clear price signals; enabling affordably priced energy services; providing equitable access to energy services; decentralizing to small-scale energy supply; lowering energy intensity (i.e., energy use per unit of GDP); researching and developing new energy technologies; ensuring transparency and participation in project siting and decision-making; offering energy education and information; preserving land and forests; enhancing the availability and quality of water; minimizing air pollution; responding to climate change/adaptation; and reducing greenhouse gas emissions/mitigation. They furthermore investigated five propositions related to the influence of culture; being green; the centrality of oil and gas; the salience of energy trade; and the necessity of affordable prices. Various intercountry comparisons were found, e.g., trade, exports and interconnectivity were important to citizens of Denmark.

Studying how energy users perceive the dimensions of energy security, Sovacool (2016) polled 2500 respondents in 11 countries including the US, Germany and Denmark. Using the dimensions of Sovacool and Tambo (2016), Sovacool tested nine literature hypotheses related to national, economic, political, professional, and epistemic cultural approaches. Water (and energy research), air pollution, security of supply, and research and development were among the highest rated dimensions; decentralization and depletion among the lowest. Results were not very different from one nation to another, and green stereotypes were found to be hardly maintained, e.g., Danes and Germans did not rate green energy systems differently from respondents from other nations. This research indicates that the public perceives the relative importance of the dimensions of energy security differently, but in a way that is not nation specific.

Sovacool and Walter (2018) examined country data from 1980 to 2010 to assess five hypotheses linking hydropower to more violent conflict, higher rates of poverty, lower economic growth, higher rates of public dept, and more susceptibility to corruption. Poverty was measured with the poverty gap; economic development with GDP per capita; debt with total debt stocks; and corruption with the World Bank Worldwide Governance Indicators (which was preferred to the Corruption Perception Index of Transparency International). There were five country classes, characterizing countries at a stage of hydropower construction, hydropower production, members of the Organization of Petroleum Exporting Countries (OPEC), low income, and countries without hydropower. Regression analysis was used to establish that hydropower construction had a positive effect and hydropower production a negative on conflict years (in a specific timeframe). Both hydropower construction and production were positively associated with the poverty gap. The authors concluded that the hydroelectric resource curse is a real phenomenon.

Laldjebaev et al. (2018) write about the vulnerability approach that focused on the risks toward the natural, technical, political and economic dimensions of energy security. Considering Tajikistan, the authors highlight energy security vulnerabilities including neglect of environmental conditions (e.g., melting of glaciers, avalanches); insufficient energy production capacity (and lack of qualified experts); unreliable and expensive energy imports; technical and economic losses caused by a dwindling power infrastructure; inadequate transparency in the power sector; lack of regional cooperation in energy and water resource sharing (which may lead to disenfranchisement and political unrest); and inadequate financial resources to address these challenges. Energy security and its vulnerabilities are discussed in the context of the World Bank (concentrating on energy efficiency, investment, trade promotion, and energy policy), the United Nations Development Program (UNDP, emphasizing renewable energy for all), and the government pathway.

In researching public perceptions in Japan, Valentine and Sovacool (2019) mention how the two oil crises of the 1970s represented the worst possible concerns. It was in part on that basis that nuclear power was framed as a path to enhanced energy security.

In the aforementioned paper by Brown et al. (2014), a Factor Analysis carried out by the authors concluded that: availability was mostly a function of oil import dependence, on road fuel intensity, and natural gas import dependence (in decreasing order of importance); affordability was a function of electricity and gasoline retail prices; energy and economic efficiency was a function of electricity use per capita, and energy per GDP intensity; and environmental stewardship was a function of CO_2 and SO_2 emissions.

In an econometric work, Valdés et al. (2016) used panel data regression for the energy sector across 21 European Union (EU) member states from 1990 to 2013 to investigate the link of energy security to renewable energy. They present an interesting causal taxonomy of energy risks, according to which geopolitical and technical factors constitute primary risks, with all other risks (e.g., related to interruption, prices, human health, and the environment) being secondary, and indicators such as energy intensity representing vulnerabilities (risk exposure). They tabulate the following dimensions of energy security (with indicators indicated in parentheses): environmental (Kyoto protocol, energy and carbon intensity), security of supply (energy imports, gas and oil dependence, the Herfindahl-Hirschman primary energy diversity index, and contribution of coal, oil, gas and nuclear to electricity generation), and competitiveness (oil, gas and coal price, and GPD per capita). In their econometric analysis, they detected nonlinearity, outliers, and multicollinearity and heteroscedasticity. They also used unit root tests to establish the presence of nonstationarity and resorted to estimation methods appropriate for the type of errors present in their panel date regressions. They concluded that energy security issues have a significant role in the deployment of renewable energy sources.

In a game-theoretic approach, Popesku and Hurduzeu (2015) examined non-cooperative and cooperative scenarios for analyzing future energy challenges for Europe. Disruptions in the Ukrainian flow of gas were analyzed as a non-cooperative game. They also modeled the European Union-Russia interactions as a Prisoner's Dilemma, where each actor was locked in trying to impose its will rather than seek a cooperative arrangement. They also discussed cooperative games among coalitions of countries, and in this context discussed how Europe attempts to secure alternative arrangements for importing gas as Liquified Natural Gas (LNG) from the Gulf or the US, or from countries of North Africa or through alternative routes without crossing Russian territory. Game theory may help enlarge or clarify the definition of dimensions of components of energy security.

3.1   The role of energy markets

In the early 1970s, energy security in major oil-importing countries was viewed mostly as an oil substitution issue, i.e., reduced dependence on foreign oil imports (Khatib, 2000). Developments in oil and gas and the emergence of global energy markets have largely changed that view. Proven reserves, stocks, and suppliers have increased; trade is flourishing; and prices have become flexible and transparent, determined more by market forces than cartel arrangement. As market forces dominate, the global energy landscape is characterized by liberalization, deregulation, and a diminishing role for the state. It is costly for a government to intervene against the market for an extended period (Khatib, 2000). In this global energy market landscape, the issues affecting energy systems have increased in number and complexity (Kucharski and Unesaki, 2015). Energy is viewed as a complex adaptive sociotechnical system of systems, with multiple interdependencies; global energy markets are a related important complex system interacting with energy security. Rising energy demand in the developing countries with an expected increase in the extraction and distribution technological infrastructure will change the global energy security landscape (Grand View Research, 2019).

Markets produce undeniable benefits to consumers (such as cost reduction, innovation, technological advances, better allocation of resources); at the same time, they appear to be able to adjust to changing circumstances more easily than governments (Khatib, 2000). Yergin (2013) considers a well-functioning energy market to be one of the 10 principles of energy security, with diversification being the most important and the most challenging one, requiring large investments in infrastructure and renewable energy (Truffer, 2014). Boosted by globalization, the liberalization and deregulation of energy markets in importing countries; the increased competition resulting from regulatory reforms; and the development of oil futures and forwards markets, have promoted energy security (Khatib, 2000).

Export markets participate in the diversification of energy resources (Kucharski and Unesaki, 2015). Khatib (2000) argues that diversity is more important for energy security than the origin of supply, with mechanisms for securing diversity including market instruments (such as payments for reserve capacity) or regulation (such as requiring the storage of a certain quantity of backup fuel supply). For energy exporting countries, the diversification of export markets can help reduce the risk of restrictive trade policies in importing countries (Kucharski and Unesaki, 2015).

Countries with rising energy exports must have reliable access to energy markets globally, and secure open sea-lanes to serve those markets (Goldwyn, 2013). Markets distant from a gas-producing region can import and use natural gas as long as they are served by a suitable port (Stringer, 2008). If such a port (or a connecting pipeline) does not exist, countries can still purchase regasified liquified natural gas (LNG) through neighboring countries, which makes relations with such a neighbor very important. LNG is not limited to transportation by pipeline. The development of spot markets, where LNG may be bought at a short notice, has added significant flexibility to the arsenal of tools available to policymakers for managing energy security. The LNG market though is a double-edged sword, as it creates new global dependencies that are vulnerable to disruption (Yergin, 2013).

Energy "*safety*" (Grand View Research, 2019) may be distinguished into short-term and long-term. Short-term energy safety is related to the ability of the system to respond to changes in the demand-supply curve while long-term energy safety is related to investments in the energy sector. Energy markets are mostly related to energy security temporalities of a very short-term to medium-term nature, where they can help enhance stability and resilience (Kucharski and Unesaki, 2015). Volatility in oil prices contributes to energy insecurity (Khatib, 2000), and cost spikes cause economic damage (Grand View Research, 2019). Markets send price signals that help adjust the demand and supply of energy, mitigating the effects of short-term shocks to the energy system (Kucharski and Unesaki, 2015). Instruments for stabilizing the oil market are multiplying and improving, e.g., strategic stocks held by oil companies and major importing countries, development and liberalization of energy markets, regional and global agreements (Khatib, 2000).

Natural disasters and black swan events may have cataclysmic impacts on energy markets and energy security. Geopolitical co-opetition and conflict also impact energy markets and energy security. Low probability high impact markets shocks include the current COVID-19 pandemic, which has seen oil prices dipping below zero ("Oil prices dip below zero as producers forced to pay to dispose of excess", The Guardian, April 20, 2020). Oil prices that low constitute a great opportunity for a country to boost its energy security by refilling its strategic reserves.

The liberalization of energy markets has empowered consumers and other actors. In fact, as decisions in free markets are made by (even small and medium) market players rather than governments, the political dimension of energy security must be reconsidered and redefined (Khatib, 2000). It is questionable whether consumers and small or medium market players are capable of selecting (or their motives can guide them to select) the best options, suggesting a need for the government to take action to protect energy security. Left on their own, markets may respond nervously to rumors or distorted information (Khatib, 2000); stability may have to be restored by the state. Also, the equity component of energy security may require government actions, e.g., to protect the interests of remote and isolated consumers. Furthermore, it is questionable whether energy markets can internalize political risk and how that affects energy security (Khatib, 2000). Visionary, bold or costly decisions, such as diversifying fuels and encouraging renewable energy, cannot be made by markets alone (Khatib, 2000). The important goal of energy security cannot be left entirely to markets; pursuing and safeguarding energy security in a liberalized market environment will likely require state guidance.

Having provided a literature background, attention now turns to methods related to energy security and the operation of energy and financial markets. On their review of methods related to *primary energy supply*, Månsson et al. (2014) noted that historical production figures, future demand forecasts, and physical supply constraints are used to develop scenarios and forecasts. The national welfare lost by declining availability of oil has been calculated in the literature. On data quality, they warn that some researchers have reported that commonly used figures on fossil fuel stocks and forecast extraction rates are overestimated. They further note that overestimating the potential of primary fuels may result in lock-in effects, while underestimating their potential may motivate investments in expensive and uncompetitive alternatives. Regarding indicators, they mention that the total stock (amount of recoverable resources) and the production rate are used in the literature, with the first being more important. The reserves to production ration is considered deceptive because it fails to account for aboveground problems and future production profiles. They also point out that there is a difference between (global) oil extraction and the fraction available for exports. Finally, they argue that the weather, seasonal patterns, climate change and technology may affect production and its variability.

On economic aspects of energy security research, Månsson et al. (2014) note that the literature often divided the global energy system into regions and analyzes the global mix of future energy sources with top-down macroeconomic and bottom-up technical models. They also suggest that the economically irrational behavior of suppliers results in inefficient oil world markets. High production costs are not framed as a security concern although their volatility and unpredictability are. The authors also note a nonlinear relationship between resource scarcity and production cost, which may cause sudden price movements. They point out that available energy storage, alternative production facilities and demand response mediate price volatility. Finally, they suggest that access, demand, and the ability to pay differ among energy users.

Turning to the review of methods related to *upstream markets and imports*, Månsson et al. (2014) note that upstream stages are primarily analyzed on long-term trends focusing on technical and below the ground issues (e.g., resource scarcity, geographical concentration of resources). For comparison, the authors write that downstream stages are analyzed on reliability, (economic) vulnerabilities, and resilience to internal and external disturbances. The authors argue that interactions among nations are shaped by foreign policy objectives. Importing energy is regarded as detrimental to national energy security because it exposes country to risks outside its jurisdiction, so import independence and less reliance on individual exporters are valid policy targets. On the other hand, while imports are a risk to energy security, they may be used (along strategic petroleum reserves) to compensate for domestic production losses. Some supplier states may have the incentive and the capacity to use energy flows as a geopolitical weapon, e.g., by restricting or cutting off the flow of energy for political reasons. Such interactions may be analyzed by game theory.

To assess the risks of supply routes, political stability and bargaining power among exporter, transit and importer countries have been examined in the literature (Månsson et al., 2014). Dependence on upstream energy markets is a related indicator. The reliability a supplier may be measured with assessed with a generic risk indicator such as the International Country Risk Guide (ICRG) or World Bank governance indicators. The authors discuss specific (i.e., diversifiable) risk, systematic (related to market) risk), and systemic risk (related to market collapse). Market collapse (as in the COVID-19 pandemic) is a systemic risk. When available information is incomplete, the best hedge option is to diversify. Diversity reduces systematic energy risk and has three dimensions: variety, balance, and disparity. As a final note on upstream markets and import, the authors note that financial portfolio theory may be used to model diversity.

On their review of methods related to *domestic markets and infrastructure*, Månsson et al. (2014) ask whether the infrastructure (e.g., electricity or gas grid) and market design are sufficient to provide an adequate level of energy security. In their review, they note that the reliability and vulnerability of infrastructure may be considered at different time periods. Although more renewable energy helps fight climate change, it may affect system reliability and volatility of prices due to its intermittent nature. Future changes under different regulations and market designs are also of concern.

On their review of methods related to *economic vulnerability*, Månsson et al. (2014) mention how excess wealth may be transferred to producer countries, welfare may be reduced, and the balance of trade may be negatively affected. Supply disturbances translate to micro scale (individual users) and macro scale (national economy) disruptions, and may result in price increases and other disruptions downstream. Reviewed studies have compared policies (such as end-use energy efficiency or replacement of oil with biofuel) to assess cost efficiency and reduce dependence on foreign oil. Security policies proposed are demand side options and fuel switching, with the capacity to switch among fuels being a proxy of system vulnerabilities. The economic consequences of a persistent decline in oil production for importing nations has also been studied.

Indicators that have been used to assess the exposure to high energy prices include the energy use by a nation or sector, spending on energy, and the energy use per capita. Price shock may be analyzed with historical price data, and its risk may be mitigated by switching suppliers and supply routes, guided by an import risk analysis. Månsson et al. (2014) mention that the direct and indirect cost of a power supply interruption for end users may be measured with the Value of Lost Load (VoLL). Finally, the authors wrote that the optimal level of reliability may be measured with: (1) surveys and interviews, e.g., willingness to pay to avoid an outage; (2) lost production and leisure time during an outage; (3) market behavior; and (4) case studies.

3.2 Incorporating qualitative techniques

To estimate an energy security index, it is possible to complement a quantitative approach with qualitative techniques such as interviews. Some pertinent examples are discussed.

Sovacool (2009) explored the proposal for the Trans-ASEAN Gas Pipeline (TAGP) in Southeast Asia, with a chronology commencing in 1975. He carried out over 100 interviews at government institutions, development banks, universities, consulting firms, energy companies, and nongovernmental organizations (NGOs). The energy policy organizational structure of ASEAN was discussed. He wrote that the factors pushing TAGP investment included economic development, foreign exchange, environmental stewardship, and energy security. Technical, economic, legal, political, social, and environmental challenges to implementation were discussed

In another work, Sovacool (2011a) conducted 64 semi-structured interviews of energy experts in related organizations. Many energy security dimensions were identified: availability, dependency, diversification, decentralization, innovation, investment, trade, production, price stability, affordability, governance, access, reliability, literacy, resilience, land use, water, pollution, efficiency, and greenhouse gas emissions. It may be argued that these dimensions are too many, not clear-cut nor well defined, corresponding to components rather than dimensions. As an example, an environmental dimension could include land use, water, pollution and greenhouse gas emissions, with a corresponding economy on the metrics used. Many metrics and indicators related to these dimensions were also proposed by the experts and were tabulated. Sovacool listed the following types of environmental damage: lead emissions; ocean oil pollution; cadmium emissions; sulfur emissions; methane emissions; nitrogen fixation; mercury emissions; nitrous oxide flows; particulate emissions; non-methane hydrocarbon emissions; and carbon dioxide emissions.

Paravantis (2019) conducted expert interviews to assess the relative importance of the seven dimension of energy security proposed in that paper. A small group of engineering, economic and geopolitical energy experts was selected, including junior and senior academic faculty (with experience in energy, environment, transportation, and geopolitics) and senior professionals (with experience in environment and water management). The interviews contained a brief semi-structured part (the results of which are reported here) and a longer structured part. During the semi-structured part, the experts were (1) asked to rate the importance of seven dimensions of energy security proposed by the author (and shown in Fig. 18.1) and (2) give their opinion on the way the dimensions were defined.

Ratings were on a scale from one to 10. The author included his own ratings in the group, deciding that little personal bias could be introduced in the framework of a semi-structured interview (Pezalla et al., 2012). The expert's average ratings of the importance of each energy security dimension is shown in Fig. 1. Physical availability was deemed to be the most important dimension (in accordance with its extensive coverage in the research literature), receiving an average rating of 8.8 (out of 10). Technology development, economic affordability and governance were next, with an average importance of 8. Social accessibility and unconventional threats received an average rating of 6.8. Finally, the natural environment was considered the least important dimension (in agreement with the lack of experts working in the non-profit sector), with an average rating of 5.8.

Some further interview findings were reported:

- Most experts tended to rate dimensions nearer their discipline as more important, reflecting a form of cognitive bias.
- A couple of experts thought that there was a little overlap among some of the dimensions, but could not suggest ways of overcoming it.
- An intelligence expert argued that data quality and intelligence should be a separate dimension.
- There was a debate as to whether the impact of conventional warfare should be included in one of the existing dimensions or create an additional war dimension; the author thought that this was accounted for implicitly through its impacts in almost all dimensions, following the usual practice of the reviewed literature.
- Finally, the author's ratings compared well with those of the other experts.

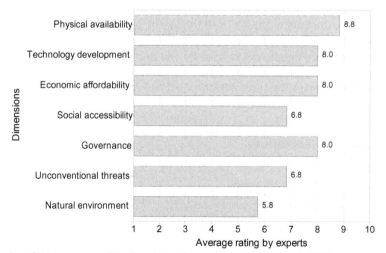

FIG. 18.1 Average expert rating of the importance of the dimensions of energy security (Paravantis, 2019).

Paravantis advises that these expert ratings be interpreted with caution because they represent nothing more than an overall sense of relative importance of the dimensions of energy security. Specific countries must have prioritized energy issues differently at certain historical milestones, e.g., OPEC versus western countries during the Oil Shocks of the 1970s; or Ukraine, Russia and the European Union during the gas crises of the late 2000s. So, the relative importance of each energy security dimension in fact depends upon the historical time frame and region or country considered.

While on the topic of interviews, how are the different dimensions of energy security perceived by different economic actors? In his paper examining seven suppositions about energy security in the United States, Sovacool (2011b) presented the following expert suppositions pertaining to energy security issues: (1) security of supply and trade; (2) energy democracy; (3) energy research; (4) energy efficiency; (5) affordability; (6) environmental pollution; and (7) climate change. Empirical research carried out by the author concluded that different dimensions of energy security are indeed perceived to be of different importance by those working in different sectors of the economy:

- The private sector considered the following four energy security dimensions to be the most important (rating over 4.5 out of a maximum of 5): (1) conducting research and development on new and innovative energy technologies; (2) providing available and clean water; (3) minimizing the destruction of forests and the degradation of land and soil; and (4) minimizing air pollution.
- Among government occupations, more (i.e., eight) dimensions were rated over 4.5, including the four of the private sector plus the following: (5) reducing greenhouse gas emissions; (6) minimizing the impact of climate change; (7) assuring equitable access to energy services to all of its citizens; and (8) informing consumers and promoting social and community education about energy issues.
- With universities, even more dimensions were rated over 4.5, including the four of the private sector plus the following: (5) reducing greenhouse gas emissions; (6) minimizing the impact of climate change; (7) informing consumers and promote social and community education about energy issues; (8) assuring equitable access to energy services to all citizens; (9) ensuring transparency and participation in energy permitting, siting, and decision making; and (10) having low energy intensity.
- The non-profit sector rated the following dimensions over 4.5: (1) providing available and clean water; (2) minimizing air pollution; (3) conducting research and development on new and innovative energy technologies; (4) minimizing the destruction of forests and the degradation of land and soil; (5) reducing greenhouse gas emissions; (6) minimizing the impact of climate change; (7) informing consumers and promoting social and community education about energy issues; (8) assuring equitable access to energy services to all citizens; (9) ensuring transparency and participation in energy permitting, siting, and decision making; and (10) having a secure supply of coal, gas, oil and/or uranium.
- Finally, those working in intergovernmental occupations rated the first two dimensions of the private sector and the following dimensions with a score over 4.5: (3) minimizing air pollution; (4) having a secure supply of coal, gas, oil and/or uranium; (5) promoting trade in energy products; technologies, and exports; (6) reducing greenhouse gas emissions; (7) informing consumers and promoting social and community education about energy issues; (8) assuring equitable access to energy services to all citizens; and (9) having low energy intensity.

Considering the perspective of the public, a couple of research publications that wrote about "*energy tribes*" but have received little attention over time. Thomson (1987) wrote of the existence of three such groups in society: business as usual, middle of the road, and radical change now. Caputo (2009) wrote of the existence of four such ways of thinking in society: egalitarianism, individualism, fatalism and hierarchy. Membership in different energy tribes reflects overlapping sets of rationality, different sets of beliefs, and different cultural values. People in different energy tribes place different bounds on what is credible/incredible, possible/impossible, sensible/foolish and rational/irrational. As a result, they have different attitudes and beliefs, and accept different solutions. Since policies can move forward only if embraced by a large majority for a long time, the existence of energy tribes means that only "*messy*" or "*clumsy*" policy solutions, combining the logic of different energy tribes, have a chance of working.

3.3 Weighting and aggregating components and dimensions

How may the different metrics, components and dimensions be aggregated into a single energy security index? One approach is to not aggregate, analyzing instead the raw indicators, possibly after making them unidirectional, converting them to a score (out of 100), and treating all of them as having the same weight (e.g., Sovacool, 2013a). Such an energy security index may be considered more of a scorecard (same source).

A simple way of aggregating 10 indicators into an easy-to-compute energy security index was described by Brown et al. (2014). Part of that work is replicated here for illustration. Relying on the dimensions, components and metrics of Sovacool and Brown (2009), the 10 variables shown in Table 18.1 (2010 indicator values) were converted to z-scores and added with

TABLE 18.1 Energy security performance index for 22 OECD countries, 2010.

Country	Oil import dependence (%)	z-Score	Petrol transport fuel (%)	z-Score	Natural gas import dependence (%)	z-Score	Electricity retail price (c/kwh)	z-Score	Gasoline price ($/L)	z-Score
Australia	21.2	−1.29	95.8	0.31	0.0	−1.40	12.5	−0.97	1.27	−1.35
Austria	82.7	0.33	88.8	−2.15	74.8	0.27	20.1	0.09	1.63	−0.38
Belgium	98.1	0.73	94.4	−0.18	99.3	0.82	16.5	−0.41	1.87	0.27
Canada	0.0	−1.84	93.2	−0.61	0.0	−1.40	7.6	−1.65	1.21	−1.52
Denmark	0.0	−1.84	98.6	1.29	0.0	−1.40	39.6	2.81	2	0.62
Finland	93.3	0.61	95.4	0.17	100.0	0.83	17.2	−0.31	1.94	0.46
France	94.4	0.64	91.9	−1.06	98.4	0.80	16.9	−0.35	1.98	0.57
Germany	92.7	0.59	90.3	−1.62	78.0	0.34	26.3	0.96	1.9	0.35
Greece	98.0	0.73	97.9	1.04	100.0	0.83	13.0	−0.90	2.05	0.75
Ireland	98.2	0.74	97.5	0.90	93.3	0.68	26.7	1.01	1.78	0.02
Italy	91.0	0.55	92.0	−1.03	90.5	0.62	30.5	1.54	1.87	0.27
Japan	96.1	0.68	97.9	1.04	90.4	0.62	20.6	0.16	1.6	−0.46
Netherlands	94.9	0.65	96.6	0.59	0.0	−1.40	24.3	0.68	2.13	0.97
New Zealand	46.4	−0.62	99.8	1.71	0.0	−1.40	16.4	−0.42	1.47	−0.81
Norway	0.0	−1.84	95.3	0.13	0.0	−1.40	16.4	−0.42	2.12	0.94
Portugal	97.6	0.72	94.2	−0.25	100.0	0.83	22.0	0.36	1.85	0.21
Spain	97.4	0.72	94.7	−0.08	99.3	0.82	21.8	0.33	1.56	−0.57
Sweden	97.4	0.72	91.8	−1.10	105.5	0.95	12.7	−0.94	1.87	0.27
Switzerland	96.2	0.68	94.8	−0.04	100.0	0.83	15.4	−0.56	1.66	−0.30
Turkey	85.4	0.40	98.1	1.11	98.1	0.79	16.5	−0.41	2.52	2.03
UK	13.8	−1.48	96.3	0.48	40.4	−0.50	23.1	0.51	1.92	0.40
United States	48.6	−0.57	93.1	−0.64	10.8	−1.16	11.6	−1.09	0.76	−2.73
Mean	70.15	0.00	94.93	0.00	62.67	0.00	19.44	0.00	1.77	0.00
Standard deviation	38.03	1.00	2.85	1.00	44.85	1.00	7.17	1.00	0.37	1.00

Road fuel intensity (gpm)	z-Score	Energy intensity (tbtu/us$ gdp)	z-Score	Electricity use (kwh/cap)	z-Score	SO$_2$ emissions (million tons)	z-Score	CO$_2$ emissions (million tons)	z-Score	Sum of z-scores
0.038	0.58	7.7	0.94	10386	0.27	2.4	1.18	424	−0.08	1.81
0.032	−0.67	5.2	−0.56	7728	−0.23	0.0	−0.44	69	−0.38	4.12
0.034	−0.26	7.9	1.06	8141	−0.15	0.1	−0.37	136	−0.32	−1.18
0.043	1.62	10.5	2.63	15841	1.31	1.4	0.50	547	0.02	0.93
0.033	−0.46	4.6	−0.93	6083	−0.54	0.0	−0.44	46	−0.40	1.30
0.034	−0.26	7.8	1.00	16185	1.37	0.1	−0.37	55	−0.39	−3.10
0.031	−0.88	5.6	−0.32	7300	−0.31	0.3	−0.24	389	−0.11	1.28
0.034	−0.26	5.3	−0.50	6666	−0.43	0.4	−0.17	793	0.23	0.51
0.034	−0.26	4.7	−0.87	5247	−0.70	0.3	−0.24	93	−0.36	−0.04
0.034	−0.26	4.1	−1.23	5449	−0.66	0.0	−0.44	38	−0.41	−0.37
0.030	−1.09	4.9	−0.75	5050	−0.74	0.2	−0.31	417	−0.09	1.01
0.045	2.04	5.6	−0.32	7801	−0.21	0.8	0.10	1180	0.56	−4.20
0.033	−0.46	7.0	0.52	6638	−0.43	0.0	−0.44	255	−0.22	−0.45
0.034	−0.26	7.6	0.88	9585	0.12	0.1	−0.37	37	−0.41	1.58
0.034	−0.26	8.0	1.12	25570	3.15	0.0	−0.44	45	−0.40	−0.58
0.034	−0.26	5.0	−0.69	4681	−0.80	0.1	−0.37	54	−0.39	0.64
0.032	−0.67	5.3	−0.50	5366	−0.68	0.5	−0.10	312	−0.18	0.92
0.036	0.16	6.8	0.40	15066	1.16	0.0	−0.44	59	−0.39	−0.79
0.034	−0.26	4.4	−1.05	7728	−0.23	0.0	−0.44	42	−0.40	1.77
0.034	−0.26	5.3	−0.50	2190	−1.28	0.5	−0.10	269	−0.21	−1.56
0.032	−0.67	4.2	−1.17	5307	−0.69	0.4	−0.17	529	0.01	3.27
0.050	3.08	7.5	0.82	12564	0.69	6.8	4.14	5637	4.34	−6.87
0.04	0.00	6.14	0.00	8935.09	0.00	0.65	0.00	519.36	0.00	0.00
0.0048	1.00	1.66	1.00	5285.49	1.00	1.48	1.00	1179.82	1.00	2.42

After Brown, M.A., Wang, Y., Sovacool, B.K., D'Agostino, A.L., 2014. Forty years of energy security trends: a comparative assessment of 22 industrialized countries. Energy Res. Soc. Sci. 4, 64–77.

signs determined by their impact on energy security: oil import dependence (%), petroleum transport fuels (%), natural gas import dependence (%), real electricity retail prices (US cents/kWh), real gasoline prices ($/liter), on-road fuel intensity (gallons per mile), energy per GDP intensity (tBTU/2005 US$ GDP), electricity use (kWh per capita), sulfur dioxide (SO_2) emissions (million tons), and carbon dioxide (CO_2) emissions (million tons). The values of the energy security index are shown in the rightmost column of the table.

It is noted that the labels of the two axes of Fig. 1 of Brown et al. are labelled identically by mistake. It is also pointed out that the results of Table 1 fail to duplicate the implied values of the energy security index used in that figure by Brown et al., likely due to numerical miscalculations in that paper.

There are more sophisticated methods of aggregating values, e.g., multiplying the dimensions, components and metrics by weights that reflect their relative importance in the energy security index. Radovanović et al. (2018) aggregated the following indicators using Principal Component Analysis (PCA): energy intensity; energy dependence; GDP per capita; final energy consumption per capita; carbon intensity; electricity prices; electricity consumption per capita; production of energy from renewable sources; and sovereign credit rating. Eurostat and Fitch ratings data were used for the values of these metrics. Such an approach relies on numerical criteria for estimating the weights of the metrics, but excludes other factors such as the subjective judgment of experts. This may justify Sovacool's reliance on expert interviews and surveys in some of his published research (Sovacool, 2009, 2011a; Sovacool and Tambo, 2016; Zhang et al., 2017a).

The energy security of China was examined in two papers by Zhang et al. (2017a, b). In one of them, China's energy policies were examined in six historical phases from 1949 to 2017. It was noted that energy diversity has been increasing, energy intensity has been declining, while China became an energy importer after 2010. In the second paper, a different set of authors turned their attention towards internal China provinces and regions. Energy security was evaluated on the following five dimensions (in italics) with the corresponding components (and metrics in parentheses):

1. *Availability and diversity* (A_1): security of supply (primary energy production per capita), energy potential (fossil fuel reserves per capita), dependency (self sufficiency), and diversification (diversity of energy consumption).
2. *Affordability and equality* (A_2): stability (stability of gasoline prices), electricity generation cost (coal-fired power tariff), electricity equality (share of electricity in total energy consumption), and gasoline affordability (quantity of gasoline bought with GDP).
3. *Technology and efficiency* (A_3): energy efficiency (energy intensity), grid efficiency (electricity transmission and distribution losses), grid reliability (average blackout hours per household), and capacity factor (utilization of power plants).
4. *Environmental sustainability* (A_4): land use (forest coverage), water pollution (wastewater emissions per capita), climate change (greenhouse gas emissions per unit of GDP), acidification potential (sulfur dioxide emissions per capita), and photochemical potential (nitrogen dioxide emissions per capita).
5. *Governance and innovation* (A_5): market potential (investment in energy industry), innovation and research (research intensity), energy and environmental management (energy savings and environmental protection).

The authors normalized and transformed the metrics into dimensionless numbers. Then they used the Fuzzy Analytical Hierarchical Process (Fuzzy AHP) and the Preference Ranking Organization Method for Enrichment Evaluations (PROMETHEE) to assign weights based on pairwise comparisons based on the judgment of experts and validated by an Error Analysis. Weights were assigned on metrics, components and dimensions. The resulting weights of the five energy security dimensions equaled 0.2964 for A_1 and A_2, 0.1588 for A_3 and A_4, and 0.0896 for A_5 (normalized to a sum of one).

After the estimation of an energy security index (so not in the context of this chapter), Principal Component (of Factor) Analysis may be accompanied by Cluster Analysis used to group countries into clusters with similar energy security characteristics. The aforementioned paper of Brown et al., 2014) used hierarchical clustering to track changes in the energy security z-scores from 1970 to 2010. Matsumoto et al. (2018) applied time-series hierarchical clustering on EU country data of three energy-security indicators (focusing on energy availability and encompassing country risks), established the presence of three country clusters, and concluded that the diversification of primary energy sources was the main driver of improvement. Their use of the Euclidean (rather than the squared Euclidean) distance measure, may have failed to penalize outlying observations although the authors remark that another disadvantage is may fail to identify similarities in the presence of a minor time lag between time series. In their review, these authors discussed national and multi-national studies and observed that few studies have analyzed energy security over the long term. They summarized the following energy security dimensions: energy availability, infrastructure, energy prices, societal effect, environment, governance, and energy efficiency. Such approaches are useful for doing comparative analysis and drawing geopolitical conclusions.

3.4 Using other indexes

Turning to the use of specific indexes, Månsson et al. (2014) discuss specific (i.e., diversifiable) risk, systematic (related to market) risk, and systemic risk (related to market collapse). Diversity has three dimensions: variety, balance, and disparity. A common method to value diversity of imports is to use modifications of indexes like the Herfindahl-Hirschman or the Shannon-Wiener index with weighting factors accounting for political stability, transport distance, etc.

The *Herfindahl-Hirschmann Index* determines the degree of a certain country's dependence on a certain supplier, and may be used as an indicator that indirectly points to the energy security of a country (Radovanović et al., 2017). The *Supply/ Demand Index* for the long-term security of supply (SD Index) (Scheepers et al., 2007) has been designed on the basis of expert assessments on all possible relevant aspects of the security of supply, and covers demand, supply, conversion, and transport of energy in the medium to long-term (Kruyt et al., 2009). It is a composite indicator (i.e., an index) that comprises 30 individual indicators, and considers the characteristics of demand, supply and transport (Radovanović et al., 2017). According to Kruyt et al. (2009), the basic difference with other indicators, is that the SD Index attempts to grasp the entire energy spectrum, including conversion, transport, and demand (taking into account that a decrease in energy use lowers the overall impact of supply disruptions).

The *Oil Vulnerability Index* (OVI) (Gupta, 2008) is an aggregated index of oil vulnerability, based on seven indicators: ratio of value of oil imports to GDP; oil consumption per unit of GDP; GDP per capita; oil share in total energy supply; ratio of domestic reserves to oil consumption; and exposure to geopolitical oil supply concentration risks, measured by net oil import dependence, diversification of supply sources, political risk in oil-supplying countries, and market liquidity. According to Radovanović et al. (2017), the OVI is a comprehensive composite indicator that manages to consider economic indicators, import dependence, and political stability.

The *Vulnerability Index* (Gnansounou, 2008) is a composite indicator which considers five indicators: energy intensity; energy import dependency, which is often high in electricity markets (Kucharski and Unesaki, 2015); ratio of energy-related carbon emissions to the total primary energy supply (TPES); electricity supply vulnerability; and lack of diversity in transport fuels (Radovanović et al., 2017). The six-factor Risky External Energy Supply (Le Coq and Paltseva, 2009) is entirely supply-oriented, and considers solely the level of diversification, with particular emphasis given to the assessment of transport safety of energy generating products (Radovanović et al., 2017).

The *Aggregated Energy Security Performance Indicator* (AESPI) (Martchamadol and Kumar, 2013) has been developed by considering 25 individual indicators representing social, economic, and environmental dimensions. The indicator (essentially an index) ranges from 0 to 10, and requires time series data for its estimation. The advantages of AESPI is that, it not only assists in knowing the past energy security status of a country, but also helps in assessing the future status considering the energy policies and plans, thus enabling monitoring the impacts of policies.

The *Socio-economic Energy Risk* is a composite index that considers the following indicators: energy source diversification, energy resource availability and feasibility, energy intensity, energy transport, energy dependence, political stability, market liquidity, and the GDP (Radovanović et al., 2017).

The *US Energy Security Risk Index* (U.S. Chamber of Commerce, 2010) is an index based on 83 individual indicators assessing geopolitical indicators, economic development, environmental concerns and reliability (Radovanović et al., 2017).

The *Energy Development Index* (EDI) (Jewell, 2011) is composed of four indicators, each of which captures a specific aspect of potential energy poverty: per capita commercial energy consumption (which serves as an indicator of the overall economic development of a country); per capita electricity consumption in the residential sector (which serves as an indicator of the reliability of, and consumer's ability to pay for, electricity services); share of modern fuels in total residential sector energy use (which serves as an indicator of the level of access to clean cooking facilities); and the share of population with access to electricity. This index was intended as a simple composite measure of the progress of a country or region in its transition to modern fuels, and of the degree of maturity of its energy end use (IAEA, 2005).

The *Energy Security Index* (ESI) is composed of two indicators (ESI_{price}, ESI_{volume}) that measure the energy security implications of resource concentration, from the viewpoint of both price and physical availability (IEA, 2007). ESI_{price} is a composite measure of the diversification of energy sources and suppliers, and the political stability of exporting countries, while ESI_{volume} is a measure of the level of dependence of natural gas imports.

In what constitutes an interesting concept, the "*energy trilemma*" is defined as balancing the trade-offs between three major energy goals, namely energy security, economic competitiveness, and environmental sustainability (Ang et al., 2015). The dimensions of energy trilemma are defined by WEC (2016a) as follows:

1. *Energy security*: Effective management of primary energy supply from domestic and external sources, reliability of energy infrastructure, and ability of energy providers to meet current and future demand.
2. *Energy equity*: Accessibility and affordability of energy supply across the population.
3. *Environmental sustainability*: Encompasses the achievement of supply and demand-side energy efficiency, and the development of energy supply from renewable and other low-carbon sources.

The *Energy Trilemma Index*, formerly known as the *Energy Sustainability Index*, was first introduced in 2009, ranking close to 90 countries. This ranking has been expanded to include 130 countries and greater detail about the performance of countries on the specific trilemma dimensions by adding a balance score, and an index watch list to indicate countries that are expected to display trend changes in the next few years (Ang et al., 2015). The Index 2.0 methodology uses a set of 34 indicators and approximately 100 data sets to rank countries on their trilemma performance (compared to 23 indicators and 60 data sets in the previous index methodology; WEC, 2016b).

Finally, the *Energy Architecture Performance Index* (EAPI) was proposed in 2010 by the World Economic Forum (WEF), and was modified the next year into the *Energy Sustainability Index* (WEF, 2014). EAPI is a composite index based on a set of indicators divided into three basic categories (energy security, energy equity, and environmental sustainability), the so-called Energy Trilemma Index (Radovanović et al., 2017).

3.5 Forecasting

Forecasting is only occasionally attempted in energy security research. Månsson et al. (2014) point out that events that occur infrequently or that have not occurred thus far are poorly (or not) reflected in historical data. The same authors also point out that the dynamic nature of energy security means that a long timeframe approach may value stability over cost effectiveness.

As Paravantis (2019) pointed out, quantitative methods are not the Holy Grail, and they should be combined with good qualitative research. As a conspicuous example, the unprecedented volatility is oil prices after 2007 shown in Fig. 18.2 (in keeping with the geopolitical unpredictability in world affairs) was predicted by David L. Goldwyn (US Department of State's Special Envoy and Coordinator for International Energy Affairs from 2009 to 2011) in a McKinsey Executive Roundtable Series in International Economics that tools place on June 21st, 2007 (Council on Foreign Relations, 2007). It is difficult to envision that any econometric time series analysis or other quantitative method would have caught that.

Forecasting related to energy security is more likely to be on target if it is informed by geopolitical expertise. The engagement of experts may facilitate the evaluation of the impact of events that are infrequent or difficult to quantify, e.g., power outages or terrorist events, on the overall energy security level of an individual country or an entire region. Using an energy security index that accounts for geopolitical dimensions and components makes setting realistic policy targets more straightforward and forecasting more likely to be on target.

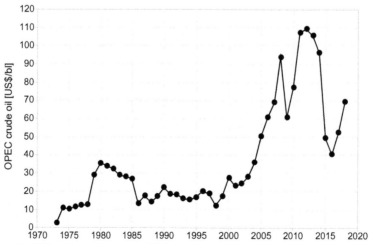

FIG. 18.2 OPEC crude oil price (in US$ per barrel; Paravantis, 2019).

4 Conclusions

This is a particularly exciting time to study the geopolitics of energy security: the global energy landscape is in the middle of a game-changing revolution in source rock resources; consumer countries have turned into producers; producer countries have turned into consumers; and the volatility of oil prices has skyrocketed in response to events that are difficult to predict in a multipolar world.

This chapter reviewed the research literature that has aimed to formulate and estimate energy security quantitatively from a geopolitical standpoint. Energy security was defined as an entity containing dimensions and components represented by metrics. Energy markets were reviewed as an important component of energy security in a changing global landscape. The complexity of energy security became clear by the number of definitions and research approaches. Reviewed works were found to analyze energy security metrics using: numerical (scoring/ranking, weighting, organizing into a matrix); statistical (z-score approaches, correlation analysis, consumer surveys); multivariate statistical (multiple regression, Principal Component Analysis, Factor Analysis, Cluster Analysis on static of time-series data); econometric (time series approaches); multi-criteria decision making (Analytic Hierarchy Process, Fuzzy Analytical Hierarchical Process, Preference Ranking Organization Method for Enrichment Evaluations); (accident) risk assessment; complexity (time series analysis coupled with path dependency and lock-in concepts, Agent-Based Models); risk assessment (covering energy, social, institutional and political factors); game theoretic; and qualitative (e.g., interviews, expert panels) methods and techniques. Qualitative approaches such as expert interviews can assist especially when information is incomplete, lacking or difficult to quantify. Public perceptions were occasionally taken into consideration. Several works were found to examine case studies of a single or a few countries; others analyzed more countries, usually located in a region (such as Europe or Asia); other studies concentrated on regions or provinces.

References

Alhajji, A.F., 2007. What is Energy Security? Definitions and Concepts. Middle East Economic Survey L, p. 45.

Ang, B.W., Choong, W.L., Ng, T.S., 2015. Energy security: definitions, dimensions and indexes. Renew. Sust. Energ. Rev. 42, 1077–1093.

Asia Pacific Energy Research Center (APERC), 2007. A Quest for Energy Security in the 21st Century: Resources and Constraints. Asia Pacific Energy Research Center, Japan.

Bambawale, M.J., Sovacool, B.K., 2011a. China's energy security: the perspective of energy users. Appl. Energy 88, 1949–1956.

Bambawale, M.J., Sovacool, B.K., 2011b. India's energy security: a sample of business, government, civil society, and university perspectives. Energy Policy 39, 1254–1264.

Brown, M.A., Wang, Y., Sovacool, B.K., D'Agostino, A.L., 2014. Forty years of energy security trends: a comparative assessment of 22 industrialized countries. Energy Res. Soc. Sci. 4, 64–77.

Caputo, R., 2009. Hitting the wall: a vision of a secure energy future. In: Synthesis Lectures on Energy and the Environment: Technology, Science and Society, Lecture #3. Morgan and Claypool Publishers.

Cherp, A., Jewell, J., 2014. The concept of energy security: beyond the four as. Energy Policy 75, 415–421.

Chester, L., 2010. Conceptualising energy security and making explicit its polysemic nature. Energy Policy 38, 887–895.

Council on Foreign Relations, 2007. Energy Security: What It Means and How to Achieve It [Video File]. https://youtu.be/kUIqF81wZJE.

Crooks, E., 2015. The US Shale Revolution—How it Changed the World (and Why Nothing Will Ever Be the Same Again). Financial Times. https://www.ft.com/content/2ded7416-e930-11e4-a71a-00144feab7de.

European Commission (EC), 2000. Towards a European Strategy for the Security of Energy Supply. Office for Official Publications of the European Communities, Green Paper, Luxembourg.

Gnansounou, E., 2008. Assessing the energy vulnerability: case of industrialized countries. Energy Policy 36, 3734–3744.

Goldthau, A., Sovacool, B.K., 2012. The uniqueness of the energy security, justice and governance problem. Energy Policy 21, 232–240.

Goldwyn, D.L., 2013. Energy & Security: Strategies for a World in Transition. Goldwyn Global Strategies LLC. Retrieved from: http://www.alaskaworldaffairs.org/wp-content/uploads/2014/07/Energy-and-Security_David-Goldwyn.pdf.

Grand View Research, 2019. Energy Security Market Size, Share and Trends Analysis Report by Application, Regional Outlook, Competitive Strategies, and Segment Forecasts, 2019 To 2025. Report ID: GVR2442.

Gupta, E., 2008. Oil vulnerability index of oil-importing countries. Energy Policy 36, 1195–1211.

International Atomic Energy Agency (IAEA), 2005. Energy Indicators for Sustainable Development: Guidelines and Methodologies. Vienna http://www-pub.iaea.org/MTCD/publications/PDF/Pub1222_web.pdf.

International Energy Agency (IEA), 2007. Energy Security and Climate Policy: Assessing Interactions. IEA/OECD, Paris.

Jewell, J., 2011. The IEA Model of Short-Term Energy Security (MOSES): Primary Energy Sources and Secondary Fuels. OECD/IEA, Working Paper, Paris, France.

Johansson, B., 2013. A broadened typology on energy and security. Energy 53, 199–205.

Jun, E., Kim, W., Chang, S.H., 2009. The analysis of security cost for different energy sources. Appl. Energy 86 (10), 1894–1901.

Khatib, H., 2000. Energy security. In: Goldemberg, J., Holdren, J., Smith, K. (Eds.), World Energy Assessment. United Nations Development Program, New York. Retrieved from: http://www.undp.org/content/dam/undp/library/Environment%20and%20Energy/Sustainable%20Energy/wea%202000/chapter4.pdf.

Kisel, E., Hamburg, A., Harm, M., Leppiman, A., Ots, M., 2016. Concept for energy security matrix. Energy Policy 95, 1–9.

Klare, M., 2008. Rising Powers, Shrinking Planet, the New Geopolitics of Energy. Metropolitan Books, New York.

Knox-Hayes, J., Brown, M.A., Sovacool, B.K., Wang, Y., 2013. Understanding attitudes toward energy security: results of a cross-national survey. Glob. Environ. Chang. 23, 609–622.

Kopp, S.D., 2014. Politics, Markets and EU Gas Supply Security. Case Studies of the UK and Germany. Springer, Berlin, Germany. http://www.springer.com/gp/book/9783658083236.

Kruyt, B., van Vuuren, D.P., de Vries, H.J.M., Groenenberg, H., 2009. Indicators for energy security. Energy Policy 37, 2166–2181.

Kucharski, J., Unesaki, H., 2015. A policy-oriented approach to energy security. The 5th Sustainable Future for Human Security (SustaiN 2014). Procedia Environ. Sci. 28, 27–36.

Laldjebaev, M., Morreale, S.J., Sovacool, B.K., Kassam, K.-A.S., 2018. Rethinking energy security and services in practice: national vulnerability and three energy pathways in Tajikistan. Energy Policy 114, 39–50.

Le Coq, C., Paltseva, E., 2009. Measuring the security of external energy supply in the European Union. Energy Policy 37, 4474–4481.

Leonard, M., Popescu, N., 2007. A Power Audit of the EU-Russia Relations. European Council on Foreign Relations, London, UK.

Luft, G., Korin, A., 2009. Energy security: in the eyes of the beholder. In: Luft, G., Korin, A. (Eds.), Energy Security Challenges for the 21st Century: A Reference Handbook. Praeger Security International, Santa Barbara, CA, USA.

Månsson, A., Johansson, B., Nilsson, L.J., 2014. Assessing energy security: an overview of commonly used methodologies. Energy 73, 1–14.

Marquina, A., 2008. The Southeast-Southwest European energy corridor. In: Marguina, A. (Ed.), Energy Security: Visions From Asia and Europe. Palgrave Macmillan, UK, pp. 54–68.

Martchamadol, J., Kumar, S., 2013. An aggregated energy security performance indicator. Appl. Energy 103 (C), 653–670.

Matsumoto, K., Doumpos, M., Andriosopoulos, K., 2018. Historical energy security performance in EU countries. Renew. Sustain. Energy Rev. 82 (Part 2), 1737–1748.

Morgenthau, H., 1985. Politics Among Nations: The Struggle for Power and Peace, sixth ed. Knopf, New York, USA.

Narula, K., Reddy, S., 2015. Three blind men and an elephant: the case of energy indices to measure energy security and energy sustainability. Energy 80, 148–158.

Paravantis, J.A., 2016. From game theory to complexity, emergence and agent-based modeling in world politics. In: Tsihrintzis, G.A., Virvou, M., Jain, L.C. (Eds.), Intelligent Computing Systems: Emerging Application Areas, Intelligent Systems Reference Library Book Series. Springer.

Paravantis, J.A., 2019. Dimensions, components and metrics of energy security: review and synthesis. SPOUDAI J. Econ. Bus. 69 (4), 38–52.

Pezalla, A.E., Pettigrew, J., Miller-Day, M., 2012. Researching the researcher-as-instrument: an exercise in interviewer self-reflexivity. Qual. Res. 12 (2), 165–185. https://www.ncbi.nlm.nih.gov/pmc/articles/PMC4539962.

Popesku, M.-F., Hurduzeu, G., 2015. Energy challenges for Europe—scenarios of the importance of natural gas prices from a game theory perspective. J. Game Theory 4 (2), 26–35.

Radovanović, M., Filipović, S., Golušin, V., 2018. Geo-economic approach to energy security measurement—principal component analysis. Renew. Sustain. Energy Rev. 82 (Part 2), 1691–1700.

Radovanović, M., Filipović, S., Pavlović, D., 2017. Energy security measurement—a sustainable approach. Renew. Sust. Energ. Rev. 68, 1020–1032.

Ren, J., Andreasen, K.P., Sovacool, B.K., 2014. Viability of hydrogen pathways that enhance energy security: a comparison of China and Denmark. Int. J. Hydrog. Energy 39, 15320–15329.

Ren, J., Sovacool, B.K., 2014. Quantifying, measuring, and strategizing energy security: determining the most meaningful dimensions and metrics. Energy 76, 838–849.

Ren, J., Sovacool, B.K., 2015. Prioritizing low-carbon energy sources to enhance China's energy security. Energy 76, 838–849.

Scheepers, M., Seebregts, A.J., De Jong, J.J., Maters, J.M., 2007. EU Standards for Security of Supply. Energy Research Center (ECN)/Clingendael International Energy Programme, Hague, Netherlands.

Sovacool, B.K., 2009. Energy policy and cooperation in southeast asia: the history, challenges, and implications of the trans-ASEAN gas pipeline (TAGP) network. Energy Policy 37, 2356–2367.

Sovacool, B.K., 2011a. Evaluating energy security in the asia pacific: towards a more comprehensive approach. Energy Policy 39, 7472–7479.

Sovacool, B.K., 2011b. Seven suppositions about energy security in the United States. J. Clean. Prod. 19, 1147–1157.

Sovacool, B.K., 2012. The methodological challenges of creating a comprehensive energy security index. Energy Policy 48, 835–840.

Sovacool, B.K., 2013a. An international assessment of energy security performance. Ecol. Econ. 88, 148–158.

Sovacool, B.K., 2013b. Assessing energy security performance in the Asia Pacific, 1990–2010. Renew. Sust. Energ. Rev. 17, 228–247.

Sovacool, B.K., 2013c. Energy policymaking in Denmark: implications for global energy security and sustainability. Energy Policy 61, 829–839.

Sovacool, B.K., 2014. What are we doing here? Analyzing fifteen years of energy scholarship and proposing a social science research agenda. Energy Res. Soc. Sci. 1, 1–29.

Sovacool, B.K., 2015. Fuel poverty, affordability, and energy justice in england: policy insights from the warm front program. Energy Policy 48, 835–840.

Sovacool, B.K., 2016. Differing cultures of energy security: an international comparison of public perceptions. Renew. Sust. Energ. Rev. 55, 811–822.

Sovacool, B.K., Brown, M.A., 2009. Competing dimensions of energy security: an international perspective. In: Working Paper #45, Working Paper Series, Ivan Allen College, School of Public Policy. Georgia Tech, Atlanta, GA.

Sovacool, B.K., Cooper, C., Parenteau, P., 2011a. From a hard place to a rock: questioning the energy security of a coal-based economy. Energy Policy 39, 4664–4670.

Sovacool, B.K., Kryman, M., Laine, E., 2015. Profiling technological failure and disaster in the energy sector: a comparative analysis of historical energy accidents. Energy 90, 2016–2027.

Sovacool, B.K., Mukherjee, I., 2011. Conceptualizing and measuring energy security: a synthesized approach. Energy 36, 5343–5355.

Sovacool, B.K., Mukherjee, I., Drupady, I.M., D'Agostino, A.L., 2011b. Evaluating energy security performance from 1990 to 2010 for eighteen countries. Energy 36, 5846–5853.

Sovacool, B.K., Rafey, W., 2011. Snakes in the grass: the energy security implications of Medupi. Electr. J. 24 (1), 92–100.

Sovacool, B.K., Saunders, H., 2014. Competing policy packages and the complexity of energy security. Energy 67, 641–651.

Sovacool, B.K., Tambo, T., 2016. Comparing consumer perceptions of energy security, policy, and low-carbon technology: insights from Denmark. Energy Res. Soc. Sci. 11, 79–91.

Sovacool, B.K., Walter, G., 2018. Major hydropower states, sustainable development, and energy security: insights from a preliminary cross-comparative assessment. Energy 67, 641–651.

Stringer, K.D., 2008. Energy security: applying a portfolio approach. Baltic Secur. Def. Rev. 10, 121–142.

Thomson, M., 1987. Among the energy tribes: a cultural framework for the analysis and design of energy policy. Policy Sci. 17, 321–329.

Truffer, P., 2014. Energy Security: 10+1 Principles. Retrieved from: https://www.offiziere.ch/?p=17175.

U.S. Chamber of Commerce, 2010. Index of U.S. Energy Security Risk: Assessing America's Vulnerabilities in a Global Energy Market. U.S. Chamber of Commerce, Washington, DC, USA.

Valdés, J., Escribano, G., San-Martín, E., 2016. Energy security and renewable energy deployment in the EU: liaisons dangereuses or virtuous circle? Renew. Sust. Energ. Rev. 62, 1032–1046.

Valentine, S.V., Sovacool, B.K., 2019. Energy transitions and mass publics: manipulating public perception and ideological entrenchment in Japanese Nuclear Power Policy. Renew. Sust. Energ. Rev. 101, 295–304.

Vivoda, V., 2010. Evaluating energy security in the Asia-Pacific Region: a novel methodological approach. Energy Policy 38, 5258–5263.

Winzer, C., 2012. Conceptualizing energy security. Energy Policy 46, 36–48.

World Energy Council (WEC), 2016a. World Energy Trilemma I 2016. Defining Measures to Accelerate the Energy Transition. WEC, London, UK. https://www.worldenergy.org/wp-content/uploads/2016/05/World-Energy-Trilemma_full-report_2016_web.pdf.

World Energy Council (WEC), 2016b. World Energy Resources. Natural Gas 2016. WEC, London, UK. https://www.worldenergy.org/wp-content/uploads/2017/03/WEResources_Natural_Gas_2016.pdf.

World Energy Forum (WEF), 2014. Global Energy Architecture Performance Index Report 2015. Switzerland http://www3.weforum.org/docs/WEF_GlobalEnergyArchitecture_2015.pdf.

Yale University, 2013. The Quest: Energy, Security, and the Remaking of the Modern World [Video File]. https://youtu.be/M_Y8Jy2JBf8.

Yergin, D., 1988. Energy security in the 1990s. For. Affairs 67 (1), 110–132.

Yergin, D., 2006. Ensuring energy security. For. Affairs 85 (2), 69–82.

Yergin, D., 2013. Energy security and markets. In: Kalicki, J.H., Goldwyn, D.L. (Eds.), Energy & Security: Strategies for a World in Transition, second ed. John Hopkins University Press, pp. 69–87.

Zhang, L., Yu, L., Sovacool, B.K., Ren, J., 2017a. Measuring energy security performance within China: toward an inter-provincial prospective. Energy 125, 825–836.

Zhang, L., Yu, L., Sovacool, B.K., Ren, J., Eli, A., 2017b. The dragon awakens: innovation, competition, and transition in the energy strategy of the People's Republic of China, 1949–2017. Energy Policy 108, 634–644.

Zhao, H., 2019. Energy security: from energy independence to energy interdependence. In: Zhao, H. (Ed.), The Economics and Politics of China's Energy Security Transition. Academic Press, London, UK, pp. 99–120 (Chapter 5).

Chapter 19

Assessing the Western Balkans power systems: A case study of Serbia

Nikolaos E. Koltsaklis

Energy and Environmental Policy Laboratory, School of Economics, Business and International Studies, University of Piraeus, Piraeus, Greece

1 Introduction

Southeast Europe (SEE) comprises a geographical region covering countries from Hungary on north to Greece on south and from Slovenia on west to Romania on east. The individual power systems of SEE countries vary significantly among themselves on their key aspects including their (electric) size, the electricity demand, the mix of installed power generating capacity, types of technology and fuels utilized in power units, and as a consequence in the resulting energy generation mix (Apostolovic and Koltsaklis, 2018). For instance, while Albania is dependent almost entirely on water resources for its electricity supply. Kosovo relies almost entirely on lignite, and others have a combination of hydro- and fossil fuel-fired electricity production. On the other hand, Greece, Bulgaria, and Romania constitute the only SEE countries that already have installed noteworthy solar PV and wind energy capacities (IRENA, 2017). Focusing on the Serbian power system, coal-based electricity generation, and particularly lignite-fired one, constitutes the dominant technology in the Serbian power sector, reporting an installed capacity of around 4 GW. Hydropower units comprise the second largest technology, in terms of power capacity, amounting to around 3 GW, as well as gas power units contribute almost 0.5 GW to the production capacity. Regarding the renewable energy sources, wind power is characterized by a significant development in the last years, recording almost 400 MW of installed capacity, while solar photovoltaics are kept at low levels with only 4 MW at the beginning of 2020 (ENTSO-E, 2020). In addition, Serbia has committed to promoting renewables to a 36.6% share in its electricity consumption by 2020 (IRENA, 2017). Regarding the future renewables' prospects, Serbia possesses noteworthy cost-competitive potential for wind power, whose total capacity could reach 5.6 GW, but this could be achieved under the condition of a lower cost of capital. Cumulative investments could be also directed to big hydropower units, mainly located on the Ibar, the Morava, the Danube as well as on the Drina River. Additional pump storage units could also provide more than 3 GW. A specific analysis regarding the techno-economic and environmental aspects of building small hydroelectric plants in Serbia was provided by Ciric (2019). The deployment of solar photovoltaics could reach almost 7 GW, only if their competitiveness is to be enhanced (IRENA, 2017). In addition, Djurdjevic (2011) assessed the potential for installing stand-alone and grid-connected solar PV energy systems for the Serbian power system.

Based on the above, the detailed and systematic modelling of a power system is of major significance for its analysis, for the understanding of its dynamics, and for the design of its energy transition roadmaps (Koltsaklis et al., 2013). The unit commitment problem is defined as the problem which determines the operational scheduling of a set of power units with the objective of meeting the projected electricity demand at minimum total cost by making use of an optimal combination of distinct power plants (Koltsaklis and Georgiadis, 2015). Alvarez et al. (2018) developed an optimization approach in order to solve the unit commitment problem considering thermal power generating units, transmission constraints, and hydraulic system constraints. The model's effectiveness is tested on a modified IEEE 31-bus power system with two pumped stations. In addition, the same authors (Alvarez et al., 2020) extended their previous model in Alvarez et al. (2018) to integrate the natural gas system incorporating pipelines, compressors, fluctuating gas loads, and line-pack. The test system is again a modified IEEE 31-bus with 2 pumped storage units and 7-node natural gas system. Focusing also on the coupling of electricity and gas networks. Yang et al. (2019) developed two mixed-integer linear programming (MILP) formulations to address the optimal power and gas flow problem. A MILP version of the unit commitment problem was provided by Feng et al. (2019) in order to address the peak load regulation problem in power systems where conventional flexibility providers such as hydropower and/or pumped-storage units are not adequate. The test system was the East China Power Grid which is China's largest regional power grid. On the other hand, Finardi et al. (2016) implemented a comparative analysis of three optimization approaches for the solution of the hydro unit commitment problem. With the objective of assessing the superiority of either unit commitment or economic dispatch approach. Cebulla and Fichter (2017) assessed how energy storage requirements are influenced by the method of power plant modelling. Based on the modelling outputs, unit-commitment was proved to be more effective in scenarios with low shares of intermittent renewable-based electricity, while economic dispatch is efficient in power systems with significant share of renewable-based electricity generation. To capture the high penetration of variable renewable energy into the power systems as well as to deal with the uncoordinated charging of plug-in electric vehicles. Yang et al. (2017) presented a unit commitment optimization framework considering multiple scenarios for renewable energy production and demand side management of dispatchable plug-in electric vehicles' load. From a similar perspective, Soltani et al. (2018) developed a stochastic multi-objective approach for the unit commitment problem considering smart grid technologies, namely plug-in electric vehicles, demand side management, storage devices such as compressed air energy storage units, and renewable distributed energy generation. Unit commitment methods have been also used in isolated power systems characterized by high seasonal variability in their electricity demand patterns. In particular, Psarros and Papathanassiou (2019) developed a MILP-based unit commitment model in order to examine the benefits from thermal units' operation in isolated systems under their technical minimum loading levels for short time periods, with the aim of providing increased flexibility to the system. Also, Zepter and Weibezahn (2019) assessed the influences of uncertain solar PV energy generation on unit commitment decisions in the German electricity market, namely with respect to total system costs and the power output of thermal power units. Szabó et al. (2019) utilized a unit commitment and economic dispatch model to investigate the future of regional market integration for power systems in the SEE, focusing on an energy transition scenario for a SEE decarbonization pathway. Also, using the EnergyPLAN tool, Batas Bjelić et al. (2013) assessed the impacts of increased wind penetration into the Serbian power system in terms of excess electricity generation, annual cost, CO_2 emissions, and share of renewable energy in the total primary energy supply. Focusing on the SEE power system, Abbate et al. (2017) presented the results of several pan-European study analyses at 2030, on the grounds that the full integration of the SEE Region with the rest of Europe comprises a key objective of the European Energy Union. The impacts and the influences of key HVDC links interconnecting Italy with the other zones of the SEE Region are also provided.

This work utilizes a methodological framework, like the one developed in Koltsaklis and Dagoumas (2018a) and Koltsaklis et al. (2018), in order to address the unit commitment problem through a co-optimization of energy and reserves market and determine the optimal annual energy mix of the current Serbian power system. In particular, it provides hourly time resolution for a whole year and implements a day by day optimization, as in the real day-ahead energy market. The days are connected among them, where information on the system's operation of the previous day passed to the next day's optimization process. Specific focus is given on the modelling of the electricity trading with the neighboring power systems. The decision variables to be determined by the mathematical model include: (i) optimal energy mix, (ii) optimal reserve provision mix per type, (iii) system's marginal price, (iv) electricity trading, and (v) and CO_2 emissions at a system-wide level.

This work is among very few works in the literature that focus on the Serbian power system; whose location is very critical for the shaping of the electricity flows within the SEE region. Through the utilization of a detailed unit commitment model and the focus on the market participants' trading strategy, the work deals with policy issues and its goal is to examine the operational, economic, and environmental influences of a power system's annual operation from a regional perspective. The outputs of this work can be utilized by all types of stakeholders in order to assess the current status and start shaping the future portfolio of a well-interconnected power system being at the beginning of its energy transition process. This is among few works in the literature proving a high level of temporal granularity and detailed power plants' modelling at a regional level.

The remainder of the paper is organized as follows: Section 2 presents the methodological part of the work, followed by the case study description in Section 3. Section 4 provides a critical discussion of the model solution, and finally, Section 5 summarizes some concluding remarks.

2 Mathematical formulation

This work presents a systematic methodological framework, based on advanced optimization techniques, for the co-optimization of energy and reserves market of a power system. For that reason, a detailed unit commitment optimization model has been employed including a series of operational, economic, and regulatory constraints for the optimal electricity market clearing.

2.1 Objective function

The objective function of the developed model refers to the total net cost minimization of the studied power system. Thermal power units u, hydropower units h (thermal and hydropower units are collectively mentioned as hydrothermal ones hu), and renewable energy units r have been considered, including also available interconnections for imports m and exports x. Each considered day is split into hourly time periods t, while the net capacity of each thermal power unit, as well as the interconnection capacity of the neighboring power systems, with both imports and exports direction, is split into several blocks b, each of which is identified based on a certain pair of quantity and price. The detailed formulation of the objective function is provided by Eq. (19.1) and incorporates: (i) energy offer cost of all thermal power generating units ($\sum_u \sum_b \sum_t C_{u.b.t}^u \cdot e_{u.b.t}$), (ii) energy offer cost of hydropower units ($\sum_h \sum_t C_{h.t}^h \cdot p_{h.t}$), (iii) energy offer cost of renewable units ($\sum_r \sum_t C_{r.t}^r \cdot p_{r.t}$), (iv) shut-down cost of thermal power units ($\sum_u \sum_t C_u^{sd} \cdot x_{u.t}^{sd}$), (v) net electricity trading cost ($\sum_m \sum_b \sum_t C_{m.b.t}^m \cdot e_{m.b.t} - \sum_x \sum_b \sum_t C_{x.b.t}^x \cdot e_{x.b.t}$), namely electricity imports offer cost minus electricity exports bid revenues (vi) Frequency Containment Reserve (FCR) with upward direction provision cost ($\sum_{hu} \sum_t C_{hu.t}^{1up} \cdot e_{hu.t}^{1up}$), (vii) automatic frequency restoration reserve (aFRR) with upward direction provision cost ($\sum_{hu} \sum_t C_{hu.t}^{2up} \cdot e_{hu.t}^{2up}$), and (viii) automatic frequency restoration reserve with downward direction provision cost ($\sum_{hu} \sum_t C_{hu.t}^{2dn} \cdot e_{hu.t}^{2dn}$).

$$
\begin{aligned}
\textit{Min Cost}^{annual} = \quad &
\overbrace{
\underbrace{\sum_u \sum_b \sum_t C_{u.b.t}^u \cdot e_{u.b.t}}_{\textit{Thermal power units}} +
\underbrace{\sum_h \sum_t C_{h.t}^h \cdot p_{h.t}}_{\textit{Hydropower units}} +
\underbrace{\sum_r \sum_t C_{r.t}^r \cdot p_{r.t}}_{\textit{Renewable energy units}}
}^{\textit{Energy offer cost}} \\[2ex]
+ \quad &
\underbrace{\sum_u \sum_t C_u^{sd} \cdot sd_{u.t}}_{\substack{\textit{Shut} - \textit{down cost of thermal} \\ \textit{power units}}} +
\underbrace{\sum_m \sum_b \sum_t C_{m.b.t}^m \cdot e_{m.b.t}}_{\substack{\textit{Electricity imports} \\ \textit{offers cost}}} -
\underbrace{\sum_x \sum_b \sum_t C_{x.b.t}^x \cdot e_{x.b.t}}_{\substack{\textit{Electricity exports} \\ \textit{bids revenues}}} \\[2ex]
+ \quad &
\underbrace{\sum_{hu} \sum_t C_{hu.t}^{R1up} \cdot e_{hu.t}^{R1up}}_{\substack{\textit{FCR provision cost} \\ \textit{with upward direction}}} +
\underbrace{\sum_{hu} \sum_t C_{hu.t}^{R2up} \cdot e_{hu.t}^{R2up}}_{\substack{\textit{aFRR provision cost} \\ \textit{with upward direction}}} +
\underbrace{\sum_{hu} \sum_t C_{hu.t}^{R2dn} \cdot e_{hu.t}^{R2dn}}_{\substack{\textit{aFRR provision cost} \\ \textit{with downward direction}}}
\end{aligned}
\tag{19.1}
$$

2.2 Constraints

2.2.1 Electricity demand balance

The electricity demand balance ensures that the total energy offer from both thermal ($\sum_u p_{u.t}$), renewable ($\sum_r p_{r.t}$) and hydropower units ($\sum_h p_{h.t}$), plus the electricity imports ($\sum_m p_{m.t}$) must meet the projected energy requirements (D_t) in each time period t plus the electricity exports ($\sum_x p_{x.t}$), as presented in Eq. (19.2).

$$
\sum_u p_{u.t} + \sum_r p_{r.t} + \sum_h p_{h.t} + \sum_m p_{m.t} = D_t + \sum_x p_{x.t} \quad \forall t
\tag{19.2}
$$

2.2.2 Operating limits

Several technical constraints have been incorporated in the mathematical model to ensure the technical feasibility of the obtained solution.

Constraint (19.3) guarantees that the cleared energy offer from each thermal power unit in each block and time interval ($e_{u.b.t}$) must not exceed its respective maximum available quantity ($ES_{u.b.t}$). Also, Eq. (19.4) explains that the cleared energy offer from each thermal unit in each time interval ($p_{u.t}$) is equal to the sum of all of its blocks ($\sum_b e_{u.b.t}$).

$$
e_{u.b.t} \leq ES_{u.b.t} \quad \forall u.b.t
\tag{19.3}
$$

$$
p_{u.t} = \sum_b e_{u.b.t} \quad \forall u.t
\tag{19.4}
$$

Analogously, Constraint (19.5) sets that the cleared energy imports from each interconnection in each block and time interval ($e_{m.b.t}$) must not surpass its respective maximum available quantity ($ES_{m.b.t}$). Also, Eq. (19.6) explains that the cleared energy imports from each interconnection in each time interval ($p_{m.t}$) is equal to the sum of all of its blocks ($\sum_b e_{m.b.t}$).

$$e_{m.b.t} \leq ES_{m.b.t} \quad \forall m.b.t \tag{19.5}$$

$$p_{m.t} = \sum_b e_{m.b.t} \quad \forall m.t \tag{19.6}$$

Constraint (19.7) describes that the cleared energy exports to each interconnection in each block and time interval ($e_{x.b.t}$) must not exceed its respective maximum available quantity ($ES_{x.b.t}$). Also, Eq. (19.8) explains that the cleared electricity exports to each interconnection in each time interval is equal to the sum of all its blocks ($\sum_b e_{x.b.t}$).

$$e_{x.b.t} \leq ES_{x.b.t} \quad \forall x.b.t \tag{19.7}$$

$$p_{x.t} = \sum_b e_{x.b.t} \quad \forall x.t \tag{19.8}$$

Constraints (19.9) and (19.10) impose the maximum and minimum operational limits for each thermal power unit, correspondingly, taking also into account the reserve provision option. More specifically, Constraint (19.9) guarantees that the sum of the cleared energy offer ($p_{hu.t}$) plus the cleared provision for frequency containment reserve with upward direction ($e_{hu.t}^{R1up}$), automatic frequency restoration reserve with upward direction ($e_{hu.t}^{R2up}$), and spinning frequency restoration via manual activation ($e_{hu.t}^{R3s}$) of each hydrothermal power unit in each time interval, must not exceed its available technical maximum (P_{hu}^{max}).

$$p_{hu.t} + e_{hu.t}^{R1up} + e_{hu.t}^{R2up} + e_{hu.t}^{R3s} \leq P_{hu}^{max} \quad \forall hu.t \tag{19.9}$$

In addition, Constraint (19.10) sets that the cleared energy offer of each hydrothermal power unit in each time interval ($p_{hu.t}$) minus its cleared provision for automatic frequency restoration reserve with upward direction ($e_{hu.t}^{R2dn}$) must be equal to or greater than its available technical minimum (P_{hu}^{min}).

$$p_{hu.t} - e_{hu.t}^{R2dn} \geq P_{hu}^{min} \cdot y_{hu.t} \quad \forall hu.t \tag{19.10}$$

2.2.3 Renewable energy production

Eq. (19.11) describes that the energy offer of each renewable energy technology in each time interval ($p_{r.t}$), must be less than or equal to an upper bound which is a function of the availability of each renewable energy technology in each time interval ($AV_{r.t}$) multiplied with its available capacity in each time interval ($IC_{r.t}$).

$$p_{r.t} \leq AV_{r.t} \cdot IC_{r.t} \quad \forall r.t \tag{19.11}$$

2.2.4 Hydropower generation

As set by Constraint (19.12), the total daily energy supply from all hydropower units ($\sum_h \sum_{t \in dt} p_{h.t}$) must not exceed a certain maximum bound (ED^{hyd}).

$$\sum_h \sum_t p_{h.t} \leq ED^{hyd} \tag{19.12}$$

In addition to Constraint (19.12), Constraint (19.13) guarantees that the aggregated energy supply from all hydroelectric power units in each time interval must be less than or equal to their total available capacity ($\sum_h P_h^{max}$).

$$\sum_h p_{h.t} \leq \sum_h P_h^{max} \quad \forall t \tag{19.13}$$

2.2.5 Energy trading

Constraint (19.14) sets an upper limit ($IC_{m.t}$), for net electricity imports, defined as the difference between imports and exports ($p_{m.t} - p_{x.t}$) from each interconnection in each time interval.

$$p_{m.t} - p_{x.t} \leq IC_{m.t} \quad \forall (m.x) \in MX.t \tag{19.14}$$

In a similar way, Constraint (19.15) sets a corresponding maximum bound ($I_{x.\,t}$), for net electricity exports ($p_{x.\,t} - p_{m.\,t}$) to each interconnection x in each time interval.

$$p_{x.t} - p_{m.t} \leq IC_{x.t} \quad \forall (m.x) \in MX.t \tag{19.15}$$

2.2.6 Ramp limits

Constraints (19.16) and (19.17) describe the ramp limits for both directions, up (RU_{hu}) and down (RD_{hu}) for each hydrothermal power unit in each time interval, defined as the rate at which a thermal power unit can increase (up) or decrease (down) its production level.

$$p_{hu.t} - p_{hu.t-1} \leq RU_{hu} \cdot 60 \quad \forall hu.t \tag{19.16}$$

$$p_{hu.t-1} - p_{hu.t} \leq RD_{hu} \cdot 60 \quad \forall hu.t \tag{19.17}$$

2.2.7 Time limits

Constraint (19.18) imposes the minimum uptime of each thermal power unit, according to which it must be dispatched in each time interval ($y_{u.\,t} = 1$) if its start-up decision has been made ($st_{u.\,t} = 1$) during the previous ($T_u^{upp} - 1$) time intervals.

$$\sum_{t'=t-T_u^{upp}+1}^{t} st_{u.t'} \leq y_{u.t} \quad \forall u.t \tag{19.18}$$

On the other hand, Constraint (19.19) defines the minimum downtime of each thermal power unit, according to which it must be out of unit commitment in each time interval ($u_{u.\,t} = 0$) if its shut-down decision has been made ($sd_{u.\,t} = 1$) during the previous ($T_u^{dn} - 1$) time intervals.

$$\sum_{t'=t-T_u^{dn}+1}^{t} sd_{u.t'} \leq 1 - y_{u.t} \quad \forall u.t \tag{19.19}$$

Also, Eq. (19.20) defines a logical correlation among the dispatch ($y_{u.\,t} - y_{u.\,t-1}$), start-up ($st_{u.\,t}$) and shutdown ($sd_{u.\,t}$) decisions of each thermal power unit in each time interval.

$$st_{u.t} - sd_{u.t} = y_{u.t} - y_{u.t-1} \quad \forall u.t \tag{19.20}$$

2.2.8 Reserve limits

Constraints (19.21)–(19.25) set the upper reserve provision limits per type (frequency containment reserve with upward direction, automatic frequency restoration reserve with both upward and downward directions, and frequency restoration via manual activation, both spinning and non-spinning) and hydrothermal power unit in each time interval.

In particular, Constraint (19.21) imposes an upper limit (RR_{hu}^{R1up}) on the frequency containment reserve with upward direction provision of each hydrothermal power unit in each time interval ($e_{hu.\,t}^{R1up}$), subject to the decision for being dispatched or not ($y_{hu.\,t}$).

$$e_{hu.t}^{R1up} \leq RR_{hu}^{R1up} \cdot y_{hu.t} \quad \forall hu.t \tag{19.21}$$

Constraint (19.22) forces an upper limit (RR_{hu}^{2up}) on the automatic frequency restoration reserve with upward direction provision of each hydrothermal power unit in each time interval ($e_{hu.\,t}^{R2up}$), subject to the decision for being dispatched or not ($y_{hu.\,t}$). Constraint (19.23) implements the same for the automatic frequency restoration reserve with downward direction.

$$e_{hu.t}^{R2up} \leq RR_{hu}^{2up} \cdot y_{hu.t} \quad \forall hu.t \tag{19.22}$$

$$e_{hu.t}^{R2dn} \leq RR_{hu}^{2dn} \cdot y_{hu.t} \quad \forall w.t \tag{19.23}$$

Constraint (19.24) imposes an upper limit (RR_{hu}^{3s}) on the spinning frequency restoration via manual activation provision of each hydrothermal unit in each time interval ($e_{hu.\,t}^{R3s}$), subject to the decision for being dispatched or not ($y_{hu.\,t}$).

$$e_{hu.t}^{R3s} \leq RR_{hu}^{3s} \cdot y_{hu.t} \quad \forall hu.t \tag{19.24}$$

Constraint (19.25) sets a maximum bound (RR_{hu}^{3ns}) on the non-spinning frequency restoration via manual activation provision of each hydrothermal unit in each time interval $(e_{hu.t}^{R3ns})$, subject to the decision for being out of unit commitment or not $(1 - y_{hu.t})$.

$$e_{hu.t}^{R3ns} \leq RR_{hu}^{3ns} \cdot (1 - y_{hu.t}) \quad \forall hu.t \tag{19.25}$$

2.2.9 Reserve requirements

Constraints (19.26)–(19.29) describe the power system's reserve requirements per type (frequency containment reserve with upward direction, automatic frequency restoration reserve with both upward and downward directions, and frequency restoration via manual activation respectively), to be met by the supply of all hydrothermal power units in each time period t.

$$\sum_{hu} e_{hu.t}^{R1up} \geq RD_t^{R1up} \quad \forall t \tag{19.26}$$

$$\sum_{hu} e_{hu.t}^{R2up} \geq RD_t^{R2up} \quad \forall t \tag{19.27}$$

$$\sum_{hu} e_{hu.t}^{R2dn} \geq RD_t^{R2dn} \quad \forall t \tag{19.28}$$

$$\sum_{hu} \left(e_{hu.t}^{R3s} + e_{u.t}^{R3ns}\right) \geq RD_t^{R3} \quad \forall t \tag{19.29}$$

The whole problem comprises a MILP model, whose objective is the total cost minimization (19.1), and subject to constraints and Eqs. (19.2)–(19.29). The proposed optimization model determines the optimal yearly energy mix of the studied power system based on a day by day iterative solution of all the dates of a year, where the solution of a specific date constitutes the input data of the next date.

3 Case study

An illustrative case study of the Serbian power system has been employed in the developed optimization framework. It was considered that the Kosovo's power system is integrated into the Sebian one. The structure of the system's condition at the beginning of 2020 has been taken as reference and is depicted in Fig. 19.1 (ENTSO-E, 2020). Lignite-fired units comprise the dominant technology in the Serbian power system with a gross capacity of around 5.2 GW. Utilizing also the country's hydro potential, hydroelectric power units follow with an exisitng capacity of around 3 GW. Thermal power units, operating with either natural gas or fuel oil, report a gross capacity less than 0.5 GW, along with a hard coal-fired unit of 125 MW. The renewable energy potential is utilized to a small extent, since these technologies report collectively a capacity of around 400 MW, where wind power accounts for almost the total.

Due to its central location, Serbia shares electricity interconnections with eight power systems including Albania, Bosnia and Herzegovina, Bulgaria, Croatia, Hungary, Montenegro, North Macedonia and Romania. Fig. 19.2 portrays

FIG. 19.1 Installed capacity of the Serbian power system (MW).

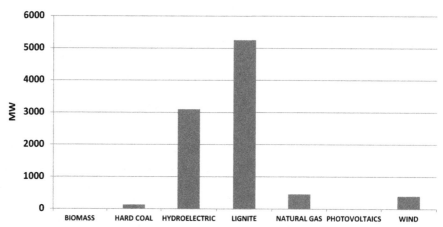

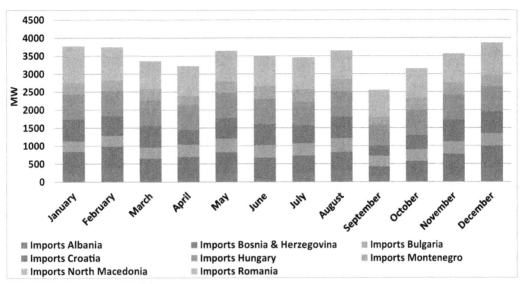

FIG. 19.2   Monthly import capacities of each interconnection (MW).

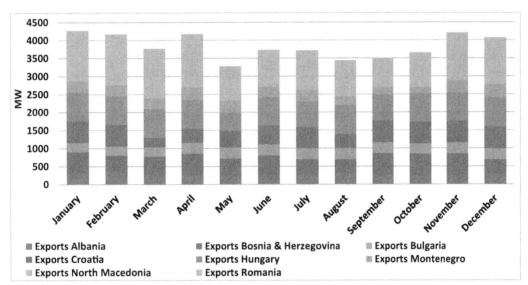

FIG. 19.3   Monthly export capacities of each interconnection (MW).

the monthly available import capacities of each interconnection with the Serbian power system, ranging from 2555 to 3861 MW in total, according to each month. Correspondingly, Fig. 19.3 presents the monthly available export capacities of each interconnection with the Serbian power system, ranging from 3280 to 4271 MW in total, according to each month. Comparing these two values, we can observe that the exports capacities are slightly higher than the corresponding import ones, reflecting the fact that the Serbian power system is used as a transit system for electricity transmission toward other systems, for instance the Greek one.

The formation of the offers (for imports) and bids (for exports) are based on the estimations for the border prices in each power system. Fig. 19.4 depicts the daily average electricity prices at the Hungarian, Romanian, Croatian and Bulgarian borders at an annual level. Although some extreme values can be observed, both peaks and minimums, most prices are in the range between 40 and 60 €/MWh. For the cases of Bulgaria, Croatia, Hungary and Romania there are available data for the power exchanges already established in these countries. For the other four remaining countries (Albania, Bosnia and Herzegovina, Montenegro, and North Macedonia), there have been made assumptions based on purchases prices of the relevant physical transmission rights between the underlying countries.

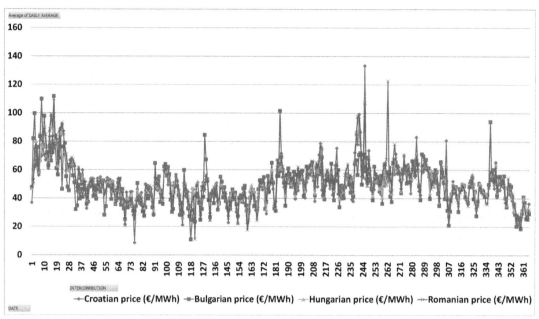

FIG. 19.4 Daily average electricity prices at the Croatian, Hungarian, Romanian, and Bulgarian borders at an annual level (€/MWh).

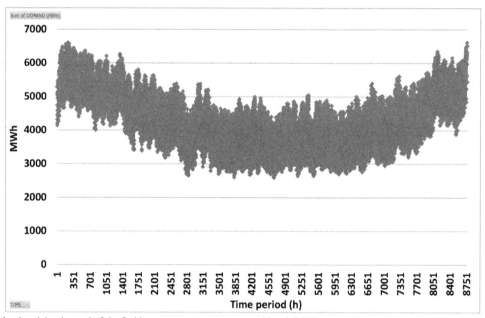

FIG. 19.5 Hourly electricity demand of the Serbian power system at an annual level (MWh).

The electricity demand of the Serbian power system equals 39.339 GWh at an annual level. The load maximum equals 6621 MW in December and the minimum 2592 MW in July. The average value equals around 4491 MW and its standard deviation amounts to around 850 MW. Fig. 19.5 shows the hourly electricity demand of the Serbian power system at an annual level. As can be observed, the largest daily values are reported during January and December, while the lowest during September and June.

4   Results

The results section contains the key modelling outputs from the implementation of the illustrative case study. The problem has been solved to global optimality making use of the ILOG CPLEX 12.6.0.0 solver incorporated in the General Algebraic Modelling System (GAMS) tool (GAMS, 2020). An integrality gap of 0% has been imposed.

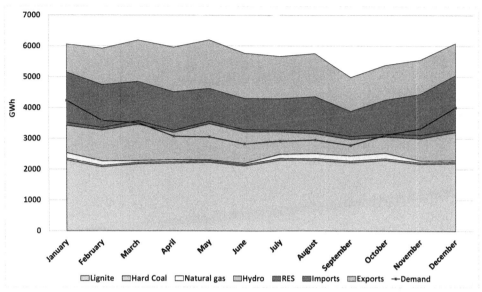

FIG. 19.6 Annual energy mix of the Serbian power system with aggregated monthly values (GWh).

4.1 Energy mix

Not surprisingly, lignite-fired power units constitute the largest source of electricity generation at an annual level, covering alone the baseload demand. Its annual generation amounts to around 26,566 GWh, accounting for almost two-thirds of the total electricity demand. Fig. 19.6 depicts the annual energy mix of the Serbian power system with aggregated monthly values. Electricity output from hydropower units amounts to 10,200 GWh, accounting for around 26% of the annual load. The remaining domestic sources of electricity generation, namely natural gas fired, hard coal-fired and renewable energy units contribute around 3000 GWh in total on an annual basis, standing for less than 8% of the yearly electricity demand. As can be observed, the share of renewable electricity generation in the Serbian energy mix is very low, at the level of 1000 GWh, underlining the space and opportunities that exist for further significant investments in this field. The role of the electricity trading is crucial for the determination of the optimal energy mix and flows. Although its net effect on the domestic energy mix is low, amounting to around 360 GWh of net exports, the absolute values of both imports and exports are quite high highlighting the role of the Serbian power system as a hub in the SEE region. It is noticeable that based on the assumptions of the examined case study the domestic generation exceeds the country's electricity requirements. A seasonality pattern can be also observed in the cross-border flows, since during the low-temperature months (November, December, January, and February) the country is net electricity importer, while during the remaining 8 months the system is converted into a net electricity exporter.

Putting emphasis on the supply side, Fig. 19.7 depicts the resulting annual energy supply balance of the Serbian power system. Among the available suppliers, lignite-fired units stand for almost half of the total electricity supply, and followed by electricity imports with 27%, hydropower units with 19%, and the remaining 5% from natural gas, hard coal and renewable energy units. The large exposure to carbon intensive energy sources underlines the need for a careful planning regarding the investment framework for renewable energy installations, especially when considered the impacts of a potential introduction of CO_2 emission pricing.

Focusing on the allocation of the electricity trading flows of each interconnected power system. Fig. 19.8 shows the annual electricity trading of the Serbian power system with each interconnection with monthly aggregated values. On an annual basis, the countries to which Serbia is net exporter are Albania, Montenegro, North Macedonia, and Romania. On the contrary, the countries from which Serbia is net importer are Bulgaria, Bosnia and Herzegovina, Croatia, and Hungary. Bosnia and Herzegovina and Hungary comprise the key countries from which Serbia imports electricity as a transit country, while Albania, North Macedonia, and Montenegro are the main countries to which Serbia exports significant amounts of electricity, the majority of which having perhaps the Greek and/or the Italian power system as destination. In terms of energy amounts, the largest quantities, both imports and exports, are directed to and from the Hungarian power system, which is the most liquid power exchange in the region and keeps also significant interconnection capacities with the Serbian power system.

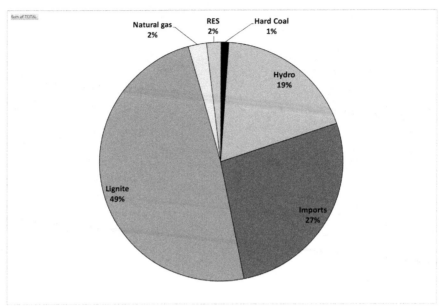

FIG. 19.7 Annual energy supply balance of the Serbian power system (%).

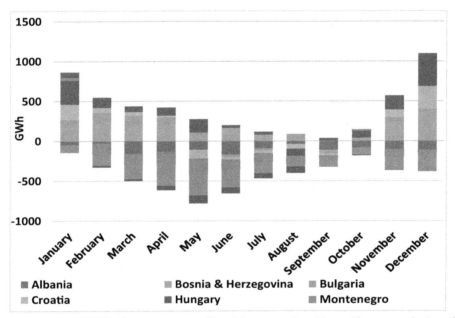

FIG. 19.8 Annual electricity trading of the Serbian power system with each interconnection with monthly aggregated values (GWh).

4.2 Economic performance

The total cost for the annual operation of the wholesale market of the Serbian power system equals around 1.4 bn €. The daily minimum net cost value amounts to around 1 m€ during a day of April when the annual daily demand low occurs. The corresponding maximum net cost value is equivalent to almost 12 m€ during a day of January when the annual daily demand peak occurs. Regarding the system's marginal price, its annual average equals 48.293 €/MWh. Fig. 19.9 depicts the average monthly values of the marginal price of the Serbian power system at an annual level. Its largest monthly average value is reported during the month of January, amounting to around 74 €/MWh. being the month with the highest aggregated electricity demand. During that month, the net electricity imports recorded their annual maximum, being equal to around 720 GWh at a monthly level (see also Fig. 19.8). The daily average maximum value equals 103.52 €/MWh during a

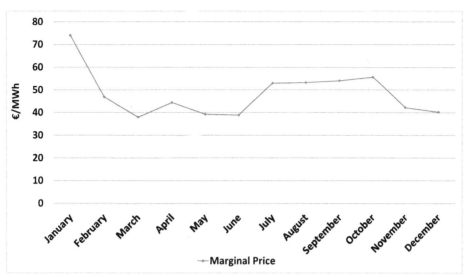

FIG. 19.9 Average monthly values of the marginal price of the Serbian power system at an annual level (€/MWh).

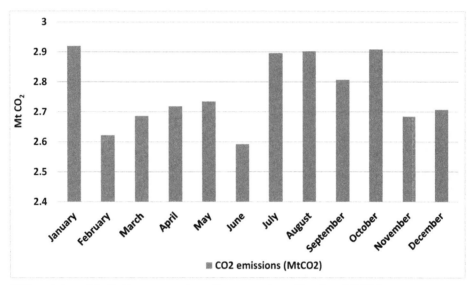

FIG. 19.10 Annual CO_2 emissions of the Serbian power system with aggregated monthly values (Mt CO_2).

day of September, the key characteristic of which was the skyrocketing price in the Hungarian power exchange, whose daily average value closed to 106.94 €/MWh. highlighting again the influence of that power market on the other electricity markets of the region. On the other hand, the respective daily average minimum value corresponds to almost 25 €/MWh during the Christmas day (25th of December), where a lot of electricity imports were recorded and the corresponding prices in the neighboring power exchanges were also at low levels.

4.3 Environmental performance

The total CO_2 emissions derived from the annual operation of the Serbian power system amounts to around 33 Mt CO_2. The key contributors of CO_2 emissions are the lignite-fired units which are assumed to have a CO_2 emission factor of 1.2 tCO_2/MWh. Fig. 19.10 depicts the annual CO_2 emissions of the Serbian power system with aggregated monthly values. The months where the largest emissions are recorded include January, July, August, and October whose values approach 3

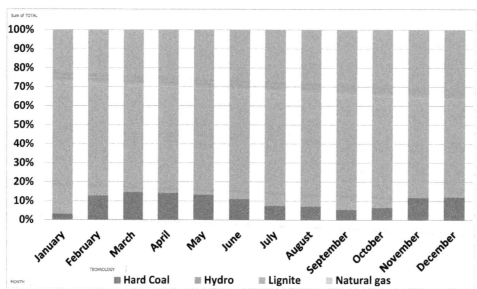

FIG. 19.11 Annual frequency containment reserve mix of the Serbian power system (%).

Mt CO_2 at a monthly level. During those months, the total domestic thermal power-based electricity generation approaches and/or surpasses the amount of 2.500 GWh. The inelastic system's dependence on the lignite-fired electricity generation has to be taken into consideration in the design of the system's future pathways in order to include alternatives for cases such as the introduction of the CO_2 emission pricing and/or the operational performance of the aging thermal power fleet.

4.4 Reserve mix

Frequency containment reserve (FCR) is defined as that type of operating reserves enabling the constant containment of frequency fluctuations from nominal value to constantly meet the power balance in the power system. Fig. 19.11 portrays the annual composition of the frequency containment reserve provision mix of the Serbian power system. As can be observed, lignite-fired units comprise the main reserve provider throughout the examined period. These units are designed for stable operation and their optimal operation does not include large deviations of their power output. Consequently, they are efficient contributors of that service, along with hard coal-fired units, whose supply is in the range 0–15% of the total during all the months of the year. Note also that the requirements for that service type are designed for upward direction.

The automatic frequency restoration reserve (aFRR) is provided continuously, both upwards and downwards, in order to restore the frequency to its nominal value of 50 Hz. This type of reserve has positive values for upward control and negative values for downward control. In addition, it is characterized by a swift response time and remains operational if necessary. Fig. 19.12 presents the annual automatic frequency restoration reserve mix with upward direction of the Serbian power system. Not surprisingly, this service is met by hydroelectric units which are characterized by very fast response times and significant ramp rates. Also, Fig. 19.13 shows the annual automatic frequency restoration reserve mix with downward direction of the Serbian power system. In the same way, hydroelectric units cover the largest amount of those requirements, with a small also contribution from natural gas-fired units, which is more time-flexible units than lignite-fired ones and they are characterized by quite high ramp rates.

In case of a noticeable deviation between supply and demand that cannot be fixed by FCR or aFRR, the transmission system operation has the option of activating flexibility sources being available as a tertiary control measure, namely frequency restoration via manual activation (mFRR). The flexibility resources differ from the FCR and aFRR balancing services on the grounds that they are deployed in a manual way and that the requested amount of energy must be activated within a quarter. Fig. 19.14 shows the annual frequency restoration via manual activation mix of the Serbian power system. As can be seen, all the types of power units contribute in the satisfaction of that service. Note also that the provision of that service is assumed to be non-priced in our case. Hydroelectric power units cover the most significant part of the relevant requirements, followed by natural gas, lignite and hard coal-fired units, correspondingly.

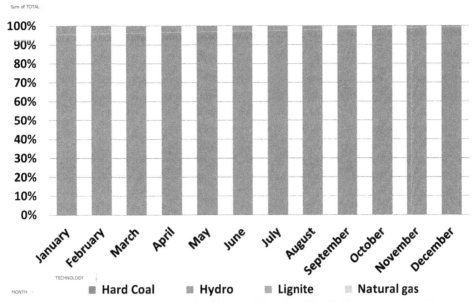

FIG. 19.12 Annual automatic frequency restoration reserve mix with upward direction of the Serbian power system (%).

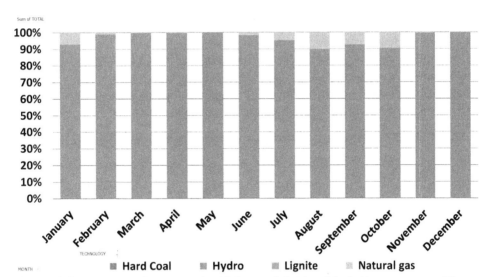

FIG. 19.13 Annual automatic frequency restoration reserve mix with downward direction of the Serbian power system (%).

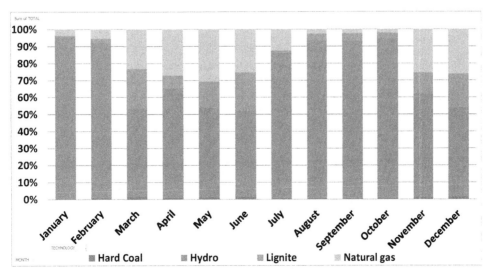

FIG. 19.14 Annual frequency restoration via manual activation mix of the Serbian power system (%).

5 Conclusions

The power sector of the Western Balkan countries finds currently itself during a transition period to be harmonized with the European electricity markets and to implement the EUPHEMIA (Pan-European Hybrid Electricity Market Integration Algorithm) model toward the internal European power market (Koltsaklis and Dagoumas, 2018b). Toward that evolution, there is a need for an in-depth analysis of the current situation in each of those power systems in order to identify the challenges that must be addressed in order to facilitate that transition.

Unit commitment models have long used in the academia in order to determine the optimal operational scheduling, typically, with a cost-optimal objective function, of a power system by satisfying a series of highly detailed technical constraints and with the aim of constantly satisfying the system's demand balance. This work makes use of a systematic approach based on mixed integer programming techniques in order to assess the relevant competitiveness, the fundamentals and the dynamics of the Serbian power system. This model implements a co-optimization of energy and reserves wholesale markets with an hourly time resolution for an annual period.

The results highlight that the Serbian power system is based on its domestic sources to cover its energy requirements, while the net effect on its trading balance, namely its imports or exports, is primarily based on the hydrological conditions affecting its hydroelectric generation. The importance of hydroelectric units is highly significant for the stability of the system and in terms of security of supply as well. The system is highly dependent on the domestic lignite reserves; however, this output does not consider its CO_2 emission pricing and must be considered in the system's future design. The model outputs underline also the influence of the Hungarian electricity market on the market prices of all the other systems of the SEE, along with the Greek and/or Italian market prices. The further installation of renewable energy units in combination with the penetration of more market participants, e.g., independent power producers with natural gas-fired units, has the potential of creating a new framework for energy exchanges.

All these must be carefully examined in the long-term energy planning, since a challenging situation could be emerged due to potential beginning of CO_2 emission pricing mechanism and closures of the aging lignite power fleet due to adverse economic conditions to refurbish, which, in a combined way, can threaten the system's security of supply.

References

Abbate, A.L., Careri, F., Calisti, R., Rossi, S., 2017. The impact of HVDC in the development of the pan-European system: focus on Italy-South East Europe ties. In: 2017 IEEE Manchester PowerTech, pp. 1–6.

Alvarez, G.E., Marcovecchio, M.G., Aguirre, P.A., 2018. Security-Constrained Unit Commitment Problem including thermal and pumped storage units: a MILP formulation by the application of linear approximations techniques. Electr. Power Syst. Res. 154, 67–74.

Alvarez, G.E., Marcovecchio, M.G., Aguirre, P.A., 2020. Optimization of the integration among traditional fossil fuels, clean energies, renewable sources, and energy storages: a MILP model for the coupled electric power, hydraulic and natural gas systems. Comput. Ind. Eng. 139, 106141.

Apostolovic, M.R., Koltsaklis, N.E., 2018. Perspectives of the further utilization of Renewable Energy Sources in the South-Eastern Europe. In: International Conference Energy and Ecology Industry. EEI. Available from: https://www.researchgate.net/publication/328341704_Perspectives_of_the_further_utilization_of_Renewable_Energy_Sources_in_the_South-Eastern_Europe. (Accessed 07 March 2020.

Batas Bjelić, I., Rajaković, N., Ćosić, B., Duić, N., 2013. Increasing wind power penetration into the existing Serbian energy system. Energy 57, 30–37.

Cebulla, F., Fichter, T., 2017. Merit order or unit-commitment: how does thermal power plant modeling affect storage demand in energy system models? Renew. Energy 105, 117–132.

Ciric, R.M., 2019. Review of techno-economic and environmental aspects of building small hydroelectric plants—a case study in Serbia. Renew. Energy 140, 715–721.

Djurdjevic, D.Z., 2011. Perspectives and assessments of solar PV power engineering in the Republic of Serbia. Renew. Sust. Energy Rev. 15, 2431–2446.

ENTSO-E, 2020. ENTSO-E Transparency Platform. https://transparency.entsoe.eu. Accessed 07 March 2020.

Feng, Z.-K., Niu, W.-J., Wang, W.-C., Zhou, J.-Z., Cheng, C.-T., 2019. A mixed integer linear programming model for unit commitment of thermal plants with peak shaving operation aspect in regional power grid lack of flexible hydropower energy. Energy 175, 618–629.

Finardi, E.C., Takigawa, F.Y.K., Brito, B.H., 2016. Assessing solution quality and computational performance in the hydro unit commitment problem considering different mathematical programming approaches. Electr. Power Syst. Res. 136, 212–222.

GAMS, 2020. GAMS—A User's Guide. Available online: https://www.gams.com/24.8/docs/userguides/GAMSUsersGuide.pdf. Accessed 07 March 2020.

IRENA, 2017. Joanneum Research and University of Ljubljana. Cost-Competitive Renewable Power Generation: Potential Across South East Europe. International Renewable Energy Agency (IRENA), Abu Dhabi.

Koltsaklis, N., Dagoumas, A., 2018a. Policy implications of power exchanges on operational scheduling: evaluating EUPHEMIA's market products in case of Greece. Energies 11, 2715.

Koltsaklis, N.E., Dagoumas, A.S., 2018b. Incorporating unit commitment aspects to the European electricity markets algorithm: an optimization model for the joint clearing of energy and reserve markets. Appl. Energy 231, 235–258.

Koltsaklis, N.E., Georgiadis, M.C., 2015. A multi-period, multi-regional generation expansion planning model incorporating unit commitment constraints. Appl. Energy 158, 310–331.

Koltsaklis, N.E., Dagoumas, A.S., Kopanos, G.M., Pistikopoulos, E.N., Georgiadis, M.C., 2013. A Mathematical Programming Approach to the Optimal Long-Term National Energy Planning. Chemical Engineering Transactions 35, 625–630. https://doi.org/10.3303/CET1335104.

Koltsaklis, N.E., Gioulekas, I., Georgiadis, M.C., 2018. Optimal scheduling of interconnected power systems. Comput. Chem. Eng. 111, 164–182.

Psarros, G.N., Papathanassiou, S.A., 2019. A unit commitment method for isolated power systems employing dual minimum loading levels to enhance flexibility. Electr. Power Syst. Res. 177, 106007.

Soltani, Z., Ghaljehei, M., Gharehpetian, G.B., Aalami, H.A., 2018. Integration of smart grid technologies in stochastic multi-objective unit commitment: an economic emission analysis. Int. J. Electr. Power Energy Syst. 100, 565–590.

Szabó, L., Mezősi, A., Paizs, L., 2019. Long-term flexibility analysis of the power sector in South East Europe. In: 2019 16th International Conference on the European Energy Market (EEM), pp. 1–5.

Yang, Z., Li, K., Niu, Q., Xue, Y., 2017. A comprehensive study of economic unit commitment of power systems integrating various renewable generations and plug-in electric vehicles. Energy Convers. Manage. 132, 460–481.

Yang, L., Zhao, X., Li, X., Feng, X., Yan, W., 2019. A MILP-based optimal power and gas flow in electricity-gas coupled networks. Energy Procedia 158, 6399–6404.

Zepter, J.M., Weibezahn, J., 2019. Unit commitment under imperfect foresight—the impact of stochastic photovoltaic generation. Appl. Energy 243, 336–349.

Chapter 20

Evaluation of capacity expansion scenarios for the Hellenic electric sector

Ioannis Panapakidis

Department of Electrical and Computer Engineering, University of Thessaly, Volos, Greece

1 Introduction

During the past decades, the electricity demand has been continually increasing in a global level (IEA, 2019a). Apart from the four traditional consumption sectors, namely the residential, industrial, commercial and agricultural, the transport sector will employ an increasing amount of electricity due to the electric vehicles (IEA, 2019b). In order to cover the increasing future demand, power system planning is utilized. It refers to a process that includes capacity scenarios formulation and evaluation. The goal is to cover the needs for electricity of the society in such a way as to meet various conditions for the exploitation of available resources and subsequently providing sufficient power supply to meet the demand at the lowest possible cost (Farrokhifar et al., 2020; Odetayo et al., 2019; Qin et al., 2019; Zhang et al., 2013).

Power system planning compares and selects between scenarios that differ in economic and technical terms (WEC, 2019). It considers various factors like the chronological evolution of the demand, macroeconomic indicators such as the gross domestic product, environmental restrictions, fossil fuel and renewable energy resources (RES) capacities, predictions for fuel prices, i.e., oil, natural gas, etc., technological development and degree of penetration of energy efficient equipment and others. Other factors that influence system planning are the need for harmonization with national and local goals for energy supply security, minimization of the environmental impact, the optimal utilization of domestic energy resources, need for a variation in energy supply, i.e., in terms of fuel categories and in terms of the geographical location of the units, minimization of production costs, environmental costs, social costs, regional and national development and economic competitiveness, introduction of technological innovations in the electricity system and others.

Power system planning is mainly composed by six phases. The first phase involves the determination of the planning period. The scope is to cover the demand until the final year of the period. The second one refers to long-term demand forecasting. The two variables under examination is the peak load and total consumed energy. The peak load determines the installed power generation capacity. The core of the planning is the third step. Here a set of scenarios is designed. The scenarios may differ in renewable energy and natural gas shares in the generation mix, different demand evolution per sector and others. There is a variety of data requirements such as the capital cost of the plants, emissions, efficiency, programmed unit decommissioning and others. In the fourth phase, the scenarios are evaluated using an appropriate software. The fifth phase refers to the evaluation of the scenarios in terms of capacity expansion cost, fuel cost, environmental impact and others. Here a sensitivity analysis can take place for the purpose of evaluating the impact of an input parameter to the results. Finally, the sixth phase refers to the adoption of the selected scenario and the preparation of its implementation (Seifi and Sadegh Sepasian, 2011). The design of the power system planning can be made by transmission system operators, energy related ministries and other governmental agencies with expertise in energy and environmental issues (Sioshansi, 2013).

IPTO SA is responsible for conducting the power system planning for the Greek energy system. From the beginning of the 1990s until today, the Greek energy system is being formed in accordance with the requirements of the national economy, the evolution of individual economic activities and the development of specific industries, consumer habits and with the European energy, environmental and development policies. The country has made the last 25 years to significantly differentiate its energy balance, thus, improving its energy security. Regarding the total final consumption in Greece, the share of RES amounted to 8% in 2016. while from 28% of the share of electricity, approximately a 5% again corresponds to RES. Therefore, the total share of RES is 13% in the total final consumption. The share of RES in gross energy consumption was to 15.30% in 2016, a rate equivalent to an increase of almost 50% compared to 2010. Respectively,

Mathematical Modelling of Contemporary Electricity Markets. https://doi.org/10.1016/B978-0-12-821838-9.00019-0

the share of electricity generation from RES was 26.5% of the total electricity production energy in 2016, while the share of non-dispatchable RES units in electricity generation amounted to 19% in 2016. This increase in shares is due to the increase in non-dispatchable production of photovoltaics and wind power and in the reduction of total electricity demand in the last decade. The exploitation of lignite was a strategic choice, despite its significant environmental impact as it is still the main domestic fuel. The great dependence of Greece on the imports of crude oil and petroleum products and the unpredictable changes in their price bring an important factor of uncertainty in energy planning policies, but also in energy security.

Today, the final energy consumption in Greece is based almost exclusively on conventional fuels. At the same time, although the penetration of natural gas has made significant progress in recent years, it still concerns only a small share of total final consumption and be far from the European average. Also, while the penetration of RES has seen a significant increase in the last decade, through the implementation of intense policy measures. Although at the beginning of this decade, the applications of RES presented high implementation rates, next a decline has been observed. There is significant room for improvement in the institutional framework to ensure the safe operation of the national energy system in conditions of high RES penetration.

The adoption of common European policies in the energy sector has already influence the decisions concerning the design and configuration of the national energy system. In particular, an increasing penetration of RES has been achieved in recent years both in electricity generation and in the final use of energy, while measures have already been implemented and policies to achieve energy saving in buildings, but also to strengthen combined power and heat generation. Greece produces a large amount of lignite that covered over the last decades a significant part of the electricity generation. The lignite was until recently a dominant fuel in electricity generation, almost representing 30% of the total production. Oil is still the most important fuel and the country depends almost exclusively on oil imports. The transport sector is the largest energy consumption sector. It is dominated by petroleum products, while much of the oil is also used in the residential sector. Significant energy consumption is also recorded by the industry and various commercial and public services consumption sectors (Georgiou, 2016; Ioakimidis et al., 2012; Institute of Energy for South-East Europe, 2019; Rampidis et al., 2010).

The scope of the present study is the exploration of future alternative scenarios for the Greek energy system. All the alternative scenarios are compared with the baseline one which corresponds to the official Ten-Year Network Development Plan (TYNDP) for the period 2018–2027, published by the IPTO SA (IPTO SA, 2018). The publication of the present TYNDP coincides with a period of continuing economic recession in the country, because of which the demand for electricity has been significantly reduced. The reduction of electricity demand. combined with the increase of distributed generation, leads to a reduction in traffic management of energy flows in the grid. Apart from covering the demand, a driving parameter for the development of the transmission system is the need to support the penetration of RES in the context of meeting national objectives for 2020. The assessment of future energy scenarios for the Greek energy sector highlights many challenges for the implementation of the national energy policy. At the same time, the recognition and comprehension of the energy related sectors that are not yet fully evolved in Greece but also those with high potential can contribute at drawing up a roadmap for approaching national goals, strengthening the domestic energy market and reduce its high energy dependence.

2 Methodology

The TYNDP 2018–2027 includes the development projects development of the energy system for the respective period, as well as the basic approach followed for their design, configuration and planning. More specifically, the TYNDP 2018-2027:

- identifies the main power transmission infrastructure to be built or to be upgraded over the next 10 years, including that necessary infrastructure for the penetration of RES,
- contains all investments already included in previous development programs and identifies new investments, where their implementation is expected to begin within the next 3 years, and
- provides technical and economic feasibility analysis for important power transmission projects those relating to international interconnections and interconnections of islands with the main interconnected system, including implementation schedule. estimated cash flows for financing the needs of the investment plans of these projects.

An additional basic parameter for the configuration of the TYNDP 2018–2027 is also IPTO's obligation to develop the necessary infrastructure for the increased penetration of RES into the energy mix of the country, as defined by the respective national policy objectives. The main factors influencing the electricity demand of the country are: (i) The economic development of the country, (ii) changes in consumer habits (e.g., air conditioning. use electricity in transport, use of energy efficient equipment, etc.), (iii) the conditions in the electricity market that define the tariffs, and (iv) various measures to support energy efficiency, protection of the environment and others. IPTO's forecasts for the evolution of energy demand are based on the available historical data of demand and in published forecasts they have prepared by other competent bodies (i.e., medium-term projections of gross domestic product, etc.). According to the TYNDP 2018–2027, for the period 2018–2027 three demand scenarios are examined, namely "Low Demand," "Baseline Demand," and "High Demand." Every demand evolution scenario is formed by adopting reasonable and consistent hypotheses, considering and the expected evolution of gross domestic product which is a determining factor in the evolution of demand. Table 20.1 presents the demand projection per scenario.

The average yearly increase rates for Low Demand, Baseline Demand, and High Demand scenarios are 0.51%, 0.91%, and 2.17%. respectively. Table 20.2 shows the three scenarios, namely "Low Peak," "Baseline Peak," and "High Demand"

TABLE 20.1 IPTO's scenarios for the demand projection.

	Scenario		
Year	Low demand (GWh)	Baseline demand (GWh)	High demand (GWh)
2018	53,100	53,400	53,490
2019	53,500	54,310	54,630
2020	54,800	55,840	56,400
2021	56,040	57,325	58,120
2022	56,270	57,750	58,750
2023	56,510	58,180	59,375
2024	58,375	60,250	61,730
2025	58,670	60,740	62,440
2026	58,960	61,230	63,150
2027	59,250	61,730	63,880
2028	59,550	62,230	64,610

TABLE 20.2 IPTO's scenarios for the peak load projection.

	Scenario		
Year	Low peak (MW)	Baseline peak (MW)	High peak (MW)
2018	9960	10,020	10,035
2019	10,040	10,190	10,250
2020	10,310	10,510	10,620
2021	10,380	10,625	10,770
2022	10,430	10,700	10,890
2023	10,470	10,780	11,000
2024	11,020	11,370	11,650
2025	11,070	11,460	11,790
2026	11,130	11,550	11,920
2027	11,190	11,650	12,060
2028	11,240	11,740	12,200

for the annual peak load projections. The prediction of the peak load is generally much more uncertain compared with the total demand. This is attributed to the fact that the peak load is highly influenced by the temperature, especially during the summer months and due to the increasing penetration of RES, a fact that increases the uncertainty of peak load prediction. The average yearly increase rates for Low Peak, Baseline Peak, and High Peak scenarios are 1.22%, 1.60%, and 1.98%, respectively.

Regarding the installed capacity, one scenario is formulated, Table 20.3 shows the installed capacity evolution per resource. The category other RES includes small hydro plants. biomass and combined heat and power. Lignite has a negative annual increase rate equal to −2.78%. implying that much amount of lignite power will be decommissioned until the end of the examined period. For natural gas, hydroelectricity, wind power, photovoltaics, and other RES the increase rates are 0.93%, 0.15%, 7.33%, 5.93%, and 9.93%, respectively.

It can be observed that no considerable addition of new units of natural gas and hydroelectricity are expected in the next decade. On the contrary other RES are expected to witness an average increment close to 10%. It should be noted that at the end of the period, the installed capacity is expected to exceed at 100% of the capacity of the base year, i.e., 166 MW. Considerable increase is also expected at wind power.

The scenarios that are considered in the present study differ in terms of increase rate of RES and Natural Gas. Thus. different rates from the official projections are examined. More specifically, the following rates are considered:

- "Base": 0%
- "Low": 5%
- "Medium": 8%
- "High": 10%

In total, 21 scenarios are examined, Table 20.4 presents the scenarios. The first letter refers to the total energy demand. The increase rates of "Low Demand," "Baseline Demand," and "High Demand" are adopted. The second letter refers to the rate increase of RES and the third letter to the increase rate of natural gas. Scenarios "IPTO_Low", "IPTO_Medium," and "IPTO_High" refer to the "Low Demand," "Baseline Demand," and "High Demand," respectively. In these scenarios, the capacity projection of Table 20.3 is regarded. Lignite plants and hydroelectricity plants do not change. The scope is to evaluate the impact of different RES and natural gas implementation rates in the system and compare their impact with the scenarios described in the TYNDP 2018–2027.

The scenarios are implemented in the LEAP software (Heaps, 2016), organized in Table 20.4. The increase rates of the four consumption sectors for the "Low Demand," "Baseline Demand," and "High Demand" scenarios are presented Tables 20.5–20.7, respectively.

TABLE 20.3 IPTO's scenario for the installed capacity (MW) projection.

	Lignite	Natural gas	Hydroelectricity	Wind power	Photovoltaics	Other RES	Total
2018	4337	4882.30	3398.70	2300	2720	166	17,804
2019	4337	5293.30	3407.70	2555	3000	174	18,767
2020	2525	5293.30	3412.70	2810	3280	180	17,501
2021	2525	5293.30	3417.70	3065	3560	210	18,071
2022	3185	5293.30	3422.70	3220	3710	275	19,106
2023	3185	5293.30	3427.70	3370	3860	325	19,461
2024	3185	5293.30	3432.70	3520	4010	325	19,766
2025	3185	5293.30	3437.70	3990	4256	375	20,537
2026	2885	5293.30	3442.70	4160	4406	375	20,562
2027	2885	5293.30	3447.70	4330	4556	375	20,887

TABLE 20.4 Formulated scenarios.

No.	Scenario reference	Total load	RES increase rate	Natural gas increase rate
1	IPTO_Low	Low	Base	Base
2	LLB	Low	Low	Base
3	LMB	Low	Medium	Base
4	LHB	Low	High	Base
5	LBL	Low	Base	Low
6	LBM	Low	Base	Medium
7	LBH	Low	Base	High
8	IPTO_Medium	Medium	Base	Base
9	MLB	Medium	Low	Base
10	MMB	Medium	Medium	Base
11	MHB	Medium	High	Base
12	MBL	Medium	Base	Low
13	MBM	Medium	Base	Medium
14	MBH	Medium	Base	High
15	IPTO_High	High	Base	Base
16	HLB	High	Low	Base
17	HMB	High	Medium	Base
18	HHB	High	High	Base
19	HBL	High	Base	Low
20	HBM	High	Base	Medium
21	HBH	High	Base	High

TABLE 20.5 Demand per sector for the "Low Demand" scenario.

Sectors (GWh)				Total
Residential	Industrial	Agricultural	Commercial	
19126.14	17,716.37	1596.12	14,661.33	53,100
19493.10	17,824.06	1107.88	15,074.43	53,500
19135.83	17,273.12	3462.21	14,928.75	54,800
19765.64	17,612.25	3105.51	15,556.14	56,040
20043.94	17,631.64	2679.13	15,914.28	56,270
20331.17	17,654.80	2238.32	16,285.22	56,510
21278.62	18,239.91	1662.23	17,194.12	58,375
21421.23	18,132.97	1657.40	17,459.05	58,670
21578.86	18,051.93	1652.25	17,677.07	58,960
21731.08	17,969.20	1647.57	17,902.19	59,250

TABLE 20.6 Demand per sector for the "Baseline Demand" scenario.

Sectors (GWh)				Total
Residential	Industrial	Agricultural	Commercial	
19234.23	17,816.47	1605.14	14,744.16	53,400
19788.25	18,094.35	1124.70	15,302.70	54,310
19499.01	17,600.99	3527.93	15,212.07	55,840
20218.87	18,016.50	3176.77	15,912.86	57,325
20571.58	18,095.48	2749.64	16,333.31	57,750
20932.47	18,176.57	2304.47	16,766.50	58,180
21962.09	18,825.83	1715.66	17,746.43	60,250
22177.01	18,772.74	1715.87	18,075.04	60,740
22409.66	18,746.94	1715.87	18,357.65	61,230
22640.67	18,721.32	1716.53	18,651.52	61,730

TABLE 20.7 Demand per sector for the "High Demand" scenario.

Sectors (GWh)				Total
Residential	Industrial	Agricultural	Commercial	
19266.65	17,846.49	1607.85	14,769.01	53,490
19904.84	18,200.97	1131.33	15,392.86	54,630
19694.56	17,777.50	3563.31	15,364.63	56,400
20499.27	18,266.36	3220.82	16,133.54	58,120
20927.79	18,408.82	2797.25	16,616.14	58,750
21362.42	18,549.91	2351.80	17,110.88	59,375
22501.57	19,288.27	1757.80	18,182.36	61,730
22797.71	19,298.15	1763.90	18,580.93	62,440
23112.37	19,334.79	1769.67	18,933.30	63,150
23429.23	19,373.37	1776.31	19,301.13	63,880

For demonstration reasons, the characteristics of LLB. MHB and HBH scenarios are presented at Tables 20.8–20.10, respectively.

In the LLB scenario, at the beginning the demand is low, starting at 53,100 GWh in 2018 and reaching 59,250 GWh in 2027. The installed capacity of RES is slightly increased by 5% compared to the values set by IPTO, while the capacity of gas units remains stable. The total installed capacity starts from 18,074.70 MW in 2018 and reaches 21,363.9 MW in 2027. In MHB scenario, the demand is moderate, starting at 53,400 GWh in 2018 and reaching 62,230 GWh in 2027. The installed capacity of RES shows a 10% increase compared to the IPTO values, with natural gas units remaining stable.

The total installed capacity starts from 18,345.40 MW in 2018 and reaches 21,840.80 MW in 2027. In the HBH scenario, the demand is high, starting from 53,490 GWh in 2018 and reaching 64,610 GWh in 2027. The installed capacity of RES is stable, and the gas units show an increase of 10% from the values set by IPTO. The total installed capacity starts from 18,292.23 MW in 2018 and reaches 21,416.33 MW in 2027.

TABLE 20.8 Characteristics of the LLB scenario.

	Lignite	Natural gas	Hydroelectricity	Wind power	Photovoltaics	Other RES	Total
2018	4337	4882.30	3410.10	2415	2856	174.30	18,074.70
2019	4337	5293.30	3419.55	2682.75	3150	182.70	19,065.30
2020	2525	5293.30	3424.80	2950.50	3444	189	17,826.60
2021	2525	5293.30	3430.05	3218.25	3738	220.50	18,425.10
2022	3185	5293.30	3435.30	3381	3895.50	288.75	19,478.85
2023	3185	5293.30	3440.55	3538.50	4053	341.25	19,851.60
2024	3185	5293.30	3445.80	3696	4210.50	341.25	20,171.85
2025	3185	5293.30	3451.05	4189.50	4468.80	393.75	20,981.40
2026	2885	5293.30	3456.30	4368	4626.30	393.75	21,022.65
2027	2885	5293.30	3461.55	4546.50	4783.80	393.75	21,363.90

TABLE 20.9 Characteristics of the MHB scenario.

	Lignite	Natural gas	Hydroelectricity	Wind Power	Photovoltaics	Other RES	Total
2018	4337	4882.30	3421.50	2530	2992	182.60	18,345.40
2019	4337	5293.30	3431.40	2810.50	3300	191.40	19,363.60
2020	2525	5293.30	3436.90	3091	3608	198	18,152.20
2021	2525	5293.30	3442.40	3371.50	3916	231	18,779.20
2022	3185	5293.30	3447.90	3542	4081	302.50	19,851.70
2023	3185	5293.30	3453.40	3707	4246	357.50	20,242.20
2024	3185	5293.30	3458.90	3872	4411	357.50	20,577.70
2025	3185	5293.30	3464.40	4389	4681.60	412.50	21,425.80
2026	2885	5293.30	3469.90	4576	4846.60	412.50	21,483.30
2027	2885	5293.30	3475.40	4763	5011.60	412.50	21,840.80

TABLE 20.10 Characteristics of the HBH scenario.

	Lignite	Natural gas	Hydroelectricity	Wind power	Photovoltaics	Other RES	Total
2018	4337	5370.53	3398.70	2300	2720	166	18,292.23
2019	4337	5822.63	3407.70	2555	3000	174	19,296.33
2020	2525	5822.63	3412.70	2810	3280	180	18,030.33
2021	2525	5822.63	3417.70	3065	3560	210	18,600.33
2022	3185	5822.63	3422.70	3220	3710	275	19,635.33
2023	3185	5822.63	3427.70	3370	3860	325	19,990.33
2024	3185	5822.63	3432.70	3520	4010	325	20,295.33
2025	3185	5822.63	3437.70	3990	4256	375	21,066.33
2026	2885	5822.63	3442.70	4160	4406	375	21,091.33
2027	2885	5822.63	3447.70	4330	4556	375	21,416.33

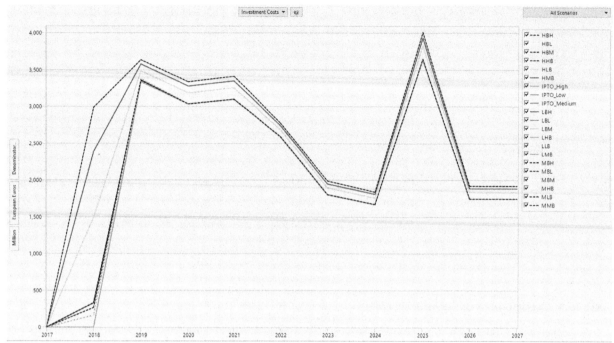

FIG. 20.1 Comparison of scenarios in terms of total capital cost.

3 Results

The results that follow refer to the comparison of the scenarios in terms of their economic and environmental impacts. The economic impact refers to the sum of the capital and operation and maintenance cost. The environmental effects include carbon dioxide (CO_2), nitrogen oxide (NOx) and sulfur dioxide (SO_2) emissions. Fig. 20.1 shows the capital cost of for each scenario. The cost is calculated based on the installed capacity added each year along with the capital costs required for each unit of power. The largest investment costs are presented in the high penetration scenarios of RES units (LHB, MHB, HHB) where the total cost for the 10-year plan reaches 27.82 b€.

The lowest cost is presented in the IPTO scenarios since there is no additional penetration of production units. Therefore, no additional capital investment costs. Gas units, even in their high-penetration scenarios, are not far behind IPTO's overall cost scenarios. In fact, low-penetration scenarios for RES have a much higher cost than high-penetration scenarios for gas plants. Therefore, RES units have higher capital costs per unit. From the figure it seems that the highest prices appear in 2025 where there is a large penetration of wind farms and photovoltaic stations. Table 20.11 presents the capital cost of each scenario per year.

Fig. 20.2 shows the cost of generated electricity for each scenario. In calculating production costs, LEAP exported results considering the cost of raw materials and fuels, the cost of capital, the cost of fixed and variable operation and maintenance, and the cost per unit of generation. In general, generation costs are lower in high-energy scenarios. The lowest generation cost is in the IPTO_High high demand scenario, with total generation costs reaching 13.39 b€. It is also worth noting that the scenarios of increased penetration of RES seem to increase costs, due to the increased initial cost of capital required for them. The highest production cost is observed in the MHB scenario, which over a decade requires 23,739.50 m€, a total of 77.20% higher than the IPTO_High scenario. Table 20.12 presents the generation cost of each scenario per year.

Fig. 20.3 shows the carbon dioxide emissions for each scenario from the power generation of conventional units. In fact, gas units produce 50% less carbon dioxide than lignite for each unit of electricity generated. As expected, most emissions appear in the scenarios of increasing gas penetration. The maximums appear in the HBH scenario due to further demand increase. Reduced emissions are shown by RES penetration scenarios with the lowest ones in the LHB scenario, where there is low power demand and at the same time the highest RES penetration. The HBH scenario produces 208.7 million metric

TABLE 20.11 Capital cost of each scenario per year (m€).

Scenarios	2018	2019	2020	2021	2022	2023	2024	2025	2026	2027	Total
HBH	329.60	3361.90	3035.40	3099.00	2589.50	1806.30	1673.80	3648.70	1743.80	1743.80	23,031.50
HBL	164.80	3374.80	3035.40	3099.00	2589.50	1806.30	1673.80	3648.70	1743.80	1743.80	22,879.60
HBM	263.60	3356.30	3035.40	3099.00	2589.50	1806.30	1673.80	3648.70	1743.80	1743.80	22,960.00
HHB	2987.00	3639.80	3338.90	3408.90	2775.90	1986.90	1841.10	4013.50	1918.10	1918.10	27,828.20
HLB	1493.50	3487.00	3187.20	3254.00	2682.70	1896.60	1757.40	3831.10	1830.90	1830.90	25,251.20
HMB	2389.60	3578.70	3278.20	3346.90	2738.60	1950.80	1807.70	3940.50	1883.30	1883.30	26,797.40
IPTO_High	–	3334.10	3035.40	3099.00	2589.50	1806.30	1673.80	3648.70	1743.80	1743.80	22,674.20
IPTO_Low	–	3334.10	3035.40	3099.00	2589.50	1806.30	1673.80	3648.70	1743.80	1743.80	22,674.20
IPTO_Medium	–	3334.10	3035.40	3099.00	2589.50	1806.30	1673.80	3648.70	1743.80	1743.80	22,674.20
LBH	329.60	3361.90	3035.40	3099.00	2589.50	1806.30	1673.80	3648.70	1743.80	1743.80	23,031.50
LBL	164.80	3374.80	3035.40	3099.00	2589.50	1806.30	1673.80	3648.70	1743.80	1743.80	22,879.60
LBM	263.60	3356.30	3035.40	3099.00	2589.50	1806.30	1673.80	3648.70	1743.80	1743.80	22,960.00
LHB	2987.0	3639.80	3338.90	3408.90	2775.90	1986.90	1841.10	4013.50	1918.10	1918.10	27,828.20
LLB	1493.50	3487.00	3187.20	3254.00	2682.70	1896.60	1757.40	3831.10	1830.90	1830.90	25,251.20
LMB	2389.60	3578.70	3278.20	3346.90	2738.60	1950.80	1807.70	3940.50	1883.30	1883.30	26,797.40
MBH	329.60	3361.90	3035.40	3099.00	2589.50	1806.30	1673.80	3648.70	1743.80	1743.80	23,031.50
MBL	164.80	3374.80	3035.40	3099.00	2589.50	1806.30	1673.80	3648.70	1743.80	1743.80	22,879.60
MBM	263.60	3356.30	3035.40	3099.00	2589.50	1806.30	1673.80	3648.70	1743.80	1743.80	22,960.00
MHB	2987.00	3639.80	3338.90	3408.90	2775.90	1986.90	1841.10	4013.50	1918.10	1918.10	27,828.20
MLB	1493.50	3487.00	3187.20	3254.00	2682.70	1896.60	1757.40	3831.10	1830.90	1830.90	25,251.20
MMB	2389.60	3578.70	3278.20	3346.90	2738.60	1950.80	1807.70	3940.50	1883.30	1883.30	26,797.40
MLB	1493.50	3487.00	3187.20	3254.00	2682.70	1896.60	1757.40	3831.10	1830.90	1830.90	25,251.20
MMB	2389.60	3578.70	3278.20	3346.90	2738.60	1950.80	1807.70	3940.50	1883.30	1883.30	26,797.40

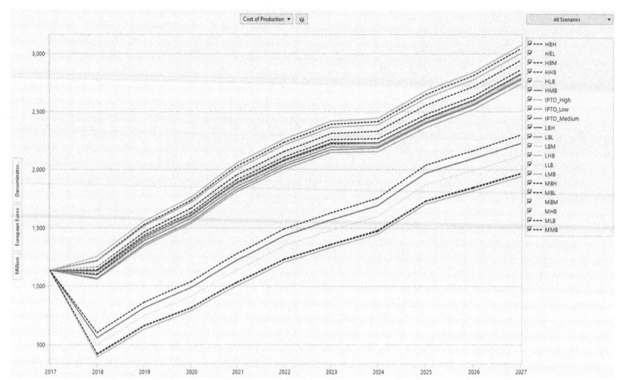

FIG. 20.2 Comparison of scenarios in terms of generation cost of electricity.

tons, 8.4% more emissions than the LHB scenario. It is worth noting that over the years there have been some strong fluctuations in the broadcasts of all scenarios. These are due to the inclusion and withdrawal of some conventional units. The first increase observed is in the year 2019 and is due to the gas unit "Megalopolis V," which was in trial operation with a limited power of 400 MW and now operates at full power 811 MW. Subsequently, the withdrawals of the lignite plants of the Amyntaio and Kardia substations lead to a significant reduction in pollutants. This is followed by the entry of the "Ptolemaida V" unit, increasing the pollution again. Finally, at the end of 2025. the withdrawal of "Megalopolis III" causes a further reduction of pollutants. All the aforementioned units refer to lignite power units. Table 20.13 presents the CO_2 emissions each scenario per year (mtons).

Fig. 20.4 shows the nitrogen oxide emissions. The results are similar to those for carbon dioxide. Most emissions occur in the HBH scenario due to high energy demand and increased gas unit penetration. Fewer emissions appear in low-demand and high-penetration RES scenarios. The scenario with the lowest emissions is LHB. which has the lowest energy demand and the highest RES penetration. The total broadcasts of the LHB scenario amount to a total of 583.40 thousand metric tons. while the HBH scenario is increased by 7.90% from the first and reaches 629.50 thousand metric tons in a decade. Table 20.14 presents the CO_2 emissions each scenario per year (mtons).

Finally, Fig. 20.5 concerns SO_2 emissions. These are produced by the combustion of lignite, unlike natural gas which does not emit at all. IPTO's high-demand scenario presents the most emissions, due to the high demand and the largest percentage of installed capacity occupied by lignite plants, as there is no additional penetration of RES and natural gas units. The difference is in the low emissions, which occur in the LBH scenario and is due to the low power demand combined with the increased gas penetration, which, as mentioned earlier, does not emit this particular chemical compound. The LHB scenario also shows very low emissions, just 0.20% more than the first, where demand is again low, with the difference that high penetration occurs in RES units. The IPTO scenario emits 1220.90 million metric tons, increased by 7.60% from the LBH scenario which emits 1134.4 million metric tons. As pointed out in previous cases for carbon dioxide and nitric oxide, the withdrawal of lignite plants in 2019 leads to a sharp reduction in pollution, which then increases again with the inclusion of the unit "Ptolemaida V" (Table 20.15)

TABLE 20.12 Generation cost of each scenario per year (m€).

Scenarios	2017	2018	2019	2020	2021	2022	2023	2024	2025	2026	2027	Total
HBH	1134.8	421.1	661.0	818.8	1035.7	1234.0	1361.0	1478.1	1736.2	1849.4	1971.5	13,701.5
HBL	1134.8	407.0	647.9	805.7	1022.7	1221.0	1348.0	1465.1	1723.2	1836.3	1958.5	13,570.2
HBM	1134.8	415.5	654.8	812.6	1029.5	1227.9	1354.9	1472.0	1730.1	1843.2	1965.4	13,640.7
HHB	1134.8	601.5	860.4	1039.4	1278.0	1489.4	1629.2	1757.9	2041.8	2167.2	2301.6	16,301.2
HLB	1134.8	497.2	745.3	913.7	1141.5	1346.4	1479.8	1602.7	1873.7	1993.0	2121.2	14,849.3
HMB	1134.8	559.8	814.3	989.1	1223.4	1432.2	1569.4	1695.8	1974.6	2097.5	2229.4	15,720.4
IPTO_High	1134.8	392.9	630.3	788.1	1005.0	1203.3	1330.4	1447.4	1705.5	1818.7	1940.9	13,397.4
IPTO_Low	1134.8	1062.0	1344.9	1538.6	1813.5	2004.3	2148.9	2159.0	2366.4	2518.5	2740.1	20,831.0
IPTO_Medium	1134.8	1066.8	1358.2	1557.0	1835.8	2028.5	2173.6	2189.4	2398.9	2554.4	2777.7	21,075.1
LBH	1134.8	1133.6	1421.0	1613.9	1893.1	2085.4	2231.6	2235.2	2440.2	2594.6	2823.0	21,606.4
LBL	1134.8	1098.2	1389.0	1582.3	1859.8	2051.4	2196.8	2203.2	2409.2	2562.6	2788.2	21,275.4
LBM	1134.8	1119.5	1406.0	1599.1	1877.5	2069.5	2215.3	2220.2	2425.6	2579.6	2806.7	21,453.8
LHB	1134.8	1255.0	1557.3	1767.4	2060.9	2265.3	2421.2	2445.9	2679.6	2841.5	3071.1	23,500.1
LLB	1134.8	1158.4	1451.0	1652.8	1937.0	2134.6	2284.8	2302.3	2522.8	2679.8	2905.3	22,163.6
LMB	1134.8	1216.3	1514.8	1721.5	2011.3	2213.0	2366.6	2388.4	2616.8	2776.7	3004.7	22,965.0
MBH	1134.8	1138.7	1435.2	1633.4	1916.8	2111.2	2260.4	2267.5	2474.8	2632.8	2864.2	21,869.8
MBL	1134.8	1103.1	1402.9	1601.3	1882.8	2076.5	2225.0	2234.7	2442.9	2599.9	2828.4	21,532.3
MBM	1134.8	1124.5	1420.1	1618.4	1900.9	2094.9	2243.8	2252.1	2459.8	2617.4	2847.4	21,714.2
MHB	1134.8	1259.6	1570.4	1785.2	2082.5	2288.8	2447.5	2475.3	2711.0	2876.1	3108.4	23,739.5
MLB	1134.8	1163.1	1464.2	1670.9	1959.0	2158.4	2311.3	2332.1	2554.7	2715.0	2943.3	22,406.9
MMB	1134.8	1221.0	1527.9	1739.5	2033.0	2236.6	2393.0	2418.0	2648.4	2811.6	3042.3	23,206.1

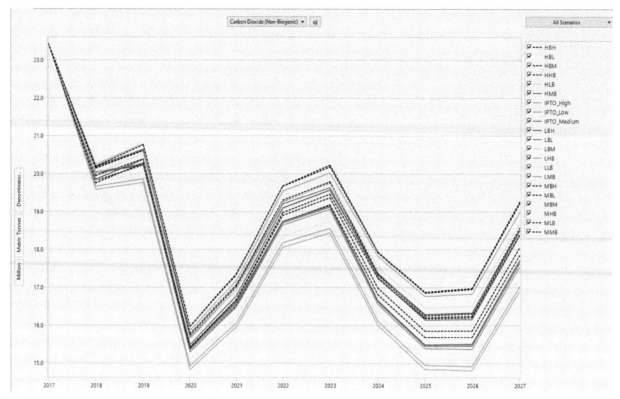

FIG. 20.3 Comparison of scenarios in terms of CO$_2$ emissions.

TABLE 20.13 CO$_2$ emissions each scenario per year (mtons).

Scenarios	2017	2018	2019	2020	2021	2022	2023	2024	2025	2026	2027	Total
HBH	23.4	20.2	20.8	16.0	17.3	19.7	20.2	17.9	16.9	17.0	19.3	208.7
HBL	23.4	20.2	20.8	15.9	17.3	19.6	20.1	17.9	16.8	16.9	19.2	208.2
HBM	23.4	20.2	20.8	16.0	17.3	19.7	20.2	17.9	16.9	16.9	19.2	208.5
HHB	23.4	19.8	20.3	15.4	16.7	19.0	19.5	17.2	16.2	16.2	18.4	202.0
HLB	23.4	20.0	20.5	15.6	16.9	19.3	19.7	17.5	16.5	16.5	18.7	204.7
HMB	23.4	19.9	20.4	15.5	16.8	19.1	19.6	17.4	16.3	16.3	18.5	203.1
IPTO_High	23.4	20.2	20.8	15.9	17.2	19.6	20.0	17.8	16.8	16.8	19.0	207.5
IPTO_Low	23.4	20.1	20.3	15.3	16.5	18.6	19.1	16.6	15.4	15.4	17.6	198.1
IPTO_Medium	23.4	20.2	20.6	15.7	16.9	19.2	19.6	17.3	16.1	16.2	18.4	203.7
LBH	23.4	20.0	20.2	15.4	16.6	18.7	19.2	16.7	15.5	15.5	17.7	199.0
LBL	23.4	20.0	20.2	15.4	16.6	18.7	19.1	16.6	15.4	15.4	17.6	198.6
LBM	23.4	20.0	20.2	15.4	16.6	18.7	19.1	16.6	15.5	15.5	17.7	198.8
LHB	23.4	19.6	19.8	14.8	16.0	18.1	18.4	16.0	14.8	14.8	16.9	192.6
LLB	23.4	19.8	20.0	15.1	16.2	18.4	18.7	16.3	15.1	15.1	17.2	195.3
LMB	23.4	19.7	19.9	14.9	16.1	18.2	18.6	16.1	15.0	14.9	17.0	193.7
MBH	23.4	20.1	20.6	15.8	17.1	19.3	19.8	17.4	16.3	16.3	18.6	204.6
MBL	23.4	20.2	20.6	15.7	17.0	19.3	19.7	17.3	16.2	16.2	18.5	204.3
MBM	23.4	20.2	20.6	15.8	17.0	19.3	19.8	17.4	16.2	16.3	18.5	204.5
MHB	23.4	19.7	20.1	15.2	16.4	18.6	19.1	16.7	15.6	15.6	17.7	198.1
MLB	23.4	20.0	20.4	15.4	16.7	18.9	19.4	17.0	15.9	15.9	18.1	200.9
MMB	23.4	19.8	20.2	15.3	16.5	18.7	19.2	16.8	15.7	15.7	17.9	199.2

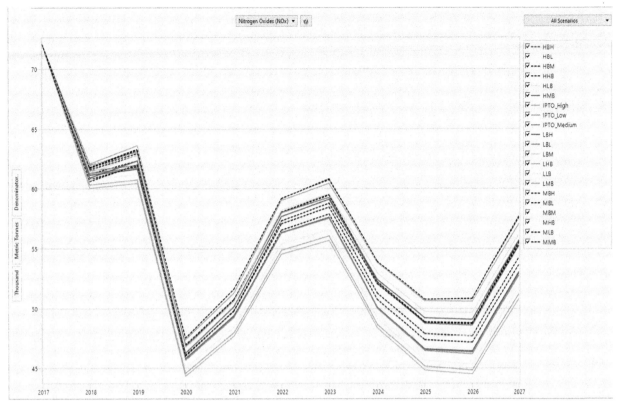

FIG. 20.4 Comparison of scenarios in terms of NOx emissions.

TABLE 20.14 NOx emissions each scenario per year (mtons).

Scenarios	2017	2018	2019	2020	2021	2022	2023	2024	2025	2026	2027	Total
HBH	72.1	61.7	63.3	47.6	51.6	59.2	60.8	53.9	50.8	50.8	57.7	629.5
HBL	72.1	61.9	63.4	47.5	51.5	59.2	60.7	53.9	50.7	50.7	57.5	629.1
HBM	72.1	61.8	63.3	47.5	51.6	59.2	60.7	53.9	50.7	50.8	57.6	629.3
HHB	72.1	60.6	62.0	46.0	49.8	57.3	58.8	52.1	48.9	48.7	55.3	611.7
HLB	72.1	61.4	62.8	46.7	50.6	58.2	59.6	52.9	49.7	49.6	56.2	619.9
HMB	72.1	60.9	62.3	46.3	50.1	57.7	59.1	52.4	49.2	49.1	55.7	614.9
IPTO_High	72.1	62.1	63.6	47.4	51.3	59.0	60.4	53.9	50.6	50.6	57.1	628.2
IPTO_Low	72.1	61.5	62.0	45.7	49.2	56.3	57.5	50.0	46.5	46.2	52.8	599.9
IPTO_Medium	72.1	62.0	63.1	46.8	50.6	58.0	59.3	52.2	48.8	48.6	55.3	616.7
LBH	72.1	61.2	61.6	45.8	49.4	56.3	57.6	50.1	46.6	46.4	53.0	600.3
LBL	72.1	61.3	61.8	45.8	49.3	56.3	57.6	50.1	46.5	46.3	52.9	600.1
LBM	72.1	61.2	61.7	45.8	49.4	56.3	57.6	50.1	46.6	46.4	53.0	600.2
LHB	72.1	60.1	60.4	44.3	47.7	54.6	55.7	48.4	44.8	44.5	50.8	583.4
LLB	72.1	60.8	61.2	45.0	48.4	55.4	56.6	49.2	45.6	45.4	51.8	591.5
LMB	72.1	60.4	60.7	44.6	48.0	54.9	56.1	48.7	45.2	44.9	51.2	586.7
MBH	72.1	61.6	62.8	46.9	50.8	58.1	59.5	52.2	48.9	48.8	55.6	617.3
MBL	72.1	61.8	62.9	46.9	50.7	58.0	59.5	52.2	48.8	48.7	55.5	617.2
MBM	72.1	61.7	62.9	46.9	50.7	58.0	59.5	52.2	48.9	48.8	55.6	617.3
MHB	72.1	60.5	61.6	45.4	49.0	56.2	57.5	50.4	47.0	46.8	53.3	599.9
MLB	72.1	61.2	62.3	46.1	49.8	57.1	58.5	51.3	47.9	47.7	54.3	608.3
MMB	72.1	60.8	61.9	45.7	49.3	56.6	57.9	50.8	47.4	47.2	53.7	603.2

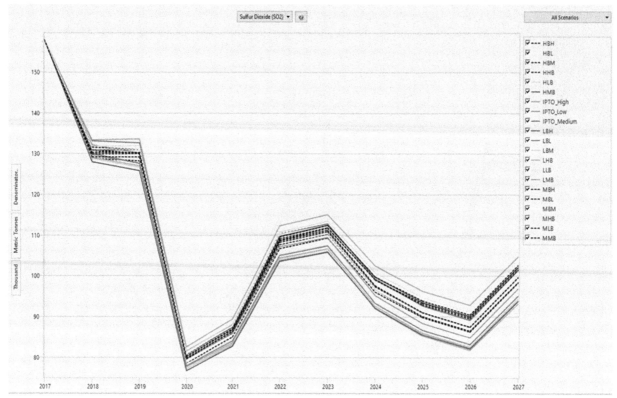

FIG. 20.5 Comparison of scenarios in terms of SO₂ emissions.

TABLE 20.15 SO$_2$ emissions each scenario per year (mtons).

Scenarios	2017	2018	2019	2020	2021	2022	2023	2024	2025	2026	2027	Total
HBH	158.0	129.1	129.2	79.6	86.4	108.8	111.8	99.1	93.3	89.9	102.1	1187.3
HBL	158.0	131.2	131.0	80.8	87.7	110.4	113.1	100.5	94.6	91.1	103.2	1201.9
HBM	158.0	130.0	130.0	80.2	87.0	109.6	112.4	99.8	93.9	90.5	102.6	1193.9
HHB	158.0	130.3	130.3	80.1	86.8	109.1	111.9	99.1	93.0	89.5	101.5	1189.6
HLB	158.0	131.8	131.9	81.4	88.1	110.8	113.4	100.8	94.6	91.1	103.2	1205.2
HMB	158.0	130.9	130.9	80.6	87.3	109.8	112.5	99.8	93.6	90.1	102.2	1195.8
IPTO_High	158.0	133.4	133.6	82.6	89.4	112.4	115.0	102.5	96.4	92.9	104.8	1220.9
IPTO_Low	158.0	132.2	130.2	79.6	85.8	107.2	109.5	95.2	88.4	84.8	96.9	1167.8
IPTO_Medium	158.0	133.1	132.6	81.6	88.1	110.4	112.8	99.3	92.8	89.2	101.4	1199.4
LBH	158.0	128.0	125.9	76.7	82.7	103.6	105.9	92.1	85.6	82.1	93.8	1134.4
LBL	158.0	130.0	127.7	77.9	84.0	105.1	107.4	93.4	86.8	83.2	95.1	1148.6
LBM	158.0	128.8	126.7	77.3	83.3	104.3	106.6	92.7	86.2	82.6	94.4	1140.9
LHB	158.0	129.1	127.0	77.2	83.1	103.8	106.0	92.1	85.3	81.7	93.3	1136.6
LLB	158.0	130.6	128.6	78.4	84.4	105.5	107.7	93.6	86.9	83.2	95.0	1152.0
LMB	158.0	129.7	127.6	77.7	83.6	104.5	106.7	92.7	85.9	82.3	94.0	1142.7
MBH	158.0	128.9	128.3	78.6	85.0	106.7	109.4	96.0	89.8	86.3	98.4	1165.3
MBL	158.0	131.0	130.1	79.8	86.3	108.2	111.0	97.4	91.1	87.5	99.7	1180.0
MBM	158.0	129.7	129.1	79.1	85.6	107.4	110.1	96.7	90.4	86.9	99.0	1172.1
MHB	158.0	130.0	129.4	79.1	85.3	107.0	109.5	96.0	89.5	85.9	97.8	1167.6
MLB	158.0	131.5	131.0	80.3	86.7	108.7	111.3	97.6	91.1	87.5	99.6	1183.4
MMB	158.0	130.6	130.0	79.6	85.9	107.6	110.2	96.6	90.2	86.5	98.5	1173.9

4   Conclusions

In this study, several alternative scenarios have been examined for the future evolution of the Greek energy sector. investigating additional cases of energy scenarios. in order to study the future state of the Greek sector, twenty-one different scenarios were examined, three of which represent the future development determined by IPTO SA for the next decade. The remaining eighteen were created based on IPTO cases, but showed some differences between them, in terms of total energy demand and future penetration of RES and gas generation units.

All cases show different results in terms of economic costs and environmental pollution. Initially, the cases of IPTO show the lowest financial cost in all cases, but they show large emissions of pollutants for the environment. On the contrary, the increased penetration of RES units shows the lowest emissions in the environment, while presenting the largest financial burden. The most favorable results appear concerning gas plants, which have low economic costs and low emissions for the environment. Furthermore, the way in which total energy demand affects economic and environmental figures has become apparent. However, some other factors must be considered for each production unit. Gas units can have very affordable results, but natural gas is an import fuel for Greece, which has a negative effect on the country's energy autonomy. Also, the variability of RES units is a challenge for the stability and proper operation of the system contrary to the benefits obtained by displacing non-environmentally friendly technologies.

References

Farrokhifar, M., Nie, Y., Pozo, D., 2020. Energy systems planning: a survey on models for integrated power and natural gas networks coordination. Appl. Energy 262 (2020), 1–14.

Georgiou, P.N., 2016. A bottom-up optimization model for the long-term energy planning of the greek power supply sector integrating mainland and insular electric systems. Comput. Oper. Res. 66, 292–312. 2016.

Heaps, C.G., 2016. Long-Range Energy Alternatives Planning (LEAP) System [Software version: 2018.1.40]. Stockholm Environment Institute, Somerville, MA, USA. https://www.energycommunity.org.

Ioakimidis, C., Koukouzas, N., Chatzimichali, A., Casimiro, S., Macarulla, A., 2012. Energy policy scenarios of CCS implementation in the Greek electricity sector. Energy Procedia 32, 354–359. 2012.

Independent Power Transmission Operator SA, 2018. Ten Year Network Development Plan. Athens, Greece.

Institute of Energy for South-East Europe, 2019. The Greek Energy Sector: Annual Report 2019. Athens, Greece.

International Energy Agency (IEA), 2019a. World Energy Outlook 2019. Paris, France.

International Energy Agency (IEA), 2019b. Global EV Outlook 2019. Paris, France.

Odetayo, B., MacCormack, J., Rosehart, W.D., Zareipour, H., Seifi, A.R., 2019. Integrated planning of natural gas and electric power systems. Int. J. Electr. Power Energy Syst. 103 (2018), 593–602.

Qin, C., Yana, Q., Heb, G., 2019. Integrated energy systems planning with electricity. heat and gas using particle swarm optimization. Energy 188, 1–12.

Rampidis, I.M., Giannakopoulos, D., Bergeles, G.C., 2010. Insight into the Greek electric sector and energy planning with mature technologies and fuel diversification. Energy Policy 38 (8), 4076–4088.

Seifi, H., Sadegh Sepasian, M., 2011. Electric Power System Planning Issues. Algorithms and Solutions. Springer-Verlag, Berlin Heidelberg, Germany.

Sioshansi, F.P., 2013. Evolution of Global Electricity Markets: New Paradigms. New Challenges. New Approaches. Elsevier Inc, Oxford, UK.

World Energy Council (WEC), 2019. World Energy Scenarios 2019. London, UK.

Zhang, Q., Mclellan, B.C., Tezuka, T., Ishihara, N., 2013. An integrated model for long-term power generation planning toward future smart electricity systems. Appl. Energy 112, 1424–1437.

Chapter 21

An ex-ante market monitoring and regulation mechanism for market concentration in electricity and natural gas markets

Athanasios S. Dagoumas

Energy and Environmental Policy Laboratory, School of Economics, Business and International Studies, University of Piraeus, Piraeus, Greece

Nomenclature

d day
f fuel/resource type f
n interconnections (entry) point
p market participant
t time period (equals to hour)
u power plant (unit)

Parameters

$BIL\_CON\_SHARE_{p,t}$	share (%) of the load represented by each market participant p in time period t, that is covered by bilateral contracts between the producer and the final consumer
$BIL\_RES\_SHARE4_{p,f,t}$	share (%) of available domestic production capacity, allocated to each recourse/fuel type, for each market participant p and time period t
$DOM\_PROD\_AVAIL_{p,f,u,t}$	domestic available production capacity for each market participant p, unit u, fuel/resource type f & time period t
$DOM\_PROD\_AVAIL_{p,f,t}$	domestic available production capacity for each market participant p, fuel/resource type f and time period t
$EXP\_AVAIL_{n,t}$	interconnection's available capacity for exports for each interconnection (entry) point type n and time period t
$EXP\_LT\_AVAIL_{p,n,t}$	long-term rights for each interconnection's available capacity for exports for each market participant p, interconnection (entry)point type n and time period t
$EXP\_SCHED\_TSOs_{n,t}$	net export schedules with neighboring TSOs (adjusting deviations & returns of emergencies), for each interconnection (entry) point n and time period t
$IMP\_AVAIL_{n,t}$	interconnection's available capacity for imports for each interconnection (entry) point type n and time period t
$IMP\_LT\_AVAIL_{p,n,t}$	long-term rights for each interconnection's available capacity for imports for each market participant p, interconnection (entry)point type n and time period t
$IMP\_SCHED\_TSOs_{n,t}$	net import schedules with neighboring TSOs (adjusting deviations & returns of emergencies), for each interconnection (entry) point n and time period t
$LOAD\_AVAIL_{p,t}$	load represented by all participants in time period t
$LOAD\_AVAIL_{p,t}$	load represented by each market participant p in time period t
$LOAD\_AVAIL_{p,v,t}$	load represented by each market participant p, for each voltage level v in time period t
$MAND\_HYDRO\_AVAIL_{p,t}$	mandatory injections by large hydro units. For each market participant p and time period t
$PEAKSAVING_{p,f,t}$	limited availability capacity factor (%) for implementing peak saving strategy in large hydro units, for each market participant p, fuel/resource type f and time period t
$PRIOR\_CAP\_AVAIL_{p,f,t}$	units in commissioning/testing operation/high-efficiency cogeneration units, for each market participant p, fuel/resource type f and time period t
$PUMP\_AVAIL_{p,v,t}$	available capacity of pumping assets per participant p, voltage level v in time period t

Mathematical Modelling of Contemporary Electricity Markets. https://doi.org/10.1016/B978-0-12-821838-9.00021-9

$\mathbf{RES\_FiT\_AVAIL}_{p,\,t}$ renewables under FiT scheme, for each market participant p and time period t

$\mathbf{RES\_FiP\_AVAIL}_{t}$ renewables under FiP scheme, for each time period t

$\mathbf{RES\_MRK\_AVAIL}_{p,\,t}$ renewables under FiP scheme or with direct participation in the market, without support scheme, for each market participant p and time period t

$\mathbf{STOR\_AVAIL}_{p,v,t}$ the available capacity of storage assets per participant p, voltage level v in time period

Variables

$CAS\_DEM_{p,\,t}$	market share indicator (%) of the total available demand capacity of each market participant p, in time period t to the total available demand capacity
$CAS\_DEM_{p,\,d}$	market share indicator (%) of the total available demand capacity of each market participant p, in day d to the total available demand capacity
$CAS\_DEM_{p,\,v,\,t}$	market share indicator (%) of the total available demand capacity of each market participant p, in each voltage level v in time period t to the total available demand capacity
$CAS\_DEM_{p,\,v,\,d}$	market share indicator (%) of the total available demand capacity of each market participant p, in each voltage level v in day d to the total available demand capacity
$CAS\_DOM\_DEM_{p,\,t}$	market share indicator (%) of the total available domestic demand capacity of each market participant p, in time period t to the total available demand capacity
$CAS\_DOM\_DEM_{p,\,d}$	market share indicator (%) of the total available domestic demand capacity of each market participant p, in day d to the total available demand capacity
$CAS\_DOM\_DEM_{p,\,v,\,t}$	market share indicator (%) of the total available domestic demand capacity of each market participant p, in each voltage level v in time period t to the total available demand capacity
$CAS\_DOM\_DEM_{p,\,v,\,d}$	market share indicator (%) of the total available domestic demand capacity of each market participant p, in each voltage level v in day d to the total available demand capacity
$CAS\_LOAD_{p,\,t}$	market share indicator (%) of the total available domestic load capacity of each market participant p, in time period t to the total available domestic load capacity
$CAS\_LOAD_{p,\,d}$	market share indicator (%) of the total available domestic load capacity of each market participant p, in day d to the total available domestic load capacity
$CAS\_LOAD_{p,\,v,\,t}$	market share indicator (%) of the total available domestic load capacity of each market participant p, in each voltage level v in time period t to the total available domestic load capacity
$CAS\_LOAD_{p,\,v,\,d}$	market share indicator (%) of the total available domestic load capacity of each market participant p, in each voltage level v in day d to the total available domestic load capacity
$CAS\_PUMP_{p,\,t}$	market share indicator (%) of the total available domestic pumping capacity of each market participant p, in time period t to the total available domestic load capacity
$CAS\_PUMP_{p,\,d}$	market share indicator (%) of the total available domestic pumping capacity of each market participant p, in day d to the total available domestic load capacity
$CAS\_PUMP_{p,\,v,\,t}$	market share indicator (%) of the total available domestic pumping capacity of each market participant p, in each voltage level v in time period t to the total available domestic load capacity
$CAS\_PUMP_{p,\,v,\,d}$	market share indicator (%) of the total available domestic pumping capacity of each market participant p, in each voltage level v in day d to the total available domestic load capacity
$CAS\_STOR_{p,\,t}$	market share indicator (%) of the total available domestic storage capacity of each market participant p, in time period t to the total available domestic load capacity
$CAS\_STOR_{p,\,d}$	market share indicator (%) of the total available domestic storage capacity of each market participant p, in day d to the total available domestic load capacity
$CAS\_STOR_{p,\,v,\,t}$	market share indicator (%) of the total available domestic storage capacity of each market participant p, in each voltage level v in time period t to the total available domestic load capacity
$CAS\_STOR_{p,\,v,\,d}$	market share indicator (%) of the total available domestic storage capacity of each market participant p, in each voltage level v in day d to the total available domestic load capacity
$CAS\_SUP1_{p,\,f,\,t}$	a market share indicator (Capacity Availability Share in Supply—CAS_SUP1) on the market share (%), for each market participant p, fuel/resource type f and time period t
$CAS\_SUP2_{p,\,f,\,t}$	the previous variable, excluding capacity from assets without market participation responsibilities, such as renewables under FiT scheme, mandatory injections by large hydro units, units in commissioning/testing operation/high-efficiency cogeneration units, as well as the net import schedules with neighboring TSOs (adjusting deviations & returns of emergencies)
$CAS\_SUP3_{p,\,f,\,t}$	the previous variable, considering a peak saving strategy for large hydro units
$CAS\_SUP4_{p,\,f,\,t}$	the previous variable, excluding capacity from thermal and large hydro units allocated to bilateral contracts
$CAS\_SUP1_{p,\,f,\,d}$	the average relevant daily market share (%) indicator, for each market participant p, fuel/resource type f & day d

$CAS\_SUP2_{p, f, d}$	the previous variable, excluding capacity from assets without market participation responsibilities, such as renewables under FiT scheme, mandatory injections by large hydro units, units in commissioning/testing operation/high-efficiency cogeneration units, as well as the net import schedules with neighboring TSOs (adjusting deviations & returns of emergencies)
$CAS\_SUP3_{p, f, d}$	the previous variable, considering a peak saving strategy for large hydro units
$CAS\_SUP4_{p, f, d}$	the previous variable, excluding capacity from thermal and large hydro units allocated to bilateral contracts
$CAS\_RES\_SUP1_{p, t}$	a marker share (%) indicator on the available supply capacity in the renewables disaggregate market, for each market participant p and time period t
$CAS\_RES\_SUP2_{p, t}$	the previous variable, excluding capacity from assets without market participation responsibilities, such as renewables under FiT scheme, mandatory injections by large hydro units, units in commissioning/testing operation/high-efficiency cogeneration units, as well as the net import schedules with neighboring TSOs (adjusting deviations & returns of emergencies)
$CAS\_RES\_SUP3_{p, t}$	the previous variable, considering a peak saving strategy for large hydro units
$CAS\_RES\_SUP4_{p, t}$	the previous variable, excluding capacity from thermal and large hydro units allocated to bilateral contracts
$CAS\_RES\_SUP1_{p, d}$	the average relevant daily market share (%) indicator, for each market participant p and day d
$CAS\_RES\_SUP2_{p, d}$	the previous variable, excluding capacity from assets without market participation responsibilities, such as renewables under FiT scheme, mandatory injections by large hydro units, units in commissioning/testing operation/high-efficiency cogeneration units, as well as the net import schedules with neighboring TSOs (adjusting deviations & returns of emergencies)
$CAS\_RES\_SUP3_{p, d}$	the previous variable, considering a peak saving strategy for large hydro units
$CAS\_RES\_SUP4_{p, d}$	the previous variable, excluding capacity from thermal and large hydro units allocated to bilateral contracts
$CAS\_SUP1_{p, n, t}$	ba market share (%) indicator for each market participant p, interconnection (entry) point n and time period t
$CAS\_SUP2_{p, n, t}$	the previous variable, excluding capacity from assets without market participation responsibilities, such as renewables under FiT scheme, mandatory injections by large hydro units, units in commissioning/testing operation/high-efficiency cogeneration units, as well as the net import schedules with neighboring TSOs (adjusting deviations & returns of emergencies)
$CAS\_SUP3_{p, n, t}$	the previous variable, considering a peak saving strategy for large hydro units
$CAS\_SUP4_{p, n, t}$	the previous variable, excluding capacity from thermal and large hydro units allocated to bilateral contracts
$CAS\_SUP1_{p, n, d}$	the average relevant daily market share (%) indicator, for each market participant p, interconnection (entry) point n and day d
$CAS\_SUP2_{p, n, d}$	the previous variable, excluding capacity from assets without market participation responsibilities, such as renewables under FiT scheme, mandatory injections by large hydro units, units in commissioning/testing operation/high-efficiency cogeneration units, as well as the net import schedules with neighboring TSOs (adjusting deviations & returns of emergencies)
$CAS\_SUP3_{p, n, d}$	the previous variable, considering a peak saving strategy for large hydro units
$CAS\_SUP4_{p, n, d}$	the previous variable, excluding capacity from thermal and large hydro units allocated to bilateral contracts
$CAS\_SUP1_{p, t}$	a market share (%) indicator for each market participant p and time period t
$CAS\_SUP2_{p, t}$	the previous variable, excluding capacity from assets without market participation responsibilities, such as renewables under FiT scheme, mandatory injections by large hydro units, units in commissioning/testing operation/high-efficiency cogeneration units, as well as the net import schedules with neighboring TSOs (adjusting deviations & returns of emergencies)
$CAS\_SUP3_{p, t}$	the previous variable, considering a peak saving strategy for large hydro units
$CAS\_SUP4_{p, t}$	the previous variable, excluding capacity from thermal and large hydro units allocated to bilateral contracts
$CAS\_SUP1_{p, d}$	a market share (%) indicator for each market participant p and day d
$CAS\_SUP2_{p, d}$	the previous variable, excluding capacity from assets without market participation responsibilities, such as renewables under FiT scheme, mandatory injections by large hydro units, units in commissioning/testing operation/high-efficiency cogeneration units, as well as the net import schedules with neighboring TSOs (adjusting deviations & returns of emergencies)
$CAS\_SUP3_{p, d}$	the previous variable, considering a peak saving strategy for large hydro units
$CAS\_SUP4_{p, d}$	the previous variable, excluding capacity from thermal and large hydro units allocated to bilateral contracts

$DOM\_PROD\_AVAIL3_{p,\,f,\,t}$	domestic available production capacity, considering a peak saving strategy for large hydro units, for each market participant p, fuel/resource type f and time period t
$DOM\_PROD\_AVAIL4_{p,\,f,\,t}$	domestic available production capacity of thermal and large hydro units allocated to bilateral contracts, for each market participant p, fuel/resource type f and time period t
$TOT\_AVAIL\_DEM\_CAP_{t}$	total available capacity for demand in each time period t
$TOT\_AVAIL\_DEM\_CAP_{p,\,t}$	total available capacity for demand for each market participant p and time period t
$TOT\_AVAIL\_DOM\_DEM\_CAP_{t}$	total available capacity for domestic demand in each time period t
$TOT\_AVAIL\_DOM\_DEM\_CAP_{p,\,t}$	total available capacity for domestic demand for each market participant p and time period t
$TOT\_AVAIL\_LOAD\_CAP_{t}$	total available capacity for domestic load for each time period t
$TOT\_AVAIL\_LOAD\_CAP_{p,\,t}$	total available capacity for domestic load for each market participant p and time period t
$TOT\_AVAIL\_PUMP\_CAP_{t}$	total available capacity for domestic pumping for each time period t
$TOT\_AVAIL\_PUMP\_CAP_{p,\,t}$	total available capacity for domestic pumping for each market participant p and time period t
$TOT\_AVAIL\_RES\_SUP\_CAP1_{p,\,f,\,t}$	the total available capacity for renewables for each market participant p, fuel/resource type f and time period t
$TOT\_AVAIL\_RES\_SUP\_CAP2_{p,\,f,\,t}$	the previous variable, excluding capacity from assets without market participation responsibilities, such as renewables under FiT scheme, mandatory injections by large hydro units, units in commissioning/testing operation/high-efficiency cogeneration units, as well as the net import schedules with neighboring TSOs (adjusting deviations & returns of emergencies)
$TOT\_AVAIL\_RES\_SUP\_CAP3_{p,\,f,\,t}$	the previous variable, considering a peak saving strategy for large hydro units
$TOT\_AVAIL\_RES\_SUP\_CAP4_{p,\,f,\,t}$	the previous variable, excluding capacity from thermal and large hydro units allocated to bilateral contracts
$TOT\_AVAIL\_STOR\_CAP_{t}$	total available capacity for domestic storage for each time period t
$TOT\_AVAIL\_STOR\_CAP_{p,\,t}$	total available capacity for domestic storage for each market participant p and time period t
$TOT\_AVAIL\_SUP\_CAP1_{p,\,f,\,t}$	the total available capacity for domestic production and imports for each market participant p, fuel type f and time period t
$TOT\_AVAIL\_SUP\_CAP2_{p,\,f,\,t}$	the previous variable, excluding capacity from assets without market participation responsibilities, such as renewables under FiT scheme, mandatory injections by large hydro units, units in commissioning/testing operation/high-efficiency cogeneration units, as well as the net import schedules with neighboring TSOs (adjusting deviations & returns of emergencies)
$TOT\_AVAIL\_SUP\_CAP3_{p,\,f,\,t}$	the previous variable, considering a peak saving strategy for large hydro units
$TOT\_AVAIL\_SUP\_CAP4_{p,\,f,\,t}$	the previous variable, excluding capacity from thermal and large hydro units allocated to bilateral contracts
$TOT\_AVAIL\_SUP\_CAP1_{p,\,n,\,t}$	the total available capacity for domestic production and imports for each time market participant p, interconnection (entry) point n and time period t
$TOT\_AVAIL\_SUP\_CAP2_{p,\,n,\,t}$	the previous variable, excluding capacity from assets without market participation responsibilities, such as renewables under FiT scheme, mandatory injections by large hydro units, units in commissioning/testing operation/high-efficiency cogeneration units, as well as the net import schedules with neighboring TSOs (adjusting deviations & returns of emergencies)
$TOT\_AVAIL\_SUP\_CAP3_{p,\,n,\,t}$	the previous variable, considering a peak saving strategy for large hydro units
$TOT\_AVAIL\_SUP\_CAP4_{p,\,n,\,t}$	the previous variable, excluding capacity from thermal and large hydro units allocated to bilateral contracts
$TOT\_SUP\_AVAIL\_CAP1_{p,\,t}$	the total available capacity for domestic production and imports for each time market participant p, time period t
$TOT\_SUP\_AVAIL\_CAP2_{p,\,t}$	the previous variable, excluding capacity from assets without market participation responsibilities, such as renewables under FiT scheme, mandatory injections by large hydro units, units in commissioning/testing operation/high-efficiency cogeneration units, as well as the net import schedules with neighboring TSOs (adjusting deviations & returns of emergencies)
$TOT\_SUP\_AVAIL\_CAP3_{p,\,t}$	the previous variable, considering a peak saving strategy for large hydro units
$TOT\_SUP\_AVAIL\_CAP4_{p,\,t}$	the previous variable, excluding capacity from thermal and large hydro units allocated to bilateral contracts
$TOT\_SUP\_AVAIL\_CAP1_{t}$	the total available capacity for domestic production and imports for each time period t
$TOT\_SUP\_AVAIL\_CAP2_{t}$	the previous variable, excluding capacity from assets without market participation responsibilities, such as renewables under FiT scheme, mandatory injections by large hydro units, units in commissioning/testing operation/high-efficiency cogeneration units, as well as the net import schedules with neighboring TSOs (adjusting deviations & returns of emergencies)
$TOT\_SUP\_AVAIL\_CAP3_{t}$	the previous variable, considering a peak saving strategy for large hydro units
$TOT\_SUP\_AVAIL\_CAP4_{t}$	the previous variable, excluding capacity from thermal and large hydro units allocated to bilateral contracts

1 Introduction

Competition policy on the power and natural gas markets is a complex and contradicting issue, as it is based on ad-hoc evaluation of each case rather than on a coherent framework applicable in all cases. The Directorate General for Competition[a] considers that "*if a company has a market share of less than 40%, it is unlikely to be dominant*", which concerns a threshold for ad-hoc and ex-post examination of potential antitrust cases. This statement defines a lower threshold of a market share that could establish a dominant position. But, market participants that have more than 40% in market share might not have dominant position, as this depends on the relative market conditions, which is a dynamic process, i.e., a participant with a market share of 45% might have a dominant position in one market, but do not have dominant position in another market even with 55% market share, or with 55% in the same market under different market conditions. This creates an uncertainty on which threshold level is acceptable by a market participant. This affects the company with high market share, as it might be conservative in its bidding strategies and tariff policies, as it might not holding a dominant position, while it also affects other market participants, as there might be a long-standing market distortion even from low threshold levels. This uncertainty might also last several years in the future, in order an antitrust case to be evaluated and closed by the Directorate General for Competition or the National Competition Authorities.

Competition policy on the energy sector is based on the legal framework of the European competition policy[b] applicable for all sectors, which concerns Articles 101 to 109 of the Treaty for the Functioning of the European Union (TFEU), the Merger Regulation (Council Regulation (EC) No. 139/2004) and its implementing rules, Articles 37, 106 and 345 of the TFEU for public undertakings, Articles 14, 59, 93, 106, 107, 108 and 114 of the TFEU for public services, services of general interest and services of general economic interest, as well as Protocol No. 27 on the internal market and competition, Protocol No. 26 on services of general interest and Article 36 of the Charter of Fundamental Rights.

According to the official document (ECDCC, 2017) of the European Commission on Competition issues, the European competition policy ensures that companies compete equally and fairly in Europe's internal market. European Competition policy is about the following four categories:

- State aid
- Mergers
- Liberalization
- Antitrust

Competition policy is horizontal across all economic sectors, including the energy sector.

The principal enforcement agency for the European competition rules is the European Commission, through its DG Competition, while the NCAs have also powers to apply the European competition policy (as well as domestic competition rules). Directorate General for Energy (DG Energy) is responsible for sectoral responsibilities in the energy sector. In case of energy the National Regulatory Authorities (NRAs), under the first, second and third liberalization package, have a key role to play in ensuring that each European country meets its targets for energy markets and implement all EU regulatory policy. Moreover, each government also implements its energy policy and regulation, considering the European competition framework.

Although the role of NRAs is crucial in regulating the energy sectors, while the role of NCAs/DG Competition is crucial for applying European competition rules, the regulatory responsibilities on the energy sector are split between authorities at different stages for competition issues.

State Aid cases concerns the cases where governments spend public money to support local industries or individual companies, giving them an unfair advantage and thus damaging competition and distorting trade. This is prohibited by Article 107 of the Treaty on the Functioning of the European Union (TFEU). However, in case of the energy sector, the government considers the Guidelines on State aid for environmental protection and energy 2014–2020 (ECC, 2014), and submits proposed ministerial decisions and regulation, in order to pass legislation into law under the approval of the DG competition.

In case on Mergers, the merger regulation gives the European Commission the power to prohibit mergers and acquisitions that threaten to significantly reduce competition. The main laws for merger decisions are the EU merger regulation and the implementing regulation. DG Competition and National Competition Authorities (NCAs), approve relevant mergers and acquisitions, before energy companies participate in the energy markers and regulated by NRAs.

In case of Liberalization, the state adopts the relevant European Guidelines in the national legislation, enrolling the NRAs with economic responsibilities to regulate the electricity and natural gas sectors, while specific responsibilities are also assigned to NRAs regarding with the organization and operation of the oil products market.

---

a. https://ec.europa.eu/competition/antitrust/procedures_102_en.html.

b. https://www.europarl.europa.eu/factsheets/en/sheet/82/competition-policy.

The term Antitrust refers to the action of preventing or controlling trusts or other monopolies. In case of Antitrust, although NRAs are enrolled with the responsibility of ensuring competition in energy markets, market participants or even citizens can create competition cases in DG Competition or the NCAs. Those cases are ex-post evaluated by Competition Authorities, creating an important lag between real-time operation of energy markets and decisions from competition authorities. This lag creates uncertainty in the market on what is allowed for market participants. Moreover, it might affect crucially the structure and concentration in the markets.

European antitrust policy is based on the following rules of the TFEU (EU, 2012):

- Article 101 of the Treaty (EU, 2008a) prohibits agreements between two or more independent market participants that restrict competition, covering both horizontal and vertical agreements, such as the creation of a cartel towards price-fixing and/or market sharing.
- Article 102 of the Treaty (EU, 2008b) prohibits firms that hold a dominant position on a given market to abuse that position.

European competition policy identifies the following antitrust competition cases:

- Anticompetitive agreements that reduce competition, whether or not the parties actually intended to restrict competition: Article 101 of the TFEU prohibits anticompetitive agreements.
- Cartels are illegal under EU competition law, where companies agree to avoid competing with each other, or agree the prices at which their products will be sold.
- A dominant position is not in itself anticompetitive, but if the company exploits this position to eliminate competition its behavior can be considered to be abusive. His is prohibited by Article 102 of the TFEU.

Dominant position and cartels can be considered of belonging in the competition issue, namely market concentration, as cartels derive from the formation of cumulative dominant position from more than one market participants. The most important task in identifying the market share of each market participant, towards indicating that a company holds a dominant position and/or a group of companies hold a cumulative dominant position, is the definition of the relevant market. Before assessing dominance, the Commission defines the product market and the geographic market.

- Product market: the relevant product market is made of all products/services which the consumer considers to be a substitute for each other due to their characteristics, their prices and their intended use.
- Geographic market: the relevant geographic market is an area in which the conditions of competition for a given product are homogenous.

Assessing market concentration is not only a problem for antitrust cases, but it also concerns the other competition categories, namely state aid, mergers and liberalization. A merger/acquisition is approved or not depending on the cumulative market share of the merging companies. The definition of the relative market, for assessing market shares, depends on the market participation status of each asset, as this might be supported under state aid support schemes, limiting their market participation obligations. Finally, liberalization process concerns the application of legislation, such as the target model that implements market coupling, eliminating/offsetting capacity concentration in interconnection points.

Therefore, the determination of market concentration is a vital pillar for the whole European competition policy. This document recognizes the need for ex-ante regulation and market monitoring on competition policy. This document does not aim to alleviate responsibilities among authorities, but to enable an Ex-ante Market Monitoring and Regulation Mechanism for Market Concentration in Power and Natural Gas Markets. This will create a clear, coherent and permanent framework for market participants and enhance competition.

This document describes that such a Mechanism could be designed by the National Regulatory Authorities for Energy and implemented by the Transmission System Operators. This mechanism could also be communicated to the Directorate General for Competition and/or the National Competition Authorities, which usually tackle market concentration cases, however in ad-hoc and ex-post manner. This mechanism could enable the establishment of a "real-time," coherent and permanent competition policy on market concentration on power and natural gas markets.

2 Generic framework of the ex-ante market monitoring and regulation mechanism

A crucial issue for the determination of the dominant position of a market participant is the determination of the relative market. We consider that besides its determination, the size of the relative market is also important, especially concerning sub-categories (disaggregate markets) of the aggregate market. The mechanism can be applied in both the supply and demand side. This chapter focuses on the supply side, which is a more complex problem. The generic idea of the mechanism is to impose ex-ante thresholds at different levels of market concentration, known to all market participants and applicable on a permanent basis. This is be applied at both the supply and demand side, as well as for both the power and natural gas markets. The mechanism has two components:

- Market monitoring mechanism for market concentration
  - Aiming to ex-ante identify when a market participant of a group of market participants have dominant position in the supply and/or the demand side.
- Regulation mechanism
  - Aiming to ex-ante identify non-competitive bidding strategies for the participant(s) with (cumulative) dominant position, in the form of non-compliance changes for market concentration.
    - It should be noted that this regulation mechanism, applied only to market participant with dominant position for its available capacity above a market concentration threshold, imposes stricter regulation compared to non-compliance charges for non-competitive bidding applied to all market participants, including market participant with dominant position, for its available capacity up to the market concentration threshold.

We continue our analysis for each of the supply and demand sides.

2.1 Defining the relative markets

A crucial issue concerning the determination of market concentration is the definition of the relative market in each of the supply and demand side, for each of the electricity and natural gas markets. Fig. 21.1 provides a classification of relative markets for both the electricity and natural gas markets.

2.2 Supply side

We identify the following four (4) thresholds for ex-ante determination of the dominant position of a market participant in the supply side.

- THRESOLD1, at the aggregate market level.
  - concerns each of the electricity and natural gas markets,
  - it considers the capacity per resource type, per market participation type,
    - i.e., for power markets: lignite, natural gas, large hydro, renewables under Feed in Tariff (FiT), Feed in Premium (FiP) schemes or with direct participation in market, per interconnections (entry) point type, as well as the capacity in bilateral contracts of market participants.
    - i.e., for natural gas markets:
  - concerns available and not installed capacity of all assets
- THRESOLD2, at the disaggregate market level.
  - concerns the available capacity for each resource type (lignite, natural gas, large hydro, renewables) for electroproduction and for each interconnection (entry) point for electricity and natural markets,

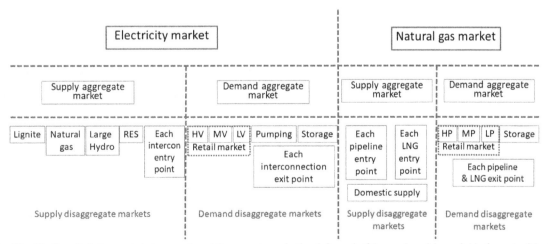

FIG. 21.1 Classification of relative market at aggregate and disaggregate market level, for each of the supply and demand side, for each of the electricity and natural gas markets. Note: HV, MV, LV refers to High, Medium, and Low Voltage customers, respectively. HP, MP, LP refers to High, Medium, and Low Pressure customers, respectively.

○ in each interconnection (entry) point, threshold concerns only long-term (yearly/monthly) explicit capacity auctions,

○ renewables are considered as an aggregated sub-category, as their participation in the market is through RES aggregators,

○ hydro disaggregate market could consider either the available capacity of large hydro or the sum of available capacity of large hydro with small hydro units, as this indicator practically shows the market share in this natural resource. Considering that small hydro units under FiP&Market participation status are represented from RES aggregators, the consideration of large hydro as distinct disaggregate market makes sense.

- THRESOLD3, on the size of the disaggregate market level compared to the size of the aggregate market level.
- THRESOLD4, on the difference between the market share in the aggregate market level in the supply side compared to the market share in the aggregate market level in the demand side.

The levels of those thresholds must be identified in a coherent manner, considering the 40% minimum threshold in market concentration acceptable by the DG Competition, which however concerns ex-post and ad-hoc evaluation. Considering that the establishment of an ex-ante threshold level is preferable, as it creates certainty on all market participants, a higher than 40% threshold could be established on the definition of dominant position. This deviation from the 40% rule could be acceptable, as it is anyway uncertain which percentage is acceptable or not by the competition authorities. The chapter proposes this regulation and market monitoring mechanism could be applicable on a permanent basis, where all participants know if they currently have or might have a dominant position in the future. This methodology also concerns the determination of cumulative dominant position and can be used in case of mergers evaluation.

We propose that a unified approach should cover aggregate and disaggregate markets, by adopting the same value for THRESHOLD 1 and THRESHOLD 2. Considering that the ex-ante regulation creating a certainty and clear rules in the market permanently, a higher value than 40% for those two thresholds could be considered, i.e., 50%.

Moreover, we consider that THRESHOLD2 on the disaggregate market should not be applied, when the size of the disaggregate market compared to the size of the aggregate market is below THRESHOLD3. We propose that a level of 2%/2.5% or 4%/5% can be applied, as a value of this threshold, depending on the value of THRESHOLD2. The reasoning of this threshold is to respond to situations, such as the followings:

- A new technology/resource type, i.e., hydrogen, enters the aggregate market, creating also a new disaggregate market. In such case, the pioneer investor will enter automatically into a dominant position status. We consider that the dominant position status can be applied, when the size of the disaggregate market is above a threshold. In case of the Hellenic electricity market, with available capacity of the aggregate market being at the level of about 12 GW, 2%/2.5% value means 240 MW-300 MW respectively, which enables the investor to mature the disaggregate market.
  ○ However, it must be clarified that exemption from non-compliance charges for market concentration does not mean that assets should not be regulated. This is the case of renewables under FiP scheme, where non-compliance charges regulation is already imposed in the Hellenic electricity market, to improve their forecasting capability. Similarly, any asset with market responsibilities can be accompanied with non-compliance charges for non-competitive bidding and supplementary by non-compliance charges for market concentration if needed.
- Interconnections with low net capacity, such as the electricity interconnection of Greece with Turkey with less than 200 MW. Although, competition should be enforced in every entry point, imposing a threshold on small capacity might lead to underuse of infrastructure. Considering also, that interconnections with explicit auctions, usually auction about 50% of their capacity as long-term (yearly and monthly), a relevant threshold is indirectly set. While, in interconnections with implicit auctions, the share of the net capacity that might be allocated to bilateral contracts allocated explicitly, is expected to be low, much lower than 50%.
  ○ Considering that Greece will implement market coupling with Bulgaria and Italy by 2021 and interconnections with other countries have low capacity, this threshold practically does not impose any restriction on the activity on any market participant in the electricity interconnections in Greece. Practically, market participant share' thresholds are imposed only to its gas interconnections.
- In case of low precipitation periods and/or accelerated climate change, large hydro units might have low availability, shrinking the size of the hydro disaggregate market. In such case, it can be argued that owing those assets does not provide a considerable relative advantage. By declaring realistic low available capacity, this threshold might enable participation without bidding strategy eliminations. On the other hand, declaring low available capacity affects also hydro participation in the balancing market, as well as in case of the establishment of capacity renumerations mechanisms. From this analysis, the determination of the actual available capacity of large hydro provides clear rules and fair treatment of those assets in all markets.

Finally, THRESHOLD4 aims to identify if a market participant is a net consumer/demander or net producer/supplier in the wholesale market, and therefore monitor and regulate its bidding behavior. It identifies the motivation of market participants in the formation of their bidding strategies. This also enables the consideration of participants that have common interests and could formulate cumulative dominant position.

We identify that a market participant can have:

- net seller (net supplier or net producer) status,
  - depending on the consideration of the total supply or total domestic production capacity respectively
- net buyer (net demander or net consumer) status
  - depending on the consideration of the total demand or total load capacity respectively

In case a market participant has a status of net buyer in the wholesale market (under THRESHOLD4), it could systematically implement a bidding strategy towards reducing wholesale prices, by systematically bidding those units at low prices, below their costs. In case a market participant has a status of net seller in the wholesale market (under THRESHOLD4), it could systematically implement a bidding strategy towards increasing wholesale prices, by systematically bidding those units at high prices. If this market participant (or a group of participants) has (cumulative) dominant position, then its (their) strategy is expected to affect wholesale prices. THRESHOLD4 could either be defined at (%) levels or at the MW levels, as the comparison among the supply and demand side could take place on the capacity levels (MW). In case it is defined at (%) levels, potential levels of THRESHOLD4 could be lower up to the value of THREHSOLD3, i.e., 1% or 2%/2.5%, depending of the value of THRESHOLD3. It is also suggested that THRESHOLD4 could be applied, considering when a market participant has a minimum market share in each of the supply and demand sides, i.e., at the THRESHOLD3 level.

2.3 Demand side

We identify the following four (4) thresholds for ex-ante determination of the dominant position of a market participant in the demand side.

- THRESOLD1, at the aggregate market level.
  - concerns each of the electricity and natural gas markets,
  - it considers the capacity per demand type (domestic load, storage, pumping), per voltage/pressure level, as well as per interconnection (exit) point for electricity and natural markets, as well as the capacity in bilateral contracts of market participants.
  - concerns available capacity of all assets.
- THRESOLD2, at the disaggregate market level.
  - concerns the available capacity for each demand type (domestic load, storage, pumping) each voltage/pressure level, as well as each interconnection (exit) point for electricity and natural markets,
  - voltage and pressure levels are considered differently, as a market participant can be allowed to change tariff policies at different levels, based on the relevant market concentration,
  - in each interconnection (exit) point, threshold concern only long-term (yearly/monthly) explicit capacity auctions,
- THRESOLD3, on the size of the disaggregate market level compared to the size of the aggregate market level.
- THRESOLD4, on the difference between the market share in the aggregate market level in the supply side compared to the market share in the aggregate market level in the demand side.

The values of THRESHOLDS1–4 are the same with the values of the relevant thresholds in the supply side. This is the reason that we don't use different names for the thresholds. The reasoning for the existence of those thresholds is the same as in the case of the supply side. THRESOLDS3 imposes a threshold on new technologies, such as the storage facilities in the electricity and natural gas markets, while the same might happen for pumping facilities in the electricity markets depending on their availability. Again, the realistic declaration of the availability of the pumping capacity of the large hydro is important, following a different pattern with hydro units' injections, namely allocating pumping demand in off-peak hours. THRESHOLD4 aims to identify if a market participant is a net consumer/demander or producer/supplier in the wholesale market, and therefore monitor and regulate its bidding behavior. This mainly concerns the supply side, especially when demand side assets are non-priced. On the other hand, in the demand side, the main interest for regulation concerns the retail, namely on whether a market participant has or not a dominant position in an aggregate or disaggregate market, under THRESHOLDS1-2, which might enable him forming competitive tariff policies generally or at specific voltage/pressure level.

2.4 Comparing supply with demand side

As mentioned above THRESHOLD4 aims to identify if a market participant is a net consumer/demander or net producer/supplier in the wholesale market. We identify that a market participant can have:

- Net seller (net supplier or net producer) status
  ○ depending on the consideration of the total supply or total domestic production capacity respectively
- net buyer (net demander or net consumer) status
  ○ depending on the consideration of the total demand or total load capacity, respectively

In case a market participant has a status of net buyer in the wholesale market (under THRESHOLD4), it could systematically implement a bidding strategy towards reducing wholesale prices, by systematically bidding those units at low prices, below their costs. In case a market participant has a status of net seller/buyer in the wholesale market (under THRESHOLD4), it could systematically implement a bidding strategy towards increasing wholesale prices, by systematically bidding those units at high prices. If this market participant (or a group of participants) has (cumulative) dominant position, then its (their) strategy is expected to affect wholesale prices.

Those status options lead to different comparison options among the supply and demand side:

- total available supply capacity with total available demand capacity, concerning assets with market participation responsibilities and excluding bilateral contracts in both sides,
  ○ considering all supply capacity from disaggregate markets, i.e., in case of the electricity market, all domestic production capacity excluding RES_FiT and commissioning units, as well as all interconnections' capacity and considering all demand capacity from disaggregate markets, i.e., domestic load, interconnections, storage and pumping,
- total available domestic production capacity with total available domestic demand capacity, concerning assets with market participation responsibilities and excluding bilateral contracts in both sides,
  ○ excluding interconnections from the figures mentioned in the previous bullet for both supply and demand sides, (in such case we consider total domestic demand capacity),
  ○ further excluding storage and pumping assets in the demand side, and therefore keeping only domestic load, as competition in the retail demand side concerns tariff formulation on the represented load (in such case we consider total domestic load capacity).

The first bullet option seems to be more appropriate, as interconnections affect wholesale prices. Theoretically, long-term rights in interconnection points can also justify vertical integration of a market participant. However, as existing noncompliance charges already regulate the bidding behavior of long-term rights, for all participants irrespective of their market shares, there is no further need for extra regulation on market concentration for those assets. Therefore, the comparison includes all assets, but specific regulation might be applied to some of them, in case a market participant has clear bidding interests and a dominant position.

In general, imposition of thresholds guarantees some standards concerning competition, but on the other hand it might lead to underuse of the infrastructure. Such is the case where there is limited participation from other participants in the auctions. Moreover, somebody could argue that considering that auctions where available to all market participants, there is no need for the imposition of thresholds in the capacity allocation process to market participants. Those cases could be exemptions from the general rule and be applied in relation to the threshold of the aggregate market, namely if a market participant violates the threshold in the aggregate market, then obligations such as capacity re-allocation/opt-out or gas release to be applied in the disaggregate market.

However, this might affect competition, as in case a market participant dominates a disaggregate market with lower cost than the other disaggregate markets of the aggregate market, and at the same time does not violate the aggregate market threshold, no rules might be applied to its market position. However, under those rules, this market participant might dominate also domestic retail market, as the energy supplied by the disaggregate market will be dominant in the whole domestic demand. This analysis can justify the need to total available supply capacity with domestic demand for capacity. It could be argued that this could also consider the available capacity of exports. However, this challenges the definition of the relative market in the supply side, as a dominant position in the supply or the demand side should concern all available supply or demand assets respectively. Mixing demand assets with supply assets complicates the definition of relative market, as practically imports interconnection capacity is offset by exports interconnections capacity. This offset is not meaningful, as energy flows in interconnections usually have a dominant pattern towards one direction, from the cheaper to the most expensive energy market. This could lead a market participant to reserve full capacity in the direction with limited flow at a very low or even zero cost, in order to offset dominant share in imports capacity and in supply capacity generally.

Therefore, supply side and demand side should be considered independently, and relevant market position shares' thresholds to be applied independently to the relative aggregate and disaggregate markets.

Following this analysis, for comparing supply and demand market shares towards identifying the market participants' interests, we consider that the supply side could consider all available capacity from production capacity assets with market responsibilities, as well as imports' interconnections capacity assets, while the demand side could concern only domestic load assets. This derives from the fact that the main reason for monitoring market concentration on the demand side is to enable or not competitive tariffs for market participants. Storage and pumping assets could be excluded from this comparison, as those assets have different interests, namely, to provide flexibility on the power system. But of course this does not mean that they should be generally regulated. When the domestic load also becomes flexible, or part of the domestic load capacity can provide demand flexibility, such as the high voltage for the electricity market, then this category can be also excluded from the market share in the demand side. This might lead to exclusion of this disaggregate market when estimating market share in the demand side, or alternatively to consider all domestic demand assets, including also storage and pumping assets, as all domestic load categories (voltage levels) become flexible.

2.5 Defining combination of market concentration in aggregate and disaggregate markets

The existence of several thresholds creates several combinations, that form different cases that could be examined, as well as indicate the disaggregate markets where regulation for market concentration could be applied. Those cases are summarized in Table 21.1. It should be noted that for some disaggregate markets, there might already exist regulation for non-competitive issues, that offset or eliminate the need for further regulation for market concentration issues.

3 Mathematical framework of the ex-ante market monitoring mechanism

This section describes the mathematical formulation of the market monitoring component of the proposed mechanism. The relevant regulation component could be examined in more detail in another study. The market monitoring mechanism is described separately for the supply and demand side. In order such mechanism to be more realistic and implementable, the methodology considers processes and public available information from the Hellenic power market. However, the mechanism could be implemented at any power market, as well as at natural gas market, adjusted on the relevant pubic available information.

3.1 Supply side

The methodology is developed towards using information included in the Day Ahead Scheduling requirements,[c] published every day in specific time schedules by the Hellenic Energy Exchange, through input provided by the Hellenic TSO. This information is supplemented by extra inputs, towards estimating different market concentration indicators. The methodology is applied to the day-ahead market, where most of the trading takes place. It also considers capacity allocated to bilateral contracts. The methodology could at a second stage be extended for intra-day and balancing markets, especially when there is considerable information from their operation. This however would require considerable further analysis and is not in the scope of this study.

The Day-Ahead Scheduling requirements include, for each hour t of the next day d:

- the available domestic capacity of each power plant u, belonging to market participant p, using fuel f (DOM_PROD_AVAILu,p,f,t)
  - the available capacity of each market participant p, using fuel f (DOM_PROD_AVAIL$_{p,f,t}$) could also be estimated
- the available capacity for imports in each interconnection n (IMP_AVAIL$_{n,t}$),
- the available capacity for mandatory injections by large hydro units MAND_HYDRO_AVAIL$_{p,\ t}$,
- the available capacity by units in commissioning/testing operation/high-efficiency cogeneration units PRIOR_CAP_AVAIL$_{p,f,t}$
- the available capacity for net import schedules with neighboring TSOs (adjusting deviations & returns of emergencies) IMP_SCHED_TSOs$_{n,\ t}$
- the long-term import capacity rights in each interconnection n per market participant p (IMP_LT_CAP$_{n,p,t}$)

---

c. http://www.enexgroup.gr/en/markets/electricity-day-ahead-market/input-data/day-ahead-scheduling-requirements/.

TABLE 21.1 Ex-ante monitoring of market concentration cases, as well as identification of cases that need ex-ante monitoring and regulation mechanism.

	Ex-ante monitoring of market concentration cases (considering combinations of thresholds being violated)						
	1	2	3	4	5	6	7
THRESHOLD1	Yes	Yes	Yes	Yes	Yes	Yes	Yes
THRESHOLD2	Yes	Yes	Yes	Yes	No	No	No
THRESHOLD3	Yes	Yes	No	No	Yes	Yes	No
THRESHOLD4	Yes	No	Yes	No	Yes	No	Yes
Cases that need ex-ante regulation (through non-compliance charges for market concentration)							
Regulation, due to THRESHOLD1 or THRESHOLD2, might be applied to:	All disaggregate markets	All disaggregate markets	All disaggregate markets	All disaggregate markets	All disaggregate markets	All disaggregate markets	All disaggregate markets
Exception due to THRESHOLD3:			Disaggregate markets not violating THRESHOLD3	Disaggregate markets not violating THRESHOLD3			Disaggregate markets not violating THRESHOLD3
Exception due to THRESHOLD4:		All disaggregate markets not vi ol ating THRESHOLD2		All disaggregate markets not violating THRESHOLD2		All disaggregate markets not violating THRESHOLD2	
Regulation applied to:	All disaggregate markets	All disaggregate markets, besides those not violating THRESHOLD2	All disaggregate markets, besides those not violating THRESHOLD3	All disaggregate markets, besides those not violating THRESHOLD3 and those not violating THRESHOLD2	All disaggregate markets	All disaggregate markets, besides those not violating THRESHOLD2	All disaggregate markets, besides those not violating THRESHOLD3

regulation in the form of non-compliance charges for market concentration, based on the proposed ex-ante market

8	9	10	11	12	13	14	15	16
Yes	No	No	No	No	No	No	No	No
No	Yes	Yes	Yes	Yes	No	No	No	No
No	Yes	Yes	No	No	Yes	Yes	No	No
No	Yes	No	Yes	No	Yes	No	Yes	No
All disaggregate markets Disaggregate markets not violating THRESHOLD3 All disaggregate markets not violating THRESHOLD2	All disaggregate markets violating THRESHOLD2	All disaggregate markets violating THRESHOLD2	All disaggregate markets violating THRESHOLD2 Disaggregate markets not violating THRESHOLD3	All disaggregate markets violating THRESHOLD2 Disaggregate markets not violating THRESHOLD3				
All disaggregate markets, besides those not violating THRESHOLD3 and those not violating THRESHOLD2	All disaggregate markets violating THRESHOLD2	All disaggregate markets violating THRESHOLD2	All disaggregate markets violating THRESHOLD2, besides those not violating THRESHOLD3	All disaggregate markets violating THRESHOLD2, besides those not violating THRESHOLD3	Nowhere	Nowhere	Nowhere	Nowhere

- the renewables' generation forecasting for renewables under FiT scheme RES_FiT_AVAILt (practically it concerns their availability)
- the generation forecast for renewables under FiP scheme not represented by RES aggregators RES_FiP_AVAILt (practically it concerns their availability)
  - ○ the generation forecast for renewables that have market responsibilities obligations (FiP&Market status in RES classification) for each market participant p RES_MRK_AVAIL$_{p,t}$ could also be estimated

All the above measures are identified at zonal level, so therefore zone z dimension can be inserted in each variable. Considering that the market splitting is not implemented in the Hellenic electricity wholesale market, the dimension z can be excluded from the analysis for the time being. Moreover, the analysis can be implemented at day level and not hour level. We suggest that the analysis can be implemented at an hourly level, but the final indicators assessing market concentration to concern average daily level. This derives from the fact that under the EUPHEMIA algorithm[d] implemented under the target model, market participants can bid using orders that concern several hours or even the whole 24h period of a day, such as the block orders. Therefore, it makes sense to consider average daily values on estimation of market concentration shares, as those aim to regulate bidding strategies through non-compliance charges.

We identify a process on estimating four (4) indicators on estimating market share in the supply side:

- Indicator 1: initially considering the available domestic production capacity for each participant, the imports interconnections capacity and the long-term capacity rights for each participant.
- Indicator 2: sequentially excluding assets with dispatching priority and without market participation responsibilities, such as renewables under FiT scheme, mandatory injections by large hydro units, units in commissioning/testing operation/high-efficiency cogeneration units, well as the net import schedules with neighboring TSOs (adjusting deviations & returns of emergencies), for each participant and in total supply.
- Indicator 3: sequentially considering a limited and more realistic large hydro availability, for each market participant and in total supply.
- Indicator 4: sequentially considering the share (%) of load of each market participant that concerns bilateral contracts, re-estimating their available capacity as well as the total available supply capacity. This Indicator is considered as the most appropriate in estimating the ex-ante market share in the supply side.

The reason for being so analytical with all those four indicators, is to enable the quantification of the effect of the different above mentioned assumptions on the available capacity of the assets, towards concluding in the suggested Indicator 4 for the market concentration in the supply side. In all estimations, capacity volumes concern MW and market share indicators concern percentage (%) levels.

3.1.1 Estimation of Indicator 1

For estimating the Indicator 1, the process is the following:

- the total available supply capacity for domestic production and imports for each time period t *TOT*_SUP_AVAIL_CAP1$_t$
- the total available capacity for domestic production and imports for each time market participant p, fuel type f and time period t *TOT_AVAIL*_SUP_CAP1$_{p, f, t}$
- the total available capacity for renewables for each time market participant p, and time period t *TOT_AVAIL*_RES_SUP_CAP1$_{p, f, t}$
- the total available capacity for domestic production and imports for each time market participant p, interconnections (entry n point) and time period t *TOT_AVAIL*_SUP_CAP1$_{p, n, t}$
- the total available capacity for domestic production and imports for each time market participant p and time period t *TOT*_SUP_AVAIL_CAP1$_{p, t}$
- a market share indicator (Capacity Availability Share in Supply—CAS_SUP1) on the market share (%) for each market participant p, fuel type f and time period t *CAS_SUP1*$_{p, f, t}$, as well as the average relevant daily market share (%) indicator *CAS_SUP1*$_{p, f, d}$
- a marker share (%) indicator (Capacity Availability Share in Supply—CAS_RES_SUP1) in the renewables disaggregate market, for each market participant p, and time period t *CAS_RES_SUP1*$_{p, t}$, as well as the average relevant daily market share (%) indicator *CAS_RES_SUP1*$_{p, d}$

---

d. http://www.enexgroup.gr/en/markets/target-model-markets/price-coupling-of-regions/.

- a market share (%) indicator for each market participant p, interconnection (entry point n) and time period t $CAS\_SUP1_{p,\,n,\,t}$, as well as the average relevant daily market share (%) indicator $CAS\_SUP1_{p,\,n,\,d}$
- a market share (%) indicator for each market participant p and time period t. $CAS\_SUP1_{p,\,t}$
- a market share (%) indicator for each market participant p and day d $CAS\_SUP1_{p,\,d}$, which stands as Indicator 1 for assessing dominant position in the supply side.

Available supply capacity for aggregate and disaggregate markets

Total available supply capacity per recourse (fuel f) disaggregate market

$$TOT\_AVAIL\_SUP\_CAP1_{f,t} = \sum_{p}\sum_{n}\Big(DOM\_PROD\_AVAIL_{p,f,t} + IMP\_AVAIL_{n,t} + RES\_FiT\_AVAIL_{p,t}$$
$$+ RES\_MRK\_AVAIL_{p,t}\Big) \tag{21.1}$$

Total available supply capacity for the renewables disaggregate market

$$TOT\_AVAIL\_RES\_SUP\_CAP1_{t} = \sum_{p}\Big(RES\_FiT\_AVAIL_{p,t} + RES\_MRK\_AVAIL_{p,t}\Big) \tag{21.2}$$

Total available supply capacity per interconnection (entry point n) disaggregate market

$$TOT\_AVAIL\_SUP\_CAP1_{n,t} = \sum_{p}\sum_{f}\Big(DOM\_PROD\_AVAIL_{p,f,t} + IMP\_AVAIL_{n,t} + RES\_FiT\_AVAIL_{p,t}$$
$$+ RES\_MRK\_AVAIL_{p,t}\Big) \tag{21.3}$$

Total available supply capacity for the aggregate market

$$TOT\_AVAIL\_SUP\_CAP1_{t} = \sum_{f}\Big(TOT\_AVAIL\_SUP\_CAP1_{f,t}\Big) \tag{21.4}$$

Available supply capacity for aggregate and disaggregate markets per market participant.

Total available supply capacity per recourse (fuel f type) disaggregate market, for each market participant p

$$TOT\_AVAIL\_SUP\_CAP1_{p,f,t} = \sum_{n}\Big(DOM\_PROD\_AVAIL_{p,f,t} + IMP\_LT\_AVAIL_{p,n,t} + RES\_FiT\_AVAIL_{p,t}$$
$$+ RES\_MRK\_AVAIL_{p,t}\Big) \tag{21.5}$$

Total available supply capacity for the renewables disaggregate market, for each market participant p

$$TOT\_AVAIL\_RES\_SUP\_CAP1_{p,t} = \Big(RES\_FiT\_AVAIL_{p,t} + RES\_MRK\_AVAIL_{p,t} \tag{21.6}$$

Total available supply capacity per interconnection (entry point n) disaggregate market for each market participant p

$$TOT\_AVAIL\_SUP\_CAP1_{p,n,t} = \sum_{f}\Big(DOM\_PROD\_AVAIL_{p,f,t} + IMP\_AVAIL_{n,t} + RES\_FiT\_AVAIL_{p,t}$$
$$+ RES\_MRK\_AVAIL_{p,t}\Big) \tag{21.7}$$

Total available supply capacity for the aggregate market, for each market participant p

$$TOT\_AVAIL\_SUP\_CAP1_{p,t} = \sum_{f}\Big(TOT\_AVAIL\_SUP\_CAP1_{p,f,t}\Big) \tag{21.8}$$

Market share (%) indicators per each disaggregate markets and market participant.

Market share (%) indicators in the total available supply capacity per recourse (fuel f) disaggregate market, for each market participant p

$$CAS\_SUP1_{p,f,t} = \frac{TOT\_AVAIL\_SUP\_CAP1_{p,f,t}}{TOT\_AVAIL\_SUP\_CAP1_{f,t}} \tag{21.9}$$

$$CAS\_SUP1_{p,f,d} = \sum_t \frac{TOT\_AVAIL\_SUP\_CAP1_{p,f,t}}{TOT\_AVAIL\_SUP\_CAP1_{f,t}} \tag{21.10}$$

Market share (%) indicators in the total available supply capacity for renewables disaggregate market, for each market participant p

$$CAS\_RES\_SUP1_{p,t} = \frac{TOT\_AVAIL\_RES\_SUP\_CAP1_{p,t}}{TOT\_AVAIL\_RES\_SUP\_CAP1_{t}} \tag{21.11}$$

$$CAS\_RES\_SUP1_{p,d} = \sum_t \frac{TOT\_AVAIL\_RES\_SUP\_CAP1_{p,f,t}}{TOT\_AVAIL\_RES\_SUP\_CAP1_{f,t}} \tag{21.12}$$

Market share (%) indicators in the total available supply capacity per interconnections (entry point n) disaggregate market, for each market participant p

$$CAS\_SUP1_{p,n,t} = \frac{TOT\_AVAIL\_SUP\_CAP1_{p,n,t}}{TOT\_AVAIL\_SUP\_CAP1_{n,t}} \tag{21.13}$$

$$CAS\_SUP1_{p,n,d} = \sum_t \frac{TOT\_AVAIL\_SUP\_CAP1_{p,n,t}}{TOT\_AVAIL\_SUP\_CAP1_{n,t}} \tag{21.14}$$

Market share (%) indicators in the total available supply capacity for each market participant p

$$CAS\_SUP1_{p,t} = \frac{TOT\_AVAIL\_SUP\_CAP1_{p,t}}{TOT\_AVAIL\_SUP\_CAP1_{t}} \tag{21.15}$$

$$CAS\_SUP1_{p,d} = \sum_t \frac{TOT\_AVAIL\_SUP\_CAP1_{p,t}}{TOT\_AVAIL\_SUP\_CAP1_{t}} \tag{21.16}$$

Indicator 1 is the indicator estimated with Eq. (21.16).

3.1.2   Estimation of Indicator 2

For estimating the Indicator 2, the process is the following:

- the total available capacity estimated for Indicator 1 is updated excluding capacity from assets without market participation responsibilities, such as renewables under FiT scheme $RES\_FiT\_AVAIL_{p,t}$, mandatory injections by large hydro units $MAND\_HYDRO\_AVAIL_{p,t}$, and units in commissioning/testing operation/high-efficiency cogeneration units $PRIOR\_CAP\_AVAIL_{p,f,t}$, as well as the net import schedules with neighboring TSOs (adjusting deviations & returns of emergencies) $IMP\_SCHED\_TSOs_{n,t}$, therefore estimating the second total available supply capacity for domestic production and imports for each time period t $TOT\_SUP\_AVAIL\_CAP2_t$
- it updates, with Eqs. (21.17)–(21.32), all the above estimated variables in Eqs. (21.1)–(21.16).

Available supply capacity for aggregate and disaggregate markets.
  Total available supply capacity per recourse (fuel f) disaggregate market

$$TOT\_AVAIL\_\_SUP\_CAP2_{f,t} = TOT\_AVAIL\_\_SUP\_CAP1_t$$
$$- \sum_p \left(RES\_FiT\_AVAIL_{p,t} + MAND\_HYDRO\_AVAIL_{p,t} + PRIOR\_CAP\_AVAIL_{p,f,t} \right)$$
$$\tag{21.17}$$

Total available supply capacity for the renewables disaggregate market

$$TOT\_AVAIL\_\_SUP\_CAP2_t = TOT\_AVAIL\_\_SUP\_CAP1_t - \sum_p RES\_FiT\_AVAIL_{p,t} \tag{21.18}$$

Total available supply capacity per interconnection (entry point n) disaggregate market.

$$TOT\_AVAIL\_\_SUP\_CAP2_{n,t} = TOT\_AVAIL\_\_SUP\_CAP1_{n,t} - IMP\_SCHED\_TSOs_{n,t} \tag{21.19}$$

Total available supply capacity for the aggregate market

$$TOT\_AVAIL\_SUP\_CAP2_t = \sum_f \sum_n \left(TOT\_AVAIL\_SUP\_CAP2_{f,t} - \text{IMP\_SCHED\_TSOs}_{n,t} \right) \tag{21.20}$$

Available supply capacity for aggregate and disaggregate markets per market participant.

Total available supply capacity per recourse (fuel f type) disaggregate market, for each market participant p

$$TOT\_AVAIL\_RES\_CAP2_{p,f,t} = TOT\_AVAIL\_SUP\_CAP1_{p,f,t} - RES\_FiT\_AVAIL_{p,t}$$
$$- \text{MAND\_HYDRO\_AVAIL}_{p,t} - PRIOR\_CAP\_AVAIL_{p,f,t} \tag{21.21}$$

Total available supply capacity for the renewables disaggregate market, for each market participant p

$$TOT\_AVAIL\_RES\_CAP2_{p,t} = TOT\_AVAIL\_RES\_CAP1_{p,t} - RES\_FiT\_AVAIL_{p,t} \tag{21.22}$$

Total available supply capacity per interconnection (entry) point n disaggregate market for each market participant p

$$TOT\_AVAIL\_SUP\_CAP2_{p,n,t} = TOT\_AVAIL\_SUP\_CAP1_{p,n,t} \tag{21.23}$$

Total available supply capacity for the aggregate market, for each market participant p

$$TOT\_AVAIL\_SUP\_CAP2_{p,t} = \sum_f \left(TOT\_AVAIL\_SUP\_CAP2_{p,f,t} \right) \tag{21.24}$$

Market share (%) indicators per each disaggregate markets and market participant.

Market share (%) indicators in the total available supply capacity per recourse (fuel f) disaggregate market, for each market participant p

$$CAS\_SUP2_{p,f,t} = \frac{TOT\_AVAIL\_SUP\_CAP2_{p,f,t}}{TOT\_AVAIL\_SUP\_CAP2_{f,t}} \tag{21.25}$$

$$CAS\_SUP2_{p,f,d} = \sum_t \frac{TOT\_AVAIL\_SUP\_CAP2_{p,f,t}}{TOT\_AVAIL\_SUP\_CAP2_{f,t}} \tag{21.26}$$

Market share (%) indicators in the total available supply capacity for renewables disaggregate market, for each market participant p

$$CAS\_RES\_SUP2_{p,t} = \frac{TOT\_AVAIL\_RES\_SUP\_CAP2_{p,t}}{TOT\_AVAIL\_RES\_SUP\_CAP2_{t}} \tag{21.27}$$

$$CAS\_RES\_SUP2_{p,d} = \sum_t \frac{TOT\_AVAIL\_RES\_SUP\_CAP2_{p,f,t}}{TOT\_AVAIL\_RES\_SUP\_CAP2_{f,t}} \tag{21.28}$$

Market share (%) indicators in the total available supply capacity per interconnections (entry point n) disaggregate market, for each market participant p

$$CAS\_SUP2_{p,n,t} = \frac{TOT\_AVAIL\_SUP\_CAP2_{p,n,t}}{TOT\_AVAIL\_SUP\_CAP2_{n,t}} \tag{21.29}$$

$$CAS\_SUP2_{p,n,d} = \sum_t \frac{TOT\_AVAIL\_SUP\_CAP2_{p,n,t}}{TOT\_AVAIL\_SUP\_CAP2_{n,t}} \tag{21.30}$$

Market share (%) indicators in the total available supply capacity for each market participant p

$$CAS\_SUP4_{p,t} = \frac{TOT\_AVAIL\_SUP\_CAP2_{p,t}}{TOT\_AVAIL\_SUP\_CAP2_{t}} \tag{21.31}$$

$$CAS\_SUP4_{p,d} = \sum_t \frac{TOT\_AVAIL\_SUP\_CAP2_{p,t}}{TOT\_AVAIL\_SUP\_CAP2_{t}} \tag{21.32}$$

Indicator 2 is the indicator estimated with Eq. (21.32).

3.1.3 Estimation of Indicator 3

For estimating the Indicator 3, the process is the following:

- the total available capacity estimated for Indicator 2 is updated considering limited availability in large hydro units,
  - considering a peak saving strategy $PEAKSAVING_{p,f,t}$
- it updates, with Eqs. (21.33)–(21.48), all the above estimated variables in Eqs. (21.17)–(21.32).

Available supply capacity for aggregate and disaggregate markets.

Total available supply capacity per recourse (fuel f) disaggregate market

$$TOT\_AVAIL\_SUP\_CAP3_{f,t} = TOT\_AVAIL\_SUP\_CAP2_{f,t}$$
$$+ \sum_{p} \left(DOM\_PROD\_AVAIL3_{p,f,t} - DOM\_PROD\_AVAIL_{p,f,t} \right) \quad (21.33)$$

where

$$DOM\_PROD\_AVAIL3_{p,f,t} = PEAK\_SAVING_{p,f,t} * DOM\_PROD\_AVAIL_{p,f,t} \quad (21.34)$$

Total available supply capacity for the renewables disaggregate market

$$TOT\_AVAIL\_SUP\_CAP3_{t} = TOT\_AVAIL\_SUP\_CAP2_{f,t}$$
$$+ \sum_{p} \sum_{n} \left(DOM\_PROD\_AVAIL3_{p,f,t} - DOM\_PROD\_AVAIL_{p,f,t} \right) \quad (21.35)$$

Total available supply capacity per interconnection (entry point n) disaggregate market

$$TOT\_AVAIL\_SUP\_CAP3_{n,t} = TOT\_AVAIL\_SUP\_CAP2_{n,t} \quad (21.36)$$

Total available supply capacity for the aggregate market

$$TOT\_AVAIL\_SUP\_CAP3_{t} = \sum_{f} \left(TOT\_AVAIL\_SUP\_CAP3_{f,t} \right) \quad (21.37)$$

Available supply capacity for aggregate and disaggregate markets per market participant.

Total available supply capacity per recourse (fuel f type) disaggregate market, for each market participant p

$$TOT\_AVAIL\_SUP\_CAP3_{p,f,t} = TOT\_AVAIL\_SUP\_CAP2_{p,f,t}$$
$$+ \left(DOM\_PROD\_AVAIL3_{p,f,t} - DOM\_PROD\_AVAIL_{p,f,t} \right) \quad (21.38)$$

Total available supply capacity for the renewables disaggregate market, for each market participant p

$$TOT\_AVAIL\_SUP\_CAP3_{p,t} = TOT\_AVAIL\_RES\_CAP2_{p,t}$$
$$+ \left(DOM\_PROD\_AVAIL3_{p,f,t} - DOM\_PROD\_AVAIL_{p,f,t} \right) \quad (21.39)$$

Total available supply capacity per interconnection (entry point n) disaggregate market, for each market participant p

$$TOT\_AVAIL\_SUP\_CAP3_{p,n,t} = TOT\_AVAIL\_SUP\_CAP2_{p,n,t} \quad (21.40)$$

Total available supply capacity for the aggregate market, for each market participant p

$$TOT\_AVAIL\_SUP\_CAP3_{p,t} = \sum_{f} \left(TOT\_AVAIL\_SUP\_CAP3_{p,f,t} \right) \quad (21.41)$$

Market share (%) indicators per each disaggregate markets and market participant.

Market share (%) indicators in the total available supply capacity per recourse (fuel f) disaggregate market, for each market participant p

$$CAS\_SUP3_{p,f,t} = \frac{TOT\_AVAIL\_SUP\_CAP3_{p,f,t}}{TOT\_AVAIL\_SUP\_CAP3_{f,t}} \quad (21.42)$$

$$CAS\_SUP3_{p,f,d} = \sum_t \frac{TOT\_AVAIL\_SUP\_CAP3_{p,f,t}}{TOT\_AVAIL\_SUP\_CAP2_{f,t}} \tag{21.43}$$

Market share (%) indicators in the total available supply capacity for renewables disaggregate market, for each market participant p

$$CAS\_RES\_SUP3_{p,t} = \frac{TOT\_AVAIL\_RES\_SUP\_CAP3_{p,t}}{TOT\_AVAIL\_RES\_SUP\_CAP3_{t}} \tag{21.44}$$

$$CAS\_RES\_SUP3_{p,d} = \sum_t \frac{TOT\_AVAIL\_RES\_SUP\_CAP3_{p,f,t}}{TOT\_AVAIL\_RES\_SUP\_CAP3_{f,t}} \tag{21.45}$$

Market share (%) indicators in the total available supply capacity per interconnections (entry point n) disaggregate market, for each market participant p

$$CAS\_SUP3_{p,n,t} = \frac{TOT\_AVAIL\_SUP\_CAP3_{p,n,t}}{TOT\_AVAIL\_SUP\_CAP3_{n,t}} \tag{21.46}$$

$$CAS\_SUP3_{p,n,d} = \sum_t \frac{TOT\_AVAIL\_SUP\_CAP3_{p,n,t}}{TOT\_AVAIL\_SUP\_CAP3_{n,t}} \tag{21.47}$$

Market share (%) indicators in the total available supply capacity for each market participant p

$$CAS\_SUP3_{p,t} = \frac{TOT\_AVAIL\_SUP\_CAP3_{p,t}}{TOT\_AVAIL\_SUP\_CAP3_{t}} \tag{21.48}$$

$$CAS\_SUP3_{p,d} = \sum_t \frac{TOT\_AVAIL\_SUP\_CAP3_{p,t}}{TOT\_AVAIL\_SUP\_CAP3_{t}} \tag{21.49}$$

Indicator 3 is the indicator estimated with Eq. (21.49).

3.1.4 Estimation of Indicator 4

For estimating the Indicator 4, the process is the following:

- the total available capacity estimated for Indicator 3 is updated excluding capacity that have been allocated in bilateral contracts
  - considering a share (%) $BIL\_CON\_SHARE_{p,t}$ of the load forecast of each market participant p $LOAD\_AVAIL_{p,t}$ is covered by bilateral contracts between the producer and the final consumer
  - the bilateral contracts of this load is covered by thermal and large hydro available capacity $DOM\_PROD\_AVAIL4_{p,f,t}$, under a recourse type allocation share $BIL\_RES\_SHARE4_{p,f,t}$
  - we consider that bilateral contracts are linked to the domestic load capacity of each participant (or alternatively its domestic demand capacity or its total demand capacity, as defined in the demand side section). This is done, as domestic load can be more easily forecasted by each participant and therefore allocate a specific share of its supply capacity to cover this load. On the other hand, supply capacity for each participant might available for electricity generation/injection, but the actual generation/injection might be more difficult to be projected, as it faces competition in the supply side.
- it updates, with Eqs. (21.50)–(21.66), all the above estimated variables in Eqs. (21.33)–(21.49)

Available supply capacity for aggregate and disaggregate markets.
Total available supply capacity per recourse (fuel f) disaggregate market

$$TOT\_AVAIL\_SUP\_CAP4_{f,t} = TOT\_AVAIL\_SUP\_CAP3_{t} - \sum_p DOM\_PROD\_AVAIL4_{p,f,t} \tag{21.50}$$

where

$$DOM\_PROD\_AVAIL4_{p,f,t} = BIL\_CON\_SHARE_{p,t} * LOAD\_AVAIL_{p,t} * BIL\_RES\_SHARE4_{p,f,t} \tag{21.51}$$

Total available supply capacity for the renewables disaggregate market

$$TOT\_AVAIL\_\_SUP\_CAP4_t = TOT\_AVAIL\_\_SUP\_CAP3_t \tag{21.52}$$

Total available supply capacity per interconnection (entry point n) disaggregate market

$$TOT\_AVAIL\_\_SUP\_CAP4_{n,t} = TOT\_AVAIL\_\_SUP\_CAP3_{n,t} \tag{21.53}$$

Total available supply capacity for the aggregate market

$$TOT\_AVAIL\_\_SUP\_CAP4_t = \sum_f \left(TOT\_AVAIL\_\_SUP\_CAP4_{f,t} \right) \tag{21.54}$$

Available supply capacity for aggregate and disaggregate markets per market participant.
Total available supply capacity per recourse (fuel f type) disaggregate market, for each market participant p

$$TOT\_AVAIL\_\_SUP\_CAP4_{p,f,t} = TOT\_AVAIL\_\_SUP\_CAP1_{p,f,t} - DOM\_PROD\_AVAIL4_{p,f,t} \tag{21.55}$$

Total available supply capacity for the renewables disaggregate market, for each market participant p

$$TOT\_AVAIL\_\_RES\_CAP4_{p,t} = TOT\_AVAIL\_\_RES\_CAP3_{p,t} \tag{21.56}$$

Total available supply capacity per interconnection (entry point n) disaggregate market, for each market participant p

$$TOT\_AVAIL\_\_SUP\_CAP4_{p,n,t} = TOT\_AVAIL\_\_SUP\_CAP3_{p,n,t} \tag{21.57}$$

Total available supply capacity for the aggregate market, for each market participant p

$$TOT\_AVAIL\_\_SUP\_CAP4_{p,t} = \sum_f \left(TOT\_AVAIL\_\_SUP\_CAP4_{p,f,t} \right) \tag{21.58}$$

Market share (%) indicators per each disaggregate markets and market participant.
Market share (%) indicators in the total available supply capacity per recourse (fuel f) disaggregate market, for each market participant p

$$CAS\_SUP4_{p,f,t} = \frac{TOT\_AVAIL\_SUP\_CAP4_{p,f,t}}{TOT\_AVAIL\_SUP\_CAP4_{f,t}} \tag{21.59}$$

$$CAS\_SUP4_{p,f,d} = \sum_t \frac{TOT\_AVAIL\_SUP\_CAP4_{p,f,t}}{TOT\_AVAIL\_SUP\_CAP4_{f,t}} \tag{21.60}$$

Market share (%) indicators in the total available supply capacity for renewables disaggregate market, for each market participant p

$$CAS\_RES\_SUP4_{p,t} = \frac{TOT\_AVAIL\_RES\_SUP\_CAP4_{p,t}}{TOT\_AVAIL\_RES\_SUP\_CAP4_t} \tag{21.61}$$

$$CAS\_RES\_SUP4_{p,d} = \sum_t \frac{TOT\_AVAIL\_RES\_SUP\_CAP4_{p,f,t}}{TOT\_AVAIL\_RES\_SUP\_CAP4_{f,t}} \tag{21.62}$$

Market share (%) indicators in the total available supply capacity per interconnections (entry point n) disaggregate market, for each market participant p

$$CAS\_SUP4_{p,n,t} = \frac{TOT\_AVAIL\_SUP\_CAP4_{p,n,t}}{TOT\_AVAIL\_SUP\_CAP4_{n,t}} \tag{21.63}$$

$$CAS\_SUP4_{p,n,d} = \sum_t \frac{TOT\_AVAIL\_SUP\_CAP4_{p,n,t}}{TOT\_AVAIL\_SUP\_CAP4_{n,t}} \tag{21.64}$$

Market share (%) indicators in the total available supply capacity for each market participant p

$$CAS\_SUP4_{p,t} = \frac{TOT\_AVAIL\_SUP\_CAP4_{p,t}}{TOT\_AVAIL\_SUP\_CAP4_t} \tag{21.65}$$

$$CAS\_SUP4_{p,d} = \sum_t \frac{TOT\_AVAIL\_SUP\_CAP4_{p,t}}{TOT\_AVAIL\_SUP\_CAP4_t} \tag{21.66}$$

Indicator 4 is the indicator estimated with Eq. (21.66).

3.2 Demand side

The estimation of the market share in the demand side, could be done either ex-post, or ex-ante, i.e., using of similar days (demand orders from similar previous days), or estimating analytically the market share in total demand and interconnection (exit) points. In case of the Hellenic power market, there exist already an ex-post evaluation is done for the demand side, through the publication at the end of each month of a relevant report on the market shares of each participant per voltage level for the previous month (HEnEX, 2020c). This report considers the demand declarations, as the ex-post settlement of actual measurements might delay several months. However, as the demand declarations are supplemented by relevant non-compliance charges to avoid non-competitive behavior, they could be considered a credible indicator. This publication could be used for allowing market participants to allow tariff policies for a voltage level, i.e., medium voltage, until their market share in this voltage level is identified as dominant in a new publication. Exceptions might be the high voltage/pressure demand side, as relevant tariffs concern confidential negotiations towards customized tariffs to the consumption pattern of each final consumer and might also concern state aid schemes, followed by different competition policy procedure.

As mentioned above, this chapter proposes an ex-ante market monitoring mechanism, using total available load capacity and excluding capacity allocated for bilateral contracts, as well as capacity in interconnections for exports and capacity for storage and pumping. Similar to the supply side, the information already available through the Day Ahead Scheduling process is the basis of the proposed process.

The Day-Ahead Scheduling requirements include, for each hour t of the next day d:

- the load forecast f (LOAD_AVAIL$_t$)
  - ○ it could extend by implementing load forecast per participant p (LOAD_AVAIL$_{p,t}$), for the participants with assets in the electroproduction side
  - ○ it could extend by implementing load forecast per participant p and voltage level v (LOAD_AVAIL$_{p,v,t}$), for the participants with assets in the electroproduction side
- the available capacity for exports in each interconnection n (EXP_AVAIL$_{n,t}$),
  - ○ the TSO also knows the long-term export capacity rights in each interconnection n per market participant p (LT_EXP_CAP$_{n,p,t}$)
- the available capacity for net import schedules with neighboring TSOs (adjusting deviations & returns of emergencies) IMP_SCHED_TSOs$_{n,t}$,
  - ○ the available capacity of pumping assets per participant p (PUMP_AVAIL$_{p,v,t}$) could also be forecasted
  - ○ the available capacity of storage assets per participant p (STOR_AVAIL$_{p,v,t}$) could also be forecasted.

Based on the above, the following volumes could be estimated, as shown in Eqs. (21.67)–(21.96):

- the total available capacity for demand for each time period t TOT__AVAIL_DEM_CAP$_t$
- the total available capacity for demand for each market participant p and time period t TOT_AVAIL_DEM_CAP$_{p,t}$
- the total available capacity for domestic demand for each time period t TOT__AVAIL_DOM_DEM_CAP$_t$
- the total available capacity for domestic demand for each market participant p and time period t TOT_AVAIL_DOM_DEM_CAP$_{p,t}$
- the total available capacity for domestic load for each time period t TOT_AVAIL_LOAD_CAP$_t$
- the total available capacity for domestic load for each market participant p and time period t TOT_AVAIL_LOAD_CAP$_{p,t}$
  - ○ considering the share of load devoted to bilateral contracts BIL_CON_SHARE$_{p,t}$
- a market share indicator (Capacity Availability Share in Load—CAS_LOAD) of the share (%) to the total domestic load capacity of each market participant p in time period t, CAS_LD$_{p,t}$, as well as the relevant indicator for day d CAS_LOAD$_{p,d}$
- a market share indicator of the share (%) to the total domestic load capacity of each market participant p, in each voltage level v and in time period t, CAS_LOAD$_{p,v,t}$, as well as the relevant indicator for day d CAS_LOAD$_{p,v,d}$

- a market share indicator (Capacity Availability Share in Storage—CAS_STOR) on the share (%) to the total demand capacity of each market participant p in time period t $CAS\_STOR_{p,\ t}$, as well as the relevant indicator for day d $CAS\_STOR_{p,\ d}$
- a market share indicator of the share (%) to the total domestic storage capacity of each market participant p, in each voltage level v and in time period t, $CAS\_STOR_{p,\ v,\ t}$, as well as the relevant indicator for day d $CAS\_STOR_{p,\ v,\ d}$
- a market share indicator of the share (%) to the total domestic pumping capacity of each market participant p, in each voltage level v and in time period t, $CAS\_PUMP_{p,\ v,\ t}$, as well as the relevant indicator for day d $CAS\_PUMP_{p,\ v,\ d}$
- a market share indicator (Capacity Availability Share in Pumping—CAS_PUMP) on the share (%) to the total demand capacity of each market participant p in time period t $CAS\_PUMP_{p,\ t}$, as well as the relevant indicator for day d $CAS\_PUMP_{p,\ d}$
- a market share indicator (Capacity Availability Share in Demand—CAS_DEM) on the share (%) to the total demand capacity of each market participant p in time period t $CAS\_DEM_{p,\ t}$, as well as the relevant indicator for day d $CAS\_DEM_{p,\ d}$
- a market share indicator on the share (%) to the total demand of each market participant p, for each voltage level v in time period t $CAS\_DEM_{p,\ v,\ t}$, as well as the relevant indicator for day d $CAS\_DEM_{p,\ v,\ d}$

Available demand capacity for aggregate and disaggregate markets.

Total available demand capacity for the domestic load disaggregate market

$$TOT\_AVAIL\_LOAD\_CAP_t = \sum_p \sum_v \left[\left(1 - BIL\_CON\_SHARE_{p,t}\right) * LOAD\_AVAIL_{p,v,t} \right] \tag{21.71}$$

$$TOT\_AVAIL\_LOAD\_CAP_{p,t} = \sum_v \left(1 - BIL\_CON\_SHARE_{p,t}\right) * LOAD\_AVAIL_{p,v,t} \tag{21.72}$$

Total available demand capacity for the domestic storage disaggregate market

$$TOT\_AVAIL\_STOR\_CAP_t = \sum_p \sum_v STOR\_AVAIL_{p,v,t} \tag{21.73}$$

$$TOT\_AVAIL\_STOR\_CAP_{p,t} = \sum_v STOR\_AVAIL_{p,v,t} \tag{21.74}$$

Total available demand capacity for the domestic pumping disaggregate market

$$TOT\_AVAIL\_PUMP\_CAP_t = \sum_p \sum_v PUMP\_AVAIL_{p,v,t} \tag{21.75}$$

$$TOT\_AVAIL\_PUMP\_CAP_{p,t} = \sum_v PUMP\_AVAIL_{p,v,t} \tag{21.76}$$

Total available domestic demand capacity for the domestic disaggregate markets.

$$TOT\_AVAIL\_DOM\_DEM\_CAP_t = \sum_p \sum_v \left(STOR\_AVAIL_{p,v,t} + PUMP\_AVAIL_{p,v,t} \right) + TOT\_AVAIL\_LOAD\_CAP_t \tag{21.69}$$

$$TOT\_AVAIL\_DOM\_DEM\_CAP_{p,t} = \sum_v \left(STOR\_AVAIL_{p,v,t} + PUMP\_AVAIL_{p,v,t} \right) + TOT\_AVAIL\_LOAD\_CAP_{p,t} \tag{21.70}$$

Total available demand capacity for the aggregate market.

$$TOT\_AVAIL\_DEM\_CAP_t = TOT\_AVAIL\_LOAD\_CAP_t +$$
$$\sum_p \sum_v \sum_n \left(EXP\_CAP_{n,t} - IMP_{SCHED_{TSOs\ n,t}} + STOR\_AVAIL_{p,v,t} + PUMP\_AVAIL_{p,v,t} \right) \tag{21.67}$$

$$TOT\_AVAIL\_DEM\_CAP_{p,t} = TOT\_AVAIL\_LOAD\_CAP_{p,t} +$$
$$= \sum_v \sum_n \left(LT\_EXP\_CAP_{p,n,t} + STOR\_AVAIL_{p,v,t} + PUMP\_AVAIL_{p,v,t} \right) \tag{21.68}$$

Market share (%) indicators per each disaggregate markets and market participant.

Market share (%) indicators in the total available domestic load capacity per voltage level v disaggregate market, for each market participant p

$$CAS\_LOAD_{p,v,t} = \frac{TOT\_AVAIL\_LOAD\_CAP_{p,v,t}}{TOT\_AVAIL\_LOAD\_CAP_t} \tag{21.77}$$

$$CAS\_LOAD_{p,v,d} = \sum_t \frac{TOT\_AVAIL\_LOAD\_CAP_{p,v,t}}{TOT\_AVAIL\_LOAD\_CAP_{p,v,t}} \tag{21.78}$$

$$CAS\_LOAD_{p,t} = \frac{TOT\_AVAIL\_LOAD\_CAP_{p,t}}{TOT\_AVAIL\_LOAD\_CAP_t} \tag{21.79}$$

$$CAS\_LOAD_{p,d} = \sum_t \frac{TOT\_AVAIL\_LOAD\_CAP_{p,t}}{TOT\_AVAIL\_LOAD\_CAP_{p,t}} \tag{21.80}$$

Market share (%) indicators in the total available domestic storage capacity per voltage level v disaggregate market, for each market participant p

$$CAS\_STOR_{p,t} = \frac{TOT\_AVAIL\_STOR\_CAP_{p,t}}{TOT\_AVAIL\_STOR\_CAP_t} \tag{21.81}$$

$$CAS\_STOR_{p,d} = \sum_t \frac{TOT\_AVAIL\_STOR\_CAP_{p,t}}{TOT\_AVAIL\_STOR\_CAP_{p,t}} \tag{21.82}$$

$$CAS\_STOR_{p,v,t} = \frac{TOT\_AVAIL\_STOR\_CAP_{p,v,t}}{TOT\_AVAIL\_STOR\_CAP_t} \tag{21.83}$$

$$CAS\_STOR_{p,v,d} = \sum_t \frac{TOT\_AVAIL\_STOR\_CAP_{p,v,t}}{TOT\_AVAIL\_STOR\_CAP_{p,v,t}} \tag{21.84}$$

Market share (%) indicators in the total available domestic pumping capacity per voltage level v disaggregate market, for each market participant p

$$CAS\_PUMP_{p,t} = \frac{TOT\_AVAIL\_PUMP\_CAP_{p,t}}{TOT\_AVAIL\_PUMP\_CAP_t} \tag{21.85}$$

$$CAS\_PUMP_{p,d} = \sum_t \frac{TOT\_AVAIL\_PUMP\_CAP_{p,t}}{TOT\_AVAIL\_PUMP\_CAP_{p,t}} \tag{21.86}$$

$$CAS\_PUMP_{p,v,t} = \frac{TOT\_AVAIL\_PUMP\_CAP_{p,v,t}}{TOT\_AVAIL\_PUMP\_CAP_t} \tag{21.87}$$

$$CAS\_PUMP_{p,v,d} = \sum_t \frac{TOT\_AVAIL\_PUMP\_CAP_{p,v,t}}{TOT\_AVAIL\_PUMP\_CAP_{p,v,t}} \tag{21.88}$$

Market share (%) indicators in the total available domestic demand capacity per voltage level v disaggregate market, for each market participant p

$$CAS\_DOM\_DEM_{p,v,t} = \frac{TOT\_AVAIL\_DOM\_DEM\_CAP_{p,v,t}}{TOT\_AVAIL\_DOM\_DEM\_CAP_t} \tag{21.89}$$

$$CAS\_DOM\_DEM_{p,v,d} = \sum_t \frac{TOT\_AVAIL\_DOM\_DEM\_CAP_{p,v,t}}{TOT\_AVAIL\_DOM\_DEM\_CAP_{p,v,t}} \tag{21.90}$$

$$CAS\_DOM\_DEM_{p,t} = \frac{TOT\_AVAIL\_DOM\_DEM\_CAP_{p,t}}{TOT\_AVAIL\_DOM\_DEM\_CAP_t} \tag{21.91}$$

$$CAS\_DOM\_DEM_{p,d} = \sum_t \frac{TOT\_AVAIL\_DOM\_DEM\_CAP_{p,t}}{TOT\_AVAIL\_DOM\_DEM\_CAP_{p,t}} \qquad (21.92)$$

Market share (%) indicators in the total available demand capacity per voltage level v disaggregate market, for each market participant p

$$CAS\_DEM_{p,v,t} = \frac{TOT\_AVAIL\_DEM\_CAP_{p,v,t}}{TOT\_AVAIL\_DEM\_CAP_t} \qquad (21.93)$$

$$CAS\_DEM_{p,v,d} = \sum_t \frac{TOT\_AVAIL\_DEM\_CAP_{p,v,t}}{TOT\_AVAIL\_DEM\_CAP_{p,v,t}} \qquad (21.94)$$

$$CAS\_DEM_{p,t} = \frac{TOT\_AVAIL\_DEM\_CAP_{p,t}}{TOT\_AVAIL\_DEM\_CAP_t} \qquad (21.95)$$

$$CAS\_DEM_{p,d} = \sum_t \frac{TOT\_AVAIL\_DEM\_CAP_{p,t}}{TOT\_AVAIL\_DEM\_CAP_{p,t}} \qquad (21.96)$$

4 Application in the Hellenic electricity market

In case of the Hellenic electricity wholesale market the following disaggregate markets can be identified:

- lignite available capacity
- natural gas available capacity
- large hydro available capacity
- renewables (wind, photovoltaics, small hydro, rest RES) available capacity
- each entry point of the interconnected countries: Italy, Albania, North Macedonia, Bulgaria, Turkey

In case of the Hellenic natural gas wholesale market the following disaggregate markets can be identified:

- interconnection (entry/exit) point's available capacity in Sidirokastron
- interconnection (entry/exit) point's available capacity in Kipoi
- interconnection (entry) point's available capacity in Revythousa
- interconnection (entry/exit) point's available capacity in Komotini of the IGB pipeline
- it is not applied to the interconnection (entry/exit) point's available capacity of the Trans Adriatic Pipeline's (TAP) in Kipoi, which has an exemption on third party access for the initial capacity of 10 bcm for 25 years (EUCD, 2013), considering its completeness within a time framework (EUCD, 2015)
  - potential exclusion of TAP concerns also capacity for THRESHOLD1

The National Energy and Climate Plan (NCEP, 2019) identifies the need for a market monitoring and regulation mechanism for market concentration issues. The proposed mechanism could support RAE to design a relevant mechanism in order to be implemented by the TSO, using inputs from the RES operator. The Hellenic Energy Exchange, being a more flexible entity, could also support the implementation of such mechanism. Fig. 21.2 provides the flow of information needed, towards implementing the proposed mechanism. The mechanism adopts an innovative approach where market participants can provide knowledge transfer, of course in a transport and robust way, for improving the forecasting capability of the RES operator and the TSO on disaggregate renewables and demand forecasting. This could be accompanied by a regulated fee, where the regulator could check and approve the robustness of the provided formulation/software.

The following analysis examines independently the power and natural gas markets, as well as the supply and demand side of each aggregate market. Considering that market concentration concerns mainly the power market, due to the market shares of Public Power Corporation S.A. (PPC), the analysis focuses on the electricity market and especially on the supply side. Moreover, market monitoring and regulation components are analyzed and discussed in different sections, focusing on the market monitoring process, as the relevant formulation of section 3 concerns ex-ante market monitoring. Ex-ante regulation is also discussed, but this would require a different study, that could incorporate its mathematical formulation. However, concerning regulation, Table 21.2 presents the disaggregate markets in the Hellenic electricity market that could potentially need regulation, in the form of non-compliance charges for market concentration, adopting the same structure of the relevant analysis done in Table 21.1.

> TSO **ex-ante** publishes Day Ahead Scheduling requirements (load forecast, interconnections' net transfer capacity, RES_FiT production, interzonal constraints, balancing services requirements, injections with priority). It also publishes available capacity of each production unit (thermal and large hydro).

> TSO **ex-ante** estimates Participants' market share in available supply capacity (Indicator 4), considering:
> - Participants' RES_FiP&Market production forecast, provided by the RES &CHP Operator (DAPEEP S.A. in Hellenic electricity market).
> - Long-term capacity rights in each interconnection, per participant
> - Available capacity allocated to bilateral contracts, per participant

> TSO **ex-ante** extends Day-Ahead Scheduling requirements publication, adding:
> - Participants' market share in available supply capacity (indicator 4), hourly or daily average
>   - It can concern only Participant with dominant position

> TSO **ex-ante** communicates to each RES_FiP&Market participant, its RES_FiP&Market production forecast
>   - It can concern only participants, operating domestic thermal and large hydro generation capacity

> **Ex-post** Knowledge transfer: Each RES_FiP&Market participant can challenge/improve DAPEEP forecasting accuracy, providing mathematical formulation and/or software
>   - One time per Participant under regulated renumeration
>   - One time per year for all Participants under regulated renumeration
>   - Unlimited/several times per participant and per year, without renumeration

FIG. 21.2 Flow of ex-ante and ex-post actions by the TSO, the RES&CHP Operator and Market Participants for implementing ex-ante estimation and publication of dominant position on total available supply capacity.

Finally, a critical issue on the analysis in the selection of the levels of the four thresholds. Different combinations could exist for the values of THRESHOLDS1–4, such as:

- 50%/50%/5%/2.5%
- 50%/50%/2.5%/2.5%
- 50%/50%/2.5%/1%
- 40%/40%/4%/2%
- 40%/40%/2%/2%
- 40%/40%/2%/1%
- other combinations

As discussed in previous sections, levels for THRESHOLD1–2 could be set at higher than the 40% minimum threshold indicated by the DG Competition, considering its ex-ante and permanent nature. The adoption of 50% could justified, considering the relevant provisions of the Law 4336/2015.[e] According to subparagraph B.2 of this law, referring to regulation on electricity sector, "from 1.1.2020, no company that is active in electricity markets in the Hellenic interconnected system is allowed to have more than 50% in total supply (generation plus imports) on an annual basis." Moreover, according to paragraph C, section 4.3, of the same law "In September 2015, the authorities will discuss with the European Commission the design of the forward electricity products auction system (NOME type), with the aim of reducing PPC's retail and wholesale market shares by 25% and falling below 50% by 2020, while the marginal prices will cover production costs and fully comply with EU rules… In any case, by 2020 no company will be able to generate or import, directly or indirectly, more than 50% of the total electricity supplied (generated and imported) to Greece." On the other hand, adopting thresholds at 40% imposes a stricter environment, further eliminating antitrust behavior. In any case, existing decisions on relevant thresholds by the National Competition Authority will not be affected, but be in place until their termination date, when they could be replaced by the new framework. Cooperation among the Regulatory Authority of Energy and the National Competition Authority might lead to re-assessment of those decisions, towards adopting the same threshold in all disaggregate markets, which would a sign of excellent cooperation among the authorities.

---

e. https://www.minfin.gr/documents/20182/455201/FekA94.pdf/de2d334d-5bd8-47e3-b201-032481c5096b.

TABLE 21.2 Disaggregate market in the Hellenic electricity market that could potentially need regulation, in the form of non-compliance charges for market concentration, based on the methodology of the proposed ex-ante Market Monitoring and Regulation Mechanism.

Disaggregate markets that potentially could need ex-ante Regulation in the Hellenic electricity market

Regulation, due to THRESHOLD1 or THRESHOLD2, might be applied to:	Lignite, natural gas, large hydro, RES, imports	Lignite, natural gas, large hydro, RES, imports	Lignite, natural gas, large hydro, RES, imports	Lignite, natural gas, large hydro, RES, imports	Lignite, natural gas, large hydro, RES, imports	Lignite, natural gas, large hydro, RES, imports	Lignite, natural gas, large hydro, RES, imports	Lignite, large hydro	Lignite, large hydro	Lignite, large	Lignite, large			
Exception due to THRESHOLD3:		Potentially lignite, large hydro, RES, imports	Potentially lignite, large hydro, RES, imports			Potentially lignite, large hydro, RES, imports	Potentially lignite, large hydro, RES, imports			Potentially large hydro	Potentially large hydro			
Exception due to THRESHOLD4:	RES, imports and potentially natural gas	RES, imports and potentially natural gas	RES, imports and potentially natural gas	RES, imports potentially natural gas	RES, imports potentially natural gas	RES, imports potentially natural gas	RES, imports potentially natural gas				Potentially lignite			
Exception due to existing noncompliance charges:	RES_FiP	RES_FiP	RES_FiP	RES_FiP	RES_FiP	RES_FiP	RES_FiP	RES_FiP	RES_FiP	RES_FiP	RES_FiP	RES_FiP	RES_FiP	RES_FiP
Regulation applied to:	Lignite, natural gas, large hydro, RES_Market, imports	Lignite, natural gas, large hydro, RES_Market, imports with potential lignite, large hydro, RES_Market, imports	Lignite, natural gas, large hydro with potential lignite, large hydro	Lignite, natural gas, large hydro, RES_Market, imports	Lignite, large hydro and potentially natural gas	Lignite, natural gas, large hydro, RES_Market, imports with potential exception of lignite, large hydro, RES_Market, imports	Lignite, natural gas, large hydro, with potential exception of lignite, natural gas, large hydro	Lignite, large	Lignite, large	Lignite, large hydro, with potential exception of lignite and large hydro	Lignite, large hydro, with potential exception of lignite and large hydro	Nowhere	Nowhere	Nowhere

4.1 Application in the electricity market

4.1.1 Supply side

4.1.1.1 Market monitoring of market concentration

The implementation of the market monitoring component of the mechanism on the supply side, requires a several assumptions concerning the evolution of installed capacity per resource type, market participation type on the domestic production capacity assets for each participant, as well as the evolution of interconnections' capacity and the relevant long-term rights for each market participant. Moreover the methodology requires specific assumptions on the large hydro availability, the assets with priority such as renewables under FiT scheme, mandatory injections by large hydro units, units in commissioning/testing operation/high-efficiency cogeneration units, well as the net import schedules with neighboring TSOs (adjusting deviations & returns of emergencies). We use as basis the National Energy and Climate Plan (NCEP, 2019). Moreover, assumption on the share of available domestic production capacity allocated to bilateral contracts. All those assumptions are provided in Tables 21.3–21.13 and Figs. 21.3–21.7, as the analysis concern the period 2020–2030, covered by the NCEP. The assumptions made in a realistic manner, but they should be considered as indicative as there might deviations from the actual power system evolution and operation.

The implementation of the formulation described in the previous section, leads to the results presented in Tables 21.14–21.15 and in Figs. 21.8–21.16. The provision of information concerning both the installed capacity, as well as the sequentially updated available capacity for indicators 1–4, enables the comparison with the final and proposed Indicator 4, as a measure for quantifying market concentration on the supply side. Moreover, results and assumptions are provided for the biggest four market participants, aiming to provide indications of potential formation of cumulative dominant position from a group of them that might have common interests in the wholesale market. The represented results are indicative, based on the assumptions presented in previous sections. The effect of hydro available capacity as well as of the bilateral contracts is important in the quantification of the final indicators. In our analysis, we have considered that all market participants allocate a certain share, i.e., 20% of their available capacity to bilateral contracts, although this seems not to be realistic, as the allocated capacity of about 85 MW indicated in Table 21.13 for each market participant 2–4, is below technical capacity of their natural gas combined cycle units.

The implementation of this mechanism in the Hellenic power market shows that, under the implemented assumptions, ending of the PPC S.A. dominant position in the supply side is linked to the de-lignitization process, as it happens in 2022 and in any case by 2023, when the decommissioning of all old lignite units will take place, when PPC market share in total available supply capacity is below the 50% threshold of the aggregate market. Considering that the mechanism is real-time and dynamic, potential non availability of partial availability of PPC units could lead to its de-characterization of having dominant position in the aggregate market earlier, even for some days in 2021. The mechanism establishes threshold not only on the aggregate market, but also on the disaggregate market. This practically means for the Hellenic power system, that a dominant position is identified for the large hydro disaggregate market. The declaration of realistic low hydro availability, the implementation of peak saving strategy in combination with scarcity pricing for the last steps of large hydro availability capacity might be the solution for tackling this issue. Moreover, the existence of a third threshold concerning the size of the disaggregate market, compared to the size of the aggregate market, might lead in several time periods the characterization of PPC as not having dominant position in this disaggregate market, especially in time periods with low precipitation, or more in the future due to the accelerated climate change effects. Moreover, the implementation of a fourth threshold on comparing the market shares of participants in the demand with the supply side, enables the understanding of the interests of market participants with vertical integration. This can also identify potential formation of cumulative dominant position, although regulation is more complex from dominant position of a single market participant. This threshold identifies that the need of regulation does not concern only market participants with dominant position but also participants with cumulative dominant position that have clear interests on distorting the market. Moreover, this threshold considers also the competitiveness of the supply assets of the market participants, towards identifying potential regulation on bidding strategies. As discussed in the next sections, there already exist non-compliance charges that offset the need for further regulation in some cases, while there exist cases where specific regulation should be applied.

4.1.2 Regulation of market concentration

The ex-ante determination of the dominant position is supplemented by a set of rules on the formation of the bidding strategies and tariff policies of the market participant. Those rules might be imposed in the form of non-compliance charges, in the similar way that Chapter 21 of the Electricity Balancing Code (ADMIE, 2019) imposes relevant clauses are applied to all market participants for not distorting the market, in a number of cases: Consequences of Illegal submission of

TABLE 21.3 Installed domestic production capacity (MW) per participant and resource type.

Installed domestic production capacity (MW) per participant and resource type

Participant Nr	Unit Nr	Fuel	Net capacity (MW)	2020	2021	2022	2023	2024	2025	2026	2027	2028	2029	2030
Participant 1	Unit 1	Lignite	274	274	274	274								
Participant 1	Unit 2	Lignite	274	274	274	274								
Participant 1	Unit 3	Lignite	283	283	283	283								
Participant 1	Unit 4	Lignite	283	283	283	283								
Participant 1	Unit 5	Lignite	342	342	342	342	342							
Participant 1	Unit 6	Lignite	273	273										
Participant 1	Unit 7	Lignite	273	273										
Participant 1	Unit 8	Lignite	289	289	289	289	289							
Participant 1	Unit 9	Lignite	271											
Participant 1	Unit 10	Lignite	271											
Participant 1	Unit 11	Lignite	280	280	280									
Participant 1	Unit 12	Lignite	280	280	280									
Participant 1	Unit 13	Lignite	255	255	255	255								
Participant 1	Unit 14	Lignite	256	256	256	256	256							
Participant 1	Unit 15	Lignite	660				660	660						
Participant 1	Unit 15	Natural gas/mixed fuel	660						660	660	660	660	660	660
Participant 1	Unit 14	Natural gas	476	476	476	476	476	476	476	476	476	476	476	476
Participant 1	Unit 15	Natural gas	550	550	550	550	550	550	550	550	550	550	550	550
Participant 1	Unit 16	Natural gas	378	378	378	378	378	378	378	378	378	378	378	378
Participant 1	Unit 17	Natural gas	417	417	417	417	417	417	417	417	417	417	417	417
Participant 1	Unit 18	Natural gas	811	811	811	811	811	811	811	811	811	811	811	811
Participant 2	Unit 19	Natural gas	147	147	147	147	147	147	147	147	147	147	147	147
Participant 2	Unit 20	Natural gas	422	422	422	422	422	422	422	422	422	422	422	422
Participant 3	Unit 21	Natural gas	400	400	400	400	400	400	400	400	400	400	400	400
Participant 3	Unit 22	Natural gas	410	410	410	410	410	410	410	410	410	410	410	410
Participant 4	Unit 23	Natural gas	433	433	433	433	433	433	433	433	433	433	433	433
Participant 4	Unit 24	Natural gas	433	433	433	433	433	433	433	433	433	433	433	433
Participant 4	Unit 25	Natural gas	334	334	334	334	334	334	334	334	334	334	334	334
Participant 4	Unit 25	Priority	128	128	128	128	128	128	128	128	128	128	128	128
Participant 4	Unit 26	Natural gas	826		826	826	826	826	826	826	826	826	826	826
Participant 3	Unit 27	Natural gas	826					826	826	826	826	826	826	826
Participant 1	Unit 28	Large hydro	3170	3170	3170	3330	3330	3330	3330	3330	3330	3330	3330	3330

TABLE 21.4 Installed domestic RES production capacity (MW) per resource and market participation type.

	Total installed domestic RES capacity (MW) per resource & market participation type	May-20	2020	2021	2022	2023	2024	2025	2026	2027	2028	2029	2030
Total	RES & Large hydro	9833	10,201	10,980	11,900	12,767	13,633	14,500	15,400	16,300	17,167	18,033	18,900
Total	Large hydro	3170	3170	3170	3330	3330	3330	3330	3330	3330	3330	3330	3330
Total	RES	6663	7031	7810	8570	9437	10,303	11,170	12,070	12,970	13,837	14,703	15,570
Total	Wind	3526	3600	3900	4200	4533	4867	5200	5600	6000	6333	6667	7000
Total	Photovoltaics	2706	3000	3450	3900	4367	4833	5300	5800	6300	6767	7233	7700
Total	Small hydro	233	233	261	270	300	330	360	360	360	377	393	410
Total	Small hydro FiT	225	225	225	225	225	225	225	225	225	225	225	225
Total	Rest renewables	198	198	199	200	237	273	310	310	310	360	410	460
Total	Rest Renewables_FiT	170	170	170	170	170	170	170	170	170	170	170	170
Total	Rest RES_FiT	395	395	395	395	395	395	395	395	395	395	395	395
Total	Wind_FiT	2468	2468	2468	2468	2468	2468	2468	2468	2468	2468	2468	2468
Total	Wind_FiP&Market	1058	1132	1432	1732	2065	2398	2732	3132	3532	3865	4198	4532
Total	PVs FiT	2571	2571	2571	2571	2571	2571	2571	2571	2571	2571	2571	2571
Total	PVs FiP&Market	135	429	879	1329	1796	2263	2729	3229	3729	4196	4663	5129

TABLE 21.5 Installed domestic production capacity (MW) per resource type.

Total installed domestic production capacity (MW) per resource type		May-20	2020	2021	2022	2023	2024	2025	2026	2027	2028	2029	2030
Total	Thermal	10,435	8573	8027	8293	7584	6697	7523	7523	7523	7523	7523	7523
Total	RES	6663	7031	7810	8570	9437	10,303	11,170	12,070	12,970	13,837	14,703	15,570
Total	Large hydro	3170	3170	3170	3330	3330	3330	3330	3330	3330	3330	3330	3330
Total	All hydro	3403	3403	3431	3600	3630	3660	3690	3690	3690	3707	3723	3740
Total	All production excluding priority units	14,706	13,212	13,445	14,631	14,789	14,768	16,461	17,361	18,261	19,128	19,994	20,861
Total	All production	20,268	18,774	19,007	20,193	20,351	20,330	22,023	22,923	23,823	24,690	25,556	26,423

TABLE 21.6 Installed interconnections' capacity (MW) for imports and exports, per entry point.

Interconnections capacity (MW) for imports		Net transfer capacity (MW)	2020	2021	2022	2023	2024	2025	2026	2027	2028	2029	2030
Interconnection 1	Total	250	250	250	250	250	250	250	250	250	250	250	250
Interconnection 2	Total	350	350	350	350	350	350	350	350	350	350	350	350
Interconnection 3	Total	700	700	700	700	700	1300	1300	1300	1300	1300	1300	1300
Interconnection 4	Total	500	500	500	500	500	500	500	500	500	500	500	500
Interconnection 5	Total	116	116	116	116	116	116	116	116	116	116	116	116
All Interconnections	Total	1916	1916	1916	1916	1916	2516	2516	2516	2516	2516	2516	2516

Interconnections capacity (MW) for exports		Net transfer capacity (MW)	2020	2021	2022	2023	2024	2025	2026	2027	2028	2029	2030
Interconnection 1	Total	250	250	250	250	250	250	250	250	250	250	250	250
Interconnection 2	Total	350	350	350	350	350	350	350	350	350	350	350	350
Interconnection 3	Total	700	700	700	700	700	1300	1300	1300	1300	1300	1300	1300
Interconnection 4	Total	500	500	500	500	500	500	500	500	500	500	500	500
Interconnection 5	Total	166	166	166	166	166	166	166	166	166	166	166	166
All Interconnections	Total	1966	1966	1966	1966	1966	2566	2566	2566	2566	2566	2566	2566

TABLE 21.7 Installed domestic supply capacity (MW) per participant, resource and market participation type.

Aggregate installed supply capacity (MW) per participant, resource and market participation type	2020	2021	2022	2023	2024	2025	2026	2027	2028	2029	2030
Participant 1	Total production capacity	9504	9193	9048	8649	8052	8342	8632	8922	9212	9502	9792
Participant 1	Lignite	3362	2816	2256	1547	660	660	660	660	0	0	0
Participant 1	Natural gas	2632	2632	2632	2632	2632	2632	2632	2632	3292	3292	3292
Participant 1	Large hydro	3170	3170	3330	3330	3330	3330	3330	3330	3330	3330	3330
Participant 1	Wind FiT	50	50	50	50	50	50	50	50	50	50	50
Participant 1	PVs FiT	50	50	50	50	50	50	50	50	50	50	50
Participant 1	Small Hydro FiT	70	100	100	100	100	100	100	100	100	100	100
Participant 1	Rest RES FiT	20	20	20	20	20	20	20	20	20	20	20
Participant 1	Wind FiP&Market	50	100	200	350	480	610	740	870	1000	1130	1260
Participant 1	PVs_FiP&Market	100	250	400	550	700	850	1000	1150	1300	1450	1600
Participant 1	Rest_RES_FiP&Market	0	5	10	20	30	40	50	60	70	80	90
Participant 1	Long-term_capacity_rights_Imports	100	100	100	100	100	100	100	100	100	100	100
Participant 1	Total prod_cap+Ltrights_imports	9604	9293	9148	8749	8152	8442	8732	9022	9312	9602	9892
Participant 2	Total production capacity	1024	1204	1384	1569	1754	1939	2124	2309	2504	2699	2894
Participant 2	Natural gas	569	569	569	569	569	569	569	569	569	569	569
Participant 2	Wind_FiT	100	100	100	100	100	100	100	100	100	100	100
Participant 2	PVs_FiT	100	100	100	100	100	100	100	100	100	100	100
Participant 2	Rest RES FiT	0	0	0	0	0	0	0	0	0	0	0
Participant 2	Wind FiP&Market	200	300	400	500	600	700	800	900	1000	1100	1200
Participant 2	PVs_FiP&Market	50	125	200	275	350	425	500	575	650	725	800
Participant 2	Rest_RES_FiP&Market	5	10	15	25	35	45	55	65	85	105	125
Participant 2	Long-term_capacity_rights_Imports	20	20	20	20	20	20	20	20	20	20	20
Participant 2	Total prod_cap+Ltrights_imports	1044	1224	1404	1589	1774	1959	2144	2329	2524	2719	2914
Participant 3	Total production capacity	1065	1170	1320	1430	1540	2476	2586	2696	2806	2916	3026
Participant 3	Natural gas	810	810	810	810	810	1636	1636	1636	1636	1636	1636

Participant		C1	C2	C3	C4	C5	C6	C7	C8	C9	C10	C11
Participant 3	Wind_FiT	100	100	100	100	100	100	100	100	100	100	100
Participant 3	PVs_FiT	100	100	100	100	100	100	100	100	100	100	100
Participant 3	Rest RES FiT	0	0	0	0	0	0	0	0	0	0	0
Participant 3	Wind FiP&Market	0	50	100	150	200	250	300	350	400	450	500
Participant 3	PVs_FiP&Market	50	100	200	250	300	350	400	450	500	550	600
Participant 3	Rest_RES_FiP&Market	5	10	10	20	30	40	50	60	70	80	90
Participant 3	Long-term_capacity_rights_Imports	0	0	0	0	0	0	0	0	0	0	0
Participant 3	Total prod_cap+Ltrights_imports	1065	1170	1320	1430	1540	2476	2586	2696	2806	2916	3026
Participant 4	Total production capacity	1422	1447	2348	2423	2498	2573	2648	2723	2798	2873	2948
Participant 4	Natural gas	1072	1072	1898	1898	1898	1898	1898	1898	1898	1898	1898
Participant 4	Wind_FiT	100	100	100	100	100	100	100	100	100	100	100
Participant 4	PVs_FiT	100	100	100	100	100	100	100	100	100	100	100
Participant 4	Rest RES FiT	0	0	0	0	0	0	0	0	0	0	0
Participant 4	Wind FiP&Market	100	175	250	325	400	475	550	625	700	775	850
Participant 4	PVs_FiP&Market	50	125	200	275	350	425	500	575	650	725	800
Participant 4	Rest_RES_FiP&Market	0	5	10	15	20	25	30	35	40	45	50
Participant 4	Long-term_capacity_rights_Imports	100	100	100	100	100	100	100	100	100	100	100
Participant 4	Total prod cap+Ltrights imports	1522	1547	2448	2523	2598	2673	2748	2823	2898	2973	3048

TABLE 21.8 Installed supply capacity (MW), under different under different combinations in considering domestic production capacity, imports' interconnections capacity and production capacity from priority units (RES_FiT and Units in Commissioning/Testing Operation/High-Efficiency Cogeneration Units).

Total installed supply capacity (MW), considering domestic production, imports Interconnections and production capacity with priority

Total	Domestic production	20,268	18,774	19,007	20,193	20,351	20,330	22,023	22,923	23,823	24,690	25,556	26,423
Total	Domestic production excluding priority units	14,706	13,212	13,445	14,631	14,789	14,768	16,461	17,361	18,261	19,128	19,994	20,861
Total	Domestic production exclude priority units, plus imports' intercon	16,622	15,128	15,361	16,547	16,705	17,284	18,977	19,877	20,777	21,644	22,510	23,377
Total	Domestic production plus imports' interconnections	22,184	20,690	20,923	22,109	22,267	22,846	24,539	25,439	26,339	27,206	28,072	28,939

TABLE 21.9 Market share (%) on total installed RES_FiP&Market capacity, per participant and resource type.

Participants' market share (%) in total installed RES_FiP&Market capacity, per participant and resource type

	2020	2021	2022	2023	2024	2025	2026	2027	2028	2029	2030
Participant 1 Wind FiP&Market	4.42%	6.98%	11.55%	16.95%	20.01%	22.33%	23.63%	24.63%	25.87%	26.91%	27.80%
Participant 1 PVs FiP&Market	23.29%	28.43%	30.09%	30.62%	30.94%	31.14%	30.97%	30.84%	30.98%	31.10%	31.19%
Participant 1 Rest RES FiP&Market	0.00%	7.69%	13.33%	14.12%	14.40%	14.55%	18.18%	21.82%	20.49%	19.59%	18.95%
Participant 1 Total	9.39%	14.94%	19.45%	22.98%	24.85%	26.15%	26.97%	27.60%	28.20%	28.70%	29.10%
	2020	2021	2022	2023	2024	2025	2026	2027	2028	2029	2030
Participant 2 Wind_FiP&Market	17.67%	20.95%	23.10%	24.21%	25.02%	25.62%	25.54%	25.48%	25.87%	26.20%	26.48%
Participant 2 PVs_FiP&Market	11.65%	14.22%	15.05%	15.31%	15.47%	15.57%	15.48%	15.42%	15.49%	15.55%	15.60%
Participant 2 Rest_RES_FiP&Market	13.89%	15.38%	20.00%	17.65%	16.80%	16.36%	20.00%	23.64%	24.88%	25.71%	26.32%
Participant 2 Total	15.97%	18.31%	19.61%	19.99%	20.23%	20.40%	20.42%	20.43%	20.65%	20.82%	20.96%
Participant 3 Wind_FiP&Market	0.00%	3.49%	5.77%	7.26%	8.34%	9.15%	9.58%	9.91%	10.35%	10.72%	11.03%
Participant 3 PVs FiP&Market	11.65%	11.37%	15.05%	13.92%	13.26%	12.82%	12.39%	12.07%	11.92%	11.80%	11.70%
Participant 3 Rest RES FiP&Market	13.89%	15.38%	13.33%	14.12%	14.40%	14.55%	18.18%	21.82%	20.49%	19.59%	18.95%
Participant 3 Total	3.44%	6.73%	9.88%	10.49%	10.88%	11.16%	11.30%	11.41%	11.54%	11.65%	11.74%
Participant 4 Wind_FiP&Market	8.84%	12.22%	14.44%	15.74%	16.68%	17.39%	17.56%	17.70%	18.11%	18.46%	18.76%
Participant 4 PVs_FiP&Market	11.65%	14.22%	15.05%	15.31%	15.47%	15.57%	15.48%	15.42%	15.49%	15.55%	15.60%
Participant 4 Rest_RES_FiP&Market	0.00%	7.69%	13.33%	10.59%	9.60%	9.09%	10.91%	12.73%	11.71%	11.02%	10.53%
Participant 4 Total	9.39%	12.84%	14.67%	15.36%	15.81%	16.13%	16.27%	16.39%	16.54%	16.67%	16.77%
Participants 1–4 Wind_FiP&Market	30.92%	43.65%	54.86%	64.16%	70.04%	74.49%	76.31%	77.72%	80.20%	82.29%	84.07%
Participants 1–4 PVs_FiP&Market	58.23%	68.24%	75.23%	75.17%	75.13%	75.11%	74.32%	73.74%	73.88%	73.99%	74.08%
Participants 1–4 Rest_RES_FiP&Market	27.78%	46.15%	60.00%	56.47%	55.20%	54.55%	67.27%	80.00%	77.56%	75.92%	74.74%
Participants 1–4 Total	61.81%	47.18%	36.39%	31.17%	28.23%	26.17%	25.03%	24.17%	23.06%	22.16%	21.42%

Continued

TABLE 21.9 Market share (%) on total installed RES_FiP&Market capacity, per participant and resource type—cont'd

		2020	2021	2022	2023	2024	2025	2026	2027	2028	2029	2030
							Participants' market share (%) in total installed RES FiP&Market capacity					
Participant 1	Total	9.39%	14.94%	19.45%	22.98%	24.85%	26.15%	26.97%	27.60%	28.20%	28.70%	29.10%
Participant 2	Total	15.97%	18.31%	19.61%	19.99%	20.23%	20.40%	20.42%	20.43%	20.65%	20.82%	20.96%
Participant 3	Total	3.44%	6.73%	9.88%	10.49%	10.88%	11.16%	11.30%	11.41%	11.54%	11.65%	11.74%
Participant 4	Total	9.39%	12.84%	14.67%	15.36%	15.81%	16.13%	16.27%	16.39%	16.54%	16.67%	16.77%
Rest partcipants	Total	61.81%	47.18%	36.39%	31.17%	28.23%	26.17%	25.03%	24.17%	23.06%	22.16%	21.42%
Total	Total	100.00%	100.00%	100.00%	100.00%	100.00%	100.00%	100.00%	100.00%	100.00%	100.00%	100.00%

TABLE 21.10 Participants' market share (%) in total installed supply capacity, under different combinations in considering domestic production capacity, imports' interconnections capacity and production capacity from priority units (RES_FiT and Units in Commissioning/Testing Operation/High-Efficiency Cogeneration Units).

Participants' market share (%) in total installed domestic capacity

		2020	2021	2022	2023	2024	2025	2026	2027	2028	2029	2030
Participant 1	Total	50.6%	48.4%	44.8%	42.5%	39.6%	37.9%	37.7%	37.5%	37.3%	37.2%	37.1%
Participant 2	Total	5.5%	6.3%	6.9%	7.7%	8.6%	8.8%	9.3%	9.7%	10.1%	10.6%	11.0%
Participant 3	Total	5.7%	6.2%	6.5%	7.0%	7.6%	11.2%	11.3%	11.3%	11.4%	11.4%	11.5%
Participant 4	Total	7.6%	7.6%	11.6%	11.9%	12.3%	11.7%	11.6%	11.4%	11.3%	11.2%	11.2%
Participants 2–4	Total	18.7%	20.1%	25.0%	26.6%	28.5%	31.7%	32.1%	32.4%	32.8%	33.2%	33.6%
Rest participants	Total	30.7%	31.5%	30.2%	30.9%	31.9%	30.4%	30.2%	30.1%	29.8%	29.6%	29.4%

Participants' market share (%) in total installed domestic capacity, excluding priority units' capacity

		2020	2021	2022	2023	2024	2025	2026	2027	2028	2029	2030
Participant 1	Total	70.5%	66.7%	60.3%	57.0%	53.0%	49.3%	48.5%	47.7%	47.0%	46.4%	45.9%
Participant 2	Total	6.2%	7.5%	8.1%	9.3%	10.5%	10.6%	11.1%	11.5%	12.0%	12.5%	12.9%
Participant 3	Total	6.5%	7.2%	7.7%	8.3%	9.1%	13.8%	13.7%	13.7%	13.6%	13.6%	13.5%
Participant 4	Total	9.2%	9.3%	14.7%	15.0%	15.6%	14.4%	14.1%	13.8%	13.6%	13.4%	13.2%
Participants 2–4	Total	22.0%	24.0%	30.4%	32.6%	35.2%	38.8%	38.9%	39.0%	39.3%	39.5%	39.6%
Rest participants	Total	7.5%	9.3%	9.2%	10.4%	11.8%	11.9%	12.6%	13.3%	13.7%	14.1%	14.5%

Participants' market share (%) in total installed supply capacity (domestic production capacity plus imports interconnections capacity)

		2020	2021	2022	2023	2024	2025	2026	2027	2028	2029	2030
Participant 1	Total	46.4%	44.4%	41.4%	39.3%	35.7%	34.4%	34.3%	34.3%	34.2%	34.2%	34.2%
Participant 2	Total	5.0%	5.9%	6.4%	7.1%	7.8%	8.0%	8.4%	8.8%	9.3%	9.7%	10.1%
Participant 3	Total	5.1%	5.6%	6.0%	6.4%	6.7%	10.1%	10.2%	10.2%	10.3%	10.4%	10.5%
Participant 4	Total	7.4%	7.4%	11.1%	11.3%	11.4%	10.9%	10.8%	10.7%	10.7%	10.6%	10.5%
Participants 2–4	Total	17.5%	18.8%	23.4%	24.9%	25.9%	29.0%	29.4%	29.8%	30.2%	30.7%	31.1%
Rest participants	Total	36.0%	36.7%	35.2%	35.8%	38.4%	36.6%	36.3%	36.0%	35.5%	35.1%	34.8%

Participants' market share (%) in total installed supply capacity (domestic production capacity plus imports interconnections capacity), excluding priority units' capacity

		2020	2021	2022	2023	2024	2025	2026	2027	2028	2029	2030
Participant 1	Total	62.2%	59.1%	54.0%	51.1%	45.9%	43.3%	42.8%	42.4%	42.0%	41.7%	41.4%
Participant 2	Total	5.6%	6.7%	7.3%	8.3%	9.1%	9.3%	9.8%	10.2%	10.7%	11.2%	11.6%
Participant 3	Total	5.7%	6.3%	6.8%	7.4%	7.8%	12.0%	12.0%	12.0%	12.0%	12.1%	12.1%
Participant 4	Total	9.1%	8.1%	12.1%	11.5%	10.7%	9.3%	8.5%	7.8%	7.2%	6.5%	6.0%
Participants 2–4	Total	20.4%	21.1%	26.1%	27.2%	27.6%	30.6%	30.3%	30.1%	29.9%	29.8%	29.7%
Rest participants	Total	17.4%	19.8%	19.9%	21.8%	26.6%	26.1%	26.9%	27.6%	28.1%	28.5%	28.9%

TABLE 21.11 Indicative hourly availability factor (%) per RES resource type, based on RES-FiT availability data.

	1	2	3	4	5	6	7	8	9	10	11	12
Photovoltaics FiT	0 00%	0.00%	0.00%	0.00%	0.00%	0.00%	1.00%	5.00%	20.00%	40.00%	50 00%	60 00%
Wind FiT	10.00%	10.00%	10.00%	10.00%	10.00%	15.00%	15.00%	20.00%	25.00%	30.00%	35.00%	40.00%
Small hydros FiT	35.00%	35.00%	35.00%	35.00%	35.00%	35.00%	35.00%	35.00%	35.00%	35.00%	35.00%	35.00%
Rest RES FiT	40.00%	40.00%	40.00%	40.00%	40.00%	40.00%	40.00%	40.00%	40.00%	40.00%	40.00%	40.00%

TABLE 21.12 Indicative hourly availability factor (%) for large hydro installations, mandatory large hydro injections

		1	2	3	4	5	6	7	8	9	10
Participant 1	Typical availability factor of large hydro (%)	10	5	5	5	5	5	5	10	20	30
Participant 1	Typical Mandatory large hydro injections (MW)	25	0	0	0	0	0	0	25	100	200
Participant 4	Units with dispatch priority (MW)	128	128	128	128	128	128	128	128	128	128
TSO	Net import Schedules with neighboring TSOs (MW)	0	0	0	0	0	0	0	0	0	0
TSO	Net export schedules with neighboring TSOs (MW)	0	0	0	0	0	0	0	0	0	0

13	14	15	16	17	18	19	20	21	22	23	24	AVERAGE
70 00%	60.00%	50.00%	40.00%	20.00%	10.00%	5.00%	1.00%	0.00%	0.00%	0.00%	0.00%	18 00%
40.00%	40.00%	40.00%	40.00%	40.00%	35.00%	35.00%	30.00%	30.00%	25.00%	20.00%	20.00%	26.04%
35.00%	35.00%	35.00%	35.00%	35.00%	35.00%	35.00%	35.00%	35.00%	35.00%	35.00%	35.00%	35.00%
40.00%	40.00%	40.00%	40.00%	40.00%	40.00%	40.00%	40.00%	40.00%	40.00%	40.00%	40.00%	40.00%

(MW), injections from units with priority (MW), net import and export schedules with neighboring TSOs (MW).

11	12	13	14	15	16	17	18	19	20	21	22	23	24	AVERAGE
40	40	20	20	10	20	30	40	60	70	80	70	40	20	28
200	200	100	100	25	25	100	100	400	700	1000	600	200	25	172
128	128	128	128	128	128	128	128	128	128	128	128	128	128	128
0	0	0	0	0	0	0	0	0	0	0	0	0	0	0
0	0	0	0	0	0	0	0	0	0	0	0	0	0	0

TABLE 21.13 Indicative hourly available capacity (MW) allocated in bilateral contracts, covered through available thermal contracts allocated to the load (i.e., 20% used in this analysis).

		1	2	3	4	5	6	7	8	9	10
Participant 1	Typical load (MW)	3960	3600	3600	3600	3600	3600	3840	4080	4320	4560
Participant 1	Share of bilateral contracts (%)	20	20	20	20	20	20	20	20	20	20
Participant 1	Capacity in bilateral contracts (MW)	792	720	720	720	720	720	768	816	864	912
Participant 2	Typical load (MW)	396	360	360	360	360	360	384	408	432	456
Participant 2	Share of bilateral contracts (%)	20	20	20	20	20	20	20	20	20	20
Participant 2	Capacity in bilateral contracts (MW)	79	72	72	72	72	72	77	82	86	91
Participant 3	Typical load (MW)	396	360	360	360	360	360	384	408	432	456
Participant 3	Share of bilateral contracts (%)	20	20	20	20	20	20	20	20	20	20
Participant 3	Capacity in bilateral contracts (MW)	79	72	72	72	72	72	77	82	86	91
	Typical load (MW)	396	360	360	360	360	360	384	408	432	456
Participant 4	Share of bilateral contracts (%)	20	20	20	20	20	20	20	20	20	20
Participant 4	Capacity in bilateral contracts (MW)	79	72	72	72	72	72	77	82	86	91

and large hydro capacity, which derives by multiplying indicative hourly load (MW) and indicative share (%) of bilateral

11	12	13	14	15	16	17	18	19	20	21	22	23	24	AVERAGE
4320	4200	3960	3840	3840	3840	4080	4440	5160	5640	5880	5520	4920	4440	4285
20	20	20	20	20	20	20	20	20	20	20	20	20	20	20
864	840	792	768	768	768	816	888	1032	1128	1176	1104	984	888	857
432	420	396	384	384	384	408	444	516	564	588	552	492	444	429
20	20	20	20	20	20	20	20	20	20	20	20	20	20	20
86	84	79	77	77	77	82	89	103	113	118	110	98	89	86
432	420	396	384	384	384	408	444	516	564	588	552	492	444	429
20	20	20	20	20	20	20	20	20	20	20	20	20	20	20
86	84	79	77	77	77	82	89	103	113	118	110	98	89	86
432	420	396	304	384	384	408	444	516	564	588	552	492	444	129
20	20	20	20	20	20	20	20	20	20	20	20	20	20	20
86	84	79	77	77	77	82	89	103	113	118	110	98	89	86

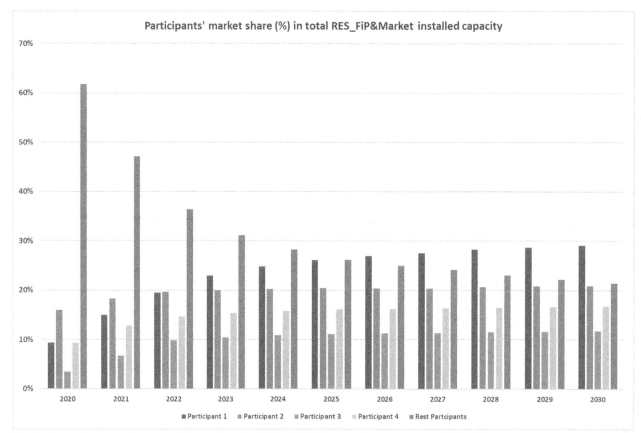

FIG. 21.3 Participants' market share (%) in total installed RES_FiP&Market capacity over the period 2020–2030.

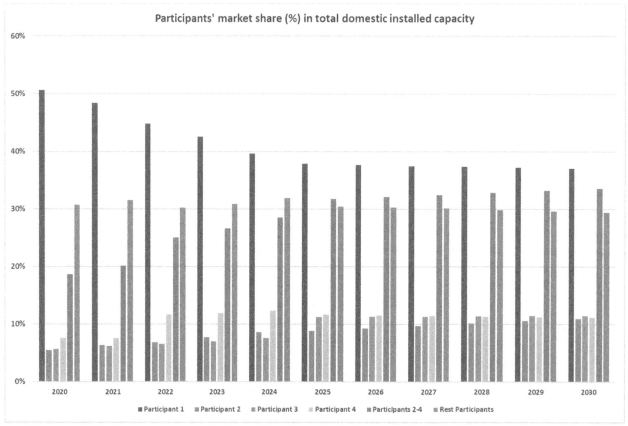

FIG. 21.4 Participants' market share (%) in total domestic installed capacity over the period 2020–2030.

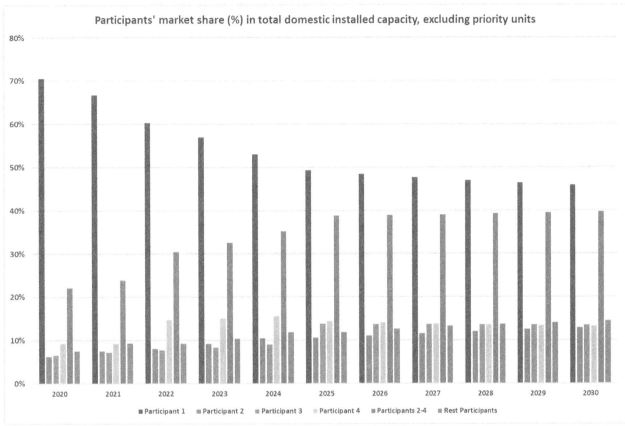

FIG. 21.5 Participants' market share (%) in total domestic installed capacity, excluding priority units, over period 2020–2030.

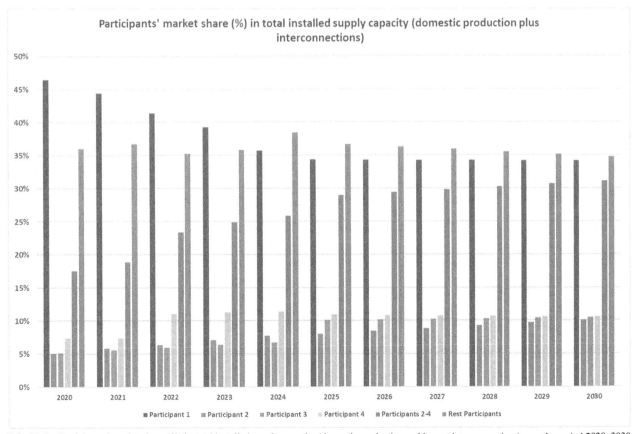

FIG. 21.6 Participants' market share (%) in total installed supply capacity (domestic production and import interconnections) over the period 2020–2030.

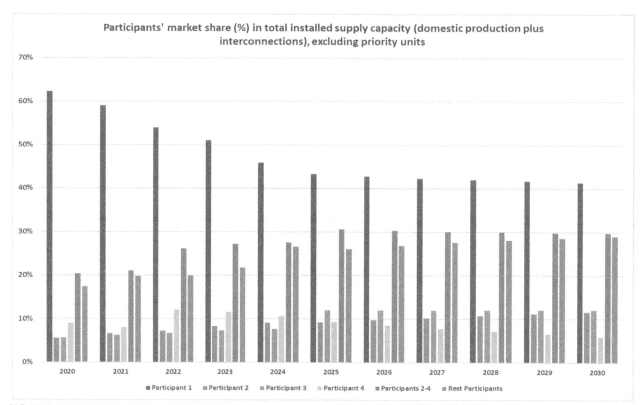

FIG. 21.7 Participants' market share (%) in total installed supply capacity (domestic production and import interconnections), excluding RES_FiT units, over the period 2020–2030.

Non-Availability Declarations, Consequences of unlawful Submission of Techno-Economic Declaration, Consequences of non-submission of Balancing Energy Offers, Consequences of not submitting Balancing Capacity Bids, Consequences of significant imbalance in the supply of Upward or Downward Balancing Energy or Energy for Non-Balancing purposes by a Balancing Services Entity, Consequences of significant systematic demand imbalances, Consequences of significant systematic imbalances in the actual production of the Non-Dispatchable RES Portfolios, Non-Compliance Charge for import/export deviations and Non-Compliance Charge for infeasible Market Schedule.

It should be clarified that the imposition of non-compliance charges for bidding strategy aim to meet different targets:

- Not allow market distortion from any market participant and power unit, through systematic non-competitive bidding of its assets.
  - This concerns imposition of non-compliance charges for non-competitive bidding for all power units from all market participants, including the available capacity up to the THRESHOD2 of the market participant with dominant position.
- Not allow market distortion from market participant with dominant position.
  - This concerns imposition of the non-compliance charges for market concentration, for the available capacity above THRESHOD2 of the market participant with dominant position, as this further capacity justifies the need for regulation on the disaggregate market for market concentration issues.
  - In such case, the non-compliance charges should be stricter, i.e., this further capacity not to be allowed to bid below MAVC every day, therefore differentiating from the logic of systematic violations.
  - This logic of imposing stricter non-compliance charges for the extra capacity, should concern bidding limitations for any disaggregate market.

For the implementation of non-compliance charges, information on the MAVC costs of each unit might be needed. According to the Article 48 of the Balancing Code (ADMIE, 2019), Producers representing Dispatchable Units with Alternative Fuel are required to submit separate Techno-Economic Declarations for the operation with both the primary and the alternative fuel.

TABLE 21.14 Daily average Participants' market share (%) in total available supply capacity, under different combinations in considering domestic available production capacity, imports interconnections available capacity, available production capacity from priority units and share of Participants' load in bilateral contracts.

Indicator 1: Participants' market share (%) in total available supply capacity (domestic production plus imports interconnections)

	2020	2021	2022	2023	2024	2025	2026	2027	2028	2029	2030
Participant 1	61.38%	59.67%	55.19%	52.86%	47.66%	45.00%	44.89%	44.79%	44.68%	44.57%	44.46%
Participant 2	4.54%	4.92%	4.99%	5.44%	5.75%	5.64%	5.82%	6.00%	6.20%	6.40%	6.59%
Participant 3	5.70%	5.99%	5.95%	6.30%	6.48%	11.44%	11.44%	11.45%	11.45%	11.45%	11.45%
Participant 4	8.19%	8.63%	13.88%	14.60%	14.93%	14.18%	14.23%	14.27%	14.32%	14.36%	14.40%
Participants 2–4	18.43%	19.54%	24.82%	26.34%	27.16%	31.26%	31.50%	31.73%	31.97%	32.20%	32.43%
Rest participants	20.19%	20.79%	19.99%	20.81%	25.18%	23.74%	23.61%	23.48%	23.35%	23.23%	23.11%
Total	100.00%	100.00%	100.00%	100.00%	100.00%	100.00%	100.00%	100.00%	100.00%	100.00%	100.00%

Indicator 2: Participants' market share (%) in total available supply capacity, excluding priority units

	2020	2021	2022	2023	2024	2025	2026	2027	2028	2029	2030
Participant 1	66.37%	64.49%	59.31%	56.84%	51.07%	47.90%	47.72%	47.56%	47.39%	47.22%	47.06%
Participant 2	4.74%	5.18%	5.25%	5.76%	6.12%	5.97%	6.17%	6.37%	6.59%	6.80%	7.00%
Participant 3	6.01%	6.35%	6.30%	6.70%	6.90%	12.33%	12.32%	12.31%	12.30%	12.29%	12.28%
Participant 4	7.85%	8.33%	14.15%	14.95%	15.32%	14.47%	14.51%	14.55%	14.59%	14.63%	14.67%
Participants 2–4	18.61%	19.86%	25.70%	27.41%	28.34%	32.77%	33.01%	33.24%	33.48%	33.72%	33.94%
Rest participants	15.02%	15.65%	14.99%	15.75%	20.59%	19.34%	19.27%	19.21%	19.13%	19.06%	18.99%
Total	100.00%	100.00%	100.00%	100.00%	100.00%	100.00%	100.00%	100.00%	100.00%	100.00%	100.00%

Continued

Indicator 3: Participants' market share (%) in total available supply capacity, excluding priority units & limited available large hydro

	2020	2021	2022	2023	2024	2025	2026	2027	2028	2029	2030
Participant 1	59.57%	57.05%	50.70%	47.26%	40.09%	37.20%	37.14%	37.09%	37.03%	36.97%	36.92%
Participant 2	5.70%	6.26%	6.35%	7.03%	7.47%	7.17%	7.39%	7.61%	7.85%	8.07%	8.30%
Participant 3	7.24%	7.68%	7.63%	8.19%	8.46%	14.88%	14.83%	14.79%	14.74%	14.69%	14.65%
Participant 4	9.45%	10.08%	17.16%	18.29%	18.77%	17.44%	17.45%	17.47%	17.47%	17.48%	17.49%
Participants 2–4	22.39%	24.03%	31.14%	33.50%	34.69%	39.49%	39.68%	39.86%	40.06%	40.25%	40.43%
Rest participants	18.04%	18.92%	18.15%	19.24%	25.22%	23.31%	23.17%	23.04%	22.91%	22.78%	22.65%
Total	100.00%	100.00%	100.00%	100.00%	100.00%	100.00%	100.00%	100.00%	100.00%	100.00%	100.00%

Indicator 4: Participants' market share (%) in total available supply capacity, excl. priority units, lim. avail. large hydro, incl. bilat. contracts

	2020	2021	2022	2023	2024	2025	2026	2027	2028	2029	2030
Participant 1	56.38%	53.53%	46.82%	42.88%	35.05%	32.38%	32.40%	32.41%	32.42%	32.42%	32.42%
Participant 2	5.36%	5.95%	6.06%	6.78%	7.25%	6.95%	7.19%	7.43%	7.68%	7.93%	8.17%
Participant 3	7.02%	7.49%	7.45%	8.04%	8.33%	15.27%	15.21%	15.16%	15.11%	15.05%	15.00%
Participant 4	9.41%	10.10%	17.75%	19.00%	19.53%	18.03%	18.04%	18.05%	18.04%	18.04%	18.04%
Participants 2–4	21.79%	23.54%	31.26%	33.82%	35.11%	40.26%	40.45%	40.63%	40.83%	41.03%	41.21%
Rest participants	21.84%	22.93%	21.92%	23.30%	29.84%	27.36%	27.15%	26.95%	26.75%	26.55%	26.36%
Total	100.00%	100.00%	100.00%	100.00%	100.00%	100.00%	100.00%	100.00%	100.00%	100.00%	100.00%

TABLE 21.15 Daily average Participants' market share (%) in total available supply capacity for the disaggregate markets, under the assumptions of Indicator 4.

Participants' supply capacity share (%) in disaggregate markets' available capacity, considering assumptions for Indicator 4

		2020	2021	2022	2023	2024	2025	2026	2027	2028	2029	2030
Participant 1	Lignite	100.00%	100.00%	100.00%	100.00%	100.00%	100.00%	100.00%	100.00%	0.00%	0.00%	0.00%
Participant 2	Lignite	0.00%	0.00%	0.00%	0.00%	0.00%	0.00%	0.00%	0.00%	0.00%	0.00%	0.00%
Participant 3	Lignite	0.00%	0.00%	0.00%	0.00%	0.00%	0.00%	0.00%	0.00%	0.00%	0.00%	0.00%
Participant 4	Lignite	0.00%	0.00%	0.00%	0.00%	0.00%	0.00%	0.00%	0.00%	0.00%	0.00%	0.00%
Participants 2–4	Lignite	0.00%	0.00%	0.00%	0.00%	0.00%	0.00%	0.00%	0.00%	0.00%	0.00%	0.00%
Rest participants	Lignite	0.00%	0.00%	0.00%	0.00%	0.00%	0.00%	0.00%	0.00%	0.00%	0.00%	0.00%
All participants	Lignite	100.00%	100.00%	100.00%	100.00%	100.00%	100.00%	100.00%	100.00%	0.00%	0.00%	0.00%
Participant 1	Natural gas	51.78%	51.78%	44.54%	44.54%	44.54%	39.08%	39.08%	39.08%	44.52%	44.52%	44.52%
Participant 2	Natural gas	11.19%	11.19%	9.63%	9.63%	9.63%	8.45%	8.45%	8.45%	7.69%	7.69%	7.69%
Participant 3	Natural gas	15.94%	15.94%	13.71%	13.71%	13.71%	24.29%	24.29%	24.29%	22.12%	22.12%	22.12%
Participant 4	Natural gas	21.09%	21.09%	32.12%	32.12%	32.12%	28.18%	28.18%	28.18%	25.67%	25.67%	25.67%
Participants 2–4	Natural gas	48.22%	48.22%	55.46%	55.46%	55.46%	60.92%	60.92%	60.92%	55.48%	55.48%	55.48%
Rest participants	Natural gas	0.00%	0.00%	0.00%	0.00%	0.00%	0.00%	0.00%	0.00%	0.00%	0.00%	0.00%
All participants	Natural gas	100.00%	100.00%	100.00%	100.00%	100.00%	100.00%	100.00%	100.00%	100.00%	100.00%	100.00%
Participant 1	Large hydro	100.00%	100.00%	100.00%	100.00%	100.00%	100.00%	100.00%	100.00%	100.00%	100.00%	100.00%
Participant 2	Large hydro	0.00%	0.00%	0.00%	0.00%	0.00%	0.00%	0.00%	0.00%	0.00%	0.00%	0.00%
Participant 3	Large hydro	0.00%	0.00%	0.00%	0.00%	0.00%	0.00%	0.00%	0.00%	0.00%	0.00%	0.00%
Participant 4	Large hydro	0.00%	0.00%	0.00%	0.00%	0.00%	0.00%	0.00%	0.00%	0.00%	0.00%	0.00%
Participants 2–4	Large hydro	0.00%	0.00%	0.00%	0.00%	0.00%	0.00%	0.00%	0.00%	0.00%	0.00%	0.00%
Rest participants	Large hydro	0.00%	0.00%	0.00%	0.00%	0.00%	0.00%	0.00%	0.00%	0.00%	0.00%	0.00%
All participants	Large hydro	100.00%	100.00%	100.00%	100.00%	100.00%	100.00%	100.00%	100.00%	100.00%	100.00%	100.00%
Participant 1	RES_FiP&Market	16.72%	19.43%	21.34%	21.76%	22.04%	22.24%	22.67%	23.03%	23.40%	23.71%	23.96%
Participant 2	RES_FiP&Market	4.34%	6.66%	8.86%	9.30%	9.59%	9.79%	10.05%	10.26%	10.33%	10.39%	10.44%
Participant 3	RES_FiP&Market	4.34%	6.66%	8.86%	9.30%	9.59%	9.79%	10.05%	10.26%	10.33%	10.39%	10.44%

Continued

TABLE 21.15 Daily average Participants' market share (%) in total available supply capacity for the disaggregate markets, under the assumptions of Indicator 4—cont'd

Participants' supply capacity share (%) in disaggregate markets' available capacity, considering assumptions for Indicator 4

		2020	2021	2022	2023	2024	2025	2026	2027	2028	2029	2030
Participant 4	RES_FiP&Market	8.72%	12.25%	14.48%	15.16%	15.60%	15.91%	16.32%	16.66%	16.76%	16.85%	16.92%
Participants 2–4	RES_FiP&Market	17.40%	25.58%	32.21%	33.76%	34.77%	35.48%	36.42%	37.17%	37.42%	37.62%	37.79%
Rest participants	RES_FiP&Market	65.88%	55.00%	46.45%	44.48%	43.19%	42.28%	40.91%	39.80%	39.17%	38.67%	38.25%
All participants	RES_FiP&Market	100.00%	100.00%	100.00%	100.00%	100.00%	100.00%	100.00%	100.00%	100.00%	100.00%	100.00%
Participant 1	Imports' interconnections	5.22%	5.22%	5.22%	5.22%	3.97%	3.97%	3.97%	3.97%	3.97%	3.97%	3.97%
Participant 2	Imports' interconnections	1.04%	1.04%	1.04%	1.04%	0.79%	0.79%	0.79%	0.79%	0.79%	0.79%	0.79%
Participant 3	Imports' interconnections	0.00%	0.00%	0.00%	0.00%	0.00%	0.00%	0.00%	0.00%	0.00%	0.00%	0.00%
Participant 4	Imports' interconnections	5.22%	5.22%	5.22%	5.22%	3.97%	3.97%	3.97%	3.97%	3.97%	3.97%	3.97%
Participants 2–4	Imports' interconnections	6.26%	6.26%	6.26%	6.26%	4.77%	4.77%	4.77%	4.77%	4.77%	4.77%	4.77%
Rest participants	Imports' interconnections	88.52%	88.52%	88.52%	88.52%	91.26%	91.26%	91.26%	91.26%	91.26%	91.26%	91.26%
All participants	Imports' interconnections	100.00%	100.00%	100.00%	100.00%	100.00%	100.00%	100.00%	100.00%	100.00%	100.00%	100.00%

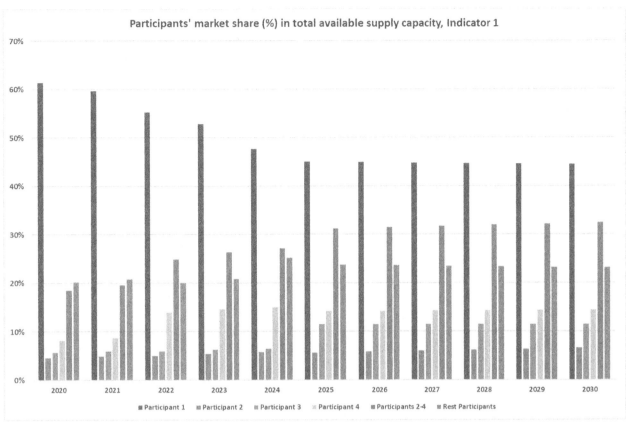

FIG. 21.8 Average indicative Participants' market share (%) in total available supply capacity, under indicator 1, over the period 2020–2030.

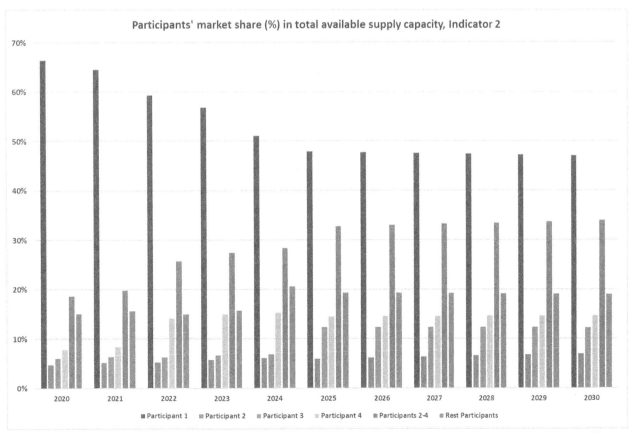

FIG. 21.9 Average indicative Participants' market share (%) in total available supply capacity, under indicator 2, over the period 2020–2030.

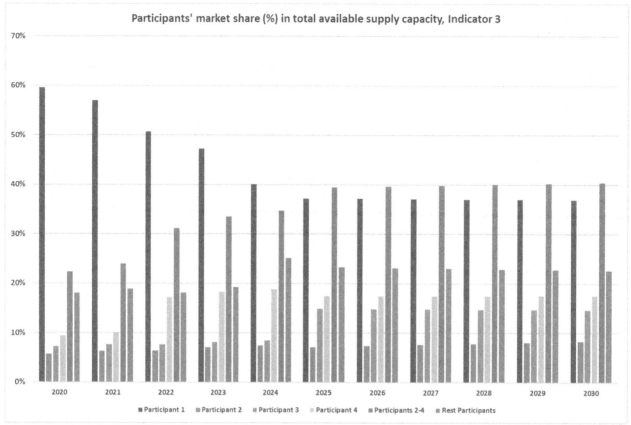

FIG. 21.10 Average indicative Participants' market share (%) in total available supply capacity, under indicator 3, over the period 2020–2030.

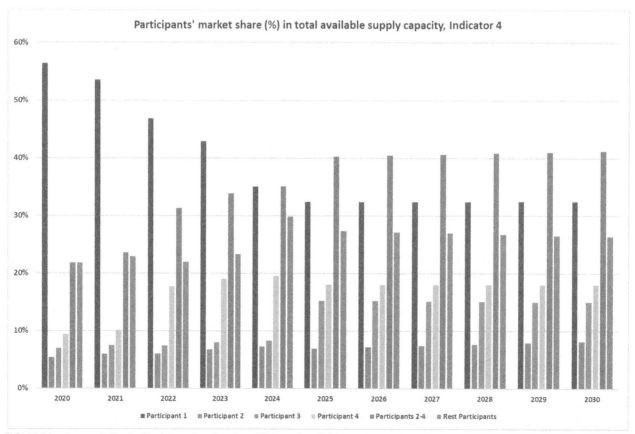

FIG. 21.11 Average indicative Participants' market share (%) in total available supply capacity, under indicator 4, over the period 2020–2030.

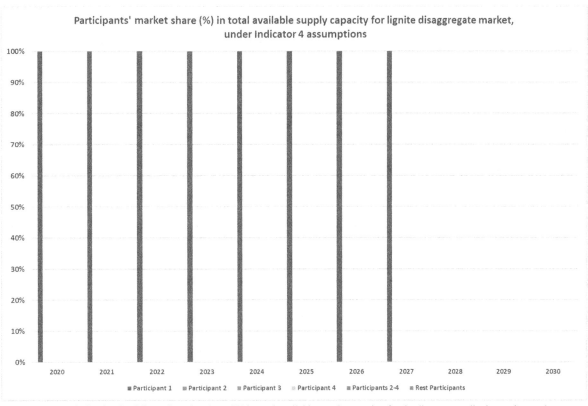

FIG. 21.12 Average indicative Participants' market share (%) in total available supply capacity, for the disaggregate lignite market, under assumptions for Indicator 4, over the period 2020–2030.

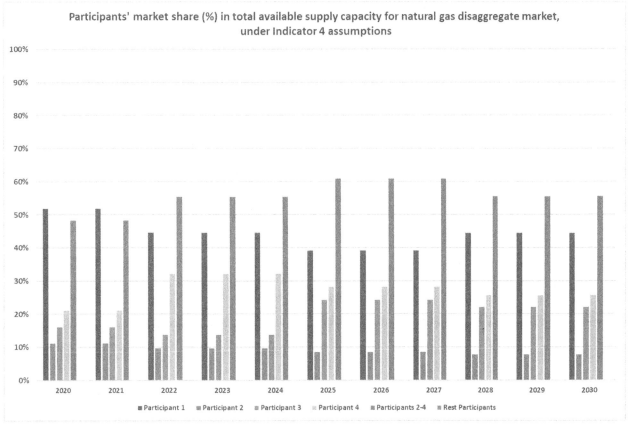

FIG. 21.13 Average indicative Participants' market share (%) in total available supply capacity, for the disaggregate natural gas market, under assumptions for Indicator 4, over the period 2020-2030.

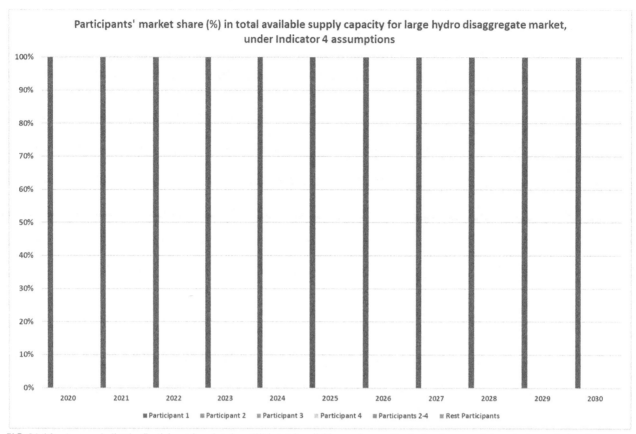

FIG. 21.14 Average indicative Participants' market share (%) in total available supply capacity, for the disaggregate large hydro market, under assumptions for Indicator 4, over the period 2020–2030.

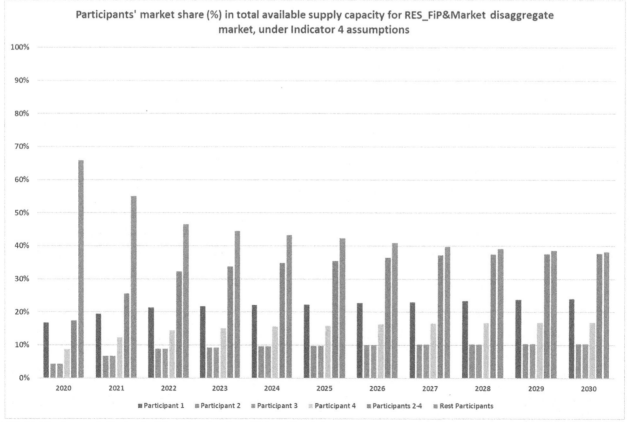

FIG. 21.15 Average indicative Participants' market share (%) in total available supply capacity, for the disaggregate RES_FiP&Market market, under assumptions for Indicator 4, over the period 2020–2030.

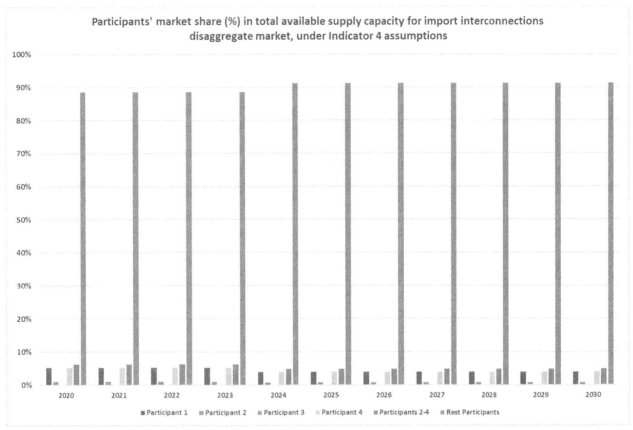

FIG. 21.16 Average indicative Participants' market share (%) in total available supply capacity, for the disaggregate import interconnections market, under assumptions for Indicator 4, over the period 2020–2030.

According to the Article 49 of the same Code, the lignite (as well as other thermal) units must provide data every day on the following Variable Cost Parameters for Thermal Generating Units:

- Fuel cost by fuel type
- Fuel lower heating value by fuel type
- Percentage composition of fuels on each capacity interval of the Specific Heat Consumption function.
- Average special cost of raw materials besides fuel for all capacity intervals of the Specific Heat Consumption function.
- Average special cost of additional maintenance costs due to operation (excluding fixed maintenance costs) for all capacity intervals of the Specific Heat Consumption function.
- Average special cost of additional labor costs due to fixed operational costs (excluding fixed labor costs) for all capacity intervals of the Specific Heat Consumption function.

Those data enable the quantification of the short-term variable cost for each unit, while there exists methodology published by the Transmission System Operator (ADMIE, 2020) on estimating the variable cost of each thermal unit, identifying among others the Minimum Variable Cost (MVC) Gumin of each unit u. Therefore, the TSO already estimates the Minimum Variable Cost (MAVC) Gp,f, d,min for each unit u, belonging to market participant/producer p, using fuel f in each time period t of day d.

The TSO can estimate the market share of each market participant and publish the market share in case a participant has a dominant position, under Indicator 4, as well as the market shares for each disaggregate market.

4.1.2.1 Lignite disaggregate market

In case of the Hellenic power system, PPC S.A. is the only one owner of lignite electroproduction assets, therefore it has 100% of the disaggregate market share. However, existing disaggregate markets might shrink, which means that a participant owning assets of a technology/resource type that is abandoned will always be considered having a dominant position.

This is the case of lignite. When all old lignite units are decommissioned, the only remaining unit, for few years 2024–2027 according the National Plan for Energy and Climate (NCEP, 2019), will be Ptolemaida V unit, with 660 MW capacity.

At the same time, DG Competition, following an energy sector inquiry implemented in 2005,[f] requested with the CASE AT.38700—Greek lignite and electricity markets from the Hellenic State on "establishing the specific measures to correct the anti-competitive effects of the infringement identified in the Commission Decision of 5 March 2008 on the granting or maintaining in force by the Hellenic Republic of rights in favor of Public Power Corporation S.A. for extraction of lignite." The DG Competition still recognizes the dominant position of PPC on extraction of lignite, as a subsequent of the non-successful open calls for selling "Lignitiki Megolopolis S.A." and "Lignitiki Melitis S.A." companies. Under the case where only Ptolemaida V exists in the period 2024–2027, the argument that a market participant (PPC) has preferable rights for the extraction of lignite might not stand, as Vevi lignite mine with relatively competitive heating value is owned by private investors. However, THRESHOLD3 does not aim to respond to cases such as dominant position on the extraction of a resource, but on the available capacity of assets using a resource type. Any obligations of the Hellenic state towards responding to CASE AT.38700 are supplementary to this mechanism. If Ptolemaida V is the only one lignite unit, it has 100% of the available capacity in this disaggregate market. But, commitments by the Hellenic State on lignite units, including Ptolemaida V, should be considered if affecting their available capacity and participation in the market.

A 5% threshold seems marginally not to be adequate to exclude Ptolemaida V from the status of dominant position for several years over the decade 2021–2030. However, in days with high renewables availability and/or partial availability of this unit and/or new added capacity investments, then this exemption might happen. Moreover, in case that PPC chooses in 2028 to replace lignite with a new technology/resource, such as hydrogen and not with an existing, such as natural gas, then this threshold enables this unit not to being considered as dominant. But this case is already mentioned above in the justification of the need of THRESHOLD 3.

For the time period, i.e., 2020–2023, where PPC has a dominant position on this disaggregate market, ex-ante regulation on the abuse can be applied, as the reason of indicating if a participant has a dominant position to inform him ex-ante on the allowed bidding strategies. This is not by imposing limits on bidding strategies, but through the ex-ante regulation of non-compliance charges in case of non-competitive behavior.

Following the Technical Memorandum of Understanding in June 2018 (TMU, 2018), mentioning that "with regard to day-ahead and intra-day electricity prices by 1 April 2019, there shall be no restrictions on price bids or price limits," the Hellenic Regulatory Authority for Energy (RAE) decided on the abolishment of the MAVC rule on units' bids for the target model, authorizing the Hellenic Energy Exchange in the Day-Ahead and Intra-Day Market Code(HEnEX, 2020a) to identify bidding limits (−500, +3000 Euro/MWh) (HEnEX, 2020b), considering the ACER 04/2017 and 05/2017 Decision on the Harmonized Maximum and Minimum Clearing Price of the Intra-Day Market, pursuant to Articles 41 and 54 respectively of the Regulation (EU) 2015/1222 (CACM).

Therefore, ex-ante monitoring should be supplemented by ex-ante regulation on imposing non-compliance charges, in case those units are used in non-competitive manner and distort wholesale market. Such rules could resemble existing non-compliance charges, ex-ante defined by RAE and implemented by the Hellenic TSO.

The abuse of dominant position, in case of expensive units, such as the lignite units, concern implementing a bidding that distorts the market and therefore changes the merit-order to the power units in favor of more expensive units (lignite). This is partially covered by imposing a level on the bilateral contracts, i.e., 20% of the load of each participant can be covered by its units, including lignite units for PPC S.A.

Potential abuse of the power of PPC lignite units means that PPC by submitting very low bids, it might affect the energy mix and wholesale prices. Submitting low bids for capacity equal to the unit's technical minimum could be justified, as a power plant aims at avoiding shutdown and start-up costs. However, this should not be systematic, i.e., happens sequentially or several times within a time period. The consideration of Minimum Average Variable Cost (MAVC), could be used in the formation of the relevant non-compliance charges.

Potential options for those charges are:

- to allow the lignite unit to bid only at least equal at tis MAVC.
  - this can concern units allocated to bilateral contracts
- to allow the first step at the technical minimum to be bid at prices below the MAVC of the lignite unit for few days within a month.

---

f. https://ec.europa.eu/competition/sectors/energy/2005_inquiry/index_en.html.

- to allow the first step at the technical minimum to be bid at prices below the MAVC of the lignite unit for few days within a month, however, the weighted average bid of the available capacity of each lignite unit must be at least equal to its MAVC.

As mentioned in the previous section, non-compliance charges are split on those concerning the available capacity up to THRESHOLD2 for non-competitive strategy, as well as stricter non-compliance charges concerning the available capacity above THRESHOLD2 for market concentration.

4.1.2.2 Large hydro disaggregate market

In such case, the market participant owns assets in the disaggregate market, that are competitive. This is the case for the large hydro units in Greece, where PPC S.A. has 100% in the disaggregate market and those units have low operating costs. In such case, the market participant should use those assets in the same way, that would have been used if owned by its competitors, namely bidding at low prices the first steps of their capacity and at higher prices the last steps, towards increasing their revenues. Moreover, those competitive assets should contribute in the overall social welfare. Therefore, large hydro units could implement a peak saving strategy, allocating their capacity in the peak hours. During off-peak hours, such as hours 1–8, the allocated available capacity can be either zero, or very low, towards providing some balancing services. A realistic scenario is that units do not provide energy such hours, as well as Frequency Containment Reserve (FCR) and automatic Frequency Restoration Reserve (aFRR) services, but only manual Frequency Restoration Reserve (mFRR) services, therefore declaring available capacity, i.e., at 5% of their Net Capacity (NCAP). Distinction among large hydro units with pumping facilities should also be made, concerning balancing services. The declaration of the available capacity is a very important and crucial issue in the mechanism, as it also affects the dominant position of PPC S.A. as a whole, their participation in the balancing services, and their renumeration in a potential Capacity Renumeration Mechanism. Those assets, having high ramping rates, are important to provide services in the needed hours, under realistic available capacity levels. Moreover, the available capacity is suggested to be bid in a way that benefits the social welfare, but also use this resource in a competitive manner. Again, bidding limits cannot be imposed, but non-compliance charges on systematic non-competitive use of those assets. Therefore, available capacity of those units could bid their capacity up to THRESHOLD2 level without bidding limitations or linked at their low actual variable cost, while for the remaining capacity non-compliance charges could be established in case of systematic bidding below their variable/opportunity cost, as estimated by a methodology by decision RAE 207/2016.[g] It should be noted that this methodology does not concern the actual variable cost of hydro units, as used for the forward electricity products auctions,[h] but reflects the opportunity cost, or "shadow price," of the water used for large hydro generation. Alternatively, this remaining capacity could be allocated through specific auctions to other market participants, namely through forward electricity products auctions. The first option seems to be more appropriate, considering the recent abolishment of those auctions. Finally, as mentioned above, large hydro units might face low precipitation periods, facilitated by climate change. This might affect their available capacity and electroproduction, as well as the size of the disaggregate market compared to the aggregate market. Declaring realistic available capacity might enable large hydro participation, without non-compliance charges.

It is important to mention that a coherent market monitoring and regulation mechanism, has the meaning of implement a coherent approach in similar cases, as abuse of dominant position in all disaggregate markets is not welcome. Competitive large hydro resource resembles to the case where an interconnection (entry) point for natural gas provides competitive energy compared to alternative disaggregate natural gas markets, i.e., Revythousa LNG terminal or the Sidirokaston entry points, under different conditions in international natural gas and crude oil markets. In such case, the mechanism similarly will identify when a participant has dominant position in the capacity of the competitive entry point and impose ex-ante regulation on abusing this dominant position. In case of natural gas entry points, the market participant with dominant position above THRESHOLD2, could:

- re-allocate the extra (from this threshold) capacity to other participants in the secondary market,
- to opt-out not using this extra capacity,
- to implement gas release programs for the volumes, concerning the extra (above threshold) capacity.

Capacity allocation concerning gas infrastructure is further analyzed in Section 2.2.2.

Similar to the capacity gas release programs, it could be argued that electricity release programs could be implemented in case of the large hydro units. This has already been implemented in case of the Hellenic power market, through the

---

g. https://www.dapeep.gr/enarxi-efarmogis-methodologias-ypolo/.

h. http://www.enexgroup.gr/en/markets/forward-electricity-product-auctions/.

Forward Electricity Products Auctions,[i] allocating lignite and large hydro electroproduction capacity. The auctions of this program have been terminated in 2019; therefore, a similar electricity release program seem not to be realistic.

Electricity release and natural gas release follow the same logic, but there exist some differences, as natural gas release concerns energy for bilateral contracts, while electricity release concerns energy for day-ahead (and other) markets, where bidding does not guarantee this energy will be produced. Therefore, regulatory coherence could be also met with other policies. Implementation of peak saving strategy together the above described bidding framework could be an option for large hydro. An indicative peak saving strategy could optimum allocate expected daily hydro electroproduction in each hour, using an optimization model that considers the demand forecast estimated by the TSO published by the Energy Exchange in the Day Ahead Scheduling requirements.[j] The estimated—by the model—hourly capacity for the provision of the expected electroproduction could be increased by a threshold (%) related to further available capacity for electricity production and by a second threshold (%) related to available capacity for the provision of balancing services (FCR, aFRR, mFRR and potential congestion management or other services in the future). The sum of those three components lead to the estimation of total hourly available capacity for the large hydro units. The key issue in large hydro seems to be the realistic declaration of their available capacity, considering the expected water inputs.

4.1.2.3 Natural gas disaggregate market

There might be a case where a market participant, has a dominant position in the aggregate market, but not in the disaggregate market. Such is the case of PPC S.A. concerning the natural gas units in the Hellenic power system. As mentioned before, the ex-ante identification of dominant position at a market aims to supplementary identify bidding strategy rules, in the form of non-compliance charges. However, in case a participant does not have a dominant position in a disaggregate market, irrespective it has or not on the aggregate market, it could be argued that it can use those assets in the same way that other participants use their assets. Therefore, not imposing any relevant limitation or non-compliance charges. This seems to be logical, but in case the market participant has a dominant position in the supply side and net consumer profile (comparing supply and demand side with THRESHOLD 4), it could implement a bidding strategy towards reducing wholesale prices, by systematically bidding those competitive units below their costs. Moreover, in case a market participant has a status of net producer/supplier (under THRESHOLD 4, comparing market share in supply and demand side), by systematically bidding those units at extreme high prices. Of course, scarcity pricing is a logical behavior, but systematic bidding in high prices should be monitored and regulated. Therefore, the need of the THRESHOLD4, as well as for relevant non-compliances charges can be justified. Therefore, although there seems not to be a need for non-compliance charges, under THRESOLDS2&3, THRESHOLD4, in combination of dominant position in THRESHOLD 1 creates the need for regulation.

As mentioned above, THRESHOLD4 enables the identification of the motivation of each market participant with vertical integration in the wholesale market and therefore to indicate potential cumulative dominant position from group of market participants with same interests.

Relevant non-compliance charge for market concentration could be imposed, where bidding strategies could be compared to the MAVC. Again, non-compliance charges for non-competitive behavior should also be in place for all market participants, including the available capacity up to THRESHOLD2 for market participant with dominant position.

4.1.2.4 Renewables disaggregate market

According to the report published by the TSO on the Balancing Market Detailed Design (ADMIE, 2017), the RES Units are categorized in terms of Market Participation in the following categories:

- 1st group (RES FiT Portfolio): This group includes RES units, for which (independently of the remuneration scheme) the TSO (ADMIE) shall be responsible for the injection forecasting (in all individual markets), LAGIE shall be responsible for the submission of the respective price-taking energy offers in the markets (Day-Ahead Market and possibly Intra-Day Market), and the TSO shall bear the balance responsibility.
- 2nd group (Dispatchable RES Portfolios or Non-Dispatchable RES Portfolios): This group includes RES units, for which (independently of the remuneration scheme) the RES Operators (RES Producers, RES Aggregators or the Last Resort Aggregator) shall be responsible for the injection forecasting and bidding in the wholesale markets, and shall bear the foreseen balance responsibility.

---

i. http://www.enexgroup.gr/en/markets/forward-electricity-product-auctions/auctions-schedule/.

j. http://www.enexgroup.gr/en/markets/electricity-day-ahead-market/input-data/day-ahead-scheduling-requirements/.

Moreover, according to the Balancing Code (ADMIE, 2019), RES units are split into two categories concerning market participation obligations:

- RES Units with Market Participation Obligation: The RES units for which a Contract for Differential State Aid Support has been concluded in accordance with the provisions of Law 4414/2016 as well as the RES units covered by the provisions of Article 3 (19) of Law 4414/2016.
- RES Units without Market Participation Obligation: RES units for which a Feed-in Tariff Agreement has been concluded in accordance with the provisions of Law 4414/2016, as well as the RES units for which a Power Purchase Agreement has been concluded in accordance with the provisions of Article 12 of Law 3468/2006 or a similar electricity purchase and sale agreement prior to the entry into force of Law 3468/2006.

In our analysis, we consider that the support with an approved State Aid scheme should be terminated by the end of the decade, especially for mature technologies such as photovoltaics and onshore wind installations, due to the rapid decrease of their levelized cost of production. Renewable units might participate in the market, without any support scheme such as FiP, like thermal and large hydro units. Cancellation of FiP schemes or the neglection of FiP schemes by RES units, might enable those units to be selective installations for other mechanisms, such as Capacity Renumeration Mechanism. Therefore, in our analysis we categorize RES units into two categories:

- RES units under Feed in Tariff (FiT) scheme, named as RES_FiT
- RES units under Feed in Premium (FiP) scheme, as well as with full market participation, named as RES_FiP&Market

We identify that Renewables should be attributed not to its owner, but to the market participant that represents them in the electricity market. This is practical, as it avoids the consideration of ownership rates in each RES unit, but as well it is fair as the role of the RES aggregators is to undertake market responsibilities for the assets they represent. Therefore, a market participant might choose its units to be represented by another market participant. This principle could concern any unit, thermal and large hydro units, as a power unit's owner might opt, under a fee, to allocate the representation of its unit to another market participant. However, although this principle avoids examining ownership status in each power plant, it does not avoid examining ownership status on market participants. Such is the case where a market participant owns and represents some thermal units and at the same has shares in a RES aggregator, including its management. The level of the shares that defines management power of company on another company is not the scope of this study but could also be regulatory defined.

Moreover, in case that a market participant or group of market participants have a net producer/supplier status, then it could implement non-competitive bidding strategies with its RES units. Therefore, non-compliance charges could also be established for those units, however a further classification of renewables should be applied, by splitting RES-FiP from RES_Market units. This derives from the fact that although both RES categories have market responsibilities, only the latter provide priced energy offers, on which specific market monitoring on bidding strategies and non-compliance charges can be applied. Moreover, existing non-compliance charges already capture the volume bidding behavior of RES_FiP units.

4.1.2.5 Interconnections disaggregate market

As mentioned above, long-term rights on interconnections capacity is already regulated through relevant non-compliance charges, which impose strict limits on their bidding behavior. Therefore, there is no need for further non-compliance charges for market concentration.

4.1.3 Demand side

The demand side is analyzed in less detail, namely it is considered that each market participant has a constant market share in the demand side. The market share in the domestic load is used in order to be compared with the market share in total available supply, under Indicator 4, leading to the results presented in Tables 21.16 and 21.17. In the whole analysis, market participants are aggregated as a sub-group, in order to show provide indications of potential cumulative dominant position. However, as shown in the results, their market interests might deviate and therefore have different bidding strategy priorities.

As mentioned before, instead of ex-ante estimation of market share in the demand side, the reports published by the Hellenic Energy Exchange could be used. Those reports are published at the end of each month on the market shares of each participant per voltage level for the previous month (HEnEX, 2020c). The difference with this report is the real-time ex-ante estimation of market concentration, rather than an ex-post market monitoring. But considering that the latter takes place with about one-month delay, it could be used as the preferred market concentration monitoring

TABLE 21.16 Indicative participants' market share (%) in total available domestic load capacity, assumed the same over the

	1	2	3	4	5	6	7	8	9	10	11	12
Total domestic load per participant (MW)												
Participant 1	3960	3600	3600	3600	3600	3600	3840	4080	4320	4560	4320	4200
Participant 2	396	396	396	396	396	396	396	396	396	396	396	396
Participant 3	396	396	396	396	396	396	396	396	396	396	396	396
Participant 4	396	396	396	396	396	396	396	396	396	396	396	396
Participant 2–4	1188	1188	1188	1188	1188	1188	1188	1188	1188	1188	1188	1188
Rest participants	792	792	792	792	792	792	792	792	792	792	792	792
Total	5940	5580	5580	5580	5580	5580	5820	6060	6300	6540	6300	6180
Market share (%) in total domestic load per participant												
Participant 1	66.67%	64.52%	64.52%	64.52%	64.52%	64.52%	65.98%	67.33%	68.57%	69.72%	68.57%	67.96%
Participant 2	6.67%	7.10%	7.10%	7.10%	7.10%	7.10%	6.80%	6.53%	6.29%	6.06%	6.29%	6.41%
Participant 3	6.67%	7.10%	7.10%	7.10%	7.10%	7.10%	6.80%	6.53%	6.29%	6.06%	6 29%	6.41%
Participant 4	6 67%	7.10%	7.10%	7 10%	7 10%	7 10%	6 80%	6 53%	6 29%	6 06%	6 29%	6.41%
Participant 2–4	20.00%	21.29%	21.29%	21.29%	21.29%	21.29%	20.41%	19.60%	18.86%	18.17%	18.86%	19.22%
Rest participants	13.33%	14.19%	14.19%	14.19%	14.19%	14.19%	13.61%	13.07%	12.57%	12.11%	12.57%	12.82%
All participants	100.00%	100.00%	100.00%	100.00%	100.00%	100.00%	100.00%	100.00%	100.00%	100.00%	100.00%	100.00%

period 2020–2030.

13	14	15	16	17	18	19	20	21	22	23	24	AVERAGE
3960	3840	3840	3840	4080	4440	5160	5640	5880	5520	4920	4440	4285
396	396	396	396	396	396	396	396	396	396	396	396	396
396	396	396	396	396	396	396	396	396	396	396	396	396
396	396	396	396	396	396	396	396	396	396	396	396	396
1188	1188	1188	1188	1188	1188	1188	1188	1188	1188	1188	1188	1118
792	792	792	792	792	792	792	792	792	792	792	792	792
5940	5820	5820	5820	6060	6420	7140	7620	7860	7500	6900	6420	6265
66.67%	65.98%	65.98%	65.98%	67.33%	69.16%	72.27%	74.02%	74.81%	73.60%	71.30%	69.16%	68.07%
6.67%	6.80%	6.80%	6.80%	6.53%	6.17%	5.55%	5.20%	5.04%	5.28%	5.74%	6.17%	6.39%
6.67%	6.80%	6.80%	6.80%	6.53%	6.17%	5.55%	5.20%	5.04%	5.28%	5.74%	6.17%	6.39%
6.67%	6.80%	6 80%	6 80%	6 53%	17%	55%	5 20%	5 04%	5 28%	5 74%	6. 17%	6.39%
20.00%	20.41%	20.41%	20.41%	19.60%	18.50%	16.64%	15.59%	15.11%	15 84%	17.22%	18.50%	19.16%
13.33%	13.61%	13.61%	13.61%	13.07%	12.34%	11.09%	10.39%	10.08%	10.56%	11.48%	12.34%	12.77%
100.00%	100.00%	100.00%	100.00%	100.00%	100.00%	100.00%	100.00%	100.00%	100.00%	100.00%	100.00%	100.00%

TABLE 21.17 Comparison of available capacity market shares (%) in supply and demand side, characterization of status of each participant (net seller/net buyer) and indication of violation of THRESHOLD4 for each market participant, over the period 2020–2030.

		2020	2021	2022	2023	2024	2025	2026	2027	2028	2029	2030
Comparison of available capacity market shares (%) in supply and demand side												
Participant 1	Total supply (Indicator 4)—domestic load	−11.69%	−14.54%	−21.25%	−25.19%	−33.02%	−35.68%	−35.67%	−35.66%	−35.65%	−35.65%	−35.64%
Participant 2	Total supply (Indicator 4)—domestic load	−1.03%	−0.43%	−0.32%	0.39%	0.86%	0.57%	0.81%	1.04%	1.30%	1.54%	1.78%
Participant 3	Total supply (Indicator 4)—Domestic Load	0.64%	1.11%	1.06%	1.65%	1.94%	8.88%	8.83%	8.78%	8.72%	8.67%	8.61%
Participant 4	Total supply (Indicator 4)—domestic load	3.02%	3.71%	11.36%	12.61%	13.15%	11.65%	11.65%	11.66%	11.66%	11.66%	11.66%
Participant 2–4	Total supply (Indicator 4)—domestic load	2.63%	4.38%	12.10%	14.66%	15.96%	21.10%	21.29%	21.47%	21.67%	21.87%	22.05%
Rest participants	Total supply (Indicator 4)—Domestic Load	9.06%	10.16%	9.15%	10.52%	17.07%	14.59%	14.38%	14.18%	13.98%	13.78%	13.59%
All Participants	Total supply (Indicator 4)—Domestic Load	0.00%	0.00%	0.00%	0.00%	0.00%	0.00%	0.00%	0.00%	0.00%	0.00%	0.00%
Characterization of status (net seller/buyer)												
Participant 1		Net buyer	Net buyer	Net buyer	Net buyer	Net buyer	Net buyer	Net buyer	Net buyer	Net buyer	Net buyer	Net buyer
Participant 2		Net buyer	Net buyer	Net buyer	Net seller	Net seller	Net seller	Net seller	Net seller	Net seller	Net seller	Net seller
Participants		Net seller	Net seller	Net seller	Net seller	Net seller	Net seller	Net seller	Net seller	Net seller	Net seller	Net seller
Participant 4		Net seller	Net seller	Net seller	Net seller	Net seller	Net seller	Net seller	Net seller	Net seller	Net seller	Net seller
Comparison with THRESHOLD 4 set at												
Participant 1	2%	Yes	Yes	Yes	Yes	Yes	Yes	Yes	Yes	Yes	Yes	Yes
Participant 2	2%	No	No	No	No	No	No	No	No	No	No	No
Participants	2%	No	No	No	No	No	Yes	Yes	Yes	Yes	Yes	Yes
Participant 4	2%	Yes	Yes	Yes	Yes	Yes	Yes	Yes	Yes	Yes	Yes	Yes

mechanism, in case the proposed in mechanism incorporates complexities, especially related to the disaggregate load forecasts per voltage level for each market participant. However, either ex-ante or ex-post, if the identification of market concentration is done per voltage level, allowing the formation of different tariff policy per voltage level, then relevant non-compliance charges should be identified, supplementary to existing non-compliance charges at aggregate domestic load level.

4.2 Application in the natural gas market

Concerning the Hellenic natural gas wholesale market, there already exist relevant actions and decisions by the Hellenic Competition Authority (HCA, 2012a, b), related to market concentration of Public Power Supplier S.A. (DEPA) and the role of Hellenic Gas Transmission System Operator (DESFA). Those decision follow a similar logic of the proposed mechanism, however imposing different thresholds, namely 55% and 40% for the Sidirokastro interconnection (entry) point through pipeline and the Revithousa LNG storage facilities, respectively. Those decisions have led to the establishment of relevant gas release schedules by DEAP that eliminate its dominant position.

Therefore, the Market monitoring in the natural gas market is not analyzed with the proposed mechanism, as the there are no further indications on market concentration of the supply or the demand side. However, monitoring capacity allocations in interconnections, the more complex nature of LNG facilities as slots and not capacity is allocated, as well as potential regulation on market concentration issues in the aggregate and disaggregate markets are discussed.

Concerning allocation capacity in gas transmission systems, the relevant regulation concerns the Capacity Allocation Mechanism Network Code—CAM NC (EUCR, 2017), established through the Commission Regulation (EU) 2017/459 by amending Regulation (EU) No. 984/2013. The CAM NC applies to interconnection points ("IP") and may apply to entry and exit points from/to third countries. The CAM NC includes also rules for determining and marketing incremental capacity, contains provisions for a capacity conversion service of unbundled capacity products, as well as for harmonizing the main terms and conditions for bundled capacity products. Incremental capacity is defined as capacity above technical capacity at an existing interconnection point, the capacity linked to the creation of a new IP, or physical reverse capacity at an existing IP where previously gas could only flow in one direction. It also incorporates requirements for offering interruptible capacity, as well as auction rules and dates for long-term capacity products. The code identifies the responsibility for the TSO to identify the maximum technical capacity for each interconnection point, available to all network users. The TSOs shall offer yearly, quarterly, monthly, daily and within-day standard capacity products. Moreover, TSOs may only offer standard capacity products for interruptible capacity of a duration longer than 1 day if the corresponding monthly, quarterly or yearly standard capacity product for firm capacity was sold at an auction premium, was sold out, or was not offered. Adjacent TSOs shall jointly offer bundled capacity products. This regulation provides the framework for capacity allocation in gas transmission system, where relevant threshold could be implemented. However, in case of existing long-term contracts reserving capacity, either bundled or unbundled, capacity re-allocation might not be feasible. Or even if it is feasible in one side of an interconnection, in case capacity is reserved in the other side of the interconnection, releasing capacity in one side might be not effective. In such case, other regulatory options, such as gas release might be implemented, to dominant position of a market participant. Moreover, although the CAM NC concerns entry points from "liquefied natural gas" (LNG) terminals, the implementation of capacity allocation is more complex compared to the pipelines' entry points, as it concerns the definition of Standard LNG Slots, the allocations of Slots through public auctions and the regasification usage rate from the LNG storage facilities. The threshold practically concerns the gas injected from the entry point, and therefore the regasification process. The disaggregate market threshold could either implemented in the Slots allocation process, or at the regasification capacity process. In the first case, a market participant that is awarded more Slots than the allowed threshold can allocate some of its Slots in the secondary market or opt out for some of them, in order not to violate the threshold, as violating it might lead to gas release requirements.

Finally, imposing exemptions on the aggregate or the disaggregate threshold levels could make sense in specific cases, such as for ensuring security of supply, where the Hellenic regulator has developed relevant Preventive Action and National Emergency Plans (RAE, 2019). In such case, the power system could acknowledge and not penalize any market participant that contributes on resolving such critical issue, even with temporal violation of market concentration issues.

5 Conclusions

Market concentration is a sensitive and contradicting issue in power and natural gas markets. This issue concerns the whole European competition policy, as it concerns liberalization process, considers assets with state aid support schemes and covers antitrust and mergers cases. Market concentration is usually tackled under Competition Authorities, through ex-post and ad-hoc evaluation of each case. This creates an uncertainty on whether a market participant is considered to have dominant position in a market, as well as on what and when is allowed for a participant to do concerning its bidding and tariffs formation strategies. The Directorate General for Competition in Europe considers that "if a company has a market share of less than 40%, it is unlikely to be dominant", however there is not specific threshold which identifies a dominant position. On the other hand, National Regulatory Authorities for Energy are responsible for the regulation and market monitoring of power and natural gas markets, however they do not tackle market concentration issues with a coherent and permanent methodology. This chapter describes an ex-ante Market Monitoring and Regulation Mechanism for Market Concentration in Power and Natural Gas Markets. The mechanism concerns the available capacity in both supply and demand sides. In the supply side, it estimates the available capacity of all market participants, considering the capacity per resource type (i.e., lignite, natural gas, large hydro, renewables), market participation type (i.e., FiT, FiP, commissioning), interconnection (entry) point type and existence of bilateral contracts. It imposes a common threshold, i.e., 40% or 50% market share, for both aggregate and disaggregate markets, namely capacity of each resource/entry point type. In the demand side, it considers load, storage and pumping as well as export interconnections. However, regulation can exclude resource/entry point types with low capacity under another threshold, i.e., disaggregate market up to 4–5% of the aggregate market. The mechanism also considers the relative size of market participants in the supply and demand side, implementing a fourth threshold. The mechanism is a coherent and permanent mechanism. The mechanism provides indicative results concerning the Hellenic power market. It can assist Energy Regulators to design clear rules on tackling market concentration ex-ante, to be implemented by the Transmission System Operators.

The implementation of this mechanism in the Hellenic power market shows that, under the implemented assumptions, ending of the PPC S.A. dominant position in the supply side is linked to the de-lignitization process, as it might take place in 2022 and in any case by 2023, when the decommissioning of all old lignite units will take place, when PPC market share in total available supply capacity is below the 50% threshold of the aggregate market. Considering that the mechanism is real-time and dynamic, potential non availability of partial availability of PPC units could lead to its de-characterization of having dominant position in the aggregate market earlier, even for some days in 2021. The mechanism establishes threshold not only on the aggregate market, but also on the disaggregate market. This practically means for the Hellenic power and natural gas systems, that a dominant position is identified for the large hydro disaggregate market and potentially for the natural gas interconnections (entry) points disaggregate markets. The declaration of realistic low hydro availability, the implementation of peak saving strategy in combination with scarcity pricing for the last steps of large hydro availability capacity might be the solution for tackling the first issue. Moreover, the existence a third threshold concerning the size of the disaggregate market compared to the size of the aggregate market, might lead in several time periods the characterization of PPC as not having dominant position in this disaggregate market, especially in time periods with low precipitation, or more in the future due to the accelerated climate change effects. Moreover, the implementation of a fourth threshold on comparing the market shares of participants in the demand with the supply side, enables the understanding of the interests of market participants with vertical integration. This can also identify potential formation of cumulative dominant position, although regulation is more complex from dominant position of a single market participant. This threshold identifies that the need of regulation does not concern only market participants with dominant position but also participants with cumulative dominant position that have clear interests on distorting the market. Moreover, this threshold considers also the competitiveness of the supply assets of the market participants, towards identifying potential regulation on bidding strategies. Finally, the implementation of this mechanism in the demand side might enable the characterizing of PPC as not having dominant position per voltage level, enabling therefore the formation of competitive tariffs in a voltage level earlier than others.

The ex-ante market monitoring mechanism enables the identification of the market concentration in a real-time, transparent, coherent and permanent manner. The incorporation of ex-ante regulation in this mechanism, similarly in a coherent and transparent manner, enables the ex-ante regulation of non-competitive bidding strategies by market participants, not in the form on imposing limits on their bids, which is anyway not allowed, but through the consideration of non-compliance charges. The implementation of this mechanism is feasible, where the role of the TSO as well as the RES operator is important for its implementation in a time framework. The market operator, being more flexible entity, could supplement the roles of TSO and RES operator. Considering that the mechanism incorporates forecasts on disaggregate volumes, such as load and renewables generation forecast per market participant; however, only for those with vertical integration, therefore four market participants in the Hellenic market, the mechanism also incorporates a knowledge transfer procedure, where market participants can provide mathematical formulation and/or software to the TSO and the RES operator, even under a regulated fee, considering that those entities justify that the improve considerable their forecasts. This might improve considerable the robustness of the mechanism. The ex-ante market monitoring and regulation mechanism could assist regulatory authority of energy in the formation of its relevant policy. The mechanism could also be extended to intraday and balancing markets, especially when there is considerable information from their operation.

Finally, the author would like to generally comment concerning regulation, as the proposed mechanism might seem as preference to over-regulation. We claim that regulation should be there to tackle issues on ex-ante, coherent, fair and long-standing manner. Regulatory interventions should be limited, allowing the market participants to compete under clear and known rules. In case there exist a chance for profit maximization, market participants will adjust their strategies in short and medium-term, using and offsetting/eliminating that chance. If that chance remains in the long-term, then it should facilitate investments. This case could also require regulation, as it might concern an improper regulated market distortion case. Therefore, the formation of coherent, fair and long-standing mechanisms should consider all main regulatory interventions. This is the case for the proposed mechanism, as it tackles an important problem, namely existing and potential (cumulative) dominant position. Another important intervention could also concern the permanent Capacity Renumeration Mechanism, which similarly will set an ex-ante and coherent environment that could potentially create the appropriate price signals for investments to all market participants. The role of permanents mechanisms is the respond in needs of the energy markets in a coherent and transparent manner. Those mechanisms should be there at a permanent basis, but might be applicable or not depending on the market conditions, i.e., when there is no market concentration, the specific non-compliance charges are not applied, or when there is adequate available capacity, capacity mechanism would lead to low or even zero prices, that do not facilitate investments.

References

ADMIE, 2019. Balancing Market Rulebook, Version 1. Available from: http://www.admie.gr/fileadmin/groups/EDRETH/Manuals/Codes/Balancing_Code.pdf. (Last assessed 15 June 2020).

ADMIE, 2020. Methodology for estimating the variable electro-production cost of thermal units. Accessible at: https://www.admie.gr/sites/default/files/users/content_user/methodologia%20thermikon%20monadon.pdf.

ADMIE, 2017. Balancing Market Detailed Design—Public Consultation. Available from: http://www.admie.gr/uploads/media/Balancing_Detailed_Design_-_Public_Consultation_201712.pdf. (Last accessed 15 June 2020).

ECC, 2014. Communication From the Commission (2014/C 200/01): Guidelines on State Aid for Environmental Protection and Energy 2014–2020 (OJ C 200, 28.6.2014, p. 1–55). Available from: https://eur-lex.europa.eu/legal-content/EN/TXT/?uri=CELEX%3A52014XC0628%2801%29. (Last assessed 15 June 2020).

ECDCC, 2017. Competition: Making Markets Work Better, Directorate-General for Communication (European Commission). Available from: https://op.europa.eu/en/publication-detail/-/publication/8200c251-aa42-11e6-aab7-01aa75ed71a1. (Last assessed 15 June 2020).

EU, 2012. Consolidated Version of the Treaty on the Functioning of the European Union (OJ C 326, 26.10.2012, p. 47–390). Available from: https://eur-lex.europa.eu/legal-content/EN/TXT/?uri=celex%3A12012E%2FTXT. (Last assessed 15 June 2020).

EU, 2008a. Consolidated Version of the Treaty on the Functioning of the European Union—PART THREE: UNION POLICIES AND INTERNAL ACTIONS—TITLE VII: COMMON RULES ON COMPETITION, TAXATION AND APPROXIMATION OF LAWS—Chapter 1: Rules on Competition—Section 1: Rules Applying to Undertakings—Article 101 (Ex Article 81 TEC) (OJ C 115, 9.5.2008, p. 88–89). Available from: http://eur-lex.europa.eu/LexUriServ/LexUriServ.do?uri=CELEX:12008E101:EN:NOT. (Last assessed 15 June 2020).

EU, 2008b. Consolidated Version of the Treaty on the Functioning of the European Union—Part three: Union Policies and Internal Actions—Title VII: Common Rules on Competition, Taxation and Approximation of Laws—Chapter 1: Rules on competition—Section 1: Rules Applying to Undertakings—Article 102 (ex Article 82 TEC) (OJ C 115, 9.5.2008, p. 89–89). Available from: http://eur-lex.europa.eu/LexUriServ/LexUriServ.do?uri=CELEX:12008E102:EN:NOT. (Last assessed 15 June 2020).

EUCD, 2013. Commission Decision C(2013) 2949 Final of 16.5.2013 on the Exemption of the Trans Adriatic Pipeline From the Requirements on Third Party Access, Tariff Regulation and Ownership Unbundling Laid Down in Articles 9, 32, 41(6), 41(8) and 41(10) of Directive 2009/73/EC. Available from: https://ec.europa.eu/energy/sites/ener/files/documents/2013_tap_decision_en.pdf. (Last assessed 15 June 2020).

EUCD, 2015. Commission Decision C(2015) 1852 Final, of 17.3.2015 Prolonging the Exemption of the Trans Adriatic Pipeline From Certain Requirements on Third Party Access, Tariff Regulation and Ownership Unbundling Laid Down in Articles 9, 32, 41(6), (8) and (10) of Directive 2009/73/EC. Available from: https://ec.europa.eu/energy/sites/ener/files/documents/2015_tap_prolongation_decision_en.pdf. (Last assessed 15 June 2020).

EUCR, 2017. Commission Regulation (EU) 2017/459 of 16 March 2017 establishing a network code on capacity allocation mechanisms in gas transmission systems and repealing Regulation (EU) No. 984/2013 (Text with EEA relevance.) C/2017/1660 (OJ L 72, 17.3.2017, p. 1–28). Available from: https://eur-lex.europa.eu/legal-content/EN/TXT/?uri=CELEX%3A32017R0459. (Last assessed 15 June 2020).

HEnEX, 2020a. HEnEx Spot Trading Rulebook: Day-Ahead & Intra-Day Markets Trading Rulebook, Hellenic Energy Exchange. Available from: http://www.enexgroup.gr/fileadmin/groups/EDRETH/Manuals/20200521_Trading_Rulebook_combined_EN.pdf. (Last assessed 15 June 2020).

HEnEX, 2020b. Maximum and Minimum Price in Orders of the Day Ahead and Intraday Markets, Hellenic Energy Exchange. Available from: http://www.enexgroup.gr/fileadmin/groups/EDRETH/Manuals/20200413_Decision_08_final_01.pdf. (Last assessed 15 June 2020).

HEnEX, 2020c. Monthly Reports on Wholesale and Retail Market Shares. Available from: http://www.enexgroup.gr/agores/analysi-agoras/miniaia-ekthesi-dieisdysis-kai-meridion-chondrikis-kai-lianikis/. (Last assessed 15 June 2020).

HCA, 2012a. Decision 551/2012 on the Case of Potential Violations of Articles 101, 102 of the Treaty for the Functioning of the European Union (TFEU) and Articles 1, 2 of Law 703/1977-3959/2011. Available from: https://www.epant.gr/files/2012/apofaseis/551_2012.pdf. (Last assessed 15 June 2020).

HCA, 2012b. Decision 555/2012 on the Case of Potential Violations of Articles 101, 102 of the Treaty for the Functioning of the European Union (TFEU) and Articles 1, 2 of Law 703/1977-3959/2011. Available from: https://www.epant.gr/files/2012/apofaseis/555_2012.pdf. (Last assessed 15 June 2020).

NCEP, 2019. National Energy and Climate Plan, Hellenic Republic, Ministry of the Environment and Energy. Available from: https://ec.europa.eu/energy/sites/ener/files/el_final_necp_main_en.pdf. (Last assessed 15 June 2020).

RAE, 2019. National Report 2019: Regulation and Performance of the Electricity Market and the Natural Gas Market in Greece, in 2018. Regulatory Authority of Energy. Available from: http://www.rae.gr/site/file/system/docs/ActionReports/national_2019. (Last assessed 15 June 2020).

TMU, 2018. Greece: Technical Memorandum of Understanding, Accompanying the MoU of the ESM Programme, 2 June 2018 (bijlage bij 21501-07,nr. 1533). Available from: https://ec.europa.eu/info/sites/info/files/economy-finance/draft_tmu_4th_review_to_eg_2018.06.20.pdf. (Last assessed 15 June 2020).

Index

Note: Page numbers followed by *f* indicate figures, *t* indicate tables, and *ge* indicate glossary terms.

Printed in the United States
By Bookmasters